WAGNER AND THE ART OF THE THEATRE

WAGNER AND THE ART OF THE THEATRE

Patrick Carnegy

Yale University Press
New Haven and London

For information about this and other Yale University Press publications, please contact:
U.S. Office: sales.press@yale.edu
Europe Office: sales@yaleup.co.uk   www.yalebooks.co.uk

Set in Minion by Northern Phototypesetting Co. Ltd, Bolton
Printed in China through Worldprint

Library of Congress Cataloging-in-Publication Data

Carnegy, Patrick.
    Wagner and the art of the theatre / Patrick Carnegy.
        p. cm.
    Includes bibliographical references (p.) and index.
ISBN 978–0–300–10695–4 (cl.: alk. paper)
1. Wagner, Richard, 1813–1883—Performances. 2. Opera—Production and direction—History.
3. Wagner, Richard, 1813–1883—Dramaturgy. I. Title.
    ML410.W13C37 2006
    782.1'092—dc22

                                                                                              2005011640

A catalogue record for this book is available from the British Library

10 9 8 7 6 5 4 3 2

Published with assistance from the Ronald and Betty Miller Turner Publication Fund.

For Jill Gomez

Wagner is to be found only within the theatre: without the theatre he is unthinkable. There is no point in bemoaning the fact.

Thomas Mann, 'An Essay on the Theatre', 1908

There is no living style in the theatre other than that of its time, whether it strikes future generations as unbearable kitsch or as greatness worthy of imitation.

Wieland Wagner, 'What Is "Faithful Representation"?' 1967

How can an artist expect that what he has felt intuitively should be perfectly realized by others, seeing that he himself feels in the presence of his work, if it is true Art, that he is confronted by a riddle, about which he too might have illusions, just as another might?

Richard Wagner to August Röckel, 23 August 1856

Contents

Acknowledgements

Many people have helped me in the preparation of this book and I am deeply grateful to them all. Among those who have generously shared their knowledge and enthusiasm for my project over many years I would particularly like to thank Mike Ashman, Richard Beacham, John Deathridge, Jill Gomez, Barry Millington and Stewart Spencer.

My early researches were carried out at the Institute für Musiktheater of the University of Bayreuth at Schloß Thurnau. They were happy days and I would like to thank the staff of the Institut and in particular Christiane Zentraf for her hospitality. At the Richard-Wagner-Museum und Nationalarchiv in Bayreuth I have been greatly helped by its director Sven Friedrich and his colleagues Günter Fischer and Gudrun Föttinger. My special thanks to Dr Föttinger for her expert help with my illustrations and for discovering answers to a host of difficult questions.

John Deathridge and Stewart Spencer read and commented on the whole book at various stages, saving me from many a pitfall and improving it with their suggestions. I have been fortunate indeed to have enjoyed the friendship and robustly forthright counsel of Professor Deathridge for longer than either of us would care to remember. The stimulus of presenting some of my ideas as talks and seminars at his invitation, most recently at King's College London, has greatly helped their development into this book. Dr Spencer alerted me to sources I might have missed, trusted me with material from his incomparable library and was indefatigable in helping me resolve the seemingly endless stream of queries thrown up by the work. His exemplary concern for exactitude in all matters Wagnerian and far beyond has done more to sustain me through the gestation of the book than I can adequately acknowledge.

I am grateful to my fellow Appian enthusiast Richard Beacham for his help with my chapter on the great Swiss theatre visionary. The chapter on Wagner in Russia would not exist at all without Rosamund Bartlett's pioneering work in this field and her generosity in sharing her findings and hard-won illustration material. She and John Barber came to my rescue in the transliteration of Russian names. The following chapter on Wagner's fortunes in the Weimar Republic has benefited greatly from the advice of John Willett and Áine Shiel. I am grateful to Nikolaus Bacht for his clarification of T. W. Adorno's knotty involvement with Wagner, and to Morris

Philipson, formerly director of Chicago University Press, for finding me a copy of Gösta Bergman's enthralling study, *Lighting in the Theatre*.

Joachim Herz has been tireless in discussing his work with me. I owe him and Kristel Pappel my thanks for the loan of photographs and much other material from his archive. My pages on his work have greatly profited from his comments. I am also indebted to the scrutiny of these pages by Marion Benz, author of an important dissertation on Herz in the context of the cultural politics of the former German Democratic Republic. Her hugely illuminating study inexplicably still awaits publication and deserves translation into English.

Hans Jürgen Syberberg, whose films have richly illuminated the labyrinthine relationship between Wagner and the German imagination, has generously answered my questions and lent rare stills from his film of *Parsifal*.

Marion Kant, formerly a dancer with the Komische Oper and co-author of a remarkable study of German modern dance and the Third Reich, has guided my ventures into the role of movement and dance in the staging of Wagner's works. She and the historian Jonathan Steinberg, both now of the University of Pennsylvania, have helped me clarify my perspective on the political aspects of the German Wagnerian theatre after the Second World War.

Frank Martin Widmaier, who worked closely with Ruth Berghaus and is now deputy Intendant of the Gärtnerplatz Opera in Munich, kindly made available to me production videos of Berghaus's Frankfurt productions of *Parsifal* and the *Ring*. Many other friends in Germany have been most helpful, among them Oswald Georg Bauer, to whose publications all students of Wagnerian stage history are permanently indebted, Monika Beer, formerly editor of Gondrom's *Festspielmagazin* (Bayreuth), and Genja Gerber of the Bayreuth Chorus.

It is a pleasure to record my thanks to the Leverhulme Foundation for a Research Fellowship, and to the Music & Letters Trust for a grant towards the illustration costs.

Yale University Press granted me the kind of say in crucial matters of the book's production that is now enjoyed by all too few authors. I am grateful to my editor Robert Baldock for sustaining my morale over a long period, to Candida Brazil for her care with the text and to Stephen Kent for his skill in designing the book and its jacket. No copy-editor could have been more scrupulous in her concern for both the letter and the sense of the text than Laura Davey. My warmest thanks to her.

My thanks to those who have given special help with the illustrations are recorded in the Illustration Credits on p. 460.

Jill Gomez has lived with this book as long as I have. We first met at the Bayreuth International Youth Festival in 1967 when she sang the role of Lora in the first performance in modern times of Wagner's first opera *Die Feen*. Since then we have heard, seen and talked endlessly together about countless Wagner performances. The book could not have been completed without her loving support; her exacting readings and re-readings have resulted in countless improvements to the style and substance of the text.

Patrick Carnegy   Elsworth, May 2006

Introduction

This book tells the story of the stage production of Wagner's operas from his own lifetime until about the end of the twentieth century. It is inevitably far from comprehensive. But landmarks do stand out, and I believe these define a coherent line of development that begins with Wagner himself. It is hard to understand, let alone enjoy, modern stagings of his works without some knowledge of the great productions that have preceded them.

There are still those who contend, with Cosima, that the composer knew exactly what he wanted, and that productions with any aim other than the perfection of Wagner's intentions are therefore nothing but intransigence and apostasy. A purpose of this book is to show that they are mistaken, not least in their understanding of what Wagner's ideas about stage performance actually were. It was not fixity but fluidity that was a guiding principle of his theatrical conceptions. The operas may have been defined by the words and music of his scores, but the composer knew only too well that performance has its necessary freedoms.

The *Ring* of Wagner's imaginings was set among the chasms and rocky heights of the Alps he loved to climb. But how could the mountains be brought onto the stage? What should his Rhinedaughters, Nibelungs and gods actually look like? The short answer is that he never really knew. As a young man in Paris he had been impressed by the pictorial illusions conjured up by the painters and machinists at the Opéra. He wanted German theatres (generally much more poorly equipped) to be able to emulate this scenic wizardry.

There were, however, aesthetic problems with whose solution Paris was not concerned. The Opéra excelled in romanticized, picture-book evocations of the historical scenes which were the lifeblood of 'grand opera'. It was precisely against this kind of opera that Wagner created his own mature works. He believed that his myth-based music dramas would rise above the limitations of grand opera, generally rooted as it was in a particular time and place. There is of course no small trace of Parisian historicity in Wagner's early 'romantic operas', his assignation of *Tannhäuser* to the 'beginning of the thirteenth century' and of *Lohengrin* to the 'first half of the tenth century'. But Paris could offer little help with the portrayal of mythological worlds, such as that of the *Ring*. A representation of 'The bed of the Rhine', perhaps, but

Nibelheim and Valhalla? Wagner turned to fashionable landscape painters, but who could help him with the costuming of his Nibelungs and his gods?

Only rarely was he content with stage production, even when he himself was in charge of it. The 'model performances' offered him in Munich by King Ludwig were, with the exception of *Die Meistersinger* in 1868, nothing of the sort; nor was he able to do significantly better with the *Ring* in 1876 in his own theatre at Bayreuth. Only with *Parsifal* in 1882 did he begin to sense solutions to the problems he had created for himself.

However much Wagner may have battled to secure the stage realizations of his mind's eye, he also knew that there could, and indeed should, be other ways of staging his operas. As he wrote in a highly significant letter to his fellow Dresden revolutionary August Röckel (23 August 1856), if works were truly great then they would admit of a multiplicity of interpretations.

At rehearsals he was never more exuberant than when his artists themselves hit on this or that way of playing their roles. And indeed by far the most influential part of his ideas about staging has had to do with how the singers should act rather than how the stage picture should look. True, he often resisted or rejected the advice of members of his production team (most notably that of his wily movement director Richard Fricke, who had vainly advised him to keep the dragon out of sight), but his oft-quoted injunction 'Kinder! macht Neues!' ('Children, do something new!') gets him exactly right. He was always the enemy of doctrinaire rigidity. It is his voice that is heard when Sachs tells Walther that he will teach him the rules but expect him to interpret them in his own way. This is by no means inconsistent with Wagner's wish to bequeath to posterity the clearest possible picture of the way he himself thought his works should be performed. I will try to show that he remained dissatisfied with even the best of what he had achieved in the theatre and looked to others to improve upon it in the future.

Although the question of what is or is not a valid stage presentation is crucial, my approach to it is practical rather than theoretical. I have not allowed myself to be unduly detained by the theoretical issues with which the subject is sometimes hedged about. Rather than get entangled in discussions of what constitutes a 'faithful' performance, I have preferred to describe what has happened on the stage, often through the eyes and minds of the director and other artists, and to attempt to explain why.

My point of view is that theatre is an ephemeral art. As Peter Brook has so well reminded us, it 'is always a self-destructive art, and it is always written on the wind' (*The Empty Space*, 1968). Plays and operas of lasting value are precisely those which inspire and invite a multiplicity of readings. Any and every performance is a three-way conversation between a text, the performers and the audience responding to it. A minor work of art admits of only a very limited range of performing possibilities. A great one is endlessly suggestive of new ones. When we speak about *Die Meistersinger* we are almost invariably referring not only to Wagner's score but also to our knowledge of how it has been performed. Interpretations become subsumed into that which they interpret. The original text is necessarily the essential starting point, but there is no way in which persistent cravings to experience a play or an opera 'as the author intended' can ever be satisfied.

I had my first taste of Wagner on stage in the touring performances by what used to be the Sadler's Wells Opera (now English National Opera) back in the late 1950s. I still cherish the vividest recollection of a *Tannhäuser* at the Coventry Hippodrome conducted by the young Colin Davis and with the Australian tenor Ronald Dowd in the title role. Soon after it was the *Ring* at Covent Garden under Solti, experienced from benches in the then upper amphitheatre that made the utilitarian seating in the Bayreuth Festspielhaus – then and now – seem positively comfortable. From the musical angle these first experiences were often intensely thrilling and, for want of knowing anything better, I was not unduly dismayed by the conventional scenery.

Visiting Bayreuth for the first time in 1967, in the privileged role of the anony-mous 'special correspondent' for the London *Times*, was a revelation. It was the year after the death (at forty-nine) of Wagner's grandson Wieland and his productions were what I saw. His rejection of pictorial scenery and concentration on the princi-pal symbols immediately seemed entirely right. As director and designer, it was mainly lighting that he used to set the stage, change its mood and atmosphere and effect seamless transitions from one scene to another. No longer was the stage vainly struggling to reproduce what was so vividly depicted in the music. It seemed rather to distil its very essence.

I found this approach infinitely more satisfactory than anything I had previously come across. But the aesthetic gulf between the traditional style of staging and Wieland's was immense. Out of the need to understand why I found it so enthralling came the work that has eventually led to this book. It was easy to discover the still remarkable fact that Wieland's simplified stage pictures had been anticipated as early as the 1890s by an obscure Swiss visionary called Adolphe Appia. But much remained unexplained, and in particular the lines of continuity that I felt sure existed between Wagner's own ideas and what seemed the radical departures of Appia and of Wieland.

In the 1960s the stage production of opera was a relatively neglected subject. Most attention was paid to the way the music was performed. Adventurous stagings were then unusual, with the result that, with certain notable exceptions, 'production' was a secondary issue. Discussion of it was largely limited to whether the composer's intentions had or had not been fulfilled. The idea that staging is not just a represen-tation of words and music but also an *interpretation* of them was barely considered – and is still heresy in certain quarters.

The writings and designs of Edward Gordon Craig and of Adolphe Appia were good starting points. The titles of Craig's famous book *On the Art of the Theatre* (1911) and of Appia's scarcely less seminal *Music and the Art of the Theatre* (first pub-lished in German in 1899) are with good reason reflected in my own title. Geoffrey Skelton's *Wagner at Bayreuth* (1965) was a richly suggestive introduction to the way the operas had been produced in the composer's own theatre. But the gaps were still immense, and until the appearance of Oswald Georg Bauer's *Richard Wagner: The Stage Designs and Productions from the Premières to the Present* in 1983 (original German edition 1982) there had been no significant attempt at a performance history with an international perspective. The focus had always been on Bayreuth and little attention had been paid to productions elsewhere.

The centenary of the *Ring* in 1976 inspired a magnificent series of commemorative volumes. Many of these provide superb documentation of Wagner's own stage practice, among them Michael and Detta Petzet's study of the performances at Ludwig II's court theatre in Munich and also those at Bayreuth (*Die Richard Wagner-Bühne König Ludwigs II.*) and Dietrich Mack's invaluable map of the first hundred years of the Bayreuth stagings (*Der Bayreuther Inszenierungsstil, 1876–1976*). The Richard Wagner-Gesamtausgabe in Munich, founded by Carl Dahlhaus in the 1960s, is engaged in the monumental project of producing critical editions of all the works. It has also published a catalogue of the compositions and sketches, the *Wagner Werk-Verzeichnis*, and is adding volumes of documentation of the works and their performance in the composer's lifetime. To date, only those for *Parsifal* (1970), *Rienzi* (1976), the first of three projected volumes on the *Ring* (1976), *Lohengrin* (2003) and *Der fliegende Holländer* (2004) have appeared, but they are indispensable for an understanding of the works and the way Wagner wanted them staged. Further volumes are impatiently awaited. The publication of Cosima Wagner's Diaries in 1978 and 1980 (German editions 1976 and 1977) has been another hugely significant contribution to the chronicling of the composer's unending battles to get the operas performed to his liking. The collected edition of the composer's letters, the *Sämtliche Briefe*, begun in 1967, is still in progress (there will eventually be some thirty-four volumes). One has to regret that only a small proportion of this core scholarship has so far been made available in English. My own indebtedness to it cannot be overstated.

The book falls into three parts. The first is an account of Wagner's ideas about the staging of his works in the light of his experiences of the theatre world of his time. For all that I believe theatre to be an art in continuous evolution, it seems to me self-evident that discussion of performance practice cannot begin without the fullest possible knowledge of the way the composer wanted his works staged and of what, as one of the very greatest theatre directors of his day, he was able to achieve for them in practice.

The one thing that emerges over and over again from what we know of Wagner's own productions is that he was acutely aware that problems remained to be solved. Protean creator that he was, he endlessly changed his mind about what he wanted, welcoming constructive suggestions from his fellow artists. A great many of his difficulties were due to an irresolvable conflict between his theatrical conceptions and his belief that the ideal stage presentation of his works could be achieved within the romantic language of the nineteenth-century proscenium stage.

It is impossible to overemphasize that for Wagner, theatre was what Appia was later to call 'l'oeuvre d'art vivant', a work of living art. Certainly he wished, as would most composers, to do everything in his power to record his intentions for posterity.

But that did not mean – *pace* Cosima and his immediate successors – that he wanted his works embalmed. The evidence shows that he did not.

The second part of the book describes what happened across the half-century following Wagner's death in 1883. There was a great deal of unfinished business. Only the *Ring* and *Parsifal* had been performed in the Festspielhaus, and only the staging of *Parsifal* had been regarded by the Wagners as remotely satisfactory. That, at least, could serve as the rock on which to found the future of the festival. The burden of Cosima's inheritance was plain: to call on everything she could recall of Wagner's own productions to establish the exemplary performances of *Der fliegende Holländer*, of *Tannhäuser* and *Lohengrin*, of *Tristan* and *Die Meistersinger*, that had so far proved elusive, and, when funds allowed, to mount a renewed assault on the *Ring*. Taken on her own terms, she had succeeded in all of this by 1901, when the Dutchman finally made landfall on the Bayreuth stage. When Siegfried succeeded her in 1907 he began, very cautiously, to look to the future rather than the past, but the real action had for some time lain elsewhere.

In the decades after Wagner's death, ideas about theatrical performance and every other kind of art underwent a massive revaluation. We now recognize this as the birth and heyday of modernism. The impact of Darwin, Marx and Freud and of the political turbulence of the period was immense. The nineteenth century's belief in 'model' performances of theatrical works came under fierce critical scrutiny. The idea of theatre as an illusory other world was replaced with one that recognized its artifice for what it was. The executive stage manager was gradually supplanted by the 'creative' stage director.

Candle and later gas lighting, whose functions had been to illuminate an intricately painted stage picture, were superseded by electric lighting, which could itself paint pictures and establish mood and atmosphere. Solid scenery replaced painted flats and drops. Bayreuth, though, saw no further than using the new technology for the old aesthetic ends, whereas theatres elsewhere were using it for wholly new ones. In Vienna in the first decade of the twentieth century, the Secessionist artist Alfred Roller and Gustav Mahler discovered new ways of staging Wagner in which the spirit of fidelity was allied to a new visual aesthetic for achieving it.

The heretical idea that the composer might not necessarily have been the ultimate authority on the best way to stage his works was argued by Appia in the 1890s but was predictably rejected outright by Cosima. Nevertheless, the ideas and designs of Appia, Craig and a number of other visionaries were those which in the long run were to influence the future course of Wagner production and do so to this day.

In Russia, they impacted on Vsevolod Meyerhold and his 1909 staging of *Tristan und Isolde* in St Petersburg. The Bolsheviks resurrected Wagner as a revolutionary people's hero, allying his works with geometric, abstract stage imagery that would set the greatest possible distance between the brave new proletarian art and the ostentatious romantic opulence favoured by the imperialist past. The cinema leaves its first significant mark on the Wagnerian stage when the great film director Sergei Eisenstein stages *Die Walküre* at the Moscow Bolshoi in 1940. Back in the 1920s in the Germany of the Weimar Republic, Wagner was still a rallying point for wounded nationalism. Most of the important energies in the arts were, however, profoundly anti-Wagnerian in inspiration. It was not until Klemperer resurrected *Der fliegende Holländer* at Berlin's Kroll Opera in 1929 that the aesthetics of modernism, particularly that of the Bauhaus, impinged on a Wagner opera, and with sensational results.

The third part of the book covers developments since the Second World War, though dips back into the Bayreuth of the 1930s in order to say something about Wieland Wagner's apprentice years. It is still extraordinarily difficult to come to a just assessment of Wagner production in Hitler's Germany, not least because the Führer was intensely interested in it and was so closely associated with Winifred Wagner's direction of the festival. But to the extent that politics and aesthetics can be unscrambled – and it is doubtful that they can in this period – the artistic achievements of Heinz Tietjen, Emil Preetorius and Wilhelm Furtwängler at Bayreuth were of an exceptionally high order. Nevertheless, from the post-war viewpoint these achievements became unavoidably tarnished, and have remained so. After the war German directors naturally sought to set the greatest possible separation between their work and that of their predecessors in the 1930s. Henceforth, the stage production of Wagner, and not only in Germany, becomes almost impossible to understand other than in a political light.

Sceptics continue to assert that Wieland's stages were 'bare' because post-war shortages left him no choice. Although much of the necessary documentation (such as his correspondence) has still not been released, my own conviction is that Wieland Wagner is telling the truth when he says that he simply had to 'clear out the rubbish' (entrümpeln) and make a completely fresh start. What better way to distance a recent past with which he himself was all too closely associated than by avoiding explicit illustrative scenery and the awkward political foreground, insisting instead that his grandfather was primarily a master of myth, of symbol and archetype, and that his work was an anticipation of depth-psychology? In 1965 Wieland presented the *Ring* as the kind of Jungian exploration of the human psyche that had been proposed so passionately by Robert Donington in his *Wagner's 'Ring' and Its Symbols* (1963).

Whereas the political horizons of Wieland's Bayreuth were very much those of West Germany's burgeoning capitalist economy, those of East Germany (a separate state until 1990) were turned towards Russia. Its strategy for distancing the recent past was, somewhat surprisingly, to resurrect the patently political Wagner of the early 1850s. Leaning on the Fabian socialism of Bernard Shaw, directors could present the *Ring* as a parable of the evils of nineteenth-century capitalism. Because of the relatively isolated situation of East Germany, Joachim Herz's brilliant Leipzig production of 1973–6 had far less influence than it deserved, and such was the political antagonism between the two Germanies at the time that it was either ignored or disparaged in the western part of the country.

By this time Bayreuth itself was ripe for more down-to-earth *actualité* in production style. Wieland's proposal of a psychological and mystical Wagner had done its work in laying the most immediately clamorous ghosts. Thirty years had passed since the war. It was time for Wolfgang Wagner to reaffirm the internationalist flag rung up by the festival in 1951 and make his grandfather's long overdue peace with the French for him by handing over the centennial *Ring* – no less – to conductor

Pierre Boulez, director Patrice Chéreau and designer Richard Peduzzi. This was a shrewd move for a great many reasons, not least because the bridge that the production built between the *Ring* as a critical expression of the mid nineteenth century and the polluted modern world of late capitalism (the Rhine dammed, Siegfried in a smoking jacket) would be seen as a piece of French rather than German iconoclasm. Highly controversial at first, it became hugely successful and because it had happened at Bayreuth gave licence to a whole new wave of 'politically relevant' stagings. Ill-informed conservative critics regarded it as reprehensibly Marxist, but what they were really objecting to was the fact that, like Herz's production, it had approached the political and ideological content of Wagner's work with a seriousness that the composer himself would have been the first to applaud. The 1976 Boulez-Chéreau *Ring* has been perhaps the last production to have generated such widespread interest (not least as a result of its filming for television and video) and such a wealth of published comment and discussion as to rank among the very greatest of landmark Wagner stagings.

I have chosen to conclude with two directors who, in their very different ways, have explored frontiers that have yet to be fully mapped. The first is Ruth Berghaus, an East German Marxist much of whose best work was done at Frankfurt, financial capital of West Germany's capitalist economy. Her stagings of *Parsifal* (Frankfurt 1982), the *Ring* (Frankfurt 1985–7) and *Tristan* (Hamburg 1988) destabilized the previously dominant notion that production should primarily be about telling the story of the opera.

In the spirit of Roland Barthes, she assumed an emancipation of the opera from the composer and his intentions. She argued that as Wagner's words and music were the bedrock of any performance, there were other things for a stage director to do than mimic or illustrate them. She believed that few works were so in thrall to their history as Wagner's, and that their reinvigoration therefore required an extremity of separation between past and present.

She left you in no doubt that the gods in the *Ring* were a despicable bunch and that the forces ranged against them were scarcely preferable. By the 1980s this idea was not new, even if her sense of comedy, of teasing the stupendous work to see how it might respond, certainly was. Scenes were often put across as an almost comical subversion of the high seriousness of the Wagnerian oeuvre. But this was never antagonistic, only rich in performing possibilities that no one else had yet discovered.

Berghaus marked the end of the era in which producers believed that their job was to make sense of the *Ring*. She inaugurated a new one in which many think this is simply no longer possible, so great is the discrepancy between Wagner's aim of creating a unified work of art and the tetralogy with all its fault lines, that he eventually completed.

Berghaus died in 1996. It was a tragic loss that a fire at the Frankfurt Opera destroyed the scenery of her *Ring* before it could be commercially filmed or seen more widely. Her work was a 'goodbye to all that', a gesture of dislocation and disavowal of a past that to the Germany of the second half of the twentieth century was as moribund as her Grail community, its 'redemption' no more than an illusion. She raises, irrevocably, the question whether a romantic Wagner can ever again be revived.

Chéreau and Berghaus have had a massive influence on the post-modern party that has followed them and are a key to unlocking some, at least, of its mysteries. Theatres all over the world, but especially in Germany, have vied with one another in uninhibited experiment, much of it not just critical but antagonistic towards the operas and the better part of their performing history. Some of it has created great theatre, true to Wagner's own restlessly regenerative spirit. I believe, though, that it is too early to discern intelligible patterns in the greater part of this work, and it is for this reason that I have chosen not to attempt to discuss it here.

As my own furthest frontier I have taken Hans Jürgen Syberberg's 1982 film of *Parsifal*, the greatest, if also the strangest, film version yet of a complete Wagner opera. It was made to a pre-recorded sound track, with some singers also performing on camera while other roles are mimed by actors. Where Berghaus had taken Wagner out of historical context, Syberberg resurrected the ghosts in order to square up to them. He believed he had to rescue Wagner from what he maintained were the 'degradations of theatre' and create a new life for him in film, the pre-eminent art form of the twentieth century.

His *Parsifal* emerged from a series of previous films – on Ludwig II, on Karl May (whose hugely popular Wild West stories were a passion of Hitler's), on the Führer himself and on Winifred Wagner – in which Syberberg had quixotically sought to elucidate, and to exorcize, the Third Reich's debasement, by appropriation, of the great romantic peaks of German culture. He identifies the sins and wounds of Klingsor, Kundry and Amfortas with those of Wagner himself, but no less of the Germany that gave rise to Hitler and that later would not take the proper steps to bury him.

Parsifal would be reborn as a reflection of the opera's relationship with its creator and with history. Syberberg turns his back on forest, temple and meadow, locating the action on, and sometimes inside, a huge studio model of the composer's death-mask. Plaster-cast heads of Aeschylus, King Ludwig, Nietzsche, Marx and the composer himself lie at Klingsor's feet as he sits on his gilded throne high on the brow of Wagner's forehead. Up to the crucial episode of the kiss between Parsifal and Kundry in Act II, the hero is a shock-headed youth, but thereafter – in the film's most arresting and puzzling idea – the role is taken over by a solemn warrior-maiden. At the end the boy and the girl are reunited, providing what Syberberg holds to be a resolution of the split consciousness represented by the two Parsifals.

Set alongside the focused political allegory of a Herz, the naked theatricality of a Chéreau, or the probing deconstruction of a Berghaus, Syberberg's film is disconcertingly regressive in its amalgam of 'innocent' storytelling, psycho-surreal invention, and parade of imagery about Wagner's entanglement with German history. It remains an unforgettable view of the composer's valedictory work in the light of its cultural and political repercussions across the first hundred years of its afterlife. It found ways of saying the unsayable about Wagner that have but rarely been equalled elsewhere. But it stands as an isolated achievement, awaiting the day when someone will pick up its challenge and once again interpret Wagner as brilliantly on film as he has been in the theatre.

PART I

CHAPTER 1

Wagner and the theatre of the early nineteenth century

The first regisseur

In 1885, two years after the composer's death, the Viennese critic Eduard Hanslick called Wagner 'the world's first regisseur', meaning what we would now call 'producer' or 'stage director'.[1] Hanslick's comment acknowledged that Wagner had made an impact on the theatre of his day extending far beyond his achievement as a composer and musical dramatist. The stage presentation of his operas had been an integral part of their conception, and the composer had passionately concerned himself with every detail of it. Characteristically he had chosen to produce his operas, leaving the conducting to others. He trusted no one but himself to get the staging right. Even if he was never satisfied with what he achieved in this direction, his insistence that singing, acting, design and movement had to be coordinated has shaped the subsequent course of opera and its resonance has been felt throughout the western theatre world. He can be praised, or blamed, for helping to invent the 'art of the director'. It is hard to make sense of the extraordinary diversity of modern opera production without recognizing Wagner as arguably its most important founding father.

In the early nineteenth century everyone understood that the director's job, whether this was undertaken by a stage manager, principal performer, librettist, composer, or whoever, was essentially to ensure the faithful execution of the stage instructions. Wagner himself generally departed from his stage instructions only when they specified something that proved technically unrealizable. This attitude was in notable contrast to the free-and-easy approach generally adopted in relation to the composer's score, which was usually cut and adapted to suit local circumstances and the singers. Arias were transposed or cut and new ones inserted – practices to which Wagner himself often contributed in his early years in the theatre. Today, the situation is reversed: the musical score is regarded as – relatively – sacrosanct, while the stage instructions are often but a point of departure for the producer's own invention.

In the early nineteenth century in Germany an 'Opernregisseur' was a lowly stage manager who arranged exits and entrances, marshalled the chorus and choreographed the ballet. Most of the preparation went into the music, and the

Kapellmeister, or conductor, exercised overall control of the staging. Once the singers had learned their roles, the little stage-rehearsal time that was allowed was given over to blocking the action and sorting out the exits and entrances. Scenery and costumes were usually chosen from stock items that saw service in any number of operas and ballets; only very rarely were they produced specially. The effects achievable with gas lighting were strictly limited and required little rehearsal. Only for exceptional repertory in the larger theatres, such as those in Paris and Berlin, where there was both the taste for lavish productions and the means of producing them, was much time available for technical rehearsal. 'Rehearsal', in the sense of a director's intensive work with the singers on characterization, acting and ensemble, was unheard of.

To Wagner's frustration, theatres in Germany and Austria were a long way behind Paris in the attention paid to stage production. It was partly for this reason, on top of the musical difficulties, that the Vienna Court Opera had in April 1863, after seventy-seven rehearsals, been defeated in its attempt to give the world premiere of *Tristan*. The gravely disappointed Wagner compared the theatre's rudimentary procedures unfavourably with those of the Paris Opéra. In an essay advising Vienna how to improve matters in the new theatre already under construction (it was to open in 1869), Wagner urged the adoption of Parisian practice. There, he pointed out, production responsibility was shared between the 'chef du chant' (chief repetiteur), the 'chef d'orchestre' and the 'regisseur', all three working to bring the musical, scenic and production aspects together.[2]

Some ten years earlier Wagner had already spelt out what he took to be the duties of the regisseur, his first advice being that he should begin (as was by no means usual practice) by studying the score: 'Most of the scenic instructions are to be found in the score at the corresponding musical cues, and with the help of the conductor the regisseur should get to know these cues quite precisely.' His other duties were to include instructing the scenic artist and holding a full 'reading rehearsal' (*Leseprobe*) attended by the singers, together with the conductor and chorus director. This *Leseprobe* was to be not just a read-through of the text but a fully animated rehearsal. The purpose of the orchestral and stage rehearsals was to bring the singing, acting and scenic technology into one accord with the orchestral contribution.[3] The whole of this prescription amounts to exactly what Wagner was to attempt at Bayreuth in 1876: the bringing together of *all* the elements.

His stage reforms, radical though they were in their time, did not spring out of the blue. If primarily a response to the needs of his own works, they were also an attack on the dominant stage practice of his time. This was basically one of grandiose divertissement, of furnishing decoration as a picturesque setting within which non-acting singers could amaze and delight. Others before Wagner had seen that this was not enough and had striven to secure stagings that would do justice to the dramatic potential of opera, and most particularly of 'serious' opera. Frederick the Great's opera adviser Francesco Algarotti had argued in his *Saggio sopra l'opera in musica* (1755) for due importance to be given to all the elements of opera and not just its vocal and musical substance. In his dedicatory preface to *Alceste* (1769), Gluck had urged the importance of words and of integrated dramatic expression as a counterblast to the prevailing 'vocal concert in costume' expectations of opera. In France the philosophes, Diderot prominent among them, had hotly debated the relative claims of words and music in the delineation of the drama. Meanwhile, opera's progress from a courtly entertainment for the privileged few to a more public and commercial enterprise had intensified an innate disposition towards the spectacular, towards any and every kind of scenic marvel that would draw in the public.

Spectacular scenery had of course been an essential ingredient in opera from its earliest beginnings in the seventeenth century, and more will be said about this shortly. But from the time of the French Revolution the cultivation of the spectacular entered a new phase in Paris. Composers, librettists and managements had become more and more resourceful in the invention of such episodes as erupting volcanoes, avalanches, storms and every kind of conflagration. These were integrated into the musical drama with varying degrees of success. The technical means of achieving such effects were, by our standards, rudimentary: the flying in and out of painted drops and flats, the use of trapdoors, and such modest variations in lighting as candlepower allowed. In their time they were extraordinary and were applauded as such. The zenith of such endeavours was the Paris Opéra around 1830, where Halévy, Meyerbeer and their colleagues wrote works exploiting the highly developed expertise of engineers and stage technicians. As we shall see, Wagner was to find this kind of theatre both an anathema and an inspiration.

Parallel developments on the German stage were in sober contrast. Its principal concern was the realization of Gluck's ideal of focused, coherent dramatic expression. The crucial innovator was to be Carl Maria von Weber, who from 1817 built up a German opera company in Dresden alongside a much better established Italian one. It was Weber who started the practice of beginning rehearsals for a new work with a *Leseprobe*, with himself as principal performer. He 'would read the text to the assembled cast, explaining details and points of meaning, and acting out the drama so vividly that at the Vienna rehearsals of *Euryanthe* he was jokingly offered a permanent job by the impressed stage manager'.[4]

It was indeed the case that the responsibility for all aspects of stage presentation lay with the stage manager, the composer concentrating primarily on securing the best possible musical performance. Weber's concern, on which Wagner was to build, was that the scenic demands of his score were faithfully realized and that they were not betrayed by the vanity of performers or the decorative values espoused by impresarios and stage managers. Weber was to die before being able to consolidate his reforms. But he bequeathed a theatrical ideal that was to inspire Wagner to attempt its fulfilment.

To do so, Wagner concerned himself with every detail of stage presentation, and this frequently brought him into collision with those whose business it had traditionally been. The authority implicit in a composer directing his own works for the stage inevitably supplanted that of a stage manager. And because Wagner's ideas about staging were an integral part of the fabric of the work and not a cosmetic varnish, his was not a task that could be undertaken by anyone else. Most important of all, it was an initiative rooted in the performer, of whom were demanded vocal characterization and acting skills that had largely been regarded as optional extras. As much as anything, it was Wagner's gift for coaxing totally committed vocal and physical performances from his singers that earned him Hanslick's description.

Theatre life in Germany in the 1820s

Wagner's reforms have been so successfully assimilated into accepted modern theatre practice that one can easily lose sight of how radical his ideas were in his time and how hard he had to fight for them. They need to be understood against the background of the theatre world in which he grew up.

If ever a composer was born into a theatrical milieu it was Richard Wagner. His father, Carl Friedrich (1770–1813), by profession a lawyer and civil servant, was an amateur actor by avocation. The Wagner home was very near the Leipzig Theatre, of which Carl Friedrich was a dedicated supporter. He named his five daughters after heroines in Goethe and Schiller. Rosalie (1803–37), who was to have an important career in Leipzig and with the Dresden Court Theatre, and Luise (1805–72) were actresses; Clara (1807–75) was briefly an opera singer, Maria Theresia (1809–14) died in infancy, while Ottilie (1811–83), to whom Richard confided his earliest dramatic efforts, abjured the stage in favour of marriage to the philologist Hermann Brockhaus. The eldest son, Albert (1799–1874), was a high tenor who was later active as a stage manager. As a member of the Würzburg Theatre company he was to secure for Richard, the youngest of the family, his first job as a repetiteur and chorus master in that same company in 1833. Albert's adopted daughter Johanna (1826–94) was to have a notable career as a singer, creating the role of Elisabeth in *Tannhäuser*.

Wagner's father died six months after Richard's birth on 22 May 1813. It was to his stepfather, the actor, dramatist and portrait painter Ludwig Geyer (1779–1821), whom his mother Johanna Rosine (1774–1848) married on 28 August 1814, that he owed his earliest experience of the theatre. The family had moved to Dresden in 1814 where Geyer had joined the Court Theatre as a character actor: he was later to smuggle his young stepson into rehearsals, and soon Richard too found himself on the stage. By his own account, he became 'a juvenile spectator from the concealed loge with its entrance from the stage'. Wagner recalled not only 'visits to the wardrobe with its fantastic costumes and all the paraphernalia of illusion' but also

> taking part in performances myself. After being terrified by *The Orphan and the Murderer* and *The Two Galley Slaves* and similar horrific works, in which I saw my father play the villains, I was obliged to appear in some comedies. In an occasional piece entitled *The Vineyard on the Elbe*, written to welcome the King of Saxony upon his return from captivity, with music by Kapellmeister Carl Maria von Weber, I recall figuring in a tableau vivant as an angel, entirely sewn up in tights and with wings on my back, in a graceful, though laboriously learned, pose.

He would have been just four and a half, the actual part not that of an angel but of Cupid. Aged seven he was to make two further appearances on the Dresden stage in

September 1820: as the boy Wilhelm in August von Kotzebue's play *Menschenhaβ und Reue* (Misanthropy and Repentance), and as one of Wilhelm Tell's two children in Schiller's drama, the other being played by his sister Clara. Their stepfather Geyer took the role of the Austrian tyrant, Geβler.[5]

Weber, who, as we have seen, had been director of the German opera in Dresden since 1817, was a regular visitor to the Geyer home. He brought *Der Freischütz* to Dresden in 1822, the year after its Berlin premiere. The eight-year-old Wagner had a model theatre in his room and immediately set about his own staging: 'It was – naturally – the scene in the wolf's-glen that the boy felt was most suitable. So out came the papier-mâché and the glue in order to produce the necessary equipment. His school-friends had to join in the work. Scenery and curtains, fireworks and animals – everything was produced.' Wagner's stepsister, Cäcilie Geyer (1815–93), 'particularly admired a great boar, which was rolled in on a plank looking with its fearful tusks horribly like the Prince of Hell in Person'.[6]

German theatre in the 1820s was unlike anything we should recognize today. Every town of any size considered it a matter of pride and duty that theatre and opera should provide both entertainment and moral sustenance. There were four principal kinds of theatre organization:

1 Troupes of touring players, similiar to those so memorably described in Goethe's *Wilhelm Meister*. Heinrich Bethmann's Magdeburg-based company, with which Wagner was to make his debut as a music director conducting *Don Giovanni* in the summer resort of Bad Lauchstädt in Thuringia in 1834, was of this kind.
2 Semi-permanent and occasionally permanent companies in municipal theatres, such as that in Wagner's home town of Leipzig. These companies were often ultimately responsible to the local princely or ducal court.
3 Small court theatres run by the potentate expressly for his court, and to which the public was sometimes, on strict conditions, admitted. No public criticism of the performances (in the press, etc.) was permitted. The Weimar Theatre where Liszt gave so many important early performances of Wagner's works, including the premiere of *Lohengrin* in 1850, was of this kind.
4 Large court theatres, such as that in Berlin. The provision of opera at these theatres, including that at Dresden, was usually entrusted to an Italian impresario.

Most smaller German theatres put on a mixed fare including tragedies and comedies, serious and frivolous opera, quasi-improvised entertainments and ballets. Vocal training in Germany, by contrast with that in Italy, was rudimentary and often non-existent. Singers were generally expected to take part in plays, while actors were expected to be able to swell the opera chorus and take singing roles.

Because theatres served relatively small populations they had to put on huge repertories in order to keep the public coming. The most frequently performed plays included those of Goethe and Schiller, and of Shakespeare in the brilliant Schlegel-Tieck verse translations (1825–33). Opera was essentially Italian, with Gluck and Mozart much in demand. German opera was far less prominent, its most popular works still largely in the Singspiel genre of musical numbers interspersed with spoken dialogue: Mozart's *Die Entführung* (1782) and *Die Zauberflöte* (1791), Beethoven's *Fidelio* (1804–14), several works by Schubert, Spohr's *Faust* (1816) and *Jessonda* (1823), and Hoffmann's *Undine* (1816). In the 1820s, Weber, and later Marschner, took important steps towards through-composed German romantic opera with *Der Freischütz* (1821), *Euryanthe* (1823), *Der Vampyr* (1828), *Der Templer und die Jüdin* (1829) and *Hans Heiling* (1833).

The grand operas that were developed from the 1820s on in Paris were the talk of Europe but in Germany could be mounted by only a very few of the larger theatres. Elsewhere the fare was provincial and wondrously variable. In opera, texts and music were cut about to suit virtuoso performers, local taste and circumstance. The singer was prime, the musical experience came next, with decor and acting a long way behind. Stage-rehearsal time was kept to the bare minimum and interest in presenting a unified, integral drama was minimal or non-existent.

The forces deployed were abysmally inadequate to the works essayed. This was particularly noticeable in opera. An orchestra of around thirty (at best), a chorus of no more than a handful and soloists drawn from a stalwart corps of actor-singers thought nothing of pitting themselves against the demands of *Don Giovanni* or romantic operas from the French repertory. It was no wonder that when it came to opera most courts vastly preferred Italian repertory sung by Italians. The cause of native, German-language opera had its supporters among the public at large but was a hard corner for composers like Spohr, Weber, Marschner and Wagner to fight on their home ground. Such performances as they secured could not – at least in this early period – have begun to do justice to conceptions that demanded very much more than melodious music beautifully sung and tactfully accompanied.

Up to 1817, the Leipzig and Dresden theatres which were to give Wagner his earliest experiences of plays and opera were served by touring companies, which often alternated between the two cities. In Leipzig, this touring system came to an end when the impresario Karl Theodor von Küstner founded a new resident opera company. Under Küstner's direction (1817–28) the Theater am Rannstädter Tor (generally known as 'Koch's Theatre', built in 1766 and seating twelve hundred) concentrated on the performance of romantic opera. It nurtured the growth of German works by Weber, Spohr and Marschner (who was artistic director of the company from 1827 to 1831) and also by Albert Lortzing (originally engaged as an actor and singer), eight of whose operas (including *Zar und Zimmermann*, 1837, *Hans Sachs*, 1840, and *Der Wildschütz*, 1842) had their premieres there. In 1850 it gave the first performance of Schumann's *Genoveva*. *Tannhäuser* and *Lohengrin* eventually arrived in the city of their composer's birth in 1853 and 1854.

When Küstner took over in 1817 the orchestra and chorus numbered twenty-seven and twenty respectively; by 1830 he had built them up to thirty-three and thirty, at which time he felt able to affirm that they were 'both as complete as one finds them in the best Court theatres'.[7] With these forces he tackled a repertory which included Gluck, Dittersdorf, Winter, Mozart, Weigl, Beethoven, Spohr, Weber, Marschner, Paisiello, Cimarosa, Cherubini, Spontini, Rossini, Grétry, Boieldieu,

Hérold and Auber. Between August 1817 and December 1818 he reports giving 374 performances of 114 works (plays, operas, ballets). In 1819 he gave 220 perform-ances of 117 works, and in 1826, 283 performances of 137 works. Küstner was not over-sanguine about such productivity; he believed that most theatres took on far too much and argued that those in smaller towns should give opera a miss and tackle only plays.[8]

Glimpses of the performer's-eye view are given by the actor Emil Devrient, who records that in the course of eleven months in Bremen in 1822 he took part in 147 performances, learning ninety-eight roles, twenty of which were operatic, and by Eduard Genast, who was engaged in the dual capacity of actor and first baritone at the Leipzig Theatre from about 1823. In his memoirs Genast makes it clear just how scarce good German singers were; for this reason actors were not generally engaged unless they could also sing in the opera chorus or take small singing roles.[9] He him-self went on to sing Don Giovanni and Caspar (in *Der Freischütz*) with Weber in Dresden. Later still, in Weimar, he took deep bass parts like that of Sarastro and, after the death of the company's first tenor Carl Moltke, somewhat improbably (if he is to be believed), even allowing for the drastic transpositions that were commonplace, the tenor role of Masaniello in Auber's *La Muette de Portici*![10]

It was therefore with good reason that, as we shall see, Weber was to complain that German singers were unlikely to excel as long as they were simultaneously expected to be all-purpose actors. Passing through Prague in 1823 on his way to Vienna to produce *Euryanthe*, Weber attended a German-language *Don Giovanni* of which he remarked, 'voices like threads … and acting that was pitiable'.[11] From 1828 economic difficulties at the Leipzig Theatre necessitated a return to performances by guest companies, including that of the Court Theatre in Magdeburg. From 1829 the Leipzig Theatre became an outpost of the Dresden Court Theatre.

German opera: Weber's company in Dresden, 1817–1826

The Dresden Theatre that the young Wagner knew had been dominated until 1817 by an Italian opera troupe directed by Francesco Morlacchi. Wagner was more excited by the complementary German company established in that year by Weber, who from 1813 to 1816 had directed and reorganized the German opera company in Prague. Under Weber the Dresden German opera rapidly became the most impor-tant company of its kind in Germany, advancing the cause of vernacular opera with performances of such works as Mozart's *Die Zauberflöte*, Beethoven's *Fidelio*, Spohr's *Jessonda* and, not least, Weber's own works, *Der Freischütz* and *Euryanthe* . Between 1822 and 1826 (the year of Weber's death), 68 per cent of premieres were of German works.[12]

In 1816 Weber had defined the German ideal as 'a self-sufficient work of art in which every feature and every contribution of the related arts are moulded together in a certain way and dissolve to form a new world'.[13] And on his Dresden appoint-ment the following year Weber published a declaration of his aims addressed 'To the Art-Loving Citizens of Dresden':

… whereas other nations concern themselves chiefly with the sensuous satisfaction of isolated moments, the German demands a self-sufficient work of art, in which all the arts make up a beautiful and unified whole.

This being the case, the present writer believes that the formation of a good ensemble is of the first importance. If an artistic production is not marred by any alien elements, it has already achieved something very valuable, namely the impression of unity. This can only be brought about by enthusiasm, devotion and the correct use of all the elements concerned.[14]

Weber set about fulfilling this programme. Composers' scores were no longer to be hacked about to serve the needs of the moment but had to be accorded a measure of respect. (Weber himself was by no means above sanctioning changes to increase a work's acceptability, particularly in the adaptation of comic opera to German taste – French and Italian works performed by the German opera company were always given in German.) Grétry's *Raoul Barbe-bleu* – the very first opera seen by Wagner, then aged five – was given with musical revision by Anton Fischer which, said Weber, 'brings the work more into line with the musical ideals of the present day, yet without prejudice to the character of Grétry's music'.[15] Nevertheless, such changes as Weber was prepared to countenance may be regarded as fidelity itself compared with the wholesale adaptations that were the order of the day.

As we have seen, Weber instigated intensive rehearsals in which new attention was paid to the text, and he encouraged singers to live rather than simply sing their characters. In a memorandum submitted in May 1817 to Count Vitzthum, an influential supporter at court, he campaigned against the use of dual-purpose actor-singers: 'the use of the organs of speech is directly harmful to those required for singing … it is a great relief to the singer to be able, as in the case of Italian works, to sing throughout'.[16]

Weber animated the chorus (who had previously either stood in lines or in a semi-circle) and 'took up the Dresden fondness for including set tableaux and made them a structural feature of his productions, conceiving them as part of the design to heighten the text at certain points instead of purely as decorative visual groupings for their own sake'.[17] He argued for the appointment of a dancing master 'responsible for training every member of the company, without exception, in the rudiments of dance and mime, for individual scenes in particular and more generally for effective grouping on the stage'.[18] Not all Weber's requests were met, but he was able to achieve a great deal. In 1821 he replaced the old machinery at the Dresden Court Theatre, and also the oil and candle lighting. He installed the best lighting then available – Argand oil lamps (invented 1780–4 by Amie Argand, a Swiss chemist) which used a glass chimney to give a smokeless clear flame of greater brightness than anything previously available. He saw his decor 'as mobile painting, playing a similarly precise expressive function, not merely as naturalistic furnishing'.[19]

Weber's approach to his singers showed a similar concern for drama. He numbered among his most valued performers the great singing actress Wilhelmine Schröder-Devrient, who in 1822 had sung Leonore in *Fidelio* in Vienna, chilling the audience by speaking rather than singing the great cry 'First kill his wife!' (Töt' erst sein Weib!)[20] Weber rated Schröder-Devrient the best of all Agathes in *Der Freischütz*, considering her 'to have outstripped all he thought he had put into the part'. As a Lieder singer she caused Goethe to revise his unfavourable view of Schubert's 'Erlkönig'. In Schumann's opinion she was the only singer who could survive with Liszt as accompanist.[21] Although certain Dresden critics censured her for 'a breach of good manners when she was seen to be actually weeping on the stage', it was precisely this intense commitment to a role which stirred Weber and the young Wagner.[22] There is little cause to doubt Wagner's assertion that Schröder-Devrient played a central role in staking out his destiny. Characteristically, he tried to pretend that his decisive experience of Schröder-Devrient was her Leonore in Leipzig in 1829: 'When I look back across my entire life I find no event to place beside this in the impression it produced on me. Whoever can remember this wonderful woman at that period of her life will certainly confirm in some fashion the almost demonic fire irresistibly kindled in them by the profoundly human and ecstatic performance of this incomparable artist'.[23]

But although there is no question of the profound effect she had on him, Wagner could not have heard Schröder-Devrient in *Fidelio* in Leipzig until December 1832. He wants us to believe that it was her performance in a *German* opera that first swept him off his feet, whereas it was her Romeo in Bellini's *I Capuleti e i Montecchi*, given as *Romeo und Julia* in Leipzig in 1834, that actually did so. He met her for the first time in Magdeburg the following year, when he conducted her in a performance of the Bellini of which the *Magdeburger Zeitung* wrote, 'when Romeo gives way to his

Primal inspiration. Wilhelmine Schröder-Devrient as Leonore in *Fidelio*. She had created a huge stir in this role in 1822 when she chose not to sing but defiantly to declaim the great cry, 'First kill his wife!' (Töt' erst sein Weib!). Her exceptional qualities as a singing actress helped confirm Wagner's intuition that opera should be a total theatrical experience.

grief beside the bier … she scaled heights which, we may say, have been reached by no other singer who has appeared here over the years: her grief was truly sublime, the tone that is hers to command did not have to be invented, given the nobility of her physical appearance'.[24]

Schröder-Devrient's heart-and-soul characterizations suggested new possibilities of stage performance and consequently of dramatic works. Wagner's dedication to finding and training singers who were prepared to act with their bodies as well as their voices may be traced directly to his experience of Schröder-Devrient. One has the feeling that her impact must have been the equivalent, in his day, of Maria Callas's in our own.

Wagner's theatrical apprenticeship

At Christmas 1827, when Wagner was fourteen, the family resettled in Leipzig, where he attended the Nikolai-Gymnasium and began to sketch a grotesque revenge tragedy, *Leubald*, whose hero he described as 'a mixture of Hamlet and Hotspur'.[25] He saturated himself in the plays and operas in the repertory of the Leipzig Theatre, which his actress sister Rosalie was to join on its reopening in 1829. '*Julius Caesar, Macbeth, Hamlet*, Schiller's plays, and at last Goethe's *Faust*, all excited and enthused me deeply. The opera was giving the first performances of Marschner's *Vampyr* [1828] and *Templer und Jüdin* [1829]. The Italian opera company arrived from Dresden and delighted the Leipzig audiences with its virtuosity'.[26] Wagner studied music at Leipzig University and at the Thomasschule, while pouring out a flood of youthful compositions. In late summer 1832 he spent four weeks in Vienna and discovered the fantastical comedies of Raimund, the outstanding comic actor of his time. In November he travelled to Prague where he attended the first performance of his Symphony in C and wrote the text for an (uncompleted) opera, *Die Hochzeit*. Back in Leipzig, his sister Rosalie's unfavourable reaction to *Die Hochzeit* prompted him to tear it up, but by the end of January 1833 he had written the text of *Die Feen*, a fairy-tale opera based on Gozzi and owing much to Weber, which was fully composed by early the following year, though never staged in his lifetime.

Meanwhile his brother Albert, then engaged as singer and stage manager in the Würzburg Theatre, secured Richard a post there as chorus master, thus beginning the years of his theatrical apprenticeship in provincial German opera houses, his duties swiftly increasing in responsibility from those of chorus master to musical director – Würzburg (chorus master, January 1833), Magdeburg (musical director, summer 1834), Königsberg (conductor, becoming musical director in April 1837) and Riga (musical director, September 1837).

As we have seen, in most German theatres opera was performed alongside plays and ballets. Thus in Würzburg Wagner's activities stretched beyond his choral duties to taking speaking parts in plays and to swelling mime groups in the ballet. The chorus under his charge numbered fifteen. In the course of Wagner's first three and a half months this modest provincial theatre put on a repertory that included Weber's *Der Freischütz* and *Oberon*, Auber's *La Muette de Portici* and *Fra Diavolo*,

Rossini's *Tancredi*, Cherubini's *Les Deux Journées*, Beethoven's *Fidelio*, Paer's *Camilla* and Hérold's *Zampa*.[27] By Wagner's own account the season also included Marschner's *Vampyr* and concluded with Meyerbeer's massive *Robert le diable*, premiered in Paris only two years before.[28]

A projected staging of *Die Feen* in Leipzig was aborted when, according to Wagner, he rejected the theatre's proposal that the sets and costumes should be drawn from its stock of oriental material: 'I fought against the insufferable turban and kaftan costumes and demanded energetically the knightly garb typifying the earliest period of the middle ages'.[29] Here we have a good example of Wagner's insistence that every detail of a work's stage presentation should be true to its composer's conception.

In 1834 he was appointed music director of a Magdeburg-based theatre troupe run by Heinrich Bethmann. Wagner had made his debut with the company on its 1834 summer tour conducting *Don Giovanni* in a wooden theatre in Bad Lauchstädt that had been built in 1802 to a design by Goethe. In *My Life* Wagner speaks of 'establishing myself as a conductor in Magdeburg by thoughtless submission to frivolous theatrical tastes'.[30] The repertory included Rossini's *Otello* and *Il barbiere di Siviglia*, Gläser's *Des Adlers Horst*, Weber's *Preciosa*, *Der Freischütz* and *Oberon*, Auber's *Fra Diavolo* and *La Muette*, Paisiello's *La molinara*, Cherubini's *Les Deux Journées*, Marschner's *Der Templer und die Jüdin* and Bellini's *I Capuleti e i Montecchi*. Wagner's spirits were lifted in April 1835 when Schröder-Devrient joined the little company for guest performances as Romeo in Bellini's *I Capuleti*, Leonore in *Fidelio*, Desdemona in *Otello* and Agathe in *Der Freischütz*.[31]

The Magdeburg period saw the completion of Wagner's second opera, *Das Liebesverbot*, based on Shakespeare's *Measure for Measure*, which was a bid to capture a portion of the Italian high ground. The circumstances of the fiasco of its first performances give an all too credible picture of a typical small-town troupe grappling with a work whose ambition exceeded both its creator's ability and the means available for its execution. In *My Life* Wagner attributes a portion of the blame for the abandonment of the second and final performance to the management's failure to have libretti available (the audience was unable to make head or tail of the plot) and to a pre-performance scrap between rival singers. But the root cause was totally inadequate rehearsal. A period of ten days was the most that could be allowed, so it was scarcely surprising that, as Wagner recalled, the singers faced the first night ill-prepared: 'The tenor Freimüller, equipped with the feeblest memory, tried to supplement the lively and engaging character of his role as the madcap Luzio by resorting to routines adapted from *Fra Diavolo* and *Zampa*, and especially with the aid of an enormous thick, brightly coloured and fluttering plume of feathers.' Wagner had relied on the loyalty of his singers and his prowess on the podium to carry the day but, as he later admitted, 'As the work was by no means a light musical comedy but rather, despite the airy character of the music, a grand opera with many large and complex ensembles, this undertaking was close to foolhardy'.[32]

By the summer of 1836 Wagner was living in Berlin, where a performance of Spontini's *Fernand Cortez* under its composer showed him just how much could be achieved by a composer prepared to involve himself – as Spontini exceptionally did – in every aspect of production. Although the singers were not in the Schröder-Devrient league, 'the exceptionally precise, fiery and superbly organized way the whole work was brought off was entirely new to me. I gained a fresh insight into the inherent dignity of major theatrical undertakings, which in all their parts could be elevated by alert rhythmic control into a singular and incomparable form of art'.[33] No less important was the part played by this experience in the conception of *Rienzi*, the grand opera on which Wagner worked from 1837 to 1840. It was a work whose dramatic strategy (cumulative development of scenes, rather than concentration on individual numbers) was principally indebted to Gluck and Spontini, rather than to the virtuoso-number operas of Auber and Meyerbeer.[34] With it he hoped to win a breakthrough in Paris, centre of the operatic world.

After a few months as musical director in Königsberg (spring–summer 1837) he took up the same post in Riga, capital of Latvia, arriving on 21 August. There he found a manager bent on pleasing his public with the lighter French and Italian repertory and a primitive theatre little better than the temporary wooden summer theatre used by Bethmann's company in Lauchstädt. Wagner's biographer Carl Friedrich Glasenapp records being told by a Riga-born cellist, Arved Poorten, that he had met Wagner in St Petersburg in 1863 and had asked him how he was ever able to conduct in such a 'Scheune' (stable, or barn). Wagner had replied that three things had stuck in his memory about this 'barn': 'firstly the steep rising stalls, rather like an amphitheatre, secondly the darkness of the auditorium, and thirdly the surprisingly deep orchestra pit. If he ever succeeded in building a theatre to his own plans, he would have regard to these three features, and that was something he had *already decided on at the time*'.[35]

This account has to be treated with caution, partly because of the second-hand reportage and partly because of Wagner's tendency, scarcely unique to him, to adjust history to suit self-mythography. Plans of the 'Theater im Mussengebäude' as it was in 1837 show the stalls area as a conventional rectangle sloping at no more than five degrees (the Festspielhaus auditorium was to slope at fifteen degrees).[36] Wagner's impression of an amphitheatre-like configuration can only have been created by the two horseshoe-shaped upper tiers. The tiny orchestra pit was four feet below stage level and divided from the auditorium by a boarded balustrade. The fact that it extended about three feet on either side into the proscenium boxes may have contributed to Wagner's recollection of it as 'surprisingly deep'. There seems to be no question, however, that the candle-lit auditorium was relatively dark as compared with the oil lighting of the stage. The auditorium candles were in two-branched sconces on the balustrades fronting the upper tiers and on the rear walls of the boxes. Economy dictated that each sconce generally carried a single candle, blazing with two only on festive occasions. In truth, the layout and conditions in the Riga theatre were not exceptional for their time. Wagner's inspiration may as likely have been drawn from his experience of any number of similiar theatres in the 1830s and 1840s.

In the summer of 1839, Wagner, deep in debt, had to flee Riga to escape his creditors. But he had had the invaluable experience of rehearsing and conducting

168 performances of twenty-five operas in Riga, including Mozart's *Figaro*, *Don Giovanni* and *Zauberflöte*, Weber's *Freischütz*, *Oberon* and *Preciosa*, Bellini's *I Capuleti* and *Norma*, Spohr's *Jessonda*, Meyerbeer's *Robert le diable* and Méhul's *Joseph*.[37] He set out for Paris, travelling via London, to seek a performance of the still unfinished *Rienzi* and the patronage of Meyerbeer. Success in opera meant success in Paris and that was Wagner's goal.

The seductions of Parisian grand opera, 1839–1842

When Wagner arrived in Paris in September 1839, hoping to secure the premiere there of the only partially completed *Rienzi*, it was the undisputed capital of the theatrical world. In the spoken theatre this was the era of Victor Hugo, Alexandre Dumas *père*, Alfred de Vigny and Alfred de Musset. The repertory at the Opéra-Comique comprised largely Italianate works by composers who included Auber, Adam, Halévy, Thomas, Donizetti, Monpou, Grisar, Bazin, Massé and Clapisson. At the Théâtre Italien, Rossini, Bellini, Mercadante and Donizetti were the staple fare.

Wagner was generally disparaging about what was on offer at the Théâtre Italien and the Opéra-Comique, with their Italian singers and fashionable audiences: 'The productions of the Opéra-Comique, because of the characteristic coldness of the acting style as well as the degenerate quality of the music produced there, had repelled me from the start. The same coldness on the part of the singers also drove me away from the Italian Opera. . . . I preferred the little theatres in which the French talent showed itself to me in its true light.'[38] His own hopes were directed at the Opéra, and although they were to be dashed it was there that he discovered much that he was later to put to good use.

The Opéra, also known as the Académie Royale de Musique, had been housed since 1821 in the Salle Le Peletier, a specially built theatre designed by François Debret and seating nineteen hundred. It had been intended as no more than a temporary home, but the Opéra remained there until the theatre burnt down on 29 October 1873. It moved into the Palais Garnier that we know today in 1875.

Despite the July Revolution of 1830, the Opéra was essentially under the control of the government, which leased out its management. Its director (from 1831 to 1835), Louis Véron, was entirely successful in his aim of making the Opéra the Versailles of the victorious bourgeoisie. As the subject matter of the popular new operas showed, the Opéra played its part in a dynamic upsurge of ideas about liberalism, socialism, emancipation and progress which were sweeping through society. Véron carried no candle for musical and artistic values as such. He was an impresario who knew what his public wanted and knew how to give it to them. The shows he put on had to have the appeal of a present-day musical, and that meant an emphasis tilted towards epic grandeur, picturesque and sensational episodes, superstar singers and, at all times, a lavishly dressed stage. These were also the values of Véron's successors Charles Duponchel (1835–40) and Léon Pillet (1840–7). Duponchel was himself a stage designer, renowned as co-creator (with Ciceri) of one of the most influential coups

The auditorium of the Paris Opéra very much as Wagner would have known it in 1839 to 1842 when he was living in the city and working on *Rienzi* and *Der fliegende Holländer*. The lithograph by Jean-Baptiste Arnout shows, on the stage, the famous ballet of the nuns, risen as ghosts from their graves, in Meyerbeer's grand opera *Robert le diable*. The spectacular scenic effects for which the Opéra was famous left a profound impression on Wagner and he sought to emulate and surpass them in his own works.

de théâtre in the nineteenth century – the sepulchral cloister setting for the ballet of the ghostly nuns in Meyerbeer's grand opera *Robert le diable* (1831).

The grand opera genre, of which Meyerbeer's *Les Huguenots* (1836), with its five acts, is a notable example, was the particular speciality of the Paris Opéra. It was a very carefully planned concoction, its scenarios limited by government decree to subjects 'drawn from mythology or history; principal subjects are kings or heroes'.[39] These subjects were only partly reflections of audience taste, for they were also carefully controlled by the authorities to mould political opinion. The master architect of this circumscribed genre, in which 'grandeur' was also commanded by the Commission de Surveillance, was the librettist Eugène Scribe. For him the scenery was at least as important as the verbal and musical drama. Words, music, singing, processions, massed crowd scenes, religious ceremonies, executions, sunrises, revolutions, sunsets and ballet were combined to maximum spectacular effect. Wagner had conceived his *Rienzi* to this formula, thereby hoping to outdo Meyerbeer, Halévy and Auber on their own ground. It is therefore important to outline something of the genealogy of this genre which Wagner sought to emulate, many of whose theatrical elements carry right through into the works of his maturity.

Reaching its apogee in the 1830s and 1840s, grand opera had its roots in the operas which flourished during the French Revolution. A prodigious totality of music, drama and scenic spectacular is already apparent in Cherubini's *Lodoïska* (1791), in whose last act Viscount Palmerston saw an old castle 'burned and blown up upon the stage with an effect of fire beyond any representation I ever saw'.[40] In the same composer's *Eliza* (1794) the snow and ice of the St Bernard Pass were suggested by three-dimensional scenery, not just by painted effects on flats and drops, thus increasing the credibility of the heroine's hair's-breadth escape from an avalanche.

There was, of course, nothing particularly novel in this delight in stage spectacle for its own sake. From its birth at the dawn of the seventeenth century, opera had always courted spectacle and effect. The sources from which Baroque opera sprang include the Florentine intermedi of the late sixteenth century (lavish musical extravaganzas given between the acts of plays) and the masques devised by Inigo Jones for the Stuart court (1605–40). In such entertainments – whose function was as much emblematic and political as artistic – prodigal marvels of stage machinery, costumes and dancing were as important as the vocal and orchestral contributions.

In the Baroque theatre scenic effects were not achieved realistically. This was not a theatre of illusion (in which the means are carefully concealed), but a theatre of artifice, of stylization, symbol and visual shorthand. The cloud machines, monsters, angry seas, never pretended that they were anything but mechanical devices. The 'scenes' painted on the moveable flats and drops were idealized depictions of Arcadia, palaces, gardens, dungeons and the like. These were portrayed using the stylized conventions of eighteenth-century representation. The spectator applauded the means by which the effects were achieved – the scene changing before his eyes – quite as much as the effects themselves.

The auditorium was often illuminated as brightly as the stage – sometimes even more so. As late as 1817, a concerned chronicler of conditions in German theatres complained that at the Court Theatre in Kassel the auditorium lighting – paid for, as he noted, by the court – was far stronger than the sparse stage illumination, which was paid for by the theatre manager.[41] The spectators were themselves very much part of the show, as was the orchestra. There was no sense of an audience sitting as a collective mass in the dark in order to immerse itself in what we would now call an illusion of 'cinematic' veracity.

But in the course of the eighteenth century, as opera became more public and less aristocratically exclusive, it renounced the esoteric conventions of courtly opera – comprehensible only to a highly educated elite – in favour of subject matter and means of more directly visceral appeal. With the rise of romantic opera, from about the 1790s on, the sophisticated artifice that had ruled from the beginnings of opera around 1600 through to the Enlightenment was gradually replaced by the portrayal of human passions and narrative adventures in historical and 'natural' settings.

The operas of Cherubini, for instance, show an interest in floods, tempests, erupting volcanoes and avalanches not as neoplatonic symbols but as manifestations of nature to be as realistically presented as the theatre knew how. The aim now was not to cultivate the sensibility of the aristocratic connoisseur but to thrill the bourgeoisie with lifelike representations of natural phenomena and of distant times and exotic places.

Cherubini and his followers sought immediate points of contact with the revolutionary aspirations of their audiences, distancing themselves from mythological and

The machinists of the Paris Opéra excelled in the depiction of the elements and especially in that of fire. The engraving, from M. J. Moynet's *L'Envers du théâtre* (1874), is a backstage view of a typical conflagration. Firemen with hoses are prominently in attendance. They were very necessary. At the first performance of *Die Walküre* in Munich in 1870 the gas flames for the magic fire around Brünnhilde very nearly set the theatre alight.

allegorical subject matter and anything dependent on the privileged understanding of a courtly, ancien-régime audience. Thus comes about the birth of 'citizens' opera', of opera as a wondrous amalgam of theatrical art and technology, as a phenomenon of and for the age of industrialization.

The popularity of historical subject matter (usually with palpable significance for the hopes and fears of the times) was powerfully evident in Spontini's *La Vestale* (1807) and *Fernand Cortez* (1809), both of which were admired by Wagner. The formula was that of an inspirational historical subject, spiced with the sensational scenic effects that a rapidly evolving new technology allowed. Thus Etienne de Jouy (Spontini's librettist) specifies that the action of *La Vestale* should be set quite precisely in 269 BC. *Fernand Cortez* features not only the obligatory processions but a dive into a lake by the heroine and the destruction of an Aztec temple. De Jouy justified the deployment of seventeen horses on strictly historical grounds.

The mood of the July Revolution, which brought Louis-Philippe to the throne, was tellingly prefigured in Auber's *La Muette de Portici* (1828) – in which Fenella's death-leap from the palace walls is accompanied by the eruption of Vesuvius in the background – and in *Guillaume Tell* (1829), Rossini's epic retelling of Swiss liberation from tyranny. At the end of the opera the storm clears to reveal the sun lighting up the glaciers on the mountains across the lake. It was 'at once a force of nature and a political allegory'.[42] Wagner surely remembered this effect both musically and scenically when he came to write the finale of *Das Rheingold*.

What was prefigured in such works – which retained their place in the repertory for decades – came to extravagant fruition in the four grand operas of Meyerbeer – *Robert le diable* (1831), *Les Huguenots* (1836), *Le Prophète* (1849) and *L'Africaine* (1865). The subject of *Les Huguenots* was the massacre of the Huguenots by the Catholics on St Bartholomew's Day in Paris, 1572. The setting for Act II was a replica of the castle, gardens and lake at Chenonceaux. Contemporaries attributed a large part of the work's success to the veracity of its historical setting and local colour.[43] *Le Prophète* was concerned with John of Leyden's occupation of Münster, 1534–5, and Halévy's *La Juive* (1835) with the persecution of the Jews at the time of the Council of Constance, 1414–18. Charles Séchan, the designer of *La Juive*, made a special trip to Constance to research its fifteenth-century art and architecture.

The effects in these works were by no means without their causes. The celebrated scene in *Robert le diable* of the nuns rising from their graves to defend the magic bough in the cloister is an early instance of a ballet sequence being integral to the drama and not merely a divertissement. Such works were fully fledged 'total works of art', if not exactly in the sense that Wagner would later recognize.

In grand opera, stage presentation assumed an importance not seen since the masques and musical entertainments of the Renaissance. The grand operas of Auber, Halévy and Meyerbeer owed a sizeable measure of their success to the brilliance of the spectacular effects around which the works were cunningly and very deliberately crafted. That such effects were an integral part of the work and not just *ad libitum* window-dressing may be gathered from the detailed staging booklets (*livrets de mise-en-scène*) which were published from 1828 on (*La Muette*) for most important Opéra productions, many of which were revived over and over again, albeit with often quite substantial changes.[44] (By 1900 *La Juive* had clocked up some 500 performances in Paris alone. *Les Huguenots* achieved 100 performances by 1839, 500 by 1872 and 1,000 by 1900.[45] *Robert le diable* had 100 performances at the Opéra within three years of its premiere and by 1835 had been seen at 77 houses in ten countries.) The *livrets de mise-en-scène* were compiled for the guidance of other houses, asserting the importance of meeting the demands of the full scenographic menu.[46]

The very limited presence of these classics of the nineteenth century on the stage of today testifies to the part played in their success by the original staging conception. We now have the technology to realize such stage effects in a manner beyond the wildest dreams of those who invented them, but on the whole have neither the funds nor the aesthetic taste to do so.

Theatre technology, 1730–1830

The appetite for ever more realistic stage effects was inseparable from the rapid development in the means for their production. The technology which made possible the sunrises, sunsets, fires, floods and cataclysms of grand opera had its origin nearly a century earlier, not on the operatic stage but in the *spectacle d'optique* entertainments which began to be popular from as early as the 1730s. The founding father of such entertainments was Jean-Nicolas Servandoni (1695–1766), whose optical performances in a darkened auditorium (a great novelty, this) at the Salle des Machines, boasting the largest stage in Paris with its depth of 43 metres, were the talk of the town. His star attraction in 1738 was 'une représentation exacte' of the interior of St Peter's in Rome based on a painting by Pannini and illuminated by a large number of lamps. The next year Servandoni claimed to have ended his show *Pandore* with 'Tremblings of the Earth, Volcanoes, Rains of Fire, Collapsing Cliffs, Thunder, Lightning and all that might serve to represent a universal disorder'.[47] Even if Servandoni achieved something less than described in his billings, it was evidently a great deal, sufficing to ensure successful seasons for him at the Salle des Machines from 1738 to 1742, and again from 1754 to 1756.

The animation in such entertainments was created by shadow plays and 'théâtre méchanique', as at the opening of the Théâtre des Récréations de la Chine (1775), where 'on the white screen, illuminated from behind, one could see comic situations with dialogues and revue songs but also sunrises and moonlight over landscape views with a magical illusion'.[48] The popularity of these theatres of optical illusion gathered momentum on into the nineteenth century. Artists such as Philippe-Jacques de Loutherbourg (1740–1812) and Louis-Jacques-Mandé Daguerre (1789–1851) designed for them, and they became an irresistible force for change in the 'live' theatres.[49]

De Loutherbourg was a German painter who exhibited at the Louvre in the 1760s. He became scenic director at Drury Lane (1773–81) under both Garrick and Sheridan and was 'particularly successful in producing the illusion of fire, volcanoes, sun, moonlight and cloud-effects, and invented strikingly effective devices for thunder, guns, wind, the lapping of waves, and the patter of hail and rain. He was the first designer to bring a breath of naturalism into the artificial scenic conventions of the day, and paved the way for the realistic detail and local colour favoured by Charles Kemble'.[50] De Loutherbourg was among the very first to put the newly invented smokeless Argand lamp (1780) to use, as in his Eidophusikon (1781–93), a tiny theatre with a stage about 6 feet wide by 8 feet deep. It advertised 'various imitations of Natural Phenomena, represented by Moving Pictures'.[51] According to an eyewitness account of a demonstration of the Eidophusikon at a private house in London, 'De Loutherbourg excelled in representing the phenomena of clouds. The lamps were above the scene and hidden from the audience – a far better plan than the "footlights" of a theatre. Before the line of brilliant lamps on the stage of the Eidophusikon were slips of stained glass – yellow, red, green, purple, and blue; thereby representing different times of day, and giving a hue of cheerfulness, sublimity, or gloom, to the various scenes'.[52]

An immolation anticipating that of Brünnhilde in *Götterdämmerung*. In the climactic scene of Auber's *La Muette de Portici* (1828), Vesuvius (at the rear of the stage) erupts and the heroine Fenella, seen centre-stage momentarily collapsed on hearing the news of her brother's death, recovers, runs to the top of the steps and leaps into the flow of lava. The drawing by Godefroy Durand is of a new Paris production in 1863.

Daguerre is principally remembered today as the inventor of the 'Daguerreotype' process of image reproduction, a precursor of the photograph. But he was also a scenic artist whose work had a tremendous impact on the technical and aesthetic development of the theatre in the first half of the nineteenth century. In 1822 he opened in Paris his celebrated Diorama, an illusionist theatre that specialized in such displays as Vesuvius in eruption and whose machinists included a director of pyrotechnics. The Vesuvius eruption was transplanted, to sensational effect, from the Diorama to the Opéra in 1828 for the finale of Auber's *La Muette de Portici*. The Diorama was an auditorium on a turntable that could be moved to face two or even three separate proscenium openings, each about 4 metres high by 7 metres wide, framing separate displays. These consisted of backdrop paintings on transparent cloths or gauzes lit by moveable coloured filters. The paintings (c. 14 m × 22 m) were rendered transparent or non-transparent depending on the lighting. The changes in the light sources and use of coloured filters permitted such effects as a 'changing play of light over the interior of Canterbury Cathedral or the romantic alpine landscape'. In the cathedral display, 'clouds and mists drifted across the sky and, all of a sudden, sunrays would strike through the stained Gothic windows drawing a pattern across the church floor'.[53] Dioramas were also opened in Berlin and London. The effects they could achieve were widely copied in traditional theatres, as in London where they were much used at Drury Lane and Covent Garden.

Daguerre worked as a scenic artist at the Paris Opéra from 1819. To him is attributed the invention of the double-painted gauze, which discloses one or other of two different scenes depending on whether it is lit from the front or back. This was used to great effect in the stagings of *La Muette* and *Guillaume Tell*. His work at the Opéra, in conjunction with that of Pierre-Luc-Charles Ciceri (1782–1868), whose skill lay in 'scenes of snow, of misty valleys dominated by candles, and of huge palace walls', laid the foundation on which the nineteenth-century theatre of illusion was built. Daguerre threw out 'the old Italian system of wings, forming corridors and denying perspective, in favour of three-dimensional scenery and such effects as clouds moving across the new panorama he installed, trees that cast actual shadows, exact historical detail in sets and costumes and photographic accuracy in landscape'.[54]

Daguerre and Ciceri were in their element devising effects for Isouard and Benincori's *Aladin, ou La Lampe merveilleuse* (1822), a work specially commissioned to show off the gas lighting that had just been installed in the Salle Le Peletier. Electric-arc lighting was first used in Meyerbeer's *Le Prophète* (1849) to create the effect of a dazzling sunrise.[55]

Electricity was to revolutionize the stage production of opera. Shown here in an engraving from H. J. Moynet's *L'Envers du théâtre* (1874), carbon-arc lighting was first used at the Paris Opéra in 1849 for the sunrise which suddenly dispels the mists over the frozen lake in Act III of Meyerbeer's *Le Prophète*. Wagner may well have taken note of Jules Duboscq's use of arc lighting to throw a rainbow over the stage in Rossini's *Moïse* in Paris in 1860. The light was refracted through a prism. A similar effect was attempted, though none too successfully, for the rainbow bridge in *Das Rheingold* at Bayreuth in 1876.

Until the 1820s it was the more populist theatres and entertainment establishments that led the way in innovative stage technology and in carefully researched historical settings and costumes. But the Opéra could not afford to lag behind. In 1827 it created the new post of stage manager and a special committee charged with the coordination of music and staging and with exploitation of the latest scenic possibilities.[56] A direct result was that librettists like Scribe and composers like Meyerbeer made sure that their operas were a showcase for ingenious three-dimensional scene changes, magical visual effects, historical costumes, mime sequences, lighting effects and whatever else might be available. Meyerbeer delighted in writing technical innovations into his works, as, famously, when the newly invented roller skates which the composer had seen on the Parisian streets inspired the Act III 'Ballet des patineurs' (supposedly skating on a frozen lake) in *Le Prophète*. One can even see this aspect of grand opera as a throwback to the fondness of the Baroque for creating an entertainment around the effects achievable by the machinists.

The lasting influence of grand opera on Wagner

How, then, did Wagner's experiences of Parisian opera influence the development of his own kind of theatre? His experiences in the city were, in fact, far more fruitful than is usually reported and than he perhaps wished to remember. He later claimed that he did not go to the Opéra 'more than four times', but in fact he saw at least ten productions between 1839 and 1842 and was eager to learn from them.[57] He wrote enthusiastically about Auber and about Spontini, whom he invited to conduct *La Vestale* in Dresden in 1844.[58] His hack work to keep the wolf from the door included making the vocal score of Halévy's *La Reine de Chypre* (1841), about which he wrote appreciatively, as also about *La Juive*.[59] Years later Cosima recorded in her diary that Wagner still took 'pleasure in the great style of [*La Juive*]' and that he praised Halévy as 'the first musical genre-painter'.[60]

Although it is Wagner's hostility to Meyerbeer as expressed in *Judaism in Music* of 1850 and *Opera and Drama* of 1851 (motivated substantially by jealousy of his success) that is remembered, he takes a very much more positive view in an earlier piece, 'On Meyerbeer's *Huguenots*', dating from the period before 1840 when he was writing *Rienzi*.[61] In *My Life* Wagner has high praise for the orchestral playing and staging of *Les Huguenots* at the Opéra: 'The production of *Les Huguenots*, which I heard here for the first time, had dazzled me very much indeed; the beautiful orchestral playing and the extremely meticulous and effective staging gave me an enticing foretaste of the great resources inherent in such well-trained artistic means'.[62]

Many of the features of *Rienzi* testify to Wagner's close study of the classics of grand opera: 'In his freeing the Romans from the tyranny of the nobles, the popular tribune Rienzi reminds one of Masaniello, the revolutionary hero of Auber's *La Muette de Portici* (1828); his prayer in Act V takes as its model the prayer of Eléazar in Act II of Halévy's *La Juive* (1835), just as Rienzi's excommunication by the papal legate in Act IV is modelled on the curse of Cardinal Brogni in the same work, while the conspiracy of the nobili (Act V) is based upon the *bénédiction des poignards* of

Meyerbeer's *Les Huguenots* (1836)'.[63] Nor did these borrowings go unremarked at the time. Berlioz reported 'a triumphal march modelled, though in no spirit of slavish imitation, on the superb march in Spontini's *Olympie*'.[64]

Of far greater importance than these 'imitations' is the originality of *Rienzi*. If Wagner probably borrowed the idea of combining the ballet with a pantomime sequence from the finale of Act III of *La Juive*, he broke with convention by moving it to the second act in *Rienzi* so that it could be a logical rather than incidental part of the drama. This sequence includes scenes of the rape of Lucretia and of Tarquinius' expulsion from Rome. It is no mere divertissement but, as John Deathridge points out, 'an allegorical mirror for the "rape" of Rome by the nobles, their overthrow by Rienzi, and, in the context of the action, a highly relevant backdrop against which the nobles attempt to assassinate Rienzi'.[65] Showpiece numbers such as the Tribune's famous prayer, 'Allmächtiger Vater, blick' herab', do not stand alone but are integrated into the dramatic flow.

In his study of Wagner's sketches and drafts for *Rienzi*, Deathridge stresses that the work does not conform to the prevalent model of 'historical' operas but is 'a didactic and somewhat pessimistic attempt to envisage the consequences of a "new state of the world" ', one in which the sheer size and weight of the dramatic effects and the music 'far exceed even the most extravagant works of Wagner's contemporaries'. The opera as a whole shows 'an uninhibited, sometimes reckless handling of traditional forms and an increasing reliance on extra-musical stimuli clearly foreshadowing the provocative originality of his mature works'.[66]

Certainly the work is not short on spectacle: the grand processions in the third and fourth acts, Rienzi – fully armed and on horseback – leading the citizens against the nobles, the brilliant choral end-of-act finales, the Act II ballet and pantomime, an excommunication scene, and the ending of the whole piece with part of the blazing Capitol collapsing and killing Rienzi, Irene and Adriano. Wagner was evidently delighted that Schröder-Devrient, playing Adriano, was intending to arrive on horseback, riding astride like a man, to rescue Irene from the flames.[67] The intended impact of such a finale looks back to *Lodoïska* as much as it looks forward to the ending of *Götterdämmerung*.

The scenic virtuosity of grand opera was to have a much more lasting impact on both the conception and the scenic intention of Wagner's mature works than its carefully calculated texts and obedient music. Indeed, a large part of his persistent ambition was to achieve in German theatres the kind of scenic magic which had so impressed him in Paris.

A few examples will suffice. In 1829, for a ballet-pantomime by Scribe, Aumer and Hérold, *La Belle au bois dormant*, Daguerre and Ciceri introduced the *panorama mobile*, 'a painted cloth which unrolled on drums to provide moving décor behind a rocking boat as the Prince journeys to the castle'.[68] This was actually a development of a technique used by de Loutherbourg in his Eidophusikon in 1786 – the representation of a changing sky by the movement of a cloudscape painted on a cloth rolled between vertical cylinders on either side of the stage, the ancestry of which is to be found in the Baroque theatre.[69] The *panorama mobile* became a feature of many subsequent Paris productions, including some that were playing during the years in which Wagner lived in the city.

This scenic technique, like much else on the Paris stage, was to be remembered by Wagner and, rechristened 'Wandeldekoration', put to use in the transformation scenes between the forest and the temple of the Grail in Acts I and III of *Parsifal*. The collapse of Klingsor's castle in *Parsifal* and the conflagration at the end of *Götterdämmerung* were coups de théâtre which may be traced back to the work of four of Ciceri's pupils – Despléchin, Diéterle, Séchan and Feuchère, active 1833–48 – who, doubtless bored by the ease with which vast wooded landscapes and distant mountain prospects could now be achieved, went in for elaborate transformations and took particular delight in 'thrilling natural cataclysms and the conflagration and collapse of mighty castles beneath them'.[70]

For a production of Rossini's *Moïse* in 1860 a rainbow extending across the stage was created by refracting an electric arc through a prism. It is possible that Wagner saw this (he had returned to Paris in 1859 and was there until 1861): it would have been a tantalizing hint that his own idea of a traversable rainbow bridge by which his gods could cross over to Valhalla might not be altogether impracticable.

From *Die Feen* to *Parsifal* stage marvels are an integral part of Wagner's conceptions. There is of course a quintessential showmanship about this, in that Wagner knew that no intellectual or spiritual drama could hold the stage unless it were also 'theatrical' in the most obvious sense. His scenic dreams and inventions owe a very tangible debt to grand opera. It showed him how the beauty of the forest and the terror of fire and tempest could be suggested as powerfully on the stage as they could in his music. He had only to harness the Parisian technical marvels to an idealistic, myth-based drama to achieve the music-theatre of his dreams.

While still in Paris, Wagner had completed *Der fliegende Holländer* (November 1841), a work whose concentration immediately declared that Wagner had looked beyond grand opera and found an unmistakable voice of his own. *Holländer* is a brilliant demonstration of how spectacular nautical events can spring indissolubly from the heart of the musical drama. Yet Wagner's very skill as a musical scene painter made the production task more difficult, not less. For the sound of the turbulent seas whipped up in his orchestra created a far more powerful mimetic representation than the scenic endeavours on stage. The evocative power of his music raised aesthetic questions as to how what was seen on stage should relate to it. Wagner was only partly aware of these questions. He never wholly answered them and they persist to this day. His lifelong quest was to find a visual language to match his words and music. The composer's fundamental belief was that the stage picture should mirror the music as exactly as possible, and for the moment the scenic virtuosity of the Paris stage offered him the best model of how this might be achieved.

When the Dresden Court Theatre eventually undertook to perform *Rienzi* (partly thanks to Schröder-Devrient's advocacy), Wagner knew that he would have to be content with a far less sophisticated stage than that of the Paris Opéra. But he was promised outstanding singers, with Schröder-Devrient as Adriano and the tenor Joseph Tichatschek as Rienzi, and would take his chance.

The Dresden Court Theatre in the 1840s

Gottfried Semper's newly built Court Theatre was among the largest and best equipped of such theatres in Germany. It opened on 13 April 1841 with Weber's *Jubel* overture and Goethe's *Torquato Tasso*. The triumphant premiere of *Rienzi* on 20 October 1842 led swiftly to the premiere of *Der fliegende Holländer* (2 January 1843) and to Wagner's appointment on 2 February 1843 as Royal Kapellmeister of Saxony. He was to remain in this post until 1849, during which time he completed and gave the first performance of *Tannhäuser*.

In Dresden he tasted success and popularity, but also saw the frustration of his first sustained attempt, taking over from where Weber had left off seventeen years earlier, to reform working conditions so that justice might be done to the performance both of his own works and of the repertory as whole. Royal Kapellmeister he might be, but his powers were far more limited than those of any present-day Generalmusikdirektor. At every turn, the changes he wanted to make brought him into collision with Baron von Lüttichau, the Royal Theatre's Intendant (general director), and the court whose uniformed functionary he was. Artistic changes necessitated administrative and political reforms which Wagner was tactless enough to press for. The story of his six years in Dresden is one of a sustained campaign to create an opera company in his own image. In an attempt to do this he sought to ensure, first, that the orchestra and singers received the training and working conditions that would enable them to give of their utmost and, secondly, that stage production was

The exterior of the newly built Dresden Court Theatre, designed by Wagner's friend Gottfried Semper and depicted under snow in 1841 in this aquatint by W. Bäßler. The premieres of *Rienzi* (1842), *Der fliegende Holländer* (1843) and *Tannhäuser* (1845) all took place in this theatre. Wagner was Royal Kapellmeister in Dresden from 1843 until 1849.

taken seriously as an integral rather than a merely decorative contribution to performance. Wagner's frustration in attempting to bring about his reforms resulted in written reports on the changes for which he was agitating, as well as detailed instructions as to how he ideally wished his works to be performed.

By the 1840s the German states had, between them, an extensive network of generously subsidized municipal, court and national theatres. But the downside of the importance generally attached to theatre as a central and indispensable part of civilized life was artistic control by bureaucrats. *Au fond*, a court supported its theatre as an expression of its values. The acute political sensitivity of post-Napoleonic Germany can be gauged from a letter from the Dresden producer and costume designer Ferdinand Heine to the artist Ernst Benedikt Kietz in Paris: 'There is not a single German court theatre, least of all one attached to a Catholic court, where stories about the church, the papacy and the clergy will get past the censor'.[71] In the case of *Rienzi* the censor did not prove implacable, Wagner agreeing to a number of minor textual changes to ensure a 'nihil obstat' for the opera.

The Dresden Court Theatre was well known for its fine actors, notable among whom was the hugely popular Emil Devrient, brother of Eduard Devrient, a former actor and singer who in August 1844 became 'Oberregisseur für Schauspiel und Oper'. (Eduard was later the author of an important five-volume history of German acting, *Geschichte der deutschen Schauspielkunst*, 1848–74, to which Wagner, who owned a copy and shared Devrient's radical ideas, devoted an essay in 1849.)[72] The plays of Goethe, Lessing, Schiller and Kleist featured prominently, while in opera Gluck, Mozart, Beethoven and Weber were among the most favoured composers. In the performance of plays and operas alike virtuoso display by actors and singers (especially Italian singers) was rated far more highly than ensemble work. Indeed, at that time the cultivation of ensemble, as seen at the Vienna Burgtheater and in Düsseldorf under Karl Leberecht Immermann, was very much the exception rather than the rule.

To keep the box office alive the Dresden repertory was large and the adequacy of rehearsal time correspondingly thin. The prompt box fulfilled a role that was central in every respect. In Wagner's first complete year as Kapellmeister there were no fewer than twenty-nine new productions: three tragedies, four dramas, nine comedies and thirteen operas and musical plays. Most productions were given no more than a few times then dropped, as happened to *Der fliegende Holländer*, though not to *Rienzi*, whose more extrovert qualities quickly made it one of the star attractions in the Dresden repertory.

The premieres of Rienzi (1842) and Der fliegende Holländer (1843)

There can be little question that Semper's theatre – despite its modern equipment – was overstretched by the technical and aesthetic demands of these operas. 'I had in mind,' Wagner said of *Rienzi*, 'only the most magnificent of theatrical conditions.'[73] The demands of *Rienzi* were extravagant enough and within ten weeks the same stage had to contain the raging seas of *Der fliegende Holländer*, the arrival and departure of a huge ghostly ship, rapid transformations between seascapes and domesticity and a concluding resurrection from the waves of the hero and heroine.

From the minute of Lüttichau's acceptance of *Rienzi* in June 1841, Wagner bombarded the conductor Carl Gottlieb Reißiger, the chorus master Wilhelm Fischer and the producer and costume designer Ferdinand Heine with instructions. Scenically Wagner secured a pale shadow of what he wanted, his elaborate ballet being travestied:

> the resources available for the ballet in Dresden did not even permit proper execution of my directions for the entrance of ancient Roman gladiators or ritual dances, as later were to be executed very well in Berlin. I had to reconcile myself shamefully to two little *danseuses* executing some silly steps, until at last a company of soldiers marched in, their shields held above their heads forming a roof of sorts to remind the audience of an ancient Roman 'testudo', only to have the ballet master and his assistant, dressed in flesh-coloured tights, leap onto the shields and turn somersaults, a proceeding which they considered redolent of gladiatorial combat. This was the instant when the house invariably exploded in applause, and I had to regard this moment, whenever it came, as the pinnacle of my success.[74]

Outstanding singing by Wilhelmine Schröder-Devrient as Adriano and Joseph Tichatschek as Rienzi helped secure huge popular acclaim, and this despite the opera's inordinate length (the first performance lasted from 6 pm to well past midnight). The management's response was to divide the work into two consecutive evenings, 'Rienzi's Greatness' (Acts I and II) and 'Rienzi's Fall' (Acts III–V, with a special prelude), but it quickly reverted to giving the work in a single span, with cuts, a practice that was usually followed elsewhere.

But for Wagner the 'success' of *Rienzi* only served to point up the gulf between the public's taste and his own emergent theatrical values as evident in the composition of *Der fliegende Holländer*: 'I became increasingly conscious of the intrinsic divergence between my inner aims and outer fortunes.' This was further underlined when Wagner travelled to Hamburg for a production of *Rienzi* organized by the theatre's director Julius Cornet:

> His one aim was to create a sensation. … The dignity of the stage presentation, a quality of which he for his part understood nothing, was utterly sacrificed to the most ludicrous and tawdry showiness, as he thought that pageantry was all that was needed to ensure my success … the sorriest part of the whole affair was the singer taking the title role, an elderly, flabby and voiceless tenor named [Josef] Wurda, who sang Rienzi with the same expression as in his favourite role, Elvino in *La sonnambula*. He was so unbearable that I got the idea of making the Capitol crumble and collapse as early as the second act, in order to bury him under the ruins, a plan which would also have eliminated several of those processions so dear to the director's heart.[75]

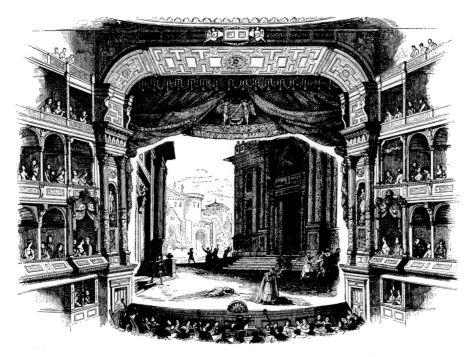

The interior of the Dresden Court Theatre, with the final scene of Act IV of *Rienzi*, as depicted in the *Illustrirte Zeitung* (Leipzig), 12 August 1843. The theatre was among the largest and best equipped in Germany.

The popularity of *Rienzi* encouraged Lüttichau to follow it up less than three months later with the first performance of *Der fliegende Holländer*, which Wagner had completed in Paris. The composer's view was that it was only Schröder-Devrient who 'rescued the work from total misunderstanding'. She had a particularly difficult time with the Dutchman, Johann Michael Wächter, an old friend of Wagner's but in no way equal to a demanding and original role that would not have been easy for its first audience to understand. In the composer's own words, 'His total incapacity in the difficult role of my spectral, suffering mariner dawned on Schröder-Devrient unfortunately only after the rehearsals were too far along to make any change. Wächter's distressing corpulence, particularly his broad, round face and the curious way he moved his arms and legs like shrivelled stumps, sent my Senta into transports of despair.'[76]

The design and staging must have been hastily cobbled together and did not even begin to do justice to what Wagner had had in mind:

the third act, in which the mightiest tempest in the orchestra was unable to disturb the quiet sea nor budge the ghost ship from its meticulous mooring, evoked amazement in the public as to how I could possibly offer, after a *Rienzi* during whose every act there was so much going on and in which Tichatschek shone in repeated changes of costumes, such an utterly unornamented, meagre and sombre piece of work. … I had to learn from what was on the whole an unsuccessful performance how much care and forethought would be necessary to assure myself an adequate representation of my later works.[77]

Nevertheless, as candid a critic as Berlioz was impressed 'by the sombre colouring of the music and by some remarkable effects of storm and wind which are an integral part of the dramatic character of the work'. Nor, Berlioz continued, had Dresden's production team laboured on *Rienzi* and *Holländer* in vain: 'Scenery, costumes and production approach the best standards achieved in Paris in works of this kind'.[78]

It was not long before Wagner was to realize that nothing less than wholesale change in the management of the theatre was a prerequisite if his works were to be performed as he intended. He submitted a radical plan for reorganization of the orchestra ('Concerning the Royal Orchestra', March 1846) – which gathered dust for a full year before being rejected – and then a 'Plan for the Organization of a German National Theatre for the Kingdom of Saxony' (11 May 1848).[79] In the latter Wagner asserted that theatre had a moral and social duty to perform and that the Royal Court Theatre should therefore be democratized as a 'National Theatre' managed not by the court but by dramatists, composers and artists. Wagner urged the establishment of a second national theatre in Leipzig, the elimination of travelling companies, a reduction in the number of performances, better utilization of the theatre

The very few surviving visual records of the premiere of *Der fliegende Holländer* in Dresden include these costume impressions of the Dutchman, Erik and Senta from the *Illustrirte Zeitung* (Leipzig), 7 October 1843. Johann Michael Wächter failed to project the demonic nature of the Dutchman's character and Wagner considered that it was only Schröder-Devrient as Senta who rescued the work from total disaster.

orchestra and schools for the training of actors, singers and instrumentalists. Two further essays in the same vein followed ('Theatre Reform' and 'More on Theatre Reform') in January 1849.[80] These writings did nothing to improve Wagner's strained relations with the court, and the consequent tension between the Royal Kapellmeister and his superiors was eventually resolved by Wagner's participation in the revolution of May 1849 and his subsequent exile from German soil.

Der fliegende Holländer was by no means a disaster, but its appeal to management and public was so much less than that of Rienzi that it received no more than four performances. Despite Wagner's best advocacy, described below, it remained far less popular than Rienzi. Some smaller theatres, however, for which the attractions of Rienzi were mitigated by its length and extravagant production requirements, were more than happy to take it up. The work was produced in Riga, Wagner's old theatre, on 22 May 1843, and in Kassel on 5 June – the first time any well-known German theatre outside Dresden had ventured on a work by Wagner. The performance was prepared and conducted by Ludwig Spohr, the composer of Faust (1816), Zemire und Azor (1819) and Jessonda (1823). Spohr made a serious attempt to follow Wagner's scenic instructions: 'two impressive sailing ships passed easily over the stage, came to anchor, rocked to and fro and then tacked about; storm clouds, moonlight, transfiguring glow, everything done with ease and as though by magic'.[81]

On 7 January 1844 Wagner himself conducted the work in Berlin. As the Royal Opera House had burnt down on 18 August 1843 the performances took place in a relatively small theatre, the Schauspielhaus on the Gendarmenmarkt (designed in chaste neoclassical style by Karl Friedrich Schinkel, 1817–21). What had been planned for the production (as recorded in a surviving sketch by the designer Karl Jacob Gerst) is vivid evidence of the way theatres improvised scenery from stock. Gerst's sketch specifies sources for the scenery as follows: the two ships were to come from the ballet Der Seeräuber, the cyclorama and masts from Oberon, Daland's room from Gretchen's parlour in Faust (a design by Schinkel) and the house in Act III from the Swiss chalet in Wilhelm Tell.[82] In the event Wagner was spared such a patchwork, as the theatre's store was also destroyed in the fire, but whatever was improvised in its stead evidently suited him well enough: 'I was most pleasantly surprised by the superb staging under the direction of the truly brilliant stage-director Blum, with the collaboration of his highly skilled and ingenious technicians.'[83] At this time, Karl Schinkel's scenic designs and the costume reforms instigated by Count Brühl put the Berlin theatre at the forefront of innovatory German theatres.[84]

In exile in Zürich in 1852 Wagner was persuaded to produce and conduct per-formances which, despite the 'wretched, crude and cramped' theatre conditions, he rated as more pleasurable than the 'infinitely clumsy and lack-lustre achievement of the technically superior Dresden theatre'. The sets were purpose built and Wagner hoped that these performances would serve as a model for larger theatres elsewhere. But it was Liszt's request for guidance as to how to produce the work in Weimar (from where Wagner was banned) that prompted the composer to produce a detailed description of his intentions. The 'Remarks on Performing the Opera Der *fliegende Holländer*' (1852) helped to ensure that Liszt's Weimar production (16 February 1853) was, despite serious deficiencies later acknowledged by Liszt, regarded as definitive for many years.[85]

That Wagner begins by asking the regisseur to study the printed instructions in the vocal or full score is evidence of the scant attention that must often have been paid to such texts. This essay, the fruit of a decade of Wagner's experiences of trying to get what he wanted for the opera, gives a very good idea of the persistent problems. Managements were still interested only in spectacular, decorative effects and had no conception of staging as an expression of the inner life of the drama. The principal musical difficulty was, not dissimilarly, that the conductor and singers should understand that the music had nothing to do with effects for their own sake but was driven from within. Schröder-Devrient was exceptional in her understanding of this. It had been a source of bitter disappointment to Wagner that at so many points, such as the above-mentioned ballet, the performances of *Rienzi* had been a betrayal of his intentions: 'Tichatschek had not for a moment been willing to lay aside his glittering manner as a heroic tenor to do justice to the gloomy, demonic strain in Rienzi's character, upon which I had placed great stress at the critical moments of the drama.... I concluded that what had really caused the success of my *Rienzi* was the result of the glorious, electrifying voice of the tirelessly exuberant singer, of the stimulating effect of the choral ensembles, and of the constant bustling activity on the stage'.[86]

Wagner's 1852 essay on performing *Holländer* is mostly concerned with characterization and with the coordination of the singers' movement and gestures with the music. He was still engaged in a struggle to have his work understood by the performers as a fully fledged drama and not merely as a succession of numbers for vocal display. He explains that Daland is a doughty sailor, not a figure of fun; Erik a stormy romantic, not a whiner; Senta a tough Nordic girl, naïve but not sentimental. But most of his remarks are about the Dutchman, the role that was hardest for his contemporaries to understand. He devotes particular attention to the Dutchman's opening monologue:

> During the deep trumpet notes (B minor) at the close of the introductory scene he has come off board, along a plank lowered by one of the crew, to a shelf of rock on the shore; his rolling gait, proper to sea folk on first treading dry land after a long voyage, is accompanied by a wave-like figure for the violins and violas: with the first crotchet of the third bar he makes his second step – always with folded arms and sunken head; his third and fourth steps coincide with the notes of the eighth and tenth bars. From here on, his movements will follow the dictates of his general delivery, yet the actor must never let himself be betrayed into exaggerated stridings to and fro: a certain terrible repose in his outward demeanour, even amid the most passionate expression of inward anguish and despair, will give the characteristic stamp to this impersonation.[87]

If such bar-by-bar instructions seem hardly likely to have inspired artists to move as naturally and truthfully as he wished, one has to remember that he was out to eliminate the habitual rhetorical posturing which was most performers' idea of 'acting'. Wagner considered, perhaps a trifle academically, that such posturing was a remnant from the Baroque theatre.

In a wonderfully striking paragraph in *Richard Wagner in Bayreuth* (1876), Nietzsche observes that Wagner finds a voice for everything in nature that had previously been content to remain silent: 'He plunges into rosy dawn, into forests, mists, ravines, mountain peaks, the terrors of darkness and into moonlight, discovering in them a secret longing: they also want to give tongue.'[88] Other composers had of course been there before him, but Wagner went further. Nature is indeed a resounding presence in *Der fliegende Holländer* and remains so in all his subsequent operas. It is there, obviously enough, not just for its own sake (as a picturesque romantic backdrop) but as representative of the psychological state of the characters and of the drama as a whole. During rehearsals for the opera's Munich premiere in 1864, Kapellmeister Franz Lachner famously complained of 'the incessant wind that blew out at you wherever you happened to open the score'.[89] How to represent nature on stage and to ally its elemental force with the human drama was always a major problem, especially as Wagner sought a totally realistic presentation of sea and storm: 'The opera's first scene has to bring the spectator into that mood in which it becomes possible for him to conceive the mysterious figure of the Flying Dutchman himself: it must therefore be handled with exceptional care; the sea between the rocks must be shown as boisterous as possible; the treatment of the ship cannot be naturalistic enough: little touches, such as the heeling of the ship when struck by an especially big wave (between the two verses of the Steuermann's song) must be very rigorously carried out.'[90]

Wagner's handwritten annotations in a copy of the vocal score used for the 1864 Munich production provide further valuable evidence of his intentions. Between the two strophes of the Steuermann's song he asks for 'The waves crashing against the ship and pushing it back somewhat'. Then, at the beginning of the second strophe, 'No waves. Calm weather and sea – Lighting in the foreground gets brighter.'[91]

Wagner had enough practical knowledge to know that gauzes and backlighting were essential aids towards ensuring that the scenery should present a 'vibrant image of nature'.[92] 'Special attention is demanded by the lighting, with its manifold changes: to make the nuances of the storm in the first act effective, a skilful use of painted gauzes, at least as far as the middle distance of the stage, is indispensable.'[93] But he could not be over-specific in his visual requirements. Referring to the scenario of the Berlin Schauspielhaus performances in January 1844 Wagner asks for 'exact observance of my scattered scenic indications, leaving to the inventive powers of the scene painter and machinist how they should be carried out'.[94]

Wagner's constant aim through the 1840s and beyond was that what the spectator saw should correspond as closely as possible with what he heard in the music. So exacting were his requirements that there was only one theatre that had the technology to begin to meet them – the Paris Opéra. As that was closed to him (until the *Tannhäuser* performances there in 1861) he was compelled to go to great lengths to try to secure the necessary conditions on German stages. But it was an elusive goal, and later experiences – particularly his efforts to find a satisfactory staging for the *Ring* – were to give him an understanding of why it was so elusive. It was a question not just of technology but also of theatre architecture, of the aesthetics of staging and of the relationship of the latter with the words and music of the score.

The premiere of Tannhäuser (1845)

Wagner's attitude to the stage performance of his romantic operas is shown nowhere more clearly than in his efforts to get *Tannhäuser* performed as he wanted. If ever a work was written to show that a romantic opera could be both a stage spectacular and a true drama from first note to last it was *Tannhäuser*. There is not a coup de théâtre that does not have a logical place in the unfolding drama of the tussle in the hero between spiritual and erotic impulses – the Venusberg bacchanale, the magical transition to the clear spring morning in the valley, the ceremony in the Hall of Song, the return of the pilgrims, the concluding chorus.

Like *Rienzi* and *Holländer*, *Tannhäuser* was written without concession to what theatres could actually manage. These works were composed for some future theatre of Wagner's mind's eye, a theatre whose capabilities were way beyond even those of Paris and Berlin, which were the best anywhere in the world. Inevitably, this created huge problems for Wagner in his struggle to bring productions into line with his dream images.

At Dresden in 1845, and as a mark of especial favour, Lüttichau did his best to accede to the composer's not unextravagant scenic demands. He ordered hugely expensive new sets from the designer Despléchin in Paris, who regularly worked for the Opéra, rather than following the usual practice of adapting stock scenery. The valley of the Wartburg was considered a successful creation, but Wagner had trouble getting the Venusberg to his liking. The French designer's first setting had been a park with statues and groves reminiscent of Versailles. This had been painted as a fresco 'on the interior walls of a wild mountain cave'. Wagner insisted on 'substantial changes, in particular on the painting out of the bushes and statues. ... The concealment of the grotto in a rosy haze, out of which the Wartburg valley suddenly emerges, had to be attempted anew with the help of a special trick I had devised for it.' The 'special trick' was probably the use of lightly painted gauzes which could be quickly flown out, or rendered transparent by being lit from behind (see Wagner's own description, quoted on pp. 37–8). When the Hall of Song failed to arrive from Paris, the scenery for Charlemagne's throne-room from Weber's *Oberon* had to be used for the premiere. (The Despléchin set eventually arrived and was used for later performances.)[95] These designs were much copied for other productions, including, as an ultimate seal of their acceptibility, the lavish Paris production of 1861. The quasi-medieval costumes were designed by Ferdinand Heine, in close collaboration with the composer.

Despite intensive coaching by Wagner, the extrovert tenor Joseph Tichatschek was at a loss to make any impression with the crucial bars sung by Tannhäuser in the Act II finale signalling his *volte face* repentance ('Erbarm' dich mein'), without which his

Tannhäuser and Elisabeth. Ink and watercolour costume drawings by Fedor Alexis Flinzer, based on Ferdinand Heine's designs (which have not survived) for the opera's premiere in 1845.

subsequent pilgrimage to Rome is, to the discerning auditor, devoid of motivation. For the second and subsequent performances Wagner had no option but to cut these bars, which were no better managed elsewhere, not even by Albert Niemann in Paris in 1861. Only once, in a single performance with Ludwig Schnorr von Carolsfeld in the Munich Nationaltheater in 1865, was Wagner to hear these bars sung 'in a shattering and hence deeply moving manner which suddenly turned the hero from an object of loathing into the incarnation of a man deserving of sympathy'.[96] Back at the Dresden premiere Wagner had been horrified by Tichatschek's insistence on crossing the stage to deliver his impassioned outburst in praise of sensual love directly into the ear of the virginal Elisabeth.[97]

Wagner was also dissatisfied with parts of the score and immediately set about making changes. No other opera of his was to be so much revised. Less than a month before his death Cosima recorded his saying that he still owed the world his *Tannhäuser*.[98] He completed his first major revisions for the Dresden performances of 1847. These were partly a response to complaints from the 1845 audience about the end of the opera. People did not understand why, in the absence of Venus herself, Tannhäuser's fevered thoughts should have turned to her. There was also perplexity in that Elisabeth's death had been merely reported by Wolfram and signalled by an off-stage chorus and flickering torchlight on the Hörselberg; the crucial part played by her death in Tannhäuser's salvation had not registered. Wagner therefore wrote new music to accompany Venus's reappearance and for the arrival of Elisabeth's bier from the Wartburg so that Tannhäuser could sink down beside it. Far more extensive revisions were to be made for the 1861 Paris production, as we shall see. And the composer continued to revise the work thereafter, right through to his last production of it, which he was to stage in Vienna in 1875.[99]

Tannhäuser was only slowly taken up by other theatres, beginning with Weimar (under Liszt) in 1849. Momentum began to build from 1852 with performances in Schwerin, Breslau and Wiesbaden. Yet again, Wagner's concern was that the inaugural performance, though under his own direction, had been in no sense a model one, but was likely to be taken as such. He was determined to do everything possible to prevent his work being travestied in performances which, in focusing only on the bewitchments of the grand effects, failed to engage the dramatic core. The score and text were not lacking in performance instructions, but these were flouted to suit the singers and stage conditions available. However badly – even desperately – Wagner needed money, he always insisted that a work should not be given at all rather than be given badly. There was still an immense gulf between the ideal performance envisioned by Wagner and what he actually got in the theatre, even when supervised by himself.

Wagner's guides to performing Tannhäuser

Once more Wagner endeavoured to help theatres understand his staging intentions by setting them out in his 1852 essay 'On Performing *Tannhäuser*: A Communication to the Conductors and Performers of This Opera' and in two documents which were used for the preparation of the opera's first performance in Darmstadt in 1853 ('Staging the Opera *Tannhäuser*' and 'Costume Description').[100] The idea for publishing these guides was doubtless indebted in some measure to the Paris Opéra's *livrets de mise-en-scène* already mentioned.

The composer had two hundred copies of 'On Performing *Tannhäuser*' printed at his own expense, and despatched them to any theatre contemplating a production. Conductor and producer, said Wagner, must work together and attend all rehearsals. The music had always to be performed with the stage action in mind, and vice versa. The orchestra had to be large enough: not immodestly Wagner urges that a minimum of four violas is required, a request eloquent of the sparse resources available in most houses.[101]

A principal problem addressed by Wagner was the failure of most singers to get inside the skin of their characters. They had to learn that there was no sharp demarcation between recitative and aria: 'declamation is at the same time singing and singing declamation'. This would become apparent only when the singer had entered fully into the psychology and motivation of the role: the character had to be lived and not just sung. The singer's understanding and delivery of the dramatic meaning was the key to solving the apparent difficulties presented by the vocal line. Wagner devotes much space to the title role and to the pivotal importance of Tannhäuser's heartfelt cry for mercy, 'Erbarm' dich mein', in the ensemble at the end of the second act. (He later complained that, despite his best endeavours, he had been unable to prevent the singers from turning the Song Contest into a succession of arias.)

The Act I Venusberg scene was not to be the familiar kind of ballet (which he had had to put up with in Dresden) but more of a mime, 'a seductive, wild and enthralling chaos of figures moving and regrouping, a chaos of emotions ranging from the tenderest contentment, languishing and yearning, to the most drunken impetuousness of exultant abandon'.[102] The rapid and silent transformation from the Venusberg to the Wartburg valley was to be effected, as at Dresden, by bringing down a succession of mistily painted gauzes at the front of the stage. When the scene has become quite indistinct, the composer continues, a huge rosy-coloured cloudscape on a canvas is lowered behind the gauze, completely obscuring the Venusberg decor. This is then quickly removed to reveal the new setting. Everything is to be coordinated with the music. The big transformation occurs when the stage suddenly darkens and first the cloud effects and then the gauzes are lifted up, revealing the new scene in the valley bathed in bright daylight. In Act II, the guests were not to enter in a formal procession, but as individuals, in a variety of costumes and each in their own time and style. The idea was 'to imitate real life in its freest and most noble forms'.[103]

Wagner's injunctions are further elaborated in 'Staging the Opera *Tannhäuser*'. Here he describes how all manner of rhetorical gesturing and empty postures were to be renounced in favour of committed flesh-and-blood acting. The whole purpose was to create a realistic picture of life. He asks that the minstrels and knightly bystanders respond to the scandalous impropriety of Tannhäuser's outburst in praise of Venus in Act II by crowding in on him with their swords, while Elisabeth throws herself in their path. Such physicality on the stage of a court opera would have been considered shocking in 1845, tolerated only because of Wagner's volcanic temperament. (As Bauer points out, the effectiveness of staging the scene in this way could be seen in Götz Friedrich's powerful Bayreuth production of 1972: see chapter 10.)[104] The costumes were to be 'medieval in style' (as were the bridles of the horses in the Act I hunting scene) and every scenic instruction faithfully observed.

But only in the rarest cases (as in Louis Schindelmeisser's Wiesbaden production, 13 November 1852) was Wagner's advice welcomed and efforts made to act upon it. In general, 'On Performing *Tannhäuser*' was counterproductive, indeed even a deterrent to performance. Newman instances the Leipzig Theatre being so dismayed by Wagner's production demands that it abandoned its immediate plan to perform the work. So wilful was contemporary theatre practice, so disrespectful of a mere composer's intentions, that the guide was disregarded as totally impracticable or, as often as not, remained unstudied. In 1864, Wagner found six copies in the basement of the Munich Nationaltheater still uncut.[105]

Wagner's idea of 'stage realism'

We have seen how Wagner insists over and over again on the imitation of 'real life in its freest and most noble forms'. He wanted this principle to direct every aspect of staging from the scenery to the acting and the vocal characterization of the singers. 'Everything on stage,' he said, 'must breathe and move with no other purpose than the most effective communication with the visual and aural perception of the spectators.' The spectator must feel as though he himself is actually on stage: he 'must live and breathe only in the work of art'.[106]

To help theatres understand how he wanted his works staged, Wagner began to issue guides to performance. This sketch of the Wartburg Valley, with ground plan and handwritten details, is from a copy by Heinrich Ploch of instructions by the composer and his trusted designer Ferdinand Heine. It was made for the preparation of the Darmstadt premiere of *Tannhäuser* on 23 October 1853. More often than not, Wagner's scrupulous descriptions were disregarded. Leipzig was so intimidated by the composer's demands that it abandoned its plans to perform the work.

In other words, the stage was to create as perfect an evocation of Wagner's imagined world as possible and the spectator was to share that illusion. As we have already seen, in *Der fliegende Holländer* Wagner wanted the first scene 'to bring the spectator into that mood in which it becomes possible for him to conceive the mysterious figure of the Flying Dutchman himself'. The detail with which Wagner describes how he wants such impressions to be achieved – leaving nothing, as one might say, to the

A characteristically idealized impression from the *Illustrirte Zeitung* (Leipzig) (c. 1853) of how the Wartburg Valley might have looked at Dresden from 1847. The drawing is of the opera's final scene, which Wagner had extensively revised. Tannhäuser sinks down on his knees at the foot of Elisabeth's bier. The shrine to the Virgin at which she had prayed is at the left.

imagination – has earned him the censure of some modern critics, who have argued the folly of pursuing historical literalism in the theatre. Such critics are correct in the truism of their assertion, but incorrect in applying it to Wagner. What he means by 'realism' and 'truth to nature' has to be understood in context.

'Stage realism' is, of course, always relative, always subject to understood conventions of representation in the same way that the illusions of reality created by painters on a flat canvas are dependent on such devices as perspective. As so much of the grand opera 'realism' of the 1830s was dependent on large-scale painting on flats and drops, its conventions were those of the romantic landscape painting of the period. The perspective and lighting of the scene were a static part of it. What was presented was a succession of fixed tableaux, changed behind closed curtains, which could not show time passing by the lengthening of shadows for the simple reason that the shadows were painted into the decor. The gas lighting permitted only the dimming or brightening of the fixed tableau that was the stage picture. And this was the accepted convention for the portrayal of the dawning day and setting sun. The acting of the soloists, the choreography of the crowd scenes and ballet and the 'special effects' of the machinists were all superimposed on the scene as set and not an organic part of it.

The boasted detail of the 'historical' and 'natural' settings was, for all the research that went into it, not in the least 'realistic'. The images created were themselves myths and fantasies designed, above all, to meet the audience's expectation of the 'grandeur' to serve which the Opéra was committed by government directive.

The tenuous basis of those images is apparent in the changes they underwent when productions were revived, as they very frequently were. When *La Muette de Portici* was revived in the 1860s, for example, the revolutionary fervour of the original production, in which a sense of historical *actualité* played an essential part, was distanced and rendered innocuous. The new scenery was at once grandiose and heavy, weighed down by the romantic pathos of neoclassical landscape with obligatory ruins. 'Realism', it will be apparent, is not short on meanings and interpretations, and it is for this reason that it should always be treated circumspectly in the context of Wagner's works and their stage interpretation.

The 'stage realism' that Wagner wanted was simply the most perfect stage representation of the worlds of myth and legend conjured up in his works. His concern was to make his images live so credibly on the stage that the audience would share them too. His scenes were not the virtuoso exercises in 'historical archaeology' on which the artists and technicians of Paris prided themselves, but pictures of what he had had in mind when composing his texts and music. His were landscapes of the imagination, unbounded by the tyranny of historical exactitude.

There can be no question that Wagner was greatly influenced by the Parisian delight in spectacle. The critical difference was that for him spectacle, at any rate after *Rienzi*, had to be an integral part of the drama. He plainly loved spectacular effects and had few rivals in depicting them in music and on stage, but his interest was always in using them to dramatize the human and metaphysical core of his work.

What Wagner sought was the total animation of his fictitious worlds. In truth, this was hardly a new ambition. Opera composers before him had wanted their creations to be as vividly realized as they had imagined them. But with Wagner a new idea of theatricality was born. Earlier composers had had fewer problems in accepting conventions of theatrical 'make-believe' that fell short of immersing the spectator in the 'total illusion' which Wagner wanted. These conventions allowed, as we have seen in relation to the Baroque, for artifice to be part of the show, for scenery to be mannered and sheerly decorative in its depictions, for acting to be rhetorical, for the spectators to be visible to each other and to the performers. Wagner's aim was that all means of creating illusion should be concealed, that the scenic depictions should use perspective to paint credible landscapes, that the singers should live their roles, and that the audience should focus its attention exclusively on the stage.

So when he talks about images that are 'true to life', 'true to nature' and so on, what he means is that they should create the illusion that the worlds he had imagined were 'for real'. In its day this was a wholly novel idea, one that made unprecedented demands on stage production, on the performers and, not least, on the attention of the audience. It met with a great deal of resistance. Wagner could only do so much in his own work with performers. But it was because the instructions in his scores were not being taken at face value that he felt it necessary to publish so many writings about performance, writings which often do no more than underline that he really means what he says in his scores. At the Karlsruhe *Tannhäuser* in 1862 he was appalled that a production by someone so familiar with his intentions as Eduard Devrient could be so far off course. In the Hall of Song, Devrient had had the ladies and gentlemen of the chorus lined up severally along the walls on either side of the stage before 'executing the regular *chassé croisé* of a quadrille and thus changing their relative positions'.[107]

In another production of *Tannhäuser*, in Munich in 1855, it seems that the regisseur August Kindermann (who also sang Wolfram) may have given Wagner the 'naturalness' he always wanted. Describing the arrival of the guests in the Hall of Song, the *Augsburger Allgemeine* wrote, 'The producer has avoided the traditional method of having the singers march on like marionettes; instead they appeared to enter as if by chance, depending on the speed with which their horses had brought them there. Having been welcomed by the landgrave, they then went to look for their seats and, thanks to the characteristic verisimilitude of the costumes and surroundings, we felt ourselves transported, as it were, into the reality of a world which had once existed centuries ago'.[108]

Wagner's explanatory writings are particularly interesting for their practical suggestions in pursuit of stage realism. He took pleasure in devising all manner of perspective stage effects and illusions. To suggest that the pilgrims in Act I of *Tannhäuser* were approaching from a distance, at their first appearance they were represented far upstage by a procession of some thirty children wearing cowls and suitably bearded. Descending the hillside path they disappeared behind the fifth row of flats, the real chorus of adult singing pilgrims finally entering in sonic splendour from behind the third row of flats. A similar subterfuge, this time in reverse, was adopted in Act III. Collapsing after her prayer, Elisabeth dragged herself painfully towards the Wartburg and was lost to sight. Some time later a tiny figure, actually a small and identically clad girl, was seen to reach the distant summit.[109] The composer's fondness for perspective effects is vividly illustrated in the drawings for *Lohengrin* that were made at his instruction by Ferdinand Heine to show how the arrival and eventual departure of Lohengrin were to be managed, once again using a child to stand in for Lohengrin when he is first seen in the distance.[110]

Wagner's 'illusions of reality' were never intended to have more than a tenuous connection with what had originally inspired them. We can see over and over again in *My Life* how Wagner's *sense* of something was always far more important for him than the 'something' itself, and this is never more true than when he had translated it into art. As a dramatist he was always dedicated to precisely that which was *not* historical, hence his argument that the true subject of drama was myth and never history. Even when his imagination caught fire from a historical subject, as it did in the case of *Die Meistersinger*, 'historical actuality' was of subsidiary importance. Around him there were many who craved the 'historical dimension' in theatrical art. Right through to the 1876 staging of the *Ring* at Bayreuth the composer found himself having to fight against them.

It was not Wagner's idea but that of the King of Prussia that in the 1856 Berlin production of *Tannhäuser* the Hall of Song should be modelled directly from that in the Wartburg. As we shall see, Ludwig II was to have similar notions about boxing art

Wagner was very fond of perspective effects. In Heine's sketch-map (1854) for the protracted arrival of Lohengrin, the letters refer to the detailed instructions which were supplied. The dotted line (b), in red in the original, is the track of a small-boy-Lohengrin look-alike drawn by an equally small swan as they cross the water at stage-rear and disappear at the right. The full-size Lohengrin enters further downstage from the same side along track (d) in a functioning small boat with an animated swan whose neck and wings both move. Similar effects with children were used in *Tannhäuser* to suggest the approach of the pilgrims from afar, and Elisabeth's disappearance into the distance towards the Wartburg after her prayer for Tannhäuser's pardon and return from Rome.

When it came to the romantic interpretation of Wagner's scenic visualizations, no one outdid King Ludwig's scenic artists in Munich. The designer for Act I of the 'model' *Lohengrin* production of 1867 was Heinrich Döll whose gouache painting of the knight's arrival dates from the following year. Döll was also responsible for Act II of *Tristan* (1865) and for Act III of *Die Meistersinger* (1868). Döll specialized in landscapes; it was quite usual for architectural scenes in the same opera to be entrusted to another artist who excelled in that particular field.

into history, but they were not shared by Wagner. It is significant that for his attempted 'model' *Tannhäuser* in Paris in 1861 he insisted on a *free* adaptation of the Wartburg Hall: history for him was but an ingredient in the construction of his own mythography. 'As soon as his creative power takes hold on him,' wrote Nietzsche of Wagner, 'history becomes malleable clay in his hands; his relationship towards it suddenly becomes quite different from that of any scholar, it becomes similar to that of the Greek towards his myths, that is to say towards something which offers material for plastic and poetic invention, performed with love and a certain shy devotion, to be sure, but nonetheless also with the magisterial right of the creator.'[111]

The Paris Tannhäuser *of 1861*

Some sixteen years after the premiere of *Tannhäuser*, Wagner was at last offered by the Paris Opéra the best means available anywhere to perform the opera. With the passing of the years, and with *Tristan* behind him, Wagner saw that the Venusberg could be evoked with more passionate music. He also hoped that an extended and suitably seductive ballet in Act I would get him off the hook for his refusal to compromise the integrity of the work by providing the Opéra's mandatory second-act ballet.[112]

The theatre could give Wagner much of what he wanted – even in excess – as witness the four horses and ten hounds which pawed the stage in the hunting scene at the first performance (the dogs were later omitted). He attended 151 of the 163 recorded rehearsals, working hard to secure a production that reflected his dramatic intentions and was not just a showcase of effects.[113] But he was up against such house professionals as Vauthrot, the chief vocal coach, who was adamant that the music and production would make little impression on the public by comparison with the virtuosity of the singers.[114] There was also a serious problem in that house rules allowed no one other than the music director Pierre-Louis-Philippe Dietsch to conduct, and it was quickly apparent to Wagner that he would fail to do justice to the score. Even the composer's most strenuous attempts to secure permission to conduct the work himself failed, and it was under Dietsch's ineffective baton that the work was launched in the French capital on 13 March 1861.

Despite the shortcomings of Dietsch and of Albert Niemann in the title role (who resolutely defied Wagner's coaching and was dismissed by Bülow as a 'toneless baritone'),[115] the staging was lavish and among the very best Wagner had ever received for any of his works. 'The production,' wrote Bülow, 'defied description – a thing of such marvellous beauty that it has to be seen to be believed. In comparison with this, everything that the German stages have done is merely puerile.'[116] But this was not enough to prevail against the wrath of a small but furiously determined section of

For the premiere of *Tannhäuser* in Dresden in 1845 the management, quite exceptionally, attempted to placate Wagner by hiring one of the Paris Opéra's top scenic artists, Edouard-Désiré-Joseph Despléchin, rather than following the usual practice of adapting items of stock scenery. Despléchin's designs were considered so successful that they were elaborated for the 1861 Paris production of *Tannhäuser*, the most spectacular yet of a Wagner opera. The artist's impression of the Hall of Song in Paris is by Emile Rouargue.

the audience. The aristocratic hooligans of the Jockey Club vented their fury against Wagner's refusal to supply the customary ballet in Act II, and this became part and parcel of a chauvinist demonstration against an alien composer of republican sentiment and his patron the Princess Pauline Metternich, wife of the Austrian ambassador. The protests continued and Wagner withdrew his score after only two further performances. It was a bitter irony that what could have been the first production to come close to the composer's intentions failed not because of the shortcomings of the performance but because of the audience's antipathy to those intentions.

Nothing could have driven it home more forcibly for Wagner that 'ideal' stage realizations were as nothing unless the audience shared his own seriousness about musical drama. It was already a sufficient cause of despair that *Tannhäuser* owed its popularity not to any understanding of the moral dilemma at its heart but to enjoyment of its more superficial, decorative qualities. Baudelaire may have seen that '*Tannhäuser* represents the struggle between the two principles that have chosen the human heart for their chief battlefield; in other words, the struggle between flesh and spirit, Heaven and Hell, Satan and God,'[117] but, wrote Newman, 'The average Parisian could not understand how the mere sound of a bell could tear Tannhäuser out of the arms of Venus.'[118] It was only with the greatest difficulty that Wagner had been able to coach the performers into even a token identification with their roles. How much greater the task of helping the audience to understand the connection between the 'effects' and their 'causes', particularly when to do so risked exposing them to uncomfortable moral choices at the core of the work. A new theatre and a new contract between audience and performers had to come into being.

CHAPTER 2

The art of the future – by royal command

A fugitive takes stock: rethinking the art of opera

Although Wagner's early operas, from *Rienzi* to *Lohengrin*, had won him renown and been widely performed, he remained deeply dissatisfied. Despite his vigorous attempts to exercise authorial control, theatre managements continued to present his works primarily for their entertainment value, thereby belittling his intentions as a musical dramatist. The terms on which he had been successful may even have prompted him to wonder whether he had yet distanced himself far enough from grand opera. Disillusioned, Wagner turned away. Between 1849 and 1850 he planned to write operas entitled *Friedrich I.*, *Jesus von Nazareth*, *Achilleus* and *Wieland der Schmied*, but such plans remained unfulfilled. The 'Jesus' of that prose sketch was as angry and revolutionary as Wagner then felt. It is familiar history that he supported Bakunin and helped man the barricades at Dresden in May 1849, which led to his becoming a fugitive and an exile from German soil for many years.

Wagner's political agitations were, at least in part, a surrogate for his frustrated artistic ambitions. But revolution and exile focused his mind on the unsolved problem of reforming the theatre and bringing a new kind of opera into being. Surely no great artist can have worked through so extensive an investigation into the basis of his work as Wagner now embarked upon. Living in Zürich, he quickly produced the essays *Art and Revolution* and *The Artwork of the Future* (both 1849), followed by the lengthy treatise *Opera and Drama* (1850–1), the far more approachable *Communication to My Friends* (1851) and a long and splendid letter to Liszt (1851) setting out his aims as a dramatist.[1] It is an extraordinary body of theoretical work, rich in contradictions and tergiversations. Vividly expressed ideas appear alongside vacuous and impenetrable ramblings. His reading was voracious but the use he makes of his material is always self-serving. History is plundered for whatever suits him. Inevitably, the readings are also wilful misreadings. Having discerned the peaks (Aeschylus, Shakespeare, Goethe, Bach and Beethoven prominent among them), Wagner can the better define his own place as their successor. History was a continually upward progress with its apotheosis in himself – a synthesis of the genius of Bach and Beethoven in instrumental music, and of the dramatic legacy of the Greeks, Shakespeare and Goethe.

Wagner argues that art can only be rescued from its function as a divertissement for the bourgeoisie through the creation of a modern equivalent of the theatre festivals of Periclean Athens. There, audience and performers had come together to marvel at the strange and terrible ways of the gods as dramatized in the tragedies of Aeschylus. The whole population took part in these festivals and not just a privileged minority (though Wagner did note, angrily, that this 'whole' population did not include the very substantial number of slaves on which its well-being and culture depended).[2] The subjects chosen for the principal festival dramas (the accompanying satyr plays were ignored by Wagner) concerned the profoundest issues of human existence, and these were presented as living myth. Aeschylus, Wagner noted, had been poet, composer and stage manager all in one. He had achieved a supreme synthesis of every artistic, moral and religious possibility.

For Wagner the important thing about myth was that its truths were true for all time. Dramas based on it were not limited as were those set in particular times and places, their significance and truths therefore limited to their particular ambience. 'The supreme characteristic of myth,' writes Wagner, 'is that its truths are perennial, and its substance, when distilled into works of art, is inexhaustible for all time'.[3] The gods and demons of mythology were the first and the most enduring inventions of human art. They are, says Wagner, the defining archetypes of human thought and feeling.

He goes on to argue that the proper subject for the nineteenth-century dramatist must also be myth. His vision is of a new kind of drama, rooted in mythical subject matter, which will restore the almost sacred relationship between author, performers and public (all as active participants) which Wagner believed to have obtained in the theatre festivals of Periclean Athens.

The heart of the new communal spiritual experience was to be the rebirth of tragedy from those myths from which the nineteenth century had most to learn. Implicit in this is a rejection of subject matter that is either historical (as favoured by Meyerbeer) or contemporaneous. In this vein, Wagner argues that the reworking of myth evident in *Don Giovanni* made it more powerful than the comedies of social critique (*Figaro* and *Così fan tutte*) with which Mozart and Da Ponte had been so successful.

Wagner hoped that myth-based drama was the most powerful means for addressing the deepest problems of the age and that it would help to bring about a new and better kind of society. This belief of Wagner's was no personal idiosyncrasy but was entirely characteristic of the German Romantic movement. Its adherents looked to art and above all to theatre – art's most public manifestation – to change society. For them, the stage was the most potent debating chamber for the central questions of man's existence.

How, then, was this new drama to be constructed? Since Aeschylus, Wagner lamented, the various arts had gone their several ways, each developing in unwholesome isolation. The time was now ripe to reunite the arts, to bring them together into a synthesis, into a Gesamtkunstwerk ('total work of art' is perhaps the least objectionable of possible translations) which would restore the Athenian spirit to the German people (for there was a vigorous nationalistic line in this too). This notion of an all-embracing work of art was by no means original. It goes at least as far back in German operatic history as the seventeenth century and was a central tenet of Romanticism, conceived in opposition to the Enlightenment's belief in clarity, separation and rational order. Wagner's 'total work of art' is his own development of a vision nurtured by Tieck, Novalis, Schelling, E. T. A. Hoffmann and others before them.

The musical contribution, he argues, is never to be formal, decorative or self-sufficient. Its function is to breathe life into myth and present it directly to the senses. The words are to be clearly audible and comprehensible at all times. To the three arts of dance, music and poetry are to be added the visual arts of architecture, painting and sculpture. Architecture will again become beautiful and useful in the construction of theatres, painting will provide the scenery, while sculpture is to be reborn in moulding the living flesh of the singing actor.

Myth and its stage representation

For Wagner stage production had an absolutely central role in the 'total work of art'. It was to be the visual and physical expression of the musical and poetic drama.[4] The marks on paper only made sense when realized in a very particular way. An intense and vivid imagining lay behind the poet-composer's notation and it was exactly that imagining that he wished to see on stage, and nothing else. This has to be read as testimony not only to the comprehensive totality (even the 'totalitarian nature') of Wagner's theatrical vision, but also to his conviction that only he could hope to realize that vision and that others would compromise and betray it.

In this he faced a fundamental problem, namely to discover a scenic language for the representation of myth. If there was one dark corner in Wagner's total vision of his works it was uncertainty about what his gods, giants and Nibelungs should look like. What he *did* know was that drama rooted in myth required a very different approach to staging from historical or topical drama. How, then, did Wagner imagine it should look on stage?

The three main Zürich theoretical treatises (*Art and Revolution*, *The Artwork of the Future* and *Opera and Drama*) are largely silent on this point. But 'Staging the Opera *Tannhäuser*' and the instructions Wagner sent to Liszt and his stage director Eduard Genast for the world premiere of *Lohengrin* in Weimar (28 August 1850) make it plain that he is still thinking in the language of romantic stage realism.[5] What he was always clear about, and it is entirely consistent with his mythopoeic credo, is that nature is the backdrop for the greater part of his dramatic foreground. And because the painter's first task was the 'inner comprehension and presentation of nature', Wagner believed that he could help him to achieve this on stage too. His idea is that the best artists of the day should no longer paint for private collectors or for the museums, but that their work should be a living and public art writ large on the huge canvas of the stage.[6]

He has little to say about stage decoration and costumes, though he is insistent on two negative points. First, that neither the scenery nor the costumes should in any way distract from the essential presentation of the drama, and secondly, that they should shun the specific historical detail that was so fashionable on the stages of his time. Flesh-and-blood characterization was for him always far more important than detailed colouration and he recognized the same approach in Mozart: 'How thoroughly Mozart understood how to give his Osmin and Figaro a national colouring, without seeking for the requisite tint in either Turkey or Spain, or even in books.'[7] Wagner's rejection of picturesque historical or ethnographic detail is no less apparent in *A Communication to My Friends*, the most important autobiographical manifesto of these years: 'The timeless nature of mythic material now made it plain that in my stagings all those small details which are indispensable in the modern playwright's presentation of convoluted historical events are totally unnecessary and that the thrust of the performance could be concentrated on a few important and decisive moments in the action.'[8] What mattered was that these decisive moments should always be absolutely clear to the spectators. The idea that such stagings would ideally require a new kind of theatre and performances under festival rather than repertory conditions first surfaces in this same *Communication*, as also in a letter of 14 September 1850 to the painter Ernst Benedikt Kietz: 'If I had [at least 10,000 talers] I would build here, just where I am [Zürich], a theatre out of boards and planks to my own design, send for the most suitable singers and arrange whatever was needed … so that I could be certain of an outstanding performance of the opera [*Siegfrieds Tod*].'[9]

But far more important for Wagner than anything scenic was, then as always, psychological and musical characterization. His principal concern is that the soloists and chorus should all live their roles, and that all gesture and movement should synchronize with the music. He talks of the singer's ability to mimic real life faithfully. By this he almost certainly means no more than the ability to conjure up 'true-to-life' impersonations of the utterly exceptional and extraordinary. What Wagner plainly wants is the kind of totally committed acting of which he himself was such a virtuoso exponent, which he recognized in Schröder-Devrient and which was an altogether exceptional occurrence on the contemporary opera stage. His sense of self-identification is patent when, in *Opera and Drama*, he elevates Molière above Racine, giving as one of his reasons the fact that Molière was an actor whereas Racine was merely a desk-bound author.

Schopenhauer on opera and its staging

Wagner's thoughts as to how the great mythical drama of the *Ring* might eventually be put on stage were of course as embryonic at this point as the work itself. The first version of the poem was completed and privately published in an edition of fifty copies by February 1853, and his next task was to compose the music. By September 1854 he had written the music for *Das Rheingold* and begun that for *Die Walküre*, and it was at about this time that the poet Georg Herwegh introduced him to the writings of the philosopher Schopenhauer. There he found both massive moral support and a challenge which helped to bring his ideas into a new and clearer focus.

What Wagner found in Schopenhauer seemed to him a confirmation of deeper, darker instincts that had been overlaid by his revolutionary fervour. Resignation and pessimism were the key to existence, not revolutionary utopianism. The world was evil and the only possible positive response to it was art, to which Schopenhauer assigned the highest value, and most especially to tragedy, the best mirror of the melancholy and dreadfulness of the human condition. Wagner's grave personal and artistic frustrations at this time only sharpened his predisposition to Schopenhauer and to the renunciatory, 'all is illusion' religion of Buddhism, to which he became powerfully drawn.

Schopenhauer argued that behind the phenomenal world, the world as it appears to our senses (or, as Wagner would have put it, the world of illusion, the world of Day), lies the inchoate metaphysical Will, which Schopenhauer identified with Kant's 'Ding an sich' (thing in itself). Mediating between the Will and phenomena are what Plato called the Ideas or Forms – independent of the laws of time, space and causality. All the arts except music are representations, metaphors of the external Ideas – incarnations of the Infinite – a notion which takes us back to Schelling's view of art as 'the infinite, finitely described'. Music, however, stands supreme in Schopenhauer's scheme in that it is the objectification not of the Ideas but of the metaphysical Will itself, of the absolute 'Ding an sich', of the bedrock of What Is. In Schopenhauer's own words, 'Music, having no connection with the Ideas, is independent also of the phenomenal world . . . . Music is by no means, like the other arts, an image of the Ideas: but an image of the Will itself, whose objectification the Ideas are. It is for this reason that the effect of music is so much mightier and more penetrating than that of the other arts; for these speak only of the shadow, music however of the essence.'[10]

The immediate and lasting impact of this line of reasoning on Wagner was to dissolve the chimera of the Gesamtkunstwerk. It dispersed the clouds of theorizing with which he had surrounded himself in setting up Drama as an absolute goal to which the several arts must be subordinate. The effect of the Gesamtkunstwerk, he later wrote, was that its constituent arts would consume and destroy each other 'in favour of the total purpose of them all.'[11]

Schopenhauer gave Wagner reasons to hold by what must have been a deep-seated instinct that music was rightfully the principal engine of drama. He was now able to acknowledge himself as the musical dramatist he had always been. 'Hear my creed,' says Wagner in 1857, when at work on Act I of *Siegfried*: 'music can never, regardless of what it is combined with, cease being the highest, the redeeming art. Its nature is such that what all the other arts only hint at becomes in it the most indubitable of certainties, the most direct and definite of truths.'[12]

This was more than a creed, for Wagner had already conceived *Tristan und Isolde*, the most completely musical of all his works. Previously he had written his texts well in advance of the music (which is not to say that musical ideas were not born with those texts, for they plainly were), but now there was little doubt in his mind that the musical idea came first. He did not even begin to find words for *Tristan* until three years after announcing to Liszt around 16 December 1854, 'I have planned in my head a *Tristan und Isolde*, the simplest, but most full-blooded musical conception.'[13] To the Princess Marie von Sayn-Wittgenstein, Wagner wrote on 19 December 1856 that while working on *Siegfried* he had slipped 'unawares into *Tristan* ... music without words for the present. There are some places, too, where I shall very likely do the music before the words.'[14]

Schopenhauer was no armchair philosopher but a man with a voracious appetite for literature and the visual arts. He spent his evenings at the theatre, opera and ballet and particularly esteemed the operas of Mozart, Rossini and Bellini. His belief in the primacy of music had implications for opera and its stage representation. For him, music's power was inseparable from the fact that, unlike most other arts, representation was not of its essence.

There had always, if unwittingly, been common ground between the philosopher and Wagner in that both were set against the 'effects without causes' of grand opera, repudiating the exploitation of lavish decoration for its own sake. It was because Schopenhauer rated opera so highly as an art form that he scourged grand opera for its rank neglect and abuse of opera's potential for getting to the heart of things. 'Grand opera,' says Schopenhauer, 'is really not a product of the pure artistic sense, but rather of the somewhat barbarous notion of the enhancement of aesthetic pleasure by the accumulation of the means, the simultaneous use of totally different impressions, and the intensification of the effect through an increase of the operative masses and forces.'[15]

Schopenhauer's whole argument on the presentation of the performing arts is that they should be non-literalistic, deliberately creating incomplete, indefinite images that seek an active response from the spectator's imagination. This view is entirely in sympathy with Wagner's own belief that only drama based on myth could strike to the core. Both Schopenhauer and Wagner – and independently of each other – had come to the conclusion that the highest form of drama and its stage presentation should be free from specific social, political or historical context. The practical implications of this were, however, far from fully apparent to Wagner. He had identified the threat of crystallizing myth into tangible history but without being able to suggest alternatives in anything other than the vaguest terms.

As we shall see in chapter 4, it was not until the 1870s that Schopenhauer's scenic strategy was explicitly reflected in Wagner's mature thoughts on the nature of his works and how he wished them to be presented in stage performance. The conception of *Tristan* (which, on the composer's own account, followed hard on his discovery of Schopenhauer) is proof enough that splendour and picturesque detail in stage action became less important for Wagner than previously – certainly in so far as they could be reckoned an intrinsic part of the work. He is now looking with a palpably more critical eye at the stage contribution to opera. Already in the Paris *Tannhäuser* of 1861 he is on his guard against the pitfalls of grandiose romantic realism, no matter how perfectly executed. He does not share the contemporary taste for historical exactitude in scenery and costumes. He recognizes, at whatever level and however imprecisely, that historicist stagings are as much a threat to the successful evocation of his mythopoeic dramas as anything sheerly decorative.

This feeling was to be even further substantiated by Wagner's experiences at the Munich Court Theatre. There, as we shall see, he was to resist the desire of Ludwig II and a great many others to follow the grand opera style by pinning Wagner's works to precise historical contexts. Beyond lay the challenge of keeping faith with his vision of the *Ring* by staging it in his own theatre at Bayreuth. The one constant factor in the development of Wagner's stage philosophy from the 1840s through to the 1870s is his realization that only a specially built theatre could provide the conditions for a performance of the *Ring* as he envisioned it.

Wagner at Ludwig II's Court Theatre in Munich

The long-term effect of Wagner's rescue from penury by the young King Ludwig II of Bavaria was the composer's realization (with the help of the king's purse) at Bayreuth of his dream of a theatre and festival for the exclusive production of his own works, and of the *Ring* in particular. But in the short term he was to pay a heavy, if somewhat unexpected, price. If, at the outset, it appeared that the composer's ambitions and the king's might converge in a triumphant first performance of the *Ring* in a new festival theatre built specially for it by Gottfried Semper on the banks of the Isar, it turned out – and painfully for both parties – that their theatrical aims were really very different.

Ludwig had inherited the throne of Bavaria on 10 March 1864 on the death of his father, Maximilian II. The new king was eighteen and had been obsessed with medieval legend from his earliest years and with Wagner's works since first hearing *Lohengrin* at the Munich Court Theatre on 2 February 1861. (He first heard *Tannhäuser* on 22 December 1862.) Within two months of his accession Ludwig had responded to Wagner's appeal (in the preface to a new version of the *Ring* poem published in 1863) for a German prince who could provide the exacting conditions he required for the performance of the *Ring*.

Those conditions, *in nuce*, were for the singers and other personnel to be trained by the composer, and for performances to be held not in any kind of German repertory theatre, but only as a festival in a specially constructed temporary building incorporating an amphitheatre-auditorium and a sunken pit so that the orchestra would be invisible to the audience. Wagner's hope was that model performances of the *Ring* would 'give the impetus to a genuinely German style of musico-dramatic production of which there is not the slightest trace at present'.[16]

In thrall to *Lohengrin* and *Tannhäuser* and to his dreams of the *Ring*, Ludwig saw himself as Wagner's saviour, paid off the composer's debts and brought him to Munich. The well-equipped Residenztheater (seating about five hundred) and Court Theatre (the Königliches Hof- und National-Theater, seating two thousand) were put at Wagner's disposal so that model performances could be given of his completed and still to be completed works. Within a month of their first meeting on 4 May 1864 the composer had produced a long-term plan which included premieres for *Tristan* and *Meistersinger* (both in 1865), the complete *Ring* (1867–8) and finally *Parsifal* (1871–2).

For the moment Wagner's long-felt need for his own theatre was laid aside, but by the end of 1864 Ludwig had determined to build not the temporary, experimental

structure mooted by the composer but a monumental festival theatre on a site overlooking the River Isar in the centre of Munich. Wagner was secretly opposed to this
but recommended Gottfried Semper, the architect already famous for the Dresden
Court Theatre (1841), with whom the composer had already discussed neo-Greek
theatre design in Zürich in the 1850s.[17] Semper was quickly summoned to Munich
to begin work. Wagner continued to urge upon the king the idea of a provisional
theatre to be constructed within the Glaspalast, a vast glass and iron exhibition hall
based on Joseph Paxton's London Crystal Palace (1850–1), for which Semper had
designed a theatre in 1856. (By the time Wagner was driven from Munich in December 1865, Semper had been working on plans for both a provisional theatre – two
versions – and a monumental theatre, all three schemes with amphitheatres and
sunken orchestra pits, as the king, though undoubtedly leaning towards the monumental theatre, had been unable to make up his mind between them.)[18]

With the architectural schemes under way, in January 1865 Wagner drew up a
revised schedule which foresaw a premiere for *Tristan* in the Residenztheater later in
the year, the completed *Ring* opening in the Semper festival theatre in August 1867,
and a grand festival in August 1873 of all the composer's works from *Tannhäuser* to
Parsifal.

Recognizing that more than architecture stood between his performance plans
and their realization, Wagner drew up a proposal for a German music school. To be
housed in a wing of the festival theatre, the school would lay the foundations for a
new and distinctively German style of both singing and acting. The project enjoyed
the lively support of the king, though not even his will and idealism were able to prevail against the political and economic pressures which prevented both theatre and

A model (1866) for the grand festival theatre which King Ludwig wanted to build for the *Ring*.
But Wagner was at heart no more enamoured of the monumental than he was of the prospect
of subservience to Ludwig and his court. The project, arguably the greatest dream-theatre of
the nineteenth century, remained unfulfilled. Its architect, chosen by Wagner, was Gottfried
Semper and the theatre's planned features of a sunken orchestra pit and Greek-style
amphitheatre were later successfully realized in the Bayreuth Festspielhaus.

school from coming into being. (Wagner rapidly lost all interest in the Semper theatre after his exile from Munich. The non-fulfilment of the theatre was a blow to the king, to its brilliant architect Semper and, ultimately, to the city of Munich. This theatre was one of Ludwig's greatest projects. Its frustration directed the king's building passion away from the enrichment of his capital and into the construction of his fantasy palaces in the Alps.)

Plainly the performances of the operas could not wait for decisions on the building plans. Wagner had to make do with yet another court theatre, though with the huge advantage, at least at first, of having the theatre's prince entirely behind him. The first of the intended model performances was a new staging of *Der fliegende Holländer* which opened on 4 December 1864. Although Wagner himself was both stage director and conductor, he was let down by technical deficiencies. The *Münchener Neueste Nachrichten* praised the painted scenery but was scornful of the small and ordinary ships, reporting that the wave effects often failed to function and that the supernatural effects in the third act were 'more a cause for mirth than terror'. The gulf between the 'model' intentions and what was actually achieved remained considerable.[19]

What the king was most eagerly looking forward to was the premiere of *Tristan* and the completion of the *Ring*. As things turned out, the *Tristan* premiere fired Wagner to complete not the *Ring* but *Die Meistersinger*, whose first night on 21 June 1868 was tainted only by the continuing public outrage about the composer's hold over the king and the scandal of his adultery with Cosima von Bülow, whose husband Hans von Bülow had conducted the premiere of *Tristan*, all of which meant that Wagner had to leave Munich in December 1865 after little more than a year. He took up residence at Tribschen, a villa overlooking Lake Lucerne, though he occasionally returned to Munich for rehearsals or performances.

Thereafter Wagner's relations with the king became severely strained, not least as a result of Ludwig's impatience to salvage for himself, and in the face of the composer's total opposition, the premieres of *Das Rheingold* and *Die Walküre* from the seemingly abandoned *Ring*. These premieres (1869 and 1870) proceeded without Wagner's personal participation (he arrived in Munich on 1 September 1869 but was barred from rehearsals) and, as he had foreseen, were far from successful, if perhaps not quite the disasters that he considered them to have been.

Ludwig's taste in art

Before discussing the Munich performances we should give some consideration to the young king's ideas about art, as these entirely determined the way in which his artists and theatre personnel set about their work. Long before he met Wagner, Ludwig had been immersed in German myths and legends. They were an inescapable part of his Wittelsbach inheritance as displayed on the walls of the castles and palaces in which he grew up. His discovery of Wagner's music and operas thrilled him profoundly because they brought his dreams to life. Just how musical Ludwig was is another matter. As a boy he was given piano lessons, but his teacher reported that the prince was unable to tell a Strauss waltz from a Beethoven sonata and blessed the day his pupil abandoned the instruction.[20] Wagner's own opinion, as expressed in 1876 to Georg Unger (the first Siegfried), was that 'the king is totally unmusical and is endowed only with a poetic temperament'.[21] Ludwig was, however, passionately fond of music. As the cabinet official Franz von Leinfelder remarked, it was capable of having 'a truly demonic effect' on him.[22] Ludwig's taste in opera was by no means restricted to Wagner, the roll-call of his 'private performances' (Separatvorstellungen) including works by Verdi, Massenet, Gluck, Mozart, Goldmark, Weber, Meyerbeer, Auber and Reinthaler.[23] But there is no question that Wagner's works affected him most of all. They inspired him to re-create life in their image, as, famously, in the uncompleted castle of Neuschwanstein, with its homage to the worlds of *Lohengrin*, *Tannhäuser* and *Parsifal*.

Neuschwanstein was, quite precisely, theatre translated into architecture, the first sketches for its exterior being the work of the scenic painter Christian Jank. Angelo II Quaglio's 1867 set for the second act of *Lohengrin* ('The court of the castle at Antwerp') was the model for the courtyard at Neuschwanstein, as designed by Jank, while the Act III bridal chamber from 1867 was transformed into the women's quarters at the Bavarian castle. Ludwig commanded that the Hall of Song at Neuschwanstein should be modelled directly from that in the newly restored Wartburg (1867). In its turn, Ludwig's Hall of Song became the model (against Wagner's wishes!) for countless subsequent stage settings for the second act of *Tannhäuser*.

But it was Ludwig's fantasy alone that created the throne room in Neuschwanstein. He had begun dreaming up settings for *Parsifal* from the moment he learnt of Wagner's plan to write the opera and, as it were, pre-empted the composer in proceeding to crystallize his own personal vision of the hall of the Grail by modelling it as a Byzantine basilica for his throne room. In the grounds of his castle at Linderhof (1870 to c. 1879) the king was able to sample at whim the disparate pleasures afforded by a Venus grotto, a Hunding hut, a Gurnemanz hermitage and a Good Friday meadow.

The one certain thing in this bewildering cross-traffic between history, stage designs and architecture is that it had everything to do with Ludwig's dream world and very little to do with the composer's own images of his works. Wagner was not afraid to voice his reservations about some of the representations of the subjects of his works which were so prolifically commissioned by Ludwig, as in the murals at Schloß Berg (*Tristan und Isolde*, 1866, and *Holländer*, 1867, both by Heinrich and August Spieß; *Lohengrin*, 1865, *Tannhäuser*, 1865, *Meistersinger*, 1866, the *Niflunga-Saga*, 1867, and *Parsifal*, 1869, all by Eduard Ille). On receipt of Ludwig's present to him of a watercolour by Ille based on *Tannhäuser*, Wagner, in thanking the king, commented that 'this style will never be free from the reproach of a certain affectation and artistic pretence, and I believe that, with my own poems and stage directions, I have demonstrated that the objects of the Middle Ages can be depicted in a more ideal, more purely human and more generally valid manner than this school of painting sets out to achieve. The painter who can match my own conception is therefore no doubt still to be found.'[24] That conception was based on his hope that the timeless kernel of myth and legend could assume some kind of modern rather than nostalgic depiction. He entertained some – perhaps not very profound – hope that, among the king's favourite painters, Bonaventura Genelli, whose style was that of a linear late classicism, might perhaps achieve something in this direction.[25]

Wagner was actively involved in the visualizations of his *Ring* poem which were commissioned by Ludwig from the historical painter Michael Echter for the Nibelungen Corridor (Nibelungeneingang) in the Residenz leading to its theatre. These thirty frescoes (1865–6) were the first point of reference for Ludwig's scenic artists in their designs for the premieres of *Das Rheingold* and *Die Walküre*.[26] The king's first artistic principle was 'fidelity to history'. He had no use for painters with too much originality. He demanded that art, which he understood only as a peep-show for bringing history to life, should conform to it. For the new production of *Tannhäuser* which, without Wagner's direct involvement, was to open on 1 August 1867, the composer wanted the 1861 Paris designs. Ludwig, however, had other ideas. His court secretary, Lorenz von Düfflipp, advised Wagner of the king's doubts: 'The hall of the Wartburg [in the Paris production] was in the Gothic style, which his Majesty regards as an unjustified anachronism because at the supposed time of the legend of *Tannhäuser* it was not the Gothic but the Byzantine style that was current.' On this occasion Ludwig gave in, but he usually had his way in such matters. In pursuit of his mania for historical exactitude he sent his stage designers to Rheims (for Schiller's play *Die Jungfrau von Orleans*), to Switzerland (for Schiller's *Wilhelm Tell*) and, very often, to Versailles (for numerous plays based on the Bourbons).[27]

At first it seemed to Wagner that Ludwig's devotion to him and the funds he made available would, at long last, enable German opera to fulfil itself at the Munich Court Theatre, triumphing over the obstacles that had proved insuperable in Dresden, Weimar and elsewhere. He had at his disposal an excellent orchestra, singers of reasonable competence and scenic artists who were among the very best of their day. Ludwig was more than willing to agree that whatever was lacking, including soloists and conductors, should be imported from elsewhere.

One of the things that must have chafed Wagner from the outset was that Ludwig's munificent provision did not totally square with the goals of the composer's theatre reform programme. What was on trial was whether, even under the most favourable circumstances, a court theatre (albeit that of an exceptionally artistic prince) could ever be wholly on the wavelength of Wagner's own vision. Conditions in Munich were scarcely likely to be conducive to the dedicated festival in a temporary theatre before an invited audience which Wagner had envisaged as part and parcel of the conception of the *Ring*.

At first, however, Wagner was more than grateful for what was on offer, and indeed it was a great deal. It made possible, particularly in the generosity of music-rehearsal time, the first performance of *Tristan und Isolde*, Wagner's first premiere for fifteen years. Previous attempts to perform the work had all floundered, notably those in Karlsruhe and in Vienna, where the production was abandoned in April 1863 after seventy-seven rehearsals. The opera, as Oswald Bauer points out, had become 'stig-

This workshop model for the Hall of Song in King Ludwig's Munich staging of *Tannhäuser* (1867) shows that his scenic artist, Angelo II Quaglio, closely followed Despléchin's designs for Dresden (1845) and Paris (1861). Ludwig was displeased that the setting was Gothic rather than Byzantine in style. The model gives a much better sense of how the scene would have looked on the stage than the artist's impression (illustrated on p. 44.)

'Dich, teure Halle . . .!' Mathilde Mallinger as Elisabeth in the Munich *Tannhäuser* (1867). Wagner thought very highly of her and she went on to create the role of Eva in *Die Meistersinger* the following year.

matized as unperformable. One Berlin newspaper rather sarcastically described the opera as an art-work only of the future since it was unperformable in the present'.[28]

The premiere of Tristan und Isolde (1865)

Not the least astonishing thing about *Tristan* is that its dramaturgy repudiates grandiose, illustrative staging, showing how far Wagner had travelled beyond his earlier romantic operas. It eschews external shows and effects, subjugating physical action to psychology and inner development. Wagner described *Tristan* not as an opera but as a 'Handlung', an unusual term the choice of which says much about the work. For although 'Handlung' generally means nothing more specific than a drama or scenic action, Wagner was using the word as the usual German translation of the Spanish word 'auto', thereby recording his palpable debt to the great Spanish dramatist Calderón de la Barca. For 'auto' was the description used by Calderón for his plays on spiritual themes, their ethos modelled on that of the medieval mystery plays. The term 'auto' indicated that a transcendental truth lay behind the immanent 'action' or tangible events.

In Wagner's 'Handlung' it is the music which carries all the action that matters, the physical movement of the characters being reduced to a bare minimum. In the composer's own words, 'virtually nothing happens [in Act II] except for music … which is made worse by the fact that I have offered the spectator practically nothing to look at'.[29] The relative importance of the stage action is so small as to inspire Paul Bekker's comment that 'Upon the stage walk sounds, not people'.[30] Tristan and Isolde are only partially 'characters' in the sense of recognizably flesh-and-blood human beings. What matters is that they embody the 'inner action', for which the vehicle is the music.

It was a fine irony that *Tristan* of all Wagner's works should be the first to receive its premiere (on 10 June 1865 – six years after its completion) in a theatre the aesthetic of which was that of Ludwig's historical realism. Not that this was of any great significance at the time, the overwhelming challenge being that of finding singers adequate to the unprecedented demands of the roles and of training an orchestra to play a score that was of extraordinary difficulty. Wagner was thrilled to discover in Ludwig Schnorr von Carolsfeld and his wife Malvina (who took the title roles) an uncanny understanding and immensely telling delivery of vocal lines which were then totally incomprehensible to most singers. The Schnorrs, together with Anton Mitterwurzer (Kurwenal), had been released as guests from the Dresden Opera through Ludwig's personal intervention with the King of Saxony.

In Ludwig Schnorr Wagner had at last found a male singer whose commitment and dramatic intensity matched those of Wilhelmine Schröder-Devrient. In the tribute he wrote following the singer's untimely death less than six weeks after the premiere, reputedly caused by a chill suffered on a draughty stage during a performance, Wagner evoked Schnorr's achievement in the hugely taxing third act: 'from the first bar to the last all attention and interest were directed towards, riveted on the singer alone … there was not a single moment, not a single word of the text

Wagner's perfect helmsman. Ludwig Schnorr von Carolsfeld in Act I of *Tristan und Isolde* at its premiere in Munich, 1865. The composer felt that he had at last discovered a male singer who could deliver the dramatic thrust of his vocal line and whose acting had the intensity of that of Wilhelmine Schröder-Devrient. This and the previous illustration (p. 57) are among the earliest photographs of singers in Wagnerian roles. They would have been taken not in the theatre but against mocked-up scenery in a studio.

that was met with inattention or distraction, rather that the orchestra completely disappeared beside him, or – more accurately – appeared to be subsumed in his delivery'.[31] Wagner himself produced the opera (in the Court Theatre, not the smaller Residenztheater as he had first envisaged), choosing as conductor Hans von Bülow, whose dedication to the composer's music survived his wife Cosima's scandalous defection to Wagner. 'With him [Bülow] a second self at my side,' wrote the composer to Friedrich Uhl in Vienna, inviting him to the premiere, 'I can attend to every detail of the musical performance and of the staging in the tranquil, relaxed, artistic atmosphere which only the sympathetic collaboration of artists who are also true friends can evoke. The care that is being lavished on the preparation of beautiful sets and extremely fine artistic costumes is such that you would think it was not a theatrical production that was at stake, but a monumental exhibition.'[32]

The sets were designed to Wagner's instructions by two of the king's best scenic artists, Angelo Quaglio (Acts I and III) and Heinrich Döll (Act II). Ludwig had argued for medieval settings, but Wagner steered them in the direction of being none too specifically early Romanesque in style, while the costume designs by Franz Seitz, the Court Theatre's technical director and costumier, were modified by Wagner into a cross between the Germanic and Romanesque. The lighting technology did not begin to do justice to the juxtapositions of Night and Day that are so central to the work. Quaglio and Döll's sets had shadows and light effects already painted in. They addressed the externals prescribed in the composer's rubrics and were virtuoso exercises in the lingua franca of romantic naturalism.

Although the first performances of an opera of such unprecedented originality must have made huge demands on the audience's understanding, the public response was by no means unsympathetic.[33] Wagner was well pleased with the settings and four performances, and most especially with his singers and with Bülow's conducting. Bülow himself reported 'the greatest success that a new Wagner work has ever had anywhere. The Schnorrs were unbelievable; all the others quite tolerable; orchestra excellent'.[34] The relatively unproblematic scenic demands had been more than adequately met. Nearly twenty years later, in writing of the first Vienna performance of 1883, Eduard Hanslick dyspeptically singled out very similar settings for praise while censuring the work itself: '*Tristan und Isolde*', he wrote, 'resembles an opera only in the visible scenery … the first act is pleasantly impressive for the pictorial effect … the overall impression of the work, despite its outstanding individual beauties, remains one of oppressive fatigue resulting from too much unhealthy overstimulation – a condition unchanged by the fact that it has been occasioned by a great genius'.[35]

The premiere of Die Meistersinger von Nürnberg *(1868)*

Six months after the *Tristan* premiere Wagner was on his way to what proved to be a highly creative exile at Tribschen. He had struggled on to complete the second act of *Siegfried*, but it was *Die Meistersinger* that he really wanted to compose. He took up the score in January 1866 and had completed it by 24 October 1867. The premiere was scheduled for the Court Theatre in the summer of 1868, and the composer agreed to return to direct the rehearsals, with Bülow conducting.

Just how 'historical' did Wagner intend *Die Meistersinger* to be? The subject matter and inspiration were, of course, Hans Sachs's Nuremberg, about which the composer had read much. But Wagner's interest, like that of so many of his contemporaries, was in creating a *myth* of old Nuremberg which corresponded to a present need that was certainly not for historical veracity. Mid-nineteenth-century Germany needed to believe in a utopian Nuremberg that would represent a bulwark of national identity against political divisiveness and the pressures of modern industrialization. Wagner, largely sharing this view, began by seeing the Nuremberg Mastersingers as material for a satyr play pendant to *Tannhäuser*, but ended by believing in them as a metaphor for his philosophy of art and the part it could play in German regeneration.

He knew the city from a number of visits, most importantly in 1861 when he arrived less than three weeks after the Deutsches Sängerfest.[36] But when it came to the stage realization of the opera, he rejected the option of archaeological exactitude (which was Ludwig's choice) in favour of whatever assisted the sheerly artistic presentation of his drama.

In 1865, however, the composer and his patron were both seized by the idea of christening *Die Meistersinger* not in Munich, as first envisaged, but in its name city. In Wagner's diary entries of 14–27 September 1865, written expressly for perusal by the king, the composer described Nuremberg as 'the home of the "art-work of the future" ', and declared that the people must be shown 'clearly and unequivocally, in golden letters of fire, what is truly German, what the genuine German spirit is: the spirit of all that is genuine, true and unadulterated'.[37] The Nuremberg plan was later abandoned in favour of a Munich premiere as part of the celebrations for the king's projected marriage to his cousin, the Duchess Sophie of Bavaria. Although the marriage never took place, the opera remained destined for Ludwig's Court Theatre. The premiere was set for 1868.

On Ludwig's initiative, and to Wagner's consternation, Angelo Quaglio and Heinrich Döll were despatched in June 1867 to do scenic fieldwork in Nuremberg. When they reported back to Wagner in Tribschen he adjusted architectural literalness to serve the higher truths of art. The Nuremberg of his opera was a product of the imagination and justice had to be done to it on its own terms, not those of historical exactitude. Working to Wagner's instructions, Quaglio (now assisted by Christian Jank in all the designs up to and including Sachs's workshop) made no attempt to recreate the interior of the real St Catherine's Church for Act I but created a composite fiction from the sketches he had made of several Nuremberg churches. Hans Sachs's famous house (destroyed in the Second World War) was plucked from the row it actually stood in and placed on a corner downstage left, opposite the rather grander dwelling of the wealthy Pogner.

Wagner's demand that the houses should be not just painted façades but practicable solid constructions was a radical departure from German stage practice and was doubtless something he wished to import from what he had seen in Paris. 'The traditional flats,' observed the *Neue Berliner Musikzeitung*, 'have disappeared in order to make room for the very embodiment of the town of Nuremberg with its houses, gables and overhangs. What one sees here are not painted houses but complete cardboard buildings, copied from real life, and streets, squares and perspectives so life-like as to deceive one into thinking them real'.[38] The Festwiese of Act III was Döll's romantic interpretation of the Hallerwiese, the traditional site for festivals held outside the city walls.

The Court Theatre, uncertain of the extent to which it could count on the exiled composer's own involvement, employed a guest stage manager, Reinhard Hallwachs from Stuttgart, to oversee the production. It also engaged a choreographer, Lucile Grahn, whose contributions to the staging included help with the street brawl at the end of Act II, and with the festivities in Act III. As things turned out, Wagner could not resist becoming involved. The opera's score is famously prescriptive of how its characters should move and behave. Wagner's remarkable mimetic gifts had, as the Vienna *Neue Freie Presse* reported on 21 June 1868, rarely been deployed to better effect:

> In a state of continuous excitement that makes one nervous Wagner [on stage, directing] accompanies every note sung with a corresponding gesture that the singers imitate as closely as they can; only someone who has seen the composer toiling and gesticulating in this way can have any idea of the multitude of nuances he wants to be conveyed. Almost every step, every movement of a hand, every

Ludwig, unlike Wagner, was a stickler for architectural exactitude. For the 1868 premiere of *Die Meistersinger* he sent Angelo II Quaglio and Christan Jank to Nuremberg to research the interior of St Catherine's Church, this drawing being one result.

It can be seen how the drawing in the previous illustration has (*at the right*) been incorporated into Angelo II Quaglio's model (1869) for the first act of *Die Meistersinger*. At Wagner's insistence, the setting was, *contra* Ludwig, not an exact replica of St Catherine's but a fictitious amalgam of features copied from a number of churches in Nuremberg.

opening door, is 'musically illustrated', and there is in *Die Meistersinger*, in particular, such a quantity of music illustrative of the singers' mime that we would
regard it as miraculous if a production of the opera that was not rehearsed under
the composer's supervision managed to introduce all the actions intended to
accompany this music. Only when Fräulein Mallinger [Eva] is singing does
Wagner suspend his instructions, listen with visible pleasure, trot to and fro …
give pleased, approving nods and smile all over his face.[39]

Again, one notes that Wagner coached intensively when needed, but was rarely hap-
pier than when singers understood his music so well that they were able both to
characterize it faithfully and bring something of their own to it.

The premiere on 21 June 1868 was enthusiastically received. So effective was the
superbly detailed, coherent production that it received unequivocal praise, even if
the music did not. If Wagner is right in his (unsubstantiated) assertion that Hanslick
knew that he had been lampooned in Beckmesser (originally 'Veit Hanslich'), then
the critic had reason enough to be antipathetic. But that feeling did not dampen his
praise for the scenic contribution and the musical performance: 'As a theatrical
experience, *Die Meistersinger* is well worth seeing, the musical presentation excellent,
the scenic incomparable. Dazzling scenes of colour and splendour, ensembles full of
life and character unfold before the spectator's eyes, hardly allowing him the leisure
to weigh how much and how little of these effects is of musical origin. … [Wagner]
has once again proved himself a born operatic producer, and brilliantly vindicates
his reputation for genius in the field of mise-en-scène.'[40]

The fact that Wagner had been allowed to watch the premiere and receive ovations
from the king's box had, from the outset, lent authority to the work's status as an
exemplar and symbol of German art. It was to meet the need of the young German
Empire born in 1871 for a work to dedicate new theatres or to celebrate patriotic
occasions; and to this day it has remained *the* German commemorative festival opera.

The premieres of **Das Rheingold** (1869) and **Die Walküre** (1870)

After the triumph of *Die Meistersinger* Ludwig ordered a premiere performance of
Rheingold as soon as it could be managed. The *Ring* was still very much a work in
progress, but *Das Rheingold* and *Die Walküre* were complete and Wagner had given
their manuscript scores as birthday presents to Ludwig in 1865 and 1866. While
wholeheartedly against any proper staging until the whole work was complete and
the appropriate festival conditions assured, Wagner had himself suggested that each
year one part of the cycle might be given a 'provisional' production in Munich, his
only condition being the refurbishment of the technical installations in the Court
Theatre, including enlargement of the orchestra pit. This refurbishment was duly
completed in 1869 and there was thus no obstacle – apart from Wagner's coolness
(he was of course still living in Tribschen) – to a performance. Supervision of
this was entrusted to Reinhard Hallwachs, who had at least worked alongside the
composer on *Die Meistersinger*.

Uneasily resigned to Ludwig having things his way, Wagner insisted that Hallwachs and other members of the production team and singers should consult with him in Tribschen. It was clear to him that the extraordinary musical and technical demands (the underwater scene with the Rhinedaughters, the transformations between the depths and mountain heights, the dwarves and giants, the thunderstorm and the rainbow bridge) stood little chance of making their desired effect without his closest personal supervision.

When the costume sketches by Hallwachs's team arrived in Tribschen, Wagner at once saw that his mythopoeic vision of the *Ring* was about to be betrayed by a characteristically Ludwigian attempt to give it historical roots. Wagner returned the sketches on 26 July 1869 not to the administration (from whom he believed they had come) but to Hans Richter, his chosen conductor, asking that he intercede for him, and insisting upon

> more detailed studies with the aim of finding characteristic costumes for this ancient Germanic world of gods. The most imaginative painters and archaeologists would naturally have to be consulted here. In general, my initial objection to the sketches I have been sent is that they show no sense of invention and that (as copies of Echter's frescoes) they include only Greek costumes … a kind of costume which reveals everything except Germanic gods. … No *gold* jewelry! that surely goes without saying in a piece where gold first has to be discovered and made known to the gods, etc.[41]

The designs were eventually prepared by Franz Seitz and Wagner was able to make some changes.

The same Echter frescoes were used by the scenic artists Heinrich Döll (scene 1), Christian Jank and Angelo Quaglio (scenes 2 and 3) as their point of departure, evidently with sufficiently good results – though Wagner himself did not see the results on stage – for the composer to consider using Döll for Bayreuth. The stage technicians were Carl Brandt, the most highly regarded German machinist of the day, and his younger brother Friedrich (Fritz).[42] When it became clear that things were not working out as Wagner would have wished, Hans Richter withdrew, as did Franz Betz (Wotan) and other principal guest singers favoured by the composer. Richter was promptly replaced by Franz Wüllner, whom Wagner considered worthless and did his best – though to no avail – to warn off. Despite Wagner's impassioned efforts to get the performances stopped, Ludwig brushed him aside. New principals were drafted in from the resident company. Rehearsal time was totally inadequate. Nevertheless, the production team was not without technical expertise and word got around that sensational effects were in preparation, so much so that Hanslick – who, as we have seen, appeared to prefer Wagner's scenic effects to his music – protested that everyone was talking 'about swimming nixies, coloured steam, the castle of the gods and the rainbow' but 'only rarely about the music'.[43] The Brandts devised swimming contraptions for the Rhinedaughters, but in the end it was ballet dancers who rode in them while the singers performed from the wings. Transformation scenes

Angelo II Quaglio's model of the final scene of *Das Rheingold*, as performed in Munich in 1878, nine years after King Ludwig had given the premiere of the work there against Wagner's wishes. The depiction of Valhalla was probably very similar to what was seen at Bayreuth in 1876 when Wilhelm Mohr remarked on 'a whole series of towers of various heights which looked like massive carriage-clocks'. At the Munich premiere the rainbow bridge was a solid construction and not the magical illusion for which Wagner had hoped.

were effected with steam suffused with coloured lighting. The best that could be managed for the rainbow bridge was a palpably solid construction that destroyed the intended magical effect.

With no one competent present to direct either the music or the staging, the result must indeed have fallen seriously short of Wagner's intentions, though level-headed eyewitnesses like the composer Peter Cornelius considered that the fuss about the staging had been overdone. The scene changes, he said, had generally worked 'with such precision that they conveyed absolutely no impression of being associated with such extraordinary difficulties'.[44] It was, in all probability, nothing to do with the production but rather the unfamiliar style of the music (especially the vocal lines, which were considered to be too much like recitative) and its inadequate performance that were responsible for the failure of *Das Rheingold* to consolidate the tremendous impression produced by *Die Meistersinger*. For Wagner's associates like Richter it must have been another demonstration that his works made scant sense when detached from his personal supervision.

Undeterred, the king issued instructions for repeat performances in December 1870, followed by the premiere of *Die Walküre*. Without knowing this, Wagner penned a howl of protest at the *Rheingold* performances as they had been described to him:

Do you want my work as I want it,
or: do you not want it like that?

In this same letter of 20 November 1869 he challenges Ludwig to tell him 'whether it was ever your serious and true intent to carry out the great plan according to which we would perform the Nibelungs and hold them up to the German world as the monumental starting-point for a new and noble period of art? … Judge then with what bitter, nay – Godforsaken feelings I had to submit to seeing your commands carried out, as you reduced this tremendous work of mine to the level of achievement of some wretched operatic repertory performed for subscribers and critics!'[45]

Wagner's objections were swept aside and *Die Walküre* was premiered on 26 June 1870 with the same conductor and production team as had been used for *Rheingold*. Lacking Wagner's personal coaching the singers evidently failed to seize the audience, who found the long and crucial second-act monologues tedious in the extreme. The spotlight fell on the prodigies achieved by the technical department. 'There was,' says Bauer, 'unqualified praise for the skill of the Brandt brothers and the storm and tempest scenes left a deep impression by virtue of their new type of lighting effects and the dramatic scudding of clouds by Angelo Quaglio. Grooms from the royal stables wearing appropriate costumes and riding real horses performed a daredevil Ride of the Valkyries.' But efforts to conjure the magic fire around the sleeping Brünnhilde nearly succeeded in setting the theatre alight: 'Since the gas

Siegmund and Sieglinde (*left*) as imagined by the historical painter Michael Echter in one of a series of thirty *Ring* frescoes for King Ludwig which were made in 1865/6 in consultation with Wagner. This is a watercolour copy by Franz Heigel as the frescoes were destroyed in the Second World War. The closeness with which the Echter frescoes were followed can be judged by the studio photograph (*right*) of Heinrich and Therese Vogl at the time of the first performance of *Die Walküre* in Munich, 1870. Someone seems to have forgotten that there should have been a sword in the tree.

flames for the magic fire were too pale to make any impact, spirit was poured into buckets and set alight, causing flames to leap several feet into the air and giving off an intense heat. The inhabitants of the surrounding houses had protested against the dangers of these pyrotechnic displays and during the performances the audience was struck by such a sense of dread and terror that the ending of the work, with all its delicacy, failed totally to make any impression.'[46] (The audience's alarm was justified: there were at least eleven hundred major auditorium fires between 1797 and 1897; the average life of a theatre or public assembly room was eighteen years.)[47]

What a bitter irony for the Wagner who had ceaselessly campaigned against opera as 'effects without causes'! As he had foreseen, the dramatic heart of the work had been entirely lost. Meanwhile the rift with the king (who was now clamouring for *Siegfried* and whose financial favours the composer nonetheless continued to enjoy at Tribschen) was all but complete. Wagner told him that he felt like a father 'whose child has been torn from his arms in order to be handed over to prostitution'.[48]

A Munich balance sheet

As we have seen, the Munich performances of his works brought Wagner face to face with the king's style of romantic realism. While this was largely what the composer himself wanted for *Tannhäuser*, *Lohengrin* and *Die Meistersinger*, he discovered that it could not do justice to so introspective a drama as *Tristan*, nor was the available technology equal to the transformations and scenic conjuring tricks required for the *Ring*. On the positive side, Ludwig was no less committed to stagings that were an integral part of the work than Wagner – such commitment being exceedingly rare in German theatres of the time – and ensured that meticulous attention was paid to every detail of the sets and costumes. But whereas Ludwig's passion for scenic illusion derived from his need for a personal time-machine in which he could relive the past and visit 'faery lands forlorn', Wagner wanted artistic images that were timeless precisely because they avoided specific historical reference – hence his constant battle against Ludwig's arguments for medieval rather than Romanesque, Byzantine rather than Gothic, and so on. Ludwig wanted art to pull him back into history. Wagner, on the other hand, wanted to bring myth and legend forward into the nineteenth century.

Ludwig shared Wagner's hopes for an idealistic form of theatre that would educate and renew the German soul, but this was always a less powerful draw for him than his own personal need for Wagner's magic carpet. He never understood why Wagner should want a temporary rather than a grand permanent theatre. Unlike the composer he was as keenly interested in a singer's physical attributes as he was in his vocal and musical ability (hence the clash over Wagner's casting his proven tenor, the portly, nearly sixty-year-old Tichatschek, as Lohengrin in June 1867). Ludwig had his own problems with the audience at his court theatres, notably the fact that it was there at all, thereby destroying the illusion of his total immersion in the performance. But these were different from Wagner's, who at all times wanted only a dedicated, out-of-town festival audience. A further disappointment for Wagner was that his plans to strengthen the whole base for the intelligent performance of opera were not fulfilled. The school for performers did not materialize, nor did he have the slightest success in his attempts to replace control over the Court Theatre by high-born court officials with control by people who were musicians and artists.

Wagner had been promised 'model performances' of his works, but although he was relatively happy with the stagings of *Tristan*, *Tannhäuser* and *Die Meistersinger* he was far from satisfied and knew that much remained to be done. He was sharply aware of the gulf between Ludwig's theatrical ideas and his own, particularly where the stage realization of the *Ring* was concerned. Ultimately the Munich experience helped Wagner define the distance between the performance aesthetic of his time in one of its most developed manifestations and whatever it was he was looking for. One thing was certain: it could only happen with not just the music and the stage under his total control but the very theatre itself.

Wagner and Ludwig were very nearly united in their love of nature and their interest in its vivid re-creation in theatrical works – as, say, in the second act of *Tristan*, the first and third acts of *Parsifal* and throughout the *Ring*. For Ludwig, the scenery for the rocky mountain heights among which the second and third acts of *Die Walküre* are set *was* the Bavarian Alps around his castles. Walking or riding in the mountains he lived the operas; seated in the theatre he expected to be transported as irresistibly into nature as into history. Wagner, too, strove to ensure that the part which his own experiences as a walker of the Alpine heights had played in the making of the *Ring* should be reflected in stage production. He had common cause with Ludwig in seeking an idealized theatrical representation of landscape and the drama of the elements.

On to Bayreuth

For some time Wagner had, of course, been looking elsewhere than Munich for his festival theatre, eventually discovering a site and friendly local dignitaries in the northern Franconian town of Bayreuth, still in Ludwig's kingdom but some 250 kilometres removed from courtly demands and princely whims. By this time Bismarck had united Germany (from 18 January 1871, when Wilhelm I of Prussia was proclaimed Kaiser at Versailles) and, as part and parcel of Wagner's ascendant aspirations for the new Reich, it must have seemed that a festival location in the more northerly Bayreuth could more readily serve the artistic regeneration of the German people as a whole than one in the Bavarian capital.

On 22 May 1872, Wagner's birthday, the foundation stone of the Festspielhaus on the Green Hill above Bayreuth was laid. The king had been invited but did not attend. Wagner battled to fund the theatre on his own, but the difficulties were immense. Finally Ludwig could bear the estrangement no longer – one should never underestimate the extent to which he identified with Wagner's festival vision; it was a dream, a purpose in his life, that he could not live without. On 25 January 1874, the king came once more to the rescue: 'No, no and again no! It shall not end like this! Help must be offered! Our plan must not be allowed to fail. Parcival knows his mission and will do everything that lies in his power.'[49]

CHAPTER 3

Staging the *Ring* at Bayreuth

The performance will lag as far behind the work as the work is removed from our own times!

Cosima Wagner, diary entry for 26 July 1876[1]

The Festspielhaus

The need for a special theatre for the production of his works – and of the *Ring* in particular – had been in Wagner's mind for a long time before Ludwig entered his life. Indeed, the whole conception of the *Ring* was indissolubly linked to that of a festival theatre dedicated to its performance. Only very shortly before his rescue by Ludwig in 1864, in his preface to the new 1863 edition of the text of the *Ring*, Wagner made it quite plain that he envisaged eventual performance only in a special theatre and under festival conditions. No existing German company could respond satisfactorily to the challenge of the work. He refers to 'the almost grotesque incorrectness of performances' by German companies. Correct performances required hand-picked singers. The auditorium would be an amphitheatre and the orchestra invisible. Nothing would be allowed to undermine the sense of total illusion created on the stage.[2]

Famously it was the Greek amphitheatre that inspired Wagner's vision of a theatre where all sightlines would be equally good. But he was no antiquarian and plundered history for his own ends. There could, for instance, be no retreat from covered theatres and artificial lighting, though it is noteworthy that the 'alternative' theatre which Semper designed for construction within the Munich Glaspalast would have put a solid roof over the stage only, leaving the greater part of the audience in daylight.

Wagner expected that his stage, unlike that of the Greek theatres, should create a perfect illusory world for the spectators, necessitating concealment of the orchestra. Such ideas may have begun to ferment in his mind at least as early as 1837–9 when he was musical director in Riga, where, as we have seen, he had been struck by the little theatre's rising stalls, the sunken orchestra pit and the relative darkness of the auditorium.

The composer's earliest practical plan for a theatre was for a strictly temporary structure whose detailed layout remained somewhat indeterminate, as may be seen in a letter from Wagner to his artist friend Ernst Benedikt Kietz, written from Paris on 14 September 1850:

> I am genuinely thinking of setting *Siegfried* [*Siegfrieds Tod*] to music, only I cannot reconcile myself with the idea of trusting to luck and of having the work performed by the very first theatre that comes along: on the contrary, I am toying with the boldest of plans... I would have a theatre erected here on the spot, made of planks, and have the most suitable singers join me here, and arrange everything necessary for this one special occasion, so that I could be certain of an outstanding performance of the opera. I would then ... give three performances – free, of course – one after the other in the space of a week, after which the theatre would then be demolished and the whole affair would be over and done with.[3]

Plans for other temporary wooden theatres followed. In July 1854 his love of the view of the mountains across Lake Lucerne from Brunnen gave him the idea of performing the *Ring* on a floating stage on the lake. It was a dream that was not abandoned until May 1856, when a storm over the lake showed only too plainly that the stage would have been even more impermanent than he had planned.

In 1861 Wagner explained to Hans von Bülow his need for his 'own theatre', one entirely different from the existing court and public theatres: 'I need a theatre such as I alone can build. It is not possible that my works should establish themselves in the same theatres where simultaneously the operatic nonsense of our time – and that includes the classics – is put on, and where everything, the presentation, the whole approach and the desired effect, is basically in direct opposition to what I desire for myself and my works.'[4]

The invisible orchestra

By 1863 the internal features of the new theatre had further crystallized in Wagner's mind: 'a temporary theatre ... perhaps just of wood. .... I have discussed a feasible plan, with an amphitheatre-auditorium and the great advantage of a concealed orchestra, with an experienced and imaginative architect [Gottfried Semper]... I would in particular lay great value on the orchestra being invisible, which could be achieved by architectural means if the auditorium were constructed in the form of an amphitheatre.' The serious-minded spectator would thus be protected from being made 'an involuntary observer of technical procedures [i.e., the movements of the players and the conductor] which should be hidden from him with almost as much care as the ropes, pulleys, struts and boards of the sets, the sight of which from the wings is well known to destroy all illusion'. Anyone lucky enough to have heard an orchestra 'through an acoustic sound-wall, purged of every trace of the non-musical sounds which the instrumentalists cannot avoid making in producing their notes', would 'realize the advantages for the singer of standing virtually directly in front of the hearer' and 'needs only to deduce how much more easily comprehensible the enunciation will be, to appreciate to the full the likely success of my acoustic and architectural proposals'.[5]

Wagner's plan for an invisible orchestra was not wholly original. Claude-Nicholas Ledoux built a theatre in Besançon (1778–84) in which the orchestra pit was partly hidden under the stage,[6] while proposals for orchestra concealment were made by, among others, de Marette, in his *Mémoire sur une nouvelle orchestre* (1775), and Karl Friedrich Schinkel in his essay 'Senkung des Orchesters' (c. 1817).[7]

The Munich festival theatre

As we saw in the previous chapter, within little more than a year of Wagner's having set out his agenda the young King Ludwig was offering to build him a theatre in Munich which would have satisfied many of his requirements. Wagner's reasons for frustrating Ludwig's plan have already been explained, but its specifications, as drawn up by Semper, are important evidence of the composer's intentions, intentions which were to carry through into the Bayreuth Festspielhaus and beyond.

Semper explained that everything in the design, as agreed between Wagner and himself, was focused on two fundamental principles:

1. Complete separation of the ideal world on the stage from the reality represented by the audience.
2. In accordance with this separation, the orchestra to be unseen, perceptible only to the ear.

The auditorium was to be modelled on 'the ancient Greek and Roman pattern with rows of seats rising step by step (*cavea*)' and the modern convention of vertical tiers of boxes was to be abandoned altogether. This scheme would enable 'all the different elements of dramatic presentation to make their effects much more easily, in particular to be equally effective for every seat in the theatre'.

Wagner's opposition to the usual court theatre layout, whose seating arrangements embodied the principle that there were many different orders in society, could not be more clearly expressed. The new homogeneous, even anonymous audience was to be separated from the stage by the sunken orchestra pit and seduced by architectural means into believing in the illusory world conjured up on the stage. The dark space between the *cavea* and the stage, Semper explained, 'creates between the two what may be called a neutral space, whose boundaries in every direction, upwards, downwards and sideways, are visible to the spectator, so that the eye can no longer measure the true distance of the stage surround rising on the far side of the neutral space, for lack of points of reference, especially if the eye is further deceived as to the distance by appropriate use of perspective and optical illusion'.[8]

The festival theatre would have been a compromise between the composer's prescriptions and the grandiose architectural statement required of a Wittelsbach building on one of the most prominent sites in Munich. If constructed, the promenade areas around the auditorium would have ensured that courtly display and social ostentation would have gone on much as before. Wagner's apprehension about these aspects of the scheme and his realization that the theatre would always be a civic monument by no means wholly in his control contributed as powerfully to its failure as the huge demand it would have made on the royal purse.

Building the 'theatre of total illusion'

As we have seen, Wagner felt that the only way to secure the core of his vision intact was to move it away from Munich, its troublesome courtiers and its less than totally compliant king. At Bayreuth, the fundamentals of Wagner and Semper's concept were translated into reality by the architect Otto Brückwald – the composer was in no position to commission Semper, who had been deeply wounded by his failing enthusiasm for and therefore effective subversion of the Munich project.

As realized at Bayreuth, Wagner's theatre was to be far removed from his early insistence – derived both from the dramatic festivals of the Greeks and from the Elizabethan theatre – that players and audience could be co-creators of the dramatic experience only if they could see and respond to each other. As expounded in a speech delivered at the laying of the foundation stone for the Festspielhaus (22 May 1872), the composer eventually concluded that 'reality should be separated from

'A theatre such as I alone can build.' Wagner and Semper's ideas were eventually realized in the Festspielhaus designed by Otto Brückwald on the Green Hill overlooking Bayreuth. This sepia photo of the west side was taken at the time of the first Festival in 1876.

ideality' and that the separation should be not just a proscenium but the 'mystic abyss', or invisible, sunken orchestra pit.[9] Wagner's thinking had developed to the point where there was no question but that the audience was a separate entity from the stage and its performers.

His new theatre was to be a machine for focusing the audience's full attention upon the stage – a demand that was quite novel in an age when a great many of the audience went to the theatre to see and be seen. It was always an absolutely central part of his programme that, through the power of his music and his theatre, the audience should be transported into his world of mythic reality. He saw that the way to achieve this was to construct as perfect a 'theatre of illusion' as he could.

All expense and effort were to go into the stage and auditorium, Wagner explained to one of his Bayreuth backers, the banker Friedrich Feustel, the utmost economy being exercised on the building itself ('*provisional* only … it should be no more solid than is necessary to prevent it from collapsing. Therefore economize here, economize – no ornamentation'). On the other hand, nothing was to be spared with 'stage machinery and scenery, and everything that relates to the ideal, inner work of art – *perfect* in every way. *No* economies here: everything as though destined to last a long time, nothing provisional.'[10]

The importance that Wagner attached to creating a totally convincing theatrical illusion for the spectator is evident in his speech for the laying of the foundation stone:

> you will find expressed in the proportions and the arrangement of the auditorium and the seats an idea, the comprehension of which will at once place you in a new relationship to the drama you will have come to see, and different from any that you have previously experienced in our theatres. Should this first impression be already pure and perfect, the subsequent mysterious entry of the music will prepare you for the unveiling and visible presentation of scenes such as you might imagine had come from an ideal world of dreams, demonstrating the most perfect illusion that a noble art can accomplish. There will be nothing 'provisional' here, to engage you with mere hints; the most up-to-date artistic resources will be used to offer you scenic and theatrical perfection.[11]

There was to be no promenade space other than the open ground outside the theatre itself. The whole setting was to be the closest approximation to that original vision of a temporary building in the middle of a meadow. Unlike most contemporaneous theatres, the action on the stage would not be set in an ostentatious frame of gilded plasterwork and footlights. At Bayreuth the classical proscenium arch would still be present, but would be doubled by a second arch set slightly forward on the line of the front of the curved shell concealing the sunken orchestra pit. Wagner's purpose was that the two arches should be a perspective device, merging the audience's field of view into the stage space and heightening the illusion that what was presented there was 'for real'. In the composer's own highly charged description, the view to the stage through the two proscenium arches 'reveals the distant scene to

This engraving from 1875 is of the Festspielhaus auditorium before the notoriously uncomfortable wood-and-cane seating was installed. It shows the decorated canvas ceiling, doubled proscenium arch and the front of the curved shell concealing the orchestra pit.

The denizens of the 'mystic abyss'. The orchestra seated for a rehearsal of *Parsifal* in the sunken pit as probably drawn by the Munich Court Orchestra official Josef Greif in 1882. The actual pit is not as steeply sloped as it is here depicted. The figure gesturing to the conductor through a removable hatch behind him is intended to be Wagner. Identifiable by his blond hair among the horn players is Franz Strauss, father of Richard Strauss.

[the spectator] with the unapproachability of a dreamlike vision, while the spectral music, rising up from the "mystic abyss" like vapours wafting up from the sacred primeval womb of Gaia beneath the Pythia's seat, transports him into that inspired state of clairvoyance in which the scenic picture becomes the truest reflection of life itself'.[12] With allowance for a degree of poetic excess, this was an extraordinarily accurate prediction of what was to be achieved in the completed Festspielhaus.

Dimming the auditorium

What went unremarked in Wagner's foundation-stone speech was the hugely important contribution to the spectators' sense of a 'vision in a dream' that would be made by dimming the lighting in the auditorium, as had already been done at the 1869 Munich premiere of *Das Rheingold* (the newly installed gas lighting was turned down to half-strength – almost certainly at the composer's instigation).[13] Remembering the advantages of the feeble ('ärmliche') lighting in the Riga auditorium, Wagner had long realized that an essential ingredient in heightening the illusion of the stage picture was that the audience should sit in relative darkness. This was novel in that in German theatres the auditorium was generally lit sufficiently well for the audience to be able to follow the action in their libretti.

Precedents for darkening the auditorium can be traced to the middle of the seventeenth century. In Venetian public theatres, the first of which opened in 1637, the auditorium was left in semi-darkness when the chandeliers were hoisted up through the proscenium arch at the start of the performance. This practice continued in Italian public theatres into the nineteenth century, the auditoria in Rome being particularly noted for their darkness.[14] The earliest theatre in which the auditorium lighting could be adjusted between 'normal' and 'dimmed' during performances was probably the Teatro Argentina in Rome, built by the Marchese Girolamo Teodoli in 1732.[15]

Audiences north of the Alps, however, were accustomed to social display in brightly lit auditoria, occasional dimming to assist moonlit stage effects coming in only from the early nineteenth century. It was the Italian Servandoni who, as we saw in chapter 1, introduced the darkened auditorium to Paris for his *spectacles d'optique* in the Salle des Machines in the mid-eighteenth century. To increase the sense of illusion, he too hoisted the chandeliers through the ceiling at the start of the performance. But this was a relatively isolated instance (another was the semi-darkened auditorium of de Loutherbourg's Eidophusikon in London, 1781–93), and the merits of darkening the auditorium were not seriously discussed until about 1800.[16]

With the increasing importance attached to 'historically correct' mise-en-scène at the Opéra from 1827, an attempt was made by Locatelli in the 1829–30 season to use a much dimmer chandelier in the auditorium, but the fashionable audience soon secured the return of the brighter illumination which their style of opera-going required.[17] Schinkel, who had worked in dioramas, also advocated dimming but with little practical consequence. The next significant step was in London at the Princess's Theatre in the 1850s, when Charles Kean plunged the spectators into darkness to enhance their appreciation of his historical settings. Kean's theatre practice was much admired by the Duke of Saxe-Meiningen, who also dimmed the auditorium in his Court Theatre. Wagner was familiar with the work of the Meiningen company. In April 1875 he and Cosima saw the duke's production of Kleist's *Die Hermanns-schlacht* in Berlin (see below). He was also well acquainted with Italian theatre practice and with Schinkel's work and ideas.

His great advantage at Bayreuth was that he had no theatre management to worry about. His intention was that the gas lighting in the auditorium should be turned down during the performance to a level such that the audience could no longer read the libretto (he advised them to study it beforehand or during the intervals), but not that they should sit in total darkness. As we shall see, total darkness was what they sat in during a performance of *Das Rheingold* on 13 August 1876 in the Festspielhaus, but this was a technical accident, rectified for subsequent performances.

The aesthetics of the *Ring* and its performance were closely intertwined with the architecture of the Festspielhaus. How would they fare together in practice?

The search for a visual world for the Ring

Having at long last achieved total control in a theatre of his own, Wagner now had a tabula rasa and some difficult decisions to make. He was no longer beholden to Ludwig's scenic artists and their predisposition to obey the historical imperative, but how was he to replace them?

The enforced Munich premieres of *Das Rheingold* and *Die Walküre* had at least had the effect of rehearsing the huge technical challenge represented by the *Ring*. But there remained the problem of finding a visual style for the scenery and costumes. While he had found much to admire in the Munich settings for *Tristan* and *Die Meistersinger*, Wagner was dissatisfied with what he had been told about those for *Rheingold* and *Walküre*. One cause of this was, as discussed in chapter 2, his aversion to the historical approach that was *comme il faut* at Ludwig's court. What he was still searching for was an aesthetic, a vision, for determining what the mythical personages and the worlds they inhabited should look like. This was supremely critical, for at every point the spectator had to be made aware of an organic, causal connection between what was seen and what was heard.

Wagner was quite unequivocal that it must be 'a matter of principle never, except in very rare cases, to transform scenic effects into purely pictorial ones'. Scenic effects were allowed to dominate only when the action is stilled, as after the giants have taken Freia away in scene 2 of *Rheingold*, when a thin mist fills the stage and the gods grow old before our eyes – then 'it is as much the scenic designer's function to aid the dramatist by providing a significant and gripping spectacle as it is the composer's to reveal the situation's inner meaning'.[18]

Wagner had not, however, given up on Ludwig's court artists as potential designers for Bayreuth, doubtless hoping that he could shape their skills to his own ends. His first choice was Heinrich Döll, who had designed or painted scenery for parts of all the Munich Wagner productions from *Tannhäuser* (1855) through

Rheingold and *Walküre* (1869–70) to *Rienzi* (1871). It was significant that the composer should turn to Döll, a landscape specialist, rather than to Angelo Quaglio or Christian Jank, who were best at architectural sets.

As we saw in the previous chapter, the first pictorial 'story-board' for the *Ring* had been commissioned from the historical painter Michael Echter by Ludwig shortly after he had signed his contract with Wagner for the completion and performance of the work, and the composer had worked closely with Echter on their composition. (Wagner later had copies of the frescoes diplayed as a narrative frieze under the gallery in Haus Wahnfried, his villa in Bayreuth.) He regarded the pictures as 'important preliminary studies for the future performance of the Nibelung work',[19] and they were used as a guide for the decor for the Munich premieres of *Rheingold* and *Walküre*. Despite Wagner's strictures on these premieres, Echter's frescoes may even have played a part in his thinking about what he hoped to achieve at Bayreuth with Döll's assistance. When Döll declined – for reasons unknown – the composer turned to the Viennese landscape painter Josef Hoffmann (1831–1904), who had been recommended by Carl Brandt, the machinist for *Rheingold* and *Walküre* in Munich to whom Wagner had entrusted the stage technology in the Festspielhaus.[20]

Brandt had pointed the composer in Hoffmann's direction because Wagner, having given up hope of finding a theatre artist capable of bringing nature to life on the stage, had come to believe that the best solution would be an accomplished landscape painter whose work could be translated into stage sets by theatre artists. In explaining his choice of Hoffmann to Ludwig, Wagner wrote that Carl Brandt, 'my principal assistant and adviser in the whole practical side of the production … a scene-builder of genius', had helped him find an architect (Otto Brückwald) to devise the extremely difficult structure, but

> was always at a loss to find the right man to recommend as a scene-designer, since what we wanted were truly artistic innovations in a new style, not merely the usual style of stage sets, however competently executed. I came upon the right man by chance. The painter Josef Hoffmann designed and painted two lots of sets for the opening of the new opera house in Vienna, for *The Magic Flute* and *Der Freischütz* (which were generally acknowledged to be excellent), although he had never worked in the theatre before, and he completely withdrew from it again afterwards. At the beginning of last year [1873] I invited him to sketch designs for every part of my work, which he completed and showed me by the autumn. Not I alone, but everyone who saw them – including the leading cognoscenti in Vienna – was delighted in the highest degree by his work: the most difficult challenge of all, the appearance of Valhalla in *Das Rheingold*, we had to wonder at as a truly inspired stroke of genius.[21]

In giving nature and landscape such an active role in the drama Wagner created huge problems both for himself and for all subsequent producers of the *Ring*. It is not only the states of mind and actions of the characters which are mirrored in the music and in the intended settings. Air, earth, fire and water are no less vital players, both in their own right and as symbolic correlatives of the characters. Wotan's anger is reflected in the thunder and lightning accompanying his appearances in *Die Walküre*. The spring moonlight flooding into the dark prison of Hunding's hut speaks for and with the lovers' transcendent ecstasy. The sunlight penetrating the dark waters of the Rhine heralds a dawning consciousness. The darkness in which the Norns spin the fate of the world, the fire surrounding the sleeping Brünnhilde and the sun she greets on her awakening are all significant elements of the drama.

Everything suggests that Wagner's ruling vision for the *Ring* settings – and it is the one described in the rubrics of his poem – was that of the wild grandeur and infinite changeability of nature. Wagner's concern to reflect the action in the mood of the weather is vividly apparent in his stage directions for the transition between the second and third scenes of Act III of *Die Walküre*, as the Valkyries depart leaving Brünnhilde alone to face Wotan: 'The Valkyries split up with a wild cry of anguish and flee into the wood; soon one hears them tearing away through the storm on their horses. The storm gradually subsides during the following scene; the clouds disperse: in the ensuing calm, evening light and finally nightfall.'[22]

And when the composer's rubrics call for 'Freie Gegend auf Bergeshöhen' (an open space on a mountain top), 'Wildes Felsengebirge' (a wild rocky mountain) or 'Nacht, Sturm und Wetter, Blitz und heftiger Donner' (stormy night, with lightning and loud thunder) he knew what he was talking about. Throughout his life Wagner was an enthusiastic mountain walker. His feeling for natural forces and the important part they play in the *Ring* are all of a piece with his experiences of the vagaries of mountain weather and his love of Alpine scenery. There, if anywhere, was the timeless landscape where his mythical heroes and villains had their home. It is far from insignificant that his first explorations of the Swiss mountains in the summer of 1851 coincided with a critical stage in his development of *Siegfrieds Tod* and *Der junge Siegfried* into the four-part *Ring*. Between 30 July and 6 August he and Uhlig undertook a strenuous walking tour from Brunnen which included a traverse of the sensational Surenen Pass. Within a few months he had added *Das Rheingold* and *Die Walküre* to his scheme. He identified certain scenes in the operas with specific mountain locations. 'He reminds me,' writes Cosima on 13 July 1878, 'that it was on this mountain [the Julierberg, near Graubünden, Switzerland, on 16 July 1853] that he visualized Wotan and Fricka: "There, where all is silence, one imagines the beings who rule there, unaffected by the passage of time." '[23] To whom could Wagner better turn for the depiction of such scenery than the monumental landscape painters who were his contemporaries?

During his search for such an artist Wagner is reported as having said, 'This could be something for Böcklin, he has the right kind of imagination,'[24] but it remains uncertain whether he actually approached the Swiss painter Arnold Böcklin, later to become famous for *The Isle of the Dead*, who was living in Munich between 1871 and 1874. We do know that Cosima later tried to interest Böcklin in designing *Parsifal*, but the artist had no patience with the composer's plans for him as a contributor to a 'total work of art'. 'The painters Böcklin and Seitz Junior [Rudolf Seitz, son of Franz Seitz, costume designer at the Munich Court Opera] decline to make me scenery and

Wagner was an indefatigable mountain walker. He envisaged the high Alpine landscape as the habitat of his gods. The Surenen Pass in Switzerland shown in this photo was traversed by the composer and his friend Theodor Uhlig on their Alpine tour of 30 July to 6 August 1851. This was a crucial time for Wagner in the crystallization of his conception of the *Ring*.

costume sketches for *Parsifal*,' recorded Cosima on 20 March 1878. 'The architect [Camillo] Sitte demands to hear the music first'.[25] Böcklin was not, however, immune to Wagner's art. In 1887, four years after the composer's death, he painted an Italian spring scene, *Sieh! es lacht die Aue*, whose title records an underlying inspiration from *Parsifal*. And Böcklin was unable to resist Bayreuth's blandishments for ever, making a posthumous debut on the Festspielhaus stage in 1977, when Richard Peduzzi, designer of Patrice Chéreau's centenary *Ring*, took *The Isle of the Dead* as a model for his revised set for the third act of *Die Walküre*.

While the composer was negotiating with Hoffmann, Cosima sent his sketches to the portrait painter Franz von Lenbach in Munich for his opinion (evidently because the Wagners were not yet wholly convinced), at the same time sounding him out as to whether Hans Makart, the luxuriantly Rubensesque painter who had got to know the composer in Vienna, 'might be any good for our purpose'.[26]

That Wagner was prepared to consider such vastly diverse styles as Döll's leafy vistas, Hoffmann's heroic landscapes, Böcklin's gloomy symbolism and Makart's voluptuous historical fantasies shows the extent to which he was flailing about. Eventually he went ahead with Hoffmann, whom he had first approached on 28 July 1872. His letter had begun by stating his belief that 'nothing worthy of the name of Germany' could be achieved in the stage presentation if this were entrusted to the usual scene painters:

> It is a question, rather, of my being able to submit designs by genuine artists to the most skilled or experienced scene painters in order to inspire the latter to produce of their best. With this in mind I have already addressed myself to a number of artists (historical painters). But my particular attention has recently been drawn to your own special achievements, my dear Sir, the character of which appears to be very close to what I am wanting. Accordingly, what I would make so bold as to ask of you now is that you might initially consider it worth your while to acquaint yourself with my poem the *Ring of the Nibelung* to the extent of its becoming sufficiently familiar for you to prepare sketches of the principal scenes both as regards the setting of the action and the shape of the dramatis personae, so that these sketches might serve as a model for further elaboration either for you yourself, should you wish to do so, or for such scene painters and costumiers as are still to be chosen.[27]

Hoffmann duly took on the job and made extensive preliminary landscape studies in the Alps – doubtless at Wagner's suggestion. The arrangement was that his designs would be translated into painted scenery by the Brückner Brothers theatre studio in Coburg, which had been recommended to Wagner by Carl Brandt. Max (1836–1919) and Gotthold (1844–92) Brückner were scenic artists at the Court Theatre in Coburg. They were sons of the painter Heinrich Brückner and supplied scenery to important theatres all over Germany.

Hoffmann travelled to Bayreuth on 28 November 1873 to present his sketches to Wagner and Brandt. Malwida von Meysenbug reported that the sketches 'greatly pleased the Master: they are the work of a true artist with a deep understanding of the poem and would produce the kind of setting on which Wagner had counted'. Cosima endorsed the approbation but also records some reservations: 'In the afternoon looked through the sketches – a fine and powerful impression, the only questionable aspect being the downgrading of the dramatic intentions in favor of an elaboration of the scenery. This is particularly disturbing in Hunding's hut, and above all in Gunther's Court, which is designed very sensibly, but is much too ostentatious.' A 'violent debate' with Hoffmann ensued, Wagner explaining how 'he turned his back on subjects such as *Lohengrin* and *Tannhäuser* in order to do away entirely with outward pomp and present human beings without any conventional frills'.[28]

Wagner also thought that the figures in Hoffmann's landscapes had been modelled too closely on those in Echter's Munich frescoes: the actual costumes were to be
the work of Carl Emil Doepler. Hoffmann made some changes at Wagner's request,
but was reluctant to make others.[29] This tension between Hoffmann's painterly
vision and the need to translate it into functional stage sets – the basic stage realization was planned to be achieved with fixed cut-outs, borders, drops and painted
gauzes – was to result in the artist's being dropped from the team. On 1 December
1874 the Wagners went to Coburg to see the first results of the Brückners' realization
of Hoffmann's designs. But Hoffmann was displeased by the translation of his
designs into scenery. Brandt and the Brückners refused to continue working with
Hoffmann and proceeded to complete the task without him.

Further changes were made, especially to comply with Wagner's desire that everything he had imagined should be animated on the stage and not just 'illustrated' in
the scenery. One instance is described in a letter from the composer to Ludwig of 6
April 1875. Wagner explains that, rejecting the idea of a painted rainbow bridge for
the gods' triumphal entry into Valhalla, he is working with Brandt to devise a real
bridge over which the gods could actually walk. He goes on to tell Ludwig that their
most difficult problem – and this was of course exactly the kind of 'historical' detail
which interested the king – was the Gibichung Hall, where they were attempting an
imaginative reconstruction of the 'hall of an ancient German hereditary king'.[30]
Hoffmann returned in 1876 to see the completed *Ring*, but Glasenapp reports that
he was far from happy with what he saw.[31]

Until a few years ago it was believed that all that had survived of Hoffmann's work
for the *Ring* were three of his models for *Die Walküre*, now in the Richard-Wagner-
Museum at Bayreuth, and in the same collection three ground plans of the stage
layout for them made later by Carl Brandt's son, Fritz jr.[32] Hoffmann's impressionistic oil paintings, on which the Brückners would partly have based their scenery, had
disappeared. The only evidence of them was the now well-known photographs that
Ludwig had had taken of them and that used to hang in the writing room of his
hunting lodge on the Schach, and fourteen photographs that Hoffmann allowed to
be published in Vienna by V. Angerer – all of course in black and white.[33] But in the
early 1990s Oswald Georg Bauer discovered a small number of Hoffmann's original
paintings in the collection of a family that may acquired them at the artist's exhibition of his work at the Altes Schloß in Bayreuth during the festival of 1876. Protracted negotiations have resulted in the acquisition of five of them, not all in good
condition, by the Richard-Wagner-Museum in Bayreuth. They are being restored
and will soon be on display in the museum.

There are no surviving photographs of what the Hoffmann–Brückner settings
actually looked like on the Bayreuth stage, the closest evidence being the photographs taken of Angelo Neumann's 1878 Leipzig production, which was modelled as
closely as possible on what had been seen at Bayreuth. It remains uncertain, however,
whether these photographs show scenes from the Leipzig production itself or clever
mock-ups created in a photographer's studio.[34]

Wardrobe worries

Remembering the trouble Wagner had had in Munich in his attempts to steer costume design away from supposedly historical models, one cannot but wonder at his choice for Bayreuth of Carl Emil Doepler (1824–1905), a professor of costume design in Berlin (and formerly costume designer at the Weimar Court Theatre, 1860–70). Whatever the reasons for his choice, Wagner's concern to put the professor on the right track is evident in a brief which quite specifically warns Doepler off following 'historical models', which was indeed the costumier's usual practice. The influence of historical painters like Kaulbach, Cornelius, Piloty and Makart on mid-nineteenth-century stage decor and costuming was considerable. Costumes were generally expected to resemble those of a specific, identifiable period. This quest for historicity was seen in its most extreme form in the productions of Franz Dingelstedt, director of the Vienna Court Opera from 1867, and of Duke Georg II of Saxe-Meiningen. Dingelstedt placed especial value on the visual impact of his productions, while Georg II, working with spoken theatre, went for historical fidelity not only in the look of the costumes but also in their materials, using, for example, real fur and heavy metallic armour.[35]

Wagner explained what he was looking for in a letter to Doepler of 17 December 1874:

> Basically what I require is nothing less than a characteristic portrait made up of individual figures and depicting with strikingly vivid detail personal events from a period of culture not only remote from our experience but having no association with any known experience. You will soon discover that you have to ignore completely the sort of picture which, following the example of Cornelius, Schnorr and others, artists have tried to put forward in portraying the characters of the medieval lay of the Nibelungs. At the same time, it will be clear to anyone who has concerned himself of late with attempts to portray the more specifically Norse myths that the artists concerned have merely had recourse to classical antiquity, which they have modified in a way which they deemed to be typically Nordic. Passing references to the costumes of the Germanic peoples in Roman authors who came into contact with these nations do not appear to have received the attention they merit.

Wagner concludes with a characteristically fuzzy appeal for creative collaboration: 'the artist who wishes to take up the subject I offer him and make it his own will find a unique field open to him in terms not only of intelligent compilation but also his own inventiveness; and I could wish for nothing more than to know that you, my very dear Sir, had made this task your own.'[36]

Wagner had begun by asking Doepler for costumes evocative of a mythical world 'not only remote from our experience but having no association with any known experience'. But in going on to mention 'the costumes of the Germanic peoples in Roman authors' he made a fatal mistake, for Doepler plunged into historical research and came up with designs encrusted with ornamental detail that were exactly the kind of decorative kitsch which the composer was so anxious to avoid. Doepler was so deeply in thrall to the historical realism of the Meiningen theatre that he modelled his *Ring* costumes directly on the Meiningen company's production of Kleist's *Die Hermannsschlacht*, which the Wagners had taken him to see in Berlin on 17 April 1875. (Kleist's play, 1808–9, is a fervent patriotic response to Napoleonic occupation, extolling Hermann as the heroic founder of the German Reich, and hence enjoying belated popularity after 1871.) The composer had already committed himself to Max and Gotthold Brückner and would have been keen to see their scenic realizations of Duke Georg's designs for Kleist's play. But the Wagners thought badly of the archaeological exactitude of the Meiningen costumes, which in their view distorted the play and 'turned it into a farce'. It was therefore all the more crass that Doepler should have slavishly followed the Meiningen style, even getting so carried away as to include in his *Ring* portfolio designs for a group of 'bards' whom he had evidently admired in *Hermannsschlacht*.[37]

It was one thing to have imagined a locale for the *Ring*, quite another to decide what its characters should look like. Wagner asked Carl Emil Doepler for costumes evocative of a timeless mythical world. The professor came up with pseudo-historical kitsch and Cosima castigated him for the 'ethnographic absurdity' of his designs. Changes were made, but the composer remained unhappy with the results.

(*On the left*) Doepler's drawing for Alberich (at one point he had been imagined in a coat with epaulettes), and (*on the right*) the stage costume as defiantly modelled by Carl Hill at Bayreuth in 1876.

Cosima's diaries make their dissatisfaction very plain: 'I am much grieved by [Doepler's figurines], revealing as they do an archaeologist's fantasy, to the detriment of the tragic and mythical elements. I should like everything to be much simpler, more primitive. As it is, it is all mere pretence.'[38] This reaction is of particular interest in suggesting that Cosima, whose interest in art and visual awareness were far more developed than Wagner's, also had a more focused sense of what the *Ring* should look like.

Cosima chronicles the battles with Doepler that continued through the final rehearsals. Thus on 28 July: 'on my request to Professor Doepler to make Siegfried's clothes a little less close-fitting and to dress Gutrune's ladies less brightly, the poor man becomes so angry and rude that I realize for the first time what a hack one is having to deal with! The costumes are reminiscent throughout of Red Indian chiefs and still bear, along with their ethnographic absurdity, all the marks of provincial tastelessness. I am much dismayed by them and also rather shocked by the professor's manner. R. is having great trouble with Wotan's hat; it is a veritable musketeer's hat!' And on 2 August: 'The costumes, particularly Alberich's, almost ludicrous – Alberich with coat and epaulettes; overwhelming impact of the work, transcending everything.'[39]

In any other theatre Doepler's efforts would have been regarded as more than adequate, if not actually superior. Indeed 'the beauty and originality of the various costumes' were praised by Richard Fricke, the very experienced ballet-master from Dessau who became a key member of Wagner's team.[40] But this was no ordinary theatre and the rightness of the composer's basic idea of non-realistic, 'timeless' costuming – a concept totally alien to his contemporaries – has been vindicated over and over again in productions after his death. It was, indeed, one of the most fertile production ideas for his own work.

The technology of romantic illusion

As we have seen, Wagner had taken on Carl Brandt (some sources give the spellings as 'Karl' and 'Brand') as technical adviser in the building of the Festspielhaus and the production of the *Ring*. Brandt (1828–81) was chief machinist at the Darmstadt Court Opera and pre-eminent among the stage technologists of his time. With the support of his brother Friedrich (Fritz, 1846–1927), he had been technical director for the 1869–70 Munich premieres of *Das Rheingold* and *Die Walküre*, although Wagner did not meet him until 1871. He was probably the only person in Germany capable of rising to the technical challenge of Wagner's stage instructions. Wagner's choice is also testimony that whatever else he thought about the enforced Munich premieres, he thought well of Brandt's central role in them.

Some thirty years of outstanding work by Brandt at Darmstadt had begun in 1849 with his arranging the movement, dances and mechanical effects for Weber's *Oberon*.[41] Brandt was particularly celebrated for his quick scene changes and pyrotechnics. Between 1857 and 1881 he modernized and reconstructed the stages in twenty-four theatres (including the Munich Court Opera and the Victoria Theatre in Berlin).

Wagner devoted himself indefatigably to working with Brandt to achieve the miracles he expected. He had both a childlike delight in the ingenuities of stage deception and an absolute belief, one wholly representative of his time, that what had been imagined should be represented literally. When fire was called for then fire it was that had to be provided – Siegfried had to forge his sword Nothung 'over a real fire with a real bar of red-hot iron'.[42] If Wagner could have had the stage flooded and the Rhinedaughters swimming and singing from underwater, that is what he would have had. He would have applauded Peter Hall and William Dudley for filling the Bayreuth stage in 1983 with a tank, naked Rhinedaughters and a huge angled mirror creating a brilliant illusion that the singers were indeed swimming around underwater. But in 1876 the Festspielhaus had to achieve its effects with clumsier means.

The ingenuities devised by Brandt and his son Fritz jr (1854–95), who took over as technical director at Bayreuth after his father's death in 1881, have often been described: the swimming machines for the Rhinedaughters; a 'big-dipper' enabling Alberich to plunge into the depths after stealing the gold; scene changes on the open stage coordinated with the music (as from the bed of the Rhine to the high mountain space and thence down to Nibelheim); and much more throughout the four operas.

Many of the more tricky effects were essayed with the liberal use of steam and lighting. These helped to mask the five scene changes on the open stage that occur in the course of the *Ring*, Alberich's transformations into giant snake and toad, and such episodes as the fight between Siegmund and Hunding (also accompanied by copious thunder and lightning). The steam was piped in though a 12-centimetre pipe from a little boiler-house 50 metres from the stage, where it was produced by two old locomotive boilers, each 3.5 metres long and 1 metre in diameter. The principal lighting was gas (the 3,066 fixed burners permitted few changes in either colour or intensity), but this was augmented by the new and experimental phenomenon of electric lighting effects devised by Hugo Bähr from the Dresden Court Theatre. Bähr (1841–1929), who described himself as 'glass painter and electric technician', was the foremost German pioneer in the new art. He designed installations for sixty-nine theatres, and his firm, riding the wave of the new medium, was to supply electric-lighting equipment to some five hundred theatres throughout the world.

Electric devices (using either limelight or carbon-arc lights) had been used for special effects in theatres since the late 1840s. One notable instance, as mentioned in chapter 1, was the creation of the sunrise for the conclusion of Act III of Meyerbeer's *Le Prophète* at the Paris Opéra in 1849.[43] But it was only with Edison's invention of the filament lamp in 1879 that full electric lighting became a practical proposition.

In 1876 electric-lighting effects were experimental, exciting and risky. Bähr devised carbon-arc lamps, sometimes projecting their intense light through glass slides (hence the very necessary skill of 'glass painter') for the creation of water effects, lightning, passing clouds, the highlighting of the handle of the sword in the tree, and so on. Light projection through moving glass slides was a technique that was to be developed over the years at Bayreuth by Bähr. Gas and electric lighting were used in combination for changes in the weather and time of day.

Wagner had given nature and landscape crucial roles in the *Ring*, but how should they be represented on the stage? He turned to the Viennese artist Josef Hoffmann whose sketches and paintings were translated into practical scenery by the theatre studio of Max and Gotthold Brückner.

The blue haze from which Erda emerged in Act III of *Siegfried* was considered successful, but the harshness of the electric lighting used to throw a shaft of moonlight onto the Wanderer's face in the first scene of Act II reportedly destroyed the carefully contrived impression of the forest round about. This was indeed a persistent limitation. While the electric-arc lamps were brilliantly successful as spotlights, the fierce white intensity of the beam destroyed the sense of illusion created by the relatively soft gas lighting playing on the pictorial flats, borders, gauzes and drops. Paul Lindau reported that 'The disproportionately strong and intensive [electric] light … obliterated all the surrounding colours and revealed the supporting constructions so that illusion was severely compromised. Instead of a tree one saw a painted canvas and instead of the sky a stretched sailcloth'.[44]

Bähr devised a special projector with prisms for producing a spectrum for the rainbow bridge. This was not new: a similiar device had been used as early as 1860 by Jules Duboscq at the Paris Opéra to create a rainbow for Rossini's *Moïse*. But it was characteristic that Wagner should have imagined not just the optical effect of a rainbow but a rainbow traversable by his all too human gods. This was a technical problem that was satisfactorily solved only in 1960, by Wolfgang Wagner and Paul

The distance between picturesque romantic fantasy and what was actually possible on stage is evident by comparing Hoffmann's Bed of the Rhine (*opposite*) with the attempt to realize it as seen from behind (*above*). Notable are not only the famous swimming machines for the Rhinedaughters but (*at centre left*) the big-dipper slide down which Alberich plunged after stealing the gold, the beam of electric light used to illuminate the gold and the row of gas lights at the very top.

Eberhardt.[45] In 1876 the effect misfired because the spectrum fell on the painted gauze behind it in such a way as to make Valhalla look transparent, while the rainbow and the bridge were palpably not one and the same.

Another challenge was the Ride of the Valkyries. Wagner wanted the impression of the warrior maidens riding through the air to be created with magic-lantern projections. This was against the advice of Brandt, who proposed repeating the Munich solution of using doubles in the shape of Ludwig's stable lads prancing real horses on a heavily carpeted floor. But Wagner persisted and five lantern slides of Valkyries in the saddle, painted by Doepler, were indistinctly projected onto the scenery.[46] For the ring of fire around Brünnhilde safety considerations prevailed and the effect was attempted, none too successfully, with steam and red electric light.[47]

None of these shortcomings should detract from the achievements of Brandt and Bähr in responding to the composer's well-nigh impossible demands, demands that could be fully satisfied only in the 'theatre of the future' and in the twentieth-century medium of film. Wagner had secured the services of the most resourceful stage technologists of his day. He in his visual imaginings and they in their inventive ingenuity stood at the watershed dividing the Baroque-based theatrical era, with its pictorial representations lit by fixed illumination, its transformations and effects produced by mechanical means, from the modern era, in which dynamic, infinitely variable electric lighting is the designer's principal medium. Brandt set the scene for a whole new era of stage design whose language was very largely that invented for it by Hugo Bähr and his fellow pioneers. The decade immediately following Wagner's death saw electric lighting replace gas in most major theatres of Europe and the United States.[48] The first theatre to be equipped with a complete electric installation was London's Savoy Theatre in 1881 (1,158 incandescent lamps, of which 824 were on stage). The bright new world of scenic possibility, offering solutions to so many of the problems Wagner set for himself, dawned cruelly late for the composer. For it was in 1882–3, the year after Brandt's death and the very last year of the composer's life, that Continental theatres first began to acquire full electric installations, the Festspielhaus following in 1888.

Movement and characterization

Although Wagner's principal strength as a producer stemmed from his gifts as an actor (Nietzsche rated him one of the greatest actors of all time), he saw he would need help in devising how his characters – everyone from gods to Rhinedaughters and sundry fauna – should walk, swim, creep and fly. In travelling around in search of singers, Wagner saw a performance of Gluck's *Orfeo ed Euridice* at the Ducal Court Theatre in Dessau in December 1872 which impressed him hugely: 'I swear that I have never experienced a more elevated and complete impression in a theatre than in this performance. . . . Everything in the production made, in each and every moment, a vital contribution to the representation: every scenic element – painting, lighting, movement, transformations – contributed to a sense of illusion so perfect that we seemed, as never before, to experience the truth of a twilight dream.'[49]

This staging, a model for what the composer hoped to achieve at Bayreuth, was the work of Richard Fricke (1818–1903), the theatre's ballet-master since 1853. In him the composer knew he had found what we would today call his 'movement director' for the *Ring*. In the first instance Fricke was engaged to 'choreograph' only the Rhinedaughters and the Nibelung slaves in *Rheingold*, but he quickly became involved with much more. Wagner had written to Fricke saying that while he had no need for a regisseur, he did want someone who knew how to arrange choreography and to help the singers with their movements.[50] As Fricke himself tells us, he did all that and himself appeared on stage as a supernumerary: 'In Act II [of *Götterdämmerung*] I play a bard who has to slaughter the sacrificial animals and in Act III, at the very end, I'm Hagen's double and have to be dragged down into the depths of the Rhine by the Rhinemaidens.'[51] Could the invention of this 'bard' have had anything to do with Professor Doepler's Kleistian fantasy?

In *Bayreuth vor dreissig Jahren* (Bayreuth Thirty Years Ago) Fricke has left us one of the most important first-hand accounts of the 1876 production, remarkable not least for the difference that clearly emerges between the composer's ideas on stage presentation and those of Fricke. Where Wagner was a literalist, Fricke believed in the power of suggestion, particularly when he thought that Wagner was asking the impossible. He suspected that even if it could be achieved the effect would be to make people laugh or otherwise undermine the seriousness of the enterprise as a whole.

This was certainly wise counsel given that the action on stage was so often fighting a losing battle with the overwhelming power of Wagner's musical evocations. Fricke was thus all in favour of the black thunderclouds, lightning and steam effects used at the end of the second act of *Die Walküre* to conceal the difficulties of staging the fight leading to Siegmund's death and its aftermath. Even though some were to complain that they were unable to see what was going on, Fricke recognized that this was far better than their laughing at a clumsy enactment.

Fricke advised that the dragon should be kept out of sight, but Wagner was adamant that it should appear. The elaborate creature was created by Richard Keene of Wandsworth in south London, who also supplied 'a car with a yoke of rams for Fricka in the *Valkyrie*, a bear, a magpie and an ousel for Siegfried'.[52] (This at least confirms that the rams were papier-mâché rather than live horn on the hoof.) The late arrival of the component parts of the dragon was a cause of massive concern to Wagner. Although Fricke was highly impressed by Keene's work when it eventually reached Bayreuth – on 12 August, the day before the first *Rheingold* – he scented trouble. 'The dragon has arrived. As soon as I saw it, I whispered to Doepler, "Into the deepest junk room with the wretched thing! Get rid of it! This dragon will be the death of us!"'[53] Not quite, but it was indeed to provoke precisely the kind of unintended mirth and derision that he had foreseen.

In discussing the difficulties of meeting Wagner's wish that the Norns should throw a real long rope to each other, Fricke counselled either that the rope should be moved by invisible wires or that the effect should be mimed: 'When you read a scene of such seriousness and essential sombreness,' he told Wagner, 'your imagination is fully engaged; but as soon as something like this is presented visually, when all our other senses are alert, the image created in our imagination risks becoming ludicrously shrunken.' Although Wagner was not, it seems, persuaded, Fricke felt satisfied that 'I had succeeded in saying this one thing to him, volatile as he is.' He reflected that he had been 'on the point of drawing his attention to other difficulties, some of them almost harder to solve, things which our imagination transforms into the most beautiful images but which, as noted, are in fact going to call the whole staging into question'.[54]

Wagner's adventurousness, his willingness to take risks, sometimes won out against Fricke's seasoned professionalism, which preferred to duck 'problems' by seeking the security of seasoned stage tricks. Fricke had wanted doubles to mime the Rhinedaughters in their 'swimming machines', with the singers vocalizing from the wings (the solution adopted at the Munich premiere). But Wagner was in love with the machines and so much so that, according to one account, when the singers playing the Rhinedaughters refused to allow themselves to be assisted into the swimming machines, the composer had himself strapped in and raised aloft. This dispelled the ladies' fears and they soon took to their machines like mermaids to water.[55] It has to be said that this testimony does not square with that of Lilli Lehmann, herself one of the three swimmers, who fails to mention any such demonstration, reporting only that it was coaxing by Brandt and Fricke that persuaded the singers to climb up into the machines, be buckled in and begin 'moving about as directed from below'.[56]

Rehearsals

Setting the scene was one thing; of even greater importance was finding the singers and instrumentalists, all of whom had to be recruited from the theatres and orchestras to which they were already contracted. Such was the dedication to Wagner of so many artists – to whom he could promise no remuneration other than their expenses – that this proved no problem. They and the technical team were called to Bayreuth between 1 July and 12 August 1875 for preliminary rehearsals.

The rehearsals of 1876 were chronicled in considerable detail by Wagner's various assistants, most notably Heinrich Porges, Richard Fricke and Julius Hey (who worked intensively as repetiteur with Georg Unger as Siegfried), by many of the singers, and by Cosima in her diary, although the intensity of the rehearsal and performance periods left her too little time to record the Wagner family's eye view as fully as she would otherwise have done (eight pages for the period of the principal rehearsals, 3 June–9 August, and barely two for the three *Ring* cycles of the first festival, 13–30 August).

Although there is an element of uncertainty as to when Porges wrote up his account (it did not begin to appear in print until 1880 and was not completed until 1896), it is of special importance in that it was compiled at Wagner's instigation. He had singled Porges out as his chronicler as early as November 1872, two years before the score was finished: 'I intend to invite you to follow all my rehearsals, just as you did for the 9th Symphony, in order to record and note down all my remarks, however intimate, concerning the interpretation and performance of our work, and in that way to establish a fixed tradition.'[57] Even after due allowance has been made for flights of airy rhetoric that play up to Wagner's self-image as the rightful successor to Aeschylus and Shakespeare, Porges provides a wealth of information about the composer's work with the singers and the orchestra. Wagner's guiding principle for stage performance is summarized by Porges as endeavouring to combine 'the realistic style of Shakespeare with the idealistic style of antique tragedy': the unison of 'an art rooted in fidelity to nature' with a more stylized form 'striving for a direct embodiment of the ideal'.[58] That, at any rate, was the theory. How did it work out in practice? How did the composer tackle the down-to-earth business of preparing the huge work for performance?

Even working with hand-picked singers, Wagner's first task was to ensure that they understood both the work as a whole and every nuance of their individual roles. This is difficult enough today, after more than a century of performances. How much harder it must have seemed when the work was new. The singers had to be taught to inhabit and project characters which were very different from the other roles in their

Working miracles for the *Ring* on stage. (*At right*) Wagner the stage director is captured at rehearsal (with probably the scenery for *Siegfried* Act II in the background) on 8 August 1875 by Adolf Menzel. (*At top left*) Carl Brandt, leading stage technologist of his time, who used steam from two locomotive boilers and lighting effects to mask scene changes made, exceptionally for this time, without the curtains being closed. (*At bottom left*) Richard Fricke, the ballet-master from Dessau who choreographed anything and everything that moved. His advice that the dragon should be kept out of sight was unfortunately not heeded.

repertory. Wagner invariably began with the psychology and motivation of the characters, believing that only when this was fully understood would verbal and musical expression make sense.

Wagner's ability both to explain and personally demonstrate the psychology of his characters won the singers' unstinting admiration. 'How he sings along with the performers,' observes Fricke, 'beating time, running round the theatre and so on! This must fulfil a very real psychological need on Wagner's part, since he clearly wants to sweat out everything that he's written. When he hears his music, he is overcome – it seems to me – by a kind of paroxysm, yet in the midst of this effusion of feelings he still feels perfectly well physically, and I'd even say that it does him good to rush around in this way.'[59] 'He could, as if by magic,' says Porges, 'assume at a stroke any role in any situation – indeed, in the rehearsals of the *Ring* he demonstrated these powers so fully it was as though he himself were the "total actor" (Gesamtschauspieler) of the entire drama.'[60]

For Georg Unger (Siegfried), as for other members of the cast, Wagner's approach to acting and vocal characterization was a considerable challenge. Unger was one of the weaker links in the cast, and his coach, Julius Hey, doubted whether he would ever catch on, but he did so well enough to get him through the performances. Amalie Materna (Brünnhilde) reported that she and her colleagues found Wagner's entirely different approach to acting a marvellous tonic after the uninspiring theatre practices to which they had long been inured.[61] The intense physical demands Wagner made on his singers are vividly described by Lilli Lehmann in her autobiography.[62]

For all Wagner's insistence in his theoretical writings on naturalness of movement and gesture in acting, Fricke spent much of his time helping the singers put Wagner's extravagant demonstrations into sensible proportion. 'Meister,' he reports himself as interrupting during a rehearsal of the second act of *Götterdämmerung*, 'we must beware of vacuous passivity and unmotivated hand- and arm-movements, but it's far worse if we do too much.' Fricke continues: 'It was altogether comical watching Wagner attempting to emphasise and underline every word by his animated behaviour and by constantly waving his arms around. I gradually assumed control, gained a proper understanding of the scene and changed virtually everything, telling him that, once those involved are standing on stage, things won't be too difficult.'[63] On other occasions, Fricke had nothing but admiration for Wagner's demonstrations: 'I had the pleasure today of admiring Wagner's skill in elucidating a character like that of Mime and explaining it to the performer. It was masterly how he was able to bring out individual details and point up the subtlest nuances!'[64] His demonstration to Josephine Schefsky (Sieglinde), a famously powerful but unimaginative singer, of how to perform the moments leading to Hunding's entrance was recorded by Lilli Lehmann (who sang Woglinde, Helmwige and the Woodbird): 'Wagner, with his bad figure, played this with overwhelmingly touching expression. Never yet has a Sieglinde known how to approach him, even approximately.'[65]

Porges records many examples of Wagner's ideas as to how the acting should be linked to the music. Here is how Fricka was to protest against Wotan's acquiescence in Siegmund and Sieglinde's incest: 'Fricka's speech, "Wie thörig und taub du dich stellst …" must be harsh and at the end she must step back a little and raise her left hand in emphasis. She should not gesticulate at the beginning of the speech, "Achtest du rühmlich der Ehe Bruch …", but only when she reveals her growing agitation at "Mir schaudert das Herz, es schwindelt mein Hirn …" As she puts her question in tones of noble indignation: "Wann ward es erlebt, daβ leiblich Geschwister sich liebten?" Fricka's movements become freer and she should lean back with arms outstretched. She holds this imposing stance for some time. At "So ist es denn aus mit den ewigen Göttern …" she strides towards Wotan'.[66] The trouble with this sort of prescription – 'she must step back', 'she should lean back' – was that Cosima, as we shall see in chapter 5, was to impose it rigidly on all subsequent Bayreuth Frickas.

All the evidence, contrariwise, suggests that Wagner's approach to acting was that it should retain, within limits, an essential element of improvisation. Porges reports both very specific instructions and many examples of Wagner repeatedly changing his mind. One day he worked on a scene in a particular way as though its problems had been definitively solved, only to take an entirely different approach at a subsequent rehearsal – to the singers', and Fricke's, despair: 'It is difficult working with Wagner since he never sticks to what he is doing. He leaps from one thing to another and cannot be pinned down to one question even though it could soon be sorted out. He wants to be his own producer (regisseur) but he lacks all the qualities necessary for this detailed work, since his mind, having the broader perspective forever in view, loses sight of all the details, so that by tomorrow he will have forgotten the moves that he worked out today. What's to be done?'[67]

Evidently his work was always suggesting new things to him. In Porges's words, 'all the extraordinary things Wagner did at the rehearsals created the impression of having been improvised: it was as though everything he demanded and himself so eloquently demonstrated occurred to him in a flash with complete lucidity just at that very moment'.[68] He altered not only blocking, stage movement and gestures, but also the musical tempi.[69] The relationship between these three crucial elements is one to which Porges paid extensive attention and it remains problematic – doubtless for all time.

What is plain is that Wagner sought to liberate the singer and never to impose his own personal characterizations. He asked only, reports Porges, that his performers must first 'subordinate themselves without reservation to the creator of the work, and thereby acquire that gift of self-abandonment (Selbstentäußerung) which, in his penetrating essay "On Actors and Singers", Wagner singled out as the basis of all dramatic talent'.[70] He believed that every artist of stature brought something inimitable to a role. Lilli Lehmann reported that he greatly prized the individual interpretations of his artists, only stepping in 'when he came upon lack of understanding or dilettantism'.[71]

Wagner's coaching of his singers included declamation, intonation, phrasing, dynamics and exhortations to the greatest clarity in presenting a character's emotions. The audibility of words was a recurring problem. What to do about this? 'Wagner,' says Porges, 'declared that the orchestra should support the singer as the sea does a boat, rocking but never upsetting or swamping – over and over again he employed that image'.[72] On the other hand, in his dealings with the orchestra and its conductor Hans Richter he often had to work hard to convince them that he was asking a great deal more of the orchestra than its usual role of tactful accompanist of the singers and the stage action!

He always insisted that the singers should address themselves to each other, preferably in profile to the audience, and that they should never sing straight out to the audience. He wanted the second scene of Act II of *Götterdämmerung*, with Siegfried, Hagen and Gutrune, to be treated as 'a kind of lively conversation on the stage to be kept wholly in the style of comic opera'.[73]

The rehearsal notes by Fricke, Porges, Hey and others make clear Wagner's insistence that gesture and movement should correspond to the tempo and expression of the music, but never be in counterpoint with it! For him, the music already embodied and cued the exits, entrances and every significant movement and gesture. But there can be no question that Wagner's insistence that the scenic action should harmonize precisely with the tempo and expression of the music created huge problems for posterity – and not just of synchrony.

Das Rheingold

Twenty-eight years after its conception, and twenty-six years after Wagner's first notion of staging it in a special festival theatre, the *Ring* finally saw its first complete performance from 13 to 17 August 1876. 'I never thought you'd pull it off' ('Ich habe nicht geglaubt, daß Sie es zustande bringen würden'), were the Kaiser's first words to Wagner on his arrival at Bayreuth railway station.[74] It was indeed perhaps the most stupendous, most improbable operatic achievement of the nineteenth century. It is little wonder that the unprecedented novelty of a four-part opera, performed in a theatre built specially for it by its composer, was the talking point of artistic Europe. What, then, were the performances actually like? The descriptions that follow are woven principally from accounts by the artists and others immediately involved. They are followed by an overview of the venture as a whole, and finally by Wagner and Cosima's own assessment and hopes for future performances.

Contrary to present-day practice and common belief, it was never Wagner's intention to extinguish *all* light in the auditorium during the performance. That this happened in 1876 was an accident. He had asked for no more than 'a pronounced lowering of the lighting', warning the audience in a prefatory note to the libretti sold in 1876 that the lighting would be too dim for reading and that the text should therefore be studied either before the performance or during the intervals.[75]

The gas lighting in the auditorium, however, had been installed so late that the mechanism for its adjustment had not been mastered by the first performance of *Rheingold*, with the result that the audience was plunged into total darkness. At later performances the lighting was successfully adjusted to a level that was merely dim. Paul Lindau, attending the second cycle, reported 'a grey half-light' which softened the transition between stage and auditorium. The gloom earned Wagner black marks here and there for reasons ranging from the impossibility of following the libretto to the exposure of lady visitors to moral danger.[76]

For the prelude, 'In the depths of the Rhine', the underwater effects were created by blue gauzes, painted darker below and lighter above, rising up and down to suggest the movement of waves. The general lighting, as already described, was gas, but watery effects were added by projecting electric light from a 'Wasserapparat', one of several devices specially invented by Hugo Bähr.[77] The flats and borders were painted with appropriate waves, ripples and subaquatic motifs. The visual effect was reported as being virtually identical to that of Döll's designs for the Munich premiere, the only noticeable difference being the addition of some tree roots among the sunken rocks.[78]

Behind the gauzes, Brandt's machines for the Rhinedaughters were in action. The impression of swimming created by their motion won general enthusiasm. 'Such was the impact of these torrents of lightning and fire, of this rumble of thunder, of this play of the waves, that it seemed as though the very elements themselves were taking part. Whoever saw the daughters of the Rhine swimming so gracefully could have had no idea that the effect was achieved with metal rods and trolleys, manoeuvred by hidden musical assistants with their scores.'[79] The girls were not actually expected to sing while 'swimming' prostrate, but were raised into an upright position a few bars before they were due to sing.[80]

Friedrich Kranich jr, who succeeded his father as technical director of the Bayreuth Festival from 1924 to 1932, was sceptical of the degree of swimming 'motion' actually produced.[81] Kranich sr, a pupil of Carl Brandt and technical director from 1886 to 1924, had been present at the 1876 rehearsals and was in a position to know: Fricke records his trying out one of the swimming machines for himself.[82]

The five scene changes on the open stage that are requested by Wagner in the course of the *Ring* – of which the first is the journey from the bed of the Rhine to the 'open space on a mountain top' – were managed by coordinating the flying in of one or more semi-transparent painted cloths to establish the new scene with the flying out of the cloths from the previous scene. This manoeuvre was partly concealed by the release of a curtain of steam from the boiler-house. As previously mentioned, steam was also used for tricky transformations like those of Alberich in scene 3 of *Rheingold*, and for masking other problem episodes. Unfortunately it tended to spread into the orchestra pit, putting instruments out of tune, and its use was accompanied by a loud hissing clearly audible in the auditorium.[83]

The complicated scene changes went well at rehearsal but at the premiere the transformation from the depths to the heights (scenes 1–2) – regarded by Fricke at rehearsal on 6 June as 'a masterpiece. . . . It defies description' – went badly wrong: a painted drop was flown out too soon, revealing shirt-sleeved stagehands at their business.[84] Brandt's urgent commands from the wings were heard throughout the auditorium.[85] There were further mishaps when Wotan (Franz Betz) dropped the Ring and twice ran off into the wings during Alberich's curse.[86]

The Hoffmann–Brückner set for scene 2, 'On the mountain heights', provoked a variety of reactions. While the *Musikalisches Wochenblatt* found it 'a serene Greek landscape, extensive, sweetly pleasant and wonderfully fitting', the critic Wilhelm Mohr was not so readily convinced: 'A flowery sward appeared, at the right of which, on the steps of a stone staircase, two people in impressive ancient costume, evidently man and wife, were asleep. On the far side of an open gorge with a river flowing through, a curious construction was revealed: a broad clump of rocks, in which a mighty tree, the World Ash, had rooted itself, and above it a four-cornered foundation, on which were a whole series of towers of various heights which looked like massive carriage-clocks or gravestones.'[87]

For the journeys to and from Nibelheim, steam was again much in evidence. The 'Riesenschlange' into which Alberich transforms himself – one of the fauna from Wandsworth – was praised by Fricke as a suitably terrifying representation, but derided by the high-minded Brahmsian Max Kalbeck as having escaped from the puppet theatre and as such unworthy of its place in so serious an undertaking as the *Ring*.[88] The appearance of Alberich's Nibelungs bringing up the treasure (actually some '44 assorted objects: oil cans, metal boxes, funnels, cake tins, buckets, watering-cans, kettles, etc.' – all props found at a local ironmonger's) was regarded as a minor tour de force, not least by Fricke who had trained thirty local gymnasts specially for this task. It is little wonder that Doepler and Fricke had some difficulty in devising a means 'of hiding Freia with the Nibelung hoard'.[89]

Donner's magic thunderstorm was managed with electric lighting effects, a thunder machine and yet more steam. The actual bridge by which the gods crossed over

The Nibelung slaves, played by local gymnasts, with their hoard – a collection of miscellaneous utensils that were found at an ironmonger's shop in Bayreuth.

to Valhalla seemed unconnected with the rainbow spectrum that was projected with only partial success by Hugo Bähr's machine. 'The rainbow, over which the gods processed to Valhalla, was so low,' mocked Hanslick, 'that one could have taken it for a painted bridge in a flower garden.'[90]

Die Walküre

The models and ground plans for the production of *Die Walküre* (the only ones that have survived from the 1876 *Ring*) suggest that, within the limits of the available technology, Wagner's printed stage directions were closely followed. But in instructing Brandt, Wagner, here as elsewhere, sought changes to Hoffmann's images either to align them more closely with the images in his mind's eye or to make them more practicable for the stage. This was evident in Act I in adjustments to the positioning of tree, hearth, table, door, etc., although the Bayreuth set was largely painted on cloth rather than a solid construct as at the Munich premiere (which took a full half-hour to strike). A beam of electric light was used to illuminate the haft of the sword in the tree. There is no record of electric lighting being used to create the moonlight effect at 'Ha, wer ging? wer kam herein?', when the rear door flies open, but we do know that part of the 'wall' above the door fell in to enhance the sudden flood of light.[91]

Franz Betz as Wotan. His vanity gave the composer a lot of trouble, but Wagner later hailed his performance as 'the grand-est thing achieved as yet in the entire field of musical drama'.

Amalie Materna as Brünnhilde with her black horse lent by King Ludwig. According to Lilli Lehmann, Materna found the committed style of acting required by Wagner very difficult but had the tremendous vocal power needed for the role.

Josef Hoffmann's own model for Act III of *Die Walküre*. It shows how the Ride of the Valkyries was suggested by the projection onto the scenery of five lantern slides painted by Carl Emil Doepler. This was preferred to Carl Brandt's idea of repeating the Munich solution whereby Valkyrie doubles, in the shape of King Ludwig's stable lads, had pranced their spirited steeds on a heavily carpeted floor.

The settings for Act II appear to have been closely modelled on Döll's Munich designs, the basic influence on both being Friedrich Preller's painting *Tötung der Rinder des Helios* from his series of Odysseus paintings which were known to the Wagners.[92] Fricka's ram-chariot, with the heads of the papier-mâché beasts wobbling pathetically as they were drawn on, was the butt of much criticism.[93] Brünnhilde's Grane was a black horse sent by King Ludwig – 'he's nine years old, meek as a lamb and keeps on nuzzling your hand in the hope of finding some sugar'.[94] But Brünnhilde appeared without Grane for the Todesverkündigung – Wagner had decided at rehearsal to leave out the horse on the grounds that it was 'distracting'.[95]

As already mentioned, Siegmund's death and the complex action at the end of Act II were accomplished with much help from the steam machinery: 'The fight between Siegmund and Hunding takes place high on the mountain peaks, shrouded in clouds and lit by occasional flashes of lightning,' wrote Fricke. 'Wotan enters at the critical moment, the sword shatters and Siegmund falls. Brünnhilde makes good her escape in order to rescue Sieglinde, who has remained below. Grane appears with Brünnhilde. Everything disappears in cloud and steam.'[96]

The Ride of the Valkyries was represented by magic-lantern projections, as described above, the consensus being that the images were not clear enough to be effective. Of Brünnhilde's ring of fire, Cosima's diary for 19 July remarks, 'Herr Brandt's "Magic Fire" magnificent,'[97] but in the performances the best that could be managed was no encircling flame but a line of spasmodic puffs of steam with red lighting at the back of the stage.[98]

Siegfried

The set for Mime's cave in the rocks in Act I of *Siegfried* was praised by Fricke as a 'triumph of decorative scene painting'.[99] Of the rehearsal on 25 June Cosima reported that 'The children liked the first act of *Siegfried* best of all – which pleases R., for it supplies proof of its folk character, whereas all the artists have up to now treated this first act as if it were quite incomprehensible.'[100] Huge rehearsal problems were caused by Siegfried's having to forge Nothung from red-hot metal over a real fire. Fricke reported that 'it finally bore the hallmark of truth and naturalness'.[101]

For Act II, the forest near Fafner's cave was created with the help of projections and transparent hangings. 'The scenery,' wrote Cosima on 26 June, 'is outstandingly beautiful, and Herr Brandt has once again worked wonders'.[102] Fricke, at rehearsal on

Mime's cave in Josef Hoffmann's painting. Richard Fricke describes how Siegfried 'worked like a Trojan and forged his sword in time with the music, before finally adding the handle and then, right at the end, splitting the anvil with it'.

Cosima Wagner had wanted the costumes to have been more primitive. Two that met her wish were the cloak worn by Betz as the Wanderer (*left*) and the animal skin worn by Georg Unger (*right*) as the young Siegfried – in *Götterdämmerung* he graduated to a hero's obligatory breast-plate, with helmet, shield and spear [*sic*].

29 June, was less convinced: 'Some splendid effects have been achieved by lighting through the cloths, but they've gone too far in having transparent borders to depict foliage hanging down from above the stage. The illusion is no longer convincing but has a jarring effect, since it is too unnatural.'[103] Whatever was eventually patched together for Fafner's draconian form was evidently far from successful, Paul Lindau describing the creature as 'halfway between a lizard and a porcupine with hairy tufts'.[104] Siegfried's mimed battle with it fared no better. Fricke's advice to keep it out of sight had gone unheeded.

At the beginning of the third act Erda emerged from a tomb-like cavern over whose entrance a dead tree appeared to have fallen – a favourite symbolic motif of Hoffmann's, and one possibly derived from Caspar David Friedrich. The curtain of fire through which Siegfried had to pass to win Brünnhilde was praised by Lindau as far more convincing than the *Walküre* flames which he had so scornfully dismissed: 'The flame-red gauze behind which the steam rose depicted the blazing fire in effective painterly fashion.'[105] Joseph Kürschner records a 'surging sea of flame which, beginning with the whole foreground, eventually spread to fill the whole stage'.[106]

Götterdämmerung

Cosima makes only the barest references in her diary to the *Götterdämmerung* rehearsals and performances – remarkable when one considers the difficulties of staging the work. Later she records her own view that Act I was perhaps too long and the Waltraute–Brünnhilde scene therefore less effective than it might have been. Wagner agreed, but never carried out his reported intention to insert 'a long pause after the introduction and begin the act with the orchestral "Siegfried's Journey" '. Thus, Cosima continues, '*Götterdämmerung* would be a repetition of the whole, an introduction and 3 parts.'[107]

Fricke reports that the problems in staging the Entry of the Vassals and the Wedding Procession in Act II were successfully solved and that 'the sets, once again, look absolutely wonderful. As expected, lack of space forced me to abandon the idea of having the Vassals wave their lances to welcome Gunther and Brünnhilde. It is sheer joy listening to 30 such voices.'[108]

Huge technical difficulties were experienced in the devising of a collapsible Gibichung Hall and in the staging of the opera's concluding scenes. Fricke had wanted Siegfried's funeral procession to proceed directly to the pyre, but Wagner rejected this suggestion in favour of Brandt's view that the procession should first disappear behind the scenery at right so that Siegfried's body could be exchanged for a dummy. The audience had been expecting Brünnhilde to leap onto Grane and plunge into the fire, only to be disappointed when she led the horse off into the wings. 'Hagen, who should throw himself as if crazed into the river,' wrote Hanslick, 'strolled into the wings on the right and turned up a few seconds later in the middle of the Rhine.' The drop showing the Rhine in flood was, Hanslick continued, badly painted with 'visibly sewn-up waves' wobbling as though they were 'the Red Sea in a provincial production of Rossini's *Moses*'.[109] Fricke reported that the final scene was 'beneath contempt. What didn't I have to listen to! How the production was torn apart! Brandt's contribution was repeatedly attacked. I had to keep quiet, though much of it was only too true. And yet, in spite of everything, it has been a great achievement and the majority of people have spoken out in support of the work.'[110]

Fricke's anonymous editor, summarizing the diary entries from 19 to 30 August (when they ceased), says that 'he was too closely bound up with the enterprise to have joined, unreservedly, in the dithyrambic praise which other writers, motivated by blind veneration, showered on the Meister. He admits that the criticism and ridicule levelled at the dragon and rainbow, to say nothing of Alberich's disappearance with the steam tarnhelm in *Das Rheingold*, were not entirely unjustified. Wagner, too, was not afraid to admit as much. "With each passing day," Fricke writes, "he feels increasingly that his work could be staged differently, he realises what needs to be removed and rejected and that I was right in everything I said. 'Next year we'll do it all differently,' he told me when we were alone together."'[111]

Impressions of the 1876 performances

Relatively few of the 1876 visitors gave much thought to how well the music and drama of the *Ring* had been served by the stage realization. The tetralogy was immediately perceived as a towering achievement. Some of the spectacular effects had come off and others had not, but this neither won nor dropped many points – the mishaps were certainly no more calamitous than commonly experienced on the stages of the time; Wagner scored handsomely just for having attempted more than anyone else.

The singers' performances varied greatly but generally sufficed to put across the burden of the work. The Rhinedaughters, sung by Lilli and Marie Lehmann and Minna Lammert, won general acclaim for their musicality and their skill in miming their subaquatic existence. Lilli Lehmann, who was a particular favourite of the composer's and went on to sing Brünnhilde, Isolde and many other roles, has left us recollections of the singers' performances which are perhaps as just an account as one could hope for. She thought most highly of Albert Niemann as Siegmund ('the intellectual power, the physical force, the incomparable expression were all glorious beyond all words to relate'), of Luise Jaide as Erda and Waltraute ('never equalled in the many productions that I have ever seen'), of Carl Hill as Alberich ('who succeeded, in the curse, in expressing the quintessence of bitterness') and of Heinrich Vogl as Loge ('acuteness, scorn, wit, envy, his exaggerated accent, that was especially suited for just this rôle, and that sounded not merely sharp but both sharp and biting, together with his incredible musical certainty combined to give the picture of the perfect Loge'). While praising Franz Betz as Wotan for his 'glorious voice and … great art', she ventures no further comment on her Berlin colleague's creation of this huge role. Lilli salutes Amalie Materna for her dedication, industry and endurance, but the unspoken thought is that she had little conception of the role as such: 'Though she possessed the tremendous voice power required for the three Brünhildes [*sic*], yet the text, language, style, and the kind of acting were entirely strange to her, and made almost higher demands upon the artist than the music itself.' She is dismissive of Josephine Schefsky as Sieglinde and Mathilde Weckerlin as Gutrune and remains silent about Friederike Sadler-Grün's Fricka, Georg Unger's Siegfried and Gustav Siehr's Hagen. Her overall impression was, nevertheless, of a great achievement: 'If we add [Eugen] Gura as a really wonderful Gunther, who invested the part with nobility, dramatic value, and vocal beauty that could not be surpassed artistically, and [Max] Schlosser's excellent Mime; the simply divine orchestra … and the admirable chorus, we have ended with the most eminent features of the performances of the Bayreuth of 1876.'[112]

Less tactful sources make it plain that Georg Unger was never truly inside the role of Siegfried, nor did he have the necessary vocal stamina. By Wagner's own account he had so little voice left for *Götterdämmerung* that Niemann volunteered to sing in place of him, an offer that Wagner refused on the grounds that while Niemann was obviously the superior artist, his 'predilection for a certain dramatic realism made me fear a break in the illusion, if the hero were to be played by two different performers on consecutive nights; I declined Niemann's offer with thanks, but lived to regret it'.[113]

Wagner himself oscillated in his views about the singers. Cosima's diaries for August and September 1876 single out for particular praise Unger's Siegfried and the performances by Heinrich Vogl, Amalie Materna and Gustav Siehr, while finding Schefsky 'inadequate' as Sieglinde and condemning Niemann and Betz for their obduracy: 'R. no longer wants the matadors Betz and Niemann; the former, in his rage at not being called before the curtain, made a downright mockery of his role!'[114]

Once the tensions and aggravations of the moment had passed, the composer acknowledged Betz's outstanding contribution in a letter of 30 November 1876, in which he strove to make up his differences with the bass – and also of course to secure his services for repeat performances in 1877. Betz is further praised in Wagner's considered retrospect (December 1878) of the 1876 festival, not least for his delivery of the Act II soliloquy in *Walküre*: 'Betz so perfectly fulfilled it that I may call his performance the grandest thing achieved as yet in the entire field of musical drama. … An arduous twelvemonth's preparation made my singer master of a style which he himself had first to invent for the occasion.' In this retrospect Wagner also singled out for special mention Carl Hill and Gustav Siehr, who 'adapted himself so completely to this character in voice, enunciation, gesture, movement, gait and bearing, that his portrayal was masterly'.[115]

There were, however, few who appreciated what Wagner and Fricke had achieved in the acting and characterization of the singers, and indeed in the animation of the action as a whole. Against the background of a general expectation that little more was required of singers than that they should stand and deliver, the sense of involvement and commitment to character must have struck many as well over the top – as indeed, if Fricke is to be believed, much of it undoubtedly was.

By most accounts (Fricke's excepted) the costumes were a disappointment, though the singers seem to have carried them off without too much embarrassment. The detailing of costumes and props prompted some to compare them with the historical realism of the Meiningen Court Theatre. The fact that the Hoffmann-Brückner settings excited little attention is a measure of their proximity to the conventional romantic naturalism of the time.

Thanks to the design of the auditorium with its uninterrupted view of the stage, the enveloping gloom and the invisible orchestra, the audience's sense of immersion in the opera was far greater than that experienced elsewhere. The effectiveness of the illusion was widely praised. The 'illusion' may have been far from perfect but was found by most visitors to have been as persuasive – within the conventions of representation accepted by contemporary audiences – as Wagner had wanted.

For Camille Saint-Saëns, who was familiar with the best productions of the Paris Opéra, 'The skill of the transition from auditorium to stage is such that one is totally unaware of an apron stage. Its disappearance is the more effective because the singers almost never approach it, but normally remain in line with the second lot of flats, where they are strongly lit from the apron and the proscenium. … Steam plays a large part in the scenic effects: puffs of white steam simulate clouds, and under red lighting it turns into the glow of fire.' Some musical detail, said Saint-Saëns, was lost in the huge orchestra pit, 'But there can be no doubt of the gain in scenic illusion.'[116] Others felt that the diminution in volume and clarity from the orchestra was too high a price to pay for the scenic advantages of its concealment.

Some found the scenic impression altogether too beguiling. It even misled so astute a critic as Hanslick into a rather crass devaluation of the mighty score:

> Never before has an opera had such an accumulation of scenic miracles to offer. Feats that have previously been thought impossible ... follow one upon the other without pause. ... But is it right that the highest ambition of a dramatic composer should be to provide a musical accompaniment to a series of magical effects produced by machines? A declared supporter of Wagner's, Karl Lemcke, in a generally favourable review of the *Ring*, deplores the deleterious influence of these 'tricks reminiscent of Bosco's Hall of Magic'. ... In fact Wagner's *Ring* comes closest, in point of theatrical genre, to magic plays and 'féeries'. The decidedly material effects deployed in it stand in a curious contradiction to the pure ideality which Wagner boasts for his work.[117]

It is strange that Hanslick should have been so distracted by the 'effects' – which he is happy to praise – as to misjudge the music as no more than a 'musical accompaniment', asserting that the work as a whole amounted to the very 'effects without causes' against which Wagner had long set his whole endeavour. One recalls Malwida von Meysenbug's comment that the composer had once implored her during a performance, 'Don't look so hard! Listen!'[118] Hanslick's position was, of course, more subtle than comes across in a single extract. His principal thrust was to reject Wagner's music-drama aesthetic as being dominated, so he believed, by theatrical rather than musical values. His praise for the 'effects' (erratically achieved, as we have seen) undoubtedly carried a measure of irony. His complaint that the music was no better than 'accompaniment' was to some extent justified by what the composer judged to be Richter's far from satisfactory conducting.

Max Kalbeck was one of the very few critics to recognize what Wagner had achieved in production and staging: 'Since Wagner's appearance on the scene, everything dependent on stage technology has taken an unparalleled upswing. That the *Ring* is stageable has been established beyond doubt; that Wagner himself has done it demonstrates his unequalled understanding of the theatre.'[119]

A very few visitors were astute enough to see that even the state-of-the-art technology of Bayreuth fell short of doing justice to what Wagner had imagined. For them, the problem was not that the effects were any kind of distraction, or that the music was unable to compete with them, but simply, as Fricke had seen, that the realization of the composer's vision was beyond the available technology. Thus the connoisseur and art collector Conrad Fiedler, in an illuminating exchange with the sculptor Adolf von Hildebrand, was unimpressed by the *Ring* as a 'total work of art', viewing it as a conception springing from Wagner's palpable frustration that the current means of theatrical presentation were hopelessly inadequate. Fiedler recognized the very thing that had totally escaped Hanslick: 'In Wagner the dramatic action and the music are not separate components; rather, it is only in the music that the dramatic action comes into being at all.'[120]

Another critic who had little time for 'gutta-percha dragons, artificial bears, realistic rams and similiar pantomime magic' was Wilhelm Mohr, who hailed Wagner's victory in the very place where, or so it appeared to him, he had sought it least – in the music. The poetry and dramatic cunning notched up no new victories, 'the new scenic miracles are actually at odds with not merely the capabilities of modern stage machinery or stage technicians but, far worse, the very nature of art itself'.[121] If this critique springs, at least in part, from a very Germanic belief in the primacy of music in opera and a corresponding suspicion of dramatic and theatrical effects, it is also of exceptional interest in anticipating that radical questioning of Wagner's ideas about the visual representation of his operas which was later to make such an impact on their stage history.

Retrospect of Wagner and Cosima

There was no room for complacent self-congratulation at the Wahnfried breakfast table, only for the composer's insatiable determination to do it better next time. The performances had fallen well short of his expectations. His remark to Fricke, quoted above, that next year he would do it all differently is more than confirmed in his letters and later writings.

Post-natal depression set in. Wagner was hugely disappointed by the failure of the press and the public at large to recognize in Bayreuth and the *Ring* the rebirth of the spirit of true German art. He felt that his lifetime's effort to create a new kind of theatre had gained no foothold. This was the mood recorded in Cosima's diary on the day of the 'Departure of Math. Maier – the last visitor': 'In the evening a long discussion about the performances and the experiences gained during them. ... Brandt's achievements far short of what one might have expected! Richter not sure of a single tempo – dismal experiences indeed! ... Costumes, scenery, everything must be done anew for the repeat performances [intended for the following year, but which shortage of money made impossible]. R. is very sad, wishes he could die! – He very comically calls Betz and N. [Niemann] theater parasites!'[122]

A year later, on 15 September 1877, in an address to the Bayreuth Patrons' Association, Wagner takes a more sober view of what had gone wrong and of his hopes for future performances: 'Some things were done carelessly, some things inadequately prepared. There was negligence of all kinds, on my part, too. Last year's performances did not measure up to my ideal. If it is to be reached in the future, I must be given a breathing space.' And he goes on to describe his plan for founding a school in Bayreuth 'for training singers, players and conductors in the correct performance of musico-dramatic works of the truly German style'.[123]

After a further year, Wagner's retrospective reflections on the festival express heartfelt thanks to Carl Brandt, the singers (especially Niemann and Betz!), the orchestra and conductor Hans Richter, while acknowledging that 'no one had more

Josef Hoffmann's painting for the closing scene of the *Ring*. The catastrophe of its execution on the stage was in keeping with the subject matter. Hanslick reported that the 'visibly sewn-up waves' on the drop showing the Rhine overflowing its banks were like 'the Red Sea in a provincial production of Rossini's *Moses*'. Wagner told Fricke, 'Next year we'll do it all differently.'

cause than ourselves to deplore the unfinished state of some of the scenery. The linden tree ... had to be hastily patched up on the spot for our second act [of *Siegfried*] ... whilst the closing scene of *Götterdämmerung* lacked the proper scenery at every performance.'[124]

What is missing from these reckonings is any sense that there might perhaps be a conflict between the nature of the work itself and the kind of scenic realization Wagner was hoping eventually to perfect for it. That was something that began to come into focus only during his work on *Parsifal* and its staging.

CHAPTER 4

Parsifal and beyond

Hier wo mein Wähnen Frieden fand/WAHNFRIED/sei dieses Haus von mir benannt

(Let this house, where I at last found freedom from Illusion, be called Wahnfried)[1]

Although *Parsifal* had been planned long before Bayreuth, its text was not finished until after the first complete performances of the *Ring*. It was the only opera by Wagner whose music was written and whose staging was imagined with the living experience of the Festspielhaus in the composer's mind. After Wagner's death *Parsifal* became the most reverentially embalmed of all his works. His injunction that performances should be restricted to the Festspielhaus was largely responsible, but it was ironic that this should have been the fate of a production in which the composer had for the first time looked beyond the pictorial romantic style for which he had previously striven.

Plainly the spiritual subject suggested a realization in softer focus than had seemed appropriate for the epic heroics of the *Ring*. '*Parsifal*,' as Oswald Bauer rightly says, 'is Wagner's most radical attempt to restore to the superficial operatic stage of his own day the dignity and expressive power enjoyed by the classical Greek theatre in its handling of themes and its association with cultic ritual, and by the mystery plays of the Middle Ages and the sacred representations of the Baroque era.' And Bauer continues, 'In his instructions for the scenery, the iconographical model of the early morality plays is transparent. On the one hand there is the Christian Grail castle, inaccessibly situated in the mountains of northern, Gothic Spain, and on the other, located on the southern slopes of these same mountains and facing Moorish Spain, Klingsor's magic garden with its tropical vegetation. In the great temple scene in Act I and in the Flowermaidens' scene in Act II, these two worlds are graphically depicted in all their polarity.'[2]

Outwardly, then, the conflict is between a corrupted Christian community and the demonic powers manifest in Klingsor, with Kundry as ambivalent intermediary, serving each in turn. Transcendence is revealed only in nature – the forest, the healing waters of the lake, the Good Friday meadow. It is the reconciling agent and healer of all wounds. But before its powers can be released, Parsifal has first to recognize nature as a benediction rather than a hunting ground, and secondly – in keeping with so many earlier morality plays – to resist seduction by a woman. The scene of the sudden disappearance of the flower garden and of Klingsor's castle when it collapses to reveal an encircling desert landscape is pure late Baroque Christian morality play. In this and in so many other instances, the scenic events are symbolic and were not in any way intended by Wagner to be presented or read as realistic.

This is also powerfully true of the work's relation to Christianity. Although Wagner had been at pains to study the Catholic rite of Holy Communion, and was very concerned that the Grail ceremonial should be entirely convincing as a religious rite, the last thing on his mind was that this should be presented *as* the Catholic Mass or confused with it. Cosima's diary records, 'He gives energetic expression to his aversion to turning the Last Supper into a theatrical performance in the Mass.'[3] Concurrent with the composition of *Parsifal* was the essay 'Religion and Art' (1880), in which Wagner argues that religion diminishes symbols by treating them as embodiments of an absolute, revealed truth.[4] His case appears to be that dogmatic interpretation is the antithesis of art, which uses symbols as a gateway to truths which go far beyond the tenets of any particular religion. If this is what he means it is a huge claim, but it at least underlines the fact that Wagner intended the spirituality of *Parsifal* to be unbounded by its Christian references.

Preparations for the 1882 premiere

Although Wagner intended that the forest and meadow (Act III) should be realistically presented – with the Good Friday blossoming as a transcendental miracle – for the magic garden and the Flowermaidens he was after something quite unrealistic. It was to be a lush, wildly overripe vegetation, the Flowermaidens emerging from the extravagantly bewitching blooms. Everything was to be the unholy conjuration of Klingsor's magic, and thus unnatural if not actually anti-nature. This was a false world and its sweetly malign seductions had to be recognized and overcome by Parsifal. Bauer even sees Klingsor's 'fleurs du mal' as 'redeemed' in the spontaneous flowering of the Good Friday meadow.[5]

From the first, Wagner was so seriously concerned about the stage realization of his *Bühnenweihfestspiel* (dedicatory stage festival play) that he wondered whether he should ever take the risk of exposing the work to any kind of stage performance. Towards the end of 1878, when he was finishing the second complete draft of Act II, his negative feelings were fed by the production disappointments of the 1876 *Ring* premiere. Cosima reports his saying 'very emphatically that he does not wish to stage *Parsifal*',[6] and other remarks to the same effect. He well knew that the rapt, mystical tone of the work had to be sustained and could be totally destroyed by the kind of scenic mishaps which had blighted the *Ring*. It was surely this apprehension which prompted his overriding new impulse towards the attenuation of romantic naturalism and the pursuit of a simpler style of staging.

Ludwig, who had long since been living the role of Parsifal, had eagerly followed Wagner's work on the text, fantasizing about the completion and production of the opera. As early as 1876 he had begun planning a Byzantine throne room for himself at Neuschwanstein (not completed until 1886, the year of his death) which was his own determined view of what the interior of the Grail temple should look like.[7] In the summer of 1877, shortly after the composer's completion of the libretto, Ludwig constructed Gurnemanz's hermit hut, setting it in a Good Friday meadow in the grounds of his castle at Linderhof. He was impatient that his scenic artists should be involved and that they should begin work without delay and indeed long before the score was finished, doubtless imagining that they would assist Wagner's own powers of visualization. He could not have been more mistaken.

In November 1878 Ludwig despatched Christian Jank and Heinrich Döll to Wahnfried to discuss designs with the composer. Wagner and Cosima were not amused: 'At 12 noon we receive the two gentlemen, discussion about the scenery for *Parsifal!* Both with their heads full of frills and vistas, R. alone putting his finger on what would be right here; he says the cupola should not be visible, only the architrave supporting it'.[8]

Evidently Wagner and Cosima had, yet again, contemplated a collaboration with an artist, for Cosima had hoped to present her husband with sample designs from such a source on his birthday (22 May). She approached Hans Makart, whom they had first met in Vienna in 1875, recording in her diary that 'Richter … brings me the happy news that Makart wants to do the sketches for the costumes and bring them here in time for the 22nd', but there is no evidence that these ever materialized.[9] In their absence, the Wagners drew inspiration for Kundry's costume from Makart's

Wagner's inspiration for the Grail temple was Siena Cathedral with its striped and soaring columns. The actual design, executed by the painter Paul von Joukowsky and the Brückner brothers, was an octagonal top-lit space whose squat columns and mosaic-clad Roman arches are more reminiscent of a Byzantine baptistery. The setting, hallowed as the one on which 'the Master's eyes had rested', remained virtually unchanged from 1882 until 1933 and is shown here in a photograph from 1930.

painting of the actress Charlotte Wolter as Messalina.[10] Arnold Böcklin, Rudolf Seitz and Camillo Sitte (also known as an architect) all declined Cosima's invitations. In many ways, Makart, the monumental Viennese painter, would have been a 'natural choice' and could undoubtedly have provided the sort of thing that most of the bourgeois theatre public would have considered fitting. But it was as well that he did not waste his time, for Wagner had already turned his back on anything other than an unmonumental realization of his insubstantial vision.

Time and again we see that Wagner's visual imagination was of a far lower creative order than his way with music and words. What he needed was an identity parade of images from which to choose. He had to fall back on recognition of what best suited his vision rather than conjuring it up directly. There can be no question that this was a massive frustration in an artist otherwise so omni-competent, and it was not until *Parsifal* that he found a painter prepared to place his own creativity unconditionally at Wagner's service.

What was clear to Wagner at this stage was that no artist or scene painter then known to him could be trusted to come up with what he wanted. The only kind of designer who was any good to him was one who would work obediently with him (he himself sketched a plan for the opening scene which clearly shows entrances and exits for Amfortas and Parsifal). It was in this frame of mind, and while staying in Naples in January 1880, that he met Paul von Joukowsky, a young painter of Russ-ian-German parentage and a pupil of Lenbach, whom he believed to be right for the task. In Wagner's eyes it did not count against him that he had never designed for the theatre before – rather it was a recommendation that he came fresh to a field almost entirely governed by conservative practice. And although he was an artist with his own independent vocation, he was not too proud to come back with sketch after sketch until Wagner was satisfied. The composer rejected at least six of Joukowsky's first coloured sketches for the magic garden as too brash: 'These colours don't go with my music. If only I could paint! I would now only like to learn how to paint.'[11] Wagner knew that he could count on the Brückner Brothers' studio to translate the sketches into scenery, and to supply those settings that he regarded as unproblematic.

With Joukowsky Wagner worked principally on Klingsor's magic garden and the Grail temple, leaving Klingsor's castle, the scenes in the forest (including the Good Friday meadow) and the transitions between forest and temple to the Brückners. The technical support was again devised by Carl Brandt. His sudden death in December 1881 at the age of fifty-three came as a great blow, but the work was con-tinued by his son Fritz, then twenty-eight, who had been part of the Festspielhaus team since 1875.

Act II was another problem altogether in that Klingsor's rocky bastion had to change into a lushly overripe magic garden, and then both castle and garden had to collapse into a barren desert when Parsifal caught Klingsor's spear and thus destroyed his magic. Virtually every scene painter of any competence would have known how to go to work on this second act; the depiction of magical fairy-tale castles – hugely popular with the public – was exactly what they were good at. But this was just what Wagner did not want. Nor did he want the kind of pedantically researched detail on which Ludwig's scenic artists prided themselves. His experiences with Jank, Döll and the *Ring*'s costume designer Doepler had shown him how historicity worked against his deeper intuition.

Not that he did not wish his scenes to be suggested by particular landscapes and buildings; he had, after all, 'discovered' Klingsor's magic garden in the gardens at Ravello in Italy and the Grail temple in the cathedral at Siena. But as in the relation of historical Nuremberg to the *Meistersinger* scenery, what Wagner wanted was *not* photographic stage facsimiles, but inspirations for his own imaginary world. The Italian locations were only a point of departure.

The aim was still to create a compelling stage illusion. With the experience of 1876 behind him Wagner wanted adjustments in the level of auditorium lighting to help manipulate this illusion, as in the creation of total darkness from the glowing of the blood in the Grail until the end of Act III. But while contemporary reports note that the auditorium lighting was markedly low, we have no evidence that it was actually extinguished towards the end as the composer had wanted.[12]

Wagner asked for the maximum contrast between the healing force of the natural world, the hermetic morbidity of the Grail temple and the conjurations of Klingsor's castle. For the transformation scenes, picturing the hero's two journeys from forest and meadow into the heart of the temple, the composer wanted the audience to experience the physical journeys, the sense of time becoming space ('Du siehst, mein Sohn, zum Raum wird hier die Zeit!'), as an inner spiritual experience. He looked for a dreamlike transition through the forest from the one scene to the other. This was accomplished by having Parsifal and Gurnemanz pretend to walk while the landscape – painted on three huge canvas scrolls running between vertical rollers on either side of the stage – moved behind them. This effect, engineered by Brandt, and found hugely effective by most who saw it, was not a wholly original invention. The Baroque theatre had used moving bands of painted cloth, often in a continuous loop, for fire and water effects, as did later pantomime and popular theatres. The earliest large-scale *panorama mobile* to appear in an opera house was probably that used at Covent Garden in 1826 for Weber's *Oberon* and it is more than likely that Wagner would have known about it. Carl Brandt's teacher Ignatz Dorn used the technique in 1836 to portray a hot-air balloon trip from Turkey to Darmstadt, while Brandt himself put it to use in 1863, also at the Darmstadt Theatre, for Aimé Maillart's comic opera *Lara*.

The only problem – as had been anticipated from the early technical discussions with Brandt (January 1881) – was that the scenery took longer to pass between the rollers than the accompanying music took to play. Wagner, who had already extended the music, was reluctantly persuaded to allow it to be repeated. When, in rehearsal, it still proved to be too short, Humperdinck composed some extra bars. Even this did not immediately solve the problem. Such were the difficulties of coordinating winding the rollers by hand that in the early performances the music tended to arrive in the Grail temple before the scenery. Wagner sanctioned the extra music required for the Act I transformation, but was against any prolongation of the music for the Act

'Here time becomes space.' To suggest a dream-like, spiritual progress for Gurnemanz and Parsifal through the forest into the temple, they pretended to walk while the scenery, on three huge canvas rolls, moved behind them. The panorama moved from left to right. The section of it frozen for the camera (*on the page opposite*) was continuous with the section (*above*) which shows the portals of the castle. This eventually opened up (*left*) into the temple. The landscape was painted by Max and Gotthold Brückner following Paul von Joukowsky's designs.

The drawing of the mechanism, used up to 1933 (*below*), was made by Kurt Söhnlein who had worked closely with Siegfried Wagner in the 1920s. The rollers were wound by hand, and later by electric motors.

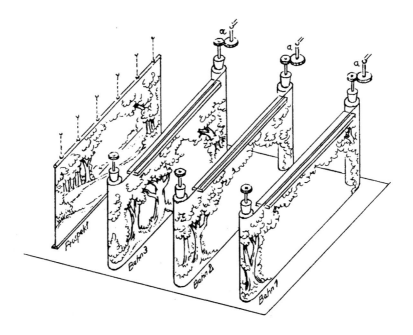

III transformation and, at the suggestion of Emil Scaria (playing Gurnemanz), the problem was solved by simply changing the scene behind closed curtains. Wagner's verdict after the performances was that the Act I transformation was too protracted. He gave instructions that this scenic journey should be drastically curtailed, and that the Act III transformation should be reinstated, but in severely abbreviated form, and this was what happened in the 1883 and subsequent performances.[13]

The creation and disappearance of the magic garden were effected by the hoisting and dropping of the gauze hangings on which the foliage was painted, the destruction of Klingsor's castle taking place in similar manner. For the catching of the spear Carl Brandt devised a fixed-wire trajectory, while at the very end of the opera, wires were again used to enable the dove to descend and hover over the Grail.

Wagner was determined that the costumes should be closely related to the settings. He was exercised anew by 'the difficulty of finding the proper costumes for nonhistorical dramas'. Cosima records his jocular apprehension: '"When I think that characters like Kundry will now have to be dressed up, those dreadful artists' balls immediately spring into my mind. Having created the invisible orchestra, I now feel like inventing the invisible theater! And the inaudible orchestra," he adds, concluding his dismal reflections in humorous vein.'[14]

Once again there was the clash between some indeterminate vision in Wagner's mind's eye and the inability of designers to produce anything not modelled on a historical example. Putting Doepler behind him, Wagner turned to Rudolf Seitz, interior designer and illustrator, son and pupil of Franz von Seitz, costume designer at the Munich Court Opera. Seitz's brief was that the costumes should above all be characterful, poetic and simple. For Kundry and the Flowermaidens Wagner was most anxious to avoid any impression of the bordello, aiming – improbable as it sounds – for what Bauer summarizes as 'a totally unreal, naively unconscious, airy and insubstantial atmosphere of seduction, both on stage and in the orchestra – in other words, what Cosima described as the "chaste" element in Wagner's art'.[15] But although Seitz did come up with designs that were freer than anything anyone had ever previously produced, the composer rejected them as either too bejewelled (Titurel) or too reminiscent of the ballet and masquerade: he told Ludwig that the long, transparent pleated skirts for the Flowermaidens were like 'indecent ball-gowns and might have been created by the famous Parisian haute couturier Worth for the demi-monde'.[16] Joukowsky was called in to make improvements and eventually the whole family became involved. Wagner's daughter Isolde supplied drawings for the Flowermaidens, the composer himself made sketches for the headgear of the knights of the Grail, and Cosima put in a great many ideas. Nevertheless, these efforts were not sufficient to rescue the costumes from being the least successful element in what otherwise proved to be a production of which Wagner felt relatively proud.

Rehearsals

It was to Wagner's advantage that he had behind him the experience of inaugurating the Festspielhaus with the *Ring*, and this time he had only a single opera to stage, not four. He had also the advantage of unprecedented forces – an orchestra of 107, a chorus of 135, and 23 soloists, including double-casting for Parsifal, Kundry, Gurnemanz and Klingsor. The production team included Richard Fricke, two conductors and nine musical assistants. Though the advance preparation had been long, there were no more than three and a half weeks for the production rehearsals, but with sixteen performances, spaced out between 26 July and 29 August 1882, it was possible to make many improvements during the run.

The composer's directions at the rehearsals are well documented in his assistants' annotations in the surviving vocal scores, including those by Felix Mottl in the published Peters edition. Of about 1,100 notes attributed to Wagner, some 360 were recorded by Mottl and 720 by Heinrich Porges and Julius Kniese. Most of the notes are about musical matters (especially those by Porges), but Mottl also records production instructions. Kniese's notes concentrate on blocking, stage movement and acting.[17]

All the notes concerning the singers bear witness to Wagner's intense concern for dramatic motivation. The external action had always to come from within. Gesture and movement had to be natural, never exaggerated, and always in time with the music. The singers were to address only each other, the single exception being Parsifal's outcry in Act II after Kundry's kiss, 'Ha! – dieser Kuß! – Verbrecherin!', which the singer was to address directly to the audience. When the singers' eyes were not on each other they were supposed to be either raised to the heavens or cast down to the earth.[18]

Wagner veered between an absolute insistence in certain matters and open-mindedness elsewhere. When in the Act III baptism scene Marianne Brandt (who shared Kundry with Therese Malten and Amalie Materna) wanted only to fall on her knees and not to bend her head to the ground as decreed by the stage rubric, Wagner held her head right down through to the end of the entire Good Friday scene. His readiness for singers to contribute production ideas of their own is instanced in the testimony of Luise Reuß-Belce, one of the original Flowermaidens. She reports that after many fruitless attempts to make her entrance ('Komm, holder Knabe!') in accord with Wagner's wishes, 'I followed my own instinct, departed entirely from the little ballet-master's [Fricke's] instructions and, following my natural instinct, ran as though terrified onto the stage. At this the Master clapped his hands and cried, "Bravo! That's how it must be done!" '[19]

Performances

The performances of *Parsifal* were on the whole considered by the composer and his audiences to have been more successful than any previous production of his, and certainly more so than that of the *Ring* in 1876. The spiritual atmosphere Wagner had looked for in the Grail scenes and the scenic and dramatic contrasts were sustained without major mishap. Felix Weingartner was among those who were deeply moved by the journey from the forest to the domain of the Grail: 'It seemed as if one were being borne aloft. At each side of the stage there were two or three pillars on which the appropriate dissolving views appeared successively until the last wall of rock disappeared and the nobly proportioned interior of the Castle of the Grail opened up before our eyes. As the C major chord resounded light flooded the majestic picture. The simplest of means had brought about an overwhelming effect.'[20] Two French visitors, Charles and Pierre Bonnier, reported that Wagner had achieved all the scenic contrasts he had wanted: in the first and third acts vertical and horizontal lines balanced each other and predominated – serene lighting, calm movements; in the second act, angular, abrupt lines and sinister shadows. 'The simple, calm silhouette of Parsifal' stood out against the luxuriant unnatural abundance of the vegetation. The Bonniers remarked that while the first scene in the Grail temple had a remote, dreamlike quality, in the second scene the action, with Parsifal as active participant, was much further towards the stage front, 'dramatic and violent'.[21]

If the presentation of the woodland nature scenes was still a rather conventional, pasteboard evocation, it was probably no worse and perhaps even rather better than pastoral representations on stages elsewhere. Wagner himself felt that it was too picturesquely literal and would have preferred the settings to have been more impressionistic.

Only the troublesome scenes in the magic garden failed to win universal acclaim, and this despite the highest praise for the music of the Flowermaidens and its performance. The general verdict was that the colouring of the huge flowers was too bright, vulgar and unreal (the latter as had been intended) and that the idea of presenting the Flowermaidens as 'singing flowers' did not come off. The harshness of the electric-lighting effects was also found detrimental. The girls' petalled costumes doubtless seemed too reminiscent of the ballet, while Kundry's Act II costume, with its loops of pearls and corsetted waist, was closer to a fashionable ball-gown than to Wagner's not wholly fanciful thought that 'she ought to be lying there naked, like a

Titian Venus'.[22] This scene has been credited by one writer as being the earliest instance of symbolism in stage design.[23]

Cosima's diaries tell a very different story from the disappointments over the *Ring* six years earlier. She records Wagner's great satisfaction with the singers ('never once did the spirit of eagerness and dedication desert the artists!', 30 August 1882; 'His delight in his artists grows ever greater in recollection', 11 September), with the production ('Everything on stage satisfies him', 29 August) and with the stage technology ('our excellent machinist Fritz Brandt, who cannot be praised too highly', 1 September).[24] Writing to Ludwig on 8 September, the composer praised the sets as 'more successful than anything I had previously experienced: in making them the Brückner Brothers were fully initiated as artists'.[25] All this encouraged the thought, often expressed by Wagner in what were to be the last months of his life, that he should stage all of his works at Bayreuth.[26]

In his published retrospect of the performances Wagner considered that his 'undeviating principle of reverent simplicity' had triumphed. Every scenic, musical and dramatic detail 'upon, above, below, behind and in front of the stage' had been perfected and each in harmony with every other, although the problem of matching the music to the moving scenery was, as mentioned above, freely admitted. The acting had been as restrained as he had hoped for, the singers everywhere clear and undemonstrative in their articulation, and the orchestra attaining 'a beauty and spirituality of expression' not encountered under everyday theatre conditions.[27]

Klingsor's magic garden at Bayreuth in 1882, the first year from which we have photographs of what scenery actually looked like in the Festspielhaus. Wagner famously claimed to have 'discovered' his model in the gardens at Ravello. Concerned that the colours should go with his music, he rejected at least six of Joukowsky's sketches as being too brightly coloured.

The costumes, as usual, gave Wagner a lot of trouble. For Kundry and the Flowermaidens he wanted to avoid any suggestion of the bordello or of 'those dreadful artists' balls'. Professional designers were rejected and the task was addressed by Joukowsky and the entire Wagner family. The results seem to have justified the composer's worst fears. Hermann Winkelmann is Parsifal surrounded by the Maidens; it had been intended that they should look like 'singing flowers'.

Because of the number of performances (sixteen) that were given in 1882, the leading roles were shared between a number of singers. Here in Act III Heinrich Gudehus kneels before the spear watched by Marianne Brandt's Kundry and Gustav Siehr's Gurnemanz. Albeit a carefully posed photograph, it suggests that in scenes like this Wagner did achieve the sense of reverential simplicity at which he had aimed.

Conscious that *Parsifal* was his valedictory testament, Wagner determined that the work should not be subjected to the abuses he feared for it if performed in theatres other than Bayreuth and under any other supervision than his own. This resolution was doubtless intensified by his feeling that he had approached the ideal perform-ance of his mind's eye and ear, an ideality that must have seemed inseparable from the unique relationship of orchestra, stage and audience in the Festspielhaus. What he could not do, try as he might – and almost up to his last letter to his king and benefactor – was prevail against Ludwig's wish to have private performances given for himself in Munich. The Bayreuth scenery was duly transported to the Munich Court Theatre and performances, for the king alone, were given on 3, 5 and 7 May 1884, with further ones in November that year and in April 1885.

From grandiose realism to 'deeds of music made visible'

The Wagner who staged *Parsifal* at Bayreuth in 1882 had travelled an immense dis-tance from the Wagner who saw *Rienzi* and *Holländer* staged in Dresden in 1842–3 and who had written *Opera and Drama* in 1850–1. The young composer had argued that stage production was an integral part of a dramatic work and should be taken no less seriously than it was at the Paris Opéra – with one crucial difference, namely that spectacle for its own sake, in which the Opéra invested lavishly, had no part in his scheme of things. There were to be no 'effects without causes'. Scenery, move-ment, gesture and vocal characterization had all to spring from the heart of the drama. All constituent elements carried equal weight and had to be held in balance with one another.

Over the course of the next twenty years, the composer's assimilation of Schopen-hauer and his experience of the historicist aesthetic at Ludwig's Court Theatre pointed him, as we saw in chapter 2, in a new direction, one to which his 1870 cen-tenary essay on Beethoven bears witness. He had come to believe that 'Music expresses the innermost essence of gesture with such immediate comprehensibility that, once it has completely filled our beings, it diminishes even the power of our sight to concentrate on the gesture, so that finally we understand it without even seeing it.'[28]

Wagner therefore now regarded the visible action as but a threshold to the hidden essence revealed in the music. By 1872 he has redefined his operas not as 'total works of art' but as 'deeds of music made visible': 'The music sounds, and what it sounds you may see on the stage before you. … I would almost like to call my dramas "ersichtlich gewordene Taten der Musik" '.[29]

This conscious emphasis on music as the prime mover in opera sowed seeds of doubt as to whether the detailed realism of the composer's early ambition was its ideal stage embodiment. The urgent question it raised was in what form 'deeds of music' should be 'made visible'. Could music, indeed, ever be anything but betrayed when subject to scenic representation? What kind of stage production would, as Schopenhauer instructed, best enable the audience to penetrate through the visible action to the hidden essence revealed by the music?

In rendering the musicians invisible in the sunken orchestra pit and in dimming the auditorium, the Bayreuth Festspielhaus had created a more perfect 'theatre of illusion' than any yet existing. But in 1876 this only emphasized the inadequacy of the machinists' and scenic artists' attempts to find a visual language for the *Ring*'s magical world of myth and psychology. Taken as a whole, the 1876 *Ring* premieres had revealed the chasm between Wagner's attempt to keep faith with a production aesthetic formulated more than a quarter of a century earlier and the ideas which had arisen from his Schopenhauerean epiphany, and which were manifest in the composition of *Tristan*, if not in its first staging. Much of his frustration in his stagings of the *Ring* in 1876 and *Parsifal* in 1882 is indeed attributable to the disparity between the theoretical position he had maintained since 1870 and his efforts to realize every detail of the original *Ring* poem.

There can be little doubt that the immensity of the practical task of realizing the *Ring* at Bayreuth kept Wagner from seeing how his new theories might come to his rescue. This is the more remarkable when one recalls the impact of Schopenhauer's influence (the principal source of the 'deeds of music made visible' philosophy) on the ever more dominant role of music in the *Ring* from *Die Walküre* on. It is only with the composition and performance of *Parsifal* that Wagner begins to see how to translate the implications of the new theory into stage practice.

In planning the production of *Parsifal* Wagner began to discover what he believed to be the right kind of 'visibility' for his musical deeds. He took steps to ensure that the acting should no longer strive quite so hard for its effects. The scenery, as we have seen, was to concern itself more with the evocation of mood, the delineation of symbol, than with the depiction of every leaf on every tree. The ethos of the Festspielhaus, temple for festivals of consecrated drama, was unequivocally vindicated in the composition and performance of *Parsifal*. But technical deficiencies and the aesthetics of pictorial representation still impaired the spiritual experience that the composer had in mind.

The Festspielhaus: theatre of the future?

Despite all Wagner's early protestations about wanting no more than a temporary, disposable theatre for his works, the Festspielhaus very quickly became a permanent monument to its creator. It was a theatre designed to function exclusively under festival conditions. It was a temple to which the faithful would wish to travel as pilgrims. It established the 'ideal' conditions under which Wagner wanted his works to be heard. It would show the world how the composer wanted his works to be performed.

Yet did he intend that his 'ideal theatre' should be copied elsewhere? Carried along by the missionary zeal of the impresario Angelo Neumann, Wagner supported his efforts to build a Festspielhaus replica in Berlin, but he did so with misgivings, for it would have compromised the singularity of Bayreuth. Wagner the cultural evangelist was at odds with the Wagner who, in his heart of hearts, wanted pilgrims to come to hear his works only in the temple exclusively dedicated to their performance. His

Shown here (*above*) in about 1930 with the original 1882 Grail temple (considerably patched up) on the stage, the Festspielhaus's raked auditorium and concealed orchestra pit influenced theatre design elsewhere, and nowhere more so than in Munich's Prinzregententheater (*opposite*), designed by Max Littmann, which opened in 1901 with *Die Meistersinger*. It was restored and reopened in 1996 with a production of *Tristan und Isolde* by August Everding.

insistence that *Parsifal* should be given only at Bayreuth and his acute displeasure at the king's determination to the contrary were eloquent of his deepest feelings about all his works.

Wagner never seems to have imagined that the Festspielhaus would be used for any works other than his own, or that its particular features would even be suited to them. The Festspielhaus was an adaptation of the classic Greek amphitheatre for his own specific needs (those of a nineteenth-century 'theatre of illusion'). Much of his theorizing about theatre design is focused on the performance of plays rather than operas. He continued to believe that comedy – which required palpable interaction between players and audience – worked best with a thrust stage (developed from Shakespeare's Globe Theatre) surrounded on three sides by the audience. Throughout the 1870s Wagner very often urges the revival of the Shakespearean stage, most especially for performances of Goethe's *Faust*. But for tragic drama – Aeschylus, Calderón, Corneille, etc. – he never wavered from his belief in the proscenium stage, capable of excluding itself from the audience and creating illusions of imaginary worlds.[30]

Even during the composer's lifetime his radical ideas about the auditorium and its relationship to the stage influenced the design of the new Dresden Opera (1871–8) built by his old colleague Gottfried Semper and his son Manfred. After his death, the Festspielhaus left its mark on the rebuilt Vienna Burgtheater (Carl von Hasenauer,

1888), and on a number of theatres by Max Littmann including the Prinzregenten-theater, Munich (1900–1), the Schiller Theater, Berlin (1905–6), the Weimar Court Theatre (1907), and the Künstlertheater, Munich (1908), discussed in chapter 5.[31] Although in some of these theatres, and in most others built before 1914, the layout of tiered boxes in a horseshoe round the auditorium generally persisted, Wagner's ideas are noticeable in closer attention to stage technology and lighting, and in the increasing tendency to slope the auditorium floor towards the stage and to lower the orchestra if not under the stage then at least below the sightlines of the spectators in the stalls.

The Festspielhaus was to become almost as famous for the unprecedented darkness of its auditorium as for its amphitheatre, sunken pit and other features. This made so successful a contribution to the 'theatre of illusion' that it quickly influenced practice in other German theatres, with the result that by 1889 most performances were given with the auditorium lighting dimmed to a quarter of full intensity.[32] In London Henry Irving was to follow suit at the Lyceum, which he had taken over in 1878, while in Paris André Antoine finally succeeded in playing in a darkened house at the Théâtre Libre from 1887.

Wagner's attitude to the 'afterlife' of his operas

Wagner wasted little energy in second-guessing what the future, when it arrived, would make of the 'artwork of the future'. To Hans von Wolzogen he writes that he has now reached the age of seventy but still cannot think of a single person whom he could entrust with the supervision of every department of an opera company.[33] And how could this be otherwise? As the creator of the works, he recognized only his own authority. To the last, he believed that works like *Tannhäuser* needed revising and that the ideal stage realization of his works (despite the huge developments he had secured between the Munich premieres of *Rheingold* and *Walküre* and the Bayreuth *Parsifal* of 1882) still eluded him.

The composer knew that what he had learnt from the *Parsifal* performances was also useful for the *Ring*, hence his asking Angelo Neumann to make amendments to the production which the impresario was to tour throughout Europe and beyond (see below). He also expected that his *Parsifal* experience would help him with that new staging for the *Ring* to which, in the final months of his life, his thoughts, as recorded by Cosima, so often turned: 'He … says he wishes for strength to stage the *Ring* once more and do it well.' And not only the *Ring*: 'In the afternoon he thinks of Bayreuth and says it would probably be a good thing if he were to stage all his works there, and they should also be staged there after his death, for they still survive, and the way in which they are done elsewhere is appalling.'[34]

Cosima's diaries for the last years show Wagner in two minds about whether their son Siegfried would eventually be able to take over at Bayreuth. 'Today [15 December 1881, when Siegfried was twelve] he again complains that nobody understands his aims, that there is nobody to whom he can entrust the realization of his works after his death. He says he does not wish to bring up Siegfried for that purpose.' Over the following year Wagner changes his mind: 'R. said he would like to stage all his works in Bayreuth, then bring Sieg. to the point where he can assume control; that would mean living another 10 years, "for at the age of 23 a man already shows what he has in him" '.[35] There is, so far as I am aware, no mention anywhere that Cosima or any other member of Wagner's family might be entrusted with control. The Wagner who once told Cosima that philosophy could only be mediated to women by men seriously underestimated what she would one day be able to do for his works.

The composer's Bayreuth productions of the *Ring* and *Parsifal* were, just as he wished, hugely influential. Such were the difficulties of staging his works that theatres far and wide were only too grateful for the Bayreuth 'models'. They had absolutely no wish to alter the productions, other than to make the operas performable on their own stages and for audiences not always as dedicated as those at Bayreuth. It was such changes that Wagner had in mind when he complained to Cosima 'about the trend of wanting to do [the *Ring*] differently from the way he did it here [at Bayreuth]'.[36]

As we saw in chapter 3, Wagner went to great pains to see that the Bayreuth productions were notated for posterity. There is certainly no evidence that he wished the performances to pass into history as no more than the memory of a 'beautiful legend'. Porges, Kniese and Mottl were entrusted with laying the foundations for a 'fixed' performing tradition, a yardstick for 'authentic' performance in years to come. Bayreuth, as Dahlhaus rightly points out, 'is the institutionalization in musical practice of a principle that the musical scholarship of the same period was documenting in the first historico-critical editions; and Wagner, the scholar among librettists, may well have been conscious of the parallel'.[37] Nevertheless, the composer reluctantly tolerated cuts and other accommodations to local circumstance without which theatres outside Bayreuth could not have put his works on at all.

In the endeavour to secure a first performance for *Tristan* in Vienna (abandoned in May 1863 after endless rehearsals), Wagner had been prepared to sanction any number of cuts and changes in the score, including the deletion of 142 bars from Tristan's part in Act III and wholesale transpositions in his vocal line.[38] For Angelo Neumann's 1878 *Ring* in Leipzig he allowed *Götterdämmerung* to be given with substantial cuts. Cosima records that Wagner

> decides after all to leave it as it is and just to make some cuts – almost the whole of the Norns' scene and a large part of the scene between Waltraute and Brünnhilde. He does this because he knows that, when badly performed, they are bound to be incomprehensible, and he would rather not sacrifice the transition to the 'Journey to the Rhine', which he knows to be effective; he would have to do this if the prologue were to be separated from the first act. Even here [in Bayreuth] the Norns' scene and the Br.-Walt. scene proved unsuccessful, he says, so how much more likely are they to fail in an ordinary theatre.[39]

On the occasions when Wagner was able to supervise stagings outside Bayreuth things could still go terribly wrong, as in May 1881 during rehearsals for the *Ring*'s Berlin premiere. Cosima reports, 'Scaria overwhelming in the scene with the Wala [*Siegfried*, Act III] – Materna [Brünnhilde] unfortunately gesticulating very strongly, making a cut ("dort sehe ich Grane") which throws Vogl [Siegfried] off, R. indignant and provoked into a very loud exclamation.' And then, 'to the *Rheingold* rehearsal, which is held with piano; the first scene just about all right, but everything else, lighting, scenery, etc., is very poor. R., depressed, says that he experienced such things in Magdeburg 50 years ago and never thought to see them repeated!'[40] His fears were not confirmed, the performances turning out well enough for him to tell Ludwig that he had returned 'fairly reassured, and even with a certain – relative – satisfaction'.[41]

On the road with Angelo Neumann

The Berlin *Ring* (Victoria Theatre, 5–9 May 1881) had been planned by Angelo Neumann, a former singer, now an impresario dedicated to securing performances of Wagner's works outside Bayreuth. The common view, and very much the composer's own, had been that the complete tetralogy could only succeed in the Festspielhaus and under festival conditions. With total determination and the requisite tact Neumann persuaded the composer (who was unable to fund further Bayreuth performances himself after 1876) to allow him to stage the *Ring* first in Leipzig in 1878, then in Berlin in 1881. The following year he was to win Wagner's permission for an extraordinary series of touring performances which were to carry the tetralogy far and wide throughout Europe in 1882–3. Neumann's endeavours are therefore of great interest as the first real trial of how well the *Ring* would fare outside Bayreuth. He had, of course, not the least desire to produce the *Ring* in any other way than Wagner's – partly because no one would have thought to do anything else, and partly because of the box-office appeal in offering a far-flung public the already famous work 'as given by the composer himself' in Bayreuth. This was not strictly true, as Neumann was never shy about making cuts and offering encores (see below).

Neumann had been a baritone at the Vienna Court Opera from 1862 to 1876, and had taken part in Wagner's 1875 productions there of *Tannhäuser* and *Lohengrin*. By 1876 he had become co-director of the Leipzig Opera with August Förster. He attended the second Bayreuth *Ring* that same year and, by his own account, imme-diately conceived 'the idea of transplanting this whole colossal undertaking to Leip-sic and giving it there next year in a complete cycle!'[42] This hope was initially dashed by Wagner, who, on 6 September 1876, wrote to August Förster, 'My work is not complete. I have learned much of its lack of finish from this first presentation. Give me time then to work it over carefully in these next few years and to present it again at Bayreuth in a more perfect form.'[43]

By January 1878, when Wagner's hopes of repeat performances at Bayreuth had faded, he was ready to sign with Neumann for complete cycles in Leipzig. At a meet-ing at Wahnfried, Neumann listened as Wagner described

> the enormous difficulties of his scenic effects, giving me minute details that proved later of the utmost value. He seemed pleased with my absorbed attention, and was especially delighted at my frank criticism of certain technical defects in the Bayreuth performances that I hoped eventually to improve under his guid-ance. Among these were the scene of the Rhine maidens, the progress to Walhalla, and particularly the Magic fire scene. This latter we afterwards staged at Leipsic so adroitly that it became a model for all later performances. The Rhine-maiden scene, however, was not perfected till 1896, when it was given at Bayreuth with an absolutely ideal finish of detail.[44]

Wagner granted Neumann the necessary rights on 21 January 1878, and the Leipzig performances, conducted by the Leipzig music director Josef Sucher, fol-lowed on 28–29 April (*Rheingold* and *Walküre*) and 21–22 September (*Siegfried* and *Götterdämmerung*). It is extraordinary how swiftly theatres could make and execute plans in those days.

The composer sent Hans Richter and Anton Seidl to assist at the rehearsals for *Rheingold* and *Walküre* – and doubtless to approve or veto the performances as they saw fit. They approved and with enthusiasm, but although the reports that reached Wagner were all positive – Liszt saying, according to Neumann, that in certain respects the performances were an improvement on those at Bayreuth[45] – the com-poser, probably on the basis of Seidl's views, felt that his intentions could be more faithfully realized. For *Siegfried* and *Götterdämmerung* he therefore urged the Brück-ner brothers upon Neumann for the scenery, together with those assistants who had worked most closely with him, in particular Anton Seidl as coach and conductor, Carl Brandt as technical director, and Fricke for movement and production. 'You will readily understand,' wrote Wagner on 21 June 1878, 'that I am most keenly interested in the production of my "Nibelungen" dramas in Leipsic, which you are pushing with such vigor. Consequently my dearest wish is to see them absolutely perfect.

Believe me when I tell you that no one (be he never so gifted and painstaking) who has not learned all these things thoroughly *here under me* in Bayreuth, can carry out my plans with absolute fidelity. ... I must beg you to follow my scenic arrangements in Bayreuth as closely as possible; with the exception of certain minor details (comparatively trifling errors).'[46]

Neumann immediately appointed Seidl to assist with the musical preparation and to help coordinate the stage action with the music. For technical and general stage management it seems that Neumann (always anxious to please Wagner, but never afraid to stand up to him) felt he was well provided for from within his Leipzig company, but he invited Fricke to attend as guest of honour. As for the scenery, Neumann had already ordered copies of it not from the Brückners but from the Lüttkemayer studio (also in Coburg) and these were what was used. For the costumes, armour and props Neumann turned to Doepler and commissioned the former head of the wardrobe at Bayreuth to execute them as she had done before. It appears that no significant changes were made, despite Wagner's obvious dissatisfaction with Doepler's efforts for Bayreuth in 1876.

The impresario Angelo Neumann proved that the *Ring* was performable not only at Bayreuth, as many had thought, but could be managed in other theatres too. He began in Leipzig in 1878, from which this scene of *Die Walküre*, Act III, with the warrior maidens encircling Wotan and the kneeling Brünnhilde, is taken.

Neumann took the *Ring* on a grand ten-month tour of twenty-five cities, included in which were the first London performances of the work (May 1882). The photographs from Leipzig 1878 are of exceptional interest as being the earliest to give an idea of how the *Ring* actually looked in performance. There is, however, an important qualification in that these images may not have been taken on the stage but on a mocked-up set in the photographer's capacious studio.

The success of the 1878 Leipzig *Ring* paved the way for Neumann to organize the 1881 performances in Berlin. Here, as we have seen, he had the benefit of the composer's presence at a number of rehearsals: 'He showed Sieglinde how to lay her head on Siegmund's lap and fall asleep. He insisted that Brunhilda, when she comes to announce the doom, must throw her right arm about the horse's neck, holding the shield and spear in her left.' As the fight between Hunding and Siegmund was not to his liking, Wagner leapt up onto the stage 'with the agility of an acrobat'. Snatching up Siegmund's sword, he 'finished the fight with Hunding on the heights at the back of the stage. Then, at a given signal, he fell with a crash close by the edge of a precipice; his head brought clearly into relief by the rise of the hill behind, and his arm hanging limp over the edge of the abyss in full view of the audience. All this with a certainty and a dashing agility that a man of twenty-five might have envied.'[47]

A rift between Wagner and Neumann opened up when, during the latter's speech of thanks at the end of the last *Götterdämmerung*, Wagner left the stage and did not return. His excuse – which Neumann did not wish to believe – was that his heart had given him a turn. But evidently certain aspects of the production had disturbed the composer – aspects of which the account of the rehearsals in Cosima's diaries quoted above had perhaps given forewarning. Wagner later wrote to August Förster, proclaiming Neumann's skill

> in drawing together an irreproachable cast: his determination to remodel the stage arrangements after the Bayreuth pattern has pleased me as well, though I could wish he would call in Fritz Brandt (an experienced technician and son of my mechanical expert, Karl Brandt) for the work.
>
> My only stipulation now is, that Herr Neumann shall appoint a new and competent stage manager who shall be thoroughly conversant with my methods. The utter lack of style and finish in the staging of my 'Nibelungen' cycle has surprised me continually in view of my constant remonstrances on the subject, which Herr Neumann has seemed not to comprehend.[48]

Förster was a master at answering this kind of letter:

> And Fritz Brandt? Certainly an exemplary man! But to make him a condition in the affair – my dear Master, I fear that is a mistake. Let me tell you – we can't be sure there's not a Mr. X.Y.Z. somewhere who could even do *better*!
> · Our interests in the enterprise are certainly the same as yours. Then why not give us some latitude?...
>
> Something of the same tenor I might say with regard to your stipulated stage manager. Where shall we find this paragon of a manager, who is he, this man who is so 'perfectly acquainted with the ins and outs of your works'? I know only one such man, but he lives in Bayreuth and his name is Richard Wagner. If you are able (and willing) to unite the professions of poet and composer, impresario and stage manager, and possibly like Sophocles be your own actor too, I think we should probably reach the ideal presentation of the Richard Wagner dramas. *Probably*, I

say, Master! For 'Close packed our heads with seething thoughts, while deeds accomplished few and far between.' I mean to say, that the theatrical profession is simply a series of compromises. Experto crede Ruperto!…

No, my dear Master – stand at your exalted post; be *you the King* – the builder – and let your labourers, carpenters, masons and draymen do the work that is apportioned to them. Small things must still be small even in the hands of the great![49]

Wagner and Neumann made up their differences, the composer subsequently telling him that he had taken this letter in good part: 'I tell you what, he can write a good letter, that colleague of yours!'[50]

By October 1881 Neumann had bought the Bayreuth scenery (the Lüttkemayer was used only for Leipzig) and had agreed terms with Wagner for the rights for a tour of the *Ring* through Germany and to England, Holland, Belgium, Switzerland, Italy, Hungary and Austria. Exceptionally for Neumann, plans to include Sweden, Norway, Denmark and the United States failed to materialize. In January 1882, the impresario was able to tell Wagner that he would be giving thirty-six cycles in nine months, promising him 'one hundred and fifty thousand Marks in royalty'![51]

It was not just Neumann's promise of royalties but his passion for the works and his resolute will which helped him to sell Wagner the idea that he would put the *Ring* on a train and tour it throughout Europe, with performances in the very run-of-the-mill theatres against which Wagner campaigned and under conditions which, smacking more of a travelling circus than of a temple of the arts, were less than ideal. Wagner was again insistent that Seidl should be involved and given 'a freer hand in the matter of the scenic arrangements than is usually given to the conductor, *for herein lies his specialty and what he has particularly learned of me!*'[52] Neumann was more than happy to take Seidl on board as chief conductor, to whom he was able to add the most outstanding Wagner singers of the day, including Therese and Heinrich Vogl, Hedwig Reicher-Kindermann, Albert Niemann and Emil Scaria. All reports suggest that the singers, who thought nothing of standing in for each other at a moment's notice, turned in some extraordinary performances.

The Richard Wagner Opera Company (Richard-Wagner-Theater) opened on 5 May 1882 with four cycles in London at Her Majesty's Theatre, then resumed in September at Breslau. Performances of the *Ring* and/or 'monster Wagner concerts' were given in more than twenty cities throughout Germany as well as in many cities abroad, including Amsterdam, Brussels, Basel, Venice, Bologna, Rome, Turin, Trieste and Budapest, finishing in Graz on 5 June 1883. News of Wagner's death on 13 February 1883 reached the company in Aachen, Neumann later giving a memorial concert on the Grand Canal in Venice, where the composer had died, on 19 April.

Whether dealing with Wagner, his opera company or the theatres where he wished to perform, Neumann was a masterly impresario. Much of his *Personal Recollections of Wagner* is taken up with accounts of his entrepreneurial prowess. Certainly the grand tour of nine countries was an extraordinary organizational feat, many of the arrangements being made once the tour was under way, the next venue often hanging in the balance. We can readily believe his claim that his may have been the largest show on the road in the nineteenth century:

> Hitherto the largest wandering theatrical troupe had been that of Meiningen; but they had only a third as many persons and appliances as we – to say nothing of their having no orchestra, with its instruments, etc. Our special train carried one hundred and thirty-four people, five freight cars full of properties, and the instruments for an orchestra of sixty. ...
>
> My petition to the [German] department of transportation for reduced rates elicited the reply that such rates could only be made to managers of circuses and menageries. So if I had only added a few elephants, lions and tight-rope walkers to my staff I might have had the benefit of this reduction! From the rates we got for our special trains, however, I am still somewhat in doubt as to whether the minister of transportation in Germany took the Richard Wagner Opera Company for something greater or less than a circus.[53]

Wagner's own views on the sawdust ring were not consistent. For although he considered Therese Vogl riding her Grane into the flames at Munich in 1878 to be no more than a 'circus trick', he gave permission to the Breslau circus director Ernst Jakob Renz for an adaptation of the Ride of the Valkyries as a showpiece for his equestrian performers.[54]

Exactly how the tour worked out in detail, how good the performances were and what their impact was on the far-flung audiences who saw them awaits further research. Neumann's own account is eloquent enough, particularly about the administrative difficulties and attendant mishaps. But he is too partisan to be a fair judge of the artistic achievement of the production. Everything that is known suggests that while the performances were outstanding musically, touring conditions ensured that the staging was a rough and ready simulacrum of the Bayreuth original. 'We admit that the managers probably did all that could be done on the stage of Her Majesty's Theatre,' wrote the *Athenaeum*'s critic of the 1882 London showing, 'but to those who remember the splendid scenery and the wonderful effects of light and shade at Bayreuth – such, for instance, as the sunset in the finale of "Die Walküre" – the presentation of the work could not be wholly satisfactory. The fight with the dragon in "Siegfried" was simply ludicrous, and more fitted for a Christmas pantomime than for a serious drama.'[55]

Circumstance, accident and the impresario's desire to avoid disappointing the public at all costs often led to happenings that were not at all in accord with the composer's wishes. Throughout the tour passages were often encored. According to Felix Adler, Mime's 'Sorglose Schmiede' was repeated three times in Bologna and a complete Erda scene was sung twice in Rome.[56] In Rome the first act of *Die Walküre* was interrupted by the late arrival of the king and queen and an obligatory performance of a royal march! In Neumann's own words, 'Seidl's feelings may be imagined when he was forced to stop his orchestra suddenly in one of the most beautiful passages of "The Valkyre" and break out into the stirring "Marcia reale" –

Hedwig Reicher-Kindermann as Brünnhilde. Undisputed star of Neumann's tour, she was also sensationally received as Erda, Ortrud, Isolde and Leonore. Neumann adored her as the 'greatest dramatic soprano of her day and generation as Schröder-Devrient had been in hers'. He was devastated when in June 1882, towards the end of the tour, she died of a fever in Trieste at the age of twenty-nine.

Angelo Neumann persuaded Wagner to allow him to take the *Ring* and other works around Europe on a chartered train with a full company, but failed to secure the preferential hire rate offered to circuses and menageries. He was not afraid to make cuts and give encores. His travelling Richard-Wagner-Theater may have been the largest road-show of the nineteenth century.

while the audience stood to applaud the King, and he stood bowing to the audience!' In London the impresario became unhappy with the tenor singing Froh. Hedwig Reicher-Kindermann (singing Fricka) noticed and volunteered to sing the lines beginning 'Wie liebliche Luft wieder uns weht' in scene 4. She was allowed to do so, and won a storm of applause.[57]

On the Italian part of the tour there were reports 'that the balance of the orchestra was faulty, the singers "mediocre", the scenery "inadequate" and damaged by too much use, and effects, such as the entry of the gods into Valhalla over a solid rainbow, often "grotesque". On the other hand, Seidl's conducting and the orchestra's playing were constantly admired, as were many of the singers, especially Hedwig Reicher-Kindermann.'[58]

Wagner did his best to keep in touch with the tour. Of particular interest is his letter to Neumann of 29 September 1882 urging production changes for Berlin (doubtless relayed via associates like Seidl) in the light of his experience of bringing *Parsifal* to the stage. He asks, yet again, for the 'greatest possible care with the staging and acting, where it will not be sufficient to rely upon traditions already existing in

Vienna and Leipzig, but where you will have to learn from the lessons that were to be gained from my recent performances of "Parsifal" in Bayreuth.'[59]

Neumann's tour was a venture scarcely less extraordinary than that of Bayreuth itself. But it was the also the antithesis of Bayreuth's dedication to being the one theatre where, under festival conditions, the *Ring* would be given 'ideal' performances before 'ideal' audiences – in short a place of pilgrimage. It was his great achievement to prove that the work was technically feasible outside Bayreuth in 'ordinary' theatres and that it could command large, and by no means necessarily 'dedicated', audiences.

That this was so only heightened the conflict in Wagner's mind between wanting to keep his works under total control at Bayreuth and his desire to be performed – in the cause of the renewal of true German art – far and wide. Neumann was the only impresario Wagner ever trusted. His obvious dedication and strength of purpose gave the composer hope that his works really could be performed beyond Bayreuth without betrayal of his essential aims. He offered at least token support to Neumann's (abortive) plan of 1881–2 to build a Wagner Theatre in Berlin, to be modelled on the Festspielhaus and designed by the same architect, Otto Brückwald, whose proposal to raise the rear section of the amphitheatre slightly above the front section and to add a second tier of boxes at the back was also approved by the composer.[60] Only in his continual efforts to secure the right to perform *Parsifal* outside Bayreuth did he fail with Wagner – just. In a disconsolate mood, the composer once talked of 'handing over *Parsifal* and the festival theatre to Herr Neumann!'[61]

Förster and Neumann's regime in Leipzig ended in June 1882 with a series of performances of all Wagner's operas, *Rienzi* to *Götterdämmerung*. In 1885 Neumann took charge of the German Theatre in Prague, reconstituting his Richard Wagner Opera Company in 1889 with Karl Muck as conductor for its final bow in St Petersburg and Moscow (11 March to 11 April), and finally Prague (22 January to 13 February 1890).[62]

The riddle and its interpretation

Wagner's much-quoted remarks about performing the *Ring* 'differently' next year and creating 'something *new*' ('Kinder! macht *Neues! Neues!* und abermals *Neues!*')[63] are far from being the anarchists' charter that some have taken them to be. His message was certainly not 'differently' in the sense of a new philosophy of staging, but rather an exhortation to find a closer approximation to his own vision. The composer's attitude to what he regarded as the inviolable substance of his works in performance and as legitimate scope for improvement, variation, invention and even interpretation is complex and problematic, but clear lines do emerge. Having done everything he could to define his intentions as exactly as possible, and to protect his works against ignorant and wilful misreadings, he remained open to the solution of unresolved difficulties.

Wagner never lost faith in his belief that theatre had its origin in improvisation and that that remained the essence of performance. He saw this not as the unbending reproduction of a blueprint but as interpretation of his words and music in the spirit of his intentions. He always welcomed imaginative interpretation from singers whose artistry he admired. In rehearsal, as we have seen, he was always improvising and changing his mind. To the dismay of his singers, his movement director Richard Fricke and his conductor Hans Richter, he was forever contradicting previous instructions, altering not only blocking and gestures but also the musical tempi.[64] In this his practice was all of a piece with his long-standing conviction, emphatically reasserted in 1871 in 'On the Destiny of Opera', that theatrical art was 'born from the spirit of free improvisation'.[65] It was, he said, mimetic improvisation which inspired what the dramatist attempted to capture on the page, and which had to be recreated over and over again in live performance. Nothing delighted him more than singers like Schnorr von Carolsfeld, Lilli Lehmann and Albert Niemann, who intuitively understood the composer's characterization and were therefore encouraged to inter-pret it in their own way. Subject only to accurate observance of his words and musi-cal notation, he never wanted any constraint on the performer's freedom to interpret a role. His overriding concern, as instanced again and again, was always for the inner, emotional life of his characters and for the psychological development of the action as a whole. It was precisely because of the supreme importance he attached to this inner life of the drama – which was entirely consonant with the music, its prime articulator – that he found it so hard to get the stage representation to his liking.

Wagner spent a lifetime wrestling with this problem. He stood on the very brink of the electro-technical-cinematic age that could have given him whatever ambience, whatever images he wanted. But the basic question is what it was that the composer hoped scenic art and technology could summon up for him. His real problem had very little to do with technology and everything to do with finding an appropriate visual language. A convincing portrayal of a stage world that was rooted in myth rather than history was as elusive as ever. Confident as he was in every other area of operatic creation – words, music, acting – Wagner admitted that, short of achieving the perfect image in his mind's eye, he did not really know what would satisfy him. Hence his exhortations that landscape painters and other artists should come to his rescue by inventing that in which he would recognize, as might a connoisseur, the visible manifestation of his musical drama.

Until about 1870 he looked for this in something akin to the romantic evocations of history, myth and legend in which Ludwig's scenic artists were so proficient. It took both the insuperable technical obstacles encountered in adapting that decora-tive aesthetic for Bayreuth and Wagner's Schopenhauerean change of focus for him to be convinced, little by little, by Fricke's counsel that, in scenery as in acting, to show less could be to suggest incomparably more.

In his staging of *Parsifal* he had taken a highly significant step back from literalistic decoration. But Joukowsky was only a partial answer, as his designs and those of the Brückners were still speaking the language of romantic naturalism. Wagner was not alone in observing that the production's success lay not in the realism of its picturesque depictions but in its atmosphere, its moods, its sense of sustained ritual gravity.

It was because he knew that 'stage realism' would not serve for *Parsifal* that Wagner had sought something truly surreal for the Flowermaidens. For the Good Friday meadow he sought 'nothing definite, just a slight haze'.[66] He had come to see how easily sets and costumes could become a fatal distraction from 'dramatic truth'. His production of *Parsifal* was testimony to his dawning realization that the singers' performances would communicate the inner drama most powerfully only in settings whose visual imagery sprang not from anything external but from the music and the innermost life of the drama. It had to be back to the world of *Tristan*: 'we go to Jouk.'s to see the cover for the Grail, which has turned out too opulent-looking. R. … says that, if people even begin to observe details such as the shrine, etc., then his aim as a dramatist is lost.'[67] Of the transformation scenes in Acts I and III he said, 'I had never meant the scenic transformation to be a decorative effect, however artistically accomplished; the idea was that the accompanying music should lead us quite imperceptibly, as if in a dream, along the "pathless" way to the Gralsburg.'[68]

Wagner's jest about inventing the invisible theatre plainly showed, as Boulez points out, that he no longer entertained any illusions about Illusion. He had painfully come to recognize that the works of his maturity were in essence a denial of the 'theatre of illusion'. By the time he wrote 'On Actors and Singers' (1872) he had quite abandoned this as the goal of stage performance. Again, Boulez goes to the heart of the matter when he says that 'In Weber and Berlioz the illusion is "credible", whereas in Wagner it is intended to destroy all illusions, in the same way as Klingsor's domain is transformed into a desert.'[69]

Had not a central tenet of Wagner's entire dramatic credo always been that drama should deal in myth, which, almost by definition, cannot be presented as an 'illusion' of anything recognizably historical or 'real' (as, say, in Ibsen)? In Goldman and Sprinchorn's summation, 'Wagner's most original contribution to dramaturgy in the nineteenth century was the perfection of … a drama that speaks to us in anagogical terms and in which the story and characters are meant to serve as medium between us and a larger, profounder, and truer world.'[70] This dramaturgy does not scorn character but uses it as the embodiment of ideas, essences, of the forces that, Wagner believed, govern the world. Against the dominant theatre aesthetic of spectacular depiction – so perfectly suited to the historical-pageant operas admired in Paris (and not only there) – the composer's search for a visual language for mythopoeic drama was always going to be difficult. If Wagner never discovered such a language he at least sensed as much and abandoned the impossible task of the exact scenic delineation of the insubstantial. But his profoundest intuition about the future life of his works had been voiced midway through his composition of the *Ring* in a letter of 23 August 1856 to August Röckel, the imprisoned friend with whom he had stood at the Dresden barricades in 1849: 'How can an artist expect that what he has felt intuitively should be perfectly realized by others, seeing that he himself feels in the presence of his work, if it is true Art, that he is confronted by a riddle, about which he too might have illusions, just as another might?'[71]

PART II

CHAPTER 5

The inheritors: Cosima and Siegfried Wagner, Gustav Mahler and Alfred Roller

The legacy

I am really only destined for painstaking industriousness and it is not granted to me to take the smallest matter lightly. And when I see how readily people rely on verve and inspiration I regard myself as a being of a quite inartistic and philistine disposition.

Cosima Wagner[1]

At Wagner's death his only clear intentions for Bayreuth were that the *Ring* and *Parsifal* productions should be perfected and repeated and that all his other works from *Holländer* on should also be performed there. He had hoped to live long enough to train Siegfried (aged thirteen at the composer's death) to run Bayreuth and direct the performances, but in his heart of hearts he must have felt that there was no one who could take up the torch he had borne.

Cosima inherited a theatre, a mountain of debts and a core of artists, assistants and supporters (like Ludwig, and the Bayreuth bankers Friedrich Feustel and Adolf von Groß) as dedicated to the Master as herself. The concept of a Festspielhaus given over exclusively to the performance of a single composer's works was unprecedented and of unlikely sustainability. It was an extraordinary achievement that she managed to overcome the financial problems, bring all Wagner's mature operas into the Bayreuth repertory and render 'permanent' a theatre that he had seen as no more than temporary. Outliving her husband by nearly half a century, by the time she died in 1930 she had run the festival herself for twenty-three years and seen Siegfried successfully take over his father's work and bring it through into the troubled heart of the twentieth century. One composer, one theatre, one family management – it was and still is a remarkable story.

The part that Bayreuth has played in the 'afterlife' of Wagner's operas and in his influence on theatre is at once central and problematic. Wagner had wanted to fix a performance tradition for his works. Cosima saw to it that that happened, but the result was the denial of that part of the composer's genius that was dedicated to change and renewal. He was not the kind of reformer who expected that the achievement of his immediate aims would render further innovation superfluous. The target was not stationary but ever on the move. Essentially, he reformed nineteenth-century theatre practice in the interest of his own works, but he also recognized that his ideals stood to benefit the larger role of theatre in the life of society and of the German people. Up to the time of his death his radical ideas and practice had left little impact on the theatre world at large – *against* whose functioning they had been conceived. It was generally thought that they were dictated by the needs of his own works and were so intimately bound up with Bayreuth and its festival theatre that there was neither point nor purpose in attempting to emulate them elsewhere. This, however, was shortly to change. Wagner's productions of his works in Berlin (*Tristan*, 1876) and Vienna (*Tannhäuser* and *Lohengrin*, 1875) together with Angelo Neumann's far-flung *Ring* tour of 1882–3 demonstrated not only the genius of the operas themselves but also that the composer's ideas about staging plainly had potential in other theatres and in other repertory. It was not long before the stage technology devised to solve the problems posed by the *Ring* and Wagner's insistence that the best operas were dramas to be *acted* as well as sung were taken up elsewhere. Theatre directors from far and wide flocked to Bayreuth to learn what they could.

When Cosima took control of Bayreuth (de facto in 1883, formally from 1885) she stood somewhere between the sunset of one theatrical epoch and the dawn of another. But for Cosima there was no choice: her self-evident task was to complete the unfinished business of staging the works at the Festspielhaus. As we shall see, this consolidation of a Bayreuth tradition was widely influential. By the same token, the 'model performances' were a provocation to agnostics and to those with other ideas about how the operas might best be staged.

Cosima's sense of her mission has earned her a less than enthusiastic press. She has been accused of fidelity to the letter rather than the spirit of Wagner's ideas and of embalming the 'artwork of the future' in the formaldehyde of the past. That these charges are substantially true should not detract from the immensity of her achievement. Seen in the context of the last two decades of the nineteenth century, her productions were extraordinarily successful. Pragmatic theatre practice, cavalier in its approach to the composer's score, was still at the door. Cosima showed that scrupulous attention to the creator's intentions could intensify the audience's pleasure in the work. It was still the exception rather than the rule that a theatre should offer a meticulously rehearsed performance, in which ensemble was as important as solo performance, and that it should solicit the total attention of the audience.

Cosima set an important example in maintaining the idea of a dedicated contract between performers and audience. She found that it was still necessary to uphold 'faithful performance' as a lesson to the innumerable theatres that imagined that Wagner's death gave them a free hand to present his operas as the sum of their highlights. This was especially true of the earlier romantic operas, *Holländer*, *Lohengrin* and *Tannhäuser*. Cosima did not rest until she had staged them all at Bayreuth in productions planned to show them as fully integrated 'dramas'.

She had not anticipated her role as both manager and artistic director of Bayreuth. Numb with grief, she largely left the memorial 1883 *Parsifal* performances to the artists who had worked with Wagner at the premiere. It was not until the rehearsals for the 1884 festival that she knew what she had to do. Fritz Brandt, the technical director, had alerted her to errors that were creeping in. She responded by having a Beckmesser-like enclosure built on the stage from where she could observe and make corrections. She did not intervene directly, choosing to send written notes to the artists, especially to Hermann Levi, the conductor, and to Anton Fuchs (Klingsor), who was rehearsing the singers. Nothing escaped her ear or eye. Hers was the authority, hers the will. To this she could add her experience of working at the composer's side for nearly twenty years and, as soon became evident, her own particular flair. Where Wagner had been excitable, impulsive, improvisatory, she was cool, watchful, analytic.

She succeeded in establishing the festival on a virtually annual basis, with *Parsifal* as its bedrock. In the last six years of Wagner's life the Festspielhaus had staged only two festivals – with three performances of the *Ring* in 1876 and sixteen of *Parsifal* in 1882. In the twenty-three years of Cosima's reign (1883–1906) there were fifteen festivals with six new productions and a total of 220 performances: *Parsifal* 119, *Tristan* 24, *Meistersinger* 22, *Tannhäuser* 21, the *Ring* 18, *Holländer* 10 and *Lohengrin* 6. It is significant that the *Parsifal* production – in which, as we have seen, the composer most closely approached the staging of his imagination – remained, essentially unaltered, as the memorial rite to its composer and touchstone for the 'Bayreuth style'.

Cosima knew that her greatest challenge lay – when she could afford it – in correcting the shortcomings of the 1876 *Ring* and creating Festspielhaus productions of operas that had had their birth in very different theatres and by no means under their composer's total control. As guides for her *Tristan* (1886) and *Meistersinger* (1888) she took every scrap of documentation from the Munich premieres (1865, 1868), which had been accounted broadly successful by Wagner, particularly in the case of *Meistersinger*. For *Tannhäuser* (1891) she was on more difficult ground. Recollection of Wagner's Vienna staging (1875) was helpful, but his input into the Paris production of 1861 had been compromised by the 'grand opera' expectations of the theatre and its public, his hopes of an ideal staging exploding into catastrophe. And the composer had remained unhappy about the score itself, cherishing right up to his death the thought of finding a definitive form for the work. For *Lohengrin* (1894) and *Holländer* (1901), with premieres stretching back to Weimar (1850, under Liszt) and Dresden (1843) and with no subsequent performances anywhere fully endorsed by Wagner, she had virtually a tabula rasa.

Under the banner of 'duty and obedience' her concern was always the realization of the composer's intentions and in a great many cases these had been more than adequately documented. There was also her own memory and that of the substantial number of associates who had taken part in or witnessed the performances of Wagner's lifetime, though the recollections of the two memory banks did not always coincide. In 1876 there had also been marked differences between the composer and herself on many production issues. 'Frau Cosima had much to say about the costumes and many other details,' reports Lilli Lehmann. 'Wagner and she were very often of quite opposite opinions, and "Wahnfried", not infrequently, was divided into two parties ... But he yielded on small points in the end, for the sake of peace.'[2]

Cosima the producer had a powerful mind and taste of her own and whenever explicit performance history failed her they came to her aid, disguising themselves as the Master's own ordinance. When the evidence faltered she could always summon up an incontrovertible 'the Master said' or 'it was decreed that'. Lilli Lehmann describes her attempts to implicate Siegfried in this game in 1896 by appealing to his memories of the 1876 *Ring*, which he had seen at the age of seven. ' "You remember, Siegfried, do you not, that it was done this way in 1876?" Whereupon Siegfried always replied, "I believe you are right, mamma." '[3]

She could not help but bring in her own ideas. Thus she sought the key to *Tannhäuser* in an academic interpretation of the conflict between the Venusberg and the Wartburg. For *Lohengrin* she invoked a tenth-century version of the legend to clarify the action as a struggle between heathen and Christian world orders. For *Holländer* she made a meticulous study of Norwegian coastal life in the seventeenth century.

There seems no doubt that she did 'rescue' these early works from their fate as 'repertory' opera, but in the process of their resuscitation as 'dramas' (in accord with the principles of *Opera and Drama*) musical values sometimes came off second best (see below). Paradoxically, the pursuit of the 'drama *not* opera' ideology sometimes had the opposite effect from that intended. The restoration of passages habitually cut in repertory performance – particularly in the more complex and protracted chorus numbers – actually underlined the indebtedness of the early works to grand opera. 'It must not be concluded,' wrote Bernard Shaw of the first Bayreuth *Lohengrin* in 1894, 'that the restoration of the omitted portions tends to make the work less operatic than the ordinary acting version. On the contrary, I was struck with the ultra-operatic effect of the restored choruses and ensembles, and could not help seeing that the managers agreed to cut them out, not in the least because they were specially Wagnerian even in the old days when that word meant something, but because they were specially troublesome.' Shaw was nevertheless all in favour of the restoration of the omitted passages: 'Telramund … from being the feebly obstructive shadow of a conventional villain as we know him, became an important and power-ful character. Ortrud shared his gain to some extent; and it is noteworthy that the scene between the two at the beginning of the second act, which has always been cut down as impossibly tedious and rather bears out that complaint in its mutilated state, was not at all tedious at full length.'[4]

Although lacking Wagner's formidable mimetic gifts, Cosima was determined in her stagecraft, curbing histrionic gesture and insisting on psychologically driven action. In stage technology she was guided by Friedrich Kranich sr, who had taken over from Fritz Brandt in 1886, introducing whatever innovations would best achieve the results she was after. For decor she continued to work happily with the Brückners and their familiar brown-hued painted scenery. Solid, practicable scenery was gradually introduced, but Cosima's was still the quintessential mid-nineteenth-century peep-show theatre of illusion, the 'reality' of the scene created by perspective painting on backdrops, flats and hangings. Although the rapid development of gas and especially electric lighting technology opened up a new horizon of possibilities,

Cosima still clung to the view that the purpose of lighting did not extend beyond illuminating the performers and scenery and, to a lesser extent, the creation of atmosphere.

The lessons of the *Ring* and *Parsifal* had taught her to be wary of Doepler's archaeological approach to costume and to seek freer, more sheerly theatrical inventions devised by the painter Hans Thoma, her daughter Daniela Thode and various others (including Josef Flüggen, Arpad Schmidhammer and Max Rossmann). Nevertheless, the spirit of historicism was still alive and well, as testified by Lilli Lehmann who was one of the Brünnhildes in 1896: 'I was told at Wahnfried that [Waltraute's] costume, together with Fricka's, was made with long sleeves of six puffs and falling over the hands, like Botticelli's pictures of Madonnas. In vain did I ask myself what Botticelli's Madonnas had to do with heathen gods.'[5] Weingartner wondered why 'Hagen and his vassals could not use bulls' horns instead of gracefully twisted metal instruments, the very look of which betrayed that they could not possibly give out the powerful notes that struck the ear? The story is that they were copied from metal horns found in Sweden which can be proved to belong to primeval ages. That may be; the purely historical has no value whatsoever on the stage.'[6] On the musical side Cosima had the support of conductors like Levi, Richter, Mottl and Seidl, and assistants like Kniese and Porges who had worked closely with the composer, and she proved herself skilful in choosing singers she could mould to her ideals.

Tannhäuser *at Bayreuth, 1891*

Cosima's attitude to staging is shown nowhere more vividly than in her 1891 Bayreuth premiere production of *Tannhäuser*. We see her on the one hand doing everything possible to fulfil its creator's own hopes for the work and, on the other, recreating it in the light of her own ideas. (She would have been shocked at the thought that there could be an element of interpretation in what she was doing.) For her, the Bayreuth production of this particular opera was a matter of especial importance; it was only the cost of the enterprise that compelled her to delay it until 1891. No other work of Wagner's had been so distorted and travestied on stages far and wide. She wanted to rescue *Tannhäuser* from the popular impression that it was a potpourri of great musical and spectacular numbers marred by an obscure and unsympathetic story. Only Bayreuth could demonstrate the coherence and force of the work as a drama. She saw her task as nothing less than 'a life-and-death struggle between opera and drama'.[7]

But first she had to decide on a version of the score, for none could be regarded as definitive. Wagner had himself produced *Tannhäuser* three times (Dresden 1845, Paris 1861, Vienna 1875) but to the very end of his life maintained that the score had yet to be given its final shape. Cosima battled for over a year to make sense of the evidence. Of necessity she had to adopt a 'critical' rather than unquestioningly 'Werktreue' stance; there was simply nothing to which she could be unequivocally 'treu' (faithful). In the end she settled for something based on the Paris version and

Wagner's subsequent revisions. As her unifying principle she took, as we have seen, the conflict between the Venusberg and the Wartburg. Obviously enough it was personified in Venus and Elisabeth, with Tannhäuser caught in the middle. But she embroidered the metaphor to represent an additional conflict between Dionysian antiquity and the Christian ideals of the Middle Ages. She enlisted academic help – from art historian Hugo von Tschudi, archaeologist Reinhard Kekulé von Stradonitz and literary scholar Wilhelm Herz – in substantiating her idea. She herself undertook research in museums and libraries in Berlin and Munich.

Great pains were taken with the choreography and mythological episodes in the bacchanale (devised by the Italian dancer Virginia Zucchi) so that it should be regarded not as a diversional ballet but as a dance with an integral role in the drama. To help with the representation of Venus, the chorus director Julius Kniese assembled some forty-four classical images (all decently clothed) of Aphrodite. The scene eventually included sixty-four sirens, naiads, nymphs, bacchantes, tritons, youths and fauns, with the Leda and Europa episodes as an allegorical mime.

In casting Elisabeth, Cosima distanced herself from the mature, heroic sopranos to whom the role was usually given, choosing instead young singers (Pauline de Ahna and Elisa Wiborg) 'not yet ruined by run-of-the-mill opera-house performance'. As she told the journalist George Davidsohn, she had sought a singer who

Cosima Wagner sought to stage her husband's work exactly as she imagined he would have wanted but inevitably interpreted it in her own way. For her expanded 'Paris' version of *Tannhäuser* in 1891 she saw the Venusberg as an incarnation of Dionysian antiquity. In the foreground, left, Tannhäuser lies in the lap of the reclining Venus, while behind them appears an allegorical mime as the Swan swims towards Leda, adrift in her pool in the woods.

The costuming and choreography of the Venusberg bacchanale has always been problematic. One can only hope that these graces, nymphs and bacchantes were more alluring in motion than in this posed grouping from 1904. The 1891 choreography had been by Virginia Zucchi but in 1904 it was reworked by the Hellenophiliac dance sensation, Isadora Duncan, who also took the part of one of the solo graces.

would not treat 'Dich, teure Halle!' as a showpiece aria, nor Elisabeth's defence of Tannhäuser as an impassioned dramatic recitative, but rather someone capable of appearing childlike and virginal. For Tannhäuser she cast Heinrich Zeller, whom she described as having 'a small but youthful voice, an intelligent sense of his role and spiritual features'.[8]

The closest attention was paid to psychological truth of expression, clarity of diction and grace of movement and gesture. Cosima was anxious to show the chorus as an active, essential participant in the drama, formed not of an anonymous mass but of individuals. Thus the guests at the Act II Song Contest, 116 in number, were given names found in the history books – 'Truchseß von Schlotheim', 'Graf von Orlamunde', etc. – separately costumed by Josef Flüggen (after exhaustive research in books by Karl Weinhold and Alwin Schultz), their movement and behaviour choreographed according to their supposed rank and station (each, on arrival, was to pay his respects to the Landgraf in his own way). Spontaneity was, however, not allowed, every gesture being strictly decreed and every movement predetermined.

In Act I, the Landgraf's hunting party numbered sixty-five, accompanied by a great many dogs but without the horses of the 1861 production, as Cosima was concerned they might be frightened by the canines. At the end of Act III she attached great importance to the role of the returning pilgrims (thirty-two older and forty

Das Szenarium nach Richard

Das Szenarium nach Isadora Duncan.

Wagner's own desire for the Venusberg was that it should show 'a chaos of emotions ranging from the tenderest contentment, languishing and yearning, to the most drunken impetuousness of exultant abandon'. These cartoons by Franz Jüttner, 'Das verbesserte Bacchanal' (The Improved Bacchanale), contrast the Venusberg according to the composer with the same scene according to Isadora Duncan. The drawings were probably inspired by the 1907 Munich staging of the opera which, as at Bayreuth 1904, was also choreographed by Duncan. It suggests that the celebrated bare-foot *danseuse* travestied Wagner's intentions by aligning them with those of the aesthetic movement. At Bayreuth her choreography was considered scandalous, but on exactly what grounds remains unclear.

younger ones, with an escort of thirty knights!) in making sense of the proclamation of Tannhäuser's redemption. The scenery was entrusted to Max Brückner, whom Cosima praised for understanding her intentions (he had had experience enough) and for 'interpreting them with freedom and imagination'.[9] On the musical side she numbered the young Richard Strauss among her assistants (he was to conduct the 1894 revival), while the conductor was Felix Mottl.

Cosima was well pleased with the production and gratified by its reception. Richard Strauss saluted her for having succeeded in rescuing the opera from its fate in court and municipal theatres, praising the contribution of Mottl and the orchestra in creating a sense of musical and scenic unity.[10] But in reiterating Wagner's view that the hardest thing in performance was to coordinate the music and staging he was very likely hinting that Cosima's concentration on the stage might unbalance the whole. Cosima herself was concerned (perhaps with justification) lest the lavishness of the production – much admired by the press – should be misunderstood as 'effects without causes', and sought to justify herself in a spate of letters and other writings. She need not have feared. Most commentators were unstinting in their praise for the production's 'truth to nature'.

Pro and contra Cosima

Cosima's *Lohengrin* (1894) and *Holländer* (1901) were planned and executed along similar lines. They were also well received, Bernard Shaw regarding the *Lohengrin* as an intelligent production 'which did not insult [the audience] with a mindless accumulation of detail'.[11] Shaw thought that this was 'probably the first time it has ever been thoroughly done at all … its stage framework is immensely more entertaining, convincing and natural than it has ever seemed before'. He goes on to praise the stage direction of the Act I finale for 'combining into one stroke a dramatic effect, a scenic effect, and a musical effect, the total result being a popular effect the value of which was proved by the roar of excitement which burst forth as the curtains closed in'.[12]

For *Holländer* she chose to suggest that the piece was more of an integrated music drama than the opera Wagner had actually written by giving it in a single-act version, despite his own preference for dividing it into three. *Tristan* (1886) and *Meistersinger* (1888) joined the Bayreuth canon very much on the terms of their original Munich premieres, but with improvements. For the *Ring*'s return in 1896 after a twenty-year absence there was new scenery by the Brückner studio, and the production benefited from a more measured approach to the solution of the still awesome scenic problems.

Throughout Cosima's reign one sees a steady movement from adhesion to the letter of the composer's wishes towards a greater freedom in response to the demands posed by the works and the possibilities she discovered in them. It is time to attempt a balance sheet of her place in stage history.

On the positive side, she consolidated the enterprise of the Festspielhaus and the festivals so that what had begun as 'provisional' soon became accepted as permanent.

The idea of perpetuating the 'authentic' performance of an opera in an authentic milieu was born, if anywhere, at Bayreuth. Cosima knew exactly which side she was on in the modern debate about what distinguishes a 'compliant' from a non-'compliant' performance in the 'afterlife' of a work that has become a classic. That this debate exists at all is partly owing to her.[13]

With hindsight we can see that there is no such thing as an ideal, perfected performance of anything, such ideality being definable only under very particular circumstances and within a very narrow time span. But to the great majority of her contemporaries it really did seem that Cosima had succeeded in staging Wagner's works as he would have wished. (Both musically and scenically the performances often left much to be desired, but they were still generally better than those given elsewhere.) She could not replicate his continually creative, totally unpredictable play with his own works, but she could hardly have served him more assiduously. To have solved the immense practical problems of staging the *Ring* as successfully as she did in 1896 was in itself a remarkable feat, to which must be added the creation of creditable first Bayreuth productions of the other major operas in his canon.

Although her point of departure was always every rubric, every written scrap, every move and image in Wagner's works and in his own productions thereof, Cosima brought theatrical skills of her own to her task. She still looked to the history books and to academics for guidance, but she was no longer quite so slavishly bound to them. She learnt how to use her research to create theatrical images which could develop a life of their own. She had a more highly developed visual sense than Wagner, working with the Brückners and with costume designers to soften garish, crude effects. In the interests of spiritualizing the action in *Tristan*, she proscribed the banal, over-pictorial 'realism' which had governed its settings at the 1865 Munich premiere. In the same cause she was tireless in restraining all unmotivated and rhetorical 'acting', movement and gesture in this and the other operas. To serve this aim, in 1892 she founded, on a modest scale and with Julius Kniese's help, a 'Stilbildungsschule' in Bayreuth for the training of performers, thus fulfilling one of Wagner's persistent but elusive ambitions. (The school was short-lived, but its notable graduates included Alois Burgstaller, who sang Siegfried 1896–7 and 1908, Hans Breuer, who sang Mime 1896–1914, and Siegfried Wagner, who first conducted at one of the school's concerts in 1893.)[14]

Psychological truth of action and expression was Cosima's constant preoccupation, as were the clear enunciation of the vocal line and its balance with the orchestra. Her blocking of the action and her treatment of the chorus as a composite of individual characters and an active participant in the drama were emulated by Max Reinhardt and other pioneers of the theatre of the twentieth century. She asserted always that stage and orchestra should be under the control of a single person, and that drama could not be successfully performed without the integration of all its elements. In the 1880s and 1890s this was still, with such rare exceptions as the Meiningen players, quite out of the ordinary. She trained Siegfried, within her terms of reference, as a more than adequate successor. Finally, and unwittingly, her cultivation of a museum aesthetic and the inflexibility of her principles were a mighty spur to those who had quite different ideas as to how, in its 'afterlife', Wagner's vision might best be served.

The defects of her authoritarian attitude must also begin the negative column on the scorecard. She believed – not without reason – that she had uniquely privileged access to the composer's intentions and took unkindly to criticism and well-informed comment alike. This was a stance that is entirely understandable in the context of the prevalent nineteenth-century belief that only the creator's intentions were of any significance. (Of course this did not mean that they were always followed – far from it!) The weakness in the position, however – and taking it on its own terms – was that it was one thing to be faithful to the letter of Wagner's wishes and quite another to be faithful to the composer's ceaselessly inventive spirit. His idea of a 'model' performance was a far more dynamic concept than Cosima's.

The Cosima who on occasion had plainly been appalled by the histrionic exuber-ance of Wagner the natural actor was not at ease with singers of personality and imagination. In obedience to the composer's own precept that acting should be coordinated with the music, her aim was to codify it so completely that all possibil-ity of error – and, one must say, of inspired invention – was eliminated. 'Madame Wagner,' said Bernard Shaw, 'is a clever stage manager; but one of the faults of her qualities is to conceive a dramatic representation as a series of tableaux vivants, and to invent attitudes for people instead of continuous and natural action, the result being that artists get stuck for ten minutes at a time into poses that become ridicu-lous after ten seconds.'[15] This regimentation of the stage successfully served the idea of performance as an endlessly repeatable, unchanging rite. It reinforced the strategy of those who saw Bayreuth as a shrine for the perpetuation of Wagner's art as a reli-gion. Cosima justified this approach as setting an example for others to follow, but in the long run it had a stultifying rather than a liberating effect. Of its essence it spoke the language of the seminary and parade ground, not of the composer's style of theatre. 'I saw and heard only wooden dolls, and I thought, with sorrow, of the year 1876, when Niemann, with a single glance and breath, gave the stamp to the whole first act,' wrote Lilli Lehmann of a 1896 *Walküre* rehearsal; and of a *Götter-dämmerung* rehearsal, 'The everlasting "standing in profile" was carried to the point of mania'; and of *Rheingold* in the second cycle, 'It made the impression on me of a play by marionettes; motions that had been imitated without force, expression, or feeling.'[16]

And what of the music? It seems clear that her mission to insist that Wagner's works were dramas (and not 'operas' with all that this word evoked of the horrors of repertory theatre) often attenuated the role of the orchestra. Wagner himself had always stressed that the conductor must at all times be closely involved in everything happening both on the stage and behind it.[17] In practice, under Cosima's overall direction, this meant being required to mute dynamics and adjust tempo and phras-ing to accommodate Cosima's ideas about the articulation of the vocal line. Her pro-duction notes as recorded in Felix Mottl's score show numerous alterations to dynamics for the purpose of making words more audible. Much of this was obviously entirely sensible adjustment of the kind that Wagner himself would have made, but one senses between the lines of Richard Strauss's long letter to Cosima of 24 August 1892 a gentle warning that there was some danger of the orchestra being asked to play second fiddle to the stage.[18]

One of Cosima's harshest critics, and from the reactionary side of the fence, was the conductor Felix Weingartner who had been a repetiteur for the 1886 *Tristan*. Even making allowance for his freely declared misogyny, his witness rings true. Musically, he rated her no better than 'an educated dilettante'. 'She interfered in details of the orchestral execution, ordered the time and the shades of expression as if she had been the most capable and distinguished of conductors; and for his part, the distinguished but all too adaptable Mottl knew no higher object than to subordinate his wishes to hers, even when it went against his convictions.' Hating the sycophantic atmosphere, Weingartner never worked again at Bayreuth, but he did return as a visitor. He found that, making a rare exception for Richter's *Meistersinger* in 1888, it had become *de rigueur* that Wagner's own forthright tempi should be sanctimoniously dragged, but reported that this had largely been rectified by the *Ring* in 1896. The musical defects that year, however, included the omission of 'whole passages' in the Valkyries' scene with 'the prompting voice of the conductor plainly audible'. In appraising the results of Cosima's concern for verbal clarity, Weingartner said that everything was 'sacrificed to pronunciation. This is carried to such lengths that the singers sometimes no longer sing but rather speak, which can only be justified in exceptional cases.'[19]

Cosima sought to lock the works into a visual aesthetic that was purely illustrative, imitating and reflecting in naturalistic scenery the imagery of Wagner's words and music. Its premiss was that there existed an exact visual translation of words and music. It was Baudelaire's 'correspondances' taken literally. That was the Xanadu pursued by Cosima. It erred in its refusal even to entertain the possibility that the exhaustive explicitness of the composer's scores might be better served not by an attempt to invent their precise visual equivalent (the path of tautology), but by discovering images and movement suggested by the music which could be in lively dialogue with it. Cosima did see the point of simplifying the scenery of *Tristan* the better to involve the audience in the psycho-drama played out in the music. But she erred in failing to see that such an approach could also benefit the *Ring* and other works. She never questioned the comprehensive authority of the creator's intentions, or the idea that the best possible staging was one which most exactly realized the stage rubrics and the images of the text.

Cosima and the reformers at the door

The glimmerings of free thought in Cosima's productions risked only minimal engagement with the new theatrical ideas that were beginning to emerge around her. So total was her dedication to perfecting the nineteenth-century aesthetic of realistic stage illusion that she could conceive of no other. Those who could she treated as heretics with the power to betray everything she meant by the 'Bayreuth style'. When Gordon Craig told her over lunch in Dresden in 1905 that the 'stage trappings at Bayreuth or anywhere else' were nothing like 'the visions [Wagner's] music conjured up', Cosima replied,

> 'And what pictures do *you* see, Mr Craig?' And I described something like the wild pampas of South America, the rushing of the wind, perhaps a prairie fire and so on.
>
> When I looked at Frau Wagner I could hardly see her face, because she had turned the same color as the table cloth, into which she seemed to be vanishing. I came to a stop, thank goodness, in time – something shot me out into reality.[20]

More significant was her rejection of the Swiss designer Adolphe Appia, whose proposals for a drastic simplification of the stage picture were to be hugely influential. Appia's ideas (which will be discussed in chapter 6) had been given powerful impetus by his negative experience of *Parsifal* at Bayreuth in 1882. He had been befriended in 1884 by Houston Stewart Chamberlain, formidable member of the Wahnfried circle whose progressive artistic ideas were in marked contrast to his extreme social and political conservatism. Appia and Chamberlain attended the 1888 festival together, in the course of which Chamberlain recommended his ideas to Cosima. She rejected Appia's suggestion that Venus (in the 1891 *Tannhäuser*) should wear white but told Chamberlain that there might be a future for him as 'costume designer and lighting consultant for Bayreuth'.[21]

Chamberlain continued to attempt to interest Cosima in Appia's ideas and sketches, hoping that she might incorporate them in the forthcoming 1896 *Ring*. But Cosima had no use for an approach so openly critical of Wagner's and her own ideas of authentic performance. In a long letter to Chamberlain she spells out a rebuttal of Appia which encapsulates her own position.[22] Her fundamental assertion is that since Richard Wagner himself produced the *Ring* in 1876 there is no further scope for invention. She is plainly appalled by Appia's insistence that all naturalistic detail and decoration should be replaced by simplified settings, with lighting the new principal agent for 'painting' scenes and creating place and mood. Appia's sketches, she says on another occasion, are reminiscent only of the pictures that the explorer Nansen had brought back from the North Pole.[23] For Appia, elaborate costuming and jewels were at all costs to be avoided; Cosima retorts that the presence of jewellery distinguishes the rank of the superior personages. The only positive assistance that Appia might be able to offer is with the lighting. By 'lighting' she meant improved illumination of performers and scenery, thus totally misunderstanding why Appia was so interested in the medium. The illumination of *trompe l'oeil* was the last thing he wanted. His vision was of the stage as an open space with changes of scene and mood created by the active use of the electric-lighting console.

Publication of Appia's *La Mise en scène du drame wagnérien* in 1895 (and of *Die Musik und die Inscenierung* in 1899) disseminated his ideas, and it was not long before others were urging them upon Cosima. They were enthusiastically

Cosima stood between the sunset of one theatrical epoch and the dawn of another. In 1896 she brought the *Ring* back to Bayreuth for the first time since its premiere in 1876. Although Max Brückner's revised scenery (*above*) for the open space on the mountain heights in *Das Rheingold* had a more solid feel to it than in 1876, there was an immeasurable distance between its romantic naturalism and the young Swiss designer Adolphe Appia's spare vision of the same scene (*opposite*). Appia had been proposed to Cosima as a designer for 1896, but she was appalled, rejecting his sketches as reminiscent of the pictures that Nansen had brought back from the North Pole.

commended by Count Hermann von Keyserling, who had been impressed by the first practical trial of Appia's ideas in the Countess de Béarn's private theatre in Paris (part of Act II of *Carmen* and extracts from Byron's *Manfred* with music by Schumann, 25 March 1903). In her patient reply Cosima carefully explained to Keyserling that 'our art' ('unsere Kunst') had no use for Appia and that the only contribution that could be made by improved technology was the better realization of the composer's ideas.[24] In speaking of Wagner as 'the creator of drama from the spirit of music' she was, unknowingly, on the same ground as Appia, whose point was always that the production must derive from the music and not from the stage instructions. The crucial difference was that while Cosima believed that music and stage instructions told the same story, Appia maintained that the latter were an aberration and that, in Schopenhauerean spirit, only the music was to be trusted.

For Cosima, as she explained to Keyserling, Wagner's ideas were comprehensive; she makes comparison with Shakespeare and Goethe, who had left only the barest indications of how their works were to be performed. Just as Wagner had built his own theatre, so 'had he also definitively determined [his works'] staging. Shakespeare and Goethe, however, have not done this.'[25] It was to Shakespeare's verbal

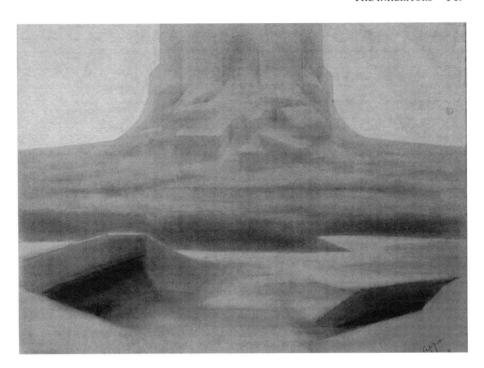

dramas and to *Faust* II and *not* to Wagner that Appia should apply his imagination. What Cosima forgot to say was that Shakespeare and Goethe had also built and run theatres, and that they and Wagner all recognized that performance had its own active, ultimately protean role in the completion of the written text.

Wagner had wanted to establish a 'fixed tradition' because he needed to defend his own imaginings against misunderstanding and perversion – he knew that the sheer ambition and complexity of his vision meant that his successors would need an unusual degree of help in realizing it. In 'fixing' a tradition he most surely did not intend to imply a ban on the freedom of intelligent performers and stage directors to contribute their own artistry and make lively contribution to the challenges he had flung down, which would doubtless stand for all time without admitting of any definitive solution. Such has ever been the essential nature of theatre.

Siegfried Wagner and the rising tide of modernism

Certainly the son's efforts to continue what the father had begun should be respected. However, the task is much more difficult than simply taking over the management of a stocking shop.

Claude Debussy, 1903[26]

The Siegfried who took over control of the festival from Cosima in 1906 had been closely schooled in the Bayreuth style, having served both as conductor (from 1896) and as assistant to his mother. Although he was more open to new ideas than

Siegfried Wagner rehearsing in 1906 under the watchful eye of his mother. The drawing from the *Berliner Illustrirte Zeitung* (13 April 1930) shows Cosima seated beside him on the stage of the Festspielhaus in the year when he took over the festival from her. Siegfried had a real interest in technical innovation, but mostly used it to refine rather than question the conservatism of Bayreuth's pictorial realism. Had he not been so subject to his formidable mother and his three older sisters, he might have succeeded in developing a more stylized and symbolic style of staging.

Cosima, his freedom of action was constrained by her longevity. Removed from the front line by a heart attack, she nevertheless retained her authority and continued to exercise a significant influence as long as she lived. Her presence at Wahnfried – invalid though she became – made itself powerfully felt right up to her death at the age of ninety-two on 1 April 1930. Siegfried survived her by only four months. He suffered a heart attack on 18 July and was too ill to attend the premiere, four days later, of a long-planned new *Tannhäuser* production that he had intended would steer Bayreuth in a more modern direction. He died on 4 August.

Given a free hand Siegfried's custodianship might have been more adventurous than it was. His achievements, like those of his mother, have received less than their due. By the time of his death the Festspielhaus had (with the exception of *Parsifal*) put the nineteenth-century means of creating illusion behind it. The scenery was now largely of solid construction, the visual imagery stylized and symbolical rather than literalistic, and lighting was beginning to play the more central role that Appia had wanted. But in one crucial respect Siegfried's Bayreuth was still locked into the nineteenth century. The rationale for his changes was always the execution of Wagner's own prescriptions. The fundamentalist Wahnfried understanding of the composer's wishes remained unshaken.

Siegfried's education could not have been more purposefully directed. His musical tutors included his grandfather Liszt, Humperdinck and Felix Mottl. For a time he studied architecture in Berlin and later travelled extensively in Asia. He developed a certain facility in drawing, particularly in sketching architectural subjects. This would enable him to provide his designers at Bayreuth (the perennial Max Brückner, and later Kurt Söhnlein) with a clearer idea of what he wanted than either his father or his mother had been able to do. But he could not long postpone submission to his hereditary destiny. As musician he was a conductor of modest accomplishment (Weingartner was distinctly unimpressed).[27] He became a prolific composer, with fourteen three-act operas, nine orchestral works and many other compositions to his name. The operas, composed 1898–1927, are mostly fairy-tale moralities to his own texts and in unoriginal late romantic idiom. In his lifetime they were extensively performed in Germany; Mahler gave *Der Bärenhäuter* (1898), his first opera, with great success in Vienna in 1899.

The young Siegfried was alert to the rising tide of impatience with nineteenth-century theatre horizons and to the winds of change in technology and in ideas about performance. If the subject of Appia was taboo in the Wahnfried salon, it was alive among the children: the fifteen-year-old Siegfried stole from his half-sister Daniela a scenic drawing by Appia: 'The Appia looks very good on my wall,' he confessed; 'would you mind if I kept it?' Her reply is unrecorded.[28]

Siegfried saw Alfred Roller's designs for Mahler's *Tristan* (1903) in Vienna and they had some influence on his renewal – a bold act indeed – of the sets and costumes for the magic garden in *Parsifal* in 1911. His sketches indicate translucent atmospheric tones reminiscent of Turner. 'For the flower garden,' he instructed Brückner, 'I want close colour coordination in orange-gold tones in all gradations through to yellow – no red – no rose-pink – no green, on the wall behind, blue.'[29] Brückner made his own feelings plain in censoring Siegfried's radicalism with a safely conservative interpretation. For the Flowermaiden costumes Siegfried turned to Ludwig von Hofmann (a Berlin artist and member of a group founded by Max Liebermann and Walter Leistikow) and for Kundry's Act II costume to Mariano Fortuny, an artist and lighting technologist of considerable importance (see chapter 6).

Siegfried was also closely acquainted with Max Reinhardt's work, which, as we have seen, was itself indebted to Wagner's ideas and to Cosima's productions. Siegfried learnt from Reinhardt's direction of his actors, and particularly from his dynamic handling of the chorus. It was, however, principally in the field of technology that Siegfried was most receptive. And here the traffic was two-way, as, from Carl Brandt onwards, the Festspielhaus had been the nursery for innovations by an outstanding succession of technical directors. As Siegfried reminded his critics in the 1920s, Bayreuth (under the redoubtable Friedrich Kranich sr) had been in the forefront of lighting development and had pioneered both the chemical production of mist and smoke effects (replacing the use of steam) and a cyclorama in place of a backdrop and even, when required, the flats forming wings. Of more specific application were Kranich's new swimming machines (from 1896), in which the singers were suspended in cradles hung from the flies and manoeuvred by wires both from the flies and from below.[30]

Between 1908 and 1930 Siegfried supervised ten festivals (there was a break of nine years between the festivals of 1914 and 1924 on account of the war and subsequent inflation) with a total of 131 performances (*Parsifal* 60, the *Ring* 21, *Meistersinger* 20, *Tristan* 13, *Lohengrin* 10, *Tannhäuser* 5, *Holländer* 2) and four new productions (*Lohengrin*, 1908, *Meistersinger*, 1911, *Tristan*, 1927, *Tannhäuser*, 1930). Over this period Bayreuth cautiously sloughed off the naturalistic camouflage of the nineteenth century and began to use solid scenery, 'creative' lighting and more stylized visual images. Attempts at exact pictorial realism (relatively successful under the soft glow of gas lighting but unconvincing under electric lighting) were replaced by growing confidence in symbolic representation.

The improvements to the 1896 *Ring* included a solid, roughly fissured rock for the Valkyries, installed in front of the Festspielhaus's first cyclorama (1906), and a new open mountain-top space (1911) for the second scene of *Rheingold*. In 1911 an even larger cyclorama was used to create, after forty lighting rehearsals, the effect of Valhalla floating above an unlimited space in which the eye could lose itself. When

Towards the end of the 1920s Adolphe Appia's ideas for the reduction of scenery to its essentials impinged tangibly on Siegfried Wagner and his designer Kurt Söhnlein, as here in the final scene of *Das Rheingold*, photographed in 1931. Technical director Friedrich Kranich jr built chunks of rock forms on three large steel trucks which were manoeuvered into new configurations for the different mountainous scenes throughout the *Ring*. Lighting no longer just illuminated the performers and scenery but was used dramatically, while mist and smoke effects were now produced by chemicals rather than with steam.

Bayreuth reopened in 1924, Siegfried had the Gibichung Hall built for the first time as a solid, collapsible structure of pillars and wooden beams. The following year Friedrich Kranich jr (succeeding his father as technical director in 1924) created a solid rock landscape on three separate stage-trucks, which could be variously assembled to suit all the *Ring*'s rocky scenes.[31] An underwater rock and the projection of light to suggest waves were added in 1928, together with a new circular Hunding hut (the only logical form, Siegfried argued, for a hut built around a tree trunk): the great door was moved from the rear to the left, enabling a more dramatic flood of moonlight when it flew open. Siegfried was proud of his new sets, arguing that they were a huge improvement on those of 1896: 'Away with all the nonsense in the previous decor. It's time for colour!! For god's sake enough of this horrible brown! I hate brown, this colour of chocolate and excrement!!'[32] But the only truly revolutionary change was his restaging of the Norns scene, which was now dominated by the silhouette of a huge fir tree against the night sky.[33] For Hans Pfitzner and the traditionalists these developments completed the artistic downfall of Bayreuth.[34]

The first new production for which Siegfried was entirely responsible (he was credited with 'Spielleitung und Inszenierung', or cast direction and staging) was *Lohengrin* in 1908, for which he designed new and more solidly practicable sets for Acts I and II. Siegfried called it 'a production for gourmets'.[35] His many simplifications concentrated attention on the interplay of principals and chorus. In Act I the use of the 20-metre-high cyclorama, curving round between two huge cut-out trees set beside the proscenium columns – and thus wrapping around the action – enabled Siegfried to dispense with the old succession of leafy top-borders hanging one behind the other. The critic Paul Schlesinger praised the 'beguiling simplicity' with which the cyclorama was painted, taking it 'as a sign that Wahnfried is also oriented towards efforts at stage reform'.[36] The uninterrupted view to the banks of the River Schelde, 'flowing' in wide turns, made possible a more credible illusion of Lohengrin's swan-borne arrival than had been previously achieved.

Cosima had already taken care to present the leading roles in *Lohengrin* as rounded characters rather than caricatures (for example, she had Ortrud portrayed as a noble survivor of heathen Europe rather than a mere evil, jealous sorceress). She had arranged that the chorus, sometimes singing with its back to the audience, and with Brabantines and Saxons clearly differentiated, should always be actively involved in the drama. By some observers the chorus had been praised as the 'best soloist' and favourable comparison made with Reinhardt's style of direction.[37] Siegfried's handling of the action was along similar lines and its effectiveness considerably enhanced by the less cluttered stage space.

He applied the same principles to a new *Meistersinger* in 1911, again using the cyclorama to great effect for the Festwiese, building a traversable bridge over the Pegnitz for the entry of the guilds and generally toning down the picturesque and sentimental in favour of a more earthy realism. In the Act I finale a crowd of people thronged the door and windows of the church, wanting to catch a glimpse of the Masters and apprentices at their secret business. In the Prügelszene (Act II finale) the women threw real water from the windows and cudgelled their menfolk in the chaos below. The Viennese critic Hermann Bahr (who had married the soprano Anna von Mildenburg in 1909) placed Siegfried's direction on the highest level, ranking his handling of the chorus in *Meistersinger*, *Lohengrin* and *Götterdämmerung* alongside Reinhardt's treatment of the bandit Roller's entry in Schiller's *Die Räuber* (Deutsches Theater, Berlin, 1908), the supplicants in *Oedipus* (Musikfesthalle, Munich, 1910) and the throng of women in *Lysistrata* (Kammerspiele, Berlin, 1908).[38]

The costumes, by Siegfried's half-sister Daniela Thode, were modelled on Renaissance portraits by Dürer, Holbein and others. As Daniela later explained, however, the costumes were not literalistic copies, as they would have been in a Meiningen production, but were adapted to serve the symbolic ends of Wagner's 'aesthetically elevated ideal world'. Thus each Master was distinguished by the colour of his particular trade. Eva's dress for the Festwiese was no longer that of a wealthy goldsmith's daughter in her Sunday best but of the 'Muse des Parnaß' of whom Walther sings.[39] This bold excursion into symbolism – presenting Eva as the idealized image of Walther's love – was way ahead of its time, even anticipating the 'play within a play' strategy of Wieland Wagner's 1963 production.

But it took the nine-year closure of the theatre imposed by the war to point Siegfried towards a production style that made more than token acknowledgement of the radical stage reform that had been in motion elsewhere since the 1890s. The scenic clear-out (Entrümpelung) and simplifications of his 1927 *Tristan*, designed by Kurt Söhnlein (1894–1985), played down realism in favour of concentration on the psychological, inner action. In Act I huge curtains enclosed a front-stage area for Isolde that could not by any stretch of the imagination be taken for a tent-like women's pavilion on the deck of a sailing ship. When the curtains parted they revealed an undecorated, almost Bauhaus-like idea of the stern of a ship. No sails or pieces of nautical tackle were to be seen save for a few token ropes. The Act II setting was condensed into the stylized silhouettes of trees at right, with steps at the rear and at the left leading up to the entrance to a circular tower. The ramparts at stage-rear were almost Appia-like in their basic, block construction. Also seemingly Appian was the way in which the lighting had more to do with the characters' states of mind than with anything pictorial. The traditional sombre hues and soft illumination were replaced by what the critic Ferdinand Pfohl called a 'symphony of colours'.[40] Act I, epitomizing the world of Day, shocked the audience with bright lighting modulating from gold-orange to an intense red. In Act II the colouring for Night moved from dark blue to pale gold, Day breaking in on the lovers with a great display of flags and torchbearers. At the end of Act III Isolde expired under the deepest of deep blue skies. Musically this production was accounted a great success (in 1930 it was conducted by Toscanini), but the lighting was condemned by traditionalists like Bernhard Diebold, who argued that only dark colours could ever be appropriate for this music.[41] They would have echoed Cosima's admonition that 'Herr Appia must not demand dark when the poem calls for light, and vice versa.'[42] Where the production fell short was that the relatively timeless settings and anti-realistic lighting failed to square with the wealth of Celtic ornamentation in the props and on the costumes, for which Daniela had stuck closely to the 1865 Munich production. Siegfried was aware of this conflict, which here, as elsewhere, he sought to resolve by the mood and atmosphere of his lighting. It was a conflict symptomatic of the tension within himself between conservative and progressive impulses.

Siegfried was certainly not a director of originality, cramped by circumstance. Fundamentally he was a conservative. But his very real interest in the new technologies awakened suppressed critical instincts in others to which he had to respond with caution, as he was weaker than the hardline traditionalists by whom he was surrounded. The ailing Cosima was an ever present conscience. Siegfried was the youngest sibling, subject to his powerful older sisters. Isolde had died in 1919, but Daniela (nine years older), Blandine (six years older) and, most conservative of all, Eva (two years older), who had married the notorious Houston Stewart Chamberlain in 1908, were still very much in evidence. Hans Mayer nicely suggests that Siegfried's true feelings towards the 'Old Bayreuth Norns' surface in his music: 'The composer who wrote a ballad for baritone and orchestra [*Märchen vom dicken, fetten Pfannkuchen*, 1913] about a "fat, greasy pancake" which becomes horrified at the sight of old women, jumps out of the frying pan and runs away must have known what he was implying here, even if he took care not to "reveal" himself.'[43]

In what were to be the last few years of his life Siegfried planned a *Tannhäuser* which he hoped would steer Bayreuth into new waters. But in the event this production, conducted by Toscanini and premiered on 22 July 1930, only a few days before Siegfried's death, was 'modern' only in its lighting and choreography. There was little novelty in Siegfried's assertion that the 1861 version had been made not just opportunistically for Paris but because Wagner, having written *Tristan*, had discovered the palette of Titian and Rubens and was thus able to fulfil musical intentions that had always been inherent in the work's conception. Like the music, the production had therefore to juxtapose 'the voluptuousness of Rubens and the austerity of Holbein'.[44]

But the visual concept was scarcely translated into practice. Söhnlein's settings were indeed painterly but had precious little to do with Rubens or Holbein. The labyrinthine caverns of the Venusberg were a recreation of the grottoes at Saalfeld and the Wartburg valley scenes a landscape inspired by the painter Hans Thoma. There was a practicable bridge in the foreground with the Wartburg in the distance, while the Hall of Song was a symmetrical Romanesque space with subdued rich-gold decoration and a view of the Thuringian mountains through the great entrance arch at the rear. How Ludwig would have loved it! The production's only distinctive features were its active lighting – usually reinforcing naturalistic atmosphere but sometimes playing against it – and Rudolf von Laban's choreography of the bacchanale.[45] In Laban's own description, 'There were no Bacchantes or fauns, no images of Leda and Jupiter or any other figure of the Graeco-Roman world of gods. It was a witchessabbath with nordic sacrificial rites and with Strömkarl, the demon of music, as the inciter dominating the whole scene. . . . the passions were not stirred up by beautiful goddesses, but were represented as innate drives.'[46] At the point at which Tannhäuser's Act II song scandalously turns to thoughts of Venus, the Hall was suddenly plunged into near-total darkness with only Tannhäuser left illuminated in the rosy red, blue and violet lighting of the Venusberg. Laban had already

Technical innovations aside, Siegfried Wagner's most adventurous contribution to stage production was commissioning the choreography of his 1930 *Tannhäuser* from Rudolf von Laban, pioneer of avant-garde 'expressive' dance. Laban, working with Kurt Jooss, banished classical allegory, creating 'a witches-sabbath with nordic sacrifical rites . . . the passions were not stirred up by beautiful goddesses, but were represented as innate drives'. The caverns of the Venusberg were modelled on the grottoes at Saalfeld.

choreographed a *Tannhäuser* bacchanale in Mannheim in 1921. Like Reinhardt and Siegfried Wagner he used his forces as a fluid mass of individuals, exploiting all available space. Inevitably his choreography was criticized as gymnastics rather than dance. Laban himself believed that Wagner's music and descriptive scenario were timeless and better realized in contemporary dance style than with nineteenth-century classical ballet (a point that Isadora Duncan had doubtless attempted to prove when, to scandalous effect, she choreographed and danced in the 1904 *Tannhäuser*). 'In this,' wrote Laban, 'Richard Wagner was ahead of his time and had anticipated a new style of movement for the stage.'[47]

From the early years of the century until his death in 1930, Siegfried's attitude was steadfastly consistent. 'I do not choose to go in one direction or another,' he said in 1907. 'My task is one of continuous development of Richard Wagner's legacy. You can't produce *Götterdämmerung* as though it were a play by Ibsen.' By 1925 he is defending his position against the modernist lobby: 'We stay true to our basic principles. We have put to use the good things among all the new achievements. But Bayreuth certainly does not exist to be hypermodern, as that would contradict the style of works whose poetry and music are not written in the cubist-expressionist-dadaist style.' Equally constant is Siegfried's defence of Bayreuth as being in the vanguard of technological innovation: 'Here in Bayreuth,' he said in 1907, 'we attach great importance to lighting, to subtle transformations of scene and to the avoidance of crude effects. I foresee a big future for Mariano Fortuny's new discoveries in lighting [demonstrated in Paris and further afield from 1902; see chapter 6]. Plainly we're in an era of rapid developments in stage technique and design and in Bayreuth we'll pay close attention to all innovations.' This did indeed happen. His claim in 1930 that he had 'been happy to adopt anything which can help to perfect the scenic instructions of my father' was nothing less than the truth. What he was not prepared to do was to consider the validity of those instructions or of his own exclusive right to their 'correct' interpretation. His attitude to those with radical ideas about the 'aesthetics of stage performance' was dismissive. As he wrote in 1907, 'Gordon Craig's ideas strike me as extraordinary, but they're not universally applicable.' And in 1924, 'We intend to have nothing to do with modern excesses, which are in contradiction to the character of the Master's works.'[48]

But while some of this made good sense, what was entirely missing was more than the barest recognition that the 'afterlife' of a work presented any kind of interpretative problem. Siegfried's assiduous cultivation of 'the Bayreuth style' exposed the problematic nature of the 'afterlife' of dramatic works of genius. 'The problems which the works of my father pose for the production team', he wrote a few months before his death, 'are now the principal difficulties in the continuing performance of the works and even more so than at the time of their creation, when they were new and not wholly understood.'[49] What he could not bring himself to recognize was that since the turn of the century the 'principal difficulties' had no longer been of a practical, technical nature but had to do with ideas suggestive that the art of performance might be different from, and complementary to, the art of the dramatist. This had long since been known outside Bayreuth and its implications put to the test – nowhere more potently than in the productions of Gustav Mahler and Alfred Roller at the Vienna Opera.

Casting off the carapace: Mahler and Roller

Although Bayreuth's idea of authenticity was occasionally questioned in the two decades following the composer's death, it was not until 1903 that a new philosophy of Wagner performance was given a practical trial in a major theatre. Its instigator was no stern critic of Bayreuth but a composer generally reckoned to have been the supreme Wagner conductor of his generation. That man was Gustav Mahler. His production at the Vienna Court Opera of *Tristan und Isolde* with designs by Alfred Roller marks the moment of liberation from the stranglehold of nineteenth-century orthodoxy. It opened up a new era in which it was seen that new solutions to old performance problems could reveal previously unsuspected layers of meaning. Thus was born the idea that there could be such a thing in an opera house as the valid, creative interpretation of a masterwork. What lent particular authority to this development was that it was driven not by a professional stage director but by a man who, like Wagner, was a great composer and conductor. The radical departure came not from scenic considerations but from concern that the production should spring from the score. There was, in truth, nothing in this notion that could not have been sanctioned by Wagner's own ideas and hopes for his works. The seeds had been planted by the composer but their germination had to be tended by his inheritors.

Gustav Mahler had first visited Bayreuth as a 23-year-old student in 1883. In the years that followed he often returned, becoming well known to Cosima and Siegfried, who were fully aware of his formidable reputation as a Wagner conductor, in Budapest as director of the Royal Hungarian Opera, 1888–91, and as music director at Hamburg, 1891–7. In Budapest he gave the first performances in Hungarian of *Das Rheingold* and *Die Walküre*, while in his first season at Hamburg there were more Wagner performances (64) than in any other house (Berlin 50, Dresden 49, Leipzig 38, etc.).[50] But anti-semitic prejudice deterred the Wagners from ever inviting him to conduct in the Festspielhaus. Cosima, supporting Felix Mottl's candidature, also opposed the confirmation of his appointment as director of the Vienna Opera in October 1897. Not that this prevented her from soliciting the composer to perform her son's operas there. Siegfried's first opera, *Der Bärenhäuter*, was duly given in Vienna in 1899 by Mahler, who, while insisting on cuts to improve the work, appears to have generally thought well of it. But despite Cosima's tireless advocacy Mahler did not perform any of Siegfried's other operas.

Bayreuth's rejection of Mahler was, in the end, no loss but its own, nor could Mahler's own fierce integrity and independence ever have been at home in such an authoritarian atmosphere. New thought about the performance of Wagner's works had perforce to come to be realized elsewhere. Yet the irony is that Mahler was a stage reformer in Wagner's own mould. He subscribed to every tenet of his theatrical reforms and his ideas about the theatre and the performance of opera – the coordination of words, music and every element in the scenic presentation. But where Wagner had concentrated on the production of his works, leaving their conducting to associates, Mahler's first avocation was to conduct them. His supervision of all aspects of the singers' performances became necessary for him when, like Wagner, he saw that the dramatist's intentions would otherwise be betrayed.

At the Budapest Opera Mahler's domination of every part of a production was remarked by Count Albert Apponyi: 'he governs with sovereign authority the stage, the action, the movements of the soloists and the chorus; so that a performance rehearsed and produced by him is in every way artistically complete. His eye extends over the entire production, the scenery, the machinery, the lights.'[51]

Cosima Wagner herself had nothing but praise for Mahler's exceptional ability as a repetiteur. While he was still at Hamburg she asked him to coach the tenor Willy Birrenkoven (a member of the Hamburg company) in the role of Parsifal, for which Bayreuth had engaged him in 1894. 'Birrenkoven', wrote Mahler to his distinguished physicist friend Arnold Berliner, 'is causing a stir in Bayreuth: Cosima and the others having no need to rehearse him *further*. By the way, he is singing in the opening performance, *not* Van Dy[c]k!' Cosima was no less pleased with Mahler's coaching of Anna von Mildenburg for the role of Kundry at Bayreuth in 1897.[52] While Mahler's direction of their expression and movement was valued by most of his leading

singers, his concern for every detail of stage business was not always welcome backstage. During Mahler's time at Hamburg his efforts were resisted all along the line by
the chief stage director, Franz Bittong.[53]

Mahler always sought to emulate Wagner's programme for the reform of theatre
management and practice – major decisions made by artists rather than state
functionaries, adequate rehearsal time, and so on. This was uphill work, especially at
a prominent house like the Vienna Court Opera with its political pressures and
repertory system (in Mahler's first season he conducted 111 performances of
twenty-three operas).[54] Mahler quickly moved to bar latecomers from taking their
seats once the music had started and darkened the auditorium. In the pit he changed
the seating so that the conductor was no longer in the middle of the band but at the
very front, with the audience behind him and all the players in front of him. He had
for some time wanted to lower the orchestra pit for Wagner performances, intending that its level should henceforth be adjustable. Emboldened by the success of
Tristan in 1903 he proceeded, against considerable opposition, to carry out his plan.
His intention had been to lower the pit by 1.5 metres, but when that was thwarted by
technical difficulties, he settled for 50 centimetres and at the same time enlarged its
area from 47 to 59 square metres.[55] His defence of his actions in an interview
published on 6 September 1903 shows how well he understood the rationale behind
the sunken pit at Bayreuth:

> The plans were designed so that the floor of the pit could be lowered or raised
> hydraulically, according to the needs of the work performed. Thus I would put the
> orchestra at the lowest possible level for certain of Wagner's works, but would
> keep the small Mozart orchestra at a normal height, and so on, as suits the work
> in question and is suggested by constant observation. There are strong arguments
> for the practice of placing the Wagner orchestra as low as possible: in some of his
> works, the orchestra is meant to sound as from a nebulous distance; in this way,
> too, the singers' voices can stand out effectively. To be sure, some passages of
> Wagner I can imagine better with a completely open orchestra – for instance, the
> Prelude to the third act of *Lohengrin*. But all in all, the public should gladly wel-
> come the lowering of the pit for the Wagner orchestra. For I think it cannot be very
> pleasant during an orchestral storm for the people in the stalls to hear the cym-
> bals above anything else, until they feel like stopping up their ears. All this will be
> changed once the music comes up from a great depth.[56]

In a second interview, three days later, he declared his belief that the orchestra was
'no longer a unit which functions independently and need pay no attention to what
is going on in the rest of the theatre. The orchestra must serve the theatre in the same
way as the other factors, such as the lighting, the full effect of which on the stage we
still do not know.'[57] Mahler went on to argue that the light-spill from the musicians'
stands in the pit was an undesirable distraction and spoilt the artistic effect of the
stage lighting. He did not win his battle in a single round, but the eventual installation of hydraulic machinery in 1904–5 (Mahler had wanted this all along) made it

possible to adjust the pit level easily and quickly, effectively silencing the residual opposition.[58] Mahler's views and practice show how Wagner's idea of a hidden pit evolved into the twentieth-century notion that opera houses should be so constructed that the relationship of stage, orchestra pit and audience should be adaptable to suit the optimum requirements for the particular work being performed.

It had continued to be the usual practice in Vienna, as elsewhere, to make substantial cuts in the operas and to give *Das Rheingold* with an interval. In September 1898 Mahler gave Vienna its first chance to hear *Götterdämmerung* as its composer had intended. Restoration of such habitual omissions as the scenes with the Norns and with Waltraute added nearly an hour to the running time. In similar fashion, Mahler's *Meistersinger* (1899) played at five hours (a gain of sixty minutes) and *Tannhäuser* (1901) at four hours (a gain of thirty minutes).[59]

Mahler's attitude to 'authentic performance' was, however, sharply critical. He did not hesitate to step in if he felt a composer had not got something quite right – as in his adjustments to Beethoven's and Schumann's orchestration. He omitted Rocco's 'Gold' aria in *Fidelio*, on the grounds that Beethoven had included it only to please his public. He exercised his composer's prerogative of 'improving' something he felt to have been less than perfectly achieved. He outraged Richter by adjusting the orchestration in the third act of *Tannhäuser*,[60] as he did Siegfried Wagner by making cuts in *Bärenhäuter*. Composers submitting scores to the Opera were given advice on improvements, their acceptance of which was a condition of Mahler's performing the work.

It remained for Mahler to address the scenic aspect of performance, and here he was on less certain ground. From his Budapest days he had always sought to eliminate everything that he considered a distraction from the unified drama of music, words and stage picture. While this was essentially a matter of his own instinct and preference, Mahler was a man of broad culture who kept closely in touch with the latest developments in literature and theatre generally. He would have followed the anti-naturalistic reforms of the avant-garde theatre in Paris, Munich and Berlin. He would have known that in Paris from 1890 to 1892 Paul Fort's Théâtre d'Art had used painters like Odilon Redon, Paul Gauguin, Toulouse-Lautrec and Edvard Munch in a quest to combine words, music and colours and thus redefine theatre as 'a pretext for the dream' – a palpably Wagnerian ambition![61] In 1893, Aurélien Lugné-Poë, encouraged by his successful premiere production of Maeterlinck's *Pelléas et Mélisande*, founded the Théâtre de l'Oeuvre. Here, too, the aim was to confound the theatre of realism, of naturalistic illusion, by using only the simplest shapes, colours and costumes. The whole emphasis was on mood and atmosphere. Once again it was well-known painters, this time Edouard Vuillard, Maurice Denis, Toulouse-Lautrec, Paul Sérusier and Pierre Bonnard from the 'Nabis' group, who created sets for important performances of plays by Claudel, Ibsen, Wilde and, in 1896, for the premiere of Alfred Jarry's scandalous *Ubu Roi*.

So by the turn of the century artists had moved into the theatre and became major innovators there. They discovered in the theatre a medium which in the nineteenth century had been the province, with very few notable exceptions such as Schinkel and

Carl Blechen in Germany, of professional scene painters. The artists' originality of vision made the stage a work of art and transformed its whole aesthetic in the process. This phenomenon extended well outside central Europe, a particularly striking example being Diaghilev's employment of Golovin, Benois, Bakst and others of the Mir iskusstva (World of Art) group for the Ballets Russes (see chapter 7).

Meanwhile in Munich Georg Fuchs and Peter Behrens, one of the foremost Jugendstil artists in Germany, were campaigning for a new theatre to embody their reforming ideas. 'Stage design', wrote Behrens in 1900, 'should be so stylized, so completely reduced to a few ornamental elements, that the whole atmosphere of the act is created simply by line and colour. The décor must not imitate nature, but should simply provide a framework for the action, a background that is both beautiful and characteristic.'[62] Fuchs published three influential books, the first of which, *Von der stilistischen Belebung der Schaubühne* (On the Stylistic Revitalization of the Stage), appeared in 1891. His lectures (from 1899) were eagerly attended and his ideas, propagated also in *Die Schaubühne der Zukunft* (The Stage of the Future, 1904) and *Die Revolution des Theaters* (Revolution in the Theatre, 1909), discussed all over Europe.[63] They were to come to fruition in 1908 in the Munich Künstlertheater, whose design by Max Littmann owed a sizeable debt to the Bayreuth Festspielhaus. Both Behrens and Fuchs were energetic publicists whose ideas were unlikely to have been overlooked by a man with Mahler's passion for the theatre.

It was Mahler's good fortune to have arrived in Vienna in the middle of an artistic ferment that was antagonistic to the conservative values of the bourgeoisie. And of course he himself was to play a major part in an artistic and intellectual movement which forged much of the spirit and temper of the twentieth century. Numbered among Mahler's new friends was Max Burckhard, who as director of the Burgtheater since 1890 had, against considerable opposition, opened up Vienna's national theatre to modern playwrights like Hauptmann and Ibsen. Burckhard, a Nietzsche-inspired visionary, revitalized the performance of the classics. His espousal of modernism exercised a palpable influence on Mahler (as also on Max Reinhardt, then a young actor with Otto Brahm's Deutsches Theater in Berlin and on the brink of his great career as a director).

Of far greater importance, however, was Mahler's close relationship with the group of artists who on 3 April 1897, the day before his provisional appointment as conductor at the Court Opera, broke away from the stranglehold of the official Academy and established themselves as the Vereinigung bildender Künstler Österreichs (Association of Austrian Artists), commonly known as the Vienna Secession.[64] The relationship was not to blossom until some years later, however, on Mahler's meeting with Alma Schindler in 1901. Until then, Mahler, according to Alma, had no 'native feeling for painting' and, so far as we can tell, little knowledge of or enthusiasm for its living practitioners.[65]

Alma was the daughter of Emil Jakob Schindler, a highly regarded landscape painter. Her own youthful accomplishments included painting, sculpture and musical composition. After Schindler's death her mother married another painter, Carl Moll, who was the second president of the Secession (1899–1901). It was at his house on 7 November 1901 that Mahler first met the 22-year-old Alma and within months they were married (9 March 1902). The director of the Imperial Opera was plunged into the very centre of the new movement in art. Its leading practitioners, most particularly Moll, Gustav Klimt, Alfred Roller and Kolo Moser, 'vied with one another to be his teacher'.[66] For his part Mahler had much to offer the Secessionists, not least in that their programme sought to dissolve boundaries between the arts. A central part of the Secessionist aesthetic was that its exhibitions were not just pictures hung on walls but 'total works of art' (Gesamtkunstwerke) in which the boldly geometric 'Kunsttempel' (designed by Josef Olbrich after a sketch by Klimt and completed in 1898), the exhibits displayed within it, music and on occasion other events all had their part to play. The 14th Secession Exhibition (April–June 1902) was focused on Max Klinger's monumental new *Beethoven* sculpture, which was set in a shrine-like enclosure by Alfred Roller with an allegorical frieze about the composer by Klimt as a supporting commentary. Mahler was invited to collaborate and at the opening of the exhibition conducted his own arrangement for six trombones of a passage from the choral movement of the Ninth Symphony.

What the Secession had to offer Mahler was exactly what he had been searching for – a wholly new approach to the scenic dimension of opera production. While wishing to dispense with the pictorial literalism of the late nineteenth century, Mahler had so far lacked a collaborator who could help him effect on the deeply conservative operatic stage a comparable revolution to that already under way in the conventional theatre. He had achieved something in this direction from 1900, when he had appointed Heinrich Lefler (a painter trained at the Academy) as head of scenic design at the Opera. Lefler quickly made a name for himself by attempting to eliminate painted flats and non-functional props, earning himself the appellation 'Raumschöpfer', or space creator. But it was not until Mahler met Roller (probably early in 1902) that he encountered a vision of how to use that space which he could fully share.[67]

By extraordinary coincidence, Roller, who had for some time interested himself in scenic design, had only recently discovered *Tristan* in traditional-style performances under Mahler's baton at the Opera. He had hated the settings and been fired to make sketches of his own which he quickly showed to Mahler. So impressed was the conductor that, recognizing the 'true visual expression' of the Wagnerian drama, and despite Roller's total lack of stage experience, he swiftly commissioned him to design new sets for *Tristan*.[68] For Roller this proved to be as decisive a turning point as it was for Mahler and, indeed, for the future course of opera production generally.[69]

The artists of the Secession had highly distinctive talents and Roller was no exception. They were united in turning their backs on the old academies in the cause of internationalism, of eliminating barriers between pure and applied art and of proclaiming the freedom of the artist to realize his own vision independently of that of 'society' and the wealthy patron. Thus the Secession invited artists from all over Europe to contribute to its exhibitions. These artists included, from France, Puvis de Chavannes, Degas, Pissarro, Renoir, Rodin, Seurat, Signac and Vallotton; from Germany, Max Klinger, Hans Thoma and members of the Munich Secession; from

Switzerland, Ferdinand Hodler; from Norway, Edvard Munch; from Belgium, Henri van de Velde; and from Italy, Giovanni Segantini. Also shown were Japanese and Russian artists and the Scottish artists Charles Rennie Mackintosh, Margaret Macdonald and Herbert and Frances MacNair (the Glasgow Four), to whom a whole 'Scottish Room' was devoted at the 8th Exhibition in November–December 1900. The uncluttered, elegant spatial layout of this room influenced Roller's designs for the next exhibition and doubtless his approach to stage design.[70]

Born in Moravia in 1864, Roller studied painting at the Vienna Academy with Eduard Lichtenfels and Christian Griepenkerl, drawing much inspiration from visits to Venice and Ravenna. A founder-member of the Secession, he became a co-editor of its journal *Ver Sacrum* in 1898, taught at the Kunstgewerbschule (School for Applied Arts) from 1900 and replaced Carl Moll as president of the Secession in 1902. Roller's graphic skills were much in evidence in the pages of *Ver Sacrum* and in posters for the Secession. With hindsight one can see his huge mural painting *Sinkende Nacht* (Nightfall) for the Klinger exhibition in April–May 1902 as very possibly inspired by the 'O sink hernieder, Nacht der Liebe' love duet in the second act of *Tristan* and thus an anticipation of the stage designs he was shortly to prepare for Mahler. This mural was on the wall behind and above the huge enthroned *Beethoven*. On the opposite wall was a complementary depiction of *Der werdende Tag* (Daybreak) by Adolf Böhm.[71]

Roller found his liberation from the dictates of academy painting in the sinuous fantasy of line, colour and tone (the style being more important than the 'faithful' depiction of a subject) and in an interest in spatial arrangement which quickly showed itself in the exhibition settings he designed for the Secession (that for the 9th Exhibition in 1901 being particularly striking in its dramatic use of space and light to display paintings by Segantini, sculptures by Rodin and other works). It was to be but a short step from here to his discovery of a new medium in the three-dimensional arena of the stage. The persistence of nineteenth-century pictorial realism on the operatic stage was indeed an urgent case for the liberation aesthetics of a Secessionist. We have seen how avant-garde theatre had been using artists as agents of scenic reform for more than a decade. Roller was the first artist of independent standing to succeed in doing the same for the operatic stage. Just as Paul von Joukowsky had, with *Parsifal*, pointed Wagner in a new scenic direction, so Roller, working with a conductor who was also a composer of genius, provided a springboard for escape from the tired visual aesthetic that was still prevalent.

Roller and Mahler's common point of departure was the elimination of anything visual that did not relate to their understanding of the music as the core of the drama. Mahler, Roller later recalled, 'had the utmost contempt for mere outward show on the stage, for any purely decorative detail, however brilliant and dazzling, that did not arise inevitably from the total conception'. Himself a master of 'decorative detail', Roller discovered an almost moral vocation in subjugating his decorative prowess to serve their joint ambition of a wholly unified stage production. This did not mean the rejection of pictorial imagery but rather its re-creation in spatial terms. The stage, said Roller, dealt not with 'pictures' but with 'space'. In his pursuit of this he would have found inspiration and support in the work of the architects most closely associated with the Secession, especially Otto Wagner and his pupil Josef Olbrich. Kurt Blaukopf even ventures the view that Roller translated Otto Wagner's 'architecture into scenic principles'.[72]

The romantic realism of the Vienna Opera's scenic style created by Carlo Brioschi up to 1886 and thereafter by his son Anton was to be superseded by simpler images. All the scenic essentials specified by Wagner would still be there, but in stylized form. Roller later recalled that Mahler had welcomed 'a stage on which everything is only intimated'.[73] The aim would no longer be the creation of a peep-show illusion but of a functional stage space inhabited by the performers.

Many of these ideas had long been advocated by Appia (including the notion that the nineteenth-century 'stage of illusion', or 'Illusionsbühne', had to be replaced by a new 'Andeutungsbühne', meaning a stage on which things should be suggested rather than shown) and were published by him in German in 1899 as *Die Musik und die Inscenierung*. This would almost certainly have been known to Mahler and to Roller. Three substantial extracts from the book were published in the *Wiener Rundschau* (15 December 1900) under the title 'Das Licht und die Inscenierung, von Adolphe Appia, Rom'. Henry-Louis de La Grange argues that Roller's own articles testify that he was acquainted with Appia's writings. He also cites an unpublished letter of Mahler's (10 July 1899) which he believes may have been written to Appia and whose contents suggest that 'Mahler also knew his writings and put some of his ideas into use in his own theatrical work'.[74]

Both Roller and Mahler were set on using the latest technology in order to paint the stage with light rather than pigment. The Opera's lighting installation, dating from 1887, was therefore improved during the *Tristan* rehearsals.[75] Light became a principal agent in the search for a visual stylization and for symbols which, in activating the audience's imagination, would deepen the musicality of its response. The dominant colour of a scene or of an entire act could determine its character, mood and atmosphere and its significance within the dramatic structure of the whole. The key to everything was Wagner's music, not his visual taste. Mahler's first principle was constant: 'It's all in the score' ('Steht alles in der Partitur').[76] But however much he was indebted to the libertarian thrust of the Secessionists, Mahler was wary of the least whiff of theatrical theory or of anything doctrinaire. He did not want to hear his productions described as 'Secessionist' but simply as serving their composers faithfully. Thus in September 1903 he is quoted as saying, 'We want to make the *light* serve the theatre in all its grades, nuances and degrees of strength. … But the matter does not end with the lighting; the whole of modern art has a part to play on the stage. Modern art, I say, not the Secession. What matters is the conjunction of all the arts. There is no future in the old standard clichés; modern art must extend to costumes, props, everything that can revitalise a work of art.'[77] This was very much what Siegfried Wagner professed for Bayreuth in 1907, the difference being that Mahler put it into practice in Vienna in 1903–7, whereas Siegfried's lip-service did not begin to be translated tentatively into action at Bayreuth until the *Tristan* of 1927.

The first fruit of the Mahler–Roller partnership was the *Tristan und Isolde* which opened on 21 February 1903, discussed below. Such was its success that Mahler appointed Roller his 'Leiter des Ausstattungswesens' (head of stage design) in place of Heinrich Lefler (who went to the Burgtheater). Together they went on to give new or redesigned productions of *Fidelio* (1904), *Rheingold* (1905), *Così fan tutte* (1905), *Don Giovanni* (1905), *Die Entführung* (1906), *Lohengrin* (1906), *Figaro* (1906), *Die Zauberflöte* (1906), *Die Walküre* (1907) and *Iphigénie en Aulide* (1907). The partnership was curtailed only by Mahler's resignation, in response to intolerable pressures at the Opera, and his departure for America in December 1907. Roller himself continued to work with Mahler's successor, Felix Weingartner, completing the *Ring* in 1909, but he felt the loss of the wholehearted support he had had from Mahler and resigned that same year. Not all the Mahler–Roller productions were equally successful, but together they amounted to a revolution in the staging of opera – and this in merely four years!

Tristan und Isolde, *Vienna 1903: 'Wie hör' ich das Licht!'*

From the surviving pictures it is not immediately apparent why Mahler's *Tristan* production struck its contemporaries as so extraordinary. Roller's settings provided every pictorial image specified by Wagner, creating credible locations on board ship, in the garden of a palace at night and at Tristan's castle in Kareol. What surprised audiences was that these settings made no attempt to be a simulacrum of the composer's 1865 production, or even of Cosima's later Bayreuth staging of 1886. It was the first time that a stage of international renown, rather than copying the authorized version, had gone back to Wagner's score and created its own new images from it. Just as Mahler had made his own interpretation of the score, so Roller made his of the stage directions.

He slewed the deck of the ship round at a slight angle. This became fully apparent only when the great sails curtaining off Isolde's quarters were pulled aside to reveal that these quarters were a kind of rear stowage underneath the upper stern deck on which Tristan was stationed at the helm. The stern itself and starboard side of the vessel were screened from view by a huge hanging sail and by the left side of the proscenium. The sea and horizon were visible only above the gunwhale on the right. And it was at this side that steps led up to the higher deck. This brilliantly simple device was as symbolically apt – the upper, light deck for Tristan, the lower, claustrophobic, dark quarters for Isolde – as it was dramatically effective. Tristan and Kurwenal could without any artifice be visible to the audience while totally out of sight of Isolde and Brangäne. Similarly, the scandal of the lovers' embrace was intensified by its being observed by the sailors, themselves unseen at the rail of the upper deck.

At the end of the act, sails and awnings were hoisted up and away to herald Marke's arrival, the king's red banner flapping against a bright blue sky while a brilliant carpet for his welcome snaked out as an intrusive gash across the forestage at the feet of Tristan and Isolde. In the second and third acts the significant innovations were the 'built' solidity of the masonry (stone terraces, tower and steps for the castle at Kareol) and a drastic pruning of the customary foliage. The overall effect was, at least from a modern viewpoint, to make the settings *more* rather than less realistically credible! There was the merest hint of Secession style in the black-and-white chequered paving of the terrace in Act II.

But what everyone was talking about was not the scenery but the way it was lit. It was Roller's new-found skill in painting with light that was the major breakthrough. For him this was a natural development of an interest in the effects of changing light that had already been demonstrated in a series of paintings of a single landscape view in different seasons and at different times of day that he had shown at the Secession exhibition in 1900.[78] There could scarcely have been a better first stage subject for Roller than an opera ruled so pervasively by the symbolism of Day and Night. For at least one member of the audience, 'the way [the stage] looked said literally what the work was about'.[79]

Quite how Roller, totally unschooled in stage technology, learnt how to manipulate the lights we do not yet know, but the results were sensational. 'Untiringly,' said Emil Lucka, 'he carried out his tests, moving from the stage to the stalls, from the stalls to the gallery, experimenting with screens, coloured discs, light-intensities, altering, improving, dealing in nuances.'[80] Roller was among the very first practitioners of 'Lichtregie', the use of the lighting console as a principal agent in the staging of opera. Among his many discoveries was the dynamic use of light in every grade of intensity, including crescendos and decrescendos between dark and light. This was the more effective because light could be thrown not onto the usual pictorial painted backdrop, hangings and flats but onto a plain cyclorama, this being among its earliest recorded uses on the stage of the Vienna Opera. 'The gradual brightening of the stage [at the beginning of acts in the later *Ring* production] … produced the most impressive effect,' wrote Egon Wellesz.[81] The low levels of intensity to which, when dramatically appropriate, Roller was prepared to reduce the lighting (as in Act II of *Tristan*) were much complained about, the general custom being a relatively high and constant level of illumination. Others, like Wellesz, were enthusiastic: 'Everything that was done had reason and meaning, always serving only to heighten the dramatic effect.'[82]

What was particularly striking was Roller's use of colour symbolism – an almost garish orange-yellow tonality for the hateful realm of Day in Act I (thus prefiguring the same idea in Siegfried Wagner's production of 1927), a deep violet velvety darkness for Act II and for the long reckoning of Act III a dull autumnal grey. In the second act the sky was alive with a thousand stars. 'Out of the Prelude … the blue night rose mysterious and this night was not the hitherto invariable, obvious, static picture, but breathed and trembled like the orchestra, the garden came alive around the lovers, getting darker or lighter with straying moonbeams and drifting shadows.'[83] Towards the end of the act, when Marke breaks in on the lovers, 'it was not the usual idiotic stage dawn that filled the sky but an excruciating greyness that made you shiver at the very sight of it'.[84]

For Julius Korngold (father of Erich Korngold and Hanslick's successor as critic for the *Neue Freie Presse*) Roller's designs for the third act were 'painted Tristan music', the colours suggesting 'weariness, illness, ruin, and imminent death'. At the end of the act, Tristan and Isolde's 'final metamorphosis and apotheosis were suggested by light effects which transformed even the neutral colours of the costumes'.[85]

Those costumes were also Roller's work. (Roller was, at Mahler's express instruction, the first head of stage design to be entrusted with scenery, costumes and lighting, responsibilities formerly divided between three people.) While his costumes were for the most part of sober practicality, a Klimt-like passion for kaleidoscopic geometric patterning broke out in the decoration of Isolde's dress in Act I, injecting a note of fashionable modernity. The Secession's love affair with abstract patterning and ornamentation was also on display in the design of Isolde's travelling chests, couch and other furniture. Mahler's direction of the action was dictated solely by the music and the psychology of the situation – that is, by the intuition that, as Thomas Mann put it, Wagner was a pioneer practitioner of depth-psychology through music.[86] Tristan did not offer his sword to Isolde for her to kill him but held its point at his chest ready for her to plunge it in.

The interrelationship between the music and the mise-en-scène – which had of course always been Mahler and Roller's goal – won high praise, as from Egon Wellesz:

> I am thinking of the warm rusty brown colour of the sail, like those used even nowadays by the fishermen of Chioggia, which stretched over the entire stage; the sombrely glowing colour of the sail seemed to reflect so perfectly the mood of the music. It is hard to begin to describe how enraptured we were. Then, in the second act, came the blue, starlit night, changing at the end into a deathly pale morning and in the third act the huge linden tree under which the wounded Tristan lay. A barren, desolate landscape just as in the music. Behind the low rampart one imagined the sea. Never had a scene made such a profound impression on me.[87]

The *Tristan* was a huge and immediate success. Dissenting voices were in the minority. Roller was variously reproached for imperfect sightlines, for failing to integrate the singers into the settings, for creating too much visual beauty and for 'his orgies of darkness'. The critic Robert Hirschfeld complained that the 'subtle pantomime' of Anna von Mildenburg as Isolde went for nothing because of what he considered to be the prevalent gloom.[88] Siegfried Wagner, attending the premiere on 21 February, also moaned about the lighting, later giving Ernst Decsey the predictable Bayreuth line: 'My father mounted the production of Tristan himself in Munich, so I'm afraid that's it and that's how it will have to stay.'[89] The singers were mostly well received and the praise for Mahler's conducting was universal.

The wider significance of the production as a 'total work of art' was recognized by the more perceptive critics. With characteristically broad sweep Hermann Bahr wrote that 'Reinhardt's aim, the same that Richard Wagner and later Appia, the young Fortuny, Olbrich and Kolo Moser cherished, has now been fulfilled for the first time by Mahler and Roller in *Tristan* and *Fidelio*. That aim is to remedy the insufficiencies of a single art, which no longer satisfies our increased dramatic demands, with resources from the other arts'.[90] Max Graf, doubtless tuning in

What most surprised the audience about the production of *Tristan* at the Vienna Opera by conductor–director Gustav Mahler in 1903 was that, quite exceptionally, it made no attempt to copy either Wagner's or Cosima's stagings of the work. Mahler and the artist Alfred Roller re-imagined Act I with the brilliantly practical and symbolic layout of a light upper deck for Tristan and claustrophobic quarters for Isolde immediately beneath it. This photo of the 1944 wartime revival in Vienna shows that it was uncannily faithful to Roller's original design.

Mahler worked as intensively with his singers as Wagner did. Erik Schmedes, the remarkably youthful-looking Tristan in 1903, is at the helm in Act I with the bearded Friedrich Weidemann as Kurwenal. Contemporary paintings of Anna von Mildenburg as Isolde show her in a richly gilded Klimt-like costume. This may have been rejected for the distinctly less flattering dress worn by her in this uncomfortable photograph, also from 1903.

somewhat overhastily to the impact of the 16th Secessionist Exhibition (17 January to 28 February 1903, and thus concurrent with the *Tristan* premiere!), which had been devoted to introducing the French Impressionists to the Viennese public, also drew attention to modern art's contribution to the Gesamtkunstwerk: 'The nervous colour-romanticism of the moderns now prevails in the new *Tristan* sets by Alfred Roller. Light and air are called upon to make music along with the Wagner orchestra.... For the first time Impressionist arts appear on the operatic stage.... The composer extends his hand to the painter. What would the master himself have said of the art of light and colour displayed in this Impressionistic *Tristan*?'[91] Graf's conclusion was that Wagner might have been astonished that his vision had inspired such an imaginative response from the world of art but also shocked that the artist appeared to be wishing to prevail in his own right. While entirely mistaken as to Roller's ambition, Graf's review does point up just how iconoclastic Roller's scenic work was generally considered to be. The idea that a stage designer could make an *original* contribution to the performance of an opera was revolutionary, and was immediately recognized as such.

Having discovered his scenic collaborator, Mahler went on to apply the Wagnerian principle of a totally unified production with the music as the ruling element to everything he performed. There was, however, one highly important variation, in that Mahler sought always to find optimum conditions for each and every opera on its own terms. In Roller's words, 'Each work of art carries within itself the key to its own production.'[92] Thus for Mozart, who, together with Wagner, was the principal focus of Mahler's attention, he was, in Egon Wellesz's recollection, 'the first to rediscover the sound of the Mozart orchestra at a time when the full sonority of the Wagner orchestra was regarded as the ideal. He performed Mozart's operas with a small body of strings, accompanying the recitatives on a harpsichord attached to the conductor's desk.'[93]

Roller described how Mahler agreed to his designs for *Don Giovanni* (21 December 1905) only 'after long reflection had convinced him of their relevance to the work's musical shape'.[94] The novelty was the square towers at either side of the stage, towards the front, which remained throughout the opera and 'between which the various changes of scenery took place'.[95] (The idea of using two permanent towers just behind the proscenium frame was mooted in Georg Fuchs's writings and was also put into practice at the Munich Künstlertheater from 1908.) They framed the action and had adjustable elements, so they could serve as parts of Donna Anna's house, a street scene, Don Giovanni's palace, a cemetery, a banqueting room, and so on. The towers were Roller's solution to the perennial problem in *Don Giovanni* of effecting a large number of scene changes fast enough to avoid undesirable breaks in the music. It was doubtless this above all else which sold the idea to Mahler. Thus the operatic debut of a set with permanent (though also changeable) features. It was the bold, functional stylization which made the greatest impression on contemporaries, the presence on the stage of items which were not part of a complete pictorial depiction but were, as on the Shakespearean stage, whatever the particular scene required them to be. This invention of the idea of a unifying, multi-purpose, non-naturalistic scenic artefact capable of symbolizing the drama as a whole was to have a huge influence on Mahler and Roller's successors in twentieth-century stage production. the perfect milieu for the Ring's untamed landscapes.

First steps to a new Ring, *Vienna 1905–1907*

When they turned from *Tristan* to the *Ring*, Mahler and Roller encountered a rather different set of problems. Their solutions show how difficult it was to hold the centre ground between stage realism and stylization in pursuit of the psychological development of the drama. Ever since his Prague and Budapest days Mahler had dreamt of creating his own *Ring* production – in Vienna he had inherited the Opera's original staging which had remained virtually unchanged since its creation in 1877–9.[96] Sketches in the Theatre Collection of the Austrian National Library show that Roller went on almost immediately after *Tristan* to plan for a new *Ring*. He imagined the second scene of *Rheingold* as a verdant open space, rocky outcrops at right, under a huge greeny skyscape with soft mauve-pink clouds. Further studies from 1904 show a Rhinedaughter with a mermaid's tail and Nibelheim with waves of bluey light and flames flaring in the background. Roller's first sketches for a project were soft-focus, almost romantic, experimenting with colour, light and atmosphere. As his ideas developed the designs became more severe and architectural.

The working sketches and their realization in the finished productions of *Das Rheingold* (23 January 1905) and *Die Walküre* (4 February 1907) show, on the one hand, Roller the painter wanting to re-create nature in the theatre and, on the other, Roller the stage designer seeking simplification and visual drama. Like Wagner, Roller was a man of the mountains. On his holiday climbs in the Dolomites he had discovered the perfect *milieu* for the *Ring*'s untamed landscapes. He put it on stage quite specifically for the second act of *Walküre* (the model almost certainly being the precipitous Val de Mezdi in the heart of the Sella massif).[97] The profile of the Valkyrie rock in the third act may well have been taken from the same locale and bears a resemblance, if reversed from left to right, to a design by Appia (illustrated in chapter 6) which had been published in 1899 in *Die Musik und die Inscenierung*.

For *Rheingold* Roller's vision was of nature before the Fall. He sought to evoke this by dressing the Rhinedaughters as mermaids, their tails covered with greenish scales, and putting garlands in Erda's floor-length tresses. The mountain-top space, also Dolomite inspired, rose in levels punctuated by banks of Alpine flowers and framed between pines and giant boulders. Nibelheim was a pitch-black cavern, filled with suppurating vapours. Roller was on less certain ground in his response to the scenic transformations so powerfully depicted in the music and to the troublesome magical effects. His attempts at such scenes as those of the swimming Rhinedaughters (awkwardly suspended in basketwork cages) and the riding Valkyries (juvenile doubles on papier-mâché horses, the Valkyries themselves entering on foot from the wings, though this was cleverly managed so that they seemed to be materializing from a stormy cloudscape)[98] did not begin to measure up to Bayreuth's solutions. Despite the installation of a huge double revolve (two discs, each 11 metres in diameter, placed side by side) the scene changes to and from Nibelheim could only be managed behind curtains.

One of Roller's aims was to eliminate anything likely to come across as puerile or risible. Hence Alberich's transformations into giant snake and then toad were masked in a gloom of vapour and black velvet drapes, while the previous wooden 'rainbow bridge' was abandoned altogether (as the curtain fell the gods were moving slowly towards the landfall of an optical rainbow projection). Like Wagner's movement director Richard Fricke, Roller believed that it was always better to appeal to the imagination rather than risk offence to the intellect. Roller's strongest suit, however, was once again as an artist painting with light. The lights, wrote Julius Korngold, 'swathe the gods in brilliance and serenity; they leave them wallowing in murky mists. The movement on the stage is frozen, as it were, into a series of pictures which are then, however, inverted with a truly inner movement by the magical changes of lighting. … The final communion between stage and music is established by Mahler's art. It is he who gives light to the orchestra. The element of tone painting, which in *Rheingold* predominates over emotional expression, is completely fused with the paintings on the stage.'[99]

Inevitably there were complaints about the 'orgies of darkness' as also about inappropriate 'symphonies of colour'.[100] But it is clear that although very low levels of illumination played their part in obscuring events better left to the mind's eye, Roller's intentions were always naturalistic and dramatic. In Nibelheim the only palpable illumination was the glow from Mime's forges, in Hunding's hut from the hearth and from a single torch on the left-hand wall. Roller re-sited the door (just as Siegfried was to do at Bayreuth in 1928) so that the moonlight streamed in diagonally, and it was only at that moment that there was sufficient light for the facial similarity of the twins to be apparent. In the second act of *Walküre* the light falling on Wotan, seemingly pinioned to the rocks like Prometheus, became progressively greyer through the course of the great doomsday monologue. At the end of the act the combatants became visible only at their emergence as silhouettes high up at the back of the stage. 'It was indescribable,' said Otto Klemperer. 'Mahler, who was his own producer, ruled over everything. I had never seen the close of the second act presented so lucidly on the stage.'[101] In the third act, the soaring flames struck by Loge from the rocks around the sleeping Brünnhilde died down into a glow around the horizon, revealing a star-spangled sky of deepest blue above.[102]

Much of the criticism of the low levels of lighting was on the grounds that the singers' expressions and gestures went for nothing, and it was supported not unreasonably by the argument that Wagner himself had always insisted on clarity of communication between performers and audience. This was the only point of disagreement between Roller and Anna von Mildenburg (Brünnhilde), who otherwise responded gallantly (if not fearlessly!) to the obstacle course presented by the solidly built sets, especially the rocky ravine of the second act of *Walküre*, where there was scarcely a level place and where footholds were few and far between. Mildenburg describes herself leaping from rock to rock like a true flying Brünnhilde (the costume had the benefit of being equipped with a pair of white wings). But there was

Alfred Roller shared Wagner's love of the mountains. His inspiration for the rocky gorge of the
second act of *Die Walküre* was the Val de Mezdi, a sensationally steep defile running into the
heart of the Sella Gruppe in the Dolomites. His watercolour sketch, made in 1903, was for the
1907 Vienna production, of which no photos are known. The Brünnhilde, Anna von
Mildenburg, described how hard it was to find a foothold on the set and how she had to leap
from rock to rock like a proper flying Valkyrie.

no question that some of Roller's sets gave unprecedented restriction to the singers'
movement, particularly as scenery did not yet generally make athletic demands on
them. There were press complaints about *tableaux vivants* with the singers as figurines. Cometh the veritable rocky gorge, cometh the need for the veritable mountain goat! If most accounts praised Roller's conciliation of realism and stylization,
this was tempered with reservation that the human element had to some extent been
subordinated to the decorative. For all the efforts Mahler must have made, and for
all the power and artistry of the vocal performances, characterization and acting
came across less strongly than the sheerly visual drama.[103] The problem of the actor's
integration into the setting remained imperfectly solved.

The debut of the art of the director

The most far-reaching legacy of Roller and Mahler's work together was their demonstration that fidelity to the protean, evanescent spirit of a dramatist's work is more
artistically fruitful than fidelity to the letter of his intentions. The right to interrogate

a work of genius and come up with answers undreamt of by its creator was established once and for all. It marks the birth, for the opera stage, of the shocking idea that production is not just the literal reading of the composer's blueprint but can be creative in its own right. As already suggested, the special authority of Mahler and Roller as iconoclasts who were themselves creators of genius undoubtedly played a major part in winning acceptance (though this has never been universal) for what was a revolutionary idea in opera production. It is perhaps remarkable that the proving ground should have been the works of Wagner, the only composer whose 'afterlife' came to be so zealously protected by his heirs. The Vienna productions were the first effective challenge to their hegemony.

Of course Mahler and Roller made their decisive first moves without stepping wholly off the carpet – nor could that ever have been possible in a theatre with the political and social constraints of the Vienna Court Opera. And the decorative elements in Roller's aesthetic never sat entirely comfortably with Mahler's more ascetic preference in scenic matters (and vice versa!). Mahler himself believed that the disciplined simplicity of their last collaboration, Gluck's *Iphigénie en Aulide* (18 March 1907), was their greatest achievement, a view shared by Bruno Walter and Lilli Lehmann.[104] Mahler was never an uncritical admirer of the Secessionists; his visual sense was closer to the philosophy of the architect Adolf Loos that 'Lack of ornament is a sign of spiritual strength!'[105] And indeed Loos, a scourge of the Secessionists, was openly scornful of what he considered to be the decorative indulgence of Roller's settings: 'There are too many coffers around. Nicely arranged. The carpet is Rudniker (Prague). I've used them too. For the entrance hall. All those cushions look nice . . .'[106]

Roller's subsequent readiness to deploy his illustrative gifts to satisfy the theatre public's perennial appetite for the pictorial (one thinks of Zeffirelli in our own day) would have been seen by Appia as a betrayal of the moral stance he demanded of the metteur-en-scène. There is certainly no question that Mahler brought out the radical best in Roller, and that after the brief golden years of their partnership the artist became to some extent, so far as his theatre work was concerned, a victim of his own versatility.

Roller stayed on to complete the new *Ring* with Mahler's successor, Felix Weingartner, but the magic had fled. An almost unbelievable trust in literal depiction is evident in Roller's complaint to Mahler (by then conducting at the Met) about Weingartner's bold and prescient idea of staging the Royal Hunt and Storm in Berlioz's *Les Troyens* (1909) 'as a dumb-show or masquerade got up by Dido in the forest for the entertainment of her guest'.[107] The down-to-earth Roller considered this imaginative idea of Weingartner's to be quite absurd. Roller, feeling himself undervalued by Weingartner, resigned his Opera post in May 1909 and took over the directorship of the School for Applied Arts. He went on to do important theatre work with, inter alia, the Burgtheater in Vienna and Max Reinhardt in Berlin, and returning to the Vienna Opera (1918–34) designed important productions of Strauss's operas. In 1920 he was a co-founder with Reinhardt, Strauss and Hofmannsthal of the Salzburg Festival and in 1934 made a belated Bayreuth debut in designing sets and costumes for Heinz Tietjen's production of *Parsifal* (see chapter 9). Roller often reverted to a pictorial, decorative style – as in his famous designs for the premiere of *Der*

Rosenkavalier in Dresden in 1911 – but the fastidious, elegant efficiency of his designs, the economy, visual honesty and truth to the musical drama that he had so momentously developed with Mahler, never deserted him. His radical modernism mellowed in the service of entrepreneurs and impresarios whose theatrical objectives were considerably less idealistic than those of Gustav Mahler.

CHAPTER 6

Adolphe Appia: the opened eye of the score[1]

Mahler and Roller's Vienna productions were, as we have seen, almost certainly inspired in part by the ideas of the Swiss theatrical visionary Adolphe Appia, and it is to him that we must now turn. Although Appia is arguably the most important architect of twentieth-century innovation in operatic production, his influence stemmed principally from his published designs and writings rather than the handful of productions with which he was associated. Totally lacking the practical and political skills of so many great theatre reformers, he was reliant on others to put his ideas into practice. Energetic entrepreneurs with their own reform agendas – Reinhardt, Copeau, Fortuny, Meyerhold, to name but a few – were not slow to assimilate his ideas into their work, often unacknowledged. Towards the end of his life he ruefully observed that 'Appia and anonymity belong together'.[2]

The few practical trials of his work – in a private theatre in Paris in 1903, at Emile Jaques-Dalcroze's Hellerau Institute in 1912–13, at La Scala with Toscanini in 1923, at Basel in 1924–5 – were, with the exception of Hellerau, no more than intimations of the performances he envisaged. He had glimpsed the promised land but was never to enter it. It was not until the 1950s – a quarter century after his death in 1928 – that his vision became manifest on stage. Perhaps it was some comfort to his shade that this should have been at Bayreuth, always the focus of his ambition, and in the productions of Wagner's grandsons, Wieland and Wolfgang.

Although Appia's reform programme had a general intent, Wagner was its *fons et origo*. He argued that the composer's own productions did not begin to do justice to his operas and that they even betrayed them. His dramatic genius had lost its way down the road of scenic realism. Appia discerned a 'profound contradiction' within his work:

> Through the medium of music he conceived a dramatic action whose center of gravity lay inside the characters. ... He wished, moreover, to place this dramatic action on stage, to offer it to our eyes; but there he failed! ... He did not conceive of a staging technique different from that of his contemporaries. A greater care and still greater splendor in the settings seemed to him sufficient. Without a doubt the actors ... were the object of his special attention; but – and this is a truly

strange fact – although he fixed their action minutely, and thus refined the deplorable contemporary operatic conventions, he then found it natural to place around and behind them painted wings and drops, whose nonsense reduced to nothing every effort toward harmony and aesthetic truth in his *productions* of drama.

… so different were his intentions from their visual realization that all his work was disfigured – to the degree that only a small majority could comprehend what it was all about. Such is still the case; and one can assert, without exaggeration, that no one has yet *seen* a Wagnerian drama on the stage.

Appia continues that in his own attempt 'to weaken, as far as possible, the Wagnerian contradiction' he took 'the *living* actor as the point of departure, placing him not before, but in the midst of planes and lines which are rightly intended for him, and which harmonize with the spaces and the time-units dictated by the music of his role'.[3] Wagner had not been aware of the disparity between his dramatic creation and his ideas for its stage production. His 'unreasonable' demands on stagecraft were due to a conflict inherent in his basic conception of drama: the rigidity of his settings stood in opposition to the infinitely supple quality of his music. The composer, Appia conjectures, had been perverted by a desire to mollify his bourgeois patrons. Appia does, however, applaud Wagner for being aware that the staging of his works was, despite Bayreuth, still in its infancy.[4] If he had truly wished to overcome high society's resistance to the new in art, Appia continues, then he might have developed the proper staging implied by his dramatic conception.[5]

Appia therefore worked out his own plan for staging Wagner's works. This was revolutionary in discarding most of the composer's own scenic instructions and proposing that his music was the only reliable guide to the scenic dimension. 'The musical score,' says Appia at his most dogmatic, 'is the sole interpreter for the director: whatever Wagner has added to it is irrelevant. . . . [His] manuscript contains by definition the theatrical form, i.e. its projection in space; therefore any additional remarks on his part are superfluous, even contradictory to the aesthetic truth of an artistic work. Wagner's scenic descriptions in his libretto have no organic relationship with his poetic-musical text.'[6] Appia regards the composer's texts (i.e., music and words) as valid for all time, but their performance as temporal. 'How,' he asks, 'can we account for the renown of a Racine or a Wagner? Is it not evident that their work is on these sheets of paper? What does it matter whether we produce their work or not, since these texts, in themselves, remain immortal?'[7]

He was thus directly opposed to Cosima's museum philosophy and it is little wonder that, despite the advocacy of his ideas by powerful friends like Houston Stewart Chamberlain and Count Hermann von Keyserling, she totally rejected him. His proposals were expressed principally in drawings, and in detailed scenarios which were more than a match for Cosima's own fastidious prescriptions. As Appia was, in effect, claiming to be in better touch with the production needs of Wagner's music than the composer, his widow or anyone else, it is not surprising that he met with resistance. But such was the force of his critique and the quality of his imagination that he was to have a hugely liberating effect on those who, like Mahler and Roller, were in search of an alternative to the conservative literalism of Bayreuth. In Appia we see Wagner's own reform programme transmuted into a true vision of the theatre of the future.

First steps

Born in Geneva on 1 September 1862, Adolphe Appia was the son of a doctor who was one of the co-founders of the international Red Cross. Dr Appia considered theatrical performance to be the work of the devil, yet his library, which became a haven for his son, was well stocked with the classics of world drama. Perhaps we should see Appia's approach to stage production as the product of his strict Calvinist upbringing. The rigorous self-denial of his scenic aesthetic, his problems in formulating it and translating it into results, may in some measure have stemmed from subconscious guilt about his ruling passion. Keyserling described him as 'extraordinarily gifted, a true artist, all eyes and ears but incapable of expressing himself… the most contemplative man I ever met'.[8] Shy and reclusive, Appia had a bad stammer and did not always write the clearest prose, a failing that the journalistically fluent Chamberlain attempted to take in hand. 'My misfortune,' said Appia, 'is that I think in German and write in French.'[9]

He studied music at conservatories in Geneva, Paris and Dresden, but it was his experience of *Parsifal* at Bayreuth in 1882 that turned him irrevocably towards the theatre. The dramatic literature which meant most to him encompassed the Greeks, Calderón, Shakespeare, Molière, Voltaire, Lessing and Goethe. In music, Wagner was the cosmic presence, the only other operas he liked being those of Gluck, Mussorgsky's *Boris Godunov* and Bizet's *Carmen*. He avoided Beethoven, had no use for Mozart, rejected even Verdi's later masterpieces, abominated Puccini and Strauss and was bored to tears by Debussy's *Pelléas*. He seems to have seen *all* drama as essentially musical rather than verbal. He did, however, distinguish between a musical text, which unfolded in a relatively fixed period of time and therefore had an exact relationship with time, and a verbal text, which was comparatively independent of time and tempo. The dramatic text, he said, has no fixed duration, but its underlying or implied music *does*.[10] To read him on Shakespeare and Goethe is almost to be persuaded that they were composers.

The formidably erudite Chamberlain, who became a close friend from 1884, played a major role in Appia's wider education. He helped him gain backstage experience at Dresden (1889–90) – most notably with Hugo Bähr, pioneer of electric lighting who, as described in chapter 3, had devised special effects for the *Ring*'s Bayreuth premiere in 1876 – and then at the Vienna Opera (1890). Appia returned to Bayreuth with Chamberlain in 1886 for Cosima's *Tristan* production, in 1888 for *Die Meistersinger*, in 1894 for *Tannhäuser*, *Lohengrin* and *Parsifal*, and in 1896 for the *Ring*.

From the first, Appia had been as overwhelmed by the music and the Festspielhaus as he was distressed by the settings. For him the latter were simply bad pictures,

The Swiss theatre-artist Adolphe
Appia, probably photographed in
1882 at around the time he attended
the premiere of *Parsifal* in Bayreuth.
He hated the 'luxury' of the representational scenery, arguing that only
simplified stagings and the creative
use of lighting could rescue Wagner's
works from his moribund visual
aesthetic. He devoted his life to
developing ideas and designs which
have profoundly influenced the
subsequent course of Wagner
production and of theatre as a whole.

vainly striving to evoke illusions of the natural world. They did not speak the same
language as the music and he soon embarked on a lifelong quest to discover its true
visual equivalent. The ascetic in Appia recoiled from the 'unusual luxury' of the
Parsifal decor. He had been impressed by the singers' movements and acting but disappointed by the 'lack of harmony between scenery and acting except in the Temple
of the Grail'.[11] He discovered a clue as to what might be needed in the Act I transformation scene. He describes how the stage was considerably darkened for the journey
from the forest glade into the heart of the temple – and in this half-light the illusion
was perfect. But when the lights came up again on the new scene, all was lost as the
knights made their entrance into what Appia dismissed as a 'pasteboard temple'.[12] He
saw that his task was to rescue Wagner's operas from the composer's visual aesthetic.
The music was timeless, the scenery no better than that decreed by fashionable taste.

While in Dresden Appia had had drawing lessons with Wagner's friend Ernst
Benedikt Kietz and from 1891 he began to sketch designs and work out bar-by-bar
scenarios for the *Ring, Tristan* and *Die Meistersinger*. In 1892 he completed a small
book, *La Mise en scène du drame wagnérien* (published in Paris in 1895, an edition of
three hundred copies). In the same year he began a much more substantial treatise,
La Musique et la mise en scène, which he dedicated to Chamberlain. It was published
in Appia's lifetime only in a German translation by Princess Elsa Cantacuzène, *Die
Musik und die Inscenierung* (Munich 1899). The original French text was not pub-

lished until 1963, the first English translation having appeared in 1962 as *Music and the Art of the Theatre*.

Appia's theories

The rationale of Appia's ideas is derived from Wagner's mature belief, underwritten by his admiration for Schopenhauer, that the music is the most important ingredient in opera. Appia quotes with approval the composer's view of opera as 'deeds of music made visible'. He argues that any attempt to bring all the arts together into a single art greater than its parts is simply nonsense. What made a painting good, or a sculpture, was sui generis. A 'total work of art' was thus the enemy of achieving a 'word-tone-drama', where the music had to be the driving force. The composer's score was the only reliable guide to what should be seen on the stage. Just as music exists in time and is quintessentially dynamic, so must the stage-picture be. But nothing could be more static than pictures painted on flats and drops. The illusion created by painted scenery was shattered as soon as an actor stepped in front of it. Scenic illusion was absurd because it showed the audience only what they were perfectly capable of imagining for themselves. The whole point of stage drama, however, was 'to render the invisible'.[13] The settings must therefore be vague and suggestive, capable of seeming to change with time even as the music does.

Appia was among the first to see that the key to the 'musicalization' of the stage picture was lighting. While Bähr and others were developing the technology of electric lighting, with the emphasis very much on 'special effects', Appia was interested in its artistic potential. He carefully distinguishes between diffused, atmospheric lighting and the 'living' light of focused spots which would move and throw shadows. He believed that the future of scenic design would lie with the lighting console and its capacity to orchestrate the play of light upon the stage in sympathy with the music. This idea had already been mooted in the *Bayreuther Blätter* in 1885 by the Spanish painter Rogelio de Egusquiza, who met Wagner in 1879, but Appia was the first to visualize what it could mean for the operas.[14] He argued that there was a powerful affinity between music and light in that both expressed the inner essence of phenomena. Chamberlain, he said, had well observed that 'Apollo was not only the god of song, but also of light'. But light could also imitate phenomena, or in other words be mimetic in suggesting fire, clouds, water, and so on, just as music could.[15]

All that was required of scenery was that it should create spaces to be brought to life by lighting and in which the actor could move and be seen and heard to best advantage. Its function was not pictorial depiction but to distil any necessary sense of specific place into its essentials. Painted surfaces were to be kept to a minimum; the set was to be of solid construction and designed primarily for the movement of the actor and the creation of atmosphere. Appia envisaged flights of steps, ramps and blocks, surrounded by the simplest hangings (drapes and, later, cyclorama) on which the light could play. Costumes were to be neither 'historical' nor reflecting current fashion (as some of Roller's did; see chapter 5) but as simple as possible, coming to life with lighting and the singer's movement, and blending with the other scenic elements.

Everything visual was to be focused on the singing-actor. His movements, gestures and vocal expression were, like the space around him, to be determined by the music. His function was, though, not to dominate the stage and play the star but to be a co-worker in the presentation of the musical drama.[16]

Designs and scenarios

The heart of Appia's work lay, as he himself insisted, not in his theories but in his bar-by-bar scenarios and drawings. The latter are not fully worked designs but impressions, always in monochrome and softly executed in charcoal, black crayon and black-and-white chalk, concentrating on structure and mood. His technique was largely 'smudging, rubbing and erasing with very little drawing'.[17] The scenarios mention neutral shades like grey and brown, but rarely green, blue or red. Stage colour was to be created only by light.

Appia's Wagner scenarios are mostly for the *Ring*, *Tristan* and *Parsifal*. A scenario (but no designs) for *Die Meistersinger* dates from 1892, but it was not until 1926 that he returned to this opera and, for the first time, to *Lohengrin*. He showed little interest in either *Holländer* or *Tannhäuser*. In the scenarios Appia carefully distinguishes between realistic and non-realistic content. Thus he considered that in *Die Meistersinger* the 'contrast between the external events and the inner meaning is central to Wagner's intention'. It therefore needed a definite, perhaps even historical setting, whereas 'la vie intérieure' of *Tristan* required settings that were stronger in mood than in any sense of time and place.[18] In *Parsifal*, the realism of the events was everywhere to be tempered or idealized, for the action was determined solely by the psychological development of the hero.[19]

Turning to the *Ring*, Appia insists, contra Cosima, that it offers 'a vast field for invention'. It cannot, he says, be staged without some compromise between realism and abstraction. For there we find 'episodic' or narrative and action-dominated passages in which 'Wotan's creatures act of their own volition'. These passages contrast with those of 'pure musical expression', when the characters behave like puppets responding to Wotan's will.[20]

The stage form of the *Ring*, he says, is a crescendo: 'its point of departure, the sacramental hierarchy of *Rheingold*, leads gradually to the confused cumulation of haphazard phenomena in *Götterdämmerung* ... the final catastrophe restores the elements of the *Rheingold* and ensures the scenic unity of the drama.' Appia considered that *Walküre* was the most difficult to stage of all the works. Any impulse to stage it realistically must be resisted, for that would completely vitiate the drama. Its settings had to be kept extremely simple, in contrast to *Siegfried*, whose 'episodic nature' permitted a degree of realism in its staging. For *Götterdämmerung* the mise-en-scène had to emphasize the mortal rather than the heroic world. The 'despotic excess' of the action suggested that the spectacle should be relatively independent of musical expression.[21]

Somewhat unexpectedly, Appia argued against symbolic interpretation of the *Ring* and in favour of *actualité* in production: 'Its significance is not symbolic; on the contrary, it is *typical* and thereby attains a preciseness which raises it well above any effect of myth. Its significance is of such a nature that we long to dress the characters as we please and place them in a situation similiar to our own.'[22] Appia's iconoclasm and prophetic instinct could hardly be more apparent than in his imagining a 'modern dress' *Ring* in the 1890s, as his later caption for his 1892 design for the second scene of *Rheingold* confirms: 'Valhalla is a structure of guilt, built upon stratagems and put together by coarse manoeuvrings. The Rhine separates it from a turf-covered summit which in Wagner is not unlike a drawing-room where the gods prattle away their time and settle – not without elegance – less than commendable quarrels. However, just as in many drawing-rooms, two doors stand menacingly: one, on the right, leads to the gloomy forges of Alberich; the other, on the left, will ultimately serve as an entrance for Erda – she whose ideas dominate the vain knowledge of the gods.'[23]

Appia was much exercised by the demands of the more spectacular scenes such as the Rhinedaughters swimming in the Rhine, the rainbow bridge, the flying Valkyries, the fight with Fafner and the collapse of the Gibichung palace with the ensuing fire and flood. He generally counselled a non-literalistic, suggestive approach, striving to avoid graphic, literalistic depiction because he did not believe in showing on stage things that were already fully described in the music. He was always far, far more interested in everything pertaining to the expression of the inner, musical life of the characters. No risk of scenic effect for its own sake, of anything becoming a scenic wonder or, by default, a mishap or disaster, must distract from the music and its embodiment in the performers.

What Appia wanted above all was to interiorize the drama, and nothing suited this aim better than *Tristan*. The main principle for producing it, he said, lay in 'making the audience see the drama through the eyes of the hero and heroine' ('à donner au public la vision qui est celle des héros du drame').[24] The scene on board ship in the first act is 'the last glimpse of the material and tangible world'. In the second act 'the threshhold is crossed and the door is closed'. When the party of König Marke enters, this is the cold voice of rational reality intruding through invisible openings. Here is how he wanted us to see the beginning of the second act:

> When Isolde enters she sees only two things: the absence of Tristan and the torch (the last trace of the first act), the reason for his absence. The mild summer night gleaming through the tall trees has lost its meaning for Isolde; the luminous view is for her eyes only the cruel space that separates her from Tristan. Yet, in spite of her extreme impatience, a fire in the depths of her soul transforms all the forces of nature into a marvellous harmony. The torch alone remains indubitably what it is: a signal agreed upon to warn away the man she loves.

> By extinguishing the torch Isolde removes the obstacle, wipes out the hostile space, arrests time. With her we are shocked at the slow death agony of these two enemies.

At last everything comes to an end. There is no time any longer, no space, no song of nature, no menacing torch, nothing at all. Tristan is in the arms of Isolde.[25]

Appia goes on to describe the lighting and its transformations in considerable detail. When the curtain opens the stage is to be dominated by

a large bright torch in the *centre* of the picture. The rather limited acting space on the stage is illuminated by a diffuse light, just enough to make the characters clearly distinguishable without entirely depriving the torch of its somewhat blinding brightness nor, above all, destroying the shadows projected by this brightness. . . .

One is only vaguely aware of the shapes which determine and circumscribe this space. The lighting creates the impression of being in the open air. One or two barely visible indications in the scenery suggest the presence of trees. . . .

When Isolde extinguishes the torch, the setting takes on a more uniform chiaroscuro in which the eye loses itself, unarrested by any line or object.

Isolde, rushing to meet Tristan, is plunged into a mysterious darkness increasing the impression of depth which the setting gives to the right half of the stage.[26]

Appia wanted to interiorize the drama, to enable the audience to experience *Tristan und Isolde* through the eyes of the hero and heroine. His charcoal and chalk drawing from 1896 illustrates his argument that when Isolde enters in Act II she is aware only of 'the absence of Tristan' and of the torch which is 'the reason for his absence'.

Appia's ideas in stage realization

This way of thinking about production does not seem so strange today, but in the 1890s it was new and shocking – we have seen how Cosima totally rebuffed its challenge to her own philosophy. Appia had to look elsewhere for a practical trial of his ideas and it was in Paris in 1903, where experimental theatre had steadily gained momentum since the 1890s, that he found a wealthy patron keen to offer him the use of her private theatre. This was the Countess René de Béarn and the original intention was to stage extracts from the second and third acts of *Tristan* with Weingartner conducting. In the end Appia had to be content with scenes from Byron's *Manfred* accompanied by Schumann's music, and extracts from the second act of *Carmen*. The pit and stage in the small theatre were remodelled at considerable expense. Appia was never a man for the practicalities of stage production and his ideas were realized with help from the designer Lucien Jusseaume (who worked with André Antoine and whose settings for the 1902 premiere of Debussy's *Pelléas* at the Opéra-Comique had earned him overnight fame) and possibly from Mariano Fortuny, the painter, photographer and electric-lighting technologist whose contribution to modern staging is discussed below.

Although it proved impossible to have a proper cyclorama or more than a handful of floodlights, all reports suggest that the visual effects – such as the dancers in *Carmen* moving between dark and light areas – were impressive. Manfred's face was picked out from the surrounding gloom by a beam of red light, and then he became a silhouette, strongly lit from behind. This was one of Appia's favourite effects and one that he wanted for the Ride of the Valkyries. Astarte appeared on the highest level of the stage floating in a silvery light that made her look quite unreal. There was always a pool of darkness preserving the distance between Manfred at the front of the stage and Astarte at the back.

Three performances were given (25, 27 and 28 March 1903) and they were attended by many theatrical personalities, including the director Aurélien Lugné-Poë and Count Keyserling, who wrote an enthusiastic review.[27] Sarah Bernhardt, who had contrived to arrive majestically late, praised the evening as 'une exquise sensation d'art'.[28] Appia was dismayed by the lack of follow-up, though some of the distinguished visitors took away ideas that they were glad to put to good use elsewhere.

The Paris showing was probably most notable for its demonstration of lighting as an active ingredient in musical production. But Appia continued to be troubled by his need to discover some principle by which to coordinate the singers' movements with the music. Having created an ideal space for the singing-actor he was left with the problem of choreographing his ideal movement within it. His meeting in 1906 with Emile Jaques-Dalcroze, composer, educationist and inventor of eurhythmics, appeared to offer a solution.

Dalcroze originally devised eurhythmics to help his students at the Geneva Conservatory of Music to overcome their difficulties with rhythm. They were exercises in the physical expression of rhythm and tempo which complemented his intensive solfège ear training. The Greek-inspired exercises were designed to cultivate a feeling for rhythm in which mind and body were instinctively at one. Advanced students were taught how to improvise a gestural interpretation of a complete piece of music. Part of the aim was to restore a sense of what Dalcroze and his followers believed to be a long-lost physical and spiritual harmony in the individual and in society at large.

It seemed to Appia that he need look no further for a solution to his problem. The exercises would help ensure that the singing-actor's every gesture and movement would flow from and be an expression of the music and of nothing else. Where Dalcroze basically saw eurhythmics as an educational aid, Appia saw that its improvisational aspect had immense potential for reforming the whole business of acting and movement in opera.

But first it was back to basics. Appia helped Dalcroze by designing 'Espaces rythmiques' for his eurhythmic exercises and they began to work closely together. Dalcroze had the energy and entrepreneurial skills that were entirely lacking in Appia. At the invitation of two wealthy social idealists, Wolf Dohrn and Karl Schmidt, he established a 'Bildungsanstalt' (cultural institute) at Hellerau, then a garden-city suburb of Dresden, with its own new festival theatre, in whose design Appia played a major part. It went one further than the Bayreuth Festspielhaus in abolishing the

Appia hoped that the eurhythmic exercises developed by Emile Jaques-Dalcroze for his music students could be used to help opera singers so that their gestures and movements would, like the stage picture, be an expression only of the music. 'Le Plongeur' (1909-10) was one of a number of 'Espaces rythmiques' which Appia designed for use by Dalcroze and his students at Hellerau, near Dresden.

proscenium arch, so that audience and performers effectively shared the same shoe-box space (c. 50 m long × 16 m wide × 12 m high). There was a rising tier of seats for an audience of 560 and a stage which could accommodate 250 performers. The sunken orchestra pit was concealed from the audience by a rampart and it could be entirely covered over when not required. The all-important lighting system, basically for diffusing light throughout the hall but with a number of spot-projectors, was designed by Alexander von Salzmann, a Russian émigré painter. Thousands of lights were concealed behind the translucent fabric covering walls and ceiling, enabling the light throughout the entire space to be varied from a central console. This system was installed with help from Mariano Fortuny.

Dalcroze and Appia did not work together on Wagner – whose orchestral and vocal demands were in any case far beyond Hellerau's resources – but in 1912 (one scene only) and 1913 (complete opera) they put on a production of Gluck's *Orfeo ed Euridice* which epitomized their ideals. The setting was linear with endless stairs and platforms. Everything was designed to focus attention on the soloists and on the chorus who, in Greek style, both sang and danced. 'Choruses,' wrote Paul Claudel, 'are no longer rows of miserable lifeless dummies, but have become flesh and blood, utterly filled and animated by the life of the drama and the music.'[29] The eurhythmic training had the aim of echoing every musical nuance in the acting and dancing and it seems that the result was a successful integration of the musical and dramatic ele-ments. Dalcroze, conducting the Dresden Opera Orchestra, cut the 'happy ending', and had the opening chorus of lament for Euridice's death repeated from the orches-tra pit.[30]

Appia was delighted by the performances, which were attended by some five thou-sand visitors including leading theatre professionals and critics from far and wide (from Russia, Sergei Volkonsky, Rachmaninov, Stanislavsky, Diaghilev, Nijïnsky and Pavlova; from Britain, George Bernard Shaw and Harley Granville-Barker; from Austria and Germany, Max Reinhardt, Hugo von Hofmannsthal, Kurt Jooss, Rudolf von Laban, Emil Nolde, Max von Schillings, Leopold Jessner and Alfred Roller; from France, Darius Milhaud, Jacques Rouché and Paul Claudel; from the United States, Upton Sinclair and Beryl de Zoete; and from Switzerland, Ernest Ansermet and Le Corbusier).[31] Appia believed that 'for the first time since the Greek era, a perfect fusion of all media of expression … has been realized'. Among the more objective observers to record positive impressions of their pilgrimage to Hellerau were Ernest Ansermet, Paul Claudel, George Bernard Shaw and Max Reinhardt. For the Ameri-can writer Upton Sinclair the whole experience was 'music made visible'.[32]

Appia again collaborated with Dalcroze on the Fête de Juin, a great pageant and patriotic folk festival held in early July 1914 in a huge hangar-like theatre by the shore of Lake Geneva. In the concluding part of the entertainment the rear curtain of the wide stage opened to reveal the spectacular view across the lake to the moun-tain landscape beyond. The outbreak of war put an end to most theatrical activities and had a paralytic effect on Appia. He re-emerged in 1921 with the publication of *L'Oeuvre d'art vivant* (The Work of Living Art), the summation of ideas which, so far as his central work on Wagner was concerned, seemed fated to remain on the page.

They had, however, come to the attention of Toscanini, in charge at La Scala again since 1920, who called Appia out of obscurity to stage *Tristan* there in 1923. As explained by Toscanini's son Walter, who had been present, 'the ideas and sketches of Appia must have appealed as a possibility of realizing the eternal love legend of Tristan and Isolde in an atmosphere of dream without dated epoch'.[33]

Thus it came about that, having entered his sixties, Appia was finally able to see his lifetime's work given a fair trial in the theatre. But it was one thing to work in the dedicated workshop of Hellerau, quite another to do so in a major public theatre. On the playbill, the realization of Appia's mise-en-scène (fundamentally the one he had conceived in 1896) was credited to 'Ernesto' (Ernst) Lert, whose recent work as director of the Frankfurt Opera had included the staging of Hindemith's *Mörder, Hoffnung der Frauen* (designs by Ludwig Sievert), and to a lighting designer called da Caramba. The moving force behind the scenes, however, was Jean Mercier, who had acted in the 1914 Fête de Juin and had been an Appia protégé from 1919. Mercier had to overcome incomprehension that anyone should want anything other than a superb concert against a backdrop of beautiful scenery. The idea of opera as an integrated, organic whole was virtually unknown in Italy. The resident team at La Scala simply did not see the point of creating different levels on the stage, or of projecting light onto plain drapes when painted scenery would have been so much more attractive.

Appia's own testimony makes it plain that his scenario was largely followed: realistic representation corresponding to Tristan and Isolde's experience of the deceitful 'vie extérieure', until the drinking of the love potion, when the staging changed to mirror only the 'vie intérieure' of the hero and heroine. The beginning of the first act took place in front of a dark red drop, thus giving the impression of Isolde's feeling of suffocation. When the curtains parted to either side they revealed the rising rear deck of a ship, but beyond there was no painted seascape, only the glow of bluish light from the Fortuny 'cupola', a kind of enclosed cyclorama that had been installed the previous year (see below). The second and third acts were very much in the style of Appia's misty evocations of 1896, with lighting setting the mood and the whole emphasis on the singers. Mercier's notes record that the opera ended with dusk fading to a night sky tinged with red, leaving the remaining human figures as silhouettes. In Appia's own description: 'Isolde, of extraordinary beauty, had enough light until the end to show the transfiguration in her face – then suddenly when she fell on Tristan, the light faded away unnoticeably into dark night.'[34]

Musically, there was no doubt about the production's success, but the reaction to the staging was mainly antagonistic. Favourable voices were in the minority: these noticed the beautiful effect of Isolde's blue costume against the red drapes in Act I, the singers in Act II fusing with the setting 'in a symphony of blue and silver', and the startling effect of Kurwenal's shadow in Act III. Others considered the production 'a very beautiful experiment', comparing the scenic style with that of Caravaggio's paintings and the effect of Act III with that of Rembrandt's etchings. But mostly there was a chorus of complaint about the unadorned abstraction, and particularly about the use of drapes and dim lighting instead of brightly lit painted scenery.[35]

Appia himself was largely happy with what had been achieved in the six performances (December 1923 to January 1924), praising Toscanini's conducting of the opera (sung in Boito's Italian translation) and the artistry of Nanni Larsen's Isotta and Stefano Bielina's Tristano: 'I consider the production to have been without precedent in the history of lyric theatre and certainly in that of Wagnerian staging.'[36] This was a view shared by Toscanini but evidently not by La Scala. It did not programme the work again until 1931, two years after Toscanini's departure, when it reinstated its old picturesque settings. For Appia, the experience was yet another dead end.

But towards the end of 1924 a long-standing plan by Oskar Wälterlin to show Appia's work in his native Switzerland came to fruition. Wälterlin, a young theatre director at the Stadttheater in Basel, had made an extensive tour of German theatres in the summer of 1922 and had alerted Appia to the fact that his designs were reproduced everywhere but rendered meaningless by the failure to synthesize the lighting and the movement.[37] It was he who urged Appia to return to the battlefield by accepting first Toscanini's invitation and then his own to stage the *Ring* in Basel.

For Basel Appia now made completely new designs that were a development of the 'Espaces rythmiques' and from which all traces of the mystic romanticism of the 1890s designs had disappeared. *Das Rheingold* reached the stage in late 1924 and *Die Walküre* in 1925. The scenery was an assemblage of platforms, stairs, ramps and a few pillars. The acting area was surrounded by drapes covering the wings and a plain blue-grey backdrop. A traveller curtain was used to cut off the upstage area so that more intimate scenes could be played in the foreground without distraction. No animals or rainbow bridge were to be seen, nor any other such pictorial indulgence. The Rhinedaughters were forbidden to make any gesture reminiscent of swimming (Appia was always against 'imitative' movement), though they were allowed, after strenuous eurhythmic preparation, to crawl and slide on the floor with slow arm movements. Their appearance and disappearance were indicated solely by bringing up and taking down the lighting. Freia's ransom was not the usual heap of jewellery and trinkets but plain gold ingots forming a solid wall in front of the goddess of the golden apples. For the second act of *Walküre* there was no rocky landscape but simply high platforms left and right, with lower ones in front and a passageway suggesting a gorge between. The dead body of Siegmund was left lying on one of the high platforms 'as though on a catafalque'.[38]

Unfortunately it seems that the lighting system and the stage technology were inadequate, so that the overall effect scarcely began to do justice to what Appia had intended. Despite this serious handicap the reaction to the scenic contribution was far more positive and understanding than it had been for *Tristan* in Milan. The voice of one particularly powerful and conservative paper, however, the *Basler Volksblatt*, was so strident as to muster the Fafner fraternity, shake the management's nerve and prohibit the completion of the cycle. 'No one,' advised the *Volksblatt*, 'will ever again dare to offer an audience of connoisseurs things like that second act of *Die Walküre* consisting of boxes and curtains and call it "a rugged Rock Pass". ... Go and see it if you want to get angry!'[39] The photographic record of that scene shows only how totally inadequate the realization of the design was – doubtless to Wälterlin's acute embarrassment – and suggests that the *Volksblatt*'s opinion was not wholly off the

It was one thing to imagine a stage setting, quite another for a reclusive dreamer like Appia to get it onto the stage. The painful discrepancy between his vision and the early attempts to realize it is apparent in this design for the end of the second act of *Die Walküre* (*above*), contrasted with the reality of its production by Oskar Wälterlin at Basel in 1925 (*opposite*). Siegmund's body lies on the high block at the rear on the left, while at stage level Brünnhilde escapes with Sieglinde.

mark. Appia was shattered by the animus of the opposition, which was led by Adolf Zinsstag, president of the Basel Wagner Society, and although he continued to dream and design – for Gluck, Ibsen, Goethe's *Faust*, *Lohengrin*, *Meistersinger* and a magnificent *Lear* project – he was a broken man and died three years later, aged sixty-five, on 29 February 1928. His ashes were buried under a huge cedar tree near the lake and mountains which had meant so much to him.

Impact and influence

Although Appia secured only the merest handful of performances, some of which were inadequate to the point of parody, by the time he died his ideas had been taken up by leading directors throughout Europe and as far afield as Russia. As already suggested, not the least remarkable aspect of Appia's role in the development of twentieth-century theatre is that its engine was theory and image rather than successful stage production. There can, of course, be no copyright in theatrical inno-

vations, nor was the wind of change blowing exclusively from Appia's direction, but his designs and theories mark the decisive break with romantic naturalism and first showed what electric lighting could do to revolutionize staging.

Although Chamberlain's advocacy cut no ice with Cosima, he used Appia as designer for his own play *Der Weinbauer* (1893–6) and created waves for ideas to which he felt a strong personal commitment. 'All your concepts are about 75 years ahead of their right time,' Chamberlain consoled Appia after Cosima's withering dismissal, 'and the mother of the kind of people who will blaze with excitement at contact with your ideas is still only a little girl who goes to school.'[40] Thanks to Chamberlain and a number of others there were people who blazed with excitement rather sooner than that, but if one accepts the view that Appia's work found its apotheosis in the New Bayreuth of 1951–66 of Wagner's grandsons, Chamberlain was not far wrong in his prediction. It was he who, believing that those likely to be most receptive would be German- rather than French-speaking, helped Appia to find in the Princess Elsa Cantacuzène a German translator for *La Musique et la mise en scène*. The translation appeared in 1899, as we have noted, as *Die Musik und die Inscenierung*. And it was almost certainly he who, now living in Vienna, secured the publication of three substantial extracts from the translation in the *Wiener Rundschau* (15 December 1900) with the billing 'Das Licht und die Inscenierung, von Adolphe Appia, Rom'.[41] Chamberlain's generously illustrated book *Richard Wagner* (1896, English translation 1897) enjoyed a wide circulation and in it he drew attention to Appia's recently published *La Mise en scène du drame wagnérien* (Paris 1895) and its thesis that 'the whole principle of the stage scenery must undergo a complete alteration'. To prevent 'a painful conflict between what is seen and what is heard', Chamberlain continues, 'the stage-picture … must be released from the curse of rigidity which now rests upon it. The only way of doing this is by managing the light in a manner which its importance deserves, that its office may no longer be confined to illuminating painted walls. … I am convinced that the next great advance in the drama will be of this nature, in the art of the eye, and not in the music.'[42]

In his account of *Tristan*, Chamberlain is of one mind with Appia's reasoning. 'The place, the scenic process are scarcely of any account at all,' he writes. 'Isolde hands the poison to her lover in "a chamber resembling a tent", the second act is in the dark, the third in the outer court of a deserted castle; the drama is so entirely within, the outer world has so completely ceased to have any meaning for Tristan and Isolde, that the surroundings are of no importance whatsoever.'[43] Brave words in 1895 from Cosima's future son-in-law! (Eva Wagner was to become Chamberlain's second wife in 1908.) Unafraid to argue with Cosima in private, he was usually fiercely loyal to her in public, his fulsome praise for her 1896 *Ring* sitting unconvincingly alongside his earlier attempts to involve Appia in its production.

Others close to Cosima were also enthusiastic about Appia's ideas, among them Hans von Wolzogen and Count Keyserling, who wrote glowingly in a Munich newspaper of the 1903 performances in the Countess de Béarn's theatre.[44] Keyserling later described Appia as 'the spiritual father of all scenic renewal from Fortuny to Preetorius'. Appia's visual world began to impinge on Bayreuth from the 1920s, as is apparent in Kurt Söhnlein's *Ring* designs of 1930–1. These were developed still further in the same direction by Emil Preetorius from 1934.

But because of its implicit challenge to Bayreuth's most sacrosanct settings, it was Appia's *Parsifal* mise-en-scène which for most people best epitomized his revolutionary stance. He had worked on it from at least 1895, and three of his designs were published for the first time in Hugo Bruckmann's Munich journal *Dekorative Kunst* in March 1908, but it was doubtless the impending release of *Parsifal* from Bayreuth's exclusive claim in 1913 that fired Appia's return to his plans for that opera, probably at Hellerau in the summer of 1912.[45] The Berlin journal *Die Scene* published three designs in its special *Parsifal* number of July–August 1913, and a mise-en-scène also appeared in *Der Türmer* in February 1914.[46] The designs inspired a number of the more independent-minded productions outside Bayreuth, though Appia was given little if any acknowledgement. Examples include the 1920 designs for the New York Met made by Joseph Urban, who had worked at the Vienna Opera under Mahler and Weingartner (see below). The archives of the Grand Théâtre de Genève include a photograph of a *Parsifal* forest scene from 1924 signed 'Louis Molina' which is a blatant copy of Appia's design.[47]

Appia always knew that his designs could only be realized successfully with the imaginative use of stage lighting. His sketches for the Valkyrie rock (the one *above* is from 1892) became the basis for countless twentieth-century versions, as in that of Emil Preetorius for the 1936 Bayreuth production by Heinz Tietjen (*below*).

Mariano Fortuny

Although there are conflicting views as to whether Mariano Fortuny helped with the 1903 Appian stagings in the Countess de Béarn's private theatre,[48] there can be no doubt that the Spanish artist, inventor and photographer made a lasting contribution to the stage realization of Appia's vision. For while Appia in the 1890s was developing his idea that light should play a dynamic part in staging, Fortuny, driven by the same ambition, was developing the technical means that would make this possible. (He was a close friend of Rogelio de Egusquiza, whose advocacy of lighting reform has already been mentioned.) The purpose was to leave behind the steady illumination of *trompe l'oeil* painted scenery and to give the director and designer the means to paint with light; indeed Fortuny the artist and photographer saw the stage as a three-dimensional painting in constant transition.

He patented his 'Système d'éclairage scénique pour lumière indirecte' in Paris in 1901. Working with motorized carbon-arc lamps he invented an enveloping canopy or curved cyclorama as a way of diffusing light (projected onto it) of variable colour and intensity throughout the stage space. In shape it resembled the unfolded hood of a pram, making a quarter of a full sphere, and it became known as Fortuny's dome, cupola or 'celestial vault'. His model of this, some 5 metres in diameter, was much admired when shown to friends in his Paris workshop in 1902. The device had its first practical trial when Fortuny installed the complete system in his reconstruction of the Countess de Béarn's theatre in 1906. It opened on 29 March with the staging of a ballet to music by Charles-Marie Widor, who was ecstatic about the Fortuny lighting: the celestial vault, which enclosed the entire acting area, was 'the canopy of the heavens, the limitless horizon, the air that one breathes, the atmosphere, life itself'. The event would be a milestone in the history of the theatre: 'For the first time … theatrical painting has penetrated into the domain of music, that is to say into "time", whereas until now it has only existed in "space"'.[49]

Later that same year the Théâtre de l'Avenue Bosquet, just along the road from the Countess de Béarn's home at No. 22, became the first public theatre to use the system (with a dome 12 metres in diameter). By the next year (1907) it had been installed in the Kroll Opera, Berlin (where it was seen by Reinhardt and copied by him for his Deutsches Theater), and within a very short time was to be found in theatres at Dresden, Duisburg, Karlsruhe, Königsberg, Stuttgart and Wiesbaden. In its perfected form, developed by Fortuny with the Berlin A.E.G. electrical company, the system consisted of a dome that was collapsible (for storage), being made of a wire structure covered with two layers of opaque fabric, and a lighting installation. Arc lamps behind and above the proscenium opening, and unseen below stage level, projected light onto the inner surface of the dome through colour-tinted glass and via revolving reflector drums, the colours and intensity being variable by remote control.[50] A conventional backdrop could also be used.

Fortuny's work, like that of Appia, was rooted in an attempt to meet the demands of the Wagnerian oeuvre. He had first visited Bayreuth in 1892 and began his experiments with stage lighting the following year. By the time Appia met Fortuny (possibly in 1902 at the latter's workshop demonstration of his dome, and certainly no later than 1903), Fortuny had already made settings for *Tristan und Isolde* at La Scala in 1901 and had worked with Gabriele D'Annunzio between 1898 and 1901 on

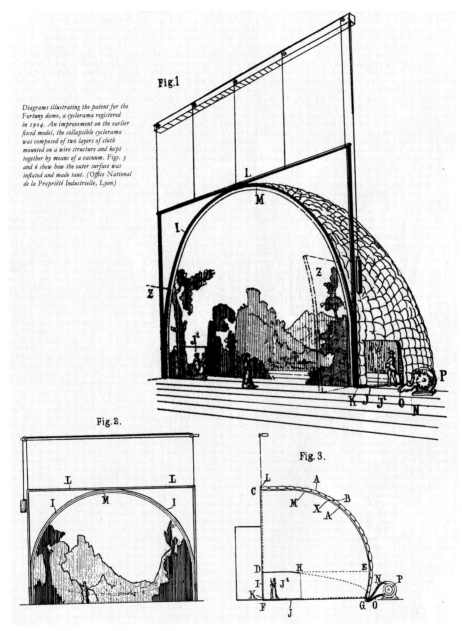

Diagrams illustrating the patent for the Fortuny dome, a cyclorama registered in 1904. An improvement on the earlier fixed model, the collapsible cyclorama was composed of two layers of cloth mounted on a wire structure and kept together by means of a vacuum. Figs. 3 and 6 show how the outer surface was inflated and made taut. (Office National de la Propriété Industrielle, Lyon)

The Spanish artist and photographer Mariano Fortuny invented a system of diffused lighting which greatly contributed to the stage realization of Appia's scenic world. Fortuny, like Appia, saw the stage space as a fluid painting. In its perfected form, Fortuny's 'celestial vault', shown here in a diagram from 1904, projected light onto the inner surface of a spherical dome, the colours and intensity being continuously variable.

a number of theatrical ventures, including an unfulfilled plan for an open-air, Greek-style national festival theatre on the shores of Lake Albano. At La Scala, Fortuny's designs had merely been an elaboration of those used in the 1865 Munich premiere of *Tristan*, with a single notable innovation, in that the audience was given the impression that it was itself inside Isolde's luxuriously draped on-deck pavilion. Fortuny's attempt to try out his diffused lighting was compromised by the impossibility of operating it fully in a theatre whose technology was relatively primitive.

Appia had immediately seen the potential of Fortuny's system and we know that they worked together in the summer of 1903 on a model for the Valkyrie rock. In a footnote to his article 'Comment reformer notre mise en scène' (May 1904) Appia recorded his hopes for Fortuny's system: 'A well-known artist in Paris, M. Mariano Fortuny, has invented a completely new lighting system based on *reflected* light. Its results are extremely successful – this excellent invention will bring about a radical transformation to the mise-en-scène in favour of lighting in all theatres.'[51]

Here is Fortuny's own account (1904) of how his system could improve the usual way of staging the second scene of *Das Rheingold*, whose

> landscapes, panoramas, borders, side-scenes, side-drops, etc, need between 75 and 100 pieces of scenery, depending on the theatre; apart from those depicting the landscape and the mountain in the distance, all the others are there solely to conceal the backdrop. With my system and my celestial vault, the amount of scenery is limited to the number of pieces strictly needed to represent the subject … four or five pieces would be enough for this scene, the illusion achieved by my lighting doing the rest.[52]

Cost-cutting aside, Fortuny's aim was very close to Appia's:

> To sum up, my system is composed of three parts: a system of lighting by means of reflection; a system of stage decoration by means of reflection, allowing for the use of a concave surface to make skies and distant views; last, and most important, a complete reform of the visual element in the theatre, because it can be said for the first time that theatrical scenery will be able to transform itself in tune with music, within the latter's domain, that is to say in 'time', whereas hitherto it has only been able to develop in 'space'. This last ability is of supreme importance for the staging of the works of Richard Wagner.[53]

What Fortuny had in mind was the depiction of such transitions as that described by Wagner at the beginning of the third scene of Act III of *Siegfried*:

> The clouds become increasingly fine and dissolve into a veil of thin pink mist which divides, the upper part floating away to reveal bright blue sky in daylight. A morning mist remains clinging to the edge of what is now seen to be the rocky summit of *Die Walküre*, Act 3, and reminds us that the magic fire is still blazing further down the mountain.[54]

Sadly, Fortuny's remarks to Appia about 'Comment reformer notre mise en scène' were construed by the latter as less than supportive (Fortuny had apparently been ironical about the article's emphasis on the pre-eminence of the performer) and this led to an estrangement. There was, in any case, a crucial divergence between the two innovators in that while Fortuny's ambition was the perfection of Wagner's theatre of illusion, Appia wanted the visual impression to be dictated solely by the music. It was unlikely that their contrasting temperaments and theatre aesthetics would have made them successful partners in reform, and Fortuny, with his major innovation in lighting technology behind him and widely adopted, moved out of the theatre after 1906 and turned his attention to textiles and fashion. Appia, for his part, reaped a lasting benefit from the Fortuny technology, which in adaptations for Hellerau and far beyond facilitated the practical application of his ideas about *Lichtregie*. The Fortuny 'celestial vault', installed at La Scala in 1922, undoubtedly made an important scenic contribution to the Toscanini–Appia staging of *Tristan* there in 1923.[55]

Austria and Germany

We have already seen how Alfred Roller applied Appian principles in Vienna. Those principles made an even stronger impact there in the 1920s and 1930s, 'when Roller worked with the stage director Lothar Wallerstein, who favored not only simplicity in his settings with emphasis on the light plot but who concentrated to a high degree on the acting singer'.[56]

Roller was but one of many artists (including Emil Orlik, Ernst Stern and Oskar Strnad) who went on to use Appian ideas in their work for Max Reinhardt, the most successful and influential early twentieth-century theatre pioneer of all. 'Wherever one looks,' says Richard Beacham, 'whether his early use of solid scenery in *The Merchant of Venice* in 1905, or in the admirable and suggestive simplicity of his designs for *The Winter's Tale* in 1906, one finds in these and a host of other productions clear evidence of the extent to which Reinhardt's stagecraft utilised the external manifestations of Appia's scenic principles.'[57] Reinhardt saw Appia and Dalcroze's work at Hellerau in 1913, and the absence of proscenium arch, the bringing together of performers and audience into a single, shared space, the use of diffused and 'formative' lighting and the eurhythmic choreography of the movement all fed into his own far more public and publicized performances. Reinhardt, however, was scarcely a faithful disciple of Appia, for the showman-entrepreneur in him drew on externals for his own spectacular ends without bothering overmuch about the totality of Appia's vision or its rationale. The word of Moses was to this extent betrayed in the theatricals of Aaron.

Palpable Appian influence is evident in Leopold Jessner's Berlin productions, such as *Othello* (1921) and *Macbeth* (1923) with their emphasis on spatial design, pervasive use of steps and levels, and active lighting plots. Jessner had also been at Hellerau in 1913 and his designers Emil Pirchan, Cesar Klein and Walter Reimann were all Appian torchbearers.[58] The Bauhaus-influenced innovations at Berlin's Kroll Opera from 1927 under Otto Klemperer (see chapter 8), which included an uncompromisingly modernist *Holländer* (1929), undoubtedly owed a sizeable debt to Appia.

French disciples

In France Appia's supporters included the composer Paul Dukas, who published enthusiastic reviews of *La Mise en scène du drame wagnérien*[59] and *Die Musik und die Inscenierung*,[60] and Jacques Rouché, who wrote a chapter on Appia in his book *L'Art théâtral moderne*.[61] Even more significant was the work of Jacques Copeau. In 1913, Copeau, dedicated like Appia to anti-realistic settings and emphasis on the actor, had founded the Théâtre du Vieux Colombier in Paris, where Shakespeare and Mérimée were often on the playbill. In the search to extend the training of his actors beyond Stanislavsky he had worked with Dalcroze, who introduced him to Appia in October 1915. They became close friends. Copeau spent the winter of 1916–17 lecturing in New York on modern theatre reforms, particularly those of Appia and himself. This paved the way for a New York season by the Vieux Colombier company over the winter of 1917–18 which was a demonstration of Appian principles and left a lasting impression on such American theatre radicals as Lee Simonson, Kenneth Macgowan, Robert Edmond Jones, Norman Bel Geddes and Donald Oenslager. After the war Copeau reopened the Vieux Colombier and in 1920 rebuilt its interior, abolishing proscenium, footlights and curtain so that, as at Hellerau, actors and audience would share the same space. To pursue his researches out of the limelight he created a theatre school at Pernand-Vergelesses, a village in Burgundy, where Appia, now preoccupied with the extension of his music-based principles into verbal drama (including projects for *A Midsummer Night's Dream*, *The Choëphori*, *Hamlet* – all with his pupil Jessica Davis Van Wyck, 1920–3 – then Ibsen's *Little Eyolf*, 1924, *Macbeth* and *Lear*, 1926–7, and Goethe's *Faust* I, 1927), became a frequent inspirational presence.

From autumn 1924 Copeau handed over control of the Vieux Colombier company to Louis Jouvet and dedicated himself wholly to the school and to touring his company. In demonstrating the successful application to spoken drama of the principles Appia had derived from Wagner, Copeau proved their enduring vitality and passed the torch to the next generation. Jean Mercier, who had worked closely with both Appia and Copeau, also played a substantial role in the dissemination of Appia's work. From 1930 to 1933 he taught and directed in Seattle, Washington, and at the University of Michigan at Ann Arbor, as well as touring with his theatre group from the Northwest to Texas. Returning to Europe, he was director of the municipal theatre in Strasbourg (1933–6) and then became director of productions at the Opéra-Comique in Paris up to the German occupation, later resuming the post until 1965. He was widely in demand as a guest producer, especially in Switzerland, where in 1947 in Geneva he once again brought Appia's conception of *Tristan* to the stage. Oskar Wälterlin, who had played such a crucial part in bringing about the Appian stagings at La Scala and in Basel, went on to become the Intendant of the Basel Stadttheater, 1925–32, and held the same position at the Zürich Schauspielhaus from

1938. After the war he directed plays and operas in Berlin, Vienna, Hamburg and
Salzburg, and in his recollections has left an important testimony to the lasting
inspiration of his work with Appia.[62]

America

America had had a first taste of Appian principles in the severely simplified staging
of *Tristan* designed in 1912 for the Boston Opera by Joseph Urban, who had been a
prominent member of the Viennese avant-garde at the turn of the century. Urban,
much influenced by Appia, had been brought over by Boston's music director Felix
Weingartner, with whom he had already worked at the Vienna Opera. Trained as an
architect, Urban had served his theatrical apprenticeship with Mahler and Roller at
the Vienna Opera, continuing to work with Weingartner when in 1907 he succeeded
Mahler as director. It was typical of the Boston *Tristan* that its first-act setting consisted of little more than a huge single sail. Between 1911 and 1913 Weingartner and
Urban's productions, more dimly lit than was usual and with every stage element
closely coordinated, created a considerable stir and, inevitably, not a little resistance.
Urban went on to become chief designer at the Met (1918–33), where his fifty or so
productions included the 1920 *Parsifal* and a *Ring* in the same year. Always less radical than Appia, and doubtless under pressure from Broadway, the prolific Urban's
work lost its edge too soon; this quality was scarcely a notable feature in the twelve
shows he designed for the Ziegfeld Follies and the many musicals on which he
worked with Romberg, the Gershwins and Richard Rodgers.[63]

Americans who had been excited by what they had seen at Hellerau and returned
home to tell the tale included the novelist Upton Sinclair (quoted above) and the
critic Sheldon Cheney, author of *The New Movement in the Theatre* (1914). Writing
in the *Musical Courier* in 1912, E. Potter Frissell was struck by Hellerau's goal of a
total artistic experience, likening its neo-Greek ethos to that of Bayreuth.[64] Other
early enthusiasts included Hiram Moderwell and also Carl van Vechten, who in 1915
bemoaned the unchanging, museum productions that were common in the United
States and throughout Europe. He argued for simplified settings, citing Appia as
pointing the way to 'the salvation of Wagner', 'the complete realization of his own
ideals'.[65] Theory blossomed into practice with Lee Simonson's 1922 designs for Paul
Claudel's *L'Annonce faite à Marie*, a play which had been premiered at Hellerau in
1913, and in Norman Bel Geddes's project, sadly unfulfilled, for Dante's *Divine
Comedy* (1921) and his setting for *Joan of Arc* (1925).[66] Donald Oenslager, believing
that the living theatre in America had to 'pick up where Appia left off', designed, in
his own words, 'a single, permanent arrangement of meaningful levels on which all
four operas [of the *Ring*] could be played, with fluid changes of locale accomplished
by the use of light'. This setting, whose grandiose, swirling, intertwining, steep
narrow stairways seem more Craig than Appia in the surviving model, symbolized
'the Life Tree of the eddas and sagas'. It was planned not for a conventional theatre
but for 'a large auditorium or convention hall'. Although never fulfilled, the project
attracted considerable attention and led to Oenslager's designing *Salome* for the Met

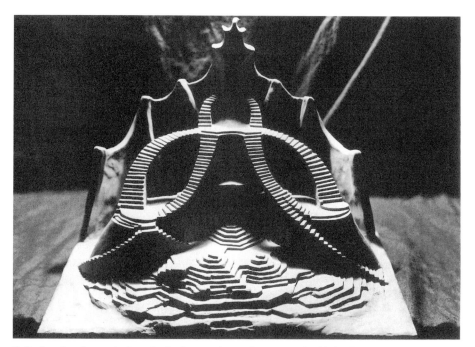

Believing that theatre in America had to continue where Appia had left off, Donald Oenslager
may have been the first to design a single permanent set on which, with lighting playing a central
role, every scene of the *Ring* could take place. The model for what Oenslager called his 'Life Tree
of the eddas and sagas' dates from 1927. The project remained unfulfilled, but Oenslager
succeeded in staging *Tristan und Isolde* on a single, unifying set in Philadelphia in 1934.

in 1934. As active in the conventional theatre and in musical comedy as in opera,
Oenslager's appetite for the Wagnerian challenge never left him. He designed a *Holländer* (1932, unfulfilled project) and a *Tristan* (Philadelphia, 1934) in which lighting and variations on a permanent set again played a major role. The staging of
Tristan, which was directed by Herbert Graf and conducted by Fritz Reiner, 'went far
beyond the traditional tastes and sensibilities of American audiences in the early
thirties', provoking opinions violently pro and contra. The designer recalls that the
audience was particularly surprised and shocked by lighting effects 'devised to
enhance the mood of the score'.[67] Oenslager's work is notable as perhaps the very first
attempt to devise single, unifying settings for the operas.

Russia

The infusion of Appia's ideas into Russia began early in the century after publication
of *Die Musik und die Inscenierung*, but the lines of influence are not always easy to
trace as the great Russian reformers were often on an autonomous parallel course. It
is likely that Stanislavsky, who used eurhythmics in the drilling of his actors, first
learnt of Appia through Prince Volkonsky, Director of the Imperial Theatres since

1899, who had himself taken part in classes at Hellerau and was a tireless advocate of eurhythmics. Stanislavsky and Volkonsky were among the international visitors to Hellerau in 1913, as were Diaghilev and Nijinsky. It was through them that eurhythmics came to leave its mark on the Ballets Russes. Marie Rambert was then an instructor at Hellerau and in November 1912 Diaghilev and Nijinsky engaged her to teach eurhythmics to the Russian Ballet. Thus it came about that eurhythmics impinged on the daring new style of choreography that was manifest with the premieres of *Jeux* and *Le Sacre du printemps* in Paris in May 1913. The mainspring of Stravinsky's music for *Le Sacre*, and of Nijinsky's choreography, was rhythm, the trouble being that Nijinsky and his dancers found it impossibly difficult. It was Marie Rambert who was entrusted with teaching them the music, earning her the not entirely friendly title of 'Madame Rythmichka'.[68] Appia, who had himself somewhat improbably donned the obligatory black tights decreed for eurhythmic exercise, could therefore claim, together with Dalcroze, to be a 'godparent of modern dance'.[69] A more active role in this direction was played by Isadora Duncan, who, as we saw, choreographed and danced in the Bayreuth *Tannhäuser* of 1904. These and other diverse attempts (Rudolf Laban and Kurt Jooss were not just visitors but also alumni of Hellerau) to solve the music-and-movement problems that were part of the Wagnerian legacy played a significant role in the evolution of modern choreography. They remind us of the Wagner who spent six hours of *Rheingold* rehearsal time attempting to coordinate the movements of the Rhinedaughters with the descending phrases on the violins,[70] and of his contention that dance was the very basis of musical rhythm and found its highest fulfilment in drama.[71]

The one common element in Vsevolod Meyerhold's diverse experimentation in the pre-war years (1900–14) is his determined anti-realism, a search for the inner core of drama and an attempt to win a response to it in the active imagination of the spectator. It was typical that after the premiere of *The Cherry Orchard* by the Moscow Art Theatre in 1904 he should remark to Chekhov, 'Your play is abstract, like a Tchaikovsky symphony. Before all else the director must get the *sound* of it.'[72] This was also a quintessentially Appian sentiment, and although we do not know when Meyerhold first came across Appia's published work he would surely have recognized a powerful affinity when he did. This must have been before his 1909 production of *Tristan* at the Mariinsky Theatre in St Petersburg and his contemporaneous essay about the opera, page after page of which echoes and endorses Appia's staging concept. Meyerhold's production of *Tristan* and the 1940 Moscow staging of *Die Walküre* by the great film maker Sergei Eisenstein, in which Eisenstein's Appian ideal was the creation of 'common spatial ground for actors and audience' (as at Hellerau and as attempted at Basel),[73] are the subject of chapter 7.

Edward Gordon Craig

It was through Stanislavsky's famous 1912 production of *Hamlet* at the Moscow Art Theatre that its designer Edward Gordon Craig eventually came into direct contact with the Swiss visionary with whom he has so often been linked. Craig had been shown three of Appia's designs in Florence in 1908 and been much impressed by them, but was led to believe that Appia, an Italian as he thought, was dead. During the final rehearsals for *Hamlet* in December 1911, Volkonsky was able to assure Craig that Appia was alive. Volkonsky showed him photographs of more designs, which in the second edition of *On the Art of the Theatre* Craig praised as 'the work of the fore-most stage-decorator of Europe.'[74] 'I must see him,' wrote Craig in his daybook for 27 December 1911, 'for I feel his work and mine are closely united.'[75]

Appia himself, however, would scarcely have been pleased by Dalcroze's report from his visit to the Moscow *Hamlet* that 'There are some wonderful things, all copied from you to such a degree that I still foam at the mouth after nine hours of insomnia.' This was probably an unjust accusation, but it was more to the point that Dalcroze complained about Craig's excessive use of spotlights: 'They accentuate and highlight, but produce shadows, grimacing and contorted silhouettes, which become a real nightmare.'[76]

The two men eventually met in Zürich in February 1914 on the occasion of the International Theatre Exhibition, when designs by both of them were on prominent display. Despite the language barrier, which they bridged with a smattering of German and by making drawings for each other on restaurant tablecloths, they found they had much in common and the meeting led to an extensive correspon-dence.[77] They hoped to collaborate in a further exhibition in Cologne, but their plans were thwarted by the outbreak of war.

The common ground between Appia and Craig included contempt for realism and an emphasis on the actor, on lighting, on movement and on a new interactive relationship between players and audience. Their differences were rooted in the fact that whereas Appia's approach was governed by music, Craig's reached back into the long and diverse history of theatre forms from around the world and was in thrall to sheerly visual drama. There was also a notable divergence in their visual aesthetics. Denis Bablet well remarks that while Craig's stage spaces are dominated by vertical lines Appia's show a preference for superimposed horizontal planes.[78]

Craig, by his own account of their first meeting, provoked Appia by asserting that 'Wagner hated the Theatre and used it as a Prostitute is used'.[79] He considered that Appia had been enslaved by Wagner and then by Dalcroze and eurhythmics. But if Appia's view of the actor was constrained by his eurhythmic perspective (see below), Craig's programme for the actor as 'Übermarionette' was scarcely more liberating, though by this he did not mean a mechanistic puppet but rather an actor totally in control of his emotions and expressive power so that he could play his part in ful-filling the director's overall conception rather than function as an individual star turn.[80] In truth, both men, as theorists, were aware of the central importance of the actor and at the same time rather terrified of him in the flesh. It was safer to talk about the ruling power of music (as Appia liked to do) or to conjure up visual images as was Craig's metier. The degree of convergence in their view of the actor is remark-able, and in both cases it was music that was the common determinant. For if Appia always had the music in mind, Craig's vision implied an abstraction of all the

The affinities between the contemporaneous designs of Appia and those of
Edward Gordon Craig are evident in the latter's 'Frozen Moment', a purely
imaginative drawing from 1907. Lee Simonson was not alone in thinking
that Craig should have concentrated his gifts on opera rather than on
spoken theatre.

elements of theatre. The actor was not to impersonate a character but to represent
an idea.[81] As he wrote in 1909, his ideal theatre would 'strive towards the condition
of music' and live 'only in the imagination'.[82]

Whatever Craig's indebtedness to Appia, his characteristic visual (and verbal)
rhetoric has not been without its delayed effect on the world of opera. There is much
in Lee Simonson's belief that Craig's 'greatest mistake' was to have forsaken opera for
spoken drama.[83] Simonson believed that Craig's 1928 concept for *Macbeth* in New
York had been cribbed from Appia's Valkyrie rock: 'I see a lofty and steep rock,' Craig
had written twenty years earlier, 'and I see a moist cloud which envelops the head of
this rock. That is to say, a place for fierce and warlike men to inhabit, a place for
phantoms to nest in. Ultimately this moisture will destroy the rock; ultimately these
spirits will destroy the men.'[84] Craig's conceptions proved too 'operatic' for the play-

The work of both Appia and Craig became an immensely rich resource for later designers.
Craig's setting for Act II of Ibsen's *The Vikings* at the Imperial Theatre in London, 1903,
anticipates Wieland Wagner's Grail temple at Bayreuth half a century later (*see page 289*).

house but flowered on the post-1945 opera stage, not least because large opera
houses and open-air arenas have been able to give them the space they always craved.
Craig's great circular configuration for Ibsen's *The Vikings at Helgeland* (Imperial
Theatre, London, 1903) is a palpable precursor of the Grail scenes in Wieland
Wagner's 1951 production of *Parsifal*.

Towards a reckoning

Appia's iconoclastic assertion was that he knew better than Wagner how his works
should be staged. It was, and is, an extraordinary claim, and if vindicated by history
still merits critical examination. His scenarios from the 1890s are every bit as confi-

dent in their dogmatics as Cosima was in her stage practice. But while both believed they were in tune with Wagner's deepest intentions, they were facing in opposite directions. Cosima's premiss was that what Wagner himself had done was right, while Appia's was that he had got it all wrong, and of these Appia's was obviously the more contentious. As we have seen, he had posited a fundamental contradiction between what Wagner had composed and how he had sought to stage it. But the trouble with his argument that 'The musical score is the sole interpreter for the director'[85] is how to distinguish a correct from an incorrect interpretation. The composer believed, by and large, in his pictorial, literalistic scenarios, while Appia was equally convinced that his anti-realistic ones were far more suitable. Ultimately there can be no logical way of deciding between these or any other claims. They are all beside the real point, which is that no single interpretation of a great work, including that of the composer himself, can be definitive. All are necessarily a product of the taste of their time, their strengths and weaknesses the proper study of criticism and debate.

We have seen how theatrical theory and practice at the turn of the century overturned the notion of 'faithful' performance in favour of directors and performers making their own creative contribution to performance. Appia's part in this is of particular interest, in that whereas his earlier work is an attempt to work out an ideal staging, towards the end of his life he comes down on the side of creating an interpretation of the moment.

Undoubtedly his work with Dalcroze played a major part in this shift. His designs undergo a notable change between what he himself called his 'romantic' phase of the 1890s and the more abstract settings which evolve from his work with Dalcroze. These are much influenced by his 'Espaces rythmiques', where the designs are determined by the needs of the actors rather than the suggestion of specific location. This principle flows over into his later Wagner settings, which are far more abstract than their predecessors. And Appia is quite plain that the music alone is to determine the actor's expression and movement, as also the stage setting for them. But hand in hand with this goes a new openness to the possibilities of production and design. In 1921, he claims no more for his designs to date than that they seek to find a 'visual evocation compatible and consistent with' Wagner's music. He knows that he has doubtless attained only a compromise so far, but one which, he hopes, comes 'as near as possible to an integral harmony that Wagner barely dreamed of, though his work bears promise of it'.[86]

From his association with Dalcroze crystallizes the idea that a dramatic text has to be continually reborn in performance. Everything in his post-Dalcroze philosophy presupposes that the text only exists in the 'here and now' moment of performance. What he now calls 'The Work of Living Art' (the highly significant title of his last book) is alive in each and every moment that it is performed, the implication being that there is freedom for performances to change, to develop, to be different from one another. He regards any attempt to pin the butterfly, whether by Bayreuth or anyone else, as misguided. The 'work of living art' is, by Appia's definition, one in process of continuous transformation.

The chantacteur

More problematic are Appia's views on the singing-actor, who he always insisted was the focus of stage production. In his writings of the 1890s, the stage space and light-ing are to exist only for the performer; his expression, gesture and movement are to be determined by the music. He is the vessel in whom the drama becomes manifest and through whom it is communicated to the audience. The actor's role is to elimi-nate his own individuality and tune in to the will of the composer. He is to acquire skill in dance and movement and thus become the perfect servant of the drama.[87] All in all, we have the impression of the 'chantacteur' (I am indebted to Jean-Jacques Nattiez for this felicitous neologism for the 'singing-actor') as a programmed puppet, not as an artist with his own personality and interpretative gifts.

To an extent this doubtless reflects Appia's unhappy experiences in theatres still largely dominated by 'star' singers. The disciplined work of the Meiningen players was dedicated to realism and thus of no interest to Appia, while Reinhardt's drilling of his actors would have seemed too concerned with external effect rather than inner truth. Appia was of course but one of many voices clamouring to chastise the still prevalent style of acting in which the text was treated as little better than a trampo-line. But in insisting that the actor's role is subservience, he approaches Craig's view (1907) of the actor as *Übermarionette*, and anticipates Oskar Schlemmer's 'Kunst-figur' (a mechanical human figure, permitting any kind of physical movement)[88] and other attempts at this time to envision a de-personalized, ritualistic performer of unlimited physical possibility. Plainly this tendency is a complex phenomenon, with theory often wildly at variance with practice.

Alongside moves to curb the actor's freedom of expression we see also a divergent emphasis on performance as a creative interpretation of the author's text. This seem-ing paradox is, of course, resolved in the burgeoning power of the director. Whether the performance is to be a free improvisation, or an attempt to find the most faith-ful stage expression for a drama, it is the director who is in the driving seat, the actors the engine and wheels responding to his touch. In 1899 Appia sees the director as an artist of the first rank who will impose overall control and unity.[89]

The greater part of early modernist theatre theory was, of course, about the role of the actor in relationship to a verbal text. Appia was virtually alone in giving con-sideration to the special role of the singer, whose text is so much more constrained than the actor's, with pitch, dynamics, phrasing and tempo all being set by the com-poser. In giving primacy of place to the music it was only logical that Appia should demand that the singer should be totally guided by it. Of course Cosima also believed this, but Appia viewed her idea of what was appropriate in gesture and movement as being determined by externals, by Wagner's words rather than by his music.

Appia's difficulty was to discover a principle whereby the singer's acting could be the physical equivalent of the music. As early as 1895 he envisaged the discovery of 'a type of "musical gymnastics" in order to train the actor in musical time and proportion'.[90] We have seen how he saw Dalcroze's eurhythmics as the answer to this problem. But what kind of answer was it? There can be little doubt that eurhythmics was used with considerable success in the 1912–13 *Orfeo* and also in the 1924–5 Basel productions of *Rheingold* and *Walküre*. Plainly the idea that eurhythmics was able to translate music into its equivalent in gesture and movement was hugely appealing to Appia, but it is hard to imagine how it could be substantiated and is scarcely realistic as an invariable principle for stage performance. There are simply too many factors involved for a prescriptive system ever to 'solve' the problems and exhaust the possibilities of acting and stage movement.

Appia himself became aware that he had been too *dirigiste* in his approach to acting. By 1921 he is speaking of the performer as a creative collaborator with the dramatist, a co-creator, an interpretative artist and not just a passive vehicle.[91] He even sees him as, in effect, the set designer: it is from him 'that the stage decoration must be born or must rise – and not from the detached imagination of the dramatist. We know now that only the living body of the actor can determine the stage space'.[92] This is a notable change from his earlier view that the settings had to be created *for* the actor. He still saw the music as imposing movements on the actor, but in now referring to his 'living body' he recognizes that the actor is a creature of flesh and blood and not just a eurhythmic puppet. Little of this seems so very novel now, but in its day Appia's insistence that the singer should be the faithful servant of the composer's expressive intentions was a necessary call to order and eloquent of the state of contemporary theatre practice. For the greater part of the twentieth century it was a commonplace requirement, and only in recent years has it been challenged by a wave of directors in whom the critical, interrogative impulse has been uppermost.

The power of the incomplete

Much of the catalytic power of Appia's ideas lay precisely in the fact that they were largely unrealized by him and that, for all their precision in certain areas, they remained vague in others. His visions were all the more attractive to other innovators because they offered a degree of freedom in their realization. Thus his beautiful idea of the transformation between Act I, scenes 1 and 2 of *Parsifal* being effected by the tree trunks of the forest becoming the pillars of the temple of the Grail – technically very difficult to achieve – remained unworked-out in detail. Nor did he leave any design for how the temple would look when the transformation was complete.[93] Rejecting Wagner and Brandt's solution of moving scenery painted on canvas, one wonders how he imagined his own transformation scene would be accomplished. 'The stone columns', he says, 'will gradually and smoothly replace the great shafts of the forest.'[94] But that is all! For all the huge emphasis he places on 'Here time becomes space' – a crucial plank in his entire stage philosophy – it is extraordinary that he failed to work out this change in any kind of detail.

Similarly, Appia has little to say about the means of accomplishing the scarcely less important transitions in Act II from the keep of Klingsor's castle to the magic garden ('Soon afterwards, the entire setting gives way to a garden, perfumed with living and full-voiced flower maidens') and thence, at the very end of the act, to a desert. Appia is a little more specific for the Act III transformation between the Good Friday meadow and the temple of the Grail: 'the forest soon surrounds [the three figures], then moves almost imperceptibly from stage right to stage left – and we are again in the temple of the Grail.'[95] This is interesting in suggesting that perhaps Appia did not, after all, rule out the use of moving scenery!

Appia's enduring achievement consists for the one part in rekindling the torch of the composer's own reforms, and for the other in demonstrating that their significance extended far beyond Bayreuth and 'carried a powerful charge' for the theatre as a whole.

Plainly, in his rejection of the whole nineteenth-century ideal of literal depiction which was the foundation of Wagner's own stage practice, Appia was pushing the boat out into new and uncharted waters. While there can be no question that Appia was in tune with the moves against picturesque realism that emerged with Wagner's own production of *Parsifal* at Bayreuth in 1882, Appia's programme was far more iconoclastic than anything that the composer himself had imagined. But in the end it is futile to measure Appia against speculation as to what the composer might or might not have sanctioned. His ideas won through because productions to which they were godparent (such as the Mahler–Roller *Tristan*, and the much later Bayreuth productions by the Wagner grandsons) were, quite simply, better than anything produced elsewhere.

Implicit in Appia's substitution of a staging aesthetic which valued the power of suggestion above that of literal depiction was, at least for the world of opera, the shockingly new idea that its production values should be fluid and subject to self-revision, development and change, not by reason of adjustment to local circumstance but simply in pursuit of the most effective realization of the composer's blueprint. In this it was inevitable that the contribution of performance should be complementary, creative and not merely re-creative. Partly this was a phenomenon created by the demand for 'afterlife' performances of works surviving their composers, but it also reflected a growing interest on the part of living composers and playwrights in the contribution that directors and designers were making to the success of their works (for example, Lugné-Poë's productions of Maeterlinck's *Pelléas*, 1893, and Wilde's *Salomé*, 1896). Kurt Weill considered that Caspar Neher's projections were a 'Bestandteil' (integral part) of *Aufstieg und Fall der Stadt Mahagonny* (1930), and as such they were among the performance materials sent to prospective producers.[96]

We have seen how Appia went beyond the tightly argued, prescriptive imperatives of his scenarios to belief in 'the work of living art'. The scenarios demonstrated the deeply serious interpretative duty of the director; the designs, spaces in which the musical drama could breathe; the theoretical writings, the need to be forever making things new in performance. That his ideas shade over into quasi-religious mystical speculation about the role of theatre was a cry from the depths of a spirit whose dreams were way ahead of its time.

CHAPTER 7

Wagner in Russia, 1890–1940

Wagner's impact in Russia from c. 1890

The story of Wagner's impact on Russian theatre in the fifty years after his death runs in close counterpoint with what happened in Germany. In some respects it lagged behind and in others it raced ahead. But just as it had taken a Swiss to make the first radical critique of the stage interpretation of Wagner's works, so it took the Russian revolutionary ferment, untrammelled by German nationalism, to experiment freely with the Appian reform programme and take it through into the age of cinema. Much that remained on the page in western Europe could be given practical trial in Russia. It was a country with its own highly energized quest for cultural and political reform, embracing in 1905 and 1917 upheavals of a magnitude not experienced in Germany until 1933 (though obviously the war of 1914–18 had its own massive impact on both countries). Wagner had a catalytic effect on Russian artistic and intellectual life, as well as becoming embroiled in political ideologies that were very different from their German equivalent.[1]

The composer's ideas fed the intuitions of both the greatest Russian theatre director and the greatest film director of the first half of the twentieth century, while his works provided an interpretative challenge on a scale to suit their gifts. The result was Vsevolod Meyerhold's *Tristan und Isolde* of 1909 at the Mariinsky Theatre in St Petersburg and Sergei Eisenstein's *Die Walküre* of 1940 at the Bolshoi in Moscow. Meyerhold's staging was the most innovative opera production in Russia before the October Revolution and was to have an impact on all forms of theatre. Eisenstein's *Die Walküre* became a landmark in Wagnerian stage history and a far from unimportant footnote in the development of cinema.

Russian Wagner fever began with the arrival in St Petersburg in 1889 of Angelo Neumann's touring company. It was the first time that Russia had seen a complete *Ring*. Four performances were given, with an extra one in Moscow at the command of the Tsar, all conducted by Karl Muck and every one sold out. The impact on the intelligentsia was immense, not least on composers such as Rimsky-Korsakov and Glazunov, on writers including Nikolai Strakhov, who strove unsuccessfully to share his enthusiasm with Tolstoy, and on Diaghilev, Alexander Benois, Nikolai Roerich and other artists of the World of Art (Mir iskusstva) secessionary movement. 'In those years,' wrote Benois, 'we were all … Wagnerians. We demanded from operatic music neither arias, *fiorituri* nor virtuosity, but moods, imagery, dramatic effects and close relationship between music and action.'[2] Diaghilev himself had been a Wagnerian since attending the Neumann *Ring* in 1889, visiting Bayreuth in 1896 and again in 1912 with Stravinsky. He wrote about the first Russian production of *Tristan* in the December 1899 issue of *Mir iskusstva*, the journal of the World of Art group which he and his friends had founded in 1898, and from that time the journal published a considerable quantity of Wagnerian material, including Nietzsche's *Richard Wagner in Bayreuth*, through to its last issue in 1904.

For the moment, the music and the ideas were more potent than what was to be seen in Neumann's production, for this was the very last bow of the travel-worn, battered replica of the 1876 Bayreuth production which had been on the road since 1882. Benois, intellectual mainspring of the World of Art movement, found Wagner's musical representations of nature as impressive of those of the painter Arnold Böcklin and considered that the Neumann scenery totally failed to do justice to them.[3] Benois had his own chance to come in on the design of Russia's first indigenous *Ring*, which opened at the Mariinsky Theatre on 24 November 1900 with *Die Walküre*. It was commissioned by Prince Sergei Volkonsky, who had been Director of the Imperial Theatres (the Alexandrinsky and the Mariinsky) since July 1899.[4] But Diaghilev was not alone in his view that Benois's 'subdued tones of grey, blue and brown' for *Götterdämmerung* (20 January 1903) failed to do justice to the grandeur of that work.[5] Benois himself considered that his production had been too detailed, too realistic, and that he had failed to 'achieve a unity of style'.[6] The cycle was eventually given three complete and sold-out performances in the 1906–7 season, and even three further cycles in the following season failed to satisfy the demand for tickets. Benois's designs for *Götterdämmerung*, executed by the artist and experienced scenic painter Konstantin Korovin, do not suggest any urgent wish to break with the Bayreuth style. 'We see a beautiful spot of northern countryside with a pile of stones … arranged like pieces of furniture,' wrote Diaghilev. 'It is here that great feats are to be accomplished, and gods and heros are to interact.'[7] There was, however, a significant departure in that a great theatre like the Mariinsky had invited designs from a real artist, who was also entrusted with the production as a whole, rather than using the conventional settings it could have provided from its own stock or studios.

Painting the stage: Diaghilev and the World of Art

Once painters of the calibre of those of the World of Art group began to work in the theatre, scenic art would never be the same again. The origin of this new direction may be traced back to 1882, when imperial control of Russia's theatres was revoked. This enabled Savva Mamontov, a railroad millionaire, to set up his 'Moscow Private Russian Opera Company', the first and most important of several such enterprises. Himself a gifted amateur sculptor, singer, dramatist and stage director, in the early 1870s Mamontov had founded an artists' colony at his estate at Abramtsevo near

Moscow which became the seedbed for the modern movement in Russian art.[8] In the winter there were theatrical entertainments at his Moscow house, his cousin Stanislavsky being among the performers. His enthusiasm for painting, music and drama helped to make him his country's most innovative theatre entrepreneur before Diaghilev. The composers he promoted included Dargomyzhsky, Mussorgsky, Borodin and Rimsky-Korsakov, and it was in his private opera company's Solodovnikov Theatre that the young Chaliapin consolidated his early renown.

Mamontov asked his painters to work not only at the easel but also in his theatre. When he inaugurated his opera company in 1883 – the year of Wagner's death – with Rimsky-Korsakov's *Snegurochka* (The Snow Maiden), the artist Victor Vasnetsov found himself painting the sets. Their exuberant fantasy was an immediate hit and set a style which was to have its apotheosis in Leon Bakst's exquisite and fantastical inventions for Diaghilev's Russian Ballet. Other artists who worked for Mamontov in the 1880s included Korovin, Levitan, Golovin and Roerich. Such was their success that from the 1890s the Imperial Theatres began to use them too, a process that was accelerated once Prince Volkonsky, who supported the aims and ethos of the World of Art, became their director in 1899. Golovin worked there regularly from 1902 and, as we shall see, his collaborations with Meyerhold from 1908 were particularly fruitful.

But although the World of Art interested itself in opera, with Benois and Golovin helping to provide sets and costumes for a sumptuous *Boris Godunov* which Diaghilev brought to Paris from the Mariinsky in 1908, it was in ballet that it discovered its true metier. Diaghilev had briefly held a minor post at the Imperial Theatres under Volkonsky but was dismissed after disagreements with his bureaucratic colleagues. From 1906 he redirected his energies into organizing art exhibitions and overwhelming Paris with Russian art, music, opera and ballet. The mainstay of his 1909 season in the French capital was to have been opera at the Théâtre du Châtelet, but when financial difficulties led to its being curtailed to a single complete opera – Rimsky-Korsakov's *Pskovityanka* (The Maid of Pskov) (characteristically billed by Diaghilev as 'Ivan the Terrible') with Chaliapin – Diaghilev expanded the season's ballet content to include four works. These were *Le Festin*, a potpourri, Fokine's *Le Pavillon d'Armide*, *Chopiniana* (later 'Les Sylphides') and *Cléopâtre*, and it was the huge success of these performances that determined the direction of his future. He formed the company that from 1911 was known as the 'Ballets Russes de Serge Diaghilev' and which in a short span conquered Europe and America. Strange, though, that the supreme achievement of Russian performing art in these years was never to be seen in the country of its birth.

Diaghilev brought to the stage a world of exuberant visual fantasy that was a thrilling departure from clichéd nineteenth-century scenery and the perfect setting for the new choreography of Mikhail Fokine. Ballet became the art in which the World of Art ideals were most closely realized. From the raw material of dance-divertissement, Diaghilev conjured a rich dramatic form, many of its ideals indebted to the Wagnerian vision of a totally integrated work of art. 'The perfect ballet,' said Diaghilev, 'can be created only by the very closest fusion of the three elements of dancing, painting and music.'[9] It was 'a medium where every gesture could be synchronized with a musical pattern, where costume and décor and dancer became integrated … a visual whole, a complete illusion, a world of perfect harmony'.[10]

But although the World of Art's guiding spirit effectively abandoned opera, many of the group's artists, particularly Benois, Mikhail Vrubel, Valentin Serov and Nikolai Roerich, persisted in their interest in Wagner. Roerich's designs for *Die Walküre* (uncommissioned project, 1907) were an attempt to invent a colour symbolism to match the music; he imagined the first act 'in black and yellow tones'. In 1912 the private Zimin Theatre in Moscow invited him to design *Tristan*, though the onset of war in 1914 again left the project on the drawing board. In the first act 'the predominant colours were to be red (symbolizing both love and destruction) and yellow (happiness and treachery), whilst in the second act, lilacs and blues were intended to convey alarm and fear'. Many other artists at this time believed in the equivalence of tones and colours, among them the symbolist Viktor Borisov-Musatov, who 'sought to convey "rhythm and equilibrium" and a "melodic fluidity" in his pictures'.[11] This was the path which was soon to lead to the birth of 'non-representational' or 'abstract' painting. Vassily Kandinsky, its central figure, famously described how, at a performance of *Lohengrin* at the Bolshoi in 1896, he had seen 'all my colours in my mind; they stood before my eyes. Wild, almost crazy lines were sketched in front of me. I did not dare use the expression that Wagner had painted "my hour" musically. It became, however, quite clear to me that art in general was far more powerful than I thought, and on the other hand, that painting could develop just such powers as music possesses.'[12]

Stanislavsky empowers the chantacteur

Exciting though these visual developments were, exotic settings, folklorist primary colours, brilliant costumes, new music and new choreography were primarily associated with Diaghilev's vibrant new world of dance. Opera was not capable of so thoroughgoing a transformation in so short a span. The problem of replacing the clichéd nineteenth-century style of performance persisted. This was very much more than a matter of design and lighting. As Appia had seen, at its centre was the credibility of the *chantacteur*, the singing-actor, a point that was obvious enough to the three most influential Russian directors of the first half of the century. Although usually thought of as men of the theatre (Stanislavsky and Meyerhold) and the cinema (Eisenstein), they were to leave a significant impact on opera too.

Konstantin Stanislavsky (1863–1938), famous primarily as the inventor of Method acting, was involved in opera in one way or another throughout his life.[13] In his youth he had studied singing with Fyodor Komissarzhevsky, who was renowned in St Petersburg as an operatic tenor under the name 'Di Pietro' and taught drama and singing from 1883 to 1888 at the Moscow Conservatory.[14] Stanislavsky put on Gounod's *Faust* with other Komissarzhevsky pupils, himself taking the role of Mephistopheles. He also directed a number of operettas, including *The Mikado* (1887), in which he played Nanki-Poo. His voice not being strong enough for a career as an opera singer, however, he had to look elsewhere. In 1886 he had become a director of the Conservatory and, already keenly aware of the problems of acting in opera, tried, unsuccessfully, to persuade it to provide acting classes for its singers. Meanwhile, he turned his attention to the spoken theatre and in 1897, together with the playwright Vladimir Nemirovich-Danchenko, founded the Moscow Art Theatre which was to become famous for its naturalistic productions. There, Stanislavsky worked intensively with his actors and his designer Victor Simov to create a 'truth to life' style which by 1901 had been applied in fifteen productions of works by, inter alios, Ostrovsky, Hauptmann, Ibsen, Tolstoy and, above all, Chekhov.[15] In both its realistic sets and its acting style it was a close equivalent of Antoine's Théâtre Libre in Paris (1887–96) and of the Meiningen players (by whom Stanislavsky was much influenced, particularly on their second Russian tour of 1890). Stanislavsky's passion for naturalism and extraneous realistic detail did, however, bring him into conflict with Chekhov, who often felt that this approach suppressed the emotional subtext.

At the Art Theatre Stanislavsky developed an acting system which laid equal stress on intellectual analysis, vocal and physical technique, and the liberation of the actor's own personality and emotions. 'We must', he said, 'understand the emotions, and have a technique to control them … the creative capacity of an actor and singer is a *science*. You have to study, develop it, as you do other forms of science.'[16] This was fine in theory, but Stanislavsky became aware of the huge difficulties of its application across the whole spectrum of drama. There was, inevitably, a tension between the part of him which saw the importance of tuning in to the 'musical' subtext of any drama (especially, say, in Chekhov)[17] and the part which sought psychological realism. Opera exposed this dilemma particularly acutely. The characters' primary means of expression was singing, scarcely a naturalistic means of communication, and it was therefore nonsensical for them to attempt to act in a naturalistic manner. Some form of stylized movement would need to be developed, one deriving from the music and not the words. The same was true for Maeterlinck and the Symbolists, where the drama lay, as it were, in what was left unsaid between the spoken lines. It was in the hope of resolving this problem that Stanislavsky started the Art Theatre's first Studio in 1902, inviting his pupil, the 28-year-old Vsevolod Meyerhold, who had already established a reputation for stylized acting, to be its artistic director.

Meyerhold and the musicalization of movement: Tristan und Isolde, *St Petersburg 1909*

Born in 1874 of German parents in Penza, a small town 350 miles southeast of Moscow, Meyerhold, too, had had his musical aspirations. He played the violin and had been interested in Wagner since he was eighteen. 'Theatre and music', wrote Boris Pokrovsky, 'existed for him indivisibly, whether he was staging Tchaikovsky, Verhaeren or Ostrovsky. The musicality of his direction was astonishing.… He did not substitute music for theatre, he turned theatre into music.'[18] From the outset of his career as actor and director he was fascinated by every kind of stylization. Although skilled in the realistic portrayal of character, he was impatient of the limits of naturalism and embarked on a lifelong search to use the inner music of dramatic texts to create a new kind of theatre. His aim was to transcend psychological realism by using symbol and stylization, dance and above all musical rhythm. Formative influences included the choreography of Mikhail Fokine and the ritualized movement of Japanese actors that he saw in 1902 in performances by the Otodziro Kawakami company. He was also excited by the World of Art group, some of whose artists he brought into the Art Theatre Studio as designers.

His two most important Studio productions were Hauptmann's comedy *Schluck und Jau* and Maeterlinck's *La Mort de Tintagiles*, for which he had a substantial score composed by Ilya Sats. The difficulties of realizing his new vision quickly became apparent. The artist-designers' atmospheric sketches, so persuasive on paper, did not translate well into stage settings. The actors found it hard to synchronize the delivery of their lines with the musical score. There was tension between the naturalistic instincts of the actors and the anti-realistic demands made on them by the texts and by Meyerhold. At rehearsals things did not work out at all as Stanislavsky had envisaged:

> Stanislavski: 'The audience won't stand for darkness very long on stage, it's wrong psychologically, you need to see the actors' faces!'

> Sudeikin and Sapunov [the artist-designers]: 'But the settings are designed to be seen in half-darkness; they lose all artistic point if you light them!'

> Again silence, broken by the measured delivery of the actors, but this time with the lights full up. But once the stage was lit, it became lifeless, and the harmony between the figures and their setting was destroyed. Stanislavski rose, followed by the rest of the audience. The rehearsal was broken off, the production rejected.[19]

It would be hard to find a more eloquent instance of the unproductive clash between Stanislavsky's actor-centred aesthetic and Meyerhold's view that the actor was but one of many elements to be integrated into a dramatic whole. Nevertheless, Meyerhold learnt much from these and other Studio productions, upon which he reflected in a number of important writings.[20]

His next significant move was the 1906–7 season he spent on tour and in St Petersburg with the company run by Vera Komissarzhevsky, the foremost Russian actress of the day. As a showcase for herself she wanted a production style dedicated to 'suggestions of things and not the things themselves',[21] and hired Meyerhold to help her achieve it. It was at about this time that Meyerhold first read Georg Fuchs's *Die Schaubühne der Zukunft* (The Stage of the Future) and began to put many of its ideas into practice in his work for Komissarzhevsky. For *Hedda Gabler* in November 1906, with Vera in the title role, he tried out Fuchs's 'relief stage' (put into practice by Fuchs at his Künstlertheater in Munich in 1908)[22] by reducing the acting area to a narrow strip about 3.6 metres deep by 10 metres wide at the extreme front of the stage.[23] But the problems of making suggestion, stylization and dramatic integration work were far from solved: Vera's *Hedda* was highly praised but Meyerhold was accused of reducing the other actors to little more than puppets. According to Vera's brother Fyodor, who himself became a notable anti-naturalistic director of both plays and operas in Russia and later in Britain and the United States, Meyerhold put stylized decor first and the actor second, whereas Vera, while sharing the same overall aim, wanted the scenery to be always dependent on the actors: 'instead of opening a marionette theatre of his own, he started, for some strange reason, to fit the real actors of my sister's Theatre into an unrealistic décor, and dressed them so that they appeared to be painted or moulded on the décor. He made them move like marionettes and speak – to use his own expression – as though "their words sounded like drops of water falling in a well".'[24]

Plainly the problems of stylization were a long way from being solved. But the important thing is that in these 'workshop years' from which modern theatre emerged, Meyerhold was drawn to every promising new idea and had, like Reinhardt, the determination to use them in his work. By the end of his twelve months with Komissarzhevsky, Meyerhold 'had staged no fewer than 13 productions of formidable complexity, shaken the staid world of the St Petersburg theatre to its foundations, and set out most of the ground rules for the rest of his creative life'.[25]

From creating a 'musical' experience from text-based drama, Meyerhold's next challenge was to find a production style for opera. The lyric stylization of spoken theatre was one thing, the theatricalization of a genre in which the composer is the dramatist quite another. And there could be no more extreme example of this than *Tristan und Isolde*, an opera that had become a talisman for the Symbolists and was to be the most demanding task of his next appointment. This was in 1908 as actor and stage director at the Imperial Theatres in St Petersburg, the enfant terrible waking up to find himself part of the tsarist establishment overnight. The rationale of the appointment was openly explained by Vladimir Telyakovsky, Director of the Imperial Theatres since 1901: 'I consider that Meyerhold, with his propensity for stirring up people, will be very useful in the State theatres. As regards his excesses, I am confident that he will curb them with us … I am even afraid that his new surroundings may turn him into a conformist.'[26] This was a prescient assessment, for although the gilded splendour of the Imperial Theatres failed to clip Meyerhold's wings, his productions in this ambience were certainly less radical than they might otherwise have been.

Meyerhold had had a foretaste of the problems of *Tristan* when he staged two extracts from it at Terioki in Finland, just over the border from St Petersburg, in July 1907. He was now to put in a year's intensive preparation, for him an exceptional amount of time, for what was to become the most significant production of the opera since that by Mahler and Roller at Vienna in 1903. Already familiar with the ideas of Craig and Fuchs, Meyerhold plunged into close study of Appia's *Die Musik und die Inscenierung*. It confirmed many of the intuitions of his own work over the previous decade, in particular his belief that opera production should follow the music rather than the sung text and verbal instructions, and that scenery, stage architecture, lighting, colours and acoustics must come together to create a unified, living presentation. These ideas are vividly set out in his essay 'Tristan and Isolde', published at the time of his Mariinsky production, which opened on 30 October 1909.[27] For Meyerhold, 'The universal acceptance of Bayreuth as the model for the staging of Wagner has given rise to the custom of giving all his works the external appearance of so-called "historical drama". All those helmets and shields gleaming like samovars, clinking chain-mail, and make-up reminiscent of Shakespearean histories [a reference to performances by the Meiningen players], all that fur on costumes and properties, all those actors and actresses with their arms bared…. And then the tedious, colourless background of historicism – which is completely devoid of mystery and forces the spectator to try to fathom the precise country, century and year of the action – clashes with the orchestra's musical picture which is wrapped in a mist of fantasy. For whatever the stage looks like, Wagner's operas force one to listen to the music.' Thus a critique, in Russian colouring, that is almost precisely equivalent to Appia's. The designer of a myth-based drama, wrote Meyerhold, should aim not 'to reproduce on the stage costumes and interiors copied from museum exhibits' but to create costumes and settings 'which persuade us that at some time in the past everything was like this. … Let the designer and director of *Tristan* take the cue for their stage pictures from the orchestra.' Meyerhold's words, however, were not exactly matched by his actual practice at the Mariinsky.

In his essay Meyerhold had addressed the task of depicting 'the deck of a moving ship in the theatre', concluding that 'All you need is one sail filling the entire stage to build a ship in the spectator's imagination'.[28] But this idea failed to carry through into the designs by Prince Alexander Shervashidze. These were based on French miniatures of courtly life at the time of Gottfried von Straßburg's epic poem and the images were particularly evident in the costumes. This 'concept' is not even hinted at in Meyerhold's contemporaneous essay on the opera. What we do know is that for the first act setting he studied French scholarly literature on medieval shipbuilding and material on the everyday life of sailors on board such a ship, and that Shervashidze produced a recreation of a thirteenth-century ship.

There was a billowing chequered sail, but also a richly curtained pavilion for Isolde at the left-hand side of the stage. To the rear was visible the base of a mast and the tall curved side of the rear deck. In the foreground on the right, above what appear to have been a group of draped coffers, ropes snaked up into the flies.

For the second and third acts Meyerhold was again trying to emulate the effect of the 'relief stage' advocated by Georg Fuchs. The point was to confine the action as far as possible to a strip across the front of the stage where actors and solid scenery could interact realistically, thus avoiding the destruction of illusion inevitable when actors approach and retreat on a deep stage flanked by *trompe l'oeil* scenery on either side. The rear hanging was to be so far behind the actors that the illusion of its painted image (mountain landscape, castle courtyard, etc.) was never compromised. But whereas Fuchs had had his Munich theatre specially built for this purpose, Meyerhold could do no more at the Mariinsky than mask the proscenium with hangings that at least spoke the same visual language as the sets. It was caparisoned on either side and across the top with hangings of a medieval lozenge pattern, while the front strip of the stage was painted with the same design. These hangings remained throughout the three acts, and in each the realistic, practicable scenery concentrated the action in the same, forward 'relief' plane.

Meyerhold refers to Wagner's stipulation of a 'Blumenbank' (flowery bank) in the second act, pointing out that this would be visually tautologous as 'the garden with the rustling of leaves blending with the sound of the horns is miraculously evoked by the orchestra. The mere contemplation of real foliage on the stage would be as flagrantly tasteless as illustrating Edgar Allan Poe.' Instead, Shervashidze provided the impressively solid-looking base of a portcullised castle entrance and tower, but with a bridge over a moat, a few sculpted tree trunks and branches, suggesting the edge of a dark forest at night, and an elevated track with rocky substratum crossing the stage front from right to left. More architectural detail than Appia would have sanctioned, but in layout close to his scheme.

'In the third act,' says Meyerhold, 'Wagner calls for a stage crammed with lofty battlements, a parapet with a central watchtower, castle gates in the background and a spreading linden tree.' Instead, Meyerhold asked Shervashidze for 'a cheerless expanse of horizon and the bare desolate cliffs of Brittany'.[29] Again, this was not exactly what emerged, but the setting certainly concentrated on the essentials. The production photograph shows at left a rocky ledge for Tristan, with weathered crags piled up behind, and at right a lowered drawbridge at the base of a castle tower. No sheltered courtyard but an exposed, extramural rocky eminence, sounding an echo of the ordeal of Prometheus. At the rear the 'cheerless expanse of horizon' is visible painted on a backcloth but, strangely, so far as one can tell from the photograph, looking more like a gently rolling landscape than a view over the sea. The 'relief stage'

'All you need is one sail', wrote the Russian director Vsevolod Meyerhold of the first act (*above*) of *Tristan und Isolde*, but for his St Petersburg staging of 1909 his designer left no detail of a medieval ship to the imagination. A notable feature of the settings for all three acts was the concentration of the action at the front of the stage. This was not for acoustic reasons but to avoid singers moving too far upstage and thus destroying the illusory world of *trompe l'oeil* scenery on a deep stage.

idea is again manifest in that the available acting area is little more than a narrow transverse strip between Tristan's stony bed and the castle drawbridge at right.

The principal distinguishing visual features were the omnipresent, gaily patterned proscenium hangings, suggesting that the opera was being enacted in a medieval tent or jousting pavilion (chiming with Meyerhold's love of circus and festive ambience), the consistent use of palpably solid scenery, and the containing of the action largely within the forward, 'relief' section of the stage. The different terraced, rocky levels, evident in Acts II and III, are eloquent of Meyerhold's protest against the 'flat surface of the stage' and his wish that it should be moulded 'as a sculptor moulds his clay'. Struck by Wagner's idea of the stage as a 'pedestal' for the living 'sculpture' of the action, Meyerhold wanted everything to serve 'as a pedestal for the actor, everything on which he leans, everything he touches, must be constructed sculpturally, with the diffuseness of painting relegated to the background'.[30]

Many attacked him for going back on everything he had previously stood for: 'The whole stage was given up to the ship on which Isolde travelled. And the ship was portrayed in every detail: there were barrels and ropes, a deck-cabin for the captain and folding stools for the crew, carpets, bales of fabric and other goods.... And the ship was fully manned. A triumph of naturalism, and this from Meyerhold who had long since been a fugitive from this style.'[31]

Alexander Benois, who followed Meyerhold's work with a discerning eye, also disapproved of the 'historical style' of the production, particularly in the light of the pains Meyerhold had been to in his *Tristan* essay to argue that drama based on myth rather than history required a non-realistic style. The naturalism of the production, as in that of Bayreuth, obscured the opera's symbolism. He had expected to see a symbolic representation of a ship, not the actual thing. Upset by this critique, Meyerhold retorted that 'the object does not exclude the symbol' and that a naturalistic ambience was a foil for the romantic inwardness of Wagner's musical vision, and for his use of stylized acting to present this.[32]

This argument fails to square with the Appian thrust of Meyerhold's essay on the opera. It comes across as special pleading on behalf of the naturalism that to some extent was imposed on him in his work for an imperial stage. Looking back some years later he said that all his productions for the Imperial Theatres had been compromises of one kind or another.[33] It seems probable that Meyerhold had had to make do with a designer who would not have been his first choice, Shervashidze doubtless being insisted on by the theatre as a safeguard against anything excessively modern. That criterion would also have been satisfied by the much more imaginative Alexander Golovin who designed all Meyerhold's other productions for the Imperial Theatres, beginning with Knut Hamsun's *At the Gates of the Kingdom* in 1908. Golovin had been a leading member of the World of Art group since 1898, and had designed *Boris Godunov* for Diaghilev's 1908 Paris season, Stravinsky's *Firebird* ballet in 1910, and a great many other important productions of the period. He had worked regularly at the Imperial Theatres since 1902.[34]

What is hardest to imagine is what was doubtless the heart of the production, namely Meyerhold's work with the singers. He was crystal clear in what he wanted.

Naturalistic acting in opera was bound to be wrong because 'people behaving in a lifelike manner on the stage and then suddenly breaking into song is bound to seem absurd'. Stylization was therefore 'the very basis of operatic art'. The actor's movements had always to be derived from the music. He must strive for 'complete control over his body'. Given that dance was 'the source of gesture in the music drama, it followed that the operatic artist should learn gesture not from the actor of the conventional theatre but from the ballet-master',[35] and here Meyerhold would have had Fokine in mind. As an actor Meyerhold was famed for his skill in movement and in February 1910 danced the role of Pierrot, alongside Nijinsky's Florestan and Karsavina's Columbine, in Fokine's Schumann-ballet *Carnaval* at a St Petersburg ball.[36] All of this is entirely in tune with Appia and Dalcroze as well as being an expression of Meyerhold's own belief in the fundamental importance of rhythm and dance. Physicality was a constant theme in all his work.[37]

Meyerhold pointed with admiration to Chaliapin as a model for what he had in mind. The renowned acting of the great bass had, he argued, been completely misunderstood as 'lifelike' because the impact of Meiningen and Stanislavsky naturalism had been so strong 'that in its radiance' the art of Chaliapin appeared to be its operatic equivalent. It had, however, to be seen 'not in the light of the Moscow Art Theatre, whose actors perform according to the laws of *mimesis*, but in the light of omnipotent rhythm'. Chaliapin was 'one of the few artists on the operatic stage who follows the composer's musical notation precisely, and imposes on his movements a design, a physical design which is always in harmony with the musical design of the score'. He knew how to balance 'on the ridge of the roof without slipping either to the side of naturalism or to the side of the operatic style which we inherited from the Italians of the sixteenth century'. As an example Meyerhold cites Chaliapin in the scene of the Witches' Sabbath on the Brocken in Boito's *Mefistofele*: 'here, not only the movements and gestures of Mephistopheles as he leads the ritual dance are rhythmical – even the movements of tense, petrified *immobility* during the frenzy convey the rhythm which the orchestra is beating out'.[38] Meyerhold's conclusion is that the totally integrated operatic performance which Wagner envisaged could not be achieved without the emergence of a new breed of singing-actor in the mould of Chaliapin, and that that called for an intensive choreographic strand in singers' training. When we recall the athletics of the composer's own work with his singers, his constant demand for a special training school, there was nothing so very new in this part of Meyerhold's programme.

What was true enough was that the singers at the Mariinsky were poorly equipped to respond to the demands Meyerhold made upon them for Chaliapin-like acting. At best he may have succeeded in curbing their routine semaphore. According to an amused friend of the director, 'He complained about the singers' usual gestures and did an imitation of them which was killingly funny.... He ordered sets to be made that were so complicated, unwieldy and dangerous for the slightest move that the unfortunate singers had to stand motionless like pedestals for fear of breaking a leg. The actors were very angry about this, but the producer rubbed his hands with delight, for he had achieved the production he wanted.'[39]

The costumes for Tristan and for Isolde in Meyerhold's production were modelled on French miniatures from the thirteenth century. Meyerhold dreamt of singing-actors like Chaliapin whose every movement was linked to the music. But his ruthless censorship of his singers' penchant for stock operatic gestures resulted only in an uncomfortably constrained style of acting.

The production's departure from the traditional Mariinsky style provoked complaints that Wagner's instructions had not been literally followed, that the thirteenth-century 'historical setting was arbitrary', and that 'the static acting did not correspond to the passion of the music'.[40] That there was a marked discrepancy between the historical and naturalistic visual feel of the production and Meyerhold's direction of the singers is apparent from an unenthusiastic diary note about the premiere by the Mariinsky's director, Vladimir Telyakovsky: 'The opera has gone very well. The orchestra and the singers transcended all the difficulties of the staging – the one interfering factor is the staging itself. Meyerhold and Prince Shervashidze are guilty here. All the main scenes of Acts 2 and 3 take place by a rock, and this is very dull. Tristan and Isolde writhe like worms by the rocks and frequently take on unnatural poses.'[41]

Reading this and other contemporary accounts at face value *and* between the lines, it is plain how disconcerting it was for Russian singers to perform without stock histrionics and on any other than a level stage in front of painted cloths. It was certainly *never* Meyerhold's aim to immobilize his performers, but it is understandable that some should have thought that to be the reason for his restraining gratuitous movement. Meyerhold's own philosophy was that 'the dramatic content is born out of the feelings of normal people, and that there are no abrupt movements or rapid crossings from one part of the stage to another. The actors are externally calm, and all their movements are gentle and lyrical'.[42]

When the production was revived in January 1910 the music director was the Bayreuth protégé Felix Mottl, who had conducted the first performance of *Tristan* at the Festspielhaus. Concerned that he should not take fright at the unconventional settings, the management arranged that his first stage rehearsal should take place in front of the scenery for the first act of *Aida*, which was on stage in preparation for that night's performance. But when Mottl was eventually allowed to see the *Tristan* scenery he could not have been more enthusiastic. 'The *Tristan* staging is unbelievable!' he wrote in his diary, enigmatically going on to add, 'One might well be in Asia!'[43]

Something of a paradox remains in that the Meyerhold who had always taken Wagnerian music drama as a model for stylized theatre was very much feeling his way when faced with the composer's own demands. He had brought rhythm and musicality to movement in the traditional theatre, but on the opera stage had settled for 'statuesque poses and sculpted groupings (each of which was designed to convey a whole musical phrase)' rather than the far more dynamic approach to movement argued for in his writings.[44] That was something that could only emerge when acting and movement became an essential part of the singer's training.

An important beginning was made in 1918 when, after the Revolution, the Bolshoi invited Stanislavsky to found an Opera Studio. The exercises he developed there for the singers (influenced in part by the work of Jaques-Dalcroze, who had given eurhythmic demonstrations at the Art Theatre in 1912) were to become an important part of his Method acting. The Studio's other purposes were research into the basis of all forms of lyric drama, and the reinvigoration of opera staging. This was manifest in Stanislavsky's many productions at the Studio, including *Werther* (1921) and *Eugene Onegin* (1922). In 1926 the Studio was detached from the Bolshoi and rechristened the Stanislavsky Opera Theatre Studio. Stanislavsky continued to work there right through to his death in 1938: the very last production he planned was a *Rigoletto* which was rehearsed and posthumously brought to the stage by Meyerhold in 1939.

Rienzi *as revolutionary agitprop*

With the advent of the Russian Revolution in October 1917, the relationship of the audience to the work performed on the stage became immensely important, though this was no more or less than Wagner had always believed. From 1911 the thrust of Meyerhold's work had been to revitalize theatre by returning to its roots in *popular*, not courtly or bourgeois, entertainment. He had found inspiration in street theatre, fairground and circus, in masks, mime, commedia dell'arte and 'cabotinage' (the improvisational skills of strolling players). His productions were anti-literary and dedicated to movement, music and popular entertainment, seen on its grandest scale in his production of Lermontov's *Masquerade* at the Alexandrinsky Theatre with a cast of over two hundred. It opened on 25 February 1917, the very day that, no more than a few miles away, the tsarist police confronted starving workers and fired the shots that precipitated the Revolution. Meyerhold's staging of Lermontov's tragedy, which had been six years in the making, was to be given over five hundred times after the Revolution. Its concern with corruption beneath a glittering façade could not have been more timely. 'It echoed,' wrote Meyerhold's Russian biographer Rudnitsky, 'like a grim requiem for the empire, like the stern, solemn, tragic, fatal funeral rites of the world which was perishing in those very days.'[45] Much of Meyerhold's work in these years should be seen as subversive of courtly and bourgeois values, and at least in part as an escape from the mounting social pressures that were to erupt in the Revolution, as can also be seen in those of his theatrical interpretations which courted the exotic, the supernatural, the mystical. Late in 1917 Meyerhold enthusiastically threw in his lot with the Bolsheviks and for a brief period in 1920–1 was head of the Theatre Department for the entire Soviet Republic.

The impact of Wagner and attitudes towards his work underwent a sea-change. The fin-de-siècle Russian interest in him as a mystical, spiritual, transcendent composer transmuted between 1905 and the early 1920s into a view of him – in both theory and theatrical interpretation – that passed over his reactionary side, intellectuals and politicians idealizing him as an opponent of capitalism and a model social revolutionary.[46] Recognizing that the shock of the 1905 Revolution had revealed the immensity 'of the gulf between the intelligentsia and the rest of the population', the symbolist writer Vyacheslav Ivanov looked to a Wagner-inspired neo-Greek theatrical revival as 'a uniting force'.[47] Writing in 1919, Ivanov saw Wagner as an inspiration for post-revolutionary synthetic art, meaning open-air performances of works presenting 'heroic deeds, myth, fairytale and legend'. Only the year before, the Bolshoi had abandoned a planned production of *Parsifal* by Fyodor Komissarzhevsky (who had emigrated) because no one was left to champion a work so religious in tone and so deficient in 'positive heroism'. No such objections were made against *Rheingold*, *Tannhäuser* and *Walküre*, all of which went ahead in the 1918–19 season.

By 1924 the 'austere and majestic form of the music drama' could be described, in a typical article, as the antithesis of bourgeois taste for 'the old operatic forms designed for amusement'.[48] The following year a 'Society of Wagnerian Art' was formed to take small-scale modern-dress productions to the masses. Two pianos stood in for the orchestra, and coloured lantern-slide projections for scenery.

Inevitably, the new political imperative had its effect on production style. Grandiose representational scenery as a symbol of the taste of the ruling elite was an obvious enough target. Theatrical artifice and imperial hegemony were illusions ripe to shatter. Between 1915 and 1918 Vladimir Tatlin, founder of Russian constructivism (which championed geometric construction, form and function against every painterly aesthetic), made designs for *Der fliegende Holländer* which, although unrealized on account of the war, were a totally new departure. Working extensively in theatre design, he was the first 'to break up the surface of the stage, building several planes tilted at different angles and intersecting each other at different levels, which opened up new and promising possibilities for the actors' dynamic and plastic movement'.[49] Tatlin's background gave him special authority as designer of this particular opera. He had been in the navy and loved sketching masts, sails and rigging. It was therefore no surprise that his design should feature 'several large masts which he intended members of the cast to climb up and down during performances, in order to exploit the full potential of both the vertical as well as horizontal space of the stage'.[50] This concept was not entirely wasted, for it became transmuted into the ascendant spiralling curves, raked ladder and net-like sails of his famous models (exhibited 1920) for a Monument to the Third International.[51] This was to have been a soaring building in glass and iron, 'dynamic, both in its outward form and inner activity'.[52] Corkscrewing up into the skies at an alarming angle to the vertical, it was to have been twice as high as the Empire State Building, thereby trumping capitalism's proudest symbol. Could this be the only recorded instance of a Wagnerian stage design ending up as a scheme for a proletarian Valhalla?

If this dream proved totally impracticable, the iconoclastic aesthetic of constructivism left its mark on the operatic stage. This was a matter not just of abstracting scenic locale into its structural and symbolic components, but of insisting that the stage picture should always be fluid, its elements forming and re-forming the stage space. Where Appia had required that the lighting should create a dynamic sense of stage space, the constructivists saw that there was no reason why the components of the set should not themselves be in a state of flux. That was what they required of art in general, with Naum Gabo's 'kinetic models' – a precursor of futuristic stage design at Berlin's Kroll Opera – and Alexander Rodchenko's mobiles dating from 1920.

It was therefore no surprise that the first new Wagner production after the Revolution, opening the second Soviet operatic season in Moscow on 5 September 1918, should have been *Lohengrin* at the former Zimin Theatre (renamed 'Theatre of the Council of Working Deputies'), with abstract settings by Ivan Fedotov. The stage was filled with cubes and cones, while Fyodor Komissarzhevsky's production arranged the chorus as static groups, creating 'a moving harmony of colours'. His characteristic aim, however, was spiritualization, with Lohengrin as a 'mystical knight' rather than a medieval warrior.[53]

But through the early Bolshevik years pressure mounted to use art to mythicize, and therefore validate, political events and social aspirations. It was for this reason that Meyerhold chose *Rienzi* for the third production of his Soviet flagship, the RSFSR Theatre No.1 (formerly the Free Theatre Company), bending Wagner's work shamelessly to the ideological needs of the moment. It was to be produced as militant agitprop, the characters sharply politicized and two new roles and some extra mime scenes added. Meyerhold's idea was that he would abolish 'scenery, costumes, and all other illusionary props which would be reminiscent of the pre-revolutionary bourgeois theatre that had entertained the ruling classes'.[54] Severely abstract designs were prepared by Georgy Yakulov. But this was a bridge too far for the Party. It was caught in the dilemma of needing to disassociate itself from bourgeois culture while being aware that the proletariat had no appetite for constructivist abstraction and craved only the discredited comforts of the old ruling class. On this occasion the problem was solved by giving Meyerhold's version of *Rienzi* in a concert performance at the Conservatory on 8 July 1921. Two years later, however (3 April 1923), Yakulov's designs were realized in a production by I. Prostorov at the former Zimin Theatre, home in 1922–4 of the most radical opera stagings in Moscow. The ideological problem of Acts IV and V (depicting Rienzi's downfall) was solved by cutting them. The designs did not paint pictures but created an arena-like space for action and crowd movement on a lavish scale, with stylized buildings, battlements and balconies rising steeply up behind it.[55] The extensive ballet-pantomime was choreographed by Inna Chernetskaya, a pupil of Isadora Duncan. A British visitor, Huntly Carter, found the production 'more left-wing than the home of classic opera had ever known … in the form of circus ideas with which the Proletkul't [proletarian] theatre had definitely associated itself. The scenery … was shaped like a circus arena, with steps at all angles and all levels, with suggestions of a trapeze and hoops and the rest of the objects and agents of circus representation'.[56] Thus another instance of the use of a populist entertainment form as an escape from bourgeois culture.

Later that same year, the sixth anniversary of the Revolution was marked by a new production of the same opera by the radical director Nikolai Petrov and designer

After the Revolution of 1917 Meyerhold and the Bolsheviks set up Wagner as a cornerstone of proletarian ideology. In 1921 Meyerhold wanted to produce *Rienzi* as militant agitprop. But the proletariat had no appetite for the aggressively anti-bourgeois designs favoured by Meyerhold and his designer Georgy Yakulov. As can be seen from this stage model, by the time their conception reached the stage at the former Zimin Theatre (1923), Yakulov had had to retreat from the furthest shores of abstraction.

The idea of 'theatre as circus' was much in vogue, and so Yakulov created a single arena, with sharply stylized balconies and buildings surrounding it.

Vladimir Shchuko. It featured the first constructivist sets to be seen in the former Mariinsky Theatre, which from December 1917 was called the 'State Academic Theatre of Opera and Ballet'.[57] But the production, premiered on 7 November 1923, was not considered a success and was given only five times. Doubtless it was too uncompromising for so grand a theatre.

The Bolshoi in Moscow, the new capital, cultivated a stronger commitment to innovation, although in the new *Lohengrin* produced by Vladimir Lossky with designs by Fyodor Fyodorovsky, which opened in March 1923, the pill of a stylized, non-representational setting was once again sweetened by spectacle on a monumental scale. A cast of some three hundred embodied the utopian optimism of the early revolutionary years. The stage rose in levels towards the back and was framed by wedge-like planes, geometric screens and rudimentary pillars and arches. Light and colour played a major role in the production's view of the work as a struggle between good and evil. As Rosamund Bartlett describes, white, silver and gold symbolized 'the qualities of goodness, innocence and purity associated with Lohengrin and Elsa', while black and dark gold colours for Telramund and Ortrud represented 'the powers of darkness'. Costumes were highly stylized, 'the futuristic-looking, spiky outfits with their elaborate head-dresses surely the most unconventional ever designed for the opera at that time'. Lossky and Fyodorovsky sought 'to create a symphony of light and colour which could merge with the symphony of sound in Wagner's score'. During the prelude the front-curtain was flooded 'with a pure silver-coloured light during the motif of the Swan-Knight ... "drowning out" the knights of darkness, but became suddenly ablaze with shades of crimson and violet at the appearance in the score of the motif of the evil Telramund, causing the image of Elsa to grow dim'.[58] The conductor, Nikolai Golovanov, was not alone in complaining that the dazzling impression detracted from Wagner's score. Huntly Carter considered it 'the most picturesque, even gorgeous [production] from the realistic-expressionist point of view that I had seen. ... I marvelled at its richness of effect and wondered how a nation that had gone through, and was still going through such unparalleled vicissitudes, could provide such a banquet of costume and colour, and how the performers working under extreme difficulties of shortage of food, inadequate housing, lack of proper everyday clothing and so on, could still give of their very best. I was struck by the reverent enthusiasm of the audience of common folk that completely filled the immense auditorium'.[59]

Some, however, regretted that the bright colours and geometric bravura of such productions compromised 'the purity of the first austere and functional Constructivist stagings'.[60] German visitors had seen nothing like it in their own country and the production became so popular that it remained in the Bolshoi repertory until the season of 1935–6.

Other Wagnerian operas were less easy to accommodate to political ideology. In 1923 the head of the state repertoire commission (Glavrepertkom) voiced his concern lest the Bolshoi, the leading Soviet theatre, should be seen to be still 'celebrating a tsar every night'. The commissars were, however, happy to advocate performances of the overtly revolutionary *Rienzi* and the *Ring*, and of the populist *Die Meister-*

singer. The guidelines were that the *Ring* was to be produced as an embodiment of Wagner's essay *Art and Revolution* and of 'the revolutionary aspirations of its time', *Die Meistersinger* as a satire of 'stagnant formalism' and as 'propaganda for living, independent art'.[61]

All works performed at this time underwent a degree of adjustment, often with new scenarios and words fitted to old scores. The 'State Academic Theatre' rechristened *Rienzi* as 'Babeuf', its hero now a leader of the French Revolution, while Meyerbeer's *Le Prophète* became the 'Paris Commune' and *Les Huguenots* 'The Decembrists'. For the same theatre's celebration in 1926 of the ninth anniversary of the Revolution, *Die Meistersinger* was the obvious choice because of 'the "agitational" scenes which occur in the work "precisely at those moments when the people are brought on to the stage and Wagner puts forward his ideas" '. The producer, Viktor Rappaport, worked hard to play down Walther's aristocratic origins, but the staging was not accounted a success. Nor was the portrayal of Walther at the Maly Opera in Leningrad in 1932 'as a sea-faring captain representing the newly emerging class of the bourgeoisie [who] defeats the old feudal structure of the Meistersinger, but is ultimately discredited by his materialist acquisitiveness'.[62]

Up to the advent of Stalin and his instigation in 1928 of his own style of 'cultural revolution' (which denounced anything avant-garde as an affront to the understanding of the common man), Wagnerian opera was at the centre of experimental design and production, partly, as we have seen, for its own sake – inspired by the needs of the works themselves and of artists to interpret them in their own way – and partly because this was a way of sidestepping ideological pressure. There can be no question that every kind of abstraction, stylization and constructivism flourished precisely because they were the antithesis of nineteenth-century bourgeois art. Sooner or later these styles, for all that they suited the ideals of intellectuals, were bound to collide with the proletarian taste to which they were supposed to appeal. And sooner or later the limits beyond which a work could not be adjusted for propaganda purposes without traducing its substance were bound to be reached and – as we have seen – clearly were.

The political imperative liked to have the crowd at the centre of the action, and this coincided with the Meyerhold-inspired desire of most producers to animate the chorus, to make the most of movement and of lighting as an active element. In all this the loser was often the solo singer, futuristically costumed, left to stand and deliver – on one occasion placed quite literally on a pedestal, as had been prescribed by Meyerhold. This was in the Bolshoi *Lohengrin* of 1923 where, 'positioned in the centre of the stage was a rectangular platform on which the soloists stood to perform their solos, like statues on pedestals'. Weighed down in their fantastical space-age armour, this was perhaps because they had no choice. (Ortrud protested at the 20-kilogramme weight of her Act I costume. The chorus's hefty shields and helmets led to their petitioning – successfully – to have the march at the start of the third scene of Act III cut.)[63]

Schooling for soloists in movement and characterization was plainly still lacking, and there were but few who felt the need for it. Even fewer would have dreamed that

As this costume model by Fyodor Fyodorovsky for the swan knight in *Lohengrin* at the Bolshoi in 1923 shows, wildly futuristic stage design flourished under the Bolsheviks. In Vladimir Lossky's production, which remained in the repertory until 1935/36, the pill of experimentalism was sweetened by lavish spectacle. The fantastical costumes effectively immobilized the soloists. They were required to sing from a rectangular platform at the centre of the stage.

the fledgling art of cinema might in any way help to resolve the manifold social, aesthetic and cultural problems of the performance of opera in a proletarian context.

Sergei Eisenstein and the myth of the moment: Die Walküre, *Moscow 1940*

With Stalin's arrival in 1928, the Wagnerian oeuvre as a whole presented so many ideological problems that its performance became narrowed to those few works that could be presented within the constraints of what was politically permissible. Censorship hardened to the point where the only safe work was *Die Meistersinger*, and, as we have seen in relation to the Leningrad performances of 1932, the 'problem' of Walther's noble lineage could be 'solved' by casting him as a seafaring captain from the ranks of the emergent bourgeoisie. The fiftieth anniversary of Wagner's death was marked in 1933 by the former Mariinsky Theatre with a production of *Das Rheingold* slanted to affirm the necessary destruction of capitalism, but Hitler's seizure of power in Germany effectively banished the composer from the Russian stage. Soviet sensibility had long felt itself threatened by the upsurge of German nationalism. Hitler's espousal of Wagner inevitably accelerated the composer's disappearance from the repertory. Spasmodic attempts to rehabilitate him, as by the musicologist Dmitry Gachev in 1937, met with little success.[64]

The tide was eventually turned by the signature in August 1939 of the German-Soviet Non-Aggression Pact, with the immediate result that Sergei Eisenstein

(1898–1948), the greatest pioneer of Soviet cinema, was commissioned to produce *Die Walküre* at the Bolshoi 'in the mutual interests of German and Russian cultures'.[65] This was to be the first production of this opera there since 1925. Eisenstein's staging was premiered in October 1940, and the story behind it remains extraordinary. In November 1938 Eisenstein had completed his vigorously anti-German epic *Alexander Nevsky*, depicting Russian resistance to Teutonic invasion in the thirteenth century. Eisenstein once called the film 'an anti-fascist engine'.[66] He was now suddenly asked to tackle part of the *Ring*, a work that had been ostracized as the epitome of German nationalism. It is scarcely any wonder that Eisenstein should have chosen to concentrate on the opera's mythic substance. Eisenstein's only excursion into opera is the first important instance of cross-fertilization between the art of the stage and the art of the screen. (He later accepted, though was prevented by illness from fulfilling, Prokofiev's invitation to stage the first performance of his opera *War and Peace*.) All this in a milieu in which Wagner's art and ideology had by now undergone protracted trial by the two most seismic social and political revolutions of the twentieth century.

The continuity of Eisenstein's work with that of Meyerhold is striking. There is a terrible pathos in that Eisenstein, while aware of Meyerhold's arrest and imprisonment in June 1939, would in all probability not have known that he had been shot in a Moscow prison on 2 February 1940, only two months before the rehearsals for *Die Walküre* began. It was Eisenstein to whom Meyerhold had entrusted his papers after the liquidation of his theatre in January 1938, and it was thanks to Eisenstein's hiding them in the walls of his dacha that these crucial documents of twentieth-century theatre history have survived.[67] Their friendship went back to the early Bolshevik years when, from 1921, Eisenstein had been Meyerhold's outstanding pupil at the State Higher Theatre Workshops in Moscow. He had shared Meyerhold's enthusiasm for rejuvenating and broadening the reach of theatre by an infusion of overtly populist entertainment forms. At the Moscow Proletkul't Theatre (where he had become head of design in October 1920) he had already made extensive use of circus techniques for *The Mexican* (adapted from Jack London) in 1921, and in 1923 was to adapt Ostrovsky's *Enough Simplicity in Every Wise Man* for the same theatre as a circus-style revue performed in an arena with the actors as acrobats and clowns. Eisenstein was Meyerhold's assistant in his Theatre Workshops production of Tarelkin's *Death* (1922), a knockabout satire on tsarist police methods, later taking over the direction of Meyerhold's projected film of John Reed's *Ten Days That Shook the World*, which he brought out in 1928, now entitled *October*. (Meyerhold actively involved himself in film only for a brief period, 1915–16, when he directed and played Lord Henry Wotton in *The Picture of Dorian Gray*. Some of his theatre techniques – such as using blackout and selective lighting of small stage areas for rapid cuts between scenes – were proto-cinematic but not pursued by him in that medium.) 'All Eisenstein's work,' wrote Meyerhold in 1936, 'had its origins in the laboratory where we once worked together as teacher and pupil.'[68]

Eisenstein was familiar with Meyerhold's essay on *Tristan*, and the piece he wrote while preparing his *Walküre* production, 'The Embodiment of Myth', is its counterpart and, in the view of Rosamund Bartlett, a tacit homage to his teacher.[69] In his essay Eisenstein carefully distinguishes the 'unreality and inaction' of *Tristan* from the movement and physicality he considered essential in any staging of the *Ring*, and his production of *Die Walküre* reflected that idea. Just as Meyerhold had done in the mainstream of his stagings (*Tristan* being the exception) and as he himself had done in his film work, Eisenstein sought to choreograph movement and gesture so that they would 'embody the content and unity of the drama'.[70] This, as we shall see, extended at key moments to having elements of the scenery move in sympathy with the music and action. Like Appia and Meyerhold, he wanted his production to spring from the score, but he departed from them in seeking not musical stylization or abstraction of the visual elements but a fully worked out visualization of a Nibelung world. Here he took up the challenge that Wagner himself had laid down but could not meet, namely of finding a credible milieu and costuming for a world of myth, unanchored in historical reality. His scenery, designed from Eisenstein's own sketches by Pyotr Vilyams, was animate, a co-actor in the drama. It was intended to suggest the mind-set of primitive peoples who 'saw the participation of the forces of nature in all their behaviour and actions'.[71] Eisenstein's view was that 'traditional' Bayreuth-style productions reflected only nineteenth-century bourgeois man's alienation from nature. They did not embody the spirit of myth and prehistory which he discerned in Wagner's music. For him the *Ring* evoked a prelapsarian state when man and nature were indivisible – though plainly this idea strangely ignores the tussle between man and nature that is evident throughout the tetralogy.

Eisenstein was not over-discerning in his understanding of the opera. He was certainly totally mistaken when, in his preliminary notes, drafted in December 1939, he concluded that *Die Walküre* is 'a historical work, and the main conflict is the shift (crossing over) from one historical period to another'.[72] As Carl Dahlhaus and John Deathridge have shown, the opera is a story of two quite distinct if interlocking myths. 'Dramatically,' writes Dahlhaus, 'there is no real connection between the divine myth [the god Wotan compelled to will his own destruction] and the heroic drama [of the Wälsung twins], although they are linked in theory. ... Siegmund's finding of the sword left for him by Wotan is as peripheral to the Wälsung drama as it is central and decisive to the future development of the dilemma in which Wotan finds himself in consequence of his "great idea".'[73]

Be that as it may, Eisenstein wanted to show a world in which man, animals and the whole of nature were inextricably intertwined. He would even have liked to ensnare the audience physically in this world. His idea was that the branches of the immense spreading ash tree, which dominated not only Hunding's hut but the entire stage, should snake out into the auditorium, thereby welding audience and performers as co-celebrants of a primitive ritual drama. But this proved no more practicable than his wish to use loudspeakers to relay the music of the Ride of the Valkyries throughout the auditorium. For Eisenstein, the great tree was the tree of life which, by the end of the first act, had grown into a 'pantheistic emblem of world creation'. The affinity of man and beast was manifest in the crossbreeds who were the 'rams' drawing Fricka's chariot and who mutely pleaded with her for Siegmund's life. Eisenstein described them as a 'chorus' of figures that are 'half-sheep, half-men, not quite domesticated animals, not quite people, who have betrayed their own passions and have voluntarily put on the yoke of the tamed instead'. At the end of Act II (also presided over by the omnipresent tree) the upstage scenery, as Rosamund Bartlett recounts, had its own cue for action:

> Two huge cliffs bathed in a reddish-orange light dominate the stage, at a height level with the upper circle. These are the cliffs on which Siegmund and Hunding do battle, and they are made to rise and fall during the fight in correlation with moments of greatest intensity in the music. Then when Siegmund is killed, the huge rock collapses with him as if lowering his body to the ground, leaving a giant crater. Even the sky enters into the fray when, with a crack of lightning, Wotan, in his alignment with the elements of air, enters the battle on a storm cloud.[74]

In all this, Eisenstein was but activating the pervasive role which the composer had already assigned to nature in his drama. In Wagner's theatre, nature was heard in the orchestra but only evoked in a painterly fashion on stage. In Eisenstein's theatre, nature has joined the cast. Tall trees flanking the stage at the end of Act III bowed down to the ground and rose up again 'as Brünnhilde was carried towards Valhalla on her rocky ledge, as if disappearing into thin air'.[75] This was also a cinematically illustrative presentation of the work's mythopoeic world, leaving little to the imagination. Nothing was referred to in music or text that Eisenstein did not try to show visually – another thwarted scheme was to use film for the depiction of Siegmund's narration in Act I. He was, however, able to use a mime group to enact the events of Sieglinde's Act I narration, 'Der Männer Sippe', during which Wotan emerged on cue from the heart of the tree and hid among various other figures in its teeming upper branches. There was, said Eisenstein, 'something Dantesque! in this tree full of characters!'[76]

Hunding was also among those escorted by pantomimic choruses. In Eisenstein's words,

> many of the characters are at certain moments enfolded, as it were, by choruses appropriate to them, from which they seem indivisible, from which they seem still inseparable, which vibrate together with them with one emotion, with one and the same feeling. Thus Hunding has been conceived as the representative of the crudest, atavistic stage of the tribe, closer to the flock, the herd, or the pack. That is why he appears surrounded by the myriapod, shaggy body of his pack, a body which when falling to the ground appears to be a pack of hounds, and which on rising to its feet appears to be Hunding's entourage – kinsfolk, armour-bearers, servants.[77]

The eight Valkyries served as Wotan's chorus, and during the Ride they were augmented by a further flight of warrior-maidens on papier-mâché steeds. To some these seemed risibly reminiscent of the fairground, but this was an idea developed with great flair more than forty years later by the Swiss director François Rochaix in his Seattle *Ring* of 1985–7. The real Valkyries and Wotan also took to the air, but on wires.

Light was an active ingredient in this syncretistic staging. 'The whole resolution of the last act,' said Eisenstein, 'was dedicated to the search for combining elements of Wagner's score with a changing light display on the stage.' He described 'that enjoyment of pathos with which the blue flame swelled to the sound of the "Magic Fire" music in the last act, sometimes echoing it, then colliding with it, then singling it out, then drawing it in, absorbing the red, the red suppressing the blue and both rising out of the crimson ocean of fire into which the whole bronze wall of the backdrop turns ... after first having turned its original silver into celestial azure – at the moment of the culminating scene of Wotan and Brünnhilde's farewell.'[78] Eisenstein goes on to reflect 'how incomparably broader, richer and overwhelming are the possibilities of this method for colour film!' – thus anticipating his plans for the unfulfilled third part of *Ivan the Terrible*. The impact of music on Eisenstein's film making is clear from the essay 'Vertical Montage' which he wrote while working on *Die Walküre*. He considered this film technique to be the equivalent of musical polyphony.[79]

Unfortunately we have only a rather cloudy picture of the Bolshoi performances, most eyewitness accounts being distorted by political and aesthetic prejudice. Prokofiev was among those who were impressed by the production, but on the whole

The world of film enters the stage in Sergei Eisenstein's direction of *Die Walküre* at the Bolshoi in 1940. During Sieglinde's telling of the story of the sword in the tree to Siegmund in Act I (at left on the higher level), Eisenstein left nothing to the imagination. He introduced a mime group (in the foreground) which enacted the events described. Had he perhaps contemplated using film? The use of film to illustrate narrative sequences had already been suggested by Friedrich Kranich jr in 1933.

For Eisenstein, man and nature were inseparable forces in *Die Walküre*. The fight between Hunding and Siegmund at the end of the second act is shown in a drawing by Eisenstein (*left*) and in a photograph of the same scene (*right*). At the bottom of the drawing are sketches for half-animal, half-human creatures who sometimes took part in the action. The rocky ledges bucked up and down with the progress of the struggle. In the photograph, Wotan can be seen descending to intervene. Brünnhilde is at the right.

it found few friends and was given only six times. The pantomimic choruses were disliked, and it was objected that Eisenstein's 'cinematic tempos' were not appropriate for the epic flow of a Wagnerian music drama.[80] Soviet critics like A. Shavedryan voiced the perennial complaint against Eisenstein's 'obscure symbolism', adding that the airborne elements failed to suit Wagner's 'heroic music'. This latter comment is doubtless explained by technical deficiencies which meant, among other things, 'that the tall cliffs of the second act squeaked as they were lowered, and that Brünnhilde, instead of giving the impression of being borne aloft on her ledge by streams of hot air, was hoisted up to Valhalla in a series of clumsy jolts'.[81] Again, one notes problems uncannily similar to those experienced by the composer at Bayreuth in 1876. But in 1940 Eisenstein had to contend with the work's unfamiliarity on the Soviet stage and a fog of prejudice and ideological expectation. All too predictable was the overheard response of two officers from the German Embassy: 'Deliberate Jewish tricks'.[82] So much for *Die Walküre*'s role in German-Soviet rapprochement.

Soviet hopes that the performances would lubricate relations between the two countries were short-lived. In June 1941 Hitler marched against the USSR and *Die*

Walküre, no longer the myth of the moment, was never revived. It was time for *Alexander Nevsky* to return to the screen.

Although it is tempting to see Eisenstein's myth-centred approach as a tactical evasion of the Teutonic nationalism with which the *Ring* had, thanks to Hitler, become inextricably associated, all the evidence suggests that this would have been his choice whatever the political circumstance. As a committed Marxist, Eisenstein identified with the anti-capitalist stance of the young Wagner, as he did with his argument that myth, and only myth, was the proper subject for tragic drama. Eisenstein's mythopoeic goals as a film maker echo those of Wagner the dramatist.

In 1932 he had spoken of wanting to film 'a kind of modern *Götterdämmerung*' about the downfall of the arms dealer Basil Zakharov and other capitalists, 'possibly with Richard Wagner's music post-synthesised'.[83] But in the case of *Die Walküre* – a stage rather than film production – Eisenstein did not seem to have regarded his work as creating any kind of pointed metaphor or allegory of contemporary events. It was to be a mythopoeic interpretation because he did not conceive of the opera in any other way, and because it was a natural part of his long-standing study of myth in all its aspects.

Shostakovich accused Eisenstein of having shamefully ignored Wagner's place in Nazi ideology.[84] But there is no evidence that Eisenstein saw anything fascistic in *Die Walküre* – quite the contrary. His preparatory notes talk only of human consciousness emerging from 'the behaviour of the primitive horde': 'The theme is human nature. The central point of the work: *Brünnhilde opens herself to human feelings*. She opens herself up to *love* in *Siegfried*. To hatred in *Götterdämmerung*. But here we have the complexity of human feelings, in which she sees how others love each other, also *compassion* and *self-sacrifice*. (*What is fascistic in this play, I wonder* ?!!!)'[85] Recalling how tightly constrained Eisenstein himself was by Stalin's ruthless control of artistic output, is it too fanciful to see his interpretation of the opera as encoding a peaceable message for the Soviet leader?

At some level he must have been happy for his production to demonstrate that nationalistic appropriation of Wagner's works was a nonsense, that *Die Walküre* should not be seen as heroic-nationalistic but only as a warning that there could be no triumph for Wotan's unruly will or for Fricka's bourgeois morality. Eisenstein believed that both were seedbeds for 'petty-bourgeois revolt – that is to say, fascism' and could have no other outcome than death and destruction.[86] This is indeed the Schopenhauerean conclusion at which Wotan himself arrives in the second act.

The visible music of myth

Eisenstein understood the music primarily in terms of the images it suggested to him – in other words, for its more obvious mimetic features. It was 'visual tangibility' which 'guided his search for the visual equivalent of the music of *Die Walküre*, and which he believed was the correct method for producing music dramas in general (and not only those by Wagner)'. 'This music,' he said, 'wants to be visible, to be seen, and the visibility must be sharply defined, palpable, frequently changing … exploding at its climax with the whirlwind of the "Flight of the Valkyries", this first day of the *Ring* dictates … visualization, objectivization, material tangibility, dynamism.'[87] Here we find an entirely different philosophy from that advocated by Appia the musician, who dreamt of stage imagery derived always from the music, never the text, and was totally against literalistic depiction. Eisenstein's concern to achieve the latter is of course reminiscent of Wagner's. It goes well beyond it in all the unscripted inventions that were intended to spell out for the audience much that the composer expected them to gather from the music alone.

In his attitude to acting, Eisenstein was more in Cosima's camp than Wagner's, wanting to predetermine every movement and gesture, cueing them quite precisely to specific bars in the score. He intended that they should communicate as 'runes', 'for the staging of the production, outwardly simple but rich in inner content, must be like these signs'. As Natalya Shpiller, who played Sieglinde, recalled, Eisenstein gave her minutely detailed instructions: 'Without taking your eyes off Siegmund, reach with your left hand over your right shoulder to the horn, take it by the middle, and in the next four bars lower your right shoulder.' Beginning to feel like a 'mechanical doll', she reports that she was able to negotiate at least some degree of freedom for her movement.[88]

Eisenstein claimed to disapprove of the traditional Bayreuth style of performance, though he probably never visited the Festspielhaus. It is more likely that he had drawn his conclusions from the various Wagner productions he had seen on his travels. The interesting difference is that although schooled in Meyerhold's principles of theatre as an improvisatory art, Eisenstein the film maker came in from a new angle. For film is about fixing a single, unique representation, requiring that rehearsal is dedicated to that end, every scene needing to be played in an identical way for each take, enabling capture from many camera angles and editing into a seamless unity. And just as literal depiction turned stale in the theatre, so it discovered a new lease of life in the cinema, its burgeoning success there only hastening its demise in the theatre. In Eisenstein's *Walküre* we can recognize a desire to import the realistic imperative from film back into opera production. Plainly this had its problems, and not least because in opera the director has less scope for invention than he does in film.

Eisenstein's interest in a fully worked out, credible depiction of a mythic fiction springs, at least in part, from his belief in the Marxist-Leninist insistence that in art everything has to speak directly and optimistically to the common man – no obscurity, no formalism, no mystic aura. In this sense he had his feet more firmly on the ground than the Hellerau visionaries, who, for all that they wanted the audience to be participants in the dramatic experience, may have taken too presumptive a view of what that audience actually *needed* in terms of vivid, visceral exposition to make that participation possible. It seems more than likely that Eisenstein's obsession with illustrative techniques in *Die Walküre* influenced Walter Felsenstein's strategy of Musiktheater (realistic music-theatre) at the East Berlin Komische Oper from 1947, to be discussed in chapter 10. It was from this strategy, and again within a Marxist cultural milieu, that there emerged pupils of Felsenstein like Götz Friedrich, Joachim Herz and Harry Kupfer, who, as we shall see, were to play a major part in the story of Wagner production after the Second World War.

CHAPTER 8

Travail and truth: Klemperer and the Kroll Opera

We have traced the spread of Appia's radical ideas from their proving grounds in Paris, Hellerau, Milan and Basel through to their adoption in America and Russia. But the number of truly significant Wagner productions between Mahler and Roller's Vienna *Tristan* of 1903 and Eisenstein's Moscow *Walküre* of 1940 was pitifully small. Bayreuth's only use for new ideas and technology, as we have seen, was to serve 'faithful' performance, and the new trail pioneered by Mahler and Roller in the earliest years of the twentieth century all too swiftly petered out.

More than twenty years and a world war later this same trail blazed into new life for four brief but hyperactive years, on the very eve of the Nazi catastrophe, when Mahler's sometime protégé Otto Klemperer became musical director of the Kroll Opera in Berlin (1927–31). It was here that the potential for reform that had been latent in opera at last exploded into a series of radical productions which put the new ideas – in wild, almost anarchic variety – into action over a sustained period. Modernism had at last erupted onto the operatic stage and in such a way as to re-engage the interest of the intelligentsia and ignite a debate about the staging of old operas and the creation of new kinds of music-theatre which rages to this day. The strands of reform and renewal were drawn together in a theatre that was altogether exceptional. What was created at the Kroll left a richer legacy to the future than most developments elsewhere. Its achievements emerged from the theatrical life of the German Weimar Republic and are best understood in that turbulent context.

In November 1918 the German Revolution effectively brought to an end both the First World War and the Wilhelmine Empire. The country's political status for the next fourteen years was determined the following July when it was declared a republic at Weimar. The first period of the Republic was marked by high hopes, political unrest and the disastrous inflation which peaked in 1923. Gustav Stresemann's stabilization of the currency ushered in a brief second period from December 1923 to October 1929 (that of the so-called 'Golden Twenties') when the arts flourished as never before. But from 1928 further economic crisis, exacerbated by the Wall Street crash of 1929, precipitated renewed social and political turmoil which led directly to Hitler's becoming Chancellor in January 1933. The upsurge of vitality in every aspect of cultural life was quickly dissipated.

Throughout the fourteen years of the Weimar Republic the theatre responded vigorously to the country's struggle to forge a democratic identity out of defeat and disgrace, and made its own contribution to the fiercely fought debates between conflicting positions. Whether in performing the classics or in the creation of new works, it is in its anger, its critical edge, its cleansing fire, that the Weimar theatre left its mark on the twentieth century.

The reaction against Wagner

Up to 1914 Wagner's impact on European culture was massive but relatively unproblematic. His work permeated the visual arts, literature, philosophy and the European intellectual climate as a whole. It was subject to endless interpretation and argument, but generally speaking did not create ideological problems of any great significance. The lines running back to Wagner seemed direct and relatively untangled, while political considerations scarcely impinged on the stage performances of his works.

Even the war failed to interrupt their momentum and indeed even contributed to it, for in 1916–17 Wagner chalked up 18.2 per cent of all operatic performances in German-speaking theatres. Although this percentage had declined to 13.9 by 1926–7, it was well ahead of Verdi at 11.3, Puccini at 7.8 and Mozart at 6.6. Wagner remained the most popular composer right through into the 1930s.[1] A far from negligible contributory factor is that for many he became a rallying point for nationalist values that were widely felt to have been shamefully betrayed in the Weimar constitution. When Siegfried Wagner succeeded in reopening Bayreuth in 1924 – it had been dark since 1914 – the flag that flew over the Festspielhaus was not that of the Republic but of imperial Germany. The official guide to the festival described Wagner as the 'Führer of German art', a prophet of National Socialism and opponent of Americanism and Judaism. General Ludendorff addressed an anti-republican rally in the town, and at the end of *Die Meistersinger* the audience rose to its feet and sang 'Deutschland über Alles'. Although Siegfried took steps to curb such displays, his half-hearted attempts to draw a line between Wagner's art and the nationalists' designs on it were ultimately doomed to fail. Nor did it help that he allowed his name, together with those of his wife and three sisters, to appear among the honorary board members of the Bayreuth League of German Youth, whose aims included inculcating 'a sense of the inseparability' of 'Adolf Hitler's cultural designs and the work of Bayreuth'.[2] The continuing popularity of Wagner's works in traditional stagings was part nostalgia for Germany's imperial past and part focus for the resistance to republicanism that was propagated by the likes of Houston Stewart Chamberlain.

The more critical and creative forces in the Weimar years were either hostile or antipathetic to Wagner. For them the nationalist and the Schopenhauerean aspects of pessimism and renunciation were equally distasteful, the prevailing styles of performance too reminiscent of the self-congratulatory bourgeois visual world of Lenbach and Makart. The case for Wagner as a subversive radical, as an artist and dramatist, had, despite isolated attempts to rescue it, all but vanished.[3] His importance now lay as a warning of what had at all costs to be shunned if the spirit of the new Germany was to find its voice.

Thomas Mann was but one of many who, by identifying Wagner with Germany's cause in the First World War, created an uncomfortable aura around his name in the painful new dawn of the Weimar Republic. Siegfried-style nationalism – as brilliantly caricatured in George Grosz's prescient 1923 drawing of Hitler in Siegfried's bearskin and with a swastika tatooed on his arm – was no small offence to the torchbearers of the fragile republican spirit.

The ascendant wave of theatre composers like Stravinsky, Busoni, Hindemith, Weill and Prokofiev fought clear, experiencing the persistence of Wagnerism as nothing but a threat. His influence lost little of its force, but took the form of 'that which was reacted against'. He was, as it were, a negative catalyst, a Mephistophelian presence engendering good work in a diametrically different direction from that of the recent past. The world that dawned in 1918 was, in Klemperer's view, one 'in opposition to Wagner'.[4] The theatrical developments which flowed from that will be the principal subject of this chapter.

Weimar theatre as background to the Kroll

Although German opera houses in the 1920s did put on a fair number of new works, they received relatively few performances (4.5 per cent in 1926–7).[5] Apart from exceptions here and there, some of which will be mentioned later, the predominant styles of staging were conservative. The ordinary theatre, on the other hand, was an adventure playground. Whether in finding new ways of performing the classics or discovering a stage language for the wave of new plays that helped the Republic carve out an identity for itself, the stage seethed with new life. 'Max Reinhardt, Leopold Jessner and Erwin Piscator managed only the most famous of over eighty "live" theatres in Berlin, which competed with more than 250 motion picture theatres, not to mention the numerous cabarets featuring the biting political satire of Brecht, Wedekind, and Tucholsky.'[6] Reform ideas that before the war had been regarded as dangerously risqué and avant-garde came into their own as writers and directors enjoyed their new-found freedoms.

There was continuity spanning the pre- and post-war years in that two of the most significant influences on Weimar theatre, the directors Max Reinhardt (1873–1943) and Leopold Jessner (1878–1945), had made their mark as innovators in the first decade of the century.[7] They had taken up the reform proposals of Appia, Craig, Behrens and Fuchs and applied them with considerable success in theatres large and small. After the war, what had been avant-garde innovation was assimilated into mainstream practice. Impresario-directors like Reinhardt were not slow to respond to the dissolution of the imperial social order. At Reinhardt's opening production for the Großes Schauspielhaus in November 1919, Germany's finest actors performed the Oresteia before 'the new republican society', the audience, 'from the chancellor down, melting into an anonymous mass unbroken by the old theatre's traditional distinctions of level'.[8] But for all its democratic façade, Reinhardt's populism was an overambitious exploitation of pre-war revolutionary ferment. It failed to recapture the freshness and impact that his work had had before the war (he claimed that at one time he was simultaneously running ten different theatres in Berlin and Vienna).[9] Disappointed by his failure to fill the aptly named Großes Schauspielhaus, he soon redirected his energies towards Vienna and the Salzburg Festival (co-founders of the festival, which opened in 1920, included Hugo von Hofmannsthal, Alfred Roller, Franz Schalk and Richard Strauss). In 1922 he abandoned the Großes Schauspielhaus to his choreographer, Erik Charell, who concentrated on operettas and revues. Part of Reinhardt was already looking to the New World, and he finally left Europe for America in 1934. Believing that 'the quality of an audience grows with its quantity',[10] Reinhardt was unsurpassed in his attempts to translate the theories of the pioneers into a theatre of universal appeal, to show how technology could be put to creative use, at the same time always seeking the closest rapport between actors and audience, between the play and the space in which it was played. But the theatre of the Weimar Republic nurtured other, less overtly commercial concerns and it is to those that we must return.

The austere figure of Leopold Jessner occupies a central role in theatrical developments which were to impact on opera production. By 1919, when he became Intendant of the lacklustre Berlin Staatliches Schauspielhaus, he had long since rejected Meiningen naturalism and had begun to rely on the kind of architectural stage space, using the simplest block-shapes, ramps and above all steps, that had been used so successfully by Appia at Hellerau. Politically well to the left and a republican member of the SPD,[11] it was characteristic that he should choose to inaugurate his regime at the Schauspielhaus (12 December 1919) with Schiller's *Wilhelm Tell*, that classic tale of the liberation of a nation from foreign tyranny and the founding of a new order. There could scarcely have been a more powerful or provocative vehicle for the expression of the outrage felt by the intelligentsia of the left at the murder of the Spartacist leaders Karl Liebknecht and Rosa Luxemburg on 15 January 1919.[12]

The dominant feature of Jessner's set for *Wilhelm Tell*, designed by Emil Pirchan, was no dream vision of Alpine lakes and mountains, but a sweep of steps leading up to platforms at the rear and sides of the stage. Although Reinhardt and others had previously adopted such a layout (stunningly anticipated by Gordon Craig in 'The Steps', a sequence of four images dating from 1905), no one had used it more effectively. The 'Jessnertreppen' were ideal for the display of crowd scenes on multiple levels. As Peter Gay well describes, this was 'a jagged arrangement of bare steps on which actors could sit, which they could climb for declamation and from which they could roll after they had been killed'.[13] Within a short time variants of the *Jessnertreppen* were to be seen on virtually every major stage in Germany.

Geßler, the Austrian tyrant, was played by Fritz Kortner, one of the Republic's most famous villain-actors, 'dressed in a glittering uniform, dripping with medals, the very type of the hateful German general; his cheeks had been rouged to a furious red, to caricature the bestial Junker'.[14] Jessner's use of light and colour symbolism in the production was as Appian in spirit as the architectural strength of the set. In his memoirs, Kortner describes how the premiere was continuously interrupted by

Appia and Craig largely fantasized about sets constructed from steps and platforms. Their ideas were powerfully turned into stage reality by the Berlin director Leopold Jessner. He rejected the romantic illusionism of the nineteenth-century stage, inaugurating his influential regime at the Berlin Staatliches Schauspielhaus in 1919 with a production of Schiller's *Wilhelm Tell*. Emil Pirchan's set replaced the traditional view of Alpine lakes and mountains with a bold sweep of steps and a dramatic opening at the rear.

nationalist demonstrations but concluded as a triumph. Kortner was not alone in finding Jessner's whole approach 'unmistakeably revolutionary and anti-nationalistic'.[15]

Jessner applied his ideas not only to Schiller and Shakespeare, but also to modern works. These, however, were not his forte and to expand the repertory in this direction he brought in Jürgen Fehling (1885–1968), who had made his name directing Ernst Toller's *Masse-Mensch* (Masses and Man) at the Volksbühne in September 1921. Fehling's particular strength was characterization, something that he was in due course to bring to his opera work at the Kroll.

Another shaping force in Weimar theatre declared itself in spring 1922 when the 24-year-old Bertolt Brecht, recently arrived in Berlin from Munich, abused the actors and created uproar while directing Arnolt Bronnen's scandalous play *Vatermord* (Patricide, the play featuring also incest between mother and son) at the Junge Bühne repertory theatre. It was, above all, Brecht's anti-naturalistic, argumentative and abrasive style which was to determine the acidic colour of a large part of Berlin theatre in the 1920s. His construction of 'epic' theatre from a sequence of narrative, self-contained scenes (harking back to Aristotle's distinction between 'epic' and 'lyrical' or 'dramatic' art) was intended to rebuff any sense of audience involvement and to appeal to the spectator's detached, critical intelligence. The idea was that it should be the very antithesis of Wagnerism, though in fact Brecht's aims differed from Wagner's in only one respect, albeit crucial. Both Wagner and Brecht strove for a theatre in which every creative element cohered. The difference lay in that whereas Wagner expected the verbal, musical and visual impressions to fuse and overwhelm the spectator, Brecht wanted the spectator to retain his sense of distance from the play and the various sensory impressions to remain distinct in his mind. Brecht's assumption was that the Wagnerian theatre-goer was passive and manipulated, whereas he solicited an active response, the spectator engaging the play with his own mind. This 'worst-case' assessment of the Wagnerian, although a recognizable pathology, did not begin to take into account the huge complex of intellectual engagement with Wagner's works evident throughout European culture since the composer's death. Brecht saw only the sycophantic ramblings and obnoxious ideology of the Wahnfried circle – whose influence is not for one minute to be denied – and failed to pick up on those reformers who, like Appia, were as insistent as Brecht himself that the spectator should complete the drama in the theatre of his own mind.

Brecht embodied a critique of bourgeois theatre entirely in keeping with the times. The astringency of his 'epic' principles of construction, teamed with Kurt Weill's music, was to create a new kind of music-theatre. Brecht and Weill's collaborations peaked with *Die Dreigroschenoper* (The Threepenny Opera, premiere Berlin 1928) and *Aufstieg und Fall der Stadt Mahagonny* (The Rise and Fall of Mahagonny, tumultuous Leipzig premiere 1930, then Berlin 1931). These works were the most brilliantly successful crystallizations, in forms that have lasted to this day, of the radical and revolutionary ideas that elsewhere often achieved no more than experimental and transient realization.

With its cabaret songs, jazz idiom, anti-heroics, political satire, spare designs and projections by Caspar Neher, *Die Dreigroschenoper* was as explosive a mix as anything invented by Piscator. This and *Mahagonny* were triumphant vindications of Brecht's 'epic'-theatre aesthetic of a 'linear chain of scenes and episodes' inviting not identification from the audience but detached, critical participation. The blows they struck against nineteenth-century opera and its prevalent mode of conservative production left a profound impression on Otto Klemperer and his Kroll colleagues and were a spur to their own reforms and innovations. Neher was among the artists they invited to help carry them out.

The impact of visual arts and influences from abroad

In the visual arts – which were to have no little impact on the theatre – the style of the times was set by the Neue Sachlichkeit exhibition at Mannheim in the summer of 1925. The cool 'new objectivity', or 'sobriety' as John Willett has so aptly translated it, marked the end of the many moods of expressionism which had been dominant since Der Blaue Reiter (active 1911–14), the Munich-based group of artists round

Kandinsky and Franz Marc, and Die Brücke (active 1905–13), the Dresden-based group led by Ernst Ludwig Kirchner, Fritz Bleyl, Erich Heckel and Karl Schmidt-Rottluff. Le Corbusier's functionalism in architecture typified the spirit of Neue Sachlichkeit. The phrase defined a mood, inspired by a determination to strip away decorative and sentimental evasion and to show things unflinchingly 'as they are', a new 'realism' that was to spread out from the visual arts into Weimar culture as a whole.

The other major engine of aesthetic change in these years was the famous Bauhaus school of applied art and design. Founded by the architect Walter Gropius in Weimar in 1919, it moved to Dessau in 1925 and later to Berlin where it was closed in 1933 by the Nazis. From 1921 it ran a theatre school and from 1923, under Oskar Schlemmer (1888–1943), dancer, artist and sculptor, was to explore extreme anti-naturalistic theatre forms centred on the actor's body (in effect Schlemmer thought of actors as essentially dancers rather than articulate characters).

Other Bauhaus artist-teachers were also interested in the theatre, not least Kandinsky, who had returned from Russia in 1923, and the Hungarian László Moholy-Nagy, who in spring 1923 became head of the basic design course at the Bauhaus. Of Moholy-Nagy (1895–1946), whose 1929 designs for Offenbach's *Contes d'Hoffmann* at the Kroll were the furthest frontier of Weimar stage design, there will shortly be more to say. Both he and Kandinsky are examples of the way in which the ferment in Berlin attracted immensely gifted innovators from far beyond German borders. Although there had been a substantial Russian presence in Berlin since the Bolshevik Revolution of 1917, it was not until the Rapallo Treaty of April 1922 that relations between Russia and Germany were freed from restrictions. This treaty was but the first of a number of international agreements which dissolved frontiers that had been effectively closed to the German Republic since the war.

The most potent external influences came in from Hungary and Russia, including the constructivism of artists like Lissitzky and Moholy-Nagy. Russian constructivists like Popova, Stepanova and the Vesnin brothers found a welcoming market for their work in Germany in fields ranging from textiles to stage design. Constructivism, whose impact on Russian theatre was noted in chapter 7, first arrived on the Berlin stage in 1922 with Friedrich Kiesler's mechanistic sets for Karel Čapek's *R.U.R.* (Rossum's Universal Robots). Stanislavsky's Art Theatre visited Berlin in 1921 and there was a big exhibition of Soviet art in Berlin in 1922. Soviet-German exchanges included the productions of six angry plays by Ernst Toller that were given in Moscow, Leningrad and Tiflis between November 1922 and the end of 1923. The visit of Alexander Tairov and his Moscow Kamerny Theatre made a huge impact on Berlin in the spring of 1923.[16] The traffic in radical stage reform was fuelled by a succession of international theatre exhibitions.

The metallic severity of the constructivists was as much to the taste of the avant-garde Weimar theatre as the decorative exuberance of Diaghilev's designers was anathema to it. The influence on German theatre from the Ballets Russes, from Viennese Jugendstil and from French and Belgian Art Nouveau was principally felt in the traditionalist world of opera and ballet, where the validity of stage design as 'decor' survived largely unquestioned. A further reason why this substantial part of German theatre life remained aesthetically cocooned was that it had its own long tradition of employing in-house scenic painters and design studios like the Brückner brothers of Coburg, who featured so largely in the early history of Bayreuth.

Film/theatre/opera

[Opera] has less to offer the eye than the film has – and colour-film will soon be here, too. Add music, and the general public will hardly need to hear an opera sung and acted any more, unless a new path is found.

Arnold Schoenberg, 'The Future of Opera' (1927)[17]

The interaction of stage and screen in the Weimar period remains an under-studied phenomenon, but its landmarks are emerging from the mist.[18] From 1923 Germany was free to import American films, and its own film industry grew so fast that in 1927 it produced 241 feature films, a total greater than that for the rest of Europe combined and only less than those for the United States (743) and Japan (407). A German radio service began in 1923 and by 1925 there were five hundred thousand subscribers; by 1930 there were more than three million, making Germany the second largest radio audience in Europe after Great Britain. Film and broadcasting were in the van of an irresistible wave, decreeing that the performing arts were no longer the property of bourgeois society but should be available to all.

The theatre director Erwin Piscator (1893–1966), ever in the forefront of the move to put technology to work in the creation of a proletarian theatre of protest and vision, was quick to seize on film's potential. In 1924 Piscator projected captions over a number of scenes in Alfons Paquet's *Fahnen* (Flags). For *Trotz alledem!* (In Spite of Everything – a rallying cry of Karl Liebknecht) the following year, a historical revue in twenty-four scenes, of the years 1914 to 1919 culminating in the deaths of Liebknecht and Rosa Luxemburg, which was staged to mark the opening of the Communist Party Congress, Piscator projected newsreel footage onto screens behind the actors. Thereafter multimedia became part of Piscator's lingua franca, a notable example being his 1927 staging of Ernst Toller's *Hoppla, wir leben!* (Hoppla, We're Alive!), in which major historical events occurring during a political prisoner's eight-year incarceration were shown on film (the production also used radio and a vast multi-level constructivist set).[19] At his Berlin Schauspielhaus Jessner used projections for Arnolt Bronnen's *Rheinische Rebellen* (Rhenish Rebels, May 1925) and film for Gerhart Hauptmann's *Die Weber* (The Weavers, February 1928). It is not hard to see why film became a potent ingredient in the realization of 'epic' theatre, and from 1927 Brecht began to work with the Piscator-Bühne to that end.

The importation of film into theatre was no gimmick but an extension of its vocabulary. Events external to the action did not need to be laboriously described but could be shown. Stage events could be in dialogue or in counterpoint with film images from the world outside. Time-frames could be compressed, expanded, chopped up and reassembled. Action, representation and reality could be presented in all manner of arresting juxtapositions.

As well as serving the cause of left-wing theatre, the affordability of film, its lack of social barriers, gave it a popularity that was also a commercial threat to the theatres and opera houses. Aesthetically it was also a major force against Wagnerian opera and its performing tradition. Visually, it could give unprecedented *actualité* to realism and to fantasy alike, and this despite its black-and-white limitation and, until 1927, its lack of soundtrack. Writing in 1930, the Berlin film critic Hans Gutmann argued that traditional opera had become obsolete because 'it doles out material that has become "old hat" to eyes that have gone to school to the cinema and [to] senses disillusioned by reality'.[20] Gutmann saw film as hastening the reform of opera and in the first instance this manifested itself in the response of living composers rather than stage directors.

As early as 1916, Richard Strauss, beginning work on his autobiographical *Intermezzo*, tells Hofmannsthal that he is intending to strip opera of its 'Wagner'sche Musizierpanzer' (Wagnerian musical armour).[21] He imagines 'cinematic pictures' in the guise of short, inconclusive scenes dissolving into orchestral interludes. No doubt his collaboration with Hofmannsthal on the contrapuntal dramaturgy of *Ariadne auf Naxos*, with its intercutting between *seria* and commedia dell'arte strands, had already pointed him in this direction.

Most other theatrically minded composers also sat up and took note of film, Schoenberg remarking in 1926 the dilemma it posed: '[Opera] can no longer take the competition of the required realism [of film, which] … has spoiled the eyes of the spectator: one need not only see truth and reality, rather also every appearance … that presents itself as reality.'[22] In other words, Schoenberg was signalling the end of the road both for opera's pursuit of naturalism (because it could not compete with cinema in this direction) and for its invocation of fantasy (because this would be judged – and found wanting – by the new criteria of cine-realism). Although the reversionary nineteenth-century dramaturgy of *Moses und Aron* (1930–2, unfinished) fails to take up this idea, the existence of film did prompt Schoenberg to write his *Begleitungsmusik zu einer Lichtspielszene* (Accompaniment to a Film Scene) – the scene is purely imaginary – which was premiered by Klemperer and the Kroll Orchestra in 1930.

Schoenberg's pupil Alban Berg believed that the sequence of short scenes in *Wozzeck* was cinematic and that the opera was eminently suitable for sound-film. In 1930 he told Schoenberg that he was totally convinced of the importance of the sound-film 'for our kind of music'.[23] It certainly played a part in the conception and construction of *Lulu* (unfinished at Berg's death in 1935), most obviously in the film sequence in Act II which shows events occurring during Lulu's year in prison.

Film techniques helped to shape Kurt Weill's style of music-theatre. The contrasted comic and tragic pantomime sequences in his one-act opera *Der Protagonist* (1926) are surely inconceivable without silent film. Weill's next opera, *Royal Palace* (Berlin 1927), with text by the Dada and surrealist poet Iwan Goll, actually includes silent film for one of its three surrealistic 'visions', in which the heroine Dejanira is seen 'in Nice, in a Pullman to Constantinople, at a ball, at the Russian ballet, flying to the North Pole, etc'.[24] Film techniques are also powerfully in evidence in Křenek's jazz opera *Jonny spielt auf*, first performed in Leipzig only a few weeks before *Royal Palace*. 'Křenek,' wrote Paul Stefan in 1927, 'offers the magic of rapidly changing scenes, which come from film; Weill imports these [filmic elements] directly: *Royal Palace* is, in this sense, probably the first film opera.'[25]

The influence of film on opera production was rather slower to take effect. At first it was noticeable in greater realism in acting and costuming. The projection of slides had been established for many years (going back to Bayreuth's magic-lantern projections for the Ride of the Valkyries in 1876, and even further beyond). By the end of the 1920s repertory operas were staged using not only film projections but 'split-screen' effects and black-and-white visual tonality. Extensive use was made of such techniques in the Berlin Staatsoper's premiere of Darius Milhaud's *Christophe Colomb* in 1930.[26] The twenty-seven scenes of Paul Claudel's libretto, moving back and forth in time, show palpable cinematic influence in their construction, and film images were projected onto a screen at the back of the stage.

If as no more than a brief digression, it is worth observing that the cinema, from its very beginning, had taken a close interest in opera.[27] Edison had at first seen his moving pictures as an accompaniment to mechanically produced sound. His experiments in synchronizing sound and image inevitably pointed him towards musical drama. As early as 1894 he made a thirty-second clip, *Carmencita*, in which the gyrations of a Spanish dancer were in all probability accompanied by a snatch of Bizet's music. Edison was not alone. In 1900 in Paris, Clément Maurice presented three three-minute films of operatic excerpts featuring Victor Maurel, who had created the role of Iago in Verdi's *Otello*. The images on screen were accompanied by more or less synchronized sound from a phonographic cylinder. The great cinematic pioneer Georges Méliès was fascinated by film's ability to make characters appear and disappear at will – just the thing for Mephisto in *Faust*, a role with which he was understandably obsessed. In 1903 he played Méphistophélès in *Faust aux enfers*, an outrageous, nine-minute reduction of Berlioz's *Damnation de Faust*, with phonographic sound. The following year he moved into more sentimental territory by condensing Gounod's opera on the same subject into a thirteen-minute feature, again with himself as Mephisto. All in all, between 1900 and 1910 there are believed to have been at least eighty attempts to synchronize cinematic images of operatic subjects with phonographic sound.

In America, following the huge success in 1903 of the Met's defiance of Bayreuth's embargo by performing *Parsifal*, the Edison Film Company – with scant regard for the Wagnerian timescale – shot a twenty-minute film of the opera. It was sold with a score of piano accompaniment and the text of a 'complete illustrated lecture'. Edison's advertisement boasted that 'In *Parsifal* we offer the greatest religious subject that has been produced in motion pictures since the [Oberammergau] Passion Play was first produced by the Edison Company....' The response was less than enthusiastic, but a print of the film survives in the Library of Congress. Evan Baker, who has seen it, reports that the acting is 'simple, direct, and with a minimum of stylized movements, although for today's eyes they resemble stereotyped grand operatic gestures such as the hands on the breast to express profound emotion, or clutching one's

Wagnerian music drama, drastically shrunk and with music reduced to a piano accompaniment, arrives on film for the first time. Following the New York Met's highly successful performances of *Parsifal* in 1903 (in defiance of Bayreuth's claim to exclusivity), the Edison Film Company shot a twenty-minute version of the opera. The Grail temple was clearly modelled on the Bayreuth setting.

hair to represent despair'.[28] Other Wagner films by other producers followed, including *Tannhäuser* (1913), *Lohengrin* (1915) and *Der fliegende Holländer* (1918).

One thing that is clear from the irruption of film into opera in the 1920s is that it confronted composer-dramatists and stage directors with a new perspective on the representation of time, of realism and of fantasy. The mythological and the exotic could be made 'real' as never before, the stuff of everyday life suborned into surrealistic fantasy. We have seen how the aesthetic problems this created were flagged up by Schoenberg. It was but a small step to treating the production not as a visual translation of words and music but as an almost abstract composition complementary to them. The consequences of this were not to be explored until after the Second World War, but they were already beginning to be felt by the end of the 1920s.

German radical opera production in the 1920s

Although Germany's leading opera houses remained largely resistant to change in their production style, a few theatres did strike out in new directions. One of these was the Frankfurt Städtische Bühnen at the time when Ludwig Sievert (1887–1966) was its head of design (1918–37). Sievert, much indebted to Appia, had already developed an anti-naturalistic approach for the *Ring* and *Parsifal* (1912–14) at

Freiburg im Breisgau, using a revolve and cyclorama and with Franz Ludwig Hörth as director. At Frankfurt, in response to the expressionist demands of works like Hindemith's *Mörder, Hoffnung der Frauen* and *Sancta Susanna* (both 1922) and *Cardillac* (1928),[29] and Křenek's *Der Sprung über den Schatten* (1924),[30] Sievert made striking use of strong colours, abstract forms and symbolism to make visible the turbulent emotional core of the music. Other adventurous productions of this time included *Ring* stagings by Saladin Schmitt and Johannes Schröder in Duisburg (1922–3), and by Franz Hörth and Emil Pirchan in Berlin (1928–9), where, in Piscator style, film was used to show the entry of the gods into Valhalla.[31]

In 1914, Ewald Dülberg, later to become Klemperer's principal designer at the Kroll, prepared designs for Hamburg's first *Parsifal* with Gauguinesque costumes for the Flowermaidens that were a palpable response to the exotic colouration of the Ballets Russes.[32] These remained unrealized because the management could not accept what would doubtless have been seen as a sacrilegious travesty of the Bayreuth version. Also rejected, probably for the same reason, was Leo Pasetti's later attempt (Munich 1924) to import the expressionist palette of Franz Marc and Emil Nolde into the second act of the same opera.[33]

The most significant developments on the operatic stage before the Kroll were arguably those associated with the art historian Oskar Hagen's revivals of Handel's operas, which had languished unperformed for more than a century and a half.[34] Hagen's Göttingen production of *Rodelinda* in 1920 appears to have been the first recorded staging of a (more or less) complete Handel opera since 1754. It was followed by *Ottone*, *Giulio Cesare*, *Serse* and other works, principally given in

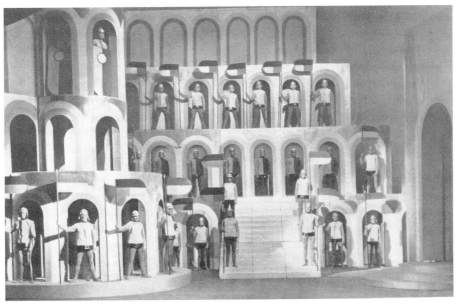

Modernistic opera design in Weimar Germany is typified by this scene from Act II of *Lohengrin* at the Hessisches Landestheater, Darmstadt 1928–9. It was directed by Renato Mordo, with designs by Lothar Schenck von Trapp.

Oskar Hagen's revivals of Handel operas after more than a century of neglect became a trial ground for new concepts in staging. The abstract forms, designed by Hein Heckroth and animated by the dramatic use of lighting, owe much to Appia, as in this scene from *Radamisto* at Göttingen, 1927. The direction of the chorus by Hanns Niedecken-Gebhard and choreographer Jens Keith is plainly influenced by the 'expressive' dance style developed by Rudolf von Laban and Mary Wigman.

Göttingen and Münster, but also in Leipzig, Halle and Berlin, so that by 1930 eleven operas had been given, and by 1939 nineteen of Handel's thirty-nine operas had been performed in Germany. Hagen's performing versions went for theatrical immediacy rather than authenticity and he himself conducted many of the performances. Such was the acclaim accorded Hagen's somewhat cavalier version of *Giulio Cesare* (with cuts, insertions and transpositions to allow a male impersonation of Cesare) that within five years it received 222 performances in thirty-four different cities.[35]

Where Handel perfectly met the mood of the time was that his operas, with their stop-go division into arias, recitatives and ensembles, were the antithesis of Wagner's continuity of dramatic development. Here was clarity of musical expression, with no pretence of realistic interaction of characters, everything being intended for straight-out delivery to the audience and no call for naturalistic representation of time and place in the settings. It would have been hard to imagine a better test-bed (other than, of course, newly composed works) for new concepts of staging, in that Handel's operas had no recent performance history. From the production photographs it is immediately evident that the ramps, platforms, steps and vigorous linear forms owed much to Appia's 'Espaces rythmiques' of the pre-war period. Equally Appian were the coordination of the lighting with the music and the colour sym-

The anti-romantic and anti-illusionistic style of Oskar Hagen's Handel stagings is evident in this photograph taken at a rehearsal of *Alexander Balus* in the Münster Stadthalle in 1926. As with Jaques-Dalcroze and Appia's work at Hellerau, the performers and the audience share the same space.

bolism, as in the reflection of the murderous progress of the action in Rodelinda's blood-red costume.

Hanns Niedecken-Gebhard, the choreographer who directed the soloists and substantial choruses, was much influenced by the innovatory 'Ausdruckstanz' (expressive dance) developed by Rudolf von Laban and Mary Wigman.[36] In the 1922 *Giulio Cesare* (given in German as 'Julius Cäsar') at Göttingen, the choreography of an entire aria was based on a single gesture, which served also as the departure point for the subsequent action. Everything about these stagings was anti-romantic and anti-illusionistic, this being particularly evident in the settings devised for performances in the Münster Stadthalle which united performers and audience in a single, shared space as at Hellerau.

While it is hard to determine the extent to which these out-and-out modernistic interpretations may have emboldened the work of Klemperer and his colleagues at the Kroll, it is more than likely that they did, and there are palpable connections, as in the Kroll's engaging Niedecken-Gebhard to produce Hindemith's *Cardillac* (30 June 1928). There was an upsurge of Handel productions in the capital during the four years of the Kroll's existence (1927–31), some of which were by Hagen and Niedecken-Gebhard.

Klemperer at the Kroll: Der fliegende Holländer, *1929*

To have been there was to have imbibed the spirit of the twentieth century.

H. H. Stuckenschmidt[37]

[The Kroll] mobilised a reserve of actuality in Wagner … which will explode today or tomorrow.

T. W. Adorno[38]

It is hard to overestimate the importance of the Kroll Opera's four years of existence for opera production in the twentieth century. But by no means was it the intention of its artistic director Otto Klemperer that the Kroll should be the adventure playground for theatre revolutionaries that to some extent, under the influence of its dramaturg Hans Curjel, it also became. Klemperer's own theatrical goals, like those of Mahler before him, were the product of an impatience with meaningless show and dramatically uninvolved singing and acting, and a wish to keep faith with the composer in the belief that he, too, would have welcomed whatever would build the best bridge between a work in modern performance and its conception in an earlier time.

Klemperer's dissatisfaction with traditional opera staging dates from his earliest work in the theatre when in 1907 Angelo Neumann took him on as a junior conductor at the New German Theatre in Prague. He had made his debut as a Wagner conductor in Hamburg in 1910 with a *Lohengrin* that had electrified the critics. The imperfections of the repertory system were painfully borne in on him two years later when he was given two and a half weeks to rehearse the complete *Ring,* which he had never conducted before.

Moving to Barmen in 1913 he conducted *Tristan* for the first time. Like every other German city, Barmen was impatient to perform *Parsifal* as soon as possible after the expiry of Bayreuth's exclusive right to the work on 31 December 1913; it managed to do so within days. For the production which Klemperer conducted on 4 January 1914 he had for the first time been able to work with a designer whose ideas on scenic reform chimed with his own. This was Hans Wildermann (1884–1954), whose sets for Hebbel's *Herodes und Mariamne,* consisting 'exclusively of curtains and cubic blocks … had been among the first in Germany to dispense entirely with painted scenery'.[39] In the Barmen *Parsifal,* 'the trunks of the trees were transformed into the pillars of the temple of the Grail. The vivid greens and blues of the forest gave way to mauves and reds as the Grail approached. The disintegration of Klingsor's castle at the end of the second act was realised by flooding the stage with a desolate grey-green light.'[40] But if the settings were a daring departure from Bayreuth, Barmen paid homage to Bayreuth practice in that the orchestra pit was covered, the performances were heralded by fanfares from the theatre's balcony, and no applause was allowed until the end of the opera. Ever more determined to take control of the stage, Klemperer put on a *Così fan tutte,* an opera that was then still largely unregarded and undervalued, in which for the first time he both conducted and produced. For this he used the very recent innovation of a 'Stilbühne', a stage curtained into sections of varying depth so that scene changes could be quickly effected without loss of continuity.[41]

In 1914 Klemperer moved to Strasbourg as deputy music director to Hans Pfitzner, whose belief in *Werktreue* had a profound and long-lasting influence on Klemperer. His first Strasbourg season followed the outbreak of war in August 1914 and a nationalistic upsurge of interest in Wagner. Klemperer's performances of *Tannhäuser*, *Die Meistersinger* and *Tristan und Isolde* were all exceptionally well received.

On becoming music director at Cologne (1917–24) Klemperer found himself up against the attitude that, in the words of his biographer, Peter Heyworth, 'opera was popular precisely because it so rarely provoked thought'. Fritz Rémond, the Intendant, was a traditionalist who in an earlier stage of his career had sung Parsifal in Bayreuth. As a stage director, his principal concern was 'to decorate the action with business'.[42] Klemperer fought hard against Rémond and the artistic constraints of the repertory system, managing to bring in demanding new works like Janáček's *Jenůfa* (its German premiere, 16 November 1918) and Busoni's *Turandot* and *Arlecchino* (26 January 1919). Disturbed by the lack of stylistic unity in a *Ring* production patched up over the years by Rudolf Hraby and Hans Wildermann, he had insisted that Wildermann should redesign many scenes. Partly under Busoni's influence Klemperer was already becoming wary of Wagner – he felt closest to *Tristan*, finding the heroic aspects of the *Ring* and the quasi-religious ambience of *Parsifal* antipathetic – and after leaving Cologne in 1924 at the age of thirty-nine he conducted the complete *Ring* only once more, in Buenos Aires in 1931. It was not until he became music director in Wiesbaden in 1924 that he found himself able to change the ways in which operas were routinely staged. The Wiesbaden Intendant Carl Hagemann (1871–1945) was himself of reforming bent and his recognition of a fellow spirit in Klemperer was plainly a factor leading to the latter's appointment.

The strength of Klemperer's base as an operatic reformer lay in the fact that, like Mahler, he was a conductor who took the keenest interest in the theatrical side of production. He needed no instruction that when the opera composer is also a consummate dramatist, every detail of production matters and the conductor has to be the force to bind them all together. Carl Hagemann, who had heard Mahler conduct *Tristan* in Vienna in 1903, considered that Klemperer was even greater as an operatic conductor:

> Mahler showed the path and the goal … it was Klemperer who first brought fulfilment. He is a disciple who has become what the teacher again and again strove for and here and there achieved: the conductor-producer, the guiding stage-artist of the opera. …
>
> Otto Klemperer has been the only living musician I have known who in the theatre conducted … exclusively for the stage. … At the piano and with models of the set before him he would try in open discussion with the producer and his assistants, the designer, the technicians, the lighting experts, the wardrobe personnel, to make clear his intentions down to the smallest detail. In the rehearsals he worked in closest partnership with the producer … and later conducted the performance as a unified work of art – not just the music, but the musico-dramatic

> *Gestaltung* as such. … Otto Klemperer … was destined to be a leader of modern music theatre.[43]

Hagemann's own role in nurturing Klemperer as a total man of the theatre is not to be underestimated. For the time he was a rare phenomenon: an Intendant-Regisseur fighting to bring about change in an essentially conservative institution. He regarded Mahler 'as the man who had achieved on the operatic stage that unity of music and drama which Wagner had sought but failed to bring about in Bayreuth'. Hagemann's own contribution to scenic renewal began about the same time. Following Roller's unitary set for *Don Giovanni* (Vienna 1905; see chapter 5), Hagemann staged *Hamlet* in Mannheim in 1907 using a single set and effecting scene changes principally through lighting. Working with Furtwängler and Ludwig Sievert in 1917 in Baden-Baden he staged a *Ring* 'with projections that represented one of the earliest challenges to the naturalism still prevailing at Bayreuth'.[44] In Klemperer, as in no other conductor, Hagemann recognized the man who could help him fulfil his Mahlerian ambitions for opera production and therefore, quite exceptionally for a theatre at that time, entrusted him with overall artistic control. For his part Klemperer had long since identified Ewald Dülberg (1888–1933) as his Roller. Dülberg was a gifted painter, woodcarver and designer of glass-paintings and textiles, theatre forming but a part of a richly varied artistic life. From his earliest years in Hamburg (1910–12) Klemperer remembered Dülberg's design-sketches for *Tristan* (never realized), which had hung in the office of the Intendant, Hans Loewenfeld. Together, Klemperer, Hagemann and Dülberg put on a *Fidelio* and a *Don Giovanni* in Wiesbaden which were landmarks in themselves and pointers to what Klemperer would shortly achieve on the more exposed stage of the Kroll in Berlin.

Klemperer had been in touch with Dülberg since 1912, when he had been impressed by his settings for Goethe's *Faust* at the Hamburg Schauspielhaus. From 1921 to 1926 Dülberg taught at the Kassel Kunstakademie and from 1926 to 1928 at the Bauhochschule in Weimar. His theatre work continued on an occasional basis, particularly at the Hamburg Stadttheater and at the Volksbühne am Bülowplatz in Berlin, where for a period he was head of design.[45] There was much common ground between Klemperer and Dülberg in that they were both pivotal figures between the old and the new. Each revered and sought to serve the nineteenth-century German cultural traditions from which they had sprung, while at the same time wanting reform and renewal. This was fired by a belief that every age had a duty to reinterpret the classics. They were deeply suspicious of novelty for its own sake, however, seeking only that which they felt to be in tune with the innermost core and spirit of the works they performed.

Dülberg was no less guarded than Klemperer in his attitude to Wagner and, like him, took his bearings on the present from composers like Busoni, Stravinsky and Hindemith. His approach to staging, again like that of Klemperer, was governed by fidelity to the music, and in this and most other respects he was a disciple of Appia. 'All my theatre work,' he said, 'springs from a longing for space … not as an end in itself but rather to make plainly visible the movement of the characters in a space designed to be moved in.'[46] The Appia who influenced Dülberg's designs was the geo-metrician of the 'Espaces rythmiques' and the Hellerau *Orfeo*, not the soft-focus visionary of the 1890s. For Dülberg, the designer's task 'was to provide a visual accompaniment to the score by means of form, colour and space'.[47] In the words of the Kroll's dramaturg and chronicler Hans Curjel, 'Dülberg effected a synthesis of cubistic abstraction, structural clarity, strongly coloured composition and lighting – not as a self-sufficient goal, but so that the scenic conception was always integrated with the course of the musical drama, with characters or groups of people whose thoughts, feelings and destinies are played out on the stage.'[48] For Dülberg there was no question of imposing stylization and abstraction for their own sake, only of finding the style from within the individual work.

These principles were powerfully evident in the *Fidelio* which opened the season in Wiesbaden on 3 September 1924. Although the producer was nominally Hagemann, Klemperer both directed the music and took an active role in the stage direction. Dülberg's sets were built of cube-like blocks and rectilinear platforms corresponding to the elemental structure of Beethoven's score and subject. Rocco's quarters were bare of domestic furniture, while there were fierce blood-red walls for the prison yard, pierced by holes, rather than doors leading to the cells. In the finale the blocks rolled away to reveal a wide and limitless open space. 'The prisoners formed an undifferentiated mass with shorn hair and whitened faces and in the finale the chorus was again deployed in static blocks, this time against a brilliant, blue background.'[49] Klemperer's conducting won high praise for its drive and sense of drama.

For its time such a stark scenic conception was extraordinary and shocking for the majority of opera-goers, but its 'revolutionary ethos' was recognized and praised by the liberal *Frankfurter Zeitung*.[50] 'Not for a moment does one have a feeling of music-making as an end in itself,' wrote another paper. 'All historical accretions, all implau-sibilities of plot and text are swept away. Myth emerges from anecdotal story, archetypes out of operatic characters. Most splendid of all, Beethoven is reborn out of the experience of our own time, fashioned out of our feeling for space and sound.'[51]

Klemperer and Hagemann were thrilled by Dülberg's contribution, and just over a year later (12 November 1925) the team staged *Don Giovanni*. This time it was the protean fluidity of the opera, its need for rapid scenic transitions within an overall dramatic unity, which suggested a staging plainly indebted to Mahler and Roller's production of 1905. Dülberg flanked the stage with 'two permanent, towerlike struc-tures whose doors, windows and balconies could be drawn into the action. The stage itself was divided into three sections, each of which could be curtained off and was used in its entirety only in the long finales of each act. Dülberg's designs avoided any suggestions of local colour beyond a stylized baroque.'[52]

Klemperer's wife Johanna Geissler sang Elvira. In the pit and on stage he worked hard to give full value to the comedy in the action. His conducting and the success of the production attracted widespread attention, not least that of Leo Kestenberg, music adviser to the Prussian Ministry for Education and the Arts (the Kultusmin-isterium), which saw theatre as a force for social education and cultural renewal.[53]

Since 1923 Kestenberg had been eager to bring Klemperer to Berlin, then the most theatrically active city in Germany. Exploratory talks that year came to nothing. But in 1926 Klemperer accepted Kestenberg's offer to be both musical and artistic director of the Kroll Opera, which Kestenberg had reconstituted as an independent company and a second home for the thriving Volksbühne, a populist theatre society founded in 1880. The Volksbühne had built its own fine modern theatre in 1914, had some eighty-five thousand members at the end of the war and by 1923 had nearly doubled that figure.[54] If its tastes were broadly for undemanding entertainment, the sheer size of the Volksbühne gives an indication of the proportion of the city's population that took an interest in theatre.

The initial idea was that extra performances for the Volksbühne could be supplied at the Kroll by the Staatsoper (State Opera), the city's principal opera house, on the Unter den Linden.[55] It was to this end that the Oper am Platz der Republik, commonly known as the Krolloper (after Joseph Kroll, architect of the winter garden built on the site in 1844, which was only later converted into a royal theatre), was reopened in 1924 as a 2,000-seat theatre. When this demand proved greater than the Staatsoper could comfortably supply, the Kroll was re-established by Kestenberg as an independent opera company, though still under the administrative umbrella of the Staatsoper.

Kestenberg's somewhat confused aim was that the Kroll should provide opera for a broad public while at the same time serving as a workshop for operatic innovation. Inevitably, it turned out that the Volksbühne's enthusiasm for *Carmen*, *Rigoletto* and *Madama Butterfly* was greater than its appetite for Hindemith, Stravinsky, Schoenberg and radical stage production. As Heyworth puts it, 'an opera by Hindemith was no more calculated to appeal to the members of the Volksbühne than a modernistic production of *Der Freischütz*'.[56] But for most of the four years of the Kroll's existence a viable balance was struck and a burning sense of controversy kept the public coming.

Kestenberg had recognized in Klemperer a conductor whose ability to give compelling performances of the classics was linked to an instinct for the music of his own time and an appetite for theatrical renewal. Klemperer's long-standing interest in the latter was further stimulated by the steady stream of conducting engagements he enjoyed in Russia following the 1922 Rapallo Treaty and the initiatives of a Soviet-German cultural association whose committee numbered Max von Schillings and Thomas Mann among its members. Klemperer visited Moscow and Leningrad every season from 1924 to 1929 and, always an avid theatre-goer, was deeply impressed by the productions of Stanislavsky, Nemirovich-Danchenko, and the avant-garde theatre led by Meyerhold, Tairov and others. The moving spirits of Soviet theatre were no less impressed by his own work, Meyerhold and Tairov joining a supper party for Klemperer after his performance of Weill's *Kleine Dreigroschenmusik* in March 1929. There can be no question that, as Peter Heyworth writes, 'Soviet avant-garde theatre undoubtedly opened new perspectives that influenced Klemperer's own approach to the stage when he became director of the Kroll Opera in 1927'.[57]

It was understandable that Klemperer, with Dülberg as his head of design, should choose to open his first season at the Kroll on 19 November 1927 with a *Fidelio* mod-

Fired by a belief that every age has a duty to reinterpret the classics, Otto Klemperer's Berlin Kroll Opera was a workshop for stage innovation. It opened in 1927 with a *Fidelio* whose designs by Ewald Dülberg were intended to echo the elemental structures of Beethoven's score. The costumes are as modern as the conception. In Rocco's quarters in the prison are (from left to right) Leonore (Rose Pauly), Rocco (Martin Abendroth), Jaquino (Albert Peters) and Marzelline (Irene Eisinger).

elled closely on his Wiesbaden staging. Dülberg, however, had now toned down the bold, almost fauve or expressionist primary colouring of the earlier production. Sobriety in an opera house, however, was seen by the overwhelming majority of conservative opera-goers in the capital as the unwelcome face of modernism and as such was resisted. There was near-unanimous press disapproval for Dülberg's sets, only Heinrich Strobel praising their 'formal strength and the subtle range of greys, blues and whites which stood in such sharp contrast to the violent colours Dülberg had used in Wiesbaden'. Some critics claimed that the production was too exactly drilled, Klemperer's conducting graceless and tyrannical.[58] By the lights of the Berlin opera cognoscenti the production was not a 'success'. What mattered, however, was that Klemperer had broken a lance for the path he intended to pursue. As that path was unprecedented, it was inevitable that his *Fidelio* should incur resentment and elicit cries that a vandal was loose in the sanctuary. But Kestenberg's support was unwavering, and by the end of the Kroll's first year Klemperer had shown that opera production could cast off its cobwebs and profit immensely from developments elsewhere in the theatre and the visual arts, which had long since left it behind.

This drew in many who had lost interest in opera or who were antagonistic to everything it had come to stand for – its moribund theatricality and its comfortable public. The Kroll's supporters included composers like Weill, Hanns Eisler, Schoenberg, Hindemith, Milhaud, Prokofiev and Roger Sessions; actors, dramatists, theatre directors and critics like Paul Wegener, Brecht, Piscator and Alfred Kerr; the artists of the Bauhaus; literati like T. W. Adorno, Walter Benjamin, Ernst Bloch and Thomas Mann; scientists like Albert Einstein; and many leading politicians and prelates. In the words of composer and critic H. H. Stuckenschmidt, who was engaged to report on the Kroll for the New York journal *Modern Music*, 'People applauded wildly, or protested with whistling and shouting, but no one was silent. Everyone was caught up. And this totally modern European theatre was impregnated with the spirit of Berlin, for only thus could such adventures have been possible or imaginable. It was epoch-making. As unforgettable and unrepeatable as the Bauhaus or, to invoke a Berlin comparison, the theatre of Erwin Piscator.'[59]

Klemperer's commitment was to vigorous *Werktreue* performances of the classics which would be 'zeitgültig' (relevant for the times), and to new productions of the best modern works.[60] In the Kroll's first twelve months its repertory included Smetana's *The Kiss*, Verdi's *Luisa Miller*, Mozart's *Don Giovanni*, Weber's *Der Freischütz*, Cimarosa's *Il matrimonio segreto*, Bizet's *Carmen*, Stravinsky's *Oedipus Rex*, *Mavra*, *L'Histoire du soldat* and the ballet *Petrushka*, Puccini's *Trittico*, Hindemith's *Cardillac* and Strauss's *Salome*. Such a cross-section of works old and new was unprecedented.

Klemperer shared the conducting with Alexander von Zemlinsky and Fritz Zweig. As Berlin's third opera house the Kroll could not hope to compete vocally with the Staatsoper and Städtische Oper, but it did not lack for good singers and Klemperer was 'more concerned with intelligence and musicality than with purely vocal attainments'.[61] On the production side those he worked with included Niedecken-Gebhard and many directors from spoken theatre, among them Jürgen Fehling (from the Berlin Schauspielhaus), Gustaf Gründgens (from Reinhardt's Deutsches Theater) and Ernst Legal, the unexciting, safe hand to whom Klemperer ceded administrative control in July 1928. Legal also produced five of the ten new productions in the Kroll's 1928–9 season.

The intention was that Dülberg, as head of design, should work on more productions than he did (these were, in addition to *Fidelio*, a Stravinsky triple bill of *Oedipus Rex*, *Mavra* and *Petrushka*, *Der Freischütz*, *Cardillac*, *Der fliegende Holländer*, *Die Zauberflöte* and *Rigoletto*), but he was already suffering from the tuberculosis from which he was to die at the age of forty-five in 1933. This opened the way for the Kroll's dramaturg, Hans Curjel, to cultivate a far closer association with artists of the avant-garde than either Dülberg or Klemperer himself – always a musician rather than an 'Augenmensch' (visual person) – would have wished. Much of the post-Dülberg design work was undertaken by his young protégé Teo Otto, who for Křenek's *Leben des Orest* (1930) worked from sketches by the surrealist Giorgio de Chirico. Otto was to become one of the most influential scenic artists of the modern

German stage.[62] Other designers from the theatre world included Traugott Müller, a close associate of Piscator, who worked on *L'Histoire du soldat* and Hindemith's *Neues vom Tage*, Caspar Neher (*Carmen*, *L'Heure espagnole*, Janáček's *From the House of the Dead*), the Viennese architect Oskar Strnad (a Křenek triple bill) and Rochus Gliese (Marschner's *Hans Heiling*), these last two names both well known in Berlin through their work for Reinhardt.

But Curjel looked to the cutting edge of innovation and was particularly keen to involve Oskar Schlemmer and Moholy-Nagy from the Bauhaus. Schlemmer's designs for Schoenberg's *Die glückliche Hand* were castigated by the composer for their failure to follow his own minutely detailed instructions (a rapprochement was achieved, but this remains a good example of a clash between a composer who knew what he wanted and an interpretative artist who knew better).[63] Klemperer's own view, which was not wide of the mark, was that Schoenberg had 'no idea of theatre, really none at all' and that it was right not to follow his instructions exactly.[64]

Moholy was responsible for the Kroll's most visually extreme production, Offenbach's *Contes d'Hoffmann*, conducted by Zemlinsky. This opened on 12 February 1929, when the public was still reeling from the hurricane of Klemperer's *Holländer*. It was as though Dr Spalanzani had invented not only Olympia but the entire production. The mechanistic, constructivist-inspired sets made use of powerful light effects and film-inserts, the scenery constantly on the move. Its props included the first functional steel furniture to be seen on an opera stage. Curjel's idea in commissioning Moholy was that 'A dream world would be evoked with modern materials. Machinery and human emotion would interact so as to reflect the ambivalence that gives the opera its special flavour.'[65]

The production was denounced by the right-wing press as cultural bolshevism and Jewish depravity. This was precisely the language of the Kampfbund für deutsche Kultur (Action Group for German Culture), which was founded at about this time in Munich by Alfred Rosenberg under Nazi auspices: its patrons included Wagner's daughter Eva, wife of Houston Stewart Chamberlain, and Siegfried Wagner's wife Winifred.[66]

Towards the beginning of the Kroll's second season the spectre of Wagner began to loom, not least because Klemperer was looking for a work which would give the house the kind of palpable success that had so far proved elusive. While Klemperer the ascetic was resistant to the rich orchestration of Wagner's later works, particularly as it came across in the lush performances conducted by Furtwängler and Bruno Walter, he took up Richard Strauss's suggestion that he should resurrect the composer's original version of *Der fliegende Holländer*. In the Prussian State Library, Klemperer and Curjel discovered the score used by Wagner himself for his performances at the Berlin Schauspielhaus in 1844, a year after the Dresden premiere. The raw vigour of the opera in which the young composer had found his own unmistakable voice was, for Klemperer, a good way of settling his differences with Wagner. Klemperer, Dülberg and their chosen producer Jürgen Fehling (working in opera for the first time) were wholly antipathetic to Bayreuth's reverential embalmings and came up with a very different view of the work.

It was inevitable – perhaps even necessary – that the production premiered on 15 January 1929, with police at the doors anticipating riots, should be assailed as a mockery of Wagner and that Curjel should be called before the Prussian Landtag (Parliament) to account for it. What other response could there have been to the first high-profile radical challenge in a German opera house to the accepted way of performing Wagner? Here was a totally unsentimental, tough-minded production of his first mature work. Its architects were not the kind of men to seek scandal for its own sake but were driven by their mission to make audible and visible the 'pure artistic core of the work'.[67]

The collision between the 'Sachlichkeit' of their approach and the Senta-sentimentality of traditional production testified to the persistence of the latter (as a refuge from the rough winds of political and cultural change) in the new theatrical era of Piscator and Brecht, of Meyerhold and Eisenstein, of the cinema, the wireless and the gramophone. Hence the outrage that the Dutchman should have been robbed of his beard, that Senta should have been a modern girl in a blue pullover and that her plait-less companions should have been mending nets rather than toying with spinning wheels. It had not helped that the philosopher Ernst Bloch had written an introductory piece arguing that to treat the opera as a nautical adventure story by Captain Marryat, but with surrealistic overtones, was as good a way as any of liberating it from the kitsch fantasy ('Traumkitsch') in which first Wagner himself and then his heirs had cocooned it.[68]

Klemperer gave the opera in three separate acts, just as Wagner had always done. Dülberg's sets again used only the most basic building blocks of ramps, platforms and steps, with the simplest of means to suggest the spars, masts and decks of the ships. The production was described by the theatre critic Bernhard Diebold:

> In the first and third acts the designs are still preoccupied with stylization. In the second act there is a complete translation of the sound world into colours.
> Senta's house is glazed like a lighthouse and stands as though surrounded by sea mist. The tar-black spars of the ghost-ship tower over the roof. The Dutchman appears from the mist and materializes in the room in the dark form of a man. No beard, no hat. A sinister man as though pictured by Th.[éodore] Rousseau: the most powerful atmosphere of the production was in the second act. Senta, as though possessed by the devil, springs up and sings the ballad. Her ecstasy possesses the whole house.

Diebold considered that although Moje Forbach was somewhat overtaxed vocally as Senta, her powerful acting conveyed an incomparable impression of heroic possession. Every gesture and action was rooted in the music, Klemperer's conducting suggesting that, like Wagner, he had sailed through the storm from Riga to Sandwike. Its directness and primal strength were in striking contrast to Bruno Walter's approach at the Städtische Oper, whose characteristically 'romantic' *Tannhäuser* turned an opera into a concert. It was 'Regie aus dem Geiste der Musik' – production from within the spirit of the music.[69]

Nor, for Heinrich Strobel, did this mean that the work had been robbed of its authentic aura: 'Clarity and directness supplanted overgrown romantic illusionism. Not that this *Holländer* was against the romantic. On the contrary, never before had the opera seemed so strange, so unreal and ghostly. It broke away from every shabby scenic gambit of the usual opera performance. ... the opera's romantic quality was achieved with contemporary means. The *Holländer* was not de-romanticized but de-operafied.' From Daland's ship emerged 'not the usual opera actors with ill-fitting slouch hats and false beards, but real seamen'.[70]

For Alfred Einstein, 'There was no Norwegian rocky shore against which the little ship had run in the storm, but rather a Hamburg pier at which Daland's boat was already moored; and from the beginning the Dutchman was standing there in the background.... Here no one was seasick other than the dear old Wagnerians.' Like everyone else, Einstein remarked the modernity of the dress and of the characters: 'Daland, the Steuermann, the Norwegian crew were just ordinary seamen, perhaps

Klemperer's *Der fliegende Höllander* at the Kroll Opera in 1929 flung down a modern-dress challenge to traditional Wagner production. Dülberg used the simplest stylized forms to represent the ships. There was outrage that the Dutchman had been shorn of his beard and that Senta was a redhead in a blue pullover. The Dutchman's ship is seen in Act III during the chorus, which was sung from the pit, of its ghostly crew.

from Lübeck or Swinemunde, at any event just Nordic seamen … the Dutchman had lost his handsome, melancholic beard, wore a black havelock and looked like a proper ghost, in other words an Ibsenesque, almost Strindbergian "man of the sea", and Senta herself was no longer a heroine (O shade of Schröder-Devrient!) but a redhead peasant girl who might have been drawn by Käthe Kollwitz.'[71] In Moje Forbach's own fascinating account, 'I wore a blue pullover, a close-fitting grey skirt of coarse cloth and a startling red wig, smoothly combed back into a knot. This was of course extraordinary, because I'd previously always worn blouses and little bodices, skirts and petticoats. But this [costume] suited Klemperer's kind of production, design, acting style and musical approach – it was, in effect, a tough Ur-Holländer.'[72]

Tough, too, on singers who, not unwillingly, went along with Fehling's intensive work to turn them into actors. He compelled them to dispense with all superfluous operatic histrionics and his blocking paid no attention to their vocal needs. Forbach describes how when singers found themselves in positions where they were unable to breathe properly, Fehling simply said, 'It doesn't matter, it's basically just a real person, a living creature,' meaning not an idealized character.[73]

The incursion of *Sachlichkeit* into operatic myth was plainly not without its problems. 'The ideology of a redemption opera is foreign to us today,' wrote Heinrich Strobel, 'but Wagner is here performed in a way that leaves the disturbing musical impression undiminished.'[74] What Strobel fails to say is whether the production ignored or transmuted that ideology, and if the latter, what it was transmuted into. He says that the production directly addresses the problem of what Wagner and his art 'have to say to us today', but he presumes rather than describes its solution.

There was also scope for difference of opinion among well-disposed critics as to whether, as Diebold thought, the action sprang directly from the music or, as in Einstein's opinion, was in dialogue with it. 'The sea, the wind,' wrote Einstein, 'the breeze of Wagner's stormy crossing from Riga to London were clearly heard in the music, but played not the slightest role in the staging. … The real stylistic break [Stilbruch] was created by such things as Dülberg's elevated living room with its transparent picture of the Dutchman … the appearance of the ghost-ship in the stage space behind this living-room … the gruesome ghostly crew of the phantom ship – once again an irruption from Strindberg, not Wagner.' All this, Einstein goes on, disturbs the harmony of the work, is unmusical, is a violation. 'Why then is it so affecting, so thrilling? It is because Wagner the dramatist of the elements, the musician of the elements, was vigorously present. … the ghostly chorus, powerful in number and sound, sang from the orchestra pit – all this had a truer, more absolute and direct effect than if enacted in the guise of "romantic opera".'[75]

Obviously enough, what was new here was that Klemperer sought to intensify the drama by giving the stage action whatever freedom it required, consistent only with the music being given full value on its own terms. It was an acknowledgement that the stage action, while still rooted in the music, could be more dramatically powerful for not echoing it slavishly but rather being in dialogue with it – a new source of dramatic tension. Plainly there were dangers in this new theatrical emphasis –

evident enough in Moje Forbach's account – but there were huge gains in the actuality of the theatrical experience: enter 'Wagner our contemporary'.

To this there could be no better witness than the pain and outrage of those – still living in the Makart era – who wanted their dreams left undisturbed and who rejected anything that reminded them of the Weimar world outside the theatre.[76] This attitude, prevalent in a sizeable portion of the Volksbühne – and critics – was nicely caught in an anonymous article mocking the protesters: 'Their understanding of Wagner is: the heroic torso of the folk-hero, a swastika in the buttonhole, old German culture and customs, grandiose gestures, a full beard, a heaving breast and long flowing blond hair, the iron fist and heil! to our dear Kaiser.' But instead of this, the writer continues, Klemperer gives us Senta as a hysterical redhead, spinning girls in woollen sweaters (not inappropriate one would have thought) and sailors looking like dockers. 'No hand-on-heart or swimming movements, no magical atmosphere, no traditional romanticism to lift the heart and banish the grey mundanity of everyday life'.[77]

As we saw in chapter 5, this was not exactly the philosophy of Bayreuth in the later 1920s. Siegfried Wagner came up to Berlin to see what all the fuss was about. After the dress rehearsal he came on stage and greeted the singers with, 'Nu, Ihr seht ja alle zum Piepen aus' ('Well, you all seem a little crazy'), to which Klemperer, offering him a chair, and punning on 'sich setzen' (to sit down), replied, 'Bitte, Herr Wagner, entsetzen Sie sich' ('Please, Herr Wagner, be enraged').[78]

Klemperer's 'zeitgültig' approach clearly unleashed a complex reaction. Klemperer and his team were not just picture-cleaning to reveal the work as the composer conceived it: they were also inevitably projecting their own concerns and images into it. The creators of the production found in it an unmystical, storytelling Wagner, a Feuerbachian utopian rather than a Schopenhauerean doom-monger, a republican revolutionary who mirrored their own impatience with burdensome cultural tradition, an angry republican tossed around by the tempests but with his feet never far from firm anchorage. That was the *actualité* of the performance. It was inevitable that it should offend those for whom the explosive power of Wagner's work had been defused into an agreeable aesthetic experience by sanctimonious tradition. Before Klemperer's production, the critical reformers had largely sought stagings that would help the musical drama speak more eloquently, more directly, than adherence to Wagner's own stage rubrics allowed. Klemperer and his team had, perhaps even to their own surprise, shown for the first time that the myths and metaphors could, with gain rather than loss, be refracted through a modern lens.

Although unintended by Klemperer and his colleagues, this also had the result of putting opera on the political agenda. That no political ideology lay behind the radical production style was self-evident and attested by a visiting Russian critic, Nikolai Malkov, who knew a thing or two about politics and theatre. Malkov considered the Berlin theatres to be backward by comparison with those in Russia, rating the Kroll's *Holländer* as 'inoffensive'.[79] Klemperer's political sympathies (fairly confused at the best of times; see Heyworth passim) were nevertheless of the left rather than the right. It was therefore no surprise that he should be accused of 'political radicalism', *Kulturbolschewismus* and worse. To the *Allgemeine Musikzeitung*, 'The clean-shaven Dutchman seemed like a bolshevist agitator, Senta a fanatical and eccentric communist woman, Erik, with his wild, tufted hair and in woollen sweater, a pimp.'[80] The political charge in Wagner's oeuvre as a whole surfaced powerfully at the Kroll, polarizing attitudes between the nationalist reactionaries at one end of the spectrum and communist revolutionaries at the other.

The Kroll's repertory and productions were, as we have seen, not at all to the taste of its Volksbühne constituency, which, as Klemperer later said, only wanted 'big singers, big arias, big applause and so on'.[81] The Kroll excited the Republic's artists and intellectuals while increasingly incurring the wrath of those who saw in it only the betrayal of the highest values of German culture. Kestenberg's great hope that education would close the gap between modernism and the public had in no way been fulfilled.[82] The Kroll became a stalking-horse for rightist attacks on the Republic. Klemperer fought hard to save it but became engulfed by the political tide of nationalism, and the theatre was eventually closed down on 3 July 1931. He joined Leo Blech and Erich Kleiber as one of the three principal conductors at the Staatsoper, where in 1933, as part of the celebration of the fiftieth anniversary of Wagner's death, he conducted a *Tannhäuser* in Kroll style, directed by Jürgen Fehling and designed by Oskar Strnad.[83] Shortly thereafter he was compelled to flee Germany, travelling first to Switzerland then to America. As for the Kroll, it suffered the ignominy of becoming the home of the Reichstag after the fire of 27 February 1933 and was later razed to the ground by the Allies.

Nothing Klemperer was subsequently to do in opera was to generate the artistic and intellectual excitement of what he had achieved at the Kroll. It was not so much a question of backsliding as of retrogressive cultural circumstance and of the catastrophic mental and physical health which all but destroyed him in America. While the Kroll was in its death throes he had already pronounced its finest epitaph: 'Whenever this approach to opera is revived, it will have to start where we have been obliged to leave off. They may shut our theatre, but the idea underlying it cannot be killed.'[84]

PART III

CHAPTER 9

Wieland Wagner: opera as mystery play

The new beginning

In chapter 6 I suggested that the ideas of Appia and Craig had to wait half a century before they came to fruition in Wieland Wagner's Bayreuth productions from 1951. While that is incontrovertibly true, Wieland's central place in twentieth-century theatrical history lies not in his application of anyone else's ideas but in his own distinctive vision. From the reopening of the Bayreuth Festival in 1951 until his death at the age of forty-nine in 1966, his artist's eye and musical sensibility created a new visual landscape. It was, in effect, an overnight revolution – offensive to traditionalists, to others a revelation. Wieland's 'empty space' stagings seemed to have discovered a way of performing his grandfather's oeuvre that solved most of the problems inherent in 'realistic' production. What was seen in the 'empty space' seemed at last to be a true visual translation of the profound mythopoeic layers of Wagner's creations. Wieland's vision sprang from his conviction that the values of myth and archetype were pre-eminent, and that the *Ring* was a profound map of the human psyche. The composer's own tortuous search for a visual world for his musical drama seemed at an end.

Wieland and his younger brother Wolfgang, aged thirty-four and thirty-one respectively, had been entrusted with the reopening of the festival after their mother Winifred had been effectively dispossessed by a denazification court. Over the festival lay the shameful shadow of the Führer's appropriation of it as a cultural flagship for the Reich. Over Wieland and Wolfgang hovered the grim truth about the 'Onkel Wolf' who had virtually been their stepfather, and the ever present strain of the proximity of their mother, unrepentant as she was of her adulation for her friend and hero. When Wieland spoke of the necessity of 'entrümpeln' – of clearing out the rubbish and making a clean start – he was speaking of more than tired old scenery, costumes and stage props.

With his *Parsifal* and *Ring* productions of 1951, he began to lay not only the political ghosts but also the myth that Wagner's works were best served by stagings in the authentic Bayreuth style as moulded by Cosima and Siegfried. Apostasy had arrived overnight on the Green Hill. Over the next fifteen years Wieland's work was never to lose its capacity to shock and surprise. Initially it met with much resistance, but by the time he died it was generally regarded as one of the most compelling and far-reaching theatrical manifestations of the twentieth century. Wagner production would never be the same again.

By the time I first saw Wieland's stagings – in 1967 – he had been dead for nearly a year. No matter how skilfully staged by those who, like the director Peter Lehmann and the great bass Hans Hotter, had worked closely with him, the productions were already history. But their impact on anyone experiencing them for the first time remained extraordinary.

First impressions and overview of the Wieland style

Wieland, famously, was dedicated to using light as a major element in production. Yet it was striking how dim the stage seemed – indeed the lighting levels were so low that they would have been impracticable in any other auditorium than the pitch-black Festspielhaus with its covered orchestra pit. But it did not take long to find one's night-vision and appreciate the new intensity this brought to listening to the music. What one saw on stage was far more closely in tune with it than was the case generally. Every sense was sharpened. What was important was the subtle effects that the muted illumination made possible. The stage was a space interfused with light that seemed to have no discernible source. And it was soon apparent that the graduations, the modulations, the shifts in mood and intensity of this light seemed to grow out of the music. One of the most wonderful images was Siegfried's awakening of Brünnhilde; it was as though she had been laid to sleep on the very rim of the earth's surface. It seemed that the great inverted dome of the sky itself had, with Siegfried, kissed her awake and inaugurated the dawn of a new world.

Elemental shapes, forms, textures predominated. This was a theatre of depth-illusion, of journeyings into a twilight world of dreams and the subconscious, the singers its shadowy dramatis personae. Specific visual imagery was kept to a minimum. It was left to the spectator's 'theatre of the mind' to complete the picture. Thus was solved the problem of dragons and rainbow bridges: they had not so much been 'left out' as consigned to a life of their own in the imagination of the audience. Wieland's concentration was on forms, structures, patterns that evoked what Jung would have called the archetypes of Wagner's cosmic vision.

Wieland always confronted the audience with the essence. In *Tannhäuser* (1961) there was no wayside shrine for Elisabeth's prayers but only a huge black cross towering out of sight behind the proscenium. His visual inventions, like those of the sculptor Henry Moore, were often inspired by rocks, geological forms, animal skulls. *Tristan* (1962) was dominated by priapic forms – in Act I the towering prow was all that remained of the ship, in Act II a totemic column with owl-like eyes, and in Act III a sharp, pierced segment – suggestive of a thorn, or the blade of an axe – presided over the agony and ecstasy of Tristan's dying. The curve of the stage floor suggested the surface of some mysterious alien planet. The cold, eerie greens and airless grey-blues created an atmosphere reminiscent of Stefan George's 'air from another planet' first breathed by Wagner in *Tristan* nearly half a century before Schoenberg in his

The idea that an elemental style of staging might correspond most closely with the musical and mythopoeic core of Wagner's works was first mooted in the 1890s. Some sixty years later the composer's grandson Wieland had the genius to translate it to the stage, as photographed here at Bayreuth in 1954. When Siegfried kissed Brünnhilde into new life from her slumber, he was also awakening a whole new era of stage interpretation.

Second Quartet. In her *Verklärung* (transfiguration) Isolde, in yellow, rose up like a new sun while the dying light behind her seemed that of the moon's terminal eclipse.

Wieland's second Bayreuth *Ring* (1965) was a perfect example of his power to evoke a subliminal world. A central raised disc, or *Scheibe*, was the unifying arena of action, with an encircling cyclorama behind. The lower part of the cyclorama, immediately behind the acting area, was kept dark so that the action sometimes seemed to be unanchored by gravity, an effect often accentuated by the use of a narrow follow spot that illuminated only a singer's head and shoulders. The eye was never lured away into the distance of a pictorial perspective, but always focused on the acting area. The blanket of darkness afforded remarkable entries for the chorus. When Hagen summoned the vassals, his own tight circle of light expanded to show that they were already there, surrounding the *Scheibe*. They, like everyone and everything else, were omnipresent, only awaiting their cue. This powerful idea was also used to dispense with the kind of entry procession for the knights of the Grail beloved of stage managers but which was anathema to Wagner and his grandson alike. The knights were heard singing while it appeared that Amfortas was alone in the temple. Then they were suddenly visible in the form of a sinister ring closing in on him from the shadows, as each man moved five paces forward to his place at the table. There was a powerful sense of the jaws of a circular vice tightening around the

Wieland always sought out the symbolic essence of Wagner's richly detailed scenarios. In his 1962 staging of *Tristan*, the ship and its prow were transmuted into a priapic form that towered over Tristan (Wolfgang Windgassen) and Isolde (Birgit Nilsson).

wounded Amfortas. The circle, though, remained incomplete until the very end of the opera, when the spear healed the wound and both the wound and the circle could close.

These great stagings of *Tristan*, the *Ring* and *Parsifal* magnificently served the more abstract, Schopenhauerean qualities of Wagner's scores. Wieland's approaches to *Holländer*, *Tannhäuser*, *Lohengrin* and *Die Meistersinger* had different strategies. But in every case he sought out what he took to be the core meaning, ridding Wagner's works of the cliché encrustations of the past and of the nationalist programme thrust upon them by the Nazis.

Die Meistersinger, 1956–1963

Bayreuth had reopened in 1951 with a conventional staging of *Die Meistersinger* by Rudolf Hartmann, but it was not long before Wieland came up with a radical treatment which dealt fearlessly with the lingering sense of unease about the misuse of which the work had proved itself capable. Wieland wanted to rescue *Die Meistersinger* from having become what he called 'a dangerous mixture of Lortzing and the Reichsparteitag'.[1] And so his production of 1956 rejected specific evocation of sixteenth-century Nuremberg in favour of a bare minimum of visual reference.

A lingering sense of unease about the Third Reich's possessive consecration of *Die Meistersinger* engendered Wieland's 1956 staging: it eliminated every trace of a timber-framed, folkloristic Nuremberg. In the second act, the intrigues of a midsummer night took place on an open raft, above which floated a floriferous sphere.

Act I revealed the congregation, posed as though in a devotional Renaissance paint-ing, singing straight out to the audience. The scandal of the production did not erupt until the second act. No trace of a timbered Nuremberg remained. The stage picture was simply that of a cobbled promontory, with a huge floral globe hung aloft and a smaller one on the right at stage level. The simplest props – cobbler's stool, worktable, etc. – sufficed for the action. The air was suffused with violet-blue light. For the Fest-wiese in Act III, there was a small stretched-canvas stage in the foreground with a steeply rising amphitheatre behind in which the full chorus was already seated. In place of processions, the entries of the guilds were mimed by a single dancer. Charac-terization played up the less agreeable side of the Masters' conservatism. Sachs was shown as a less than wholly honourable manipulator of the action. He had, in the words of Wieland's daughter Nike, been 'transformed from a Nazi Kreisleiter into a psychoanalyst who directed this play of psychological undertones, guiding the erotic urges of Eva and Walther into matrimony and the destructive forces of the citizens into harmless excesses'.[2] The effect of the whole was summed up by Walter Panofsky as 'a mystery play about the secret of creative inspiration'.[3]

It created a furore, until then a most unusual phenomenon at Bayreuth, but understandable in that this was the first time that the picturesque scenery had been totally removed. It was *Die Meistersinger* not only without nineteenth-century romantic ideas about the German Renaissance but also without sixteenth-century Nuremberg.

Returning to the opera in 1963, Wieland restored it to the sixteenth century but now as a play, or series of plays, within a play, the framework being that of a Globe-style galleried wooden theatre in which the Nurembergers enacted the opera as a coarse comedy, as an entertainment staged by mechanicals.[4] Wieland's rationale was that Wagner's comedy 'had no need of the conventions of illusionistic opera-theatre'.[5] His approach therefore owed something to Brecht's theory of presenting a sequence of actions rather than representing them as 'real'. The curtain was replaced by a front-drop with the title inscribed in Richard Wagner's hand together with his signature. The church was signified by a triptych altarpiece (copied from a Lukas Cranach original), later obliterated by flying in a screen on which the rules of the *Tabulatur* were set out. The galleries and ground plan of the wooden O lent them-selves readily to the intrigues of Act II. Act III began with a relatively conventional set-up for Sachs's parlour. This was flown out for the 'Festwiese', leaving the theatre ready for the rough-and-tumble of a Bruegel-like peasant dance which evolved into a conga, with the girls from Fürth drawing the entire company into a single human chain. Fanfares from trumpeters on papier-mâché horses heralded the arrival of the guilds. 'The whole impression,' wrote Walter Panofsky, 'was that of an improvised farce like the play of Pyramus and Thisbe presented by Peter Quince to the court.'[6] But eventually the knockabout comedy stopped. After Sachs's address, a drop hid the wooden theatre from view and the chorus, now in earnest, sang their praise of Sachs straight out into the audience from the front of the stage.

Wieland's Masters were a stalwart aspirant-bourgeoisie embodying the spirit of German art. For Geoffrey Skelton, this textually accurate presentation of the Masters

In his second *Die Meistersinger* in 1963, Wieland satirized the nationalistic aura by having the Nurembergers enact the opera as an irreverent comedy in a Globe-style galleried theatre. In this scene from the finale, Eva (Anja Silja) sits surrounded by the Nine Muses, with Jess Thomas in the centre just below her as Walther.

defused 'the taint of nationalism from Sachs's words [in his closing address], or rather what Sachs's words are usually taken to mean'. Sachs, indeed, came across as 'propounding a thought of irreproachable liberalism, almost indeed of pacificism. It is not through its warriors that a nation shows its greatness, he says, but through its artists.'[7] Some pined for the more spiritualized treatment of 1956. They felt less than comfortable with the idea that art may be more at home in a rumbustious, earthy context than on some more elevated plane. But there could be no question that the effect of both productions was to exorcize the malign spirits of the past and to show that *Die Meistersinger* was more than an anthem to German nationalism. 'Wieland,' observes Nike Wagner, 'managed to offend both the conservatives who believed that art should reinforce traditional German values … and the liberals who favoured art that was formally exquisite and apolitical.'[8]

Wieland had travelled a long way from the sets and costumes he had designed as a 26-year-old for the 1943/4 Bayreuth staging by Heinz Tietjen, described in the official propaganda as 'a talisman and contribution to victory'.[9] To understand the significance of Wieland's work after 1951 we must go back to the story of its emergence from his apprentice years, when his talent was nurtured under the flag of the Führer. For obvious reasons, Wieland himself drew a veil over a past he was anxious to put behind him, but as his reaction against it was a formative influence on his mature work, it is not to be ignored.[10]

Winifred and her artistic team

At Siegfried's death in 1930 control of Bayreuth passed to his 33-year-old widow
Winifred. She had known Hitler since 1923 when she had first invited him to visit
Wahnfried. He was to become a frequent visitor and an increasingly close friend of
the family, later providing the money and Führer-support which helped the festival
to survive and flourish.[11] Her choice of artistic collaborators was shrewd. As music
director she engaged Wilhelm Furtwängler, conductor of the Berlin Philharmonic,
who although already renowned as a Wagnerian had not so far performed at
Bayreuth. As artistic director she appointed Heinz Tietjen (1881–1967), conductor,
producer and, since 1927, Generalintendant (general director) of the Prussian State
Theatres.[12] This established a bond between the Berlin Staatsoper and Bayreuth
which meant that the festival could draw on the pick of the Staatsoper's singers and
instrumentalists, probably then the finest in Germany.

Tietjen was a safe pair of hands – and no mean chameleon. He had risen to eminence as a socialist in the Weimar Republic, yet within years became the most powerful theatre administrator in the Third Reich. He was so skilled an operator that the
denazification process was only able to classify him as a 'kleiner Mitläufer', or minor
collaborator.[13] After the war he re-emerged as Intendant at the Hamburg Opera. A
hatchet was buried when he invited Wieland Wagner to stage his first *Lohengrin*
there in 1957, Wieland reciprocating by inviting Tietjen back to Bayreuth to conduct
the Bayreuth version of this production. But at the Festspielhaus in the 1930s he
worked principally as a producer, while Furtwängler and superlative singers gave
musical performances of legendary quality.

On the scenic side, Winifred and Tietjen moved resolutely beyond the simpler,
more painterly, but still excessively reverential style of Siegfried into uncharted
waters. The designer they chose was Emil Preetorius (1883–1973), who made his
Bayreuth debut in 1933 with designs for the *Ring* and *Die Meistersinger*.

Preetorius had a passion for classical and oriental art. He had begun as a Jugendstil artist specializing in book illustration and design, producing the jacket for the
first (limited) edition of Thomas Mann's *Herr und Hund* (his story about his dog,
Bauschan) in 1919. It was at Mann's suggestion a couple of years later that Bruno
Walter engaged Preetorius to design *Iphigénie en Aulide* for the Munich Opera. This
was his first venture into the theatre, where he was to enjoy considerable success in
the 1920s in Dresden, Munich and Berlin, leading to his invitation to Bayreuth.

His *Ring* designs of 1933–42 were a resourceful compromise between the imperatives of Bayreuth's canonical literalism and the freer, consciously symbolic shapes
and spaces advocated by Appia in the 1890s, which Preetorius softened with naturalistic detail. After the war he designed a *Ring* for Rome (1953–4) and for Karajan at
the Vienna Opera (1958–60), though in each case without any significant change to
his pre-war style.

Winifred's appointments of Tietjen and Preetorius were not at all what the Party
would have wished. Indeed, they were regarded with suspicion as, under Winifred
and Hitler's protective patronage, they ploughed a furrow that was freer and more

When Siegfried's widow Winifred took over the festival in 1930 she chose Furtwängler as her music director and an equally strong production team. At rehearsal with her (from left to right) are technical director Paul Eberhardt, producer and conductor Heinz Tietjen, and the designer Emil Preetorius.

imaginative than the mainstream of ideologically correct, 'naturalistic' theatre production in which nothing adventurous was permitted. Goebbels's policy was aptly characterized as 'One Reich, one Folk, one Staging Style'.[14] Although the very fact that Tietjen and Preetorius sustained important artistic positions under the Reich implies a degree of complaisance that could not have been blameless, their political pedigrees were nothing but an embarrassment.

Both men had been active Social Democrats and Tietjen had been openly anti-Nazi in the closing years of the Weimar Republic. Goebbels hated him but was unable to remove him as head of the Prussian State Theatres as that appointment lay in the gift of Goering, whose dislike of Goebbels was certainly a contributory factor in his continued support of Tietjen. Alfred Rosenberg, the Party's cultural ideologue, protested against Winifred's appointment of Tietjen as artistic adviser to Bayreuth on the grounds that he was a Social Democrat and hence unacceptable, but Winifred stoutly defended her choice.[15] Preetorius had been a member of the Union to

Combat Anti-Semitism (Verein zur Abwehr des Antisemitismus) and was denounced as such by the *Völkischer Beobachter*. Tietjen, Preetorius and Furtwängler secured exemption from the Führer for a number of exceptional Jewish musicians: Schnorr, Kipnis, List and several others were allowed to sing at Bayreuth long after they had been banned from appearing elsewhere in the Reich (most of them gradually withdrew to more hospitable pastures abroad).[16] Preetorius had the courage to maintain his Jewish friendships for the duration of the Reich.[17]

The productions of Heinz Tietjen and Emil Preetorius

The huge attention attracted by Hitler's involvement with Bayreuth has obscured the achievements of Tietjen and Preetorius. In reality the artistic break between the Bayreuth of Cosima and Siegfried and that of Winifred, Tietjen and Preetorius was as great as that between the latter and the New Bayreuth of Wieland and Wolfgang Wagner. The essence of the new start made in 1933 was that, after a year in which the theatre had been dark, it broke decisively with the attitude of unconditional reverence for Wagner's own stage aesthetic. Tietjen and Preetorius, tempered in the cauldron of Weimar experimentalism, knew that Bayreuth, fifty years after Wagner's death, had to move on. Their scarcely daring idea was that provided one kept faith with certain essentials, certain fixed points in the dramaturgy, there was much that needed to be done to make Wagner's works more compelling for new audiences. 'Our efforts,' they said, 'are aimed at detaching the production, the stage set and the costumes … from the traditional sphere of historicism and naturalism, and at penetrating to its core substance, the musical drama.'[18]

This impulse arrived at Bayreuth at the same time as the Nazis – and it was Hitler's own enthusiasm for Wagner and interest in stage production which helped bring it to fruition. As Frederic Spotts points out, 'The paradoxical effect of Hitler's patronage was to make the Festival the only cultural institution in the Third Reich independent of Nazi control.'[19] Bayreuth, previously the epitome of nationalistic values, became a cradle of theatrical innovation, even if within a relatively conservative frame. This was a terrible blow to the traditionalists. When Walter Dirks observed in 1938 in the *Frankfurter Zeitung* that Bayreuth's scenic renewal had placed it in the same league as the world's leading stages, to the guardians of the Grail this was nothing but a betrayal of the true spirit of Bayreuth. They had looked to Hitler to deliver Bayreuth from any descent into the outrageous experimentalism of the Weimar period, only to discover that it was surging in under his patronage! Winifred supported Tietjen and Preetorius in their efforts to cultivate an artistic path quite other than that of the state-decreed 'naturalism'.[20]

A Jungian at heart, Preetorius anticipated Wieland Wagner in seeing the *Ring* as embodying 'archetypes of eternal events' and seeking to avoid any historical sense of time and place.[21] His response to Wagner's mimetic evocations of nature in the music (which he recognized as perhaps the major scenic problem to be solved) was to complement them with theatrical suggestions rather than pictorial illusion. Preetorius set out his ideas in the article 'Zum Szenenproblem in Bayreuth', published in the

1933 programme book.[22] Renewal, he says, is essential because the old naturalistic-illusionistic style of staging could never do justice to the complex magic of the operas. Nevertheless, a degree of naturalism was indispensable in showing the waves of the Rhine, the thunderstorm and rainbow bridge, the moonlight breaking into Hunding's hut, the forest murmurs in the second act of *Siegfried* or the twig from which Siegfried cuts his pipe, Brünnhilde's steed Grane, or the swan in *Lohengrin*. Nor was it enough to imagine that geometric forms like cubes could represent a rocky wasteland in *Götterdämmerung* or the castle courtyard in *Lohengrin* – such things had to be palpably present. And such alien modernizations as abstract forms or beardless heros were not to be allowed. That would be going too far.

What was needed was the elimination of superfluous detail. The effect of such decorative detail in the costumes of the gods, for instance, was to diminish their humanity. Renewal could only come from within. It had to be remembered, insisted Preetorius the classicist, that Wagner's great model was Greek tragedy. The designer's aim must therefore always be to create a symbolic world, a mirror in which man would recognize himself. The operas were parables, metaphors of cosmic truths, and their representation should be ahistorical. The designer's task was to bring the multi-layered *Ring* 'under a single artistic span and to weld it into the kind of unity that alone can reveal the breadth and immensity of the Wagnerian conception, concentrating its richly coloured diversity into an all-embracing symbol'.[23]

These were the principles on which Preetorius, together with Winifred and Tietjen, was attempting the scenic renewal of Wagner's works, and they were no less applicable to the works of Gluck, Mozart or Weber. Keenly aware of the context in which he would be read, Preetorius signs off by saying that this task was part of a great national undertaking to secure for the Festspielhaus, now and in the future, its vital role as a resounding testimony to German genius and German aspiration.[24]

In a later essay, Preetorius considers that while Wagner's work is 'symbolic in its essential existence' the designer should never oversimplify or over-stylize, 'still less should he venture into the field of abstraction … he must always remain on the terra firma of concrete images'. The problem was to reconcile apparently contradictory elements in order to secure 'a harmonious interplay between symbol and illusion, dream and reality, inner vision and outward nature, forcing them together to form an overarching compositional whole'.[25]

Whereas Siegfried and Söhnlein's solid scenery had resembled clumsily moulded rock piles with cast-in visible steps for the singers' safety, Preetorius created more geologically credible rock forms with a stratified, horizontal emphasis. Something of this was owed to Appia, most noticeably his Valkyrie rock (illustrated in chapter 6). For the third act of *Tristan* in 1938, Kareol's castle wall and the sheltering tree were moved to the extreme left-hand margin of the stage, opening up the foreground as a huge, plain rocky ledge. At the rear this blended almost imperceptibly into the sea and sky beyond. Preetorius developed the projection of skyscapes more effectively than ever before, so that the sky and land forms were subtly bound together achieving, through stylization and simplification, a greater realism than had been attained by even the most perfectly painted cloths.

Preetorius's use of light was based on his belief in 'a muted palette avoiding direct colour contrasts but using colour values to create the most varied changes of mood, more especially through the medium of light which, in its mysterious affinity with sounds, has the power to change and to effect such changes'.[26] His lighting plots, developed with the Festspielhaus's technical director, Paul Eberhardt, revelled in strong dramatic effects, as in the darkening of the stage when the giants abduct Freia, the towering image of Valhalla still glowing incandescently at the rear.[27] In the second act of *Götterdämmerung* (1938), the chiaroscuro lighting and sky effects established a superbly ominous atmosphere, the scene framed at the front of the stage by silhouettes of vassals, facing in to stage centre.[28]

Where Preetorius did use strong colour contrasts was in his costumes – for Wotan and Fricka, blue; for Freia and Froh, pale green; for Donner, dark brown; for Loge, light red. In design they were in romantic storybook style, with Alberich and Mime as Rackham-like caricatures with bushy black beards. In *Götterdämmerung*, Siegfried addressed the Rhinedaughters wearing a winged helmet and there was chain-mail armour for Tristan, Lohengrin and Parsifal.[29] There was much consternation that Amfortas was (*pace* Preetorius's manifesto of 1933) shorn of his beard – in this case as part of the wish to dechristianize the ethos of the work. The heroines wore long medieval-style gowns with braided decoration, and with waist-length plaits for both Elsa and Ortrud.

Tietjen's strength as a director lay not in any originality of approach but in his skill in bringing orchestra, voices and production together into a powerful dramatic unity – still a relative rarity in the 1930s. His gods suppressed physical agitation and anger, affecting a tense, almost statuesque sense of calm authority, while his human heros were allowed a freer, more natural and individualistic expression. Sub-humans were histrionic caricatures. For such scenes as the finale of *Siegfried* or Brünnhilde's immolation, a powerful sense of pathos in vocal expression and physical movement was the style.[30]

Tietjen had a Reinhardt in him in his fondness for large-scale effects. Wieland and Wolfgang's sister, Friedelind, considered Tietjen 'a very great stage director' but was sorry 'when he fell a victim to the lavishness of the Reinhardt school. He was not satisfied unless he had at least 800 people and a dozen horses milling around on the stage. Comparing his manner with Father's I was finally convinced that many of his productions were too elaborate and a departure from the inner meaning of the music dramas.'[31] Against Cosima's handling of the chorus as a group of distinct individuals, Tietjen reverted to de-personalized mass blockings. Siegfried had already inflated Wagner's 1876 Gibichung chorus of 26 to 64, but Tietjen expanded this to 101 in 1933.[32] In *Parsifal*, 48 Flowermaidens blossomed on stage (Wagner had wanted 24), while the Festwiese chorus and extras in *Die Meistersinger* numbered no fewer than 800 in 1933.[33] For *Lohengrin* in 1936 there were more than 300 retainers in each procession in Act II, escorted by 70 noble pages carrying burning torches. All told, this production required 800 new costumes.[34] Such lavishness would not have been possible without Hitler's subvention and the Führer was not displeased to see his money spent in this way. Alfred Einstein, the discerning critic of the *Berliner*

Tageblatt, who generally admired Tietjen's work, ticked him off for inappropriately transferring the luxuriance of big-city opera to a small-town festival theatre – the Berlin style imposed on little Bayreuth. But he had high praise for the 1933 *Meistersinger*, remarking the beauty of its evocation of old Nuremberg, with subtle lighting effects.[35]

H. H. Stuckenschmidt rated this same production of *Meistersinger* as better than that at the Berlin Staatsoper. He considered that Tietjen had developed into an outstanding Wagner producer and that this *Meistersinger* was the best thing he had done. The settings were magical, the high point being Act I, when every detail meshed with the music – one of the truly great pieces of dramatic production.[36] Reviewing the 1933 festival, the famous record producer Walter Legge wryly noted the Hitler mania in Bayreuth and the Aryan embarrassment that apart from Frida Leider, Lotte Lehmann and Rudolf Bockelmann, most of the outstanding singers were either foreign or Jewish, or both. He goes on to praise Tietjen and Preetorius's stagings as 'the great delights of the festival'. 'Those of us who have watched with interest the development of Emil Preetorius as a scenic artist and of Heinz Tietjen as a producer have been astonished by the dramatic strength and stark realism of the scenery and the dramatic significance and beauty of grouping of these Bayreuth productions. ... For Preetorius and Tietjen give dramatic truth, and Wagnerian dramatic truth will outdo any other form of theatrical art.' Legge puts this achievement into perspective when he writes that 'We in England, accustomed to Covent Garden's badly painted cloths and inadequate stage machinery ... have little idea of the advance in operatic staging that has taken place in Central Europe during the past twelve years.'[37]

It is likely that Tietjen and Preetorius would have developed their approach even more boldly without the pressure exerted not by the Party, from whom they were effectively insulated by Hitler, but by Daniela, Eva and the equally conservative Wagner Societies, who were insistent that everything specified in Wagner's scenic instructions should be shown on stage.[38] Looking back after the war, Tietjen spoke of the Fafner fraternity's resistance to attempts by himself and Preetorius to evolve a new tradition by drawing the best of the old tradition 'fruitfully into our efforts of renewal', efforts in which lighting and stage technology had played a major role.[39]

The Führer and the festivals

The complex story of Bayreuth in the Reich is understandable only in the light of Hitler's immense personal enthusiasm. Behind his back dissenting subordinates may have done their best to curtail the spread of the contagion, but on parade at Bayreuth dutiful appreciation was the order of the day. The Chancellor's passion for Wagner went back a long way. As a boy he had steeped himself in his works at the theatre in Linz. 'In that hour it began,' he famously told Winifred Wagner in 1939, referring to his intense first experience there of *Rienzi*.[40] He had the good fortune to see the great Mahler-Roller Wagner productions at the Vienna Opera just before and after Mahler's departure for New York in December 1907, and was deeply impressed by them. He saw *Tristan*, *Holländer* and *Lohengrin* on a visit in 1906, and drawings by him of Roller's designs for Acts II and III of *Tristan* in the ground-breaking 1903 production have come to light in a sketchbook of 1925.[41] In September 1907 he moved to Vienna hoping to study painting and architecture at the Academy of Fine Arts (it turned him down), and is recorded as attending something like ten performances each of *Lohengrin* (his favourite opera at that time) and *Die Meistersinger* in his first year in the city.[42] Hitler's interest in stage production began in these Vienna years, when he spent his days dreaming of rebuilding Vienna and his evenings in the cheapest seats at the Opera.

From 1923, as we have seen, Hitler was often Siegfried and Winifred Wagner's guest at Bayreuth. His architect and later Minister for Armaments, Albert Speer, wrote that 'It seemed to a musical layman like myself that in his conversations with Frau Winifred Wagner he displayed knowledge about musical matters in detail; but he was even more concerned about the directing.'[43] His passion for grandiose architecture and military display spilled over into a concern for stage design that was rare among political leaders. Baldur von Shirach, head of Hitler Youth, from 1941 Gauleiter of Vienna and later Albert Speer's fellow prisoner in Spandau, recalled 'Hitler's amazing knowledge of stagecraft, his interest in the diameter of revolving stages, lift mechanisms, and especially different lighting techniques. He was familiar with all sorts of lighting systems and could discourse in detail on the proper illumination for certain scenes.'[44] No wonder that he should have laid out nearly 2.4 million francs for the purchase of the personal archive of Edward Gordon Craig.[45]

Just as he chose Speer to fulfil his architectural dreams, Hitler's preferred designer for the realization of his stage fantasies was Benno von Arent, who was given the unprecedented role of 'Reich theatre designer' (Reichsbühnenbildner). The Chancellor himself once prepared coloured-crayon sketches for *Tristan* and gave them as an inspirational aid to Arent. He did the same for the *Ring*, making sketches for its every scene during a three-week period in which he had an exceptionally demanding political schedule.[46] For a new Nuremberg *Meistersinger* to mark the opening of the 1935 Party rally he commissioned sets and costumes from Arent and himself vetted the preliminary sketches. Here the Festwiese was an undisguised celebration of 'das Volk', with martial blocking and avenues of Party banners, from which only the swastikas were missing. He 'considered what sort of lighting would do best for the moonlight scenes at the end of the second act. He went into ecstasies over the brilliant colours he wanted for the final scene on the Mastersingers' meadow, and over the romantic look of the little gabled houses opposite Hans Sachs's cobbler's shop'.[47]

Hitler at one point suggested that Benno von Arent should replace Preetorius, but he stopped short of insisting.[48] However much Winifred may have worshipped Hitler, she was her own woman, and indeed this was one reason why the Führer, in his turn, thought so well of her. Wolfgang is entirely credible when he asserts that 'She would never have considered employing a designer like Benno von Arent … who botched the festival meadow in *Die Meistersinger*'.[49] Politically she would have had no problem with Arent. It just happened that, artistically, she chose to back Preetorius.[50]

Hitler's own theatrical taste was that of a romantic conservative, in thrall to coups de théâtre and stirring effects. Speer, writing in *Spandau: The Secret Diaries*, considered him 'a genius of dilettantism', lacking any sense 'of the dualistic nature of romanticism, its inner conflicts and decadence. Nor did he understand its serenity. He knew only its dark side, its destructive urge and its popularized debased forms....'[51] This is surely as shrewd a verdict on Hitler's artistic pretentions as one is likely to come across. It pinpoints precisely why the Hitler image of Wagner was so perverted and one-dimensional, missing out on the complexities, the inner contradictions and everything that goes to make his art that of the tragedy of the human condition and not of the triumph of the Aryan enterprise.

Although it is widely accepted that Hitler's Bayreuth left nothing but an ugly stain on the stage history of Wagner's works, the facts do not support so simplistic a view. It is easy enough to establish a measure of common ground between Nazi ideology and what went on in the town of Bayreuth, more difficult to come to a fair assessment of performances in the Festspielhaus.

The fact that supreme artistic achievements can thrive under political barbarism is a puzzle set for all time. In the case in hand it is explicable, at least in part, by a German propensity to elevate art to the status of a religion, to place it beyond moral and political responsibility, to regard its values as self-sufficient and transcendent. That was the attitude both of the politically *engagés*, like Houston Stewart Chamberlain and Winifred Wagner, and of those like Furtwängler, Tietjen and Preetorius whose political opinions were attuned, rather as Wagner's had been, to their artistic goals. The charge of moral irresponsibility persists – a subject disturbingly treated by Thomas Mann in *Doktor Faustus*[52] – but the supreme artistic achievements remain, quite tangibly in Furtwängler's recordings from the period, less obviously in the quiet revolution of many of Tietjen and Preetorius's productions.

The area of common ground between Winifred, her artistic team and Nazi ideology is relatively easy to define. It included a preference for a romantic-heroic style of vocal declamation, acting and visual imagery – one that was by no means confined to Bayreuth or even Germany in the 1930s. It was the norm wherever Wagner was performed.

Empathy with the nationalistic thrust of much of Wagner's work – something that is incontrovertibly there – was felt both by Bayreuth's artistic directors and the Reich's ideologues, though not always in the same way, or to the same degree. But certainly Winifred and her team saw *Die Meistersinger* as a hymn to the Germanness of German art just as Hitler did.

Looking back from 1966, Wieland Wagner would profess extreme distaste for the sentimental nationalism of Tietjen's Bayreuth staging of *Meistersinger*, as we shall see. But that was how the work had been produced all over Germany since at least 1924, when it had reopened Bayreuth after the ten-year closure occasioned by the First World War.[53] The 1933–4 production was, as noted above, praised by observers like Einstein, Stuckenschmidt and Legge, who were certainly no friends of the Party. Embarrassment with such a style of stage presentation became widespread only after 1945.

What happened in *practice* was that the Nazi ethos did not generally impose itself upon the style of performance, but was content to identify – selectively – with those historical and mythopoeic echoes which it saw as precursors of its own endeavours. It did not worry overmuch about deciphering the rest of the story. Hitler himself hated political demonstrations inside the theatre and took steps to stop them. The 1934 *Meistersinger* audiences found in their programmes a card reading, 'The Führer wishes to see an end to the singing of "Deutschland über Alles" or the "Horst Wessel Lied" and similar demonstrations at the close of the performances. There is no finer expression of the German spirit than the immortal works of the Master himself. Gruppenführer Brückner, Adjutant to the Führer.'[54]

A notable exception to the willed separation of art and overt nationalism was the political emphasis in the 1936 *Lohengrin*, planned to celebrate the thousandth anniversary of the death of King Heinrich, the first German monarch (AD 876–936). The pre-echoes of the Reichsidee were most obvious in the scenes involving the king. In Act III, King Heinrich's stirring address about the supremacy of the German sword and the eradication of the threat posed by the hordes from the east ('Nach Deutschland sollen noch in fernsten Tagen/Des Ostens Horden siegreich nimmer ziehn!') was delivered to the assembled company from horseback. At the very end the swan transmuted into Gottfried as the new 'Führer', clad in the same chain-mail armour that Lohengrin had worn. The settings for Act I and for the end of Act III, shadowed by immense spreading trees, evoked the classic primeval German landscape, like illustrations to some sanctified place of primitive judgement described by the Brothers Grimm. In Act II the Burghof was framed by claustrophobic stonework, with a view to the rear of fortified towers and battlements, triumphantly described by the *Dresdener Nachrichten* as 'symbols of the human will to arms'.[55] A critic from the Swiss *Neue Zürcher Zeitung* discerned that the production had actualized the 'mystic-political' significance of the work, noting that the habitually cut passage in the Grail narration (a cut sanctioned by Wagner himself and invariably made even in Bayreuth) had been reinstated. The audience was left in no doubt that the Brabantine army would follow Lohengrin and that the hordes from the east would never be victorious.[56]

Hitler attended three performances of what was by all accounts an outstanding production (conducted by Furtwängler and Tietjen), was moved to tears and magnanimously offered the entire production and performers to Covent Garden in honour of Edward VIII's coronation. The offer was declined, not on the grounds of what might have been seen as the audacity of invoking King Heinrich as a forebear of the House of Windsor, but simply because Edward declared he was bored by opera.[57]

Bayreuth's own missionary zeal – doubtless also a push to win back the foreign visitors who had deserted in droves – was proclaimed in five articles in the 1938 *Festspielführer* under the heading 'Richard Wagner und das Ausland'. But few were deceived. Ernest Newman's contribution candidly observed that 'Naturally a good deal in Wagner that is of the highest importance to the German mind calls forth rather less response in the foreigner. … It is not to be expected that, for the foreigner at any rate, Wagner's views on politics, religion, social and racial matters should have

Tietjen was a follower of Max Reinhardt in his liking for lavishly filled stages, as in the final scene of *Lohengrin* in 1936 for which 800 new costumes were required. Hitler adored the production and offered it to Covent Garden for the coronation of Edward VIII. The offer was declined on the grounds that Edward found opera boring.

quite the significance that they have for the Germans.'[58] No question that those views were adapted to the political message of the moment. The festival programme books, for instance, often prefaced by photographs of the Führer-patron (the ones in the 1934, 1936 and 1939 programmes are credited to 'Wieland Wagner'), strenuously sought to show that Wagner's works were the artistic expression of the German will to power. 'Be alert, you young Siegfrieds, be aware of deeds undone, be on your guard against the Hagen in your soul!' advised Karl Hermann in 'Bayreuth und Deutschlands junge Generation'.[59]

But matters on stage, with the important exceptions of *Lohengrin* and to a lesser extent *Meistersinger*, did not dance to that tune. Indeed, Winifred kept at bay not only Hitler's own impassioned notions about production but also Party pressures to secure 'Gleichschaltung' (alignment) between the political rally and the stage. Suggestions that German icons should be imported into the productions – for example, that the Gibichungs' shields should be emblazoned with swastikas – were successfully resisted.

The supporters of Benno von Arent may have recognized no essential distinction between the stage management of a Nuremberg rally and that of a Wagner opera, but Winifred, Tietjen and Preetorius held out for the difference. They were insistent that the works should not be demeaned by narrowing the interpretative perspective. By all means celebrate the overt nationalism in *Lohengrin* and *Die Meistersinger* – it could hardly be more explicit in their sung texts – but it was still Bayreuth's job to maintain the values of art as art, as a metaphor for the universal human condition.

And this was unequivocally so in the other works performed under the Führer's patronage – *Holländer*, *Parsifal*, *Tristan*, the *Ring*. It was evident in the nature symbolism of Preetorius's scenery and in his relatively timeless, simplified costumes. Siegfried, Brünnhilde and Wotan were put across not as Germanic stereotypes but as heroic human beings.

Parsifal, 1934–1937: Wieland gets his first break

As an admirer of Roller, Hitler cannot have been too disappointed by Preetorius, whose sets plainly owed much to the Vienna-based artist. Nor was Roller himself forgotten, for when Bayreuth's venerated *Parsifal* could no longer be patched, it was the seventy-year-old Roller who was called on to be the designer for a new staging in 1934 by Tietjen. He had declined a previous invitation from Siegfried but, old and ailing though he now was, responded positively to Winifred. It has been suggested that the idea came from Hitler himself,[60] but Wolfgang's account seems more credible: 'The fact that [Roller's] employment by my mother accorded with Hitler's wishes was a fortunate coincidence. When Hitler eventually got a chance to speak with Roller, it emerged that an acquaintance had once given him a letter of introduction to Roller requesting the latter's help in getting him accepted by the Vienna Academy of Art, but that he, Hitler, had been too diffident to make use of it.'[61]

There can be no question that Winifred was very glad of Hitler's support for her Roller initiative, against which a massive protest was organized by Daniela and Eva and all those passionately opposed to any tampering with the sacred sets 'on which the eyes of the Master had reposed'.[62] The signatories included Toscanini, Ernest Newman, the ex-Tsar Ferdinand and Richard Strauss, who nevertheless went through with the painful task of conducting the sacrilegious production. As it turned out the protesters had a point, for Roller's sets, developed from those he had made for Vienna in 1914 (which Hitler much admired),[63] were plagued with constructional problems, while his scheme for lighting them was bungled. The images in the scenic transformation between the forest and the Grail temple were not correctly synchronized. The pillars of the temple which Roller had intended as slender columns ascending to infinity were executed as relatively thick and squat. Klingsor's tower, a magnificent design based on a sketch by Appia of 1912, failed to collapse, as did the magic garden. The absence of the traditional cupola in the temple outraged the old Wagnerians, while even Winifred had to confess that the magic garden was 'a disaster'.[64] Roller himself felt badly let down and looked forward to correcting the mistakes the following year, but he was to die (21 June 1935) before that could happen. The production remained a shadow of what it might have been.

Its shortcomings opened the way for revisions that, in 1936, were to give the 19-year-old Wieland Wagner his (uncredited) Festspielhaus debut. It was Preetorius who added capitals to the columns and a round arch to suggest the grievously missed cupola, but Wieland whose designs – he claimed he had knocked them off in an hour – replaced Roller's for the Good Friday meadow.[65] His relatively conventional treatment was good enough to persuade Winifred and Tietjen that he could be entrusted with entirely redesigning the Roller staging. For the 1937 festival the sets were three-dimensional realizations based on paintings by Wieland; it was only later that he began to work with models.

As Wieland had to miss vital rehearsals through being called away on military manoeuvres, he was unable to fine-tune his work. What he had been able to do, with the help of Paul Eberhardt, was establish a Bayreuth first in effecting the transitions between forest and temple by means of projected slide-paintings. Eberhardt designed a variable-speed device by which three different slides were projected through a single lens. The ability to vary the speed meant that the operator could coordinate the scenic transformation exactly with the conductor's tempo.[66] Wolfgang reports that the rollers used until 1933 for winding the old travelling landscape cloth across the stage (see chapter 4) ended up as piles supporting his chicken hut in a field just outside Bayreuth.[67]

Wieland dutifully restored the Romanesque temple and cupola (which reminded one visitor, Hans Schüler, of 'a luxurious Turkish bath').[68] This was a solid architectural construct in red, gold and black, but the scenes in the forest were indeed painterly conceptions translated to the stage – in Act I, handsome groups of beech tree trunks framing a view to a large lake and mountains beyond, and in the first scene of Act III, a high mountain pasture, Gurnemanz's hut at left, scattered fir trees to either side and clouds hanging in the distant valley behind. Not arrestingly original but highly accomplished naturalistic images.[69]

The press response was respectful and largely positive, but Aunt Daniela, who had withdrawn from Bayreuth in high dudgeon at what she considered to be the betrayal of the Master's works, was not amused. Not, at any rate, by what she had *heard* about the colours of the costumes (mostly still by Roller; Wieland had made new designs but few were used, possibly on the grounds of expense), the increased number of Flowermaidens and sundry other deviations from holy writ. Wieland's response was that he was happy to listen to her advice, provided she first came to a performance. More importantly, this letter of Wieland's also made plain what had not been at all obvious, namely that he was thinking seriously about his future role in the festival.[70] In November 1937 Hitler released Bayreuth's heir apparent from military service after one year, enabling him to stretch his wings by designing sets for two of his father's operas – *Sonnenflammen* in Düsseldorf and *Der Bärenhäuter* in Cologne, both given in 1938.

Studies in Munich: productions in Altenburg and Nuremberg

In the same year Tietjen offered Wieland an eight-year apprenticeship at the Berlin Staatsoper but, perhaps already perceiving that he needed to come in from his own angle, he turned it down in favour of going to Munich as an art student under the Moravian-born artist Ferdinand Staeger.[71] He worked hard at his painting and made good progress. Until this time his musical education had been in the hands of Tietjen, but from spring 1940 his mentor was Kurt Overhoff (1902–86), a Viennese composer-conductor who had worked with Roller and Strauss at the Vienna Opera.[72] Overhoff taught Wieland score-reading and conducting, even persuading him to take up the baton for the overture to *Der fliegende Holländer* at a concert in Heidel-berg, an experience Wieland felt no desire to repeat. The truly productive work was the bar-by-bar, line-by-line study of his grandfather's works. Overhoff's searching analysis and understanding of the music in relation to the drama were to be a major influence on the apprentice designer-director.[73] During the four years Wieland was to spend in Munich he also made the most of his contacts at the Nationaltheater with the conductor Clemens Krauss, the director Rudolf Hartmann and the designer Ludwig Sievert, who produced the settings for *Der Freischütz* there in 1940. On emerging from his studies Wieland was invited to design *Der Meistersinger* in Nuremberg in 1942, a frustrating experience which made him resolve that hence-forth he would design only where he could also direct.

He was now able to begin to put this into practice, for in early 1943, while the war was plunging Europe into a darker and darker night, Wieland was appointed chief opera producer at the small Landestheater in Altenburg, near Leipzig, with Overhoff as musical director. It was Goebbels who had helped find this job for Wieland, the perfect out-of-the-limelight proving ground – if also something of a deep end. His very first task was to produce the *Ring*, in parallel with which ran a commission to stage the same work in Nuremberg, to say nothing of designing *Die Meistersinger* for Tietjen at Bayreuth that summer. Little visual evidence of the Altenburg and Nurem-berg productions survives, but written reports suggest that Wieland the artist was already searching for new visual solutions.[74] He later claimed that the existing Altenburg *Ring* scenery had been in such a wretched state that he had simply dis-pensed with as much of it as he could, giving the impression that this had prefigured his later 'empty space' Bayreuth stagings. But if Ernst Lüsenhop, then artistic direc-tor at Altenburg, is to be believed, the stage was far from bare, Wieland's recollection perhaps being a piece of the self-mythography for which his grandfather had set such a masterly precedent – the rearrangement and even sheer invention of the past in order to suit the story of the moment. What is not in dispute is that Wieland tried to minimize illustrative scenery and to use lighting to link the moods of the stage picture to those of the music.[75]

Lüsenhop kept the theatre closed for a full week before the opening of *Götter-dämmerung* so that Wieland could fine-tune his lighting.[76] He was rapidly moving away from scenery as decor, as pictures painted on canvas, or even built in the round, to Appia's idea that the designer should be painting with light in a largely empty stage space, light as music's closest equivalent. Wieland studied Appia and Craig, as also the work of Roller and Oskar Strnad for the Vienna Opera. Through his con-tacts with Sievert in Munich he would have learnt of Sievert's long-standing interest in light as the shaping force in scenic design, which went back to his part in a 1912–14 *Ring* in Freiburg. Sievert had remained an important designer, but the con-straints of the time muted the experimental streak that had been so characteristic of his work at Freiburg and during the Weimar years (see chapter 8).

Wieland and Overhoff were of one mind in seeking to allow the stage picture to be determined by the music, to visualize its moods and colours. This inevitably led to press complaints that too many of Wagner's rubrics were being ignored or traduced, as indeed they were. The Valkyries had no breastplates or helmets, just body-hugging costumes and long hair free to blow every which way, one or two trees made do for a forest, while the Norns remained rooted to the spot without benefit of fir tree, stone bench or rock, and with no breaking of their rope. On the much larger stage in Nuremberg, Wieland seems to have had more scope for powerful visual simplification. A review of his *Walküre* there (30 June 1943) discovered a 'quality of genius' in the mountain scenery for Act II, praising the genuinely unearthly character of a huge rock on the left, with its steep, jagged high walls. In Act III Wieland used the theatre's wide cyclorama to create a vast open view from the mountain top past the branches of the obligatory fir tree to distant peaks on the horizon, a closing image of Brünnhilde's fate 'brought out into the wide world, which does after all play a prominent role in the drama'.[77]

Wieland's programme note for this production describes the basis on which he was then planning his work: 'Wagner's composition sketches show quite clearly that during the process of creation he heard the sound and at the same time saw the stage action vividly in his mind. In consequence the happenings on the stage must be made to correspond exactly with the music.'[78] While Wieland fails to support his view with any evidence from the composition sketches (it would be hard to find), his conclusion is not seriously at variance with the Bayreuth tradition, in which gesture (in other words, acting) was precisely synchronized with the music. Implicit in it is the very un-Bayreuth view that Wagner's stage instructions are of secondary importance, as Wieland goes on to spell out: 'The nature of the dramatic action demanded by each musical motive is not of course specified, and it cannot be defined according to one particular style. Thus the producer is at complete liberty to seek new forms of expression, in line with the personality of the singer concerned.'[79]

This is not entirely correct, for Wagner's remarks on performing *Der fliegende Holländer* and Porges's transcription of the *Ring* rehearsals in 1876 (see chapters 1 and 3) make it plain that the composer *did* believe that every musical motive specified a particular dramatic gesture. The important part of Wieland's argument is that stage action is always an *interpretation* of the core meaning, not that meaning itself: even the composer was only an interpreter of his own musical drama. This, as we have seen, was not at all Cosima's view. In declaring his opposition to a single definitive performing style Wieland was asserting his right to diverge from the Bayreuth tradition. He was claiming the right, for himself and his singers, to make fresh interpretations whose only allegiance was to the score. This is a more forthright version of Winifred's own philosophy. She herself had created something of a furore in 1931 when she let it be known that she was happy for conductors to play the music in their own way rather than slavishly follow tradition.[80]

Wieland's intensive work at Altenburg and Nuremberg began to make waves, earning him an invitation from Karl Böhm to produce the *Ring* in Vienna. To honour the seventy-fifth anniversary of the birth of his father Siegfried in 1944 Wieland staged *An allem ist Hütchen schuld* in Altenburg (later given also in Bayreuth's Markgräfliches Opernhaus), while his brother Wolfgang, who had taken up Tietjen's offer of an apprenticeship at the Berlin Staatsoper, staged *Bruder Lustig* there. Later in the summer Wieland provided largely conventional designs for Tietjen's new *Meistersinger* at Bayreuth.[81] But with the intensification of the war the German and Austrian theatres were closed and Wieland's Nuremberg *Ring* remained incomplete, his Vienna commission unfulfilled. In the final phase of the war he was put to work in a secret military research unit in Bayreuth that was trying to devise an optical anti-aircraft tracking system. There he spent much time drawing on the scientists' expertise to invent new theatre-lighting systems with the help of models. Whatever else came out of this unit it was not enough to prevent American bombers devastating a large part of Bayreuth in the closing months of the war, including on 5 April 1945 about a third of Haus Wahnfried. Miraculously the Festspielhaus and Markgräfliches Opernhaus remained untouched.

The 'creative black years'

For Wieland the end of the war marked the beginning of what he called his 'creative black years'. Living in Winifred's house at Nußdorf on the Bodensee he began to come to terms with the truth about 'Onkel Wolf', lying low until his own future and that of the Festspielhaus came into focus. In 1947 he stayed at Richard Strauss's villa in Garmisch with Overhoff, who was tutoring Strauss's grandson, the composer himself then still in exile in Switzerland. Wieland and Overhoff embarked on an intensive study of *Tristan*, the early fruits of which included Overhoff's monograph on the opera, 'a musical and philosophical interpretation' in which the author acknowledges his indebtedness to Wieland's ideas.[82] This joint work was later to underwrite Wieland's 1952 Bayreuth production of *Tristan*. Strauss himself had once promised to go through Wagner's works with Wieland, and it remained a source of deep regret that Strauss died (in 1949) before this could happen.

Although Wieland's upbringing had been within an intellectual milieu that was relatively liberal, much had been kept from him. What he had been able to discover about the radical theatre reformers of the earlier part of the century had been in the context of the disapproval of anything the Reich's representatives considered subversive. But Wieland already had the courage of his rebellious convictions. Wolfgang reports that at a meeting with Hitler his artist-brother expressed great concern about the Nazi denunciation of all modernist and Jewish art as 'entartet', or 'degenerate', and about the 1937 *Entartete Kunst* exhibition in Munich. Had not Goebbels himself put on a substantial exhibition of Edvard Munch, one of the pilloried artists, a few years earlier? Hitler, evasive, responded that 'after a phase of self-discovery, art of that kind would be able to be shown in Germany once more'.[83] This is a far more conciliatory response than that recorded by Speer on the occasion of Hitler's last visit to Bayreuth in 1940, appropriately enough to see the reworked *Götterdämmerung*: '[Wieland] began talking enthusiastically about the kind of art that was in those days regarded as "degenerate". Hitler listened … with barely concealed irritation, and on the drive back his full anger erupted. … He could not suspect that already, in Wieland Wagner, the foundation for a Wagner renaissance was being laid, with the result that today [1962] the works have been brilliantly resurrected.'[84]

Now was the time to make good, Wieland scratching a living for himself and his young family by selling his paintings, while catching up with Freud, Jung and Adler, with Klee, Picasso and the modernists. He plunged into Brecht, his reading in Greek theatre and mythology loosening the Teutonic emphasis that had been part of his schooling and exciting his interest in the Greek elements in Wagner's work. He was strongly drawn by modern reworkings of classical subjects, especially those by the French dramatists, including Giraudoux's *Electre* (1937), Sartre's *Les Mouches* (1943) and Anouilh's *Antigone* (1944).[85]

Wieland's intellectual discoveries opened up new perspectives on what he had been trying to achieve in his theatre work. There was now no question that he had been on the right track in his rejection of conservative staging, in his concentration on the music and on light as the designer's most important tool. Virtually all of this was to be found in the predecessors he most valued, in Mahler and Roller, in Klemperer and the Kroll. From Appia and Craig (who had also impressed his father) he gleaned much, though he claimed to reject Appia's later espousal of geometric, virtually abstract settings. In actual fact, Appia's idea that the production was only the interaction of empty space, lighting and the singing-actor was more powerfully evident in Wieland's post-1951 productions than the visual symbolism of Appia's work in the 1890s. Wieland's wariness of the latter was doubtless due to its all too palpable influence on Preetorius, from whom, as from Tietjen, he had reason enough to dissociate himself.

Quite how early Wieland's aversion to Tietjen and Preetorius manifested itself may not be known until further documents are released. But in distancing his own stagings from those of Tietjen and Preetorius – and with every justification – Wieland underestimates their tangible achievements and influence on him. It was unfair of him to dismiss Preetorius for his 'Japanese tea-garden style'[86] and the Tietjen productions as being more interested in psychology than musical drama. (After all, Wieland himself was scarcely uninterested in psychology; indeed, what were his many attempts to uncover and present archetypal images – as in the 1962 *Tristan* – but manifestations of Jungian psychology?)

It made little sense for him to praise Kurt Söhnlein's 1927 designs for *Tristan* as the first stylized scenery at Bayreuth while dismissing Preetorius's Valkyrie rock as no more than an improved version of what had been on the stage in 1876![87] And it was this very design of Preetorius's which, as noted above, was a mirror-image realization of Appia's sketches from the 1890s. The work of both Söhnlein and Preetorius was marked by a refreshing concentration on stylized, simplified forms, forms which, differently from the 1876 scenery, were solid constructions whose appearance, like that of the stage as a whole, could be changed dramatically by lighting. But it is easy to see why Wieland the radical took issue with the rapprochement with tradition advocated by Preetorius in 'Zum Szenenproblem in Bayreuth' (summarized above).

Wieland's attitude to Tietjen was more ambivalent. Tietjen had fostered his talent and given him his first opportunities. He had kept the Wagner family show on the road through difficult times. But Tietjen had also been a 'kleiner Mitläufer'. In

Wieland's eyes he had not done enough to resist the Party's aesthetic demands. He had succumbed to over-inflated chorus numbers and to the Germanic spin put on *Lohengrin* and *Die Meistersinger*, and had been happy that Wotan should still seem to be king of the castle at the end of the third act of *Die Walküre*, whereas, Wieland argued, he was already the dispossessed, powerless Wanderer: 'He continues to act as though he rules the world … but every moment shows that his supremacy is over. In himself he has already become the Wanderer.'[88]

There was also the classical Oedipal situation for both Wieland and Wolfgang – Tietjen as a paternal figure whom they had to demolish. (Some believe he may have been Winifred's lover.)[89] Their antagonism was only sharpened when, after 1937, Winifred dropped Furtwängler and Tietjen became, in effect, both artistic director and principal conductor. The politicking by which Tietjen managed to remain at the helm through the war years and into the future is well documented.[90]

In truth, it is exceedingly hard to get any clear perspective on this highly competent musician and man of the theatre. In piloting his course – and that of the Prussian Theatres and Bayreuth – from Weimar radicalism, through the years of nationalistic triumphalism and defeat, to his post-war work as Intendant in Hamburg, Tietjen tacked and cut his cloth according to the wind. Had he not done so, Bayreuth would most likely have fallen into less competent hands, rendering the task of its eventual rehabilitation even more difficult. It is unrealistic to imagine that 1930s' Wagner production could have been more radical and imaginative than it was. The long-term effect of Tietjen's cultural realpolitik and manoeuvring was beneficial to the cause of Wagner production. At the very least it provided the Wagner grandsons with something to react against, a springboard for the plunge into the iconoclasm that came with the opening of the 1951 festival.

The 1951 reopening

The formula for Bayreuth's future thrashed out between the Allied Occupation and the Wagner family, whereby Winifred the legal owner ceded control to her sons, was completed in 1949. That left a bare two years to prepare for the reinauguration of the festival in 1951. It was agreed that Wolfgang would be responsible for administration and finance while Wieland would be artistic director. The festival would reopen with productions of the *Ring* and *Parsifal* by Wieland and of *Die Meistersinger* by Rudolf Hartmann, Intendant of the Munich Opera and a friend from Wieland's student years in that city.

We have seen that, as early as his 1943 programme note for *Die Walküre* in Nuremberg, Wieland had perceived the need for a total change in the way Wagner was performed. Now that he had the Bayreuth stage and the eyes of the world upon him, he felt it advisable to nail his colours to the mast with 'Tradition and Innovation', a mission statement published in the 1951 festival book.[91] Here he reaffirmed Appia's argument that production should be true to the music, but not necessarily to Wagner's stage instructions. Realizing that a major task would be to combat prejudice about Bayreuth's duty to put on 'faithful' performances, he reiterated his belief

The architects of Bayreuth's revolutionary break with its past. Wieland (left) and Wolfgang Wagner, the composer's grandsons, are seen here in 1954. Three years earlier they had reopened the Festival after Winifred had been denazified and compelled to cede control to them.

that while 'the works of Richard Wagner tolerate no change' their stage interpretation is necessarily 'subject to change': 'To avoid change is to transform the virtue of fidelity into the vice of rigidity. Ultimately it spells death.' Wieland compares Wagner's works to the *Iliad*, the *Divine Comedy* and the plays of Shakespeare. He contends that their texts are inviolable but that their interpretation is subject to change. That these works are inexhaustibly protean, continually revealing new aspects of themselves, is proof of their immortality. He reminds his readers how 'tragically disappointed' Wagner was with his own stagings, citing his revealing lines to Ludwig II: 'Everyone thinks he can outdo me by better and more beautiful things, while I am only striving for a definitive something, a certain poetic effect, but no theatrical pomp. Scenery, for instance, is invariably designed to be looked at for its own sake, as in a panorama, but I want only a subdued background to characterize a dramatic situation.' Wieland attributes Wagner's failure to secure satisfactory stagings not to the technical limitations of his time but to the inherent impossibility of reproducing on stage an ultimately unrealizable vision. He concludes that 'Today, after seventy-five years of improving our technical methods to an incredible point of perfection – the development of lighting undoubtedly represents the peak of scenic design – we must still admit that the stage can, at its best, provide only a sparse reflection of that which is triumphantly conveyed from the orchestra pit.' The path to the future therefore 'lies neither in an attempt to employ all the most modern devices in achieving a movie-like realization of Wagner's dream, nor can it be found in a reversion to former "tried and trusted" methods. ... Wagner's heritage must not be embalmed and made into a museum piece through misconceived loyalty. His timeless validity must be proved anew at every revival.'[92]

How could this philosophy be put into practice? The one thing Wieland knew was that he had to clear the stage and trust the Appian strategy of doing as much as possible with as little as possible.

Parsifal, 1951–1966

Of Wieland's inaugural productions of the *Ring* and *Parsifal* it was, inevitably, his treatment of the latter which was the most provocative. No other work had been so closely associated with the Bayreuth tradition. The new staging effected by Tietjen, Roller and Wieland from 1934 had, as we have seen, provoked furious opposition. The annual *Parsifal* ritual had come to an abrupt end in 1939 and the work had since been but seldom performed. Wieland told Goléa, 'It's always a thorn in the flesh of the powers that be – not just the religious [authorities] but also the Nazis. Hitler had effectively banned *Parsifal*. A similiar mentality prevailed in the GDR after the war. That was why *Parsifal* was no longer performed there.'[93] The time was ripe for a production that would make a decisive break with the past.

True to his intentions, Wieland approached *Parsifal* through an analytic scenario which he set out as 'Parsifal's Cross: A Psychological Pattern'. This was a diagram showing how the opera's events moved towards and then away from the peripeteia of Kundry's kiss, and were symmetrically related to each other.[94] But what struck most visitors in 1951 was not the psychology of the production but its mystic spiritual aura. In the dim, soft light the eye had to search for the barest intimations of place – four dull-gold vertical brushstrokes indicating the pillars of the Grail temple, a spider's web tracery for Klingsor's domain – and for the shadowy forms of the singers. The work had been transformed into a dream play.

In 'Tradition and Innovation' Wieland explained that the staging of *Parsifal* required 'mystical expression of a very complex state of the soul, rooted in the unreal, grasped only by intuition',[95] and this was what he provided. The impact of the production was as well described by its enemies as by its friends: 'a symphony in gloom, a formless play of patterns and shadows which dispenses with individual dramatic relationships, confines itself exclusively to symbols and thereby becomes wearisome.'[96] Those in the other camp, like Ernest Newman, would not have faulted the description, insisting only that the whole effect was not 'wearisome' but 'magical'.[97]

This *Parsifal* was a persuasive demonstration of Appia's old contention that light was the closest sensory equivalent to music and that the designer's task was to paint with light in an empty space. From Alfred Roller on, many designers were of the same opinion, as we have seen, their efforts handicapped only by technical limitations. Where Wieland could go so much further was that in Paul Eberhardt he had already found a supremely gifted lighting specialist, one with whom he had worked on *Parsifal* in 1937.[98] To the eye of Wieland the artist, seeking to reflect the shades, colours, luminosities of the music, was added Eberhardt's technological know-how. Eberhardt

With his 1951 production of *Parsifal*, most tradition-bound of all Wagner's works, Wieland immediately declared his belief in a theatre of the spectator's imagination. Designing principally with light, Wieland sustained a mystic spiritual aura in which the architecture of the Grail temple, seen here in 1968, was barely suggested. The knights did not process; they arrived at their places as a suddenly visible ring closing in to the table from the surrounding darkness.

had worked at the Festspielhaus since 1932 and from 1934 to 1966 was its technical director. He rebuilt the theatre's electrical installation in 1933 and from then on kept it at the forefront of technological development. He was among the first to exploit the potential of xenon lighting to suffuse the stage with light of no apparent source. When American troops arrived at the Festspielhaus in 1945, it was an anxious Eberhardt who was there to greet them, explain the derelict barn-like structure which had miraculously escaped the severe bomb damage, and plead for its preservation.[99]

Eberhardt recognized that Wieland's sense of colour was exceptionally acute. They spent hour after hour together, Wieland playing the music at the piano while Eberhardt, at his lighting console, tried to find the luminous equivalent. In a tribute to Eberhardt on his retirement in 1966 Wieland looked back to the times when they used to sit 'for weeks on end in the still chilly auditorium, feebly warmed by electric fires', busying themselves 'with the nuances of a shade of green or blue, a filter mixture, or the exact musical plan for a lighting transition: always trying and trying again'. Wieland goes on to describe the crucial difference between the aesthetics of the old and new Bayreuth: 'I confronted you with something new: the empty room, whereas before, up to the last festivals before the war, you had been illuminating decorations which in form, volume and colour filled the stage of themselves. My stage rooms could only become the musical spaces I had envisaged for the Wagnerian musical drama through the medium of your light – and lighting changes.'[100]

To illustrate just how extreme the change had been, Wieland quoted the reply of Hans Knappertsbusch, the conductor of *Parsifal*, to those who wondered why he had consented to conduct so disgraceful a production: he had imagined, right up to the dress rehearsal, that the stage decorations were still to come. Henceforth the conductor in the pit was to have his stage counterpart in the man at the lighting console, orchestrating the stage picture in accord with the music. It was Baudelaire's 'correspondances' come to life in the theatre, with music and light working indistinguishably on the senses.

The Ring, 1951–1965

In the 1951 *Ring*, a fair amount of representational scenery and props remained. The Valkyries were equipped with helmet, shield and spear, Fafner was a reptilian dinosaur and Brünnhilde was laid to sleep under the branches of a tree. But the basic acting area was a tilted rectangle and the costumes, stylized production and lighting were those of the new direction. The mood was that of a Greek tragedy, no traces remaining of the *Ring* as a Germanic saga. Nor was there anything in the least romantic about the stark chiaroscuro of the lighting, seen at its most dramatic in the second act of *Die Walküre* when Brünnhilde appeared from the back of the stage framed in a vertical shaft of light dividing the sheer black walls at either side. This, as Dietrich Mack suggests, was no longer a scene from nature but a narrow prison, symbol of Wotan's entrapment, with the blinding cleft of light at the rear offering the only hope of escape from 'das Ende' (the end of it all). Where Preetorius had created stylized evocations of nature, Wieland's images were metaphysical ciphers.[101]

In the following years the remnants of naturalistic scenery were quickly dispensed with. Embarrassed by his palpable compromises with traditional production, Wieland later tried to suppress photographs of the 1951 production. By 1952 all that remained of Hunding's hut was a central ash trunk – there was no roof, no hearth, no door to fly open. By 1953 the action, ever more Attic in inspiration, was taking place on a large, gently tilted disc. Movement was restricted, the singers kept their distance from one another, addressing themselves to the audience rather than to each other. Wotan had two good eyes but no helmet, and he and Brünnhilde had by now lost their armour. No attempt was made to square the sung text with the visual impression, Wieland being happy to accept inconsistencies created in his concentration on a single vision.

By 1957 the tree trunk in Act I of *Walküre* was no longer so lonely; to it had been added an open triangle of roof beams, plainly symbolic of the Hunding-Siegmund-Sieglinde relationship. Valhalla, initially an abstract play of light on the encircling cyclorama, became a projected image of plate-like walls, rising up layer after layer behind each other.[102]

In 1951 the Gibichung Hall in *Götterdämmerung* had been built of geometric box forms, with steps, strong verticals, everything rectilinear and the whole impression

Wieland's first Bayreuth *Ring* (1951-58) invoked the world of Greek tragedy rather than that of Germanic myth. In *Die Walküre*, photographed in 1952, Brünnhilde first appeared before Wotan in a dramatic vertical shaft of light, the whole effect being reminiscent of Jessner's *Wilhelm Tell* in 1919 (see p. 238). The timeless simplicity of the costumes is striking as Brünnhilde (Martha Mödl) seeks to comfort Wotan (Hans Hotter) in the second scene of Act II in 1953.

Two very different approaches to the oaths on the spear in the second act
of *Götterdämmerung*. In 1957 (*left*) the emphasis was on the powerful
grouping of the Gibichungs around the central open space. For the same
scene in his new *Ring* in 1965 (*opposite*), Wieland's imagery is that of
archetypal symbols, as in the three presiding totemic forms.

reminiscent of an Appia 'Espace rythmique' of c. 1909.[103] At the end of Act III, no logs
were piled up, no Hall collapsed. The conflagration of Valhalla and flooding of the
Rhine were lighting effects, leaving as the final image a halo of light floating above
the empty disc.

Wieland's first Bayreuth *Ring*, taken as a developed entity, was uncompromising
in its visual economy. The stage images were concentrated in elemental forms, suggested by the music but not in any sense illustrative of the natural phenomena of air,
fire, earth and water depicted in it. Economical with its visual markers, it was a production for those who already knew the work, but who Wieland hoped would rediscover it by focusing on the music and exercising their imaginations. It was a step
towards making new connections between music and the subconscious.

By the time Wieland returned to the *Ring* in 1965, he felt that the way forward lay
in inventing more overtly symbolic images. 'With hindsight,' he told Walter Panofsky, 'my path that began in 1951 with many compromises led irresistibly from the
diffusely lit empty stage to abstract, sculptural forms and "modern" colouration.'[104]
In search of the kind of archetypal forms he had admired in Lipchitz and Moore, he
invited Moore's collaboration in his new *Ring* – an exceptional step for a producer

who had always believed he had to be his own designer and vice versa. (Moore's
influence on Wieland was already apparent in the pierced totemic shapes that dominated all three acts of his 1962 *Tristan*.) When the sculptor declined – he reportedly
found no point of contact between Wagner's art and his own – Wieland had no
option but to go it alone. The pitted, honeycombed, geological forms he devised
were as though crystallized from primeval lava and slime and seemed a homage to
the great sculptor.

For Wieland these images were markers in his furthest exploration of the *Ring* as
a portrayal of the deepest layers of the psyche. He liked to think of his scenic visualizations as 'Traumbilder' (dream pictures); they were an attempt to translate the
musical ciphers of the *Ring* into archetypal images.[105] One striking example was the
piling up of the hoard in *Das Rheingold*. The gold blocks brought on by the
Nibelungs, when assembled, were suddenly seen as an icon of female fecundity.
African fetishes, stone-age fertility effigies and the famous 'Venus von Willendorf'
fed into his brilliant solution: woman-in-the-flesh exchanged for her equivalent in
cold gold.

Wieland's long-standing interest in his grandfather's indebtedness to the Greeks
also manifested itself again. The Festspielhaus's amphitheatre had of course been
Hellenic in inspiration, though the theatre was also characteristically nineteenth-
century in its double proscenium arch. Since 1951 Wieland had always tried to suggest a Greek ambience on the stage too. The tilted, disc-like arena which he so often
used as his playing area from 1953, sometimes dubbed a 'Weltenscheibe' (world
disc), would have been recognized by the Greeks as a version of the orchestra where
their chorus danced and sang. But for the 1965 *Ring* Wieland concentrated the action

When the last piece of the hoard was piled in front of Freia in the 1965 *Das Rheingold*, the gold was suddenly revealed as a symbol of sexuality and fecundity.

on the level surface of a smaller disc, about 11.3 metres in diameter and raised about 1.8 metres above the stage floor, generally known simply as the 'Scheibe'. 'It is,' said Wieland, 'nothing else but the buskin of the ancient Greek theatre, on which human beings were raised up in the literal sense of the word. ... It fulfils the practical function of concentrating the action – which I know can easily fall apart on a stage as large as ours – and reducing the distance between the individual players as far as possible.'[106]

In the Tübingen scholar Wolfgang Schadewaldt Wieland discovered a renowned classicist who not only supported these ideas but helped him in their elaboration, especially in the parallels that could be drawn between the *Ring* and Greek tragedy. Schadewaldt gave three lectures in Bayreuth in which he drew attention to parallels such as those between the Orestes–Electra and Siegmund–Sieglinde recognition scenes and between the characters of Hercules and Siegfried.[107] Wieland himself told Goléa that he saw Siegfried as 'Prometheus, the first man to stand up to the gods in order to make men independent of them, who was therefore punished', and the daughters of the Rhine as the Oceanides.[108] These were ideas which he put to good use in the direction of his singers.

The circular disc, seemingly afloat in a sea of blackness, was the ground on which the gods, men and dwarfs, now more sharply delineated than in the first *Ring*, played out a drama that was seen as much through Jungian and Freudian eyes as through those of classical antiquity. Wieland certainly shared Thomas Mann's perception of

Wagner as a forerunner of Freud in that his music is a psychological exploration of character. (The influence of Mann's powerful 1933 essay 'The Sorrows and Grandeur of Richard Wagner' is everywhere evident in Wieland's thought and work.) 'Depth-psychology,' Wieland believed, 'is the modern equivalent of the folk-tale, the saga, religion.'[109]

Elemental material like leather gave a suitably primitive feel to the costumes, but their cut and textures allowed for the clear delineation of character. In conversations with Goléa, Wieland showed that his mind had not been exclusively focused on myth and antiquity – more immediate inspirations lay to hand. He described Alberich as a 'bloody fascist and slave dealer', Nibelheim as 'the first concentration camp' and Nothung as 'an atomic bomb'.[110] Kirsten Meyer, playing Waltraute, said that Wieland had told her to imagine she had just escaped from Hitler's bunker. 'She thinks, "I have the secret of saving the world", and steals out of that Valhalla, where all are standing still just waiting for the moment when everything explodes.'[111]

Schadewaldt had drawn Wieland's attention to the weather as a principal player in the Aeschylean and Wagnerian drama. This was reflected in the ever changing moods and skyscapes of Wieland's lighting direction, which exchanged the soft hues and transitions of his first production for stronger, more saturated colours and sharper contrasts, as in *Siegfried* Act III, where the great bowl of light above Brünnhilde's sleeping form was of an intense, luminescent blue which, at Siegfried's arrival on the disc, magically emerged from the enveloping red glow that had been the fire around the rock. The idea of the watery subconscious, its seductions and instability, was established from the very beginning of *Das Rheingold* by a near unfathomable darkness, out of which dim light picked the mermaid-like forms of the Rhinedaughters, played by actresses with mermaid-like figures. They were seen reclining far apart, first in this crevice and then in that, while the real singers sang from behind the scene. This, exceptionally for Wieland, was a naturalistic evocation of the bed of the Rhine.

The ensuing scene on the mountain into which it dissolved set the style for the remainder of the cycle: a geological form or forms rising up behind and dominating the transactions of the psyche conducted on the *Scheibe*. Valhalla was a scaly cliff, slashed by diagonal grooves and considered by some to be an evocation of Wall Street, though Wieland himself said he had in mind 'the Tower of Babel, token of corrupt power and the disaster it must inevitably bring with it'.[112] Wotan and Brünnhilde's great encounter in the second act of *Die Walküre* was backed by another rough-hewn rock wall. This time physical interaction, in the shape of an embrace, took place between the god's super-ego and his will. The irreconcilable conflict between the male and female instincts was at least to this extent made physical in a production in which a restrained, coolly Brechtian mode of gestic acting predominated. Thus Wieland treated the first scene of Act II of *Walküre* not as a personal intervention by Fricka, 'but as a soliloquy presented as a dialogue between Wotan's will and his moral self'.[113] The following scene, however, in which Wotan is dealing with Brünnhilde as his anima, his secret will, was played as an eye-to-eye interaction between the two during which Wotan actually embraces Brünnhilde.

Wieland's mastery of a stage on which things are suggested rather than shown is well illustrated in his treatment of the dragon in *Siegfried*. In the 1951–8 *Ring* he had experimented first with a physical creature emitting clouds of steam and collapsing after Siegfried's thrust, and later with nothing but clouds of steam. Convinced, after all, that the dragon is not 'a dispensable prop',[114] Wieland's solution in 1965 was to suggest the vastness of the dragon-figure by letting its eyes stand for the whole. But the idea was more subtle than that, for already in the first act of *Siegfried* the mouth of Mime's cave resembled the skull of an immense beast. When Mime told Siegfried about Fafner's existence, the skull became animate, light glinting though its eye sockets, its mouth breathing steam. In the second act the eyes glinted from behind the honeycomb-like rock lattice where the creature had barricaded itself. This idea, like many in this *Ring*, had been tried out in Wieland's Cologne production of 1962–3, and was described by him to Walter Panofsky in 1964: '[The eyes] glow sometimes here, sometimes there in the dark and should seem so numerous as to suggest a Hydra, being finally extinguished when it dies.'[115] Thus it was when I first saw the Bayreuth production in 1967 – arguably the most satisfactory solution to the dragon problem ever seen. Everything essential about the creature was there – the power, the terror – everything that can reduce it to a risible prop was absent.

In the second act of *Götterdämmerung* three totemic images presided over the swearing of the deadly oaths on the spear point, the Gibichungs being shadowy figures in the dark circle around the disc, spectators rather than participants in the action. For Walter Erich Schäfer, who gave Wieland his Stuttgart theatre as a 'winter Bayreuth' and another proving ground for his productions, nothing better illustrated the great arc of Wieland's development from 1951 to 1965 than this scene – Wieland's progress from the ascetic, cubistic forms of the early modernist stage through to a nightmare world of psychic transactions shadowed by archetypal images and symbols.[116] At the end of the 1965 *Rheingold* there was no triumphant progress of the gods into Valhalla, only their descent from the circular arena into the darkness around it, with Fasolt's body left on the stage as a reminder of the efficacy of Alberich's curse. By the end of the cycle Schäfer was convinced that the pessimism of Wieland's first *Ring* had turned into a nihilistic vision. Whereas in the first *Ring* the tragedy had been softened by the aesthetic beauty of the presentation, the stillness in the closing bars of the second intimated nothing but despair. Wieland himself saw it as the downfall of the world ('der Weltuntergang'), the inevitable consequence of Wotan's power politics, agreeing with Goléa that it was an end without promise of a new beginning ('ein hoffnungsloser Untergang').[117] The production was not without its loose ends and would certainly have been developed by Wieland had he lived, but Dietrich Mack justly wrote that the logic of the production as a whole won out over any quibbles about the execution of many details within it. This was a *Ring* which all future stagings would have to take as their point of departure.

Der fliegende Holländer, *1959*

Wieland's 1959 staging of *Holländer* was, for him, a rare foray into theatrical realism. Its narrative directness seemed indebted to the 'music-theatre' aesthetic of Walter

Felsenstein's Komische Oper in Berlin, founded in 1947. With hindsight it can be seen that its style of robust comedy was a forerunner of the 1963 *Meistersinger* discussed above. The 1955 production of *Holländer* by Wieland's brother Wolfgang had been characteristic of the early years of New Bayreuth – an austere, disciplined beauty of the strongest, simplest shapes and a visual symphony of light, space and air celebrating liberation from the past. In 1959 it was Wieland's turn and he stepped back from Wolfgang's poetic abstraction into a theatrical realism where character and physical movement were of central importance.[118] In Act I there was no shore but simply the planked deck of Daland's ship with its guardrails and rope ladders vanishing aloft. At the climactic chorus 'Mit Gewitter und Sturm' the men were clustered round the wheel in a tight protoplasmic ball, lurching and swaying together – an extraordinary image of a ship driven before the wind.

The Dutchman's ship was a projection emerging from the darkness. It enveloped Daland's deck, its prow a monstrous ribcage with the Dutchman seemingly pinioned upon it – no pale ghost but a wild man. It was as though the blood-red firmament had broken open and thrust the cursed vessel to shore – a magical image of extraordinary power.[119] No less striking was the moment in Act III when, in response to the sailors' challenge ('Seeleut'! Wacht doch auf!'), the masked figures of the Dutchman's crew rose up like grey lemurs out of the sea behind the maniacally dancing Norwegian sailors, singing full out to the audience and, spectrally phosphorescent, trampled them to the floor while advancing threateningly towards the audience.

Wieland used the original 1843 Dresden version of the score, but with some of Wagner's later softening changes and with short pauses inserted between the three acts. Daland sported a vulgarly striped sailcloth suit and a rakish top hat. Wieland saw him as avarice personified, like a character from Balzac. In action he reminded Walter Panofsky of 'a performing bear, a malevolent clown, even a Nordic descendant of Pantalone'.[120] If this should suggest the caricature that Wagner specifically warned against, in Josef Greindl's performance Daland emerged as a figure scarcely less powerful than the Dutchman. For K. H. Ruppel the overall effect was poised somewhere between the grotesque realism of Dickens and the expressionist colouring of Nolde. With George London (initially) as the Dutchman, Anja Silja joining as Senta in 1960 (in Panofsky's words 'a somnambulist harbouring a secret animus in her heart')[121] and Wolfgang Sawallisch conducting, this staging transported the opera to a wholly new plane of seriousness and importance. It was rich in comedy, and pointed the way towards the demythologizing productions which were later to treat the opera as a drama of social realism.

That would never have been Wieland's own way. For him the theatre was, above anything else, a place of ritual, of magical invocation; the whole point of dramatic art was to defy the gravitas of real life. Thus Daland's domain into which the legendary sailor arrived from out of the blue was not the historically precise seafarer's home which Cosima had sought to construct, and which Joachim Herz was to create on stage at the Komische Oper in 1962, and on film in 1964,[122] but an exaggerated presentation – Daland's striped clown's suit and stovepipe hat, the gross breasts of the coarsely clad spinning wenches, the earthy simplification of the parlour in Daland's house into a space as primeval and inhospitable as Hunding's hut. For even

'Mit Gewitter und Sturm': for the climactic chorus in Act I of *Der fliegende Holländer* in 1959, Wieland created an extraordinary image of a ship driven before the wind by grouping the crew around the wheel in a lurching protoplasmic ball. Seated in front of them are Georg Paskuda as the Steuermann and Josef Greindl as Daland.

here, in the theatrical realism of his *Holländer*, Wieland's real interest was always in mining the depths of the drama, not in trafficking with its surface. His fundamental vision of Wagner's works was always that they were mystery plays. Nowhere was this more evident than in his productions of *Lohengrin* (1958–62) and *Tannhäuser* (1954–6).

From realism to mystery play: Lohengrin, *1958–1962*

'Wagner's theatrical style,' Wieland told Geoffrey Skelton in 1962, 'cannot be thought of in terms of stage realism. All his works are – I should almost say – subject to the laws of the mystery play, and mystery plays have different laws from realistic opera.'[123] Historically, the term 'mystery play' is more or less synonymous with 'miracle play', both generally denoting plays on biblical themes which emerged in the thirteenth and fourteenth centuries as a means of teaching and celebrating the doctrines of Christianity. They evolved thoughout medieval Europe in such varied forms as the English mystery play, the French *mystère*, the Italian *sacra rappresentazione*, the Spanish *auto sacramentale* and the German *Mysterienspiel*. Common to all forms was the depiction of man's fall and redemption, especially the salvation of his soul through the miraculous power of the Resurrection and of the Host. Wagner was no

Anja Silja as Senta in
1960. Walter Panofsky
described her magnetic
performance as that of 'a
somnambulist harbouring
a secret animus in her
heart'.

Christian in any ordinary sense of that word, but it is clear that his myth-based
operas were mystery plays at least in that they so often feature miraculous moments
which are crucial to the action. Absolutely central to Wagner's dramas is the irruption of the magical, fairy-tale fantastical into 'ordinary' life: the sudden arrival of the
Dutchman's ship, the apotheosis of the Dutchman and Senta, Tannhäuser's redemption by the death of Elisabeth, Lohengrin's arrival and departure – and that is just to
cite examples from the three early operas. These episodes are at the heart of Wagner's
works. Wieland was entirely right in his view that from the very beginning their
scenic potential had remained unfulfilled because of 'realistic' stage representations
which followed Wagner's own. 'If I think in realistic terms,' said Wieland, 'I must tell
myself that Lohengrin sailed through the Straits of Dover in a boat pulled by a swan
– actually in fact from the direction of Spain along the coast of France, through the
Straits of Dover; he then turned off into the river Schelde, and the unfortunate swan
had to tow him upstream all the way to Antwerp. I just do not believe it, and nowadays you could not make an audience believe it.'[124]

'Either,' said Wieland, 'I must produce a realistic work – and I did just that with
The Flying Dutchman – or I must produce a mystery play, and that has its own

special laws.' For Wieland those laws dictated that in *Lohengrin* the chorus should comment on the action, not take part in it. He positioned them as a concerted mass, singing straight out to the audience from relatively static positions in a shallow amphitheatre. They looked down onto a circular orchestra-arena at stage front where all the significant action between the principal characters took place. The chorus did not turn to greet the arrival of the swan, nor process across the stage in Acts II and III. The point, said Wieland, was that 'one cannot really localize miracles. As far as I am concerned, a miracle takes place everywhere at once, before and behind the spectator.' In addition there was a purely practical reason: 'The Swan chorus is one of the finest choral pieces that Wagner ever wrote, and I find it horrible when this whole piece is sung towards Lohengrin standing at the back of the stage just for the sake of conventional stage realism. On top of that I do not like the chorus to turn their backs on the audience when miraculous things are happening. It does not help the miracle at all, but rather weakens its effect.'[125]

The same reasoning led to the omission of all incidental actions prescribed by Wagner, Wieland even bringing down the curtain during the dawn transformation in Act II to obviate any need for superfluous business. This he explained as follows:

> according to Wagner's stage instructions, several things happen during the dawn transformation: the gate is opened, maidens go to the well (it used to be done that way in Bayreuth once), water is scooped up, a whole lot of men come in. And what do they do? In the good old German way they clap each other on the shoulder, they shake hands. And none of it has anything at all to do with *Lohengrin*. The music is not suited to it either. In a realistic work there is no reason why I should not let the maidens go to the well and the char-women scrub the steps of the church. It could look very nice. But none of it has a place in Wagner's mystery plays.[126]

The swan was a projected silvery image that emerged from nothing by becoming progressively brighter: it was not a physical arrival, the approach and mooring of an aquatic conveyance, but the materialization of a miracle. And this epiphany was echoed in the second act by Elsa's appearance, as Lohengrin's bride, in the same place at the back of the amphitheatre and her slow descent down a processional carpet towards the audience. The first scene of this act had been played around a pagan altar erected on the *Spielscheibe* at the front of the stage, circumscribed by darkness. Wieland had first devised 'the Ortrud-Telramund confrontation … as a slow cross-ing of the stage, then decided to leave it completely static, with the characters at the opposite sides of the stage so that the music would dominate everything'.[127] When the curtain rose after the 'dawn interlude', the chorus were again in their fixed positions as narrators of the action, not participants. There was no physical distinction between the kemenate and the minster, between which the bridal procession sup-posedly takes place. The minster was, however, symbolically present in a misty stained-glass image of the Virgin seen behind Elsa as she walked down the staircase, and in a broad ring of little towers and Gothic arches suspended over the arena like

In the second act of Wieland's *Lohengrin*, which he interpreted as a mystery play, the chorus did not participate in the action but were narrators singing from fixed positions. There was no bridal procession to the minster. Elsa (Anja Silja) entered from the same place from which Lohengrin had materialized in the first act, advancing slowly down the staircase towards the audience. This photograph dates from 1962.

a mystic crown. Panofsky describes the moment at the end of the second act, when at Elsa's 'Hoch über alles Zweifels Macht soll meine Liebe stehn!' Lohengrin sank to his knees before her. Observing this, Ortrud circled the rapt pair as though entrapping them in a magic ring.[128]

Act III began with the light picking out a bridal chamber that was merely a bench set in front of a semi-transparent floral hanging, behind which the chorus became visible. Lohengrin and Elsa seemed as alone as Tristan and Isolde in their own flowery bower.

In the characterization, Elsa was not a virginal figure but a sensual creature fired with passion for Lohengrin from the moment he appeared. Lohengrin himself remained a silvery presence, a shining image of the Grail's messenger from another land. Ortrud was the voice of Elsa's dark self, wanting to unmask the mysterious saviour.

The overall impression was that of a grave ceremonial enactment, almost a sacred oratorio. But there was no question that Wieland, well aware that the composition of

Lohengrin in the mid-1840s coincided with Wagner's first serious engagement with Aeschylus, had taken his interpretative cue from the Greek theatre. Wieland was convinced that Wagner had himself looked at the Lohengrin legend with the eyes of a Greek, and it was Panofsky's view that Wieland's production, in its materialization of a medieval mystery in a classical guise, had realized the composer's own dream of a symbolic unity between Greek and German culture.[129]

Tannhäuser, *1954–1964*

While there was nothing exceptional in Wieland's view of *Tannhäuser* as a drama of *eros* versus *religio* in the context of medieval Christianity, his three realizations of it (1954, 1961 and the major revision thereof in 1964) showed his genius for distilling the essence of the drama. In each case the action was played out on the open area of the stage floor, surrounded by the simplest box-like walls, textured and beautifully lit, but without any romantic perspectives or suggestions of nature, other than a small number of mop-head artificial trees. In 1954 the floor in Act II was a chequered chessboard, though Wieland was too subtle to move his singers around like chess pieces. From 1955 an immensely tall, slender cross, downstage left, was present in all three acts. It was at the foot of this cross, not at a modest wayside shrine, that Elisabeth prayed, and from where she simply withdrew, slowly disappearing into the far distance. Later in the same act, the appearance immediately behind it of the vision of the Venusberg – like the interior of an immense mussel or oyster with Venus as its pearl – was an unforgettable statement of the central tension.

The orgies to which Tannhäuser was drawn – and of which until 1964 he was merely a spectator – were not the hothouse of sensuality evoked by Wagner's music, especially in the Paris version which Wieland tailored to his own needs, but rather desperate couplings reminiscent of Bosch or Dante in which, especially as choreographed by Maurice Béjart in 1961, sex and death were one and the same, the dancers spread-eagled together on the floor like starfish, or caught up in a huge net as though ready for the cauldron.

Wieland's Tannhäuser sinned not from weakness but from strength. His tragedy was that of a restless romantic, an equivocating, Hamlet-like figure, as appalled by the erotic fatigues of Venus as by the moral order of the Wartburg, sinning against both and denied absolution by the supreme spiritual authority. Wieland saw Tannhäuser as closely related to Tristan in his conflict between honour and a forbidden love and to Parsifal in his search for redemption.[130]

Wagner himself wanted the members of the chorus to behave not as a mass but as distinct individuals, asking that the entry of the guests into the Hall of Song should be 'throughout true to life in its noblest and freest forms'.[131] Wieland, however, characteristically went for stylized groupings and choreography that symbolized the chorus's collective role in the drama.

Here it is important to acknowledge the largely unsung contribution of Wieland's wife Gertrud Reissinger to the movement in his productions. Trained at the best modern dance school in Munich, she was steeped in the expressive dance style of the

In *Tannhäuser* from 1955 all three acts were dominated by a huge cross. In the third act it became the 'wayside shrine' at which Elisabeth prayed.

1920s. Her daughter Nike points out that in contrast to Wieland's 'predominantly symmetrical approach to direction and design, she loved to make use of diagonal lines, and frequently emphasised movements on unstressed beats of the bar to achieve a kind of "choreographic syncopation"'. Nike goes on to describe how in the 1954 *Tannhäuser* 'the rhythmic sexuality of her "Bacchanal" shocked the audiences: her penitent pilgrims dragged themselves asynchronously across the stage, and the guests at the singers' contest entered the hall of the Wartburg with movements some-how gliding above the music'.[132] The guests were seated in banked tiers, the segre-gated men and women facing each other from the sides of the stage across the great chequered hall. In response to Tannhäuser's blasphemous outburst, the men re-formed as a diagonal phalanx behind the Landgraf and the other minstrels, with Tannhäuser trapped downstage right, Elisabeth dramatically interceding for him by running against the advancing line of the phalanx.

By 1961, the banked tiers had disappeared, the guests now lining the walls at either side and to the rear of the great central space in which Elisabeth's throne, on a dais, occupied the position where Venus, played by the black singer Grace Bumbry, had taken up her commanding stance in Act I. As the angry guests moved in from either side, like the jaws of a vice closing in on the errant minstrel, Elisabeth stepped down from her throne, holding them apart with her 'Haltet ein!' Best of all was the 1964 configuration, in which the guests, now divided into blocks, formed a semicircle around the central singing arena, Elisabeth on a stool at the front of the stage with her back to the audience. The break-up of the tight seating pattern was freer and more spontaneous, suggesting that Tannhäuser's outburst had generated not so much solid resistance in the courtiers as anarchy.

The treatment of the pilgrims also changed. In 1954 they had advanced across the stage in Act I as a solid mass, with tonsured heads, each clutching a crucifix and bent earnestly forward under the weight of sin. Seven years later they progressed in groups of three, each bearing a large penitential cross. Their stylized movement was now that of a strange ritual dance, expressing the masochistic ecstasy of their sinful burden. The concluding apotheosis, signalling Tannhäuser's salvation through the intercession of the saintly Elisabeth, developed from a pyramid of golden-haloed heads seen in silhouette, to the same arranged in great circles ringing the rear of the stage, a vision of the cherubim and seraphim of the heavenly host.

By framing the opera's central conflicts within the formal structures of a mystery play, Wieland succeeded in making them timeless in a way never attempted before. It was right that the riddles within the work should find expression in a way that kept faith with them as serious, perennial issues. In concentrating on the mythic essence behind the 'romantic opera' façade, Wieland had restored the sense of timeless tragedy proper to the work.

The critical reception

Criticism of Wieland came from two principal groups. The first were those who continued to believe – as many still do – that Wagner's ideas about how his works were to be performed were inviolable. Numbered among this group were those for whom Wagner and the conservative Bayreuth tradition represented something important about the Germanness of German art, about a sacred German identity. These people felt betrayed that the composer's own grandsons had thrown all that over, insisting that his work spoke with a universal, supranational voice.

The second group were those who fell under the spell of Wieland's work but were perplexed by inconsistencies, loose ends and the editing-out of anything that failed to fit the vision. It was only from this group that there emerged a critique of any value, and Wieland was always ready to engage with it and, up to a point, explain himself. The greater part of this critique centred on Wieland's omissions, all the things that his 'dramaturgy of the invisible stage', as Hans Mayer so well put it, chose to leave invisible.[133] Typical was the reaction of the London publisher Victor Gollancz, reporting on the 1965 Ring for the Observer. Gollancz considered that while Wieland had been brilliantly successful in creating 'a general atmosphere of the primitive or immemorial' he had 'wilfully failed' in his representations of 'the actual dramatic situation'.[134] Why, he asked, had Wieland ignored many of Wagner's instructions, particularly where crucial symbols and symbolic moments were concerned? Why was there no rainbow bridge in Das Rheingold, no great door flying open in the first act of Die Walküre? Why did the gods go down at the end of Rheingold? Gollancz came in from the angle of robust common sense, his point being that the omissions contravened the composer's instructions and sold his drama short. Surely the magnificent single-mindedness of the productions would not have been compromised by the inclusion of the missing items? Gollancz put his objections to Wieland in person and was answered with arguments that will by now be familiar: it was anti-dramatic for the staging to recycle nineteenth-century effects that were now clichés and for it slavishly to follow the music. Wieland courteously welcomed Gollancz's critique while defending the right of his generation to reinterpret Wagner's work for a modern world in which theatre could no longer behave as though cinema and television did not exist.[135]

Some accused Wieland of being an 'abstract' producer, meaning that he wanted to have nothing to do with the nineteenth-century aesthetic of naturalistic illusion, or the leaf-for-leaf representation of nature. It was a charge that he always denied.[136] But no matter how clearly he explained his Appian principles of eliminating the merely picturesque in the interests of serving the deepest levels of the musical drama, this cut no ice with those whose prejudices were an essential part of their Wagnerolatory.

The argument about unhelpful omissions was developed (more subtly) by Robert Donington, whose Jungian analysis of the *Ring*, *Wagner's 'Ring' and its Symbols* (1963), although quite independently conceived, reads almost as a screenplay for Wieland's productions. In subsequent writings, Donington was disturbed by the absence of symbols he considered essential and wondered why Wieland sometimes introduced new symbols of his own.

Wieland's reply to such criticism was that the only symbols that mattered were those in the music. It was not the job of the staging to be a visual echo of the music, but rather to omit distracting secondary detail and concentrate the imagination on essentials. If the great door can be heard flying open in the music, why show it on the stage? That, for Wieland, was boring, deadly theatre; for Gollancz and Donington, to omit it was the perverse passing up of the chance to strengthen the musical effect with the precise visual event envisioned by Wagner. Ultimately there can be no adjudication between these two positions.

For my own part, I did not regret the omissions in question, finding Wieland's visual images always richly resonant, the lighting all that one could wish for by way of the stage picture reflecting the music. To be freed from the suspension of disbelief necessitated by invariably unsuccessful attempts to portray the detail of Wagner's stage rubrics was nothing but gain.

Another bone of contention was Wieland's attitude to the music, Gollancz and others complaining that he often ignored on the stage 'the plain demands of the orchestra'.[137] Wieland himself claimed never to have deviated from the production principle he hammered out with Kurt Overhoff in the 1940s, namely that the producer's work should always be rooted in the score but beyond that should be free in its stage interpretation. But one man's idea of being true to the music is not necessarily another's, not least because of the inherent difficulties in talking about it. The ground gets even stickier when Wieland, challenged in the 1960s that he was not always as true to the music as he claimed to be, retorted that his best guide was no longer the music but the dramatic ideas that lay behind it.[138] While there is no doubt that Wagner did compose like that – the words and the music inspired by an underlying dramatic idea – Wieland could claim no more privileged access to that source than anyone else and his defence is little more than sophistry. His approach to the music's role in the complete performance was critical, not deferential – rather obviously so when he cut the 'deutsches Schwert' chorus in Act III of *Lohengrin*, doubtless for political reasons, or the little Gutrune scene in the third act of *Götterdämmerung* in 1965 because he found it 'boring'.

Wieland and the chantacteur

Certainly Wieland always liked to work with a certain tension between the music and the stage production. Nowhere was this more striking than in his direction of the singers. He was never interested in action for its own sake, but only in the movement of the soloists and chorus as a choreography of the 'inner action', of what was happening in the characters' hearts and minds:

> The great danger of Wagner's works is the over-suggestiveness of the music, which simply compels definite gestures, and these then become conventionalized. I take the view that the psychological situation gives rise to the gesture and at the same time to the music. That is to say, it is not the music that gives rise to the gesture, but the psychological situation and the actor's interpretation of it foremost. The music expresses what the singer thinks and feels. It is not the other way round. The singer should not simply react to the music. That is to my mind a ballet style – the style of 1910, which unfortunately persists because in most opera houses there is not sufficient time for rehearsals.[139]

This is a diametrically opposite approach to that of Wagner himself, who had wanted all stage movement exactly coordinated with the music.

Wieland's concentration on the operas as myth, as a reincarnation of Greek tragedy, implied an anti-naturalistic style of acting. It was more important to him that the stage characters should represent Ideas rather than people of flesh and blood. He wanted them to be in touch with and communicate the archetypes embodied in them with as little 'real-life' distraction as possible. This was the enactment of a ritual drama, not the presentation of a heightened slice of life. In distancing himself from the Bayreuth tradition of naturalistic interaction between characters (cultivated by Tietjen as much as by Siegfried and Cosima), Wieland, in his first Bayreuth period, kept the singers well apart from each other, asking them to sing not to each other (as Wagner had wanted) but directly, or at least obliquely, to the audience. The point was that characters should not interact realistically but rather soliloquize, behaving as though they were engaged in profound self-analysis (which of course they are). They were sleepwalkers in their own drama, and the style of vocal expression also reflected this.

This presentation of character was much criticized in the 1951–8 *Ring* as 'Wieland's oratorio style', as the intellectualizing of production.[140] In the 1965 *Ring*, movement was noticeably freer, with the blocking now less symmetrical and with tangible contact between characters, as in Wotan's embracing Brünnhilde in the second and third acts of *Die Walküre*.

Much less remarked was Wieland's insistence that singers should understand and deliver their words as intently as their music (he found that this was all too rare, even among native German speakers). For him, as for Wagner, the text and the music were indissoluble. Clear articulation of the words and their meaning was often hard to combine with a beautiful sound, and both were essential. The principal thing, Wieland told his singers, was that they should never sacrifice expression of the underlying emotion to tonal quality. It was also less important for them to retain eye contact with each other than that they should sustain the projection of the characters' feelings to the audience. Thus, as Anja Silja records in her memoirs, in the duet between herself as Senta and the Dutchman in the second act of *Der fliegende Holländer*, 'Each of us sang not to each other, but to ourselves as though engaged in an inner monologue. At the end we moved slowly together, but were still emotionally in our private worlds, Senta enraptured, the Dutchman hesitant, full of doubt.'[141]

Silja, a singing-actress who took major roles in many of Wieland's later productions (and who became his mistress), gives a vivid picture of the way he worked: 'He wanted to know what, during Wotan's great monologue in the second act of *Walküre*, was going on not just in Wotan ... but also in Brünnhilde. Wieland often concentrated on the singers who were on stage but not singing. It was significant that he ignored all leitmotives. He always said: "Either you react before or after the music, but never with it." Today many directors do the opposite, everything always beautifully synchronized – and that's terrible.'[142]

When Silja says that he ignored leitmotives she means that he forbade any attempts to coordinate action with them or to illustrate them – thus no spear was ever to be lowered (or even raised) in synchrony with its motive. Jess Thomas, a favourite tenor of Wieland's, told me of his quandary when singing Parsifal: Wieland had ruled that he should not raise his spear during the baptism in the third act,[143] while Knappertsbusch, conducting, had insisted that he should. As the moment approached he grew more and more terrified as he felt he had to follow the conductor. Just as he was about to lift the spear darkness swallowed him up. Lighting was always Wieland's first and last weapon.[144]

The journey into the interior

In Wieland's trajectory from the ascetic, geometric modernism of the early 1950s through to the symbolic ciphers of a decade later, the one clear thing is that this was a great interpretative artist's journey into the interior of Wagner's works. The aesthetics of traditional stage production had become moribund, the politics of such productions impossible in a Germany struggling to exorcize guilt and find a new identity. Wieland had the genius to see that he had to dive below the tarnished surface, to work from the timeless core of Wagner's works and emerge only with images of universal significance. In treating them as mystery plays, and as maps of the cliffs and chasms of the human mind, he came up with the most potent realizations yet of Wagner's mythopoeic music dramas; the *Ring* not as a dream of world domination, but as an interpretation of that dream, a pathology of its roots. It was a revelation of Wagner as the musician of the inadmissible subconscious, a confirmation of the

Schopenhauerean composer whose music embodied the most secret purposes of the Will. 'Wagner opened up a new and higher dimension in the theatre,' Wieland told Panofsky. 'He invokes not the world of actorish make-believe, but the dream image, the subconscious – visually and, above all, musically. … Who besides Wagner has ever written music that can persuade an audience to accept without demur as tragic necessities such things as incest, adultery and filicide, to take only three examples from *Die Walküre*?'[145] Wieland animated the dream images on the stage, creating with them a theatre of beauty and power that was also a resurrection of the sense of the miraculous in Wagner's works.

Wieland's legacy

Much of the vitality of Wieland's work lay in its divergence from traditional production. Much of the excitement was that of iconoclasm. There had been iconoclasm before, as in the stagings of Mahler and Klemperer. But Wieland's innovations were more politically momentous in that the challenge to orthodoxy was mounted in the composer's very own theatre in the immediate post-war context.

Wieland himself saw his work as an open-ended quest, not the perfection of a single vision. No one could have been more self-critically aware of how swiftly the revelation of today hardens into the cliché of tomorrow. He would have been the first to point out that even archetypal images are only approximations to absolutes, visual metaphors that are for ever dissolving and re-forming.

It was not his fault if in some quarters his productions came to be seen as no less definitive, no less exemplary, than his grandfather's own efforts.[146] He (and his brother Wolfgang) were keenly aware of the danger that New Bayreuth might become 'a new kind of anachronism'.[147] His inspired use of a circular playing space for the *Ring*, at once the epitome of his indebtedness to Greek theatre and an omnipresent visual symbol of the work as a whole, became, as he complained, the new common language of Wagner production: 'The *Weltenscheibe* which I introduced in 1951 has since been copied almost ad absurdum on all the stages of the world. One is almost ashamed to see it nowadays. It has become the common thing.'[148]

In due course new production strategies did emerge, the best of which bore out Wieland's own commitment to ceaseless experiment and renewal. Many of these were to address a problematic element that was inseparable from the very success with which Wieland had depoliticized his grandfather's works and put Bayreuth's Nazi past behind it. For in his determination to liberate Wagner from the taint of nationalism, Wieland overcompensated. This was especially evident, as we have seen, in both his stagings of *Die Meistersinger*. It was a strategy that extended also to the music. Wieland's chosen conductor for the 1956 'ohne Nürnberg' production was the Flemish André Cluytens, whom he repeatedly implored not to conduct 'in a German way': 'Anything but German, you understand?'[149] Doubtless he said something similar to Thomas Schippers, the young American conductor of the 1963 production. For *Parsifal*, he reminded his chorus master Wilhelm Pitz, 'No unnecessary crescendos and decrescendos, no marcatos, everything mystical but not German and not

Christian Democratic'.[150] Even an admirer like the producer's daughter Nike had to ask, 'for how long can one experiment with squaring a circle, with de-Germanising a German work of art?'[151] Wieland's emphasis on the Greek rather than German affinities, on the universality of a psychological reading of myth, had cut the operas adrift from their historical anchorages. He had effectively de-historicized them, ridding them not only of unacceptable aspects of their performance history but also of the political and ideological roots which are an intrinsic part of their meaning.

Wieland had created the impression that one could burrow down through the uncomfortable accretions of history, and of Wagner's own preachments, to discover untainted, Ideal forms of the works. No such pure, inviolate forms could, however, exist. History cannot be rubbed out but only manipulated. That was what Wieland, like every other stage interpreter, had to do and did. There were both political and artistic reasons for doing so and it was fortunate that they reinforced each other.

We have seen how Wieland had invoked Freud and Jung to support his psychological approach to stage interpretation. But the missing historical element is most clearly apparent in his calling on Schadewaldt to provide, in his Bayreuth lectures, an intellectual underpinning for the 'Greek dimension' of his staging strategy. It was, however, an underpinning that was far from sound. Schadewaldt had of course been well aware that Wagner had made use of the Greeks for his own nineteenth-century purposes, but he chose to do less than justice to the full scope of those purposes. He spoke of the way the composer had moulded Greek elements in order to help him speak 'to the subjective situation of the torn, worldless, and desperate individual in an age which has lost its old ties but not formed new ones'[152] – a formulation that would have found a sympathetic echo in the Bayreuth of the 1950s and early 1960s. But Schadewaldt culpably underplayed the extent to which Wagner had actually subsumed the Greeks into a Germanic ideology.

It is hard not to agree with John Deathridge's view that Wieland, albeit for understandable reasons, had perpetuated

the myth that Wagner's dramas could be seen through the lens of the Greeks, with their origins in the more problematic nationalist corners of German Idealism greatly diminished, and cleansed of their immediate past in pre-war Bayreuth. Once cumbersome beings in the service of German nationalist ideology, they shed their skins, so to speak, to metamorphose into creatures of sublime beauty and universal truth. With the support of Schadewaldt's lectures on Wagner and the Greeks, they became essentially works without a palpable history, despite the clamour in the wings, which can still be heard, that they are nothing of the sort.[153]

The history of Wagner's works cannot in truth ever be kept down. The way in which it resurfaced in East Germany and eventually reasserted itself at Bayreuth after Wieland's death will be the subject of the next chapter.

CHAPTER 10

The political imperative

> By his creation of an art intoxicated with the past and the future, the author of the *Ring* did not transcend the age of bourgeois culture in order to exchange bourgeois values for a totalitarianism that destroys mind and spirit. The German spirit signified everything to him, the German state nothing.
>
> Thomas Mann, 'Richard Wagner and *Der Ring des Nibelungen*' (1937)[1]

The politics of Wagner's life, works and performance history are so intertwined as to defy attempts to separate them. Encoded in the works is a political programme full of contradictions. By the end of his life its social-revolutionary aspect had all but disappeared. It was not the 'people' who turned up for the supposedly 'democratic' Bayreuth festivals of 1876 and 1882 but princelings from abroad, the power brokers of the young German Empire and, yes, a sprinkling of composers, artists and cognoscenti.

Wagner's own politics, those intrinsic to his works, and the political interpretations that have been made of them, whether in themselves or in performance, are by no means the same. In this chapter I am primarily concerned not with the political qualities of the operas (a huge and difficult subject) but with the political significance that has been read into them in the theatre. Most particularly I will discuss their stage performance in the former Marxist state of East Germany, which existed from the end of the Second World War until 1990. It is a complex story whose strands include the denazification of Wagner, the impact of the anti-Wagnerians Brecht and Felsenstein, and the development by Joachim Herz and Götz Friedrich of productions which, arguably for the first time, were critically alert to the operas as an expression of their composer's political views.

The promulgation of Wagner as a man of the right – and of the left

After Wagner's death the ultra-conservative Germanic nationalism of Cosima and her Wahnfried circle tightened around the composer and his works. Wagner's protean revolutionary spirit was corralled into an ideological mould that may have been inspired by him but was far from his own complete story. The unequivocal chauvinism and anti-semitism of the Wahnfried evangelists projected onto Wagner a more extreme conservatism than he had himself espoused. The composer's name served as a rallying cry for the discontents of the fledgling German Empire. Wagner became the focus for nationalist energies which welcomed the war of 1914. In the press he was acclaimed as an epitome and guarantor of Germanness. All too soon, Hitler would be marshalling the composer to the same end.

But the right did not have it all its own way. Marx and Engels may have had no use for Wagner, but there were others who did take seriously the revolutionary socialism of the young composer. Among them was a Viennese group led by Engelbert Pern-erstorfer who, turning a blind eye to Wagner's jingoistic response to the Prussian siege of Paris in 1870–1, celebrated him as a socialist artist.[2] Nietzsche, appalled by the later Wagner's self-aggrandisement and Germanomania, spoke out tartly for his subversive, revolutionary side, inconveniently reminding him of his indebtedness to the now reviled France that had been nursery to the radical anarchism of his form-ative years. But this critique had as little effect on the mainstream stage interpreta-tion of the operas as Bernard Shaw's insistence, in *The Perfect Wagnerite* (1898), that the *Ring* was an allegory of the evils of nineteenth-century capitalism. Shaw was a Fabian socialist who knew he was on to something important, but the wit with which he decoded Wagner's mythologizing did no service to a view of the *Ring* that had no tangible impact on stage performance until three-quarters of a century later.

It was not until the 1920s backlash against Wagner that there appeared stagings which sought to resuscitate the composer's political and artistic radicalism. These included Klemperer's 1929 *Holländer* at the Berlin Kroll Opera (discussed in chap-ter 8). But, as liberal intellectuals warned, Wagner remained vulnerable – as he always had – to absorption into nationalistic ideology. Writing in 1928, Bernhard Diebold vigorously defended the democratic, liberal impulse in his works against their nationalistic appropriation.[3] This warning was courageously reinforced by Thomas Mann in his lecture, 'The Sorrows and Grandeur of Richard Wagner', deliv-ered in Munich on 10 February 1933 at the very time when Hitler was seizing power.

Meanwhile, in Russia the Bolshevik Revolution of 1917 had adopted Wagner as a like-minded forerunner (as described in chapter 7). This was largely thanks to the enthusiasm of Anatoly Lunacharsky (1875–1933), an intellectual who had been writing about Wagner since 1902 and who, on 26 October 1917, was appointed 'People's Commissar of Public Education'. Lunacharsky extolled Wagner's vision of an anti-bourgeois art that would inculcate social values in the populace. He consid-ered that *Art and Revolution* was an important counterpart to the Communist Man-ifesto, both being products of the 1848 revolutions. He saw to it that a translation of Wagner's essay was one of the first publications (1918) of his commissariat.[4] This coercion of Wagner as a Bolshevik was matched with productions whose geometric modernity was designed to set the greatest possible distance between the re-invented Wagner and the one that had been celebrated amidst the lavishly upholstered decor of the tsarist yesteryear. When Moscow's first post-Revolution opera season opened on 5 September 1918 with an abstract-futuristic production of *Lohengrin* at the 'Theatre of the Council of Working Deputies', directed by Fyodor Komissarzhevsky, it was prefaced with a speech by Lunacharsky in which he extolled the part that Wagner would be playing in the creation of the new Soviet society. Lunacharsky was by no means alone in his advocacy, the great pianist Mariya Yudina recalling that Wagner's 'music embodied the spirit of the first revolutionary years'.[5]

This phase of wildly experimental productions was less than totally successful in its education of the proletariat and was short-lived. After Lenin's death in 1924, Stalin swiftly rose to power. Doctrinaire Marxism began to bite and Wagner was soon denounced as an imperialist, as an artist incomprehensible to the masses, and his works vanished from the boards. Lunacharsky resigned his position in 1929. He continued to commend Wagner as a forerunner of the people's revolution, but now carefully distinguished Wagner's earlier 'progressive' period from the later one in which the revolutionary had become a reactionary, the rebellious petit-bourgeois a crippled figure, 'a poisoned Siegfried' who had kissed the Pope's slipper and, as Nietzsche said, had in *Parsifal* knelt at the foot of the Cross.[6]

Elsewhere, productions in radical spirit were few and far between. In the Bayreuth of the 1930s Winifred Wagner, as we have seen, resisted the overt politicization of production, but there and elsewhere in Germany the theatre was, if not compliant, in no way out of tune with the cultural ideology of the Reich.

First steps in Wagner's post-war rehabilitation

When the dust began to settle after the war, there could be no doubt that the ideological battle for Wagner had so far been won by the right – and so overwhelmingly that the hope for a future purged of danger from the resurgence of fascism could not help but regard Wagner with suspicion. An art that had served as a cultural focus for the Third Reich was not going to have a smooth passage through denazification. Nevertheless, it was surprising how very quickly Wagner was back on the boards in Germany, especially when we remember that virtually every one of its larger theatres had been razed to the ground or severely damaged. At the end of the war the country had been divided into sectors by the Allies, the Western Sector (which in 1948 became the Federal Republic of West Germany) under Allied occupation and the Eastern Sector (which in 1949 became the GDR, or German Democratic Republic) under the Soviets. Because of their antagonistic political regimes, with West Germany established as a capitalist democracy and East Germany evolving into a Marxist socialist state, there were to be two very different approaches to the denazification and rehabilitation of the composer.

The first post-war performance of Wagner in East Germany was a *Tannhäuser* given on 24 February 1946 in an improvised theatre in Chemnitz. Operas like *Der fliegende Holländer* and *Tristan*, which are comparatively free from overt nationalistic content, soon followed.[7] The central part played by *Die Meistersinger* in Nazi pageantry militated against its overhasty reappearance, but for some ten years after the war both Germanies looked forward to eventual reunification, and this hope placed the nationalism of *Die Meistersinger* in a new light which hastened its rehabilitation. The national element, especially in *Meistersinger* and *Lohengrin*, could be cultivated not in the triumphalist sense of the Nazis, but as speaking for the unity, the generic oneness of the German people and for the supremacy of their art. The historical realism of *Die Meistersinger*, its credible characters and blend of wistful resignation, comedy and progress from the rule book of a moribund old order to the hope of a flowering of new art forms, judged and acclaimed by the people rather than the cognoscenti, needed no apology and could cause but minimal residual embarrassment in either Germany. Wagner, like Bach, Handel and Beethoven, was invoked as a symbol of national unity. It was in this spirit that the Staatsoper, in the Soviet-controlled Eastern Sector of Berlin, broke the tacit taboo and gave the first post-war performance of *Die Meistersinger* at Christmas 1948. It was as enthusiastically received as the one with which Bayreuth reopened its doors in 1951.[8] From 1968 Bayreuth's programme books began to cite Wagner's own statement in *Art and Revolution* that the 'national element' in a work 'must be no more than an ornament, an added individual charm, and not a confining boundary'.

Bayreuth's *Meistersinger*, as we have seen, was in comparatively traditional style, and it was only Wieland Wagner's productions of the *Ring* and *Parsifal* that declared a total break with the recent past. The long overdue aesthetic need for a new direction coincided with the political need for a style of production that would look away from a narrowly Germanic Wagner towards a universal one. Bayreuth had to be seen to be addressing the world at large. The dragon of Nazi misappropriation had to be laid to rest. In its place new appropriations appeared. As Nike Wagner remarks, 'Wieland's reinvention of his grandfather as a "Western European" rather than a German chimed well with the political climate of Adenauer's Federal Republic, which placed great emphasis on the shared cultural heritage of Western Europe.'[9] Cynics said that the bare stage spoke only of a straitened budget (and that the proper naturalistic decor would soon be back). But time soon proved them wrong. The depth-psychology and the symbols were there to stay. The strategy was that of wiping the slate clean and the productions barely concerned themselves with the operas' political penumbra. The plain intent of New Bayreuth's slogan of 'Hier gilt's der Kunst' (Our concern is art) – which had also been used by Siegfried Wagner in the 1920s – was depoliticization. Discussion of the political aspects of the composer, his works and their abuse was not encouraged. A poster blatantly declared, 'In the interests of a smooth operation of the festival we request visitors kindly to refrain from conversations and discussions of a political nature on the Festspielhaus hill.'[10] In the same spirit, West Germany as a whole chose to ignore the East's strategy of disassociation, one which, in its efforts to square Wagner with Marxist-Leninist politics, was certainly no less remarkable.

East Germany and the cultural politics of socialism

The Soviet zone of East Germany, within whose borders lay Wagner's birthplace of Leipzig, was no less interested than its western counterpart in the rehabilitation of the composer. But it had a very different political perspective which (especially from the late 1950s) took its cultural bearings from Moscow. One of its central precepts was that culture was political and should contribute to the socialist purpose of the state.

To this end the GDR leant on strict Marxist cultural ideology as promulgated in 1934 by Stalin's cultural commissar Andrei Zhdanov. The directive was that art in all its forms had to shun the 'formalism' of expressionism and abstraction, of pessimism and nihilism. It had instead to be 'socially realist', appealing to all by being readily comprehensible and uplifting in its portrayal of heroic deeds and happy endings. Theatre directors were urged to avoid the manifold errors of 'formalism'. Looking towards Russia for practical exemplars as well as for theory, the SED (Walter Ulbricht's Sozialistische Einheitspartei Deutschlands, or Socialist Unity Party) adopted Stanislavsky as one of its models for theatre production. The aristocratically inclined Russian director's philosophy of the actor's total identification with his role, of finely detailed naturalism, became a point of departure for socialist theatre in general and, in particular, for the theatrical realism developed by Walter Felsenstein at his Komische Oper in East Berlin.[11]

From the socialist viewpoint, New Bayreuth's productions, while undoubtedly successful in laying the ghosts, perpetuated only a Wagner for the bourgeois connoisseurs of the capitalist West. Symbolic and depth-psychological presentation was akin to formalism and was incomprehensible and inaccessible to the ordinary man or woman. Was there not another Wagner to be rescued, one which, by being available to all at modest prices, could contribute powerfully to the cultural health of the state and to its international standing?

East Germany had two powerful figures on whom to construct a socialist theatre, but they had entirely different, even divergent approaches, and were united only in their antipathy to Wagner. It was very much as it had been in the Weimar aftermath of the First World War, the most important directors turning their backs on Wagner as an epitome of retrogressive nationalism. Nevertheless, both Walter Felsenstein and Bertolt Brecht were to play a crucial role in the emergence of distinctively East German styles of new Wagner production.

Walter Felsenstein (1901–75), born in Austria, had been a leading director of opera and plays in the 1930s, largely in Freiburg, Cologne, Frankfurt and Zürich. In 1947 he constituted the Komische Oper with the declared aim of demystifying opera by presenting it as meticulously rehearsed 'music-theatre' and opening it up to all with massively subsidized seat prices. Felsenstein used the term 'Musiktheater' to describe a style of production that has had an immense influence. The basic idea, he says, is to treat an opera as a real drama in which 'the first and most important stage director is the composer'.[12] Music-theatre differs from spoken theatre in that the vocal expression springs from a different psychological motivation: 'The singing actor must prove to me that he has no choice but to *sing* the line.'[13] It is the antithesis of treating opera (and musicals too) as 'concerts in costume'. The plot is always taken seriously and intensively rehearsed as an ensemble drama of real-life people. Where the plot of an opera is itself fantastical, as say in Offenbach's *Orpheus in the Underworld* or Britten's *Midsummer Night's Dream*, then the realism becomes 'fantastic realism'. Wieland Wagner described Felsenstein as the master of 'magical realism'.[14] The acting has always to be an expression of the music and the singers are expected to act as convincingly as they sing. Hence Felsenstein's preference for the term 'singing-actor' and for referring to the chorus always as 'chorus soloists' (Chorsolisten).

An important objective is that everything should be understandable by a popular audience, operas always being sung in the vernacular. Felsenstein often made new translations and sometimes added extra action in order to explain what might otherwise be obscure to the uninitiated. 'Everything', says Felsenstein, 'must be shown quite concretely.'[15] Although never used by him, the appellation 'realistisches Musiktheater' has gained a certain currency – as, for example, in the Akademie der Künste's publications relating to Joachim Herz's Leipzig *Ring* of 1973–6 (see p. 420, note 54 below). Herz himself, who worked closely with Felsenstein, says that the principles of music-theatre 'can be reduced to one basic law: that of the truthfulness of the action'.[16] Herz has sometimes varied the usage, as in 'Die realistisch-komödiantische Wagner-Interpretation 1960–1976', the title of a lecture given in Salzburg on 3 March 1983. This was translated by Stewart Spencer as 'Wagner and Theatrical Realism 1960–1976', 'theatrical realism' (with the musical medium understood) being perhaps the best English shorthand for an elusive German concept.[17]

Felsenstein's ideals had an important precedent in those of Klemperer's Kroll Opera in the closing years of the Weimar Republic. As we saw in chapter 8, the Kroll was also an attempt to make opera available to ordinary people, not just with inexpensive tickets but by creating an experience that was dramatic in the fullest sense. At the demise of the Kroll – under political pressure from the ascendant nationalist right – Klemperer had defiantly announced that although the theatre was being shut down, the ideas it stood for could not be destroyed. When they resurfaced at the Komische Oper after the war there could have been no more powerful symbolic link back to the Kroll than Klemperer's conducting *Carmen* there in 1948. This was so successful that Felsenstein invited Klemperer to be his music director, but as Klemperer was then happily ensconced at the Opera in Budapest he declined.

Between 1927 and 1943, Felsenstein directed six Wagner productions, including in 1934 a *Tannhäuser* in Frankfurt designed by Caspar Neher, but thereafter had nothing to do with him.[18] His antipathy to the composer is attributable partly to personal preference, partly to the indelible association with the Third Reich, and partly because most of the operas were simply on too large a scale for successful performance at the Komische Oper with its 1,260 seats. There was doubtless another reason, in that Wagner's mythical subject matter was never going to lend itself to Felsenstein's kind of theatrical realism. Wagner's error in his own production strategy had been to seek 'realism' in the presentation of his mythical beings. Felsenstein would not have wished to repeat the mistake by squandering the coinage of his realistic approach where its purchasing power was likely to be negligible. The extraordinary thing, nevertheless, was that it was from this approach that Felsenstein's disciples Joachim Herz, Götz Friedrich and Harry Kupfer were to develop new ways of staging Wagner. These were very different from those of Wieland Wagner, but were to be no less successful in exorcizing the recent past and discovering aspects of the operas that had been all but ignored.

The other major influence on Herz, Friedrich and Kupfer was to come from the exactly opposite direction, namely from the critical objectivity of Bertolt Brecht (1898–1956), the second great shaping force in GDR theatre. Brecht's ideas about opera and its production, manifest in his collaborations with Kurt Weill (especially in *Aufstieg und Fall der Stadt Mahagonny* and in the notes accompanying that work, in which he distinguished his 'epic' theatre from the traditional 'dramatic' variety),[19] were the antipode to those of Felsenstein (and of Stanislavky).[20] Brecht wanted to subvert theatre as illusion, as a manifestation in which actors identified with their roles and the audience with the action as though it were real. The audience was to be confronted with scenes that would disconcert and make them think – a theatre that was a workshop for the forging of ideas which would change men and society for the better.

Felsenstein was as fundamentally against 'interpretation' in production as Brecht was in favour of it. Brecht wanted his Berliner Ensemble, founded in 1949 after his return from exile in America, to be 'a force for social change', but he disputed the official policy of socialist realism, as also the Party's blanket censure of avant-garde art.[21] These were dissents which the Party was prepared to tolerate only because of Brecht's high standing in the world at large. Brecht believed that the theatre should always be ready to challenge the foundations of society, the Party decidedly did not. The opera he wrote with the composer Paul Dessau, *Die Verurteilung des Lukullus* (The Condemnation of Lucullus, 1951), was by no stretch of the imagination a work of socialist realism and was duly censured for this failing.[22] Neither Brecht nor Felsenstein were ever members of the Party, and only Felsenstein could be said to be in tune with its cultural strategy (though this was through his own conviction and totally without coercion). In effect, Felsenstein was seeking to reclaim the bourgeois art of opera for the socialist state by cutting through the mystique and presenting it as living drama, played in the vernacular and as comprehensible to the man in the street as a good play or film.

The rise and fall of Wagner in the East in the 1950s

The antipathy – even opposition – of Felsenstein and Brecht towards Wagner, not to mention that of composers like Hanns Eisler and Paul Dessau, who condemned Wagner as subversive of socialist culture, did nothing to prevent an upsurge of performances of his works in the 1950s.[23] A central part in the rehabilitation of Wagner in the East was played by the Landestheater (the former Ducal Theatre) in Dessau, which prided itself on a long tradition of dedicated Wagner performances. Dessau's Intendant Willy Bodenstein opened his rebuilt theatre in 1949 with the democratic slogan 'Vom Hoftheater zum Volkstheater' (From court theatre to people's theatre). His declared aim was a new perspective on Wagner's work, 'free from the misinterpretations and falsifications of fascism' and communicating it to 'a new public, to the manual workers and agricultural labourers who are the creative brains of our Republic'. Bodenstein's direction aspired to a rigorously disciplined fidelity of which Cosima would totally have approved. This persisted even when, in 1956, Bodenstein

hired a new designer, Wolf Hochheim, who had inhaled, if not too deeply, the rari-
fied air of New Bayreuth. Bodenstein staged twenty Wagner productions in eight
years (1949–57), effectively bidding to establish Dessau as a 'Bayreuth for the GDR'.
Karl Schönewolf, one of the GDR's best-known music critics, daringly urged the
exchange of production ideas between Bayreuth and Dessau.[24]

By the end of the decade Wagner's operas were the most frequently performed in
the repertory, with theatres like that in Weimar uninhibitedly presenting the *Ring*
and *Parsifal*. But at the same time this phenomenon began to come under ideological scrutiny, much of it directed against mystical, abstract styles of production which
percolated in from New Bayreuth, not only in Dessau but also elsewhere. This was to
be seen, for example, at the Berlin Staatsoper, where the producer Erich Witte (who
as a singer had in 1952 and 1953 played Loge in Wieland Wagner's *Ring*) moved in
the Bayreuth direction, as notably in his *Lohengrin* of 1958, with designs by Heinz
Pfeiffenberger. The production was viciously attacked in the officially sanctioned
theatre journal *Theater der Zeit* as symptomatic of dangerous modernist tendencies
at the Staatsoper, and there were condemnations of the cultivation of Wagner as neo-
Nazi, proto-fascist, etc. etc. Such pressures brought to an end Bodenstein's brave and
well-supported ventures in Dessau. No official Party directives were issued, but such
assaults put Intendants on their guard, both as to production style and to the
inadvisability of programming the *Ring*, *Tristan* and *Parsifal*, all now proscribed as
ideologically incorrect 'problematische Spätwerke'. Nor were the earlier works any
longer entirely safe.[25]

In Halle in 1958, for example, a *Tannhäuser* already in rehearsal was replaced by
Der fliegende Holländer, the reason given being that as 'the church plays no accept-
able role in socialism' no work should be performed in which 'Catholicism was glo-
rified'. In the same year a certain Heinz Bär doubted whether Wagner's works as a
whole could have anything to do with 'the aims of our cultural revolution' and called
for a ban on their performance.[26] Some apologists spoke up for the *Ring* as showing
the necessary destruction of capitalist values, but the prevailing view was that it had
nothing to do with dialectical materialism and amounted to cultural pessimism.

Eastern opposition to the 'problematic late works' and to the aesthetics of New
Bayreuth was encapsulated in a 1958 article in *Theater der Zeit*: Wagner, it suggested,
does not show us real people, only mythologies on two legs – New Bayreuth had let
the cat out of the bag in this respect. In his operas, the author went on, things do not
change or develop but remain as they are. The action offers no positive outcome, the
characters are always in the wrong, salvation exists only in the hereafter. Wagner's
music is dedicated only to mystification. It is the music of the unconscious and irra-
tional, leading to the dehumanization of the listener. In reality it is 'the resounding
antechamber of fascism'.[27] The SED concluded that Wagner's works as a whole
were 'ideologically problematic' and sought, through articles in *Theater der Zeit*, to
prescribe how performances could be shaped to be supportive of the socialist
national culture.[28]

By the time the Wall went up in 1961, the state's hold on every aspect of life was
all but total. The hope of eventual reunification, which had been strong in the early

years, had disappeared and Ulbricht's GDR turned its back against the West, as affirmed in his notorious pronouncement that 'Everything links us to the victorious Soviet Union and not to the imperialistic Federal Republic'.[29] The cultural policy of the 'sozialistische deutsche Nation' was now enforced strictly by the Party instead of loosely as before. Compliance was generously rewarded – subsidy levels in the theatre were as high as 90 per cent. And the policy did seem to draw in a broader audience, one survey (albeit in *Theater der Zeit*) claiming in 1969 that 20–30 per cent of audiences were working-class.[30]

Restrictive cultural directives reached their furthest point with the stern measures passed in 1965 by the Plenum of the Central Committee of the SED. These were censorious of all experimental, non-conformist and potentially subversive theatre. In practice this meant Brechtian appropriation (Aneignung) at its most rigorous, with Shakespeare 'performed in such a way as to bring out the social and economic background of his plays, specifically the emergence of the Elizabethan bourgeoisie from the feudalism of the Middle Ages'.[31]

Life became difficult for those musicians and theatre men who clung to their conviction that Wagner not only deserved a place in the socialist state but could make a positive contribution to it. These included such notable Marxist intellectuals as Ernst Bloch and Hans Mayer. Both were passionate Wagnerians, critical of the composer's absorption into nationalism, and indefatigable in their efforts to rescue the revolutionary and utopian content of his work. Both men bolstered the case for Wagner as a positive force in the socialist state. Where Bloch interested himself principally in Wagner as a transcendental visionary, Mayer built on Shaw's interpretation and saw the composer's works as a critique of nineteenth-century capitalism – ideas that both developed from and fed into the theatre work of Herz and Friedrich.

But the views of the professors were tough going for the political supremos, so much so that they came to be regarded as ideologically suspect, if not dangerously subversive. It did not help that Bloch and Mayer, whose Marxism was in both cases supported by humanistic ideals utterly foreign to the cultural commissars, were intensely interested in New Bayreuth and nourished by its vision. Bloch was actually in Bayreuth as a guest of Wieland when the Wall went up and decided not to return. Hans Mayer was to follow in 1963.

What were East German directors interested in Wagner to do? Neither traditional stage production (with its fascist associations) nor the modernism of New Bayreuth was safe to build on.

By the late 1950s, as we have seen, the GDR had become antagonistic to what it considered the political incorrectness of Wagner's 'late works', and was generally wary of the composer. But towards the end of the decade the prospect of the 150th anniversary of Wagner's birth in Leipzig in 1813 began to loom and with it pressure to integrate the composer into the cultural heritage of the GDR. There was also the rebuilt Leipzig Opera to open in 1960, and the authorities could not resist the more or less inevitable choice to do so with *Die Meistersinger*, a work still largely above socialist suspicion. Few works would have been easier to cast as a Volksoper and exemplar of socialist culture – protracted choral ensembles, mass festivity, 'ordinary'

people rather than gods and mythological heroes, a happy ending. (From the opposite angle it had of course been equally easy for National Socialism to claim the opera
as its own!)

Resurrection: Joachim Herz and Die Meistersinger, Leipzig 1960

The task of staging the 1960 *Meistersinger* fell to the 36-year-old Joachim Herz, who
had been appointed as the Leipzig Opera's new director of opera the previous year.
Born in 1924, Herz was proud to have attended the Kreuzschule in Dresden where
Wagner had once been a pupil. From an early age he had been enthusiastic about
Wagner's works and had attended many performances in Dresden under Karl Böhm.
He studied music and directing (with Heinz Arnold) at the Musikhochschule in
Dresden and had already produced seven operas by the time he was taken on at the
Komische Oper as assistant to Felsenstein on *Die Zauberflöte* and as stage director in
his own right (1953–6). When he arrived in Leipzig in 1957 as director of productions (Operndirektor) he already had many outstanding stagings to his credit, covering a broad spectrum from Mozart through Verdi and Puccini to Britten, but so far
there had been no Wagner. His approach was always that of music-theatre, as previously described, but because of Felsenstein's antipathy to Wagner, Herz had not as
yet had the chance to apply it to his works, and he was eager to do so. As his designer
for *Die Meistersinger* he chose Rudolf Heinrich, with whom he had already worked
on five productions in Berlin.[32]

Where, in Herz's words, Wieland Wagner placed the spiritual content of an opera
at the centre of his interpretation, Herz wanted to concentrate on the human drama.
He was realistic in his treatment of character but also anti-illusionistic in that, bringing in what he had learnt from Brecht, he expected the audience to be critically
active, and not just passive spectators. He had seen Wieland's 1956 production and
had been impressed, but not convinced. Indeed, he considered it to be the absolute
antithesis to his own kind of theatre. He objected to its lack of palpable physical context, of the constraints which explain why the characters behave as they do, especially
in Act II. In his view, the huge open promontory may have given physical expression
to the boundless love of Walther and Eva, but it failed to suggest the bourgeois pressures that resisted it – how, for instance, the relationship of Sachs's house to the
narrow alleys enables Sachs to overhear and then foil their plan to elope. This sense
of resistance, Herz argued, was essential to the drama. The clash between the individual will and social constraint was for him an essential ingredient. And he disliked
Wieland's tendency to choreograph the chorus as a mass rather than as a collection
of distinct individuals.

For his own setting, said Herz, there were three possibilities: 'the theatre of illusion
cultivated by Wagner himself; the symbolic dream world cultivated by New
Bayreuth; and finally the realistic style of production in which we are interested here
in Leipzig.'[33] Herz and Heinrich wanted to present the work as a 'Kunstkomödie', a
comedy about the conflict between tradition and innovation in art. Politically, it was
important that the Leipzig *Meistersinger* should be at the furthest remove not only

from the nationalistic style favoured by the Nazis, but from Wieland's Bayreuth spiritualization. There was, moreover, the problem of the intrinsic Germanness of the work. Herz and Heinrich, reasonably enough, wanted the opera's milieu to be recognizably that of sixteenth-century Nuremberg. But the Party officials were equally keen that the opera should not be associated any more than was necessary with a city that was now in the West. How, therefore, to find a setting?

In 1958–9 Herz and Heinrich had been in Moscow for guest performances by the Komische Oper of Felsenstein's *Contes d'Hoffmann* and Herz's *Albert Herring*. The visit coincided with an international festival of puppet theatre and Heinrich was greatly struck by the auditorium used by the puppeteer Sergei Obrastszov, which was surrounded by Renaissance-style tiered balconies. This provided the inspiration for framing the action of *Meistersinger* within a galleried Globe-style theatre. The basic elements of the set were two wooden galleries, each of two tiers, ranged down either side of the stage. In Act I they were used to suggest the nave of a church of late medieval ambience undergoing reconstruction as a Protestant 'preaching-church' of the kind favoured by the Reformation. But here, as throughout, there was no attempt at historical accuracy. The stage language was that of seeking audience acquiescence in a 'let's pretend' style of theatre far removed from that of nineteenth-century illusion. In Act II the galleries became the balconies of houses giving onto the River Pegnitz, which, making an uncanonical debut in this act, and duly labelled in the Brechtian manner, flowed down the length of the stage. The theatre's Intendant, Karl Kayser, was worried as to what Ulbricht might think, but in the event the reference to Nuremberg went unremarked and the General Secretary of the Party appeared to have been enthused by the whole production.[34]

Much of the action took place on bridges thrown across the river to connect the walkways on either side. Beckmesser sang his serenade from one bridge, while under it were Walther and Eva, hiding in the boat with which they hoped to make their escape. It was there that they were discovered and apprehended by Sachs. Pogner and Sachs's houses were on opposite sides of the river. For the first scene of Act III, the workshop of Sachs the down-to-earth cobbler and mediator was on the stage floor, the library of the poet and philosopher up a few steps on a higher level. During the 'Wahn' monologue the troubled 'Schuster und Poet dazu' restlessly moved between the two levels of his psyche. When this scene was struck for the Festwiese, the galleries were finally revealed as part of an open-air theatre, with a raised trestle-stage standing in the centre ready for the song contest. The guild entry processions were necessarily constrained, their particular songs being acted out in mime on the little stage as the populace, some two hundred strong, packed into the galleries. Throughout the production, highly effective use was made of a forestage spreading out beyond the proscenium and drawing the audience closely into the action.

Herz's chorus were the kind of people whom the Masters, grudgingly or not, were happy to co-opt as judges of the song contest. This was emphatically not what was seen on the stage in nationalistic productions, nor, for that matter, in Wieland's production. Herz's 'chorus' were not only individuals who shared the Masters' dedication to art but an essentially peaceable community, not the rather brutal and

Joachim Herz disputed the bare-stage minimalism of Wieland Wagner's 1956 *Meistersinger*. For his own 1960 production in Leipzig he introduced a new sense of theatrical realism into the staging of Wagner. He was the first to perform the opera in a Globe-style theatre, an idea which Wieland gratefully took over when he produced the work again in 1963. In the final scene of Herz's Act III, Walther (Gustav Papp) sings the Prize Song on a trestle-stage set up on the floor of the galleried theatre.

disorderly one shown in the many contemporaneous productions which attempted to de-idealize the model German community of the nationalists. The Prügelszene at the end of the second act was not the traditional all-out riot in which ugly emotions are unleashed, but a midsummer carnival with maskers. All enjoyed the licence of Midsummer Day to make fun of their neighbours. Aggressive emotions were civilized, tamed – even turned into art – by being expressed in uninhibited comic behaviour, underwritten by Wagner's playful use of fugal procedures.

In this community living for and through art, the principal characters were not antagonists but rather complementary figures in a comprehensive picture of what art is and how it develops – the perennial tension between the Academy and the Secession, between tradition in the person of Beckmesser and innovation in that of Walther, with Sachs and the people as mediators. Herz saw the opera as showing a process of integration, working towards a utopian unity of 'art and life, of artists and society, of those who create art and those who enjoy it'. It is this that he took as the subject of Sachs's 'ehrt eure deutschen Meister!' exhortation – the sacred contract between artists and their public, between innovation and tradition, which must always be in a state of change and renewal.[35]

Troubled by the inconsistency between Beckmesser's respectable standing as town clerk and elected Marker of the Mastersingers and his behaviour in first purloining and then mangling the Meisterlied which he believes to be by Sachs, Herz attempted to make this more dramatically plausible. For him, Beckmesser is 'the most intelligent of all the Masters, but mulish … also the most German, insisting on his theory'. His efforts to woo Eva are driven more by his desire not to be outdone in song by Walther than by love of the lady.[36] Herz took the bold step of going back to an early draft of the opera in which Beckmesser does not mangle the words of Walther's song. Instead he has correctly memorized the text, but makes a nonsense of it by trying to fit the rapturous love lyric to the stiffly regimented melody of his Act II serenade. Everyone readily understands that he has failed not because he has gone mad, but because he has committed the Masters' cardinal sin of not matching the tune to the words. After his humiliation Beckmesser did not, as was usual, flee the stage or take refuge in the crowd. Sachs crossed the stage to shake his hand and offer collegiate sympathy. The point was to present Beckmesser not as a parody of pedantic impotence (which was what Wagner probably intended), but as a credible representative of a type found in most societies. Nor was Sachs over-idealized; after his oration in praise of sacred German art, he modestly stepped back into the ranks of the Masters, allowing the choral acclamation to be heard as though directed to them all.

This balancing of the claims of the protagonists upon our sympathies was a distinctive feature. If at first sight the democratization of the structured society portrayed in Wagner's text looks like compliance with the political context within which Herz was working, closer inspection shows the production to have been nothing of the kind. Herz's community of distinct individuals, whose opinions carried equal weight and who zealously guarded their traditions while being receptive to innovation, was exactly what the GDR was not. This was palpable dissent from the GDR's dirigiste regime, in which the state dictated what everyone should and should not like.

Herz's vision foresaw a peaceful community, united not by politics but by its informed dedication to art. He sought to show how things might be, and could not pretend, as the Party did, that utopia had already arrived. He looked for a Sachs who was a people's hero and a Stolzing who was a revolutionary genius, both winning out over Beckmesser the conservative pedant. Ideologically, Beckmesser had to be the enemy. The commissars objected that he had not been shown as an incarnation of anti-socialist ideas about art, as a proponent of formalism.[37] Herz had shown a society in which divergent points of view were not suppressed but talked through and resolved. His *Meistersinger* was a timeless, universal metaphor for the transactions between art and society, between cultural tradition and innovation.

The reviews in the state-controlled press applauded the production for its lucidity, its presentation as a genuine people's opera, its fidelity to the populist core of the work and its being a convincing socialist interpretation.[38] It was also praised by men of the liberal left like Ernst Bloch and Walter Jens, in particular for its exoneration of Beckmesser. The commissars, put out by Herz's refusal to simplify the debate about art and society into one about heroes and villains, had to value what they could in the production.[39] They could not dismiss it, if only because it had given them something that, apart from the waggish allusion to the Pegnitz, was very definitely 'ohne Nürnberg', and because it was distinctively different from the 'mystic falsifications' of Wieland Wagner. Herz was rewarded with the coveted National Prize.

But it was praise through gritted teeth. Privately the officials were seething. In their confidential official reports they slated the production for its 'equivocation' and its failure to demonstrate that Wagner's ideal art-dedicated community was alive and flourishing in the GDR.[40] Ironically, it was the production's radical and heretical features that best demonstrated that the GDR was culturally far healthier than it had any right to be under the muddled strictures of official policy. Herz distanced himself from the ideological debate and from the 'Leipzig versus Bayreuth' polemic. He was interested only in discussion of the artistic differences between Wieland's *Meistersinger* and his own, not in the politics of the two conceptions. West Germany, for its part, and with one notable exception, studiously ignored the Leipzig production (no mention even in specialist opera and theatre journals), proving itself as culturally paranoiac as the East.[41] Wieland Wagner came to see it, was impressed, and took over the idea of a Globe-style setting as the starting point for his next production of the opera, in 1963 (see chapter 9).

Herz's Holländer *on stage and on screen, 1962–1964*

The popular success of the Leipzig *Die Meistersinger* was instrumental in winning a more positive attitude towards Wagner. The fruitful application of the Musiktheater philosophy to his work was not lost on Felsenstein when he saw the production. The experiment had to be worth trying at the Komische Oper and he invited Herz to direct *Der fliegende Holländer* there in 1962, this of all Wagner's operas being the one best suited to the populist ethos and modest size of the theatre. The production went down so well that Herz recreated it in his own Leipzig theatre, was invited to direct it in Moscow, and ended up making a film version which appears to have been the very first of a more or less complete Wagner opera. Here was a work by the revolutionary young Wagner which offered, inter alia, a brisk wind to blow away misconceptions about the composer's political viability, a critical view of bourgeois existence, and a picture of an individual discovering redemption in self-denial.

How could Herz make credible to a modern audience the relationship between Senta and the Dutchman? Did a piece based on legend have to be set in a timeless milieu? Wagner's own answer, said Herz, was a resounding 'no'. The composer was not simply narrating a story but showing us people who keep a legend alive by telling it over and over again and are stunned to find themselves suddenly experiencing it for real. What the spectator needed to see on the stage was the impact of a legendary figure on everyday bourgeois reality. Herz decided he should be a survivor from the great age of exploration and circumnavigation, a Vasco da Gama or Magellan (not, indeed, so far from Wagner's prescription that he should wear a 'black Spanish costume').

Herz sought to make the fable as tangible as possible – a 'real' situation broken into by adventures and phantoms from another world.[42] He depicted Daland and his

Directing *Der fliegende Holländer* at the Komische Oper in Berlin in 1962, Herz set the work around the time of its composition. He interpreted it as the impact of a legendary figure on a bourgeois community. Daland's home was that of a prosperous shipowner, his parlour furnished with striped wallpaper and a boudoir grand for Senta to accompany herself. As Senta (Christa-Maria Ziese) sang her ballad, the walls became transparent and it seemed as though the raging sea and the Dutchman were already in the room.

family as a prosperous 1840s shipowner's household, with a parlour finely furnished with a boudoir grand piano, striped wallpaper and candelabra. Senta and her companions were well-to-do young ladies in tea gowns, spinning to pass the time while singing favourite songs – things they enjoyed rather than with which they identified. Senta, however, whose fantasies have been nurtured by the nautical memorabilia tastefully displayed in the room – model ships in glass cases, charts, a small portrait of the Dutchman on the wall – identifies totally with her ballad. As she sings, the walls become transparent and the sea is seen to roar and rage outside. She conjures it into becoming her new, liberating reality. Daland's ship was no rough fishing vessel, but a sleek schooner with auxiliary steam-powered paddle-wheel.

Herz argued that the Christian notion of damnation versus redemption had almost as little significance for an audience in the 1960s as it had had for Wagner in the 1840s. He therefore reconstructed it as bourgeois constraint versus freedom to break out into a life of your own. The 'redemption' sought by the Dutchman is that of becoming truly human, meaning to love and be loved by a real woman rather than by the 'angel' which he at first takes Senta to be. The usual view of the end of the opera is that the Dutchman surprises Erik wooing Senta, concludes she is unfaithful and angrily sails away to his doom. But, Herz reminds us, this does not square with

Wagner's text. What the Dutchman overhears is Erik's cavatina bemoaning her rejection of his love. The Dutchman realizes, for the first time, that she is a fallible woman, not an angel, and may therefore one day slip from the grace of the fidelity she has sworn. If this should happen, she would be lost, and it is to save her from this fate that, abandoning his last hope of human love, he so precipitately departs. Herz's view is that it is in making this renunciation that, unsuspectingly, he finds his own redemption, an idea also stressed in Wieland Wagner's 1959 production (see chapter 9). Senta does not need to jump into the sea to kill herself; she dies because she can no longer live without the Dutchman, thus picking up on Wagner's own bizarre observation that sensitive Norwegian girls are especially prone to cardiac arrest.[43] The couple's farewell is that of two idealistic lovers, each sacrificing for the other.

In Berlin Herz followed Klemperer's 1929 Kroll Opera production in using the original 1843 ending. In Leipzig, however, the *Tristan*-style epilogue of 1860 with harp and the transfigured Senta motive was played, Herz distancing himself from it by refusing to show any representation of the lovers' physical apotheosis and offering only the projection of an abstract image.[44] This met with a furious objection from Karl Kayser, who said that religious people would be shocked, meaning they would be deprived of an ending in which the Dutchman found salvation and he and Senta bodily resurrection. 'Who,' asked Herz, 'are these people?' 'That's me, these religious people!' replied the atheist, socialist, Central Committee member. Herz relishes the irony that beneath the Party dogma – which should in theory have favoured a non-transcendent ending – the expectations of an erstwhile Christian culture were still very much alive.[45]

Plainly such an interpretation fitted well with social aspirations in the GDR in the early 1960s and with the cultural climate in Moscow. Herz's production there on 14 May 1963 commemorated the 150th anniversary of Wagner's birth.[46] It was the first *Holländer* at the Bolshoi since the 1904–5 season, and the first Wagner production to be given there since Eisenstein's staging of *Die Walküre* in 1940, as well as the first time a foreigner had directed an opera at the Bolshoi. Herz was allowed what was for him an incredible eleven weeks of rehearsal, considered a relatively short time in that theatre.

At the Bolshoi the more thoroughgoing Party ideology had no problems with the unredemptive ending. But the translator, Kurt Sanderling, had wanted to eliminate the 'angel' from the Russian translation in which the opera was sung, a move successfully resisted by Herz. Socialism, the director wryly comments, had no problems with Satan. What the company lacked in Wagnerian stage experience it had made up for in real life: quite a few members of the male chorus had served in the Red navy. Primitive scene-change technology (and an appetite for ice cream and shampanskoye) meant two intervals, rather than the continuous 'Bayreuth version' given in Leipzig.

But Herz's conception of the opera had its apotheosis not on the stage but in the black-and-white film version he made for DEFA (the GDR's state film company) in 1964, the composer's score being fairly painlessly shortened to the 102-minute span of this 'Film nach Wagner'. Herz's aim was to make a real film (i.e., not to film a stage performance but to make a film from Wagner's text and music) that would open up opera 'to people who have a horror of it'.[47] Although the film is made with actors rather than the singers who are heard on the soundtrack, the synchronization is so good that the spectator is never aware that this is the case.

Four weeks were spent pre-recording the music with the Leipzig Gewandhaus Orchestra and Leipzig Opera Chorus under Rolf Reuter, with each singer's voice on a separate track. The use of four-channel stereo sound (for the first time in European film making, claims Herz) enabled the 'voices' to issue from the separate cast of miming actors wherever they happened to be in screen-space. The Dutchman's ghostly crew was heard as though from the rear of the cinema. An even sharper visual separation between Senta's prison of her real world and her fantasy life was accomplished by using normal screen size for the former, the image broadening out into wide format as Senta's dreams take wing.

As the film begins, Senta is reading the legend of the Flying Dutchman to herself from an old book. A door mysteriously creaks ajar, there is an ominous ghost-story

Herz developed his conception of *Der fliegende Holländer* into a brilliant film version (1964) in which the central action is shown as Senta's dream. Actors mimed to a pre-recorded soundtrack. On location, lights, camera and director are seen in pursuit of Senta (Anna Prucnal).

When the wind swings round at the end of the first act, in the film Herz has Senta (Anna Prucnal) run out along the jetty and excitedly wave farewell to Daland's ship.

atmosphere. Senta presses her face to the wooden shutters, listening to the wind, its whine rising in pitch until it blends into the D minor music of the overture which breaks in like the seas raging within her. As she begins to dream, the eye of the camera takes us in cinemascope out through the shutters into the waves beyond. It pulls back into the reality of the prosperous bluff Daland confronting his preoccupied daughter, who retreats back to her room with the small portrait of the Dutchman she has taken down from the wall. As the Dutchman's theme is heard in the orchestra, the camera closes in on the portrait, the image dissolving into the sea and sky, then capturing the silhouette of the Dutchman's ship with its tattered sails driven before the wind. Once again a close-up of the portrait, and a cleverly patched transition from the overture into the middle of the Dutchman's monologue ('Wie oft in Meeres tiefsten Schlund') as a voice-over. We soon see him, an unheroic, rather slight figure, pulling on ropes and anxiously bustling about because his crew, incapacitated by fatigue or disease, are lying below decks, little better than corpses. At times he is seen to sing, at times his voice is heard only on the soundtrack (inner soliloquy). As the monologue ends the screen image is again that of the portrait, which Daland snatches from Senta as the Dutchman's torpid crew are heard echoing his despair.

Thereafter the film moves cleverly between Senta's home life and her fantasy, the transitions marked by such expedients as Senta being transported by what she sees reflected in water or in the flames of the huge stone fireplace. Reality and dream modes are chillingly juxtaposed when in Act III the Dutchman's crew, eventually

Senta (Anna Prucnal) pleads with the Dutchman (Fred Düren) not to leave her. He has overheard Erik's claim that she's broken her promise to be true, and is therefore poised to depart. Erik (Herbert Graedtke) looks on. The still is from the promotional brochure for the film.

goaded from their sleeping sickness, rise up like Golems to stare in through the windows at the Norwegians' celebration party for Senta's betrothal. With its low camera angles, chiaroscuro lighting and against-the-light shots of Senta and the Dutchman moving through a wind-ravaged nautical burial ground – it is there, O Liebestod!, that they first embrace – or climbing a slope rising up from the rocky seashore, the film owes as much to the 1920s films of Murnau and Pabst as it does to those of Bergman, not least *The Seventh Seal* (1957).

The contrast between the Norwegians partying in the bright lights of Daland's mist-girt chalet and the expressionist flavour given to the supernatural is vividly evident when, in response to the challenge flung at the Dutchman's ship by the Norwegians, the tarred grimace of its gargoyle figurehead momentarily re-composes into a semblance of Senta's face.

Senta dreams the story through to the bitter end of the Dutchman's departure. As his ship sinks beneath the waves she is seen running out along a jetty; there is no jump but her image dissolves into the foaming sea and the film returns to reality. She awakens from her dream-death lying in front of the cold hearth whose flames had once fired her fantasy. What she has experienced in her dream gives her the courage to change her life.[48] As the harp of the 1860 version is heard in the orchestra, she once again takes down the Dutchman's portrait from the wall, leaves the house and, with the sun catching her smiling face, walks cheerfully out along the beach with new-found resolution.

The film develops the socialist realism of Herz's stage production while using all the camera's techniques to weave a supernatural aura around it. It is very much in keeping with the opera-as-film that Herz casts Senta's fantasy-Dutchman not as a gaunt operatic hero but as a rather ordinary, put-upon fellow in need of her love. This makes the stranger more credible as a guest in Daland's house, his relationship with Senta at once real and disconcerting. The burden of the phantasmagoric is diverted onto his ship and crew, the Dutchman himself more browned-off barge-man on the Elbe canal than defiant circumnavigator, his voice on the soundtrack, like those of the other characters, much lighter than one would expect – all part of Herz's turning his back against operatics in the interest of creating a film in which the music and the action would seem to be causally intertwined. This remains extraordinarily close both to the way Wagner composed and to his ideas as to how his works should be performed.

Harry Kupfer's version of 'Senta's dream', Bayreuth 1978

Herz's emphasis on Senta's dream world as a key element in the interpretation was widely copied. In 1975 in San Francisco Jean-Pierre Ponnelle offered a variation on this theme, staging the principal events of the opera as dreamt by the Steuermann. But the most exciting 'dream' interpretation after Herz was that at Bayreuth in 1978 by Harry Kupfer. Like Herz, Kupfer had been a Felsenstein pupil, and he was glad to acknowledge that the Herz film had been the source of his own 'Senta's dream' stage production.

Where Herz had chosen Stanislavsky-style realism for Daland's bourgeois milieu, Kupfer and his designer Peter Sykora used constructivist, surrealistic, even expressionist means to move swiftly between Senta's real and fantasy worlds. The walls of her prison flew asunder or reassembled in the twinkling of an eye. Senta was on stage from the very beginning of the overture. The Dutchman's picture suddenly fell off the wall. Clutching it to her, Senta climbed a metal stair to a vantage point by a window from where, in constant view of the audience, she observed the dream-action as it rapidly unfolded. The fantasy Dutchman conjured up by Senta was her dark counterpart. But the chains from which he hung inside the cradling fingers of his vessel were, unlike hers, self-forged. They were those of a Prometheus bound by his own 'mind-forged manacles'; through Senta's power he cast them off and stumbled ashore to tell his tale.

At the beginning of Act II, still clutching the picture of the Dutchman, she stepped down from her platform into the real world of the spinning session. The crucial moment was that of her father's arrival with a stranger, the light streaming in so powerfully from behind him that she could not tell who he might be. As in Heine, she anxiously kept checking the portrait in the hope that *this* could be him. When the stranger moved forward the red-sailed ship loomed up again and it was the Dutchman who stepped down from its prow to take the stranger's place in the room and in her imagination. Fantasy and reality had become interchangeable. The ship remained, transforming itself into a love-bower, its rigging strewn with flowers.

In Act III Erik's protestations suddenly made it clear to her that her fantasies were neurosis and that she had put herself beyond all chance of future happiness with him. Leaping from her high window she crashed to her death on the ground, still clutching the picture. A small group gathered uncomprehendingly around the body – Erik was the only one to kneel to mourn her. Kupfer explained the tragedy as the triumph of the mundane over the dreams and fantasies that spring up in protest against it. 'Whether she jumps from a cliff or from a window is immaterial – the only important thing is that there's no longer any role for her.'[49]

Much of the power of Kupfer's production (also captured on video) lay in exceptionally swift transitions between reality and dream modes – and in fostering a Pirandello-like sense of suspension between the two modes. Kupfer's use of stage wizardry was a modern means of realizing Wagner's own intentions for the work as a 'dramatic ballad', effecting cuts of filmic rapidity between scenes and within scenes, thus (correctly) denying that the work is a developmental drama based on the working out of conflict.

Herz's dream interpretation of *Der fliegende Holländer* has been hugely influential. At Bayreuth in 1978, Harry Kupfer's Senta (Lisbeth Balslev) was a deeply-disturbed psychotic, clutching the Dutchman's picture to her breast and observing the action from a high vantage point from which she eventually crashes to a very mortal death. The walls of the set were those of Senta's prison, dramatically flying asunder and reassembling in a trice, thus effecting exceptionally fast transitions between reality and dream. From left to right at deck level in Act I are Daland (Matti Salminen), the Steuermann (David Kuebler) and the Dutchman (Simon Estes).

The sheer verve of Kupfer's production, its psychological acuity and the magnetic performances by Lisbeth Balslev and Simon Estes made this a staging which deservedly attracted a huge wave of critical approbation.[50] Inevitably the bleakness of Senta's suicide, however logically justified, was not to everyone's liking but, as Kupfer said, he wasn't in the business of providing the audience with the 'untroubled pleasure of an apparent catharsis'.[51]

The politics of re-politicizing the Ring, Leipzig 1973–1976

The success of Herz's *Holländer* – which was consolidated by his 1965 productions of *Lohengrin* in Leipzig and *Tannhäuser* in Frankfurt – opened the way for the *Ring* that he staged in Leipzig from 1973 to 1976 with designs by Rudolf Heinrich. At that time the *Ring* was still officially categorized as a 'problematic late work' and performances of it were not encouraged. Indeed, between 1960 and 1974 there was only a single performance of the complete cycle in the GDR and only a few isolated performances of *Die Walküre*.[52] The objection lay not in its revolutionary, anti-capitalist sentiments (those of the Wagner who had conceived it) but in the idea that *Götterdämmerung* is a bleak tragedy, offering no hope for the future. The suggestion was that despite the resurgence in the closing bars of the rapturous melody first sung by Sieglinde to Brünnhilde in the third act of *Walküre*, the destruction of the corrupt lords of ownership and misrule was not balanced by a positive view of a future for liberated humanity.[53]

From the outset Herz's project, which in effect re-politicized the *Ring*, was itself politically embattled. He was surrounded by those who believed that the only way to tackle the *Ring* was to box it into the ideology of the socialist Republic. Karl Kayser characteristically suggested that Herz should make Siegfried an unattractive, even repulsive figure, but Herz ploughed his own furrow, answering Kayser with the musical point that Siegfried's music was written not for a character tenor but for a heroic one. Herz had to fight determinedly against those like Kayser and even the theatre's Chefdramaturg, Christoph Hamm, who thought that the *Ring* should emerge not only as critical of capitalism but as supportive of utopian socialism.[54]

The Ring as an allegory of the nineteenth century

Herz's interpretation of *Der fliegende Holländer* had been partly influenced by Thomas Mann's essay 'Ibsen and Wagner' (1928). It was in the light of this, of Mann's other writings on the composer (including 'The Sorrows and Grandeur of Richard Wagner', 1933, and 'Richard Wagner and *Der Ring des Nibelungen*', 1937) and of Bernard Shaw's *The Perfect Wagnerite* (1898) that Herz wanted to approach the *Ring*.[55] A no less important inspiration was Wagner's impressions of industrial London as seen from a boat trip on the Thames in 1877 and reported by Cosima: 'This is Alberich's dream come true – Nibelheim, world domination, activity, work, everywhere the oppressive feeling of steam and fog.'[56]

The Mann and Shaw texts were well known to the cognoscenti in the GDR, one of whom, Hans Mayer, had written an influential essay, 'The *Ring* as a Bourgeois Parable', that had been published by Wieland Wagner in the 1966 Bayreuth yearbook.[57] The fact of this publication showed that the West, too, was beginning to take a renewed interest in the political subtext of the tetralogy. Common to these writings was the wish to understand Wagner as a product of his own time and his operas as a mask for advancing against its injustices.

Herz had long been familiar with Shaw's robust view of the *Ring* as an allegory of the evils of nineteenth-century capitalism and felt that a stage interpretation might be attempted along the same lines. Shaw had ripped away the masks of gods and Nibelungs, exposing them as typical industrial overlords and underdogs. The tarnhelm, wrote Shaw, 'is a very common article in our streets, where it generally takes the form of a tall hat. It makes a man invisible as a shareholder, and changes him into various shapes, such as a pious Christian, a subscriber to hospitals, a benefactor of the poor, a model husband and father, a shrewd, practical, independent Englishman, and what not, when he is really a pitiful parasite on the commonwealth.'[58] What is extraordinary is that no one had attempted to stage the *Ring* in this way before. In the context of the GDR, it would be hard to imagine an approach more compliant with its political and social objectives, though the problem of the work as a fatalistic tragedy – Wagner's original revolutionary impulse having been negated after his Schopenhauerean epiphany, or so ran the argument – remained.

Herz, following Carl Dahlhaus, disputed this argument as simply not corresponding to a close reading of both text and music.[59] Wotan's despair in the second act of *Die Walküre* and his resignation in the third act could not be wrapped up as 'Schopenhauerean' but were entirely characteristic of someone who had been used to power and who had to face giving it up. Wagner's first conception, as Dahlhaus had controversially argued, was 'also his last'. At the end of *Götterdämmerung* the destruction of the worlds of both Wotan and Alberich was, said Herz, plainly a fulfilment of Wagner's original revolutionary intention (the radical rejection of *every* kind of political structure founded on coercion, slavery and the rejection of love). The conflagration and cleansing flood witnessed by the survivors may *perhaps* lead to new knowledge and understanding, perhaps even to a utopia. But, Herz said, the ending was certainly not a concrete political sketch or manifesto for a new world, nor did it have any explicit connection with the political aspirations of the GDR. The principle of hope, here as elsewhere, remained paradoxical, even in the view of a Marxist like Ernst Bloch.[60] Herz further maintained that the *Ring* was fundamentally a work of art and not a political manifesto.

So much for theory. In practical terms Herz was keen to see if the principles of theatrical realism which he had used in his productions of *Meistersinger*, *Holländer*, *Lohengrin* and *Tannhäuser* would also work for the *Ring*. How would the mythological personages of the tetralogy respond to being represented primarily as humans? They would have to be shown as recognizable people caught up in the social and political drama of the mid-nineteenth century. Thus, the first scene of Act II of *Die Walküre* would show not confrontations between Wotan, Fricka and Brünnhilde on a wild rocky mountain, but a family quarrel in the grandiose memorial hall of a feudal baron, replete with marble busts of his heroic ancestors.

Nevertheless, and here Herz would be departing from Felsenstein, he would be seeking not to substitute one illusionistic style of theatre for another, but to use Brechtian tactics. It would be a theatrical montage of historicity and fantasy, soliciting the audience's critical engagement with the tetralogy. It would not be a *complete* transposition of the *Ring* into the period of its creation. Not a realistic invocation of the nineteenth century, but the theatrical quotation of elements from it. 'We didn't put the *Ring* into the nineteenth century, but we saw that its characters and social classes were those of the nineteenth century.' It would be true to the Brechtian strategy of making a story strange, of putting it in quotation marks, in order to bring us closer to it so as to understand it more clearly.

For Herz, Wotan and Alberich personified two different kinds of power that were typical of the development of society in the nineteenth century: governance based on agreed contracts, and the brutal imposition of authority untroubled by concern for law or human rights. Like Shaw, Herz saw Wotan's grand scheme as an attempt to impose a revolution from above, a transformation of the social structure initiated by the powerful existing order, but thwarted because that order could not accept the concomitant diminution of its own power.[61] For Alberich, on the other hand, power

Wagner's revolutionary politics in the *Ring* were rediscovered in Herz's Leipzig staging of 1973 to 1976. It updated the work to Wagner's own time, much as Bernard Shaw had suggested in 1898. But working in communist East Germany, Herz had to fight off pressure to align the great tragic drama with utopian socialism. In the scene of the piling up of the gold in *Das Rheingold*, Fasolt and Fafner were supported by a crowd of worker-giants dressed like dockers in 1848. Rudolf Heinrich's settings were not stage pictures intended to create illusions but Brechtian theatrical artifice (note the bare stage surround and exposed lights).

meant the unlimited piling up of wealth in a world devoid of purpose or love. The essential dramatic conflict was between the hereditary regime of Wotan and the gods on the one hand and those who developed and profited from the capitalist exploitation of industrialization on the other. This latter group included not only Alberich, representative of the ruthless managerial class, but also the Gibichungs as the newly rich factory owners.

Against this despoiled and corrupted world arose the counter forces of Siegmund and Siegfried, heroes either too subject to the gods or simply too weak and deficient to overcome that world, and of Brünnhilde and Sieglinde, whose melody ('O hehrstes Wunder!') soars, at the very end, over the destruction of the values symbolized by Valhalla and Nibelheim. Humanity, shown in the ordinary people whom Wagner calls onto the stage after the conflagration and flood, survives, and the reassertion of the Sieglinde melody in the orchestra seems, for Herz, not only to refer to Brünnhilde, but also to be an elegiac reminder of Sieglinde's tragically unfulfilled hope that her son Siegfried would redeem the world.

Herz's scenario: theatrical realism and Wagnerian mythography

Rudolf Heinrich's scenic concept owed much to the collage and photo-montage ideas of Brecht and *his* stage designers. The bare side walls of the stage house were occasionally visible, the floods and spots of the lighting often undisguised, and the floor sometimes undressed. All the images were visual markers, awaiting completion in the imagination of the audience. Anachronisms were necessarily very much part of the anti-illusionism of Herz's stagecraft. Where this created a problem for Herz's wish to be both true to Wagner's text *and* realistic, as in the sword and spear weaponry, it was solved by treating such items as reliquaries from ages gone by, as talismans to swear on or by. The 'sword in the tree' in Act I of *Die Walküre* was a prized exhibit in Hunding's parlour. The costumes (a mixture of military uniforms, high bourgeois fashion, working men's clothes, etc.) delineated the layers of the nineteenth-century social order, but also included purely theatrical elements. Again, the actuality of the historical combined with the timeless to create a theatrical fantasy. All the costumes looked old and dirty or torn, as though their wearers no longer cared about them.[62]

Herz applied the kind of close analysis of character and motivation that was typical of theatrical realism. Who *were* the 'giants' and how could they have managed to build Valhalla? Obviously two would not be enough, and so Fafner and Fasolt became the leaders of two teams of master masons (forty-five in all, the whole male contingent of the Leipzig chorus, their costumes actually modelled on a photograph of dockers from 1848).[63] The quarries from which the stone had been taken were plainly visible in the background as photograph blow-ups on linen sheets. The Nibelungs were divided up into Alberich, the factory boss with attendant body-guards, and, as can be seen from Heinrich's captions on his costume sketches, 'Prohlen' (proletarian slave workers, previously 'unemployed') led by Mime, Alberich's chief engineer. Nibelheim is a labyrinth of caverns filled with toiling men

Rudolf Heinrich's costume designs (for the Leipzig *Ring*) caption Alberich and his bodyguards (*above*) as 'Bosse' (factory bosses) and the Nibelungs (*below*) as 'Prohlen' (proletarian slave-workers).

and foundry furnaces. The picture, said Herz, corresponds to Friedrich Engels's classic description of the condition of the working classes in England. This Alberich has renounced life and love not only for gold, but also for ceaseless productivity, his great discovery being that manpower can be turned into mass production. In him Herz saw the principle of unending toil and the rejection of pleasure, his only purpose the eventual ousting of the unscrupulous gods.[64]

The Nibelung workers are not natural dwarfs, but have become bent double through hard labour.[65] Herz treats them as ripe and ready for rebellion. When Alberich's back is turned they appear to be plotting how to seize him.[66] Mime's forge in *Siegfried* is a huge automated machine, seemingly defunct until Siegfried accidentally presses something that sets it in motion. It produced the sword for Siegfried while he sang, one of many ideas taken over by Patrice Chéreau for his 1976 Bayreuth production (see chapter 11).

The Nibelungs' capitalist overlords dwell in a Valhalla that, when seen for the first time at the end of *Rheingold*, is a stately pile modelled on elements from the Palais de Justice in Brussels, the Emperor's Staircase of the Burgtheater in Vienna, the Galleria Vittorio Emanuele in Milan, and the Germania Niederwalddenkmal on the Rhine: 'an eclectic façade of late bourgeois sterility in the final phase of the gods' imperial power; stolen architecture paid for with stolen money.'[67] In the spectacular

The Valhalla into which the gods ascend at the end of *Das Rheingold* in the Herz production was an eclectic composite of well-known grandiose buildings from the nineteenth century. In Rudolf Henrich's words, 'stolen architecture paid for with stolen money'. Although not visible in the photograph, the rainbow bridge was a spectrum woven into the carpet along which the gods process. Images of cheering crowds were projected onto the walls at the sides of the stage.

sequence in which it burned and crumpled into the ground at the end of *Götter-dämmerung*, the photo-images also took in elements of the domes of the Capitol in Washington and of the Panthéon and Opéra in Paris, as well as a reference to the steel and glass cupola of the Gibichung Hall. The rainbow bridge was a spectrum woven into the carpet on which the gods stepped up into their palace. Valhalla's imposing interiors, rich in the pompous decorative pretence of the Wilhelminian Gründerzeit (c. 1870–3), came into their own as the setting for Wotan's quarrel with Fricka in the second act of *Die Walküre*.

Fricka, obviously enough, was Wotan's conscience and the stern moral guardian of bourgeois society; Donner, 'the principle of fascism: not discussion and argument but the violent exercise of power'; Froh, a kind of 'Minister of Culture', the cultural front for Wotan's power politics; Freia, the spirit of love and creation, abused and downgraded by the pursuit of wealth and power. Loge embodied 'the intellect, which can be used and misused. He serves both Wotan and Alberich. He is not primarily a force of nature [fire] but stands for scientists whose technical discoveries create more and more power over nature.' His make-up was modelled on that of the ambivalent character Vice in the medieval morality plays.[68]

How had Siegmund come to arrive at Hunding's hut? His flight from Hunding's men was portrayed in mime during the prelude to Act I of *Walküre*,[69] the nearly empty stage contrasting starkly with the solid comforts of the Hundings' living room – massive table, veneered sideboard – the home of a well-to-do landowner. In Heinrich's words, 'You could equally well use this setting for an Ibsen play.'[70]

At the start of the third act, the eight soloist Valkyries were supplemented by thirty-two dancers, all in furious motion and with an emblematic effigy of the war goddess Bellona, in the style of Hitler's favourite sculptor Arno Breker, hanging above them. It was an image of war as a classic means by which ruling classes maintain and impose their control. Herz describes this as 'the Donner principle', pointing to the dominance of the Donner motive in the prelude as Siegmund flees his pursuers.[71]

The fire around Brünnhilde's rock was a large group of dancers with swirling flame-coloured veils, their faces made up to resemble Loge's. The idea was that the 'fire' was animate and could think for itself – in Act III of *Siegfried* the dancing flames recognized that Siegfried had no fear of them, and formed up protectively around Brünnhilde's rightful partner. The same dancers (the entire corps de ballet of the Leipzig Opera) were also mobilized, oriental style, to animate the writhing body of the dragon – a kind of mechanical worm that might have been produced in Alberich's factory.

In order to show that the actions of the principals impacted upon the world at large,[72] Herz sometimes supplied a social context, either with actors or with photo-images, or even with both together, as in the progress into Valhalla at the end of *Rheingold*. The images of the quarry were replaced by photographs of cheering crowds; this, says Herz, is what the gods were *imagining*, but their procession was actually being watched by the assembled giants and Nibelungs, all wondering, 'And now what will happen to us?'[73]

The costumes of Fricka (Renate Härtel) and Wotan (András Faragó) in Act II of *Die Walküre* clearly identify them with the ruling class of Wilhelminian Germany.

While they were waiting for Siegfried's emergence with the ring from Fafner's cave, Alberich and Mime were both accompanied by their minders (or 'mafias' as Herz liked to call them) – an idea taken from one of Wagner's early sketches. Again, says Herz, the question posed for the Nibelungs is what Siegfried and his power with the ring will mean for them. Siegfried himself has no idea of this power, though of course the Nibelungs are only too conscious of it, and Herz showed this in the action. He had Siegfried hold up the ring admiringly, and when he moved it from side to side the Nibelungs and their attendants, caught in its mesmerizing spell, moved with it like iron filings responding to a magnet.

Herz de-heroicized Siegfried, depicting him not only as the would-be destroyer of the old order, but also as Thomas Mann's 'little fellow who wields the slapstick in the fairground booth'.[74] Siegfried's departure from Brünnhilde to undertake 'new deeds' was unmasked as no more than the pathos of empty heroism, of a Don Quixote. The journey down the Rhine became the progress of a populist hero and putative freedom fighter. It was a tangible image of Siegfried in the real world. The throng of hopeful people cheering him on included women and children. Herz felt it important to show that the ordinary inhabitants of the world had once believed that the Siegfried who had slain the dragon could be their champion.

The steel and glass cupola of the Gibichung Hall symbolized the technical progress made between the world of *Rheingold* and that of *Götterdämmerung*. The Hall was not classically grand like the interior of Valhalla in Act II of *Walküre* but the fashionable home of a nouveau-riche family. Double doors at the rear opened to reveal a Jugendstil winter garden, into which Gutrune enticed Siegfried. The massive steel conference table declared that this was also the nerve centre of a business empire. Gunther – pale inheritor of Wotan's feudal might – was plainly totally dependent on the new powers of capital and industry. The Gibichungs and Hagen were shown as representative of the new social strand, made wealthy by the factories they owned. The Gunther-Hagen relationship was that between aristocrat and newmoney capitalist, between a Kaiser and a Krupp.[75] When Siegfried arrives in this industrialized modern world it is as a shocking anachronism – a survivor from the age of single combat seen as the revolutionary hope of the nineteenth century, just as Herz's Dutchman had been a survivor from the age of Magellan!

The settings for the second act of *Götterdämmerung* plainly declared that the age of coal and steam had given way to that of electricity. The early nineteenth-century milieu of steam and sweat in Nibelheim had evolved into the Gibichungs' cleanly efficient electrical generating station – a temple to the power that now rules and enslaves the world.

In one important respect, the production did carry specific allusions to Germany's imperial and perhaps even more recent past. The second part of the second act of *Die Walküre* was played between the ruined columns of some great building, as though suggesting that the End desired by Wotan in his long despairing narration had already come about. Many in the audience could not have helped but experience the scene as taking place within the bombed remains of a German city at the end of the war.

The staging of Siegfried's Funeral March, after the removal of his body, evoked similar associations. In an unscripted appearance, Wotan was seen walking sorrowfully along an avenue of high stone plinths surmounted by imperial eagles, all monuments to fallen heroes. It was Herz's characteristic response to Hamlet's question as he leaps into Ophelia's grave to vie with Laertes in mourning her, 'What is he whose grief bears such an emphasis?' The music, Herz decided, represents no one else's grief but Wotan's, the grave being that of his great hope for the world.

At the very end, as the painted backdrop of the great temple of Valhalla began to collapse, the ninety men and women of the chorus in ordinary working clothes came onto the stage to witness its destruction. When the fire and flood had abated, the Rhinedaughters swept down from above in their gondolas to reclaim the ring – symbol of man's exploitation of man and of his servitude to accumulation – which transmuted into a dreamlike golden web that drifted about like a veil before floating up and away into the flies with the Rhinedaughters. 'We do not,' said Herz, 'intend that this image should mean "gold for all" in the sense of a shareholding in Volkswagen with every worker a little capitalist, but only that it should be a fantasy of something new, beautiful and warmly human.'[76]

In the cold grey light, and now on a bare stage against a backdrop of white curtains, the people were still watching and waiting. It was a tabula rasa, an image which neither affirmed nor denied the note of hope sounded in the music. The future, said Herz, is open and no one can predict what will happen. Although very much what Wagner himself had intended, this image, as we shall shortly see, was not one calculated to win the endorsement of suspicious Party officials, though both the image and the production as a whole were, by and large, enthusiastically received by the broad mass of the public.

Reception

The Leipzig *Ring* was highly acclaimed in both the Eastern and the Western press. There was appreciation for the conductor Gert Bahner and the Leipzig Gewandhaus as having dispensed 'with luxuriousness of sound and sheer volume, and thus musically added conviction to the basic concept of the production'.[77] For some of the singers there was less than total approbation, though there was high praise for Karel Berman as Alberich, András Faragó as the *Walküre* Wotan, Günter Kurth as Loge and Siegmund, Sigrid Kehl as Brünnhilde, Gertrud Oertel as Waltraute and Fritz Hübner as Hagen. But the staging was hailed as a triumph to set against the work of Wieland Wagner, and a socio-political corrective to psychologizing and abstraction. 'Leipzig,' pronounced a leading Dresden paper, 'has overtaken Bayreuth. The hub of Wagner interpretation has moved from the FRG to the GDR.'[78] Other Eastern papers wrote that the Herz production was 'the valid interpretation of the *Ring* from a Marxist perspective' and that it was 'a touchstone for the socialist approach to Wagner'.[79]

The Western press, which, with a few exceptions, had ignored previous productions in the East, was drawn to notice the Leipzig *Ring* and thought highly of it. Its critics tended to be less interested in the politics of the staging than in the music-theatre treatment of Wagner's mythopoeic material. Paul Moor in the *New York Herald Tribune* compared the intensity of its 'realism' to that of a documentary film.[80] Writing in the Munich journal *Kürbiskern*, Oskar Neumann noted that 'nothing was smuggled into the *Ring* that was not there already in the nineteenth century, nothing that was not there in the text and music – and at the same time there is so much new and important to discover that had been buried or tainted, that when measured against it other attempts to rehabilitate and give *actualité* to Wagner seem very limited if not actually regressive'.[81]

Opera magazine's correspondent in East Germany, Eckart Schwinger, wrote of *Das Rheingold* that 'Seeing on the vast Leipzig stage what this social-psychological, far-seeing thinker really meant at the time of conception of this work, done in such an enlightening and fantastic way, completely demythologized and for the first time done as realistic music-theatre, one cannot imagine it interpreted in any other way, especially as it corresponds so well with the music.' When the *Ring* was completed, Schwinger found that 'The clarity and consistency with which Herz and Heinrich had carried through their original concept, and the contemporary dimension they brought to the tetralogy as an intellectual and realistic "game" against the bourgeoisie, were truly impressive. … Once again, the socio-revolutionary aspects of the *Ring* had been critically interpreted and cogently argued in visual terms.'[82]

Little of this carried any weight with the GDR's cultural authorities. They were disconcerted that the already suspect work and its production had failed to endorse their official policies. The biggest thorn in their flesh was the 'open ending', which they considered confirmation of Herz's lack of Marxist historical perspective. It was not enough that the director had opened up Wagner's critique of capitalism and awareness of the class struggle. He had sinned in adopting a *purely* historical approach, and in failing to interpret the work as demonstrating that capitalism carried within itself the seeds of its own destruction, and in showing that the ending represented the triumph and new dawn of the proletariat and of utopian socialism. The voices raised against Herz included not only that of Karl Kayser but also that of the Leipzig theatre's equally doctrinaire Christoph Hamm. The Chefdramaturg complained of the failure to introduce 'our historical perspective' and to show the 'oppressed classes', which for Hamm included not only the Nibelungs but also Siegmund and Siegfried, as anything other than a passive, inarticulate mass.[83]

It was characteristic of Herz that he defended himself vigorously. In this he was supported by his production dramaturg Eginhard Röhlig, who insisted that Wagner had written 'no didactic work of political economy'.[84] It was wrong, said Herz, taking up the argument, to impose the political philosophy of the present on an essentially nineteenth-century work. He pointed out that Kayser himself had often argued against those critics who found ideological fault with the classics of the opera repertory, saying, 'We can't send the composer to the Party's school'. Wagner, Herz continued, had diagnosed the social evil of capitalism but had not deduced from it any practical plan of political action for its amelioration. The *Ring* was neither a Marxist dramatization of history, nor a retrogressive, pessimistic and apocalyptic view of history. It was not an anticipation of Marxist world-revolution but an artist's unpolitical vision and hope for a future free from slavery, alienation and the abuse of power. The tetralogy did not embody an optimistic belief in historical progress.[85]

With hindsight, these views are unexceptionable, but it took courage to stand up for them in the GDR of the 1970s, and, to give the other side its due, respect for Herz as an artist was such that the ideological debate was conducted openly and later published.[86] The question remains whether there is anything to decode in his avowedly non-political realization of Wagner's politically loaded work. Looking back in 1991 after the fall of the Wall and the reunification of Germany, Eginhard Röhlig saw it as, generally speaking, demonstrating the collapse of the designs of an arrogant and powerful elite on society, and also, specifically, as a dramatization of a critical view of the GDR as it was![87] This is something that Herz himself would wish to deny, though he would not deny that his allegiance to the work and its creator inevitably brought him into conflict with a certain 'powerful elite' who wanted art bent to their own purpose, as is evident enough in the way he defended himself against them. In the long run his views and his production have been vindicated as a landmark in Wagner interpretation, while the arguments brought by his accusers appear more and more absurd.

The lasting influence of Joachim Herz

Until relatively recently many West German commentators have either ignored the Herz Wagner productions, or patronized them as products of Marxist political pressure, arguing that they were constrained by the socialist-realist diktats of the GDR.[88] But a detailed study of the cultural pressures on Herz and his consistently combative response to them shows that these arguments do not hold water. What can certainly be said is that everyday life in the GDR cannot but have sharpened any artist's political awareness, and that in Herz's case it put him in touch with the political dimension of Wagner's works, which until then had tended to be either perverted or evaded. The Nazi appropriations of Wagner had been answered by a production of the *Ring* that had engaged fearlessly and honestly with it as an expression of the composer's politics in their historical context. Yet Herz had also kept a balance between the *Ring* as a political parable and as a work of art of universal, timeless resonance. His production was certainly a fulfilment of T. W. Adorno's prophecy that Klemperer's Kroll *Holländer* of 1929 had 'mobilised a reserve of actuality in Wagner … which will explode today or tomorrow'.[89] It was surely for this reason that, despite the animadversions of the ideologues, Wagner's 'problematic late works' now began to be rehabilitated and to find favour again. The press changed its tune. The *Ring*, typically, was now described as 'a grandly impressive image of the redemption of the world from the ruinous effects of gold'. *Tristan* was revalued as 'an exercise in recovering a sense of the truly human in inner emigration'. *Parsifal*, once totally taboo, was hailed as a work in which Wagner had set 'brotherly love and compassion, grounded in an equal-rights community, against the Bismarck regime's containment and suppression of the exploited masses'.[90]

This climate was not to last for long, however. Party officials became suspicious of burgeoning liberal tendencies in the arts and clamped down on what they considered to be 'concessions to Western ideology'. One result was that the wave of immensely gifted stage directors who had been nurtured by Felsenstein and Brecht (though in very disparate proportions) – Joachim Herz, Götz Friedrich, Ruth Berghaus and Harry Kupfer – increasingly began to work in the West.[91] Herz hoped that his Leipzig *Ring* would open the way for approaches along similar lines, and in the West it did indeed do so, patently influencing stagings by Luca Ronconi (*Die*

Walküre and *Siegfried*, Milan 1974–5) and Patrice Chéreau (Bayreuth 1976).[92] But it was to have no real successor in the East. Attempts to perform the work at Schwerin, Dessau and Magdeburg were abandoned for technical or artistic reasons (often failure to find suitable singers), as was Ruth Berghaus's production at the Berlin Staatsoper in 1979, after her *Rheingold* had been viciously attacked as too progressive and experimental. (The Berghaus *Ring* eventually came to fruition in the West at the Frankfurt Opera, 1985–7, as we shall see in the next chapter.)

As things turned out, the first impetus for the re-politicization of West German production was to come not from Herz but from another East German director and Felsenstein pupil, Götz Friedrich, whose 1972 *Tannhäuser* at Bayreuth created shock waves that were to travel far and wide.

Götz Friedrich's Bayreuth Tannhäuser, 1972

The West German opera houses of the 1960s were largely in thrall to Wieland Wagner, regarding the East with suspicion. A few, however, liked to exploit the frisson associated with artists from the wrong side of the Iron Curtain. The invitations they issued to these artists also reflected a fascination with Marxism among West German intellectuals. The *Wirtschaftswunder* was beginning to make the capitalist Federal Republic prosperous, but in the universities Marxism was still esteemed as a powerful explanatory tool. When student dissatisfaction with materialism and inflexible professorial authority erupted throughout Western Europe in 1968–9, its discontents were also echoed in the theatres, notably in repertory and styles of production that were critical of bourgeois values and the status quo. Hence the interest in the socialist interpretative slant of the East.

It is, however, unlikely that this in itself would have been the reason why Wolfgang Wagner, five years after his brother's death, turned in this direction, though it has been too little remarked that Bayreuth, a mere 63 kilometres from the border with the Ostblock, took a sympathetic interest in those countries and its artists. Until 1967 those artists could usually get the necessary permission to take part in the festival, whether on stage or behind the scenes. (After 1967 this was possible only if, like the bass Theo Adam, they were of international standing.)[93] Bayreuth's International Youth Festival, founded and run by the festival's press chief, Herbert Barth, welcomed and financed hundreds of students from the GDR, Czechoslovakia, Poland, Hungary, Rumania and other Ostblock countries to join with those from Western Europe in making music, dance and opera together, and provided them all with cheap seats for the Festspielhaus.

Wolfgang would certainly have known of the remarkable work going on in the East and been aware that its distinctive difference might be a good way to break the New Bayreuth mould. He may also have had his own personal reasons for wishing to see a radical break from the hegemony of his brother's style of production. That was exactly what happened when in July 1972 Götz Friedrich's *Tannhäuser* irrupted as iconoclastically upon the Festspielhaus stage as Wieland's first productions had done twenty years earlier.

Wolfgang's gamble was a risky one. Friedrich had never previously directed a Wagner opera and would therefore, as Friedrich himself put it, be coming neither 'Bayreuth-impaired' nor 'Bayreuth-initiated'.[94] He had made his mark at the Komische Oper in its characteristic repertory – *Bohème* (1959), *Fra Diavolo* (1960), *Tosca* and *Così* (1961), *Salome* (1963), *Jenůfa* (1964), *Il ritorno d'Ulisse* and *Trovatore* (1966), *Der letzte Schuß* (Matthus, 1967), *Aida* (1969), *Porgy and Bess* (1970) and *Don Quichotte* (1971). He had also worked in the West, particularly in Bremen (*Rigoletto*, 1963, *Ariadne auf Naxos*, 1964, *Forza del destino* and *Carmen*, 1965, *Don Giovanni* and *Bohème*, 1966, *Salome*, 1967, *Figaro*, 1968) and Copenhagen (*Boccanegra*, 1968, *Il ritorno d'Ulisse*, 1969, *Eugene Onegin*, 1970, *Trovatore*, 1971).

Coming to Wagner for the first time, as Herz had done in 1960, there was everything to play for. For both directors the composer's works were not part of an awesome hermetic tradition, but simply operas like any others. That they were abjured by Felsenstein may also have been an attraction.

Friedrich had seen only two of Wieland's productions and declared that he had been as much irritated as impressed: 'the permanent half-darkness, the displacement of concrete human action into the far distance. I thought it must be possible to achieve a concretization of the human action which Wieland never found.' But he also saw no reason why the suggestive power of symbolism should not be combined with telling a dramatic *human* story. Some of his critics suggested that he had sought a confrontation with Wieland, but there is no evidence that that was so and Friedrich was undoubtedly telling the truth when he said that he hoped his own work would be regarded as a continuation and development of Wieland's. 'When I came to Bayreuth I brought with me what I'd learnt from Felsenstein about handling people on the stage. On the bare boards I sought to find a connection between intensive human action (Super-Aktion) and intensive stylization (Superstilisierung) – but my task was certainly not that of the exorcist or of the storm trooper.'[95]

This, then, was the historic moment when the narrative realism of East German music-theatre impacted in Bayreuth on Wieland Wagner's mystic world of dreams and symbols. *Tannhäuser* was no longer a mystery play but the story of an artist's journey 'through inner and outer worlds, in search of himself'. Act II presented such a starkly confrontational picture of an artist's struggle against society that many failed to notice that in Act III the scenario had changed into that of the individual's struggle with himself (his loneliness, sense of exclusion and isolation). It was a scenario with which, as a regisseur, Friedrich felt a special identity, projecting into Tannhäuser his own sense of the 'terrible, beautiful aloneness' of the director and the fragility of the line 'between success and disaster'.[96]

The Landgraf (Hans Sotin) and his courtiers were feudal brutes who had to be carried to the hunt in cumbersome sedan chairs by sweating servants. These servants were, of course, dismissed so that prodigal minstrels could be discreetly welcomed home. In the second act, the armed intervention of the knights (here, in effect, the court police) after Tannhäuser's sacrilegious invocation of Venus carried unmistakable echoes of fascist brutality. Such elements were heir to Jürgen Fehling's 1933 production at the Berlin Staatsoper. Fehling had anticipated Friedrich in presenting the

Venusberg as a terrifying nightmare, and in the naked violence of the knights' assault on Tannhäuser. After four performances the Nazi Kampfbund had insisted that the production be removed and the previous naturalistic one reinstated.[97]

Friedrich's playing area, designed by Jürgen Rose, was a seven-sided planked plat-form, set just above stage level for the first and third acts. When at the opening of Act II the curtains parted for 'Dich, teure Halle', the platform had been lifted up and, to sensational effect, was reached by a great angulated ramp of steps sweeping up across the width of the stage – seemingly an apotheosis of the *Jessnertreppen* described in chapter 8. At the very front of the stage was a ramp built out over the orchestra pit which was used exclusively by Tannhäuser and the shepherd boy. It softened the proscenium's otherwise sharp demarcation between stage and audience, drawing the audience into the action while encouraging them to view it critically – not that they needed any encouragement.

During the overture a distraught Tannhäuser (a role shared by Hermin Esser and Hugh Beresford) rushed onto the open stage, miming his flight from the chill hypocrisy of the Wartburg court to the enervating pleasures of the Venusberg. He pressed his minstrel's harp to his brow and stared through its strings as though they were the bars of a prison. Venus was his muse, his inspiration, but also held him in thrall, filling him (in the opera's Catholic context of Mariolatry) with guilt and, when the pilgrims returned, with the impulse to expiate it by joining them. As the overture passed into the Venusberg, the lighting revealed great threads spanning up from the stage behind Tannhäuser as though they were the strings of a giant harp. Behind this appeared a fantasy image of Venus in a red glow. The scene was played as Tannhäuser's fevered fantasy, even a nightmare, passing in the minstrel's imagi-nation from ecstasy to the horror of three giant skeletal images of death.

The acting was unflinchingly realistic and, when the action demanded, more brutal than had previously been seen at Bayreuth. For the first time at Bayreuth, Venus and Elisabeth were played by the same singer (Gwyneth Jones), suggesting that sensuality and spirituality can coexist. Where Wieland had seen in Elisabeth an 'ecstasy of asceticism' that was the very opposite of Venus, Friedrich saw Venus as the hidden, inner self of the unhappy young girl.[98] When the joyous pilgrims returned from Rome, bearing a huge cross decorated with holy images, there was an unfor-gettable moment when Elisabeth impulsively ran through the procession from pil-grim to pilgrim, frantically searching for Tannhäuser, then collapsed in despair when she found he was not among them. Wolfram, shown as a benign but imaginatively barren official court minstrel, offered to escort her, but she crawled away on her knees.

In this third act, after the failure of his pilgrimage to Rome, Tannhäuser once again invoked his muse. Friedrich had her appear in the guise of an old woman with wrin-kled skin and withered breasts, her body surmounted by a skull. As the apparition crumbled and Wolfram announced Elisabeth's death (at first illustrated by a huge projected death-mask of her face, later dropped), all that could be seen was Tannhäuser's crooked finger thrust aloft, a valedictory gesture perhaps of repen-tance, perhaps of defiance, spotlit in a narrow shaft of light. Then the darkness was shattered by an explosion of light. The chorus that was suddenly revealed, praising the miraculous grace that had been accorded to Tannhäuser (who lies dead in their midst, his arms outstretched as though crucified), was one not of devout pilgrims but of ordinary people in their working clothes – the last word seemingly left with the proletariat.[99]

It was here that Friedrich most strikingly secularized the religiosity. The idea was that salvation and grace were not to be regarded as gifts from above, but had to be won by each and every man for himself – and that the hope of doing so is something that we all carry inside ourselves.[100] Inevitably, this ending was construed by many in the audience as an East German teaching the Christian Western world a socialist lesson, and there was a furore in the auditorium that had not been experienced since the early years of Wieland's productions. Offence was also given by the presentation of the Landgraf's court in the second act. Elisabeth, de-sentimentalized, was not the dutifully radiant daughter of the house but the counterpart of Tannhäuser, in that she too seemed like a prodigal returning to a home where she could only cling to her memories. The guests, demarcated by costume and rank, entered under the watchful eye of the knights, threateningly kitted-out in black. The decorations were festive, with flags in the colours of the Federal Republic. Tannhäuser's protestation that Venus rather than the Virgin was the true goddess of love was viciously repulsed by Biterolf, representing the true nature of this society. The realism of the scene in which Elisabeth saves Tannhäuser from the knights – although in tune with Wagner's own instructions ('With drawn swords all advance on Tannhäuser, who defiantly stands his ground; Elisabeth throws herself between them') – was too uncomfortable for many in the audience. Friedrich's interpretation of Wagner's rubrics showed just how potent they could still be.

This was, however, an interpretation of the scene, and indeed of the opera as a whole, that departed from Wagner's own conception in many important respects. As Stewart Spencer points out, there is no evidence that the composer himself regarded the Wartburg court in a critical light. The anti-institutional slant in production can be traced back to 1909–10 (a severely expressionist design for Act II by Rochus Gliese) and was also a central feature of Jürgen Fehling's 1933 Berlin staging.[101] But it was not until Friedrich that this began to be the normative presentation of the Landgraf's court. It is compliant with Wagner's dramatic intentions only when Tannhäuser comes across not as an apostle of free love martyred by society, but as suddenly overcome by a sense of real guilt, to which the knights aggressively respond. This was certainly so in Friedrich's staging, Tannhäuser being pre-eminently an artist battling against himself, clashing with the Wartburg society but not just a libertarian victimized by that society.[102]

Some critics saw the violence at the Song Contest as an invocation of police brutality in the Third Reich or in modern East Germany; others saw the men's sombre black attire and the long coloured dresses of the women in the same scene as an unkind reflection of the fashionable Festspielhaus audience. At the end of the premiere the right-wing Bavarian leader Franz Josef Strauss rose from his seat and walked out. Letters in the press demanded that the festival's Federal and Land

Theatrical realism from East Germany arrived as sensationally on the Bayreuth stage in 1972 as Wieland Wagner's spare iconoclasm had in 1951. In Act II of Götz Friedrich's *Tannhäuser*, seen here in the 1978 revival, Elisabeth (Gwyneth Jones) stands between the errant minstrel (Spas Wenkoff) and the naked swords of the court. Friedrich secularized the religiosity, creating a storm among those in the audience who felt outraged that an East German seemed bent on teaching the Christian world a lesson in secular socialism.

subsidies should be withdrawn. Strauss subsequently wrote to a Sunday newspaper protesting that while the final chorus may have been sung superbly it looked like the 'workers' militia choir of the state-owned "Red Locomotive" works at Leipzig'.[103]

Friedrich claimed that he had been concerned only to portray the structures of contemporary society (taking care not to suggest which), and that the uniforms of the knights were not intended to be reminiscent of the SS, later changing them into something more neutral. He similarly claimed that he had not intended the final chorus to be a gospel proclaimed by the proletariat.

The fierce controversy generated by the premiere followed the familiar Bayreuth pattern, mellowing through the revised revivals of subsequent years (up to 1978) into acclamation. What had at first been seen as an otiose Eastern politicization of the work – and indeed of the Bayreuth stage – rightly emerged, as Herz's productions had done, as a long overdue reinvigoration of social and political concerns that had mattered intensely to the composer himself. Friedrich's emphasis on the individual's accepting responsibility for himself was a constant element in his work and in his earlier productions had a palpably East German flavour. But this element was also implicitly critical of a state like the GDR. The utopianism of the vision was socialist, but the accent on self-determination against the controlling power of the state was a protest against the East German regime.

Friedrich's *Tannhäuser* was also an attempt to secularize the work, to explore what its notions of sin, redemption and grace might mean to modern man. This was a process that Friedrich was to take even further in his 1982 centenary *Parsifal* at Bayreuth. Here he interpreted redemption as the discovery of a new sense of individual and collective responsibility. At the end the knights were joined, doubtless for the first time anywhere, by a group of women, supposedly symbolizing 'the dawn of a new society that might possibly put an end to the inherent conflict between the sexes in the opera'. Wolfgang Wagner found this stimulating 'because the range of potential associations seemed so wide'.[104] Whether these associations illuminated the opera in any way was another question. Friedrich's assault on the opera's Catholic penumbra would have been regarded as normal in East Germany, but in the West it came across as a challenge to its capitalist and nominally Christian foundations.

Götz Friedrich's London Ring, *1974–1976*

One of the great advantages for a director working in the West was that his work could be debated openly. Friedrich thrived on this and the Bayreuth *Tannhäuser* became a turning point in his career. He had wanted to return to the GDR as director of the Komische Oper, but when denied the job he turned his back on the East and settled in Hamburg, first as Oberspielleiter (director of productions) and then as Chefregisseur (chief producer). In 1974 he staged *Tristan* for the Netherlands Opera and in the same year embarked on the *Ring* at Covent Garden, with Colin Davis as conductor and Josef Svoboda (sets) and Ingrid Rosell (costumes) as his designers. It was his first encounter with the tetralogy and he extended his narrative style of theatre to meet the challenge of its complex and inconsistent dramaturgies.

In retrospect it seems to have been more or less inevitable that the three most influential reinterpretations of the *Ring* for its 1976 centenary were the work of directors who were not West Germans – Joachim Herz in Leipzig, 1973–6, Götz Friedrich in London, 1974–6, and the Frenchman Patrice Chéreau in Bayreuth, 1976.

Obviously enough, the two East German directors shared a sharpened awareness of the *Ring*'s political dimension. Both acknowledged a debt to Bernard Shaw's *Perfect Wagnerite*. Friedrich's approach was more disparate than Herz's. Some of his ideas were palpably derived from Marx. He described Wagner's use of myth as an expression of his 'artistic alienation from the reality of nineteenth-century Europe', seeing this as a source of the *Ring*'s timelessness. For Wagner, myth had been a mask with which to advance upon contemporary problems. For us, Friedrich argued, it required remodelling so that the *Ring* could address the problems of the following century, as well as those of the past and of the future. It should, in short, be seen as a time-machine.[105] The *Ring*, he said, could only be a drama of the here and now. Where does it take place, he asked? In Iceland, in the north of Sweden, in nineteenth-century Germany, in the vicinity of some presidential palace, or in a distant galaxy? No. 'If the place of action must be stated it is the stage of Covent Garden.'

The *Ring*, he argued, was not a dramatization of events in antiquity, nor of those of Wagner's Germany, nor of those of the world today, but a theatrical fusion of all three time-frames. If the production could successfully relate these three periods to each other then a further perspective would emerge, that of a glimpse into a better future.

This notion derived from the characteristically Eastern emphasis on a social revolutionary Wagner forging a path to utopia, as opposed to the Western view that his political prognostications were of little significance. Nevertheless, both parties could agree that Wagner's work embodied a condemnation of the heedless pursuit of wealth. In Friedrich's words, the incontrovertible precondition for *Rheingold* was 'the move by the gods into a Valhalla paid for by stolen gold which seals the end of their once meaningful work "on earth". Now there is only the threat of power without love.'[106]

Friedrich's emphasis on the here-and-now immediacy of his presentation specifically rejected the identification of Wagner's characters with living people, or indeed with those of any other particular period. It recognized – how could it not? – that the heads of modern government had a precursor in Wotan, the technicians of Cape Canaveral in Fasolt and Fafner, the instigators of modern revolutionary movements in Alberich, and the proletariat in the Nibelungs. But, continued Friedrich, it would be crass to mute the resonance of myth by pinning it to specific reference to historical figures. The startling contemporaneity of the *Ring*'s images 'should not tempt us to follow the fashionably sure-fire path of typical gimmickry, for instance portraying Wotan as Nixon or seeing a likeness to Chinese destiny in the saga of the Nibelungs.... Even the more appropriate assumption that Valhalla is a sort of millionaires' skylab of the future, into which they withdraw from the earth, or that the Gibichungs' Hall should look like Orwell's 1984 should not lead someone to make it into a science-fiction musical.'[107]

Contemporary, then, but without contemporary reference. The theatrical language, on the other hand, he wanted to be unashamedly modern. Svoboda designed a hydraulically activated square platform that rose and fell, heaved and tilted, to create images of a world in crisis that were purely dramatic, not representational. 'The stage is the world,' explained Colin Davis, 'so we have a platform which represents the world and what goes on over and beneath it.'[108] In mounting the *Ring* on a revolving quadrilateral platform, Friedrich may have chalked up a first in thus attempting to square its eternal circle.

What he did *not* do was suggest that the work was a unified entity. In accord with the principles of Brechtian immediacy, which abjured any comfortable sense of closure or of transcendental order behind the action, Friedrich treated each opera as an individual drama – in Barry Millington's excellent description, '*Rheingold* as a mystery play viewed ironically through modern eyes, *Walküre* as typical nineteenth-century psychological theatre, *Siegfried* as black comedy and *Götterdämmerung* as the last stage of a glittering civilisation doomed to decline'.[109]

Friedrich's stage spectaculars never allowed those watching to forget for one instant that they were just that. At the start of *Rheingold*, the platform was tipped up

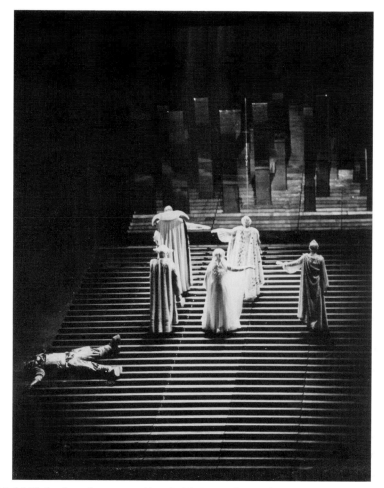

Götz Friedrich's fondness for steps, evident in his Bayreuth *Tannhäuser*, was used even more dramatically for the gods' ascent into Valhalla at the end of *Das Rheingold*, Covent Garden 1974–6.

to reveal its mirrored underside, in which were reflected the Rhinedaughters moving on the horizontal subfloor of the stage, thereby creating the illusion that they were soaring up and diving down in the watery depths. (This effect was even more successfully achieved in the 1983 Bayreuth production designed by William Dudley and produced by Peter Hall.) When Wotan, invoking Erda, stood on the platform's forward edge, again reared high above the stage, and she emerged from the blackness far below, the great chasm between them could not have been more physically telling. Where the technology at Bayreuth had always been an invisible presence, here it was undisguised, even a palpable actor in the drama.

In Friedrich's *Tannhäuser* the singers had fully inhabited their characters; in his *Ring* they sometimes addressed themselves directly to the audience. This is already scripted in Loge's part in *Rheingold*, where he shares his indiscretions about the gods with anyone who will listen.[110] But Friedrich extended it so that, for example,

Alberich launched his complaint against Wotan's violent theft of the Ring straight out into the auditorium, warning us, said Friedrich, that the Nibelungs were about to take part in world events.[111] When Wotan left the flame-girt mountain top at the end of *Walküre*, he stepped down to the very front of the stage, defying the audience to brave his spear point, pass through the fire and claim Brünnhilde.

A further disassociating effect was the use of masks, as by Fricka in Act II of *Walküre*, the face of the singer (Josephine Veasey) being plainly visible behind the quasi-carnival mask she held up on a stick in front of her. Thus even the character was presented as an indissoluble mixture of artifice and reality. Related to this alien-atory device were the huge glass lenses used in the Gibichung Hall. Suspended near the front of the stage, when a singer closely approached them from behind they projected an immensely magnified close-up of his face into the auditorium.

These dislocations and deconstructions of our perceptions of the characters were further intensified as a result of the emphasis (the Felsenstein legacy again) on lucid narration. Siegmund entered during the prelude to *Walküre* (just as Friedrich's Tannhäuser had done during the overture) and, on the furiously heaving platform, acted out the flight that had brought him exhausted to Hunding's hut. The Hund-ings, as William Mann pointed out in *The Times*, 'cook, serve, eat and clear away supper, and sit on chairs at a table near a stove, because the play alludes to all of this'.[112] Some of Wagner's instructions were followed more literally than they may ever have been before. At the end of *Götterdämmerung*, Wotan, the Valkyries and heroes were plainly visible in Valhalla while it burnt.

Ingrid Rosell's costuming of the gods was fantastical and emblematic. They tended to wear white, Wotan with a huge winged collar – a motif taken up in the Valkyries, who resembled birds of prey, unholy angels of death scavenging the charred corpses of fallen heroes and despatching them to Valhalla. The giants were space-fiction astronauts with ray guns. Hunding was slender, spruce, well dressed and an amiable enough host. Siegmund was an uncouth man of the woods, at first glance no rival for Sieglinde's affections.

No matter how exotic, exaggerated or stylized the costuming, the characters behaved, often very movingly, like real people. There was a wonderful moment in the Todesverkündigung when Brünnhilde, who had materialized as an apparition on a rocky eminence, opened her arms to Siegmund and revealed 'great enfolding wings'.[113] In *Götterdämmerung*, William Mann remarked 'Brünnhilde's natural, touching approach to Siegfried when she sees him at the wedding and assumes that he will respond to her loving embrace – his impassivity motivates her vengeful design thereafter: she would not plot his death if she had not tried to win him back'.[114]

After the tired traditionalism of previous *Ring* productions at Covent Garden this one certainly broke new ground. The theatricality of the great world-platform heav-ing and tilting to suit the scene was strikingly effective. Gods, human heroes and Nibelungs felt closer to us than they had seemed in a long while. But the wish to spell things out realistically sometimes jarred with the mythological dimension. Friedrich's idea of finding a synthesis between the underlying myths, Wagner's engagement with them, and the here and now of 1976 was not realized in practice, nor any prophetic epiphany attained. Myth and modernity shook hands, but the production conveyed little sense of the *Ring*'s roots in the mid-nineteenth century.

In some quarters the production was praised for its political awareness, but this may well have been prompted more by knowledge of Friedrich's East German origins than by what actually happened on stage. The production was accompanied by programme-book material that included extracts from Shaw's *Perfect Wagnerite* and Hans Mayer's 'The *Ring* as a Bourgeois Parable' as well as Friedrich's own 'Utopia and Reality'. But the politics of the production were really no more than those of the work as Wagner conceived it. Hans Mayer was not alone in observing that Wieland had 'de-historicized' the *Ring*, obliterating its roots in the nineteenth century. Friedrich talked of exposing those roots again, but in practice his excavation was no more than superficial.

The decisive breakthrough into reinterpretation of Wagner's political dimension had arrived with Friedrich's *Tannhäuser* and Herz's *Ring*. These were the two landmark productions which showed how theatrical realism could be used to create a sense of Wagner's relevance to the political and moral questions of past and present alike. By the end of the 1970s political concepts of one kind or another were the norm in stagings across Europe, many of them going way beyond Herz's essentially *Werktreue* approach. Wagner was used as a stalking-horse not only for social and political purposes but also for every kind of modern angst.

In the years between 1976 and Friedrich's next *Ring* (Berlin 1984–5, seen also in Japan 1987, Washington 1989, and London 1989–91) he became increasingly interested – as did many other directors, including Patrice Chéreau (whose Bayreuth centennial *Ring* is the subject of the next chapter) – in staging the tetralogy as an anticipation of the problems of the late twentieth century, and particularly those of man's exploitation of the environment. The rape of nature is, after all, a central topic in the *Ring* as Wagner conceived it, and it did not require too much imagination to discern its intimations of ecological catastrophe. Chéreau and Peduzzi's dam on the Rhine and caged Woodbird were one response from this angle, and it was taken further by Friedrich in his Berlin *Ring*. He picked up on Chéreau's argument that to connect fully with a modern audience, the production must engage that audience's concern, or potential concern, about the threat of nuclear immolation, of ecological and cosmic catastrophe. Friedrich's idea was to treat the tetralogy as a series of linked events, connecting through the time-tunnel (his set for all four operas) with any moment in history (past or future) when Wotan-like behaviour might precipitate similar consequences.

The action was confined within a huge receding tunnel. This was initially modelled on the Washington D.C. subway and on Henry Moore's drawings of the London Underground when used as a refuge in the Second World War. As in a play within a play, the characters were condemned to re-enact the events which had brought them to their incarceration. Designed by Peter Sykora, this *Ring* was an 'endgame' showing what human beings had done to their history and natural environment. In Friedrich's words, the time-tunnel was a visual metaphor for 'the imprisonment of people who have shot up the heavens'. Its purpose, as Sykora said, was to create a purgatorial space with associations 'reaching from the early Christian catacombs to an atomic waste-storage area'.[115] The time-tunnel concept was first designed for the considerable stage depth of the Deutsche Oper Berlin, and its suggestiveness was diminished in the subsequent reworking necessitated by the shallower stages in Japan and at Covent Garden. Taken as a whole, this *Ring* failed to generate the excitement of its Covent Garden predecessor and seemed to have remained stuck in its tunnel between stations.

The idea of a perspective vanishing into infinity behind the stage was used far more successfully on the immensely deep Bayreuth stage in 1988 by yet another Felsenstein pupil, Harry Kupfer. He and his designer Hans Schavernoch built a 'Weltstraße', or street of world history, vanishing into past and future some fifty metres behind the proscenium. Schavernoch's images evoked the nightmare of man battling to find a future in a world where all that remained of nature was the Wanderer's pathetic mechanical yo-yo that stood in for the Woodbird. Brünnhilde's sacrifice was diminished by being 'quoted' as a spectacle staged for groups watching it on television sets. Unnoticed, two children with flashlights slipped away, seeking escape from under the slow descent of a guillotine curtain. For Kupfer and Schavernoch the *Ring* had turned on its darkest side.

CHAPTER 11

Our uncomfortable contemporary

By the time of the 1976 centenary of the *Ring*'s first performance, the embarrassment with Nazi Wagner had shaded over into a more general unease about what should perhaps be called the composer's uncomfortable side, most notably his nationalism and anti-semitism. Of course Wagner the progressive revolutionary had also been resurrected and that too became part of the context of expectation and possibility in the last quarter of the twentieth century.

What was new was that whereas the task of a Joachim Herz or Götz Friedrich had been to put the political content of the works back on the agenda, their successors saw their job as critical engagement. A rising tide of accusations levelled against Wagner in numerous publications fed into the stage interpretations of this period, and continues to do so even now. Wagner's popularity goes from strength to strength, but it is accompanied – if not universally – by an insistent conscience about his darker side, and a feeling that productions have to deal with it. And here 'political correctness' has often found itself in conflict with the old chestnut of 'fidelity'. As Jean-Jacques Nattiez, one of the shrewdest and most insightful commentators on Bayreuth's centennial *Ring*, has mischievously pointed out, if you believe that Wagner's opinions are dramatized in his works, then 'an authentically Wagnerian *Ring* would turn Alberich and Mime into repulsive Jews'.[1] Thus the rationale behind productions that have attempted to combine fidelity to the substance with criticism of it – a hugely difficult task. There opens up a kind of *via dolorosa*, or at least a *via negativa*, setting out to own up to and atone for the political sins of the composer and those who have abused his works for their own ends.

Producers like Friedrich and Kupfer had begun the process of refracting Wagner through a modern lens. In doing so they demonstrated that Wagner's belief in the timeless universality of myth was absolutely right. The world had moved on and its new problems were echoed in the *Ring* and other works no less powerfully than those of the mid-nineteenth century had been. As Boulez has argued, 'it is impossible to interpret the past with any degree of profundity except by setting out from the present, filtering it through a genuinely up-to-date way of thinking'.[2]

The Bayreuth centennial Ring, 1976

Of all the productions of the last quarter of the twentieth century that showed that the *Ring* could be read as a story of the modern world, it was Bayreuth's centennial staging of 1976 which created the greatest stir and had the most significant influence. Its creators, the French team of Pierre Boulez, Patrice Chéreau and designer Richard Peduzzi, ended the hegemony of German production, and this was something that happened at Bayreuth and by invitation of the composer's grandson Wolfgang. Had the production taken place elsewhere its impact would surely have been far less. For Wolfgang to have chosen a French team to mount the centennial production of the *Ring* was itself a reaffirmation of Bayreuth's international aspirations.

One can only applaud Wolfgang's decision to use Boulez, whom Wieland had sought out to conduct his *Parsifal* in 1966, as a pivotal figure between the now classic radicalism of New Bayreuth and the shape of things to come. But who would be the right producer to work with him? Approaches were made to Ingmar Bergman and Peter Stein, neither of which worked out, and in the end it was Boulez's sister, Jeanne, who proposed Patrice Chéreau.[3] A disciple of Giorgio Strehler, director of the Piccola Scala in Milan, Chéreau had until that time been known principally for his work at the Théâtre National Populaire in Paris. He had directed only two operas, *Les Contes d'Hoffmann* at the Paris Opéra and *L'italiana in Algeri* for the Spoleto Festival. These had both attracted attention for the powerful acting and characterization from the singers which had also been Strehler's trademark, and which were to be such a notable feature of Chéreau's *Ring*. With this slender experience in directing opera, Chéreau more or less met Boulez's half-serious requirement that the director he was looking for should be coming fresh and unprejudiced to the task. Together, they embarked on a sophisticated attempt to rediscover Wagner from 'first principles'.

The new Bayreuth *Ring* had affinities with Herz's Leipzig production, but this went largely unremarked in 1976. In all probability the affinities were no more than coincidental, for Chéreau and his team are not known to have seen anything of the Leipzig *Ring*. Both productions were variations on the Shavian view of the tetralogy as an allegory of nineteenth-century capitalism. The distinction was that whereas Herz kept his staging consistently 'in period', Chéreau in *Götterdämmerung* brought the action forward so that at its end the immolation of the old order is witnessed by people who might have been part of a post-1945 workers' revolution. He wanted the *Ring* to be understood in relation not only to the period of its genesis but to the later part of the twentieth century. He would refashion Wagner's own reforged myth and give it a contemporary resonance. Through the *Ring* flowed traffic between mythic antiquity, Wagner, and the audience of the moment, all of which was important if we were to experience it to the full. In Boulez's words, 'A work of art is a constant exchange between past and future, which irrigates it as it irrigates us.'[4] The production's visual references actually reached much further back than the nineteenth century, as in the Baroque costuming of the gods in *Rheingold*, but Wagner's world was its principal point of departure.

Fragments of industrial machinery and of grandiose nineteenth-century architecture reminded us that the work had roots in that period, but the dam across the Rhine, the dinner jackets in the Gibichung Hall and the *On the Waterfront* setting for the end of *Götterdämmerung* all told us that the *Ring* was no less about the world of 1976.

Chéreau saw it as an allegory of the modern world – certainly of that world in relation to the nineteenth century. The bridge that he built between a sense of Wagner in his own age of industrial triumph and human degradation and the black-tie milieu of the wealthy in the Bayreuth audience was responsible for much of the hostility with which the production was initially received. Siegfried in a dinner jacket at the Gibichungs' villa could hardly have been more provocative.

An allegory for modern times

For Chéreau the E flat prelude so often eulogized as a depiction of nature before the Fall, of a river running out of Eden, spoke only of the fantasy of an industrial world that had long since harnessed the waters for its own ends (just as Wotan had constrained natural man, in the shape of the giants, to labour for him without just reward). And so the opening image, deeply shocking at the time, was of the concrete buttresses and steel catwalks of a hydroelectric dam across the Rhine – its daughters, equally un-innocent, touting for custom in a froth of scarlet petticoat.

In no doubt 'that Alberich and, even more so, Mime, are figures Wagner uses to represent the Jews', Chéreau wanted to rehabilitate them as dramatic characters.[5] The theory was that they should come across as evil not because they were Jews, but because this was the only road left open to them by Wotan's obduracy; his criminality was that of those who enjoy power and make up the rules to suit themselves, theirs was that of the downtrodden. Chéreau spoke of 'the tragic greatness of two lives made up of humiliations, the impossibility of living within the framework of the world willed by Wotan and the energy of despair of two beings'.[6] Heinz Zednik gave an outstanding performance as Mime that, as Chéreau himself said, was 'funny and tragic – close to a caricature, and grave and feeling – clownish like Charlie Chaplin and overwhelmed like a humiliated people'.[7] Zednik's Loge, with its playful echoes of Quasimodo, Cagliostro and other manipulative figures, was no less brilliant; both roles were the veritable apotheosis of the art of the *chantacteur*.

When in the second scene we were introduced to the Wotan family, they were the aristocracy of 1848, 'a ruling class' whose lust for power and possessions had embroiled them in crime. They were discovered bivouacking in the open alongside their luggage, looking for all the world as though they had just been evicted by bailiffs. Valhalla, the new home which Wotan had to be woken up to see, was shown as the façade of a fortress-like bank or mansion.

The idea of nature exploited by industrial power was sustained in the copious smoke and steam of Nibelheim, and in the clouds of the same that were released by Donner (from a huge hamper, part of the voluminous luggage awaiting the move

For the centennial *Ring* at Bayreuth in 1976, Patrice Chéreau and his designer Richard Peduzzi immediately announced their disenchanted modern perspective with a Rhine brutally dammed for some industrial purpose. Alberich (Zoltan Kelemen) is seen here with the Rhinedaughters (Ilse Gramatzki, Yoko Kawahara and Adelheid Krauss) in the first scene of *Das Rheingold*.

into the gods' new home) as a 'thunderstorm' by which to erase the dirty deeds that had paved the way to Valhalla.

The first two acts of *Die Walküre* were dominated by Chéreau's continuing preoccupation with industrial machinery. It was a preoccupation that had a critical slant, as though reproving Wagner for his professed distaste for the mechanical inventions on which the wealth of his patrons and his own comforts were so critically dependent. Hunding's hut became a kind of factory yard (intended by Peduzzi as a space neither inside nor outside)[8] with a beam-engine towering up at one side, and the neoclassical pillars of the owner's mansion (Hunding's?) at the other. An antiromantic note was sounded in that all that remained of the tree was a stump so wretched that it seemed surprising that Hunding had not long since had it uprooted.

In the second act Fricka confronted Wotan in what one presumed to be his laboratory in Valhalla. He was wearing very much the kind of brocaded housecoat that Wagner himself liked to wear. This served him as a magician's cloak – and also as a symbol of his gift for self-deception.

The idea was in part an acknowledged borrowing from E. T. A. Hoffmann, whose influence on Wagner has been insufficiently remarked. At the beginning of Wotan's renunciation scene in the second act of *Die Walküre*, there was an unmistakably Hoffmannesque moment when, disgusted at himself for losing the argument with

Although the Chéreau *Ring*'s pivotal visual reference was Wagner's own time, its mythography moved freely across the centuries. In *Das Rheingold*, some of the gods were in Baroque costume, as in the 1978 revival with Froh (Siegfried Jerusalem) and Donner (Martin Egel), seen (at the left) in front of the giants (Matti Salminen and Heikki Toivanen). Wotan (Donald McIntyre) is listening intently to Heinz Zednik's Loge (whose outfit was modelled on that of the manservant Riff Raff in the 1973 *Rocky Horror Show*). Fricka (Hanna Schwarz) is on the right.

Fricka, Wotan draped his housecoat over his dressing mirror in an attempt to hide the true reflection of what he had become.

Donald McIntyre's Wotan was a geophysicist, exploring the earth's motion with the help of a Foucault pendulum (indicator of the earth's rotation about its axis), perhaps dreaming of discovering some means of having the earth dance to the tune of his desires. But the earth also has a will of its own, memorably shown by the pendulum's spherical plumb bob circulating maddeningly like some kind of torture until Wotan impulsively stopped its motion as a first gesture in his new resolve to expedite 'das Ende'. His sense of self-disgust was further exacerbated by his angry compliance in Siegmund's death. There was a deeply affecting moment when, having successfully engineered his murder, Wotan tore across the stage and cradled the body of his dying son in his arms.

The Valkyrie 'ride' featured a number of well-behaved ponies, led on foot by the warrior-maidens, delivering heroic corpses not for apotheosis in Valhalla but simply for a dust-to-dust burial in a walled cemetery, complete with headstones and senti-

In the second act of *Die Walküre*, Wotan (Donald McIntyre), clutching a deliberately anachronistic spear, was a scientist bent on discovering the secrets of the earth's motion. His self-deception extends to trying to obliterate the image of himself which he sees in the huge dressing mirror behind him. Brünnhilde (Gwyneth Jones) kneels at his feet.

mental effigies. In 1976, Brünnhilde was laid to sleep on the slopes of a mini-Matterhorn, thereafter changed for the better to the ruins of a chapel loosely modelled on Böcklin's *Isle of the Dead*.

Chéreau's Wotan was a criminal self-deceiver. He 'cannot bear real freedom – conscious freedom – as it impeaches his power'.[9] His tragedy was to realize this too late: Siegfried's was that the 'freedom' which is the purpose of (or rather Wotan's purpose for) his existence is illusory. Thus Chéreau seized every opportunity to show that at each critical juncture Siegfried is to all intents and purposes programmed by Wotan. In truth, said Chéreau, the character is only interesting because he is obscurely aware of 'the swindle which presides over his existence and his life: a feeling of a lack which he harbours like an inward and secret wound (and this wound is, on the other hand, also his true freedom) which he doesn't speak of but which manifests itself in a kind of sad gravity'.[10] This was how Chéreau had his Siegfrieds (René Kollo, Jess Thomas and Manfred Jung) play the role – always suggesting an awareness of an obscure wound gnawing away within the character. And indeed the production as a whole showed a profound empathy for the pain at the heart of all the characters. The kind of acting Chéreau wanted was one 'creating contradictions for [the singers] – gaps in their thought – changes of mind – a sensuality and a confusion – demanding of them that they have the violence and the cruelty of history in their bodies and in their singing. I want the torments and the wounds to be engraved in their flesh – that the loneliness be felt and not just acted out.' 'Yes, the *Ring* is violent and brutal. Wotan is

Wotan takes his leave of Brünnhilde after laying her to sleep in a ruined sanctuary which seemed a late echo of Böcklin's *Isle of the Dead*. This sanctuary was a later replacement for Peduzzi's 1976 setting which had been the lower slopes of a mini-Matterhorn.

brutal and unjust – like Lear who drives away Cordelia. It's a violence which is everywhere, which inhabits the characters and eats away at them.'[11] This was manifest in the exceptional brutality of the killings and in the bloodcurdling cries uttered by those who had the ring wrested from them.

In the first act of *Siegfried*, Mime's cave was a walled factory yard with a rectangular pit surrounded by metallic mesh decking. Above the treetops seen behind the rear wall, the flywheel of a huge steam engine was visible. At the back of the yard was a substantial shrouded object and when the Wanderer left Mime after the quiz session, this was revealed as an automatic drop-forge, a present for Siegfried to help him remake the sword. The miraculous forge, a technology beyond that of Mime's dreams, helped Siegfried put Nothung back together almost without dirtying his hands.

In the second act the dragon was a monster on a wheeled cart, manipulated as though a puppet by visible assistants, an idea (suggested by Boulez) taken from the kinds of dragon used in oriental dance and ritual displays. After Siegfried had delivered the mortal blow, the cart disappeared back into the steam and in its place stepped forward the dying Fafner in his original guise as a giant, addressing Siegfried face to face before crashing down dead. The Alberich and Wanderer who had been watching events were clad in identical attempts at disguise. The Woodbird discovered by Siegfried was not a free creature in the branches overhead, but – presumably a second essential present from Wotan – was a mechanical toy clicking away in a droll little cage hanging from a tree branch. The bird repaid Siegfried for her release by showing the way to the fire-and-mist-shrouded mausoleum where Brünnhilde awaited her awakening.

We did not arrive in the recognizably modern world until *Götterdämmerung*, where the Gibichung Hall resembled the ostentatious villa of an industrial baron. Franz Mazura's Gunther looked like America's President Ford. He and Gutrune (Jeannine Altmeyer) were in evening dress waiting for cocktails. It was, however, a ménage that did not run to servants, relying on half-brother Hagen, in shabby lounge suit and with loosened tie, to fetch them drinks and fix them up with spouses. Siegfried arrived wearing traditional forest-hero gear, but by the second act was sufficiently well assimilated to sport a tuxedo for his wedding to Gutrune.

Chéreau saw Brünnhilde as the 'real loser' in the *Ring* and Gwyneth Jones brought out both the youthful impulsiveness and nobility of the character and the pathos of her humiliation in *Götterdämmerung*. Unforgettable in this vein was her entry as Gunther's reluctant bride. In an image inspired by Baudelaire's albatross, captured by sailors, she was tugged in by Gunther in a billowing white dress with her head, hidden by her long hair, hung low and her free arm, in its huge sleeve, trailing like the grounded bird's useless wing.[12]

The third act found us back at the dam for Siegfried's last chance to give up the ring, but the waters had now dried up. Siegfried was viciously killed on the downstream riverbed, his Woodbird having been caught and killed by Hagen's men, as also

The deeply shamed Brünnhilde (Gwyneth Jones) appears like Baudelaire's wounded albatross as Gunther (Franz Mazura) in black tie presents his bride to the assembled Gibichungs in the second act of *Götterdämmerung*.

The intensity of the acting in the Chéreau *Ring* is captured in this revival when in *Götterdämmerung* Brünnhilde (Gwyneth Jones) threatens Siegfried (Manfred Jung) with the point of the spear, its shaft held behind her by Hagen (Karl Ridderbusch).

Wotan's ravens. Hagen, in one vivid account, 'bounded like a bear across the stage, snatched up his spear, rammed it with incredible phlegmatic delight and brutality into Siegfried's back – plunging the weapon repeatedly into the twisting body on the ground'.[13]

There was no march, with Siegfried lifted aloft and borne solemnly away; rather the body was left at the front of the stage, a drop quietly descending behind as 'ordinary' people (emphatically not Hagen's henchmen) filed on from the wings to observe and then go their way. Where Herz had asked the audience to imagine the music as Wotan's mourning for his grandson, Chéreau and Boulez simply invited us to look on, like those on stage, and let the theatre of our own imaginations engage with the music.

This handing over of the 'meaning' to the spectator was also the production's solution to the very end. The ordinary working people and their children, representatives of what Chéreau describes as 'a humanity which is enslaved and manipulated',[14] who had witnessed Brünnhilde's sacrifice and the immolation of the old order, turned around and remained looking out into the audience, as though suggesting that what happened next would depend on what we ourselves made of the music's recapitulation of Sieglinde's hope that love may yet redeem the world.

Chéreau asked us to experience the ending as the Greeks did the oracle at Delphi:

> The Redemption motive is a message delivered to the entire world, but like all pythonesses, the orchestra is unclear and there are several ways of interpreting its message.... Doesn't one hear it, shouldn't one hear it with mistrust and anxiety, a mistrust which would match the boundless hope which this humanity nurses and which has always been at stake, silently and invisibly, in the atrocious battles which have torn human beings apart throughout the *Ring*. The gods have lived, the values of their world must be reconstructed and reinvented. Men are there as if on the edge of a cliff – they listen, tensely, to the oracle which rumbles from the depths of the earth.[15]

Thus Chéreau's rounding off of his production brilliantly picked up on Wagner's own image that his orchestra should, in the Greek sense, be the chorus commenting on the action as well as, from the profundity of its hidden pit, its interpreter and judge.

The impact and significance of the 1976 Ring

It is not hard to understand why this *Ring* should have had such a huge impact. Like most landmark productions it was initially found shocking because it disrupted a prevailing orthodoxy. Here was a production which took on the awkward corners of the composer's dramaturgy, denied itself the comfort of taking the work's unity and closure for granted and tackled it scene by scene as an epic rather than as a seamless music drama. Chéreau brought out less than comfortable aspects of the *Ring* which had been all but forgotten. The booers at the premiere seemed especially aggravated that Chéreau should have made 'so many illuminating, often unkindly truthful points about the *Ring*'.[16]

Certainly it was a critical interpretation, but the 'criticism' emerged from what was a close and knowledgeable reading of the text and music. It was an interpretation that honoured the massive complexity, the many-sidedness of the work, and which engaged with the internal contradictions at its heart. Chéreau felt no need to pretend that the *Ring*'s difficulties did not exist or to edit them out. He presented them for what they are, and thereby only enriched the work.

Many German Wagnerians, scandalized that Wolfgang Wagner should have chosen a French team for the centennial production, looked on it as the revenge of the French for the composer's own disparagement of their country and its culture. There was also vociferous opposition from some of Boulez and Chéreau's fellow countrymen, who had brought their whistles into the Festspielhaus along with their prejudices. Some attacked the staging as 'political', even as Marxist, but in truth it was among the least political of modern times. In essence, Boulez and Chéreau plucked the *Ring* out of the field of political football and handed it back to the theatre, a world where everything may be put on trial but where no verdicts are ever final. It was exactly the kind of theatrical art in which Wagner himself was most at home and most himself.

At the time it did seem that sheer theatrical effectiveness had been more important for this *Ring*'s creators than anything else, but it was not long before the intelligence of the reading began to be appreciated. And if it recast the *Ring* in a modern mould, what else could it honestly have done? To have made the work more shocking and violent than it had been for many years, and from within rather than without, had merely been to restore the charge it had once had. And it did so on the terms set by the work itself rather than those of any imposed ideology. The only politics that interested Chéreau and his team were those intrinsic to the *Ring* as a work of art and not as a political manifesto. They were true to Boulez's perception that Wagner was always primarily theatrical, 'a man who dramatized the conflicts of his day and used them to his own advantage, as a means of nourishing his own work'.[17]

Ruth Berghaus in Frankfurt

Nearly a decade passed before the appearance of the next significant landmark in stage interpretation of Wagner. All it had in common with the Boulez-Chéreau *Ring* was that its chemistry was that of the juxtaposition of elements generally considered antipathetic. The unexpectedness of a French team working in Bayreuth was now matched by that of an East German Marxist (and disciple of Brecht) directing in Frankfurt, financial powerhouse of West Germany's capitalist economy. Ruth Berghaus, like her colleagues Götz Friedrich and Harry Kupfer, had been working in the West since the 1970s, Berghaus making her Western debut in 1974 with *Il barbiere di Siviglia* in Munich. She, like them, brought with her ideas deriving from Felsenstein, Brecht and the aesthetics of socialist realism. What was new about Berghaus's stagings of *Parsifal* (Frankfurt 1982), the *Ring* (Frankfurt 1985–7) and *Tristan* (Hamburg 1988) was an analytic inquisition whose severity was matched by what sometimes came across as an almost comical subversion of the high seriousness of the Wagnerian oeuvre. It certainly seemed like the ultimate Brechtian interrogation of Wagner. But there was very much more to Berghaus than that. We have seen how West and East German approaches to putting Nazi Wagner behind them differed hugely. In Berghaus's work in West Germany the contraries meet and its consequent strangeness should not perhaps surprise.

The idea of rehabilitating works that seemed lost through overfamiliarity, clichéd presentation or political taint by making them seem strange was far from exclusive to Berghaus. It had, for example, been central to the *Ring* produced by Ulrich Melchinger and designed by Thomas Richter-Forgách in Kassel (1970–4). In this a surrealistic juxtaposition of images from ancient Egyptian (or possibly Nordic) deities to Pop Art and space-age technology deconstructed any sense of unity or specific context. In the Ride of the Valkyries robot-like figures that might have been invented by Oskar Schlemmer exercised in an arena surrounded by totemic images, possibly representing horses. The magic fire was a huge neon halo hovering over the sleeping Brünnhilde. In white and silvery spacesuits the Norns were in charge of the electronic circuit board of the world-brain. The Gibichung Hall parodied the grandiosity of Hitler's favourite designer, Benno von Arent. The Gibichung vassals were in red uniform jackets with riding-breeches and jackboots. This was a production which mastered the oppressive past by debunking it, strenuously insisting that the audience should contemplate Wagner's mythology as a fantasy of the Star Wars present.

This kind of approach was intensively developed during Michael Gielen's regime as musical director at the Frankfurt Opera, with considerable input from his Chef-dramaturg, Klaus Zehelein, who had studied with Adorno and Horkheimer. From 1977 to 1987 Gielen worked with a group of directors and designers (including Alfred Kirchner, Christof Nel, Hans Neuenfels, Erich Wonder, Axel Manthey) who shared his aim of challenging the prejudices of the Frankfurt audience.

The Gielen directorate's own prejudices were those of the left. This was evident from the outset in its mounting the world premiere of Luigi Nono's *Al gran sole carico d'amore* in June 1978. Zehelein, impressed by Berghaus's *Elektra* at the East Berlin Deutsche Staatsoper in 1967, had wanted her to stage the Nono. But when the GDR authorities refused her permission to travel it was directed by Jürgen Flimm, with Karl-Ernst Herrmann as designer. In staging the operatic classics that were the backbone of the Frankfurt repertory, Gielen's strategy was one of modernist appropriation. For him the first thought was not 'what Handel wanted' but 'what Handel might want now'. And even that had to yield to the imperative of 'what interests *us* … what *we* want'.[18] Gielen's concern was to probe the works he performed for hidden meanings, for interpretative angles that squared with his own political stance.

The strategy worked at several different levels. Believing that the intrinsic impact of classic operas had been softened by too many 'museum' performances, Gielen and his collaborators set out to restore their dramatic immediacy, their sense of dangerous *actualité*. The most notable instance of this was Neuenfels and Zehelein's anti-colonialist staging of *Aida* (1981) set in a Cairo museum. Radames, a grey-suited and over-romantic archaeologist-connoisseur, addressed 'Celeste Aida' to a statuette in a display cabinet. Aida herself turned out to be a put-upon *Gastarbeiter*, a foreign 'guest worker' scrubbing floors and doing the dishes. The triumphal march was a goose-stepping burlesque of a Nazi parade performed before a stage audience in evening dress sitting in boxes similar to those of the auditorium.

It can well be imagined how this went down with the audience. Protest was vociferous and attendance slumped. The strange thing was that the city's right-wing (CDU) administration stood by Gielen. Eventually he drew in a new audience who were attracted by the very iconoclasm that had repelled those who had voted with their feet. By the end of his tenure (1987) Gielen had a hugely enthusiastic following.

Doubtless one explanation for the city's support of Gielen was a common wish to stake out the greatest possible distance between the present and the uncomfortable recent past. If there could be one word for the strategy of disassociation and renewal it would be 'Durchbrüche' (breakthroughs), which was used as the title of the booklet commemorating the achievements of Gielen and his iconoclasts.[19] Gielen's radical reappraisals were a resurgence of the aggressively experimental productions fostered by the Russian Revolution (see chapter 7) and later in the 1920s by Klemperer's Kroll Opera in Berlin (see chapter 8). In Russia, too, there had been a pressing need to bury a still threatening past, to break the mould of opera as an expensive diversion for the ruling elite and to make it seem futuristic and even utopian. Many crucial elements in the stage language of new Frankfurt had been prefigured in the avant-garde modernism of the 1920s, and especially in that of the theory and practice of Oskar Schlemmer's theatre workshop at the Bauhaus.

Dominant in this was the idea of theatre as choreography, and it is highly significant that the Ruth Berghaus who was to astonish Hamburg and Frankfurt with her Wagner stagings in the 1980s began as a dancer. This remains an essential clue to her work in opera, obsessed as it was with movement and gesture. She had trained as a dancer and choreographer with Gret Palucca at her school in Dresden (1947–51). Palucca's work had itself come out of the revolutionary 'expressive dance' aesthetic of the 1920s and had been banned in 1936 after Hitler had pronounced it too 'intellectual'.[20] When Palucca reopened her school after the war, her objective was, in her own words, to ignite in the younger generation the 'longing to revolutionize creative forms so that they reflect and express the great political and technological upheavals of today'.[21]

Brecht was also a major influence on Berghaus, as were the aesthetics of socialist realism and the dialectical agenda of T. W. Adorno and the Frankfurt School. In 1954 she married the Marxist composer Paul Dessau, whose operas she later directed. Berghaus began her career as a choreographer working in cabaret, plays, opera and films, and in 1964 sprang to fame with her direction of the battle scenes in the Berliner Ensemble's production of Brecht's version of *Coriolanus*. She worked at the Berliner Ensemble from 1964 and after Helene Weigel's death in 1971 directed it until 1977.

Berghaus's first work in opera was as what we would now call a 'movement director' at Felsenstein's Komische Oper; it was she who had choreographed the chorus in Joachim Herz's 1964 film of *Der fliegende Holländer*. Her first opera production (jointly with Erhard Fischer) was Dessau's *Die Verurteilung des Lukullus* (1960) at the Deutsche Staatsoper and this was followed in the same house by her own stagings of three Dessau premieres (*Puntila*, 1966, *Lanzelot*, 1969, *Einstein*, 1974), *Elektra* (1967), *Il barbiere di Siviglia* (1968), *Der Freischütz* (1970) and *Die Fledermaus* (1975). In all of these she sought to extend into opera the principles of Brecht's 'epic' theatre, central to which was the abnegation of Wagner's goal of a seamless Gesamtkunstwerk.

In 1977 she left the Berliner Ensemble to work again at the Staatsoper, where she produced *La clemenza di Tito* (1978), *Das Rheingold* (1979), *Idomeneo* (1981) and *Cenerentola* (1983). Berghaus was also in demand more widely, her notable productions including *Il barbiere di Siviglia* (Munich 1974), *Don Giovanni* (Welsh National Opera 1984) and *Wozzeck* (Paris 1985). But it was in Michael Gielen, with whom she worked in Frankfurt from 1980, that she was to find her most sympathetic collaborator. Their work included stagings of *Die Zauberflöte* (1980), *Die Entführung aus dem Serail* (1981), *The Makropoulos Case* (1982) and *Les Troyens* (1984) which are talked about to this day.

Parsifal, *1982*

Berghaus's first Wagner production in the West was her Frankfurt *Parsifal* of 1982, conducted by Gielen.[22] This being the centenary of the work's first performance, it was impossible for a new staging not to stake out a position vis-à-vis the opera's aura and history. And in that history there was much to engage Berghaus's interest: the opera's association with its composer's theories of regeneration for the Teutonic race, its vision of an elect community of German manhood revenging itself on a semitic adversary, the sanctimonious awe in which the work was held, Hitler's idea of reserving it for the consecration, in victory, of his thousand-year Reich,[23] even Wieland Wagner's attempt to revalidate its gospel of redemption, healing and renewal – all these were provocation enough for a director of Berghaus's background and temperament. For her there was no question but that from first to last the Grail community remained a moribund, masculine and misogynistic society, its 'redemption' no more than an illusion. She saw the opera as an endgame in which the knights were held spellbound within the glowing red circle that in Axel Manthey's design represented the Grail. Each knight had with him a suitcase packed for a journey, but it was equally clear that none of them was going anywhere. The blind schoolmaster Gurnemanz – presented as a Tiresias-like figure – taught that they could be saved only by a 'pure fool', but that seemed far from certain. In Act I this Gurnemanz was discovered with chalk and pointing stick at a blackboard – on which was spread-eagled 'knowledge' in the shape of an open book – attempting to indoctrinate young squires who, with their shorts, shirts and ties, looked as though they might have graduated from the Hitler Youth.

When the 'pure fool' materialized he was in a red romper suit, red symbolizing for Berghaus not socialism but rather the blood of the reborn anarchic life-force. As the action developed, Walter Raffeiner's Parsifal never lost his sense of being a child in an alien grown-up world, his helmet, shield and spear no more than playthings. Crowned king, he moved slowly forward into the glowing circle of the Grail, but the concluding image was of Parsifal beginning to shiver, perhaps even to freeze, as he inherited the icy mantle of all who must wield power.

To emphasize Kundry's apartness she was played by the black singer Gail Gilmore. Not for the first time, Kundry was Woman as men like to think of her – wild beauty, whore and serving maid. The production was profoundly sympathetic to her and especially in bringing out what Berghaus believed was her unfulfilled wish – seen as an expression of Wagner's interest in the transcendent qualities of androgyny – to be both Man and Woman. (The androgynous theme, but applied to the character of Parsifal, was also to be a central feature of Hans Jürgen Syberberg's film version of the opera made in the same year.) When Parsifal took off his armour Kundry tried it on and offered to fight for him. She ran hither and thither as though seeking

Working in Hamburg and Frankfurt in the 1980s, Ruth Berghaus subjected Wagner to a brilliantly idiosyncratic Brechtian interrogation. In her centennial *Parsifal* (1982) she engaged fearlessly with the dark side of the work, presenting the Grail community as totally moribund. In the first act, Kundry (Gail Gilmore) is seen with the almost mummified Amfortas (John Bröcheler). Behind them is the blackboard used by the blind Gurnemanz for his instruction of the young squires.

a new role that no one would find for her. At the end, unable or unwilling to follow Parsifal into the magic circle, she quietly prostrated herself on Titurel's coffin, perhaps dead, perhaps not.

Much in the production was, like most things by Berghaus, difficult to understand, not least in its tripartite colour symbolism of red, yellow and blue, all three colours being found only in Kundry's costume. The conception of the Grail community as irretrievably doomed flung down a challenge to the composer's own view and its sanctification by the racist ideologues of Wahnfried. Kundry and Parsifal opened up a fissure (literally carved like a gash across the set) which represented both the community's wound and the hope of its being healed through the discovery of a connection back to the external world. Wagner's quasi-religious mystery play became a Beckettian tragicomedy in which the wise fool could bring no lasting panacea because whatever wisdom he could offer was incompatible with the roseate glow of self-induced intoxication favoured by the fated community.

Certainly the religiosity of the piece would have been anathema to Berghaus's Marxist socialism. The impact of her iconoclasm on this talisman of Wagnerolatory was of course hugely controversial. It had powerful political repercussions in a West Germany still anxious to atone – if necessary by self-flagellation – for its persistent sense of guilt about Wagner.

The Ring, 1985–1987

Berghaus's deliberate disassociation of the stage action from the composer's own intentions was central to her production philosophy. For her there would have been no point in a reading of the score and text that did not question those intentions in order to attack preconceptions generated by more than a hundred years of performances good and bad. And because few works were so in thrall to their performance history as Wagner's, their reinvigoration required an extremity of separation between past and present. Theatrical value, for Berghaus, lay precisely in the tension that could be set up between the intrinsic, even over-explicit theatricality of Wagner's music and a new theatricality that was free to question and comment on it. This was an essential feature in all her productions, no matter who the composer, and it informed every aspect of the Frankfurt Ring she devised with Gielen, the dramaturg Klaus Zehelein and the designer Axel Manthey between 1985 and 1987.

At this time the Boulez-Chéreau Ring was still the one in everyone's mind. But for Berghaus the intensity of its realistic acting and its passionate humanity were a provocation. The tetralogy had become all too credible in its actualité – indeed it had been 'modernized' so effectively that it was easily broken up and shown on British television as a serial in ten instalments. Popularization, yes, but to Berghaus's mind there may also have been betrayal in the packaging of the work for relatively painless

For Ruth Berghaus, the Ring was a labyrinth which she explored with probing playfulness. In the piling up of the hoard in Das Rheingold in 1985, the giants (Manfred Schenk and Heinz Hagenau) are grey-suited factory foremen dwarfed by huge puppet-effigies of themselves. The masks are those behind which the gods, deprived of their elixir in Freia's golden apples, had taken refuge when the goddess (June Card) was abducted.

home consumption. New obstacles had to be created, a higher level of resistance found which, as in the transmission of electricity, would enable greater power to be drawn from the source of energy that was Wagner's work of art.

Contra Wieland, whose characters were abstract archetypes, contra Chéreau, whose were living flesh and blood, Berghaus's characters were iconic stalking-horses for her analytical critique. This was almost literally so in the case of the *Rheingold* giants – factory foremen in grey suits, dwarfed by a pair of carnival-style puppet effigies towering behind them, their papier-mâché faces those of put-upon honest artisans. In the third scene the Nibelung workers were shown by cluster-groups of quasi-African white masks, appearing and disappearing at five cavernous holes in the rear wall and at one point seeming to weep. Berghaus's characters were figurines, automatons, often figures of fun and slightly absurd – much of this not inappropriate for a work in which hardly anyone, with the notable exceptions of Siegmund, Sieglinde and Brünnhilde, is free to act of their own volition. They were not characters with whom anyone could readily identify, thus securing the Brechtian objective of presenting them as though at arm's length. As people they were weirdly unreal, even anti-real, and the drama that Berghaus chose to unfold was not so much of humans as of ideas about them. They were ciphers and semiotic signs signifying hidden truths. Berghaus took it for granted that the *Ring* was indeed an impenetrable labyrinth. Much of her production suggested that Wagner's characters had been denatured and set loose on the stage to discover who they actually were. Boulez once said that the interpretation of a great work of art consists in discovering a new mystery within the unfathomable mystery that is the essence of the work, and that is certainly as good a way as any of approaching Berghaus's *Ring*. For her own part, Berghaus said that for her 'every work of art is a puzzle. And of course you try to solve the puzzle. But if you succeed then it is no longer a work of art.'[24]

Axel Manthey's scenography provided a collection of brightly coloured toys on the Frankurt stage's huge revolve, ready to be used by the characters in their self-discovery and their reconfiguring of the riddles in the work. The Rhinegold was a golden ball that rolled very slowly forward out of the depths. Erda was a grey-suited lady rolling before her a globe of the Earth. Under their absurdist balloon-like skirts, the Norns had other globes that might have represented the solar system or even the universe as a whole. The Rhinedaughters were clad in tight cocktail gowns and moved up and down in a circular trajectory like glamorous marionettes. The bases of their flared skirts glowed red at moments of alarm.

Berghaus's method, in its probing playfulness, was to deal as lightly as possible and yet as purposefully as a forensic scientist or psychoanalyst with the textual imagery and its quiddities. The self-destructive behaviour of the gods was cleverly manifest in the way they stalked awkwardly about on their palpably built-up boots (as if a parody of the *kothurni* worn by the principal actors in a Greek tragedy) – the source of their superior stature being also that of their clumsiness. When Freia was abducted and they lost their elixir, the immortal gods stepped down from their lifts ('came down to earth') and held up large scowling masks to signal their displeasure.

In the first act of *Die Walküre*, Sieglinde was in a tight-fitting red gown with a cumbersome train – natural woman enslaved by seriously unnatural man in the shape of Hunding, who stomped around in a suit of golden armour. Siegmund wore a moss-green velveteen tracksuit. When Hunding retired for the night, Sieglinde re-entered in a long white shift, dragging in the red gown which she and Siegmund tore to pieces. At the cue for the door to fly open, the whole hut rose up into the flies leaving brother and sister vulnerably alone on the open stage with the tree trunk. It was typically Berghausian use of the scenery to add to, or comment on, Wagner's own symbolism, reinforced at the end of the act when Siegmund and Sieglinde disappeared behind the patently phallic tree, up which they were seen to climb as the curtain fell.

At the beginning of the second act, Fricka had to deal with a Wotan who was already attempting to evade his responsibilities as leader of the gods by prematurely affecting the long dark coat and gangster trilby of his Wanderer role in *Siegfried*. She slowly stripped him of his all too transparent disguise, then hung the power-boots of his divinity roughly around his neck by their laces before handing him over to Brünnhilde.

Siegfried's killing of Fafner was Berghaus at her best. In response to Siegfried's horn call, a mask-like fragment of a huge mouth and blotchy red lips – reminiscent of the traditional Greek mask-representation for 'tragedy' – came slowly forward from the rear. It was of course both Fafner's cave and his mouth, into which Siegfried climbed to despatch him. The moment of the fatal sword thrust was signalled by the

Brünnhilde (Catarina Ligendza) exults in her nursery games with Wotan (Wolfgang Probst) at the beginning of the second act of *Die Walküre* in Frankfurt, 1986.

mask rotating through ninety degrees. Siegfried re-emerged from the mouth, while the dying giant, in the same suit that he had worn in *Rheingold*, crawled out from under the mask, which receded again when he died. The magic really began when, after Siegfried had killed Mime, the little boy playing the Woodbird (he wore a single wing on his arm like a shield) pushed the clumsy Siegfried in his baggy white suit towards the red curtain that now filled a large circular aperture at the back of the stage – yet another image of Fafner's cave. At the Woodbird's command, the curtain was drawn, revealing the cave mouth as the threshold through which Siegfried is reborn as he and the Woodbird walk hand in hand into the dazzling light of the future. In Berghaus's own words, 'The killing of the dragon also signifies "escape from home", "release from mother". The mouth therefore is a good image, as it is also an image of the way into the body and the way out again.'[25]

Much play was made with symbolic props, prominent among which was a plain wooden kitchen chair associated with Fricka and domesticity. The performers were sometimes confronted with physical challenges, like the negotiation of a narrow ledge across a steeply sloping surface, that were devised to be complementary to the psychological ones imposed by Wagner's text and music. At her entrance in the second act of *Die Walküre*, Brünnhilde had already tried on the Wotan-trilby (symbol of criminality) for size as she bestrode his crawling form as her nursery hobbyhorse. Later, in the Todesverkündigung, she borrowed Fricka's chair to signal her complicity in Fricka's insistence that Siegmund has to die. By the end of the second act of *Götterdämmerung* it was in a trilby that she joined the oath that Siegfried must die, but it seemed culpably, even risibly superfluous that she should arrive for her immolation carrying at least three such hats – perhaps tokens of all the felonious deeds for which she was about to atone?

The tension, even sense of contradiction, that was sometimes set up between stage action and music is perhaps best exemplified by the treatment of Siegfried's Funeral March. His body was not solemnly borne aloft but brutally kicked aside by Hagen's men. 'In that this contradicts the stage instructions,' said Gielen, 'it will increase the audience's consciousness of the greatness of the music. You will find such a dialectic in all Berghaus stagings.' (This of course assumes an audience equally well adjusted to a dialectical response....) In his conducting of the passage Gielen naturally took care to avoid any sense of bombast or grandiloquence. He was also keen to suggest, perhaps wishfully, that the Funeral March 'expresses Wagner's personal disappoint-ment that at the time of the completion of *Götterdämmerung*, all those humanistic ideals held by the young revolutionary of 1848 had gone to the devil'.[26]

Where Berghaus had the men appear as pitifully ridiculous in their crimes and deceptions, the women fared rather better, though Catarina Ligenza's Brünnhilde was anything but heroic and, as we have seen, her own implication in Wotan's web, however unwitting, was emphasized throughout. In all this it must be remembered that Berghaus's Brechtian intention was not to flesh out characters with whom we would empathize but rather to hold them up for critical approbation. At the immo-lation, Siegfried's body was present not on a funeral pyre but on the ground at the front of the stage. Berghaus said she could not allow 'Brünnhilde to stand there unless Siegfried, and not the horse Grane, is there with her, dead and unobserved in the foreground. His body is all that is left to her and it is this that she addresses. Brünnhilde's loneliness in front of the burning Valhalla, however one does this, has to be understood in this context.'[27]

Thinking choreographically, as though the characters were mute, Berghaus gave them a semaphore sign language. The Rhinedaughters pointed fingers at their temples, or straight up in the air to command attention (as did other characters). Fingers were also used to count out the points being made on the fingers of the other hand. Hands were raised to cover one side of the face, perhaps to suggest that the other half had other thoughts, or that inner wisdom was at work – an extension of the idea that Wotan's blinded eye gave him special insight. The use of the same gesture by Siegmund and Sieglinde seemed to emphasize that each was the missing half of the other. Berghaus explained that 'the Wälsung siblings are able to discover each other in this way because they have learnt [the gesture] from their father. This hiding of an eye is a sign of love, and it is then taken over by the Woodbird as a sign of his leading Siegfried astray. In reality he is a bird of death not a sweet little songster.'[28]

For Berghaus the development of the motif of Wotan's single eye, its extension to other characters and especially to his progeny, was crucial as representing a fatal lack of external perspective, with the corollary that no one (with the single exception,

At the end of the second act of *Siegfried*, the mouth of Fafner's cave was suddenly revealed as the threshold through which the Woodbird (Christian Fliegner) must lead Siegfried (William Cochran) on towards Brünnhilde.

Berghaus believed, of Brünnhilde) can ever have a true picture of the world as it actually is – it is seen only 'as man wants to see it'.[29] In *Götterdämmerung* this idea was recapitulated in the closing image, which was of Gutrune going to a prominently displayed telescope and looking through it into the audience. 'I give Gutrune the possibility, using one eye and the medium of technology, to look out into everything. For me this represents the boundlessly hopeful but also monocular and terrible prospect into infinity.'[30]

All this added up not so much to a coherent view of the *Ring* as to a view of its deconstruction. Berghaus left one in no doubt that the gods were a despicable bunch and that the forces ranged against them were scarcely preferable. But by the 1980s these ideas were hardly new, even if the sense of comedy, of teasing the stupendous work to see how it might respond, certainly was.

All coherence gone?

The Berghaus production marked the end of an era in which producers believed they could make sense of the *Ring*. Many have since come to think that this is simply no longer possible, and even that it has never been possible, so great is the discrepancy between Wagner's aim of creating a unified work of art and the fault lines in the completed work itself. Until Berghaus, as Mike Ashman has well said, even the most experimental producers had 'maintained a referential narrative visual framework, using either present-day or nineteenth-century equivalents for necessary symbols and scenery'. Ashman rightly sees in Berghaus a transposition to the theatre of the emancipation of literature from authorial intent, as proposed by Roland Barthes in *Writing Degree Zero*.[31] Certainly, Berghaus destabilized the previously dominant notion that production should primarily be about telling the story of the opera.

Was Berghaus really, in heart and soul, the Marxist people's artist that her affiliation with Brecht and Dessau would suggest? For the abstruseness of her work could not have been at a further remove from the scrupulously explanatory realism of Felsenstein and the Komische Oper. It was an art for connoisseurs, not at all for the uninitiated. No aspect of her productions could conceivably be described as socially realist, socially aware or reaching out to a broad audience. Certainly Berghaus showed not the least concern for narrative clarity. On the contrary, her work was arcane, obscure, more a commentary on the problematic aspects of the operas than a direct engagement with their substance. It turned its back on 'intelligibility' and was, in truth, only understandable – and then no more than partially – by those who knew the works extremely well.

The puzzle she created often seemed like a sequence of elaborate footnotes, fascinating in themselves, from which one had to try to reconstruct the missing text. This was, of course, to miss Berghaus's point that the 'text', in the shape of Wagner's words and music, should always be palpably present; there were other things for a stage director to do than merely mimic or illustrate it. She assumed a total Barthesian emancipation of the opera from its composer and his intentions. 'You must,' she said, 'expose and then break free from the intentions in a work so that the spectator can make his own picture.'[32] Berghaus seemed to cultivate a semiological extravaganza, a deconstruction proofed and defiant against reconstruction.

With the important exception of her portrayal of the Grail community as something far more negative than had been imagined by the composer, the real politics of Berghaus's work had little to do with her critical interrogation of Wagner. Her open-ended reading of the *Ring* was not unusual and was well within the envelope of Wagner's own ideas about the work. No, its lasting significance has to do with the extremism of her work, its provocation of controversy. This began with an assault on the values of the conservative opera-goer. It was a 'goodbye to all that', a gesture of dislocation from and disavowal of a past that was as moribund and despicable as her Grail community. It revelled in discovering and suggesting discontinuities, in effecting Brecht's 'separation of the elements' in opposition to Wagner, who had sought unity and coherence, whether in his early Gesamtkunstwerk theory or in the later Schopenhauerean vision in which music became pre-eminent.

Her task was not to strain for a new coherence – only to exhibit the findings of her analysis. It was enough that this should connect with 'what interests *us* … what *we* want', and this was still, at root, that the ghosts of Nazi appropriation should be banished. Hence Gielen's unlingering tempi, his anti-heroic phrasing, hence the seemingly light-hearted spirit in which Berghaus wielded her scalpel – the gods tottering on their lifts, Parsifal and Siegfried in their baggy suits, Brünnhilde with her trilbies. Possible, perhaps, but scarcely compatible with Wagner's own ideas, which had in any case been removed from the agenda. (His own maladroit jokiness, arguably far less pleasant, was of a different order.)

Obviously we cannot know whether Wagner would have enjoyed Berghaus's jokes, her burlesque of his scenario. But he would probably have complained that her interpretation was one for the head rather than the heart. And he might have found her critical irony subversive of an indispensable rhetoric – as though the high poetry of Othello's speeches or Prospero's farewell had been negated by an actor's over-zealous attempt at a streetwise vernacular. What Berghaus does raise, irrevocably, is the question of whether a romantic Wagner can ever be revived.

The dramaturgy of fragments, of disassociation, of the surreal, of psychology and absurdism, was fundamentally one of burying the past. It denied that there could be any useful dialogue with old-style *Werktreue* theatrical production. It was a way not so much of coming to terms with the still troublesome ghosts as of pretending that they simply could not be there.

Whether Wagner could be reinstated 'as himself' and his works as the quintessence of nineteenth-century German romanticism has been the seemingly quixotic project of the film director Hans Jürgen Syberberg. Unimpressed by, indeed contemptuous of, modern stage interpretations, Syberberg believed that it was his calling to succeed where the theatre had failed. In many ways his film version of *Parsifal* is the antithesis of Berghaus's stage production, both dating from the same centenary year of 1982. Where Berghaus had sought to revitalize Wagner by making him strange, even to the point of taking him out of historical context, Syberberg insists on reinstating that context as forcefully as possible. Berghaus denied the existence of the ghosts; Syberberg resurrects them in order to square up to them, and in his view this clears the way for the recovery of *Parsifal* as a fairy-tale dream opera. Whether or not he succeeded is a question to be taken up later, but his film of *Parsifal* remains one of the most extraordinary interpretations ever inspired by a work of Wagner's.[34]

The lamentations of Hans Jürgen Syberberg

Richard Wagner! A Black Stone fallen from the sky to the earth with eternal yearning for the heavens, for the lost paradise of the angels, the paradise that bears the guilt for the sin of the world, when Adam and Eve were guilty.

(The actor André Heller, in Wagner's cloak, at the end of Syberberg's *Hitler: Ein Film aus Deutschland*, 1977)[33]

Syberberg abhorred what he considered to be the critical, anti-romantic interpretations of Chéreau and Berghaus (and of many other directors!), which he blamed on the dominance in Germany of Marxist intellectuals like Bloch, Adorno and Marcuse. He attacked the intellectuals and their disciples for making 'guilt into a trade which was fatal to the imagination'. They had criminalized everything the Nazis had touched, 'especially almost all of our romantic heritage, from Hölderlin to Richard Wagner', and had inculcated self-hatred in the Germans.[35] Syberberg believed that their philosophies of rescue, their re-invention of Wagner in the image of modern guilt about him, amounted to betrayal. He was far from being so naïve as to imagine that the operas could be resurrected 'on their own terms' and without regard to their cultural and political history, but he vehemently believed that a new interpretative strategy for dealing with that history had to be found.

Certainly such a strategy had to begin with facing up to the Nazi legacy. One could not pretend that the Furies were not there; they had to be understood, answered and assimilated. The lingering sense of guilt, of contamination, had to be worked through. The due processes of exorcism, painful though they were, had to be activated. Syberberg summed all this up in what he called 'Trauerarbeit', or the work of mourning.[36] He saw his work as an essential contribution to that task, and it culminated in his *Parsifal*.

Syberberg was not alone in his passion to explore the Wagner–Hitler nexus. What he attempted to do through film, the artist Anselm Kiefer did in his own medium. Kiefer, too, has a mission to reconstruct the foundations of German mythology and self-identity. When he makes a picture of the rough floorboards of his studio hut, it is Hunding's hut that he has in memory – the planks hewn from the sacred German forest – and the hilt of Nothung sticks out from the floor. The Weltesche (world ash tree), core image of the *Ring*, is also a pivotal subject for Kiefer, as in his painting *Yggdrasil*. In other works he depicts trees with bare branches and blasted trunks similar to those in paintings by Caspar David Friedrich. The tarnished images are there sometimes in irony and always for mourning. In Kiefer's *Die Meistersinger von Nürnberg* twelve straw men are shown in a desolate Nuremberg landscape. The men are of straw because of their extreme vulnerability to the historical echoes

summoned by the painting – not just Wagner's Nuremberg but that of the Nazi ral-
lies and of the trials of the Nazi leaders. In 1977 Kiefer published a book of photographs of old railway tracks, calling it 'Siegfried's Difficult Way to Brünhilde' [sic].
That was also the difficult path towards reclaiming the nobler part of the German
soul on which he and Syberberg were both bent.

It seemed to Syberberg that all the usual processes of analysis and critical discussion – even if they could be mobilized – could never be enough, and would most
likely become inextricably bound up with their horribly serious subject. His hope lay
in the un-German strategy of using satire and irony to discredit the barbarous
appropriations and get them laughed out of court. This was, of course, to follow in
the footsteps of those like Heine and Nietzsche who had also both loved and
despaired of the Germans' uses of their culture. With Kleist, and quite specifically,
Syberberg believed that there was a possibility of return to paradise but that this
could be accomplished only by circumnavigating a fallen world and finding the back
gate to the Garden of Eden.[37]

Fighting against the singularity of socio-political interpretation (as in Herz and
Chéreau, for example), Syberberg wanted rather to *expand* Wagner's mythic resonance, to explore his work, as Wieland had done, primarily as psycho-drama, but in
his case as a drama not only of the universal psyche, but also quite especially of that
of the twentieth-century German nation (and in that sense there was no way he
could avoid being political). He believed that in order to do this he had to rescue
Wagner from the theatre and find a new life for him in film, the pre-eminent art
form of the twentieth century. His *Parsifal* emerged from a series of previous
films in which he had sought to elucidate and exorcise the association between the
romantic peaks of German culture and their debasement by the Third Reich.

It was doubtless the centrality of Wagner to his films about Ludwig II, Karl May
and Hitler that pointed him towards meshing his own directorial talents with those
of the Master of Bayreuth. Perhaps Syberberg saw that his obsession with the
Wagner–Hitler nexus would eventually call for some kind of exorcism and that there
could be no better medium for this than *Parsifal* – interpreted, as we shall see, as
Wagner's valedictory confession. Syberberg's film therefore locates the action of the
film in no forest or castle of the Grail, but on and sometimes inside an immensely
enlarged studio model of the composer's death-mask.

The films that showed the way to Parsifal

Born in 1935, Syberberg spent his childhood on his father's estate in Pomerania in
eastern Germany. The evolution of his distinctive theories of film as 'the music of the
future' – theories that were to culminate in his *Parsifal* – may be traced from 1953
when he met Brecht and made the only existing film record of him rehearsing
(*Mutter Courage* and other plays) on stage.[38] In that same year Syberberg moved
from East to West Germany and in 1956 wrote a thesis on Dürrenmatt. Between
1963 and 1965 he made more than eighty short television films and a long film in
which Fritz Kortner rehearses Schiller's *Kabale und Liebe*. And then in 1972 came

Ludwig: Requiem for a Virgin King,[39] which marked the beginning of a fascination with Wagner that was to become ever more obsessive.

Both Ludwig and Wagner are apostrophized as subversives, as incarnations of the inherently romantic German spirit scandalously emasculated and cheapened by commercial exploitation. Those who have done this have seen their mystique, their irrationalism, as a dangerous phenomenon, a threat to the order of a modern democratic state. Thus Syberberg shows Ludwig rendered harmless as a 'kitsch-king', travelling at night with his dreams in his sleigh through the snowscape of the Alpine forests to the music of the love duet from the second act of *Tristan*, or wandering in ermine through the mists to the music of Siegfried's arrival on the mountain top to awaken Brünnhilde.

Through these mists also strides an effeminate, almost androgynous Wagner, proclaiming that he was always a revolutionary and the creator of the protest music of the nineteenth century. Against a backdrop of the 1876 Bayreuth setting for the opening of *Rheingold*, three parody Rhinedaughters foresee that 'das Ende' will be brought about by 'the pressure to produce' and 'environmental pollution'. Ludwig is the positive side of German irrationalism and his fate a warning of how easily, if it is denied, that irrationalism can turn diabolical. 'Ludwig lives a fairy-tale life for us,' says a Bavarian peasant woman. 'Do you want to kill what's best in us?' The German soul requires its breathing space, and without it there could be only catastrophe. Ludwig himself observes that even if the people kill him, someone else will come along with the same kind of dreams – the obvious implication being that dreams which had a romantic innocence in him would be diabolical in their Hitlerian incarnation. As the film comes to its close, Syberberg has his Ludwig, like the Bourbons he so admired, guillotined by the mob, then ironically resurrects him, still in ermine but yodelling like the vulgar entertainer to which he had been so disgracefully reduced.

Syberberg's interest in the significance of apparently marginal material resulted in an accompanying film in which Ludwig was seen through the eyes of his cook.[40] These explorations of Germany's infatuation with Ludwig were followed by a study of another source of escapist fantasy, little known outside Germany, namely Karl May, the author of hugely popular Wild West adventure stories. May was much admired by Hitler who, passing over the writer's inconvenient pacifism, allegedly commended the stories to his generals as a recipe for victory at Stalingrad.[41]

These films had all been cast in the form of fantastical, fictionalized documentaries, so it was no surprise that Syberberg should next seek to substantiate his ever growing interest in Wagner's impact as mythographer of the modern German soul by persuading Winifred Wagner to talk on camera about her infatuation with Hitler and his role in the Bayreuth of the 1930s.[42] Here, at last, Syberberg had found a key player who was prepared to give, willingly and proudly, an unapologetic account of what had happened and how it had stayed with her as something that was overwhelmingly positive and not for one minute to be regretted. Siegfried's widow calmly extolled Hitler's patronage of the festival and professed her undying allegiance to him and to the ideals of National Socialism. For a Bayreuth that for twenty-five years had striven to lay its ghosts and was preparing to reassert itself in 1976, centenary of the *Ring*, as an international rather than a Germanic phenomenon with a French production of the tetralogy, the Winifred film could not have been more embarrassingly timed.

The director first used the word 'Trauerarbeit' at the end of the Winifred film, where a shot of a smiling Syberberg is captioned, 'This film is part of Hans Jürgen Syberberg's *Trauerarbeit*', disconcertingly suggesting a degree of ironical detachment in the film maker himself. The *Trauerarbeit* continued with *Hitler: A Film from Germany*, an immensely long (seven hours) cinematic essay about the Führer's hold over Germany that is at once an interrogation of the past and a castigation of the present.[43]

The story unfolds as an elaborate collage of quotation and allusion in which historic film-clip footage is set against images of a young girl attempting to bring under control her puppet dolls of Hitler and his cronies. In an undisguised studio space the child – actually Syberberg's nine-year-old daughter Amelie – wanders through the junk shop of German history. Sometimes she cradles her Hitler-dog puppet, sometimes she abuses it. Betweentimes, major players in the Reich launch into self-justificatory apologias. No less eloquent are monologues by the likes of Himmler's masseur and Hitler's valet, and by the tour guides of today as they show the public over Berchtesgaden – 'the German Disneyland on the holy mountain near Berchtesgaden', explains the Director of Tourism in the fourth part of the film, 'We Children of Hell', 'an amusement park with special movie showings'.[44] At the end of the second part, the child of today, the child of the cine-age, is seen swathed in celluloid; at the very end of the film, music from *Fidelio* signals the dawn of freedom, but it is not a prospect she is ready to face. She folds her hands in prayer, covers her ears, closes her eyes as though to blot out the nightmare landscape she has traversed. She has been through the world but not been able to find the way back to paradise.

Through all this threads Wagner's music on the soundtrack. As the film opens, the prelude to *Parsifal* accompanies the title credits, and soon it is heard again beneath an extract from Hitler's 1932 speech urging the necessity of a single united party and the need to be prepared to sacrifice all, including one's life, for the greater German cause. And then, soon, music from *Rienzi* (which tells of the rise but also eventually the catastrophic fall of the Roman people's Tribune), as Hitler, now a clown, declares the necessary death of democracy. Much later the Verklärung from *Tristan* accompanies an evocation of mystic oblivion, and the Funeral March from *Götterdämmerung* sounds as a lament for fallen Germany.

A key repeated image is that of a victorious Hitler in a Roman toga rising up out of Wagner's own tomb to the music of the *Rienzi* overture. Syberberg suggests that Hitler was inordinately proud that his name would be for ever associated with Wagner's (as the Hitler puppet declares in the film's third part, 'So long as Wagner's music is played, I will not be forgotten'), and perhaps even that if he had to perish he would take Wagner down with him in a diabolical love-death. (The historical Hitler actually did this, for the autograph full scores of *Die Feen*, *Das Liebesverbot* and *Rienzi*, fair copies of *Das Rheingold* and *Die Walküre*, and other manuscripts all disappeared with him in the bunker.) Through the film there also resounds an echo of a favourite theme of Thomas Mann's, namely that Hitler was a pathological miscarriage of the artistic impulse, an instance of the evil that results when the dreams of art are translated into real-life politics. The film is everywhere in thrall to Wagner's inspirational influence on Nazism.

Against this, Syberberg posits hope of renewal in Beethoven's *Fidelio*, Mahler's Second Symphony ('Resurrection') and Mozart's D minor Piano Concerto, extracts from which round off the first three parts of the film. The plain implication is that beyond Wagner there awaits an unsullied saving Eden of other music, and perhaps most especially that of Mozart. The Elysium of Mozart's music, of Goethe's poetry, of Brentano's folk poetry, of Runge's fairy-tale paintings and of Caspar David Friedrich's symbolic landscapes is seen as that which has to be reclaimed. And it has to be reclaimed precisely because it was not only in Wagner but in the very soil of German Romanticism that National Socialism had professed to find its roots. As tellingly cited in the film, Goebbels was totally smitten with his 'secret mission, the propaganda of a steel-clad Romanticism'.[45]

The film insists that Germany will have to be honest in accepting the Nazi uses of Romanticism before the *Trauerarbeit* can be completed and the romantic legacy reclaimed. The film is also relentlessly self-referential and self-regarding in its implied assertion that Wagner would have been a film maker if he could, that it was film and not music that was the artwork of the future, and that both Hitler and Syberberg are the composer's filmic heirs. Hitler, it is suggested, was a failed and frustrated artist, displacing his ambitions into the political sphere and the creation of a monstrous film production called *The Third Reich*. As Ellerkamp, Hitler's projectionist who 'knew his most secret desires, his dreams, the things he wanted beyond the real world', remarks, 'Yes, the man who controls the cinema controls the future. There is only one future, the future of the cinema, and he knew that.... I know he was really the greatest, the greatest film-maker of all time.'[46] The clear implication is that it was in Hitler's scenography of the Third Reich that Wagner's notion of the 'total work of art' found its apotheosis.

A critique of the Hitler film

Syberberg's *Hitler* is perhaps more successful as a sustained assault against Germany's wilful blindness towards its past, an exposé and critique of perceptions, than as an exorcism of the horrors. Syberberg is a satirist of genius but cannot entirely escape the charge of becoming part of the problem himself. Who but a German would address a topic of overwhelming national importance by making a seven-hour film about it that could hope to get only a very occasional showing attended by the initiated? For the film comes perilously close to being the very alliance between high culture and barbarism which it seeks to discredit. And what hope of this or any other film or work of art cleansing the doors of perception and providing 'innocent', uncontaminated access to the romantic soul of German art?

If anything the effect of Syberberg's *Hitler* was to inflate the problems that persisted in relation to the understanding and enjoyment of Wagner's art. Never before had the extent to which Hitler had drawn inspiration from Wagner been so suggestively explored, but the 'recovery' of an unsullied Wagner seemed, if anything, even more remote.

The way lay open for a swing in Syberberg's attitude to Wagner. In the Ludwig and Hitler films he had been mesmerized by the composer's hold over two very different kinds of romantic dreamer. One comes away with the feeling that Wagner was to blame for the catastrophes of both men. But then Syberberg compels himself to undergo the severest trial of his *Trauerarbeit*, namely to conduct the interviews with Winifred Wagner and there learn the truth about the Wagner–Hitler equation from the survivor who had been closest to it. The result of this was to make him think that Wagner was more sinned against than sinning, and to wish to rescue him by making a film of the opera in which the composer most intimately confronts himself and his art.[47] After the *Confessions of Winifred*, why not the *Confessions of Richard* in the shape of a version of his last opera? Syberberg had reason to believe that film might be able to take over from where, in his view, the stage had foundered.

Wagner's true medium?

There was actually little new in this thought, which, long before the invention of film, is already prefigured by Wagner himself, albeit jokingly, in his wish for an 'invisible stage' – a wish that could, at a pinch, be interpreted as capable of satisfaction by a 'visible screen'. A negative view of such a notion is apparent in Nietzsche's contention that Wagner's music is itself so intrinsically theatrical that the kind of stage representation for which he strove (with a naturalism that could indeed be anachronistically described as 'cinematic') was superfluous, cheapening and crudely sensationalist. Syberberg fancifully writes of Nietzsche's anger that Wagner could have allowed himself to dream 'that his Bayreuth was really a Hollywood'.[48]

Adorno uncharitably rebuked Nietzsche for having 'failed to recognize the artwork of the future in which we witness the birth of film out of the spirit of music'[49] – a development, he might have added, that he himself lamented. For Adorno the cultural dialectician is really putting his own words into Nietzsche's mouth as he simultaneously recognizes and condemns an intimation that film would become the artwork of the twentieth century, a medium certainly reaching far more people than the music drama could ever do. In 1937–8, Adorno observes that 'it is precisely the religious *Parsifal* that makes use of the film-like technique of scene-transformation that marks the climax of this dialectic [i.e., Wagner's readiness to avail himself of the technology of the nineteenth century while at the same time denouncing it]: the magic work of art dreams its complete antithesis, the mechanical work of art'.[50] For Adorno, this was not at all a desirable dream. His remarks expose what he considered to be the composer's self-delusion in creating a transcendental, mystic art while at the same time seeking to substantiate it on the stage with clumsy mechanical means that would one day evolve into technologies that would subvert it even more effectively. Syberberg, on the other hand, takes the opposite point of view: only film could now rescue Wagner from the degradations to which his art had been subjected across a century of theatrical performance.

Strategies for translating opera into film

The relationship between opera and film has of course been problematic from the outset. The film maker has always striven to use scenic realism and close-up to draw the viewer into the action, but this creates an unresolvable tension between the artifice of characters singing and the realism craved by the camera, a disparity only magnified by close takes on the singers' faces. Most generally, as Syberberg has himself described, the strategy has been 'to film the ways of staging opera in the theatre, but using cutting and other filmic tricks to make popular films for the masses'[51] – in other words, the Hollywoodization of opera. Directors like Zeffirelli and Losey have never pretended that their opera films were capturing a stage performance, choosing instead to film in exotic 'real' locations and make 'real' for the viewer what can only be imperfectly shown or suggested on the stage. Other directors like Karajan, Götz Friedrich and Ingmar Bergman have used film to capture as closely as possible a pre-existing stage performance, giving the viewer not only close-ups but other perspectives not available from a single seat in a theatre. In the case of Bergman's *Magic Flute* the response of the theatre audience and glimpses of goings-on backstage are incorporated into the whole. Yet another approach is that exemplified by Peter Brook's three 'Story of Carmen' films, which drastically cut and edited not just the original scenario but also the music itself.

In all such filmic transpositions, the greatest care would have been taken to synchronize the movements of a singer's or actor's lips with the voice on the (usually) pre-recorded soundtrack – although the camera rarely stays with the singer but tries to picture whatever it is he or she is singing about. But there exists another kind of experimental film, such as those made by Carmelo Bene, Werner Schroeter and others, in which there is no attempt at synchronization of what is heard and what is seen and the imagery has only the most tangential connection with the opera in itself.

None of these approaches was right for Syberberg, who wanted to get right away from previous production strategies. Syberberg's answer was not to use film 'Hollywood style' for the depiction of forest, Klingsor's castle and the temple of the Grail, or to create such magical effects as the transformations between forest and temple, but to supply what he argued Wagner himself had really wanted, namely images not illustrative of the music, but rather inspired by it.

It is inconceivable that the composer would have chosen the same images as Syberberg (nor is that important), but he would doubtless have applauded Syberberg's determination that the camera and the editor should allow themselves to be directed by the music, refusing the endemic cinematic temptation to woo the spectator's attention by constantly changing the image. 'The director's task,' says Syberberg, 'was to work with slow movements of actors, heads, faces, camera and lighting.' There would be long continuous takes of up to nine minutes and an interdict against edits for purely visual reasons. Everything would correspond as far as possible with Wagner's 'unendliche Melodie' and its rhythms.[52]

The death-mask: Parsifal *as the confessions of Richard Wagner, and of Germany*

In his Hitler film Syberberg had told the story of a monstrously perverted quest for a political Grail: at its opening the words 'Der Gral' in fractured, block letters slowly move into focus over music from the prelude to the opera, an image given again at the very end, but this time with the word 'Gral' repeated in several different languages. In the *Parsifal* film the quest is to rediscover the dream of a redeeming Grail.[53] The sins and wounds of Klingsor, Kundry and Amfortas are identified with those of Wagner himself and also of the Germany that gave rise to Hitler and would not take the proper steps to bury him. Kundry's seduction of Amfortas and the incurable wound inflicted by Klingsor represent Germany's seduction by evil (and its inability to make good its moral damage).

This then would be a film that rejected realism in favour of a psychological exploration of the opera, of its roots in Wagner's mind, and of its historical afterlife. The opera would be reborn in the light of its relationship with its creator and with history. Thus it was that Syberberg conceived of placing its action on the composer's death-mask, representing what he calls a physiognomic panorama of Wagner's soul.[54] This scenic idea also recapitulated Syberberg's earlier use of the same mask to cue the final stages on the journey towards Hitler at the beginning of the second part of his previous film. That association is no more than marginal in the *Parsifal* film, but it is nevertheless implicit in it. The film, said Syberberg, 'would be an adventure in the head, a vision'.[55]

How, then, does the action relate to its locale on the craggy landscape of the 15 m × 9 m model of Wagner's death-mask, in which the height from the studio floor to the tip of the nose was 4.5 metres? The mask is but seldom seen in its entirety, the individual scenes taking place in appropriate areas of its physiognomy. At the beginning, when trumpet fanfares herald the dawning day, the 'Gralsburg' that is revealed is that of Wagner's own head, with behind it a projection of Caspar David Friedrich's *Kreuz im Gebirge*, one of the most famous images of German Romanticism. A cornucopia of such projected 'quotations' is found throughout the film. At first seen flying like a witch on a horse-model of the sort used for Valkyries in nineteenth-century Bayreuth, an Ophelia-like Kundry soon emerges from a pool that is later revealed as the socket of Wagner's eye. For Gurnemanz's instruction of the squires, the location moves to the cleft of the chin. For the transformation scene, a rift appears in the skull as Gurnemanz sets out to guide Parsifal into the labyrinthine passages of its interior which lead to the temple of the Grail.[56] At this point the hero is a shock-headed youth (Parsifal I), but after the crucial episode of the kiss between Parsifal and Kundry in Act II – and for reasons that will emerge – the role is taken over by a solemn warrior-maiden (Parsifal II).

The significance of Syberberg's choice of physiognomic location is not always clear, as when he describes how Gurnemanz leads Parsifal I 'through the north-south cleft of the chin towards the lips'.[57] A girl representing the 'solo voice from on high' stands sentinel-like upon Wagner's forehead. Klingsor's gilded throne is also placed

Hans Jürgen Syberberg's full-length film version of *Parsifal*, also marking its centenary in 1982, was the antithesis of Ruth Berghaus's stage interpretation. Syberberg revelled in the problematic historical context of the work, hoping to exorcize the ghosts and recover its romantic soul. He placed Klingsor's throne on the brow of the huge death-mask of Wagner which serves as the set. Syberberg's fondness for cultural reference is seen in the waxwork heads of the kindred magicianly figures, Wagner, Ludwig II, Nietzsche, Marx and Aeschylus, that lie at Klingsor's feet. He was both acted and sung by Aage Haugland; Kundry was played by Edith Clever, miming to the voice of Yvonne Minton.

on the composer's brow. When he tries to throw the spear, the effort is too great and he and the throne both crash to the ground on the bridge of Wagner's nose. Kundry is discovered in deep sleep in the eye socket and the skull begins to split open again as the psychological journey continues. The Flowermaidens do not dance but are loitering whores, soliciting for custom from niches in the rocky interior of the skull.

For Parsifal's return to the domain of the Grail and the flowering of the Good Friday meadow, Syberberg found the playing area afforded by the skull too small. He therefore mocked up a separate enlarged section in which an eye socket becomes a pool for the baptisms, with a waterfall flowing down from the bridge of the nose. On the edge of the pool, in the shadow of Wagner's nostrils, is an oasis of greenery and flowers as in a medieval herb garden.

There is a surprising addition to the physiognomic landscape in the shape of an octagonal stone fountain with twelve waterspouts and an angel with outstretched wings holding two pitchers from which water also flows. This was modelled on a fountain in Van Eyck's great altarpiece in Ghent and is intended as the antithesis to the projection of Bosch's vision of hell shown during the seduction scene in Act II.

The resolution in the temple of the Grail takes place in a strange and very cold-looking wasteland. When Parsifal declares, 'Enthüllet den Gral, öffnet den Schrein!' ('Uncover the Grail, open the shrine!'), the skull, seen in profile, moves apart at the fault line under the nose. Through the gap distant icy mountains are glimpsed and in the gap male and female Parsifals, at last united, embrace. For Syberberg this is a resolution of the split consciousness seen in the two Parsifals. The vision of Amfortas and Kundry lying dead alongside each other, and of the Parsifals embracing, effectively provides a utopian apotheosis 'of this work of joyous renunciation and of desolation'.[58]

In none of the golgothan settings is the anatomy assertive or intrusive and it is certainly never incongruous. More immediately arresting – and sometimes puzzling – is the accretion of knowing allusions to paintings, sculptures, temples and ruins thereof, to places associated with Wagner and his writing of the opera, such as the window of the room in the Palazzo Vendramin in Venice where he died, and to the stage settings from 1882. The visual concept is basically so strong and simple that it quickly seems natural, never detracting from the essence of the opera.

Principal images of the film

It is characteristic of Syberberg's imagery that the Amfortas-wound is treated as representative of a whole array of other wounds. Abstracted from Amfortas's body, his wound is on public view as a suppurating pathological exhibit, carried about on a cushion by two female pages whom one is tempted to call 'Wundemädchen'. It is at once a symbol of a mortally ill monarchy and an object of public shame. It is Germany's unassuaged shame and guilt, an object of fascination and horror until it can be healed. Syberberg also intends it as a symbol of original sin and paradise lost, and of course as the wound in Christ's side pierced by the lance. There is also an intentional visual reference to a reliquary from a devotional medieval painting. Behind Titurel, as he lies down to die in his living tomb beneath the throne of Amfortas (modelled on that of Charlemagne in Aachen Cathedral), are photo-projections that are supposedly of wounded warriors awaiting attention in a field hospital. For this is a film that gathers wounds as it rolls; they bleed for mankind and for everything that needs to be healed. Towards the end of the third act the wound has become a smouldering fire of red blood on a bed next to Amfortas's, on which Kundry will soon lie down alongside him.

The images of the Grail are similarly varied. They include projections of Joukowsky's 1882 Grail temple (also shown in ruined form) and a huge crystal which girls load onto a trolley and bring into the temple. At the beginning of Act III, as an image of the goal of Parsifal's journey, the Grail is a model of the Tree of Life, set at the centre of a maze and the whole enclosed in a glass sphere. At the end, during the closing bars, it has become a model of the Festspielhaus, which, cradled in Kundry's arms, is intended to signify a Bayreuth at last redeemed from misinterpretation, from its guilt and ghosts.[59]

Characterization

Gurnemanz, as acted and sung by Robert Lloyd, is a comparatively youthful figure, not bearded and patriarchal but clean-shaven, dark-haired and lighter and more lyrical of voice than usual. Because the opera is imagined as a psycho-drama where time has become space, he does not visibly age between the first and third acts. Amfortas, sung by Wolfgang Schöne, is acted by the conductor Armin Jordan, the gaunt features of whose aquiline profile successfully hold the camera in the long takes of his anguished outpourings. He lies on his litter with sweaty matted hair, sickly pallor and blackened teeth as he is borne to the pool. His profile, surely deliberately, is close to that of Wagner himself. In the temple of the Grail he sits in a toga like an ailing Roman emperor on his throne.

Syberberg is not the first director to have been so mesmerized by Kundry that the opera becomes the story of her redemption rather than that of Amfortas. A more original touch is that she and Amfortas are conceived of as the female and male halves of a single suffering self. They are bound together by her enforced seduction of him and by the wounds thereby inflicted on them both. Both are Klingsor's victims. In the scenes in the temple of the Grail, Kundry is usually close to Amfortas and at the end she expires on a bier laid next to his as though they were husband and wife, a pair brought together by sin and now absolved and reunited in death. It could be the story of Wagner's extramarital liaisons and his wishful resolution of the pain and guilt produced by them. As seen by Syberberg it is also the story of Germany's seduction by an evil that had raped the feminine spirit of Romanticism.

After the shooting of the swan, Parsifal I (the boy) first appears leading in a white horse, but without a bow, the latter soon to be shown as a huge crossbow, set up as a symbolic instrument of wounding (and, says Syberberg, of Parsifal's desire to throttle Kundry) which is passed by Gurnemanz and Parsifal on their way to the temple of the Grail. In the second act Parsifal passes unscathed through the ranks of the Flowermaidens, remaining innocent of his sexuality until Kundry reawakens memories of his mother Herzeleide. When her kiss simultaneously awakens his sexuality and overwhelming feelings of shame and guilt, his place is taken by Parsifal II (the girl). At the moment when Wagner says that Parsifal 'falls into a complete trance', a full-frontal photographic projection of the death-mask appears at the rear and from it steps forward the girl, from whose mouth is heard the tenor voice of Rainer Gold-berg proclaiming, 'Es starrt der Blick dumpf auf das Heilsgefäß' ('My gaze is mes-merized by the holy vessel'). Parsifal I briefly joins voice with her before dissolving into soft focus and disappearing.

It is the rather serious girl Parsifal who sets off on the long restitutional journey back to the Grail and who in Act III, in her leather helmet and jerkin, is rapturously received by Gurnemanz and Kundry. The scenes of her reception and the baptisms that follow are the most touching and beautifully handled in the whole film. The spear transmutes into a crucifix and it is with this that she arrives back in the temple of the Grail. But at the line 'Nur eine Waffe taugt' ('Only one weapon will serve') Parsifal I reappears with the necessary spear. Every wound is healed, though Amfortas and Kundry, as we have seen, die of their cure. The two Parsifals share the closing lines as a duet before they embrace in the cleft that has now opened up at the heart of the death-mask – the animus and anima now healed and whole at last.

Syberberg's logic for dividing the role is not wholly easy to fathom.[60] At the end of the prelude, the camera closes in on the male and female Parsifals wrapt closely

The crucial moment after Kundry's kiss when Karin Krick's female Parsifal II (left) takes over the difficult mission from Michael Kutter's Parsifal I. In Jungian terms, the idea is that the redemptive journey has to be undertaken by the anima because the animus can go no further. From the mouth of both Parsifals resounds the tenor voice of Rainer Goldberg.

together in silent communion before Parsifal I gently breaks free and departs. He leaves Parsifal II behind to dream, Syberberg's idea being that while one Parsifal dreams the other enacts the dream, the roles being reversed at the point of Kundry's kiss.[61] Syberberg speaks of the double act being necessary in order to present the idea of paradisiacal creatures, presumably meaning Parsifal as both Adam and Eve, a very strange spin on Wagner's conception of the 'reiner Tor' (pure fool), which is surely Rousseauesque rather than biblical.[62]

Syberberg says that the moment of changeover after the kiss is not just about the sexuality of our two poles, male and female, or the bringing together of the feminine and the masculine, but about overcoming 'the primeval principle of seduction which is so near and dear to us'.[63] He then goes on to observe that the female Parsifal arrives so that the yearning and pain in the heart of the male Parsifal can begin to be 'resolved on another level'.[64] His Jungian interpretation of the character as a whole is certainly at the furthest remove from any Christian perspective on the opera. An essential ingredient is Syberberg's insistence that Parsifal must be seen through Kundry's eyes. The pain of her double rejection by Parsifals male and female is emphasized. What emerges from the film itself, as distinct from Syberberg's account of it, is that Parsifal's animus, the masculine principle, is on its own powerless to

Kundry (Edith Clever) attempts to seduce Parsifal II (Karin Krick): 'Redeem the world, if this is your destiny: make yourself a god for an hour, and for that let me be damned forever, my wound remain unhealed!'

bring the therapeutic journey through the psychic labyrinth to a successful conclusion in repentance and baptism (the terms are unavoidable), for this journey is
essentially that of the anima alone. Kundry's wound and that of Parsifal are healed
simultaneously in the extraordinarily powerful moment in the third act when the
returning female Parsifal kisses Kundry. One further point must be made. Just as
Syberberg builds up the role of Kundry, so he needs a female Parsifal in order to substantiate his thesis that the opera is about Wagner's soul, about the soul of Germany,
and that this psyche is quintessentially feminine. 'The adventure of this Parsifal is a
journey through Woman. Woman as fundamental image of the world and of life –
for music itself is feminine.'[65]

More mundanely, it is clear that Syberberg had no very high opinion of the ability of the tenor physiognomy to reflect the spiritual progress of Parsifal, preferring
the unwrinkled faces of a youthful male and female. The same thinking guided his
choice of the actress Edith Clever for the role of Kundry rather than its singer Yvonne
Minton, who was nothing short of looks for the part. Only the face, he argued, especially in close-up, could hope to show everything embodied in the character. An
actress was needed to realize things that could not be managed with any singer. It did
not matter if there was a certain discrepancy between voice and face. The music was
the driving expressive force and it would dissolve any seeming discrepancies. Certainly these are considerable in that neither of the two youthful Parsifals is able to
convey the masculine ardour of Rainer Goldberg's tenor rendition. The crucial
moment when, under the petrified gaze of Wagner's mask, the girl steps forward to
replace the boy is certainly very strange. Karin Krick's face is too blank, too newborn,
and when her voice emerges as that of a full-blooded tenor the effect comes across
as odd rather than magical.

Syberberg's somewhat tortuous theorizing is really saying little more than that he
wanted faces that fitted his own conceptions of the characters; that the youthful face
of Lloyd and the rugged complexions of Hans Tschammer and Aage Haugland were
fine for Gurnemanz, Titurel and Klingsor respectively, but that he wanted his chosen
actors for the other roles.[66]

No question that many of the most touching moments are those involving
Kundry. At the beginning of the seduction scene she is seated on a high throne with
a starry sky all around her – a 'Queen of the Night', says Syberberg. As she tells Parsifal I the story of his birth, she becomes Herzeleide, cradling in her arms the puppet
of the child Parsifal seen in Act I. Syberberg exploits to the full the ambivalence of
Wagner's characteristic presentation of erotic love and love of the mother. Kundry's
words are hugely significant for Syberberg's attempt at an expiation of Germany's
guilt: 'Bekenntnis/ wird Schuld in Reue enden,/ Erkenntnis/ in Sinn die Torheit
wenden.' ('Confession turns guilt into remorse, understanding changes folly into
enlightenment.')

Syberberg directs the Good Friday reunion of Kundry and Parsifal as a recapitulation of their encounter in Act II. It is handled with immense tenderness as they
again look into each other's eyes. When the seated Parsifal II greets the flowering of
the meadow, Kundry lays her head on her knee. The whole scene of reconciliation,

In the Good Friday baptism scene, the healing waters begin to flow. Gurnemanz (Robert Lloyd) with Parsifal II (Karin Krick).

absolution and baptism is filmed with a rapt, unflinching concentration on its redemptive power. For Syberberg this scene was of central significance in his project to cleanse and redeem Wagner for his sins and for those trespassed against him. And does this not indeed chime precisely with Gurnemanz's 'Das dankt dann alle Kreatur,/ was all da blüht und bald erstirbt,/ da die entsündigte Natur/ heut ihren Unschuldstag erwirbt.' ('Thus all creation gives thanks for everything that blossoms and soon dies – absolved from sin, nature regains its state of innocence')? As the bells begin to toll the figures advance towards the camera and disappear out of focus.

Cinema versus theatre

Although we can imagine Wagner using film to realize scenic imaginings that could perhaps only be fulfilled in this way, it is doubtful that he would have approved of Syberberg's approach. He had written *Parsifal* to dedicate the Festspielhaus and to be performed nowhere but there. The idea of turning it into a film that could be seen anywhere in the world and at any time would doubtless have appalled him, though he would surely have approved the deeply touching intimacy of the characters' dealings one with another, as they can never register in this way in the theatre. He might well have objected to the portrayal of Parsifal by a young boy and a young girl backed by the voice of a Heldentenor, though his interest in androgyny and in the interaction of the masculine and feminine principles suggests that he might also have been fascinated. But as Jean-Jacques Nattiez points out, Wagner's conception of androgyny is actually very different from Syberberg's.[67]

The question remains whether, as posited earlier, film can be a satisfactory medium for the operas, and if so on what terms. There is an argument which suggests that the music drama could properly be 'made visible' only with the help of a medium that had yet to come into being, and that that medium, quite precisely, is film. Wagner, runs this argument, would have made film if he had been alive today. Hence Susan Sontag's suggestion that 'Wagner's fantasy of the invisible stage was fulfilled more literally in that immaterial stage, cinema' – and that fantasy was of course provoked specifically by the composer's frustrations in staging *Parsifal*.[68] It is certainly what Syberberg himself believes, but it will not hold water as a philosophy suggesting that theatre is obsolete and that film is its successor and the 'artwork of the future' to which Wagnerian opera had once aspired.

Syberberg asks that his film should 'be seen in the light of the laughable and painful images of the past hundred years of the opera's history',[69] thus apparently writing off the entire stage production history as worthless, with not a single exception cited to the contrary – no Wieland Wagner, no Herz, no Berghaus, though settings of various Wagner operas by Wieland and by Chéreau are quoted in the course of the film.

Syberberg's disparagement of stage performance appears to apply not only to 'traditional' productions but *also* to those which have sought to engage with the social and political dimension of Wagner's works and to perform him as our uncomfortable but always inspiring contemporary. He makes no acknowledgement that great theatre work has been produced by his contemporaries, and that they too have sought to lay the ghosts, to find new ways of bridging the gap between the works as an expression of the composer and his century and the works as they reflect and refract modern concerns, modern perspectives, the world as we see it today. Set alongside the political interpretations of a Herz, the naked theatricality of a Chéreau, or the probing deconstruction of a Berghaus, Syberberg's film is extraordinarily retrogressive in its amalgam of 'innocent' storytelling, psycho-surreal invention and contingent imagery about the opera's entanglement with German history. In effect he sets up a dialectic between the innocence of *Parsifal*'s integrity as a work of art and its painful relations with Wagner's life and what history has subsequently made of it.

Syberberg opens the shrine. In the concluding scene, Parsifal II has returned the holy spear (transformed into a crucifix) and healed Amfortas's wound. The full profile of Wagner's death-mask becomes visible for the first time. The mask slowly splits apart to reveal the male and female Parsifals finally united.

It is mistaken of Syberberg not to acknowledge that film also has its limitations as a Wagnerian medium. He writes that 'It is only in myth as an act of human cultural will that we get hold of our history, unabashed'.[70] Yes, certainly, but whereas film crystallizes myth, freezes a particular view of it, only theatre has the transformational fluidity to help it develop, grow, change. The composer's own view of a myth-based theatre was that this was the most potent way for myth to renew itself and continue to speak eloquently to successive generations by tuning in to the different mental horizons of those generations. A film of an opera, in framing a single interpretation and perpetuating it on celluloid, exhibits all the pathos of a work of art in Benjamin's 'age of mechanical reproduction'. It acquires an instant immortality, but at the price of being born locked for ever into its historical moment. The real way in which, unabashed or not, we can reclaim that part of our history which is bound up with Wagner is not through even the most searching, suggestive film but through the reinterpretation and recreation of his mythopoeic operas over and over again in the evanescent medium of stage performance – and of course by continuing to make new films too.

Syberberg's *Parsifal* is not to be evaluated on the criterion of comparison with stage performance. It is simply a film that demonstrates that the film medium has a far greater potential for Wagner than had previously been realized. It stays with the music and the words, while being amazingly free and inventive. It discovers potentialities within the work that are not accessible to stage performance. It expands Wagner without betraying his essential core. It opens up a new and different seam of interpretative possibility. What is certainly not established is the thesis (if it really is that) that film, not the stage, is the only authentic medium for the production of Wagner's works.

Requiem for a lost paradise

Au fond Syberberg knew that he was rounding something off with his *Parsifal*, not pioneering a path to future interpretation. This *Parsifal*, he says, 'seems like a distant memory from the past ... we end with the distant sound of Kundry's voice ["Schlafen – schlafen – ich muβ"] and the sound of bells, like an echo of our memories of the culture that has disappeared, and of our life and the history of mankind and its adventures, slowly disappearing into the darkness of the final fade-out'.[71] It is really a requiem for the work and for Wagner, a farewell and an embalmment with all honours and profound feeling of a strain of art that, in his view, belonged to the past and defied revival without mortal damage. For all his invocation of a paradise, and of the hope of finding a return thither through its back gate, Syberberg's real belief was that the game was over, and that no such miracle could ever happen. 'The film,' writes Syberberg, embodies 'reflections of a post-Hitlerian existence and fragments of memories from Germany before our end arrives.'[72]

Redemption might indeed be possible for Parsifal, for Wagner and for the effects of his legacy, but the atonement and forgiveness could properly lead only to a longing for silence and oblivion. Syberberg's sentiments at the end of the film are those of Kundry's 'Let me only rest ... I must sleep', recapitulated from the first act. The temple of the Grail has become an icicled tomb, the Festspielhaus a frozen exhibit cradled by Kundry. Saved, perhaps, but with scant promise of a future.

Does Syberberg succeed in winning through against Hitler and the uncomfortable side of Wagner? The trouble is that in the Hitler and Winifred films he had dwelt with such exhaustive intensity on Wagner as an inspirational force in Nazi ideology as perhaps to energize rather than exorcise the demons. Could it not be that it was his awareness of this danger that steered him towards making his *Parsifal*? It would be a film in which everyone would be redeemed – Germany in the shape of Amfortas and Kundry, Wagner for his own manifold sins, and finally the film maker himself for having overindulged an obsession with the Third Reich's roots in Romanticism, and for having imagined that history can ever be unwound and the 'purity and innocence' of pre-Hitlerian culture (which assuredly never existed as such) restored.

Yet in his desire to exonerate Wagner he surely does, at least partially, succeed, for Syberberg rightly shows a *Parsifal* whose message of redemption and restitution is the antithesis of everything the Nazis stood for. In this sense they are exposed, yet again, as uncomprehending Wagnerians, as promulgators of a Wagner who never existed. To do this Syberberg perhaps needed his 'other level' of fairy tale and dream awareness – not to engage as some productions have done with the alleged anti-semitic and nationalistic content of the work, but to ignore it and return to the opera's mythopoeic genesis.

Trust the story, trust the music, and trust me to resuscitate the sleepwalking innocence of a transcendental work of art. The uncomfortable material is there, but it is shown as the detritus along Parsifal's route. It is shown as precisely that which Parsifal has to overcome and leave behind before he is able to find his way back to the Grail. Not for Syberberg a savage youth who discovers the error of his ways, but two ethereal creatures who remain uncannily pure and are, on this 'other level', a reproach and redemptive 'correction' to the world about them, whether within the narrative of the film, or by metaphorical implication in the society against which it was launched. Syberberg does not confront the charges of bad faith levelled at Wagner and the opera, insisting rather that they are irrelevant to his contention that *Parsifal* is a great work of art, a metaphor which subsumes the dross that may have gone into its making and that has dogged its hundred-year history into something transcendent, inspiring and even redemptive.

Having conceived his *Parsifal* 'against everything that surrounds us today',[73] Syberberg knew full well that 'in our pluralistic consumer-democracy' the film would be 'as unwelcome as is the Hitler film to the children of the Hitler generation'.[74] In Germany (which was the target of his cultural critique) that indeed turned out to be the case. In the East, from where he came, his films were condemned for accusing the socialist state of being a reincarnation of the Third Reich. In the West he was denounced for being 'proudly nostalgic for the Hitler Youth, dreaming of an idealistic, ecological and anti-Semitic fascism'.[75] In both parts of Germany his insistence on a *Trauerarbeit* that involved shaking skeletons which people believed were better left in the cupboard, and his castigation of mass culture's devaluation of the sacred cultural heritage, won him few friends. The French, however, took a very different view, seeing in him 'the German the French have always wanted – an iconoclast and a romantic'. They were excited by his films (admirers included Michel Foucault, Gilles Deleuze, Bernard Sobel) and believed that he really was exorcizing 'the currents which made Hitler possible'.[76] They helped finance his films and gave him an intellectual support base, so that it is no surprise that he should have made Paris his home for many years. Interest in his work was stimulated across the English-speaking world by the impassioned but by no means uncritical advocacy of the American writer Susan Sontag.

Syberberg's films are immensely worth revisiting, not just as documents of the essential process of laying the ghosts of Nazi appropriation, of coming to terms with the entanglement of Wagner's works with twentieth-century history, but for their superabundant imagery and, in the *Parsifal* film, the depth and resonance of Syberberg's imagination as an artist. For all that the film comes across as a requiem for the composer rather than staking out a path to his future, it stands as an isolated achievement, awaiting the day when someone will pick up its challenge and again interpret Wagner as brilliantly on film as he has been in the theatre.

Over the horizon

The interpretations of Wagner with which this chapter has been concerned have shown three very different approaches to the historical task of reinventing the composer as our uncomfortable contemporary. Beyond the zone of palpable 'relevance' has been glimpsed a future in which the operas are rediscovered as mythopoeic, magical and ultimately mysterious. Taking a swipe at the cruder production assaults by 'political adventurers' – which have largely gone unrecorded in these pages – Boulez suggested that perhaps this 'purification through infamy' had been necessary in order that Wagner's myths and symbols 'could take on their true meaning and escape the chance circumstances of their origins'.[77]

Chéreau and Boulez effectively brought to an end the Germanic hegemony. They did not neglect the intrinsic political content of the *Ring*, but regarded the work critically with its flaws and discontinuities freely on show. Their interpretation powerfully demonstrated its timeless modernity. Berghaus's production marked the end of a long era in which directors had allowed themselves to imagine they could make coherent sense of the *Ring*. It was a 'writing degree zero' approach in which authorial 'intentions' were set at naught. At the opposite extreme from Chéreau, the characters were not flesh and blood but rather ciphers entrusted with the task of decoding themselves. The *Ring* was a labyrinth in which we were all lost and would never find the way out. In part, the production was a response to the sheer descriptiveness of the music, setting up an inquisitorial theatricality which wanted to question and comment on it. The production's avant-garde extremism made people wonder whether a route could ever be found back to a 'romantic' Wagner – a challenge taken up by Berghaus's fellow countryman Syberberg. Setting out from opposed perspectives, both directors came up with centennial productions of *Parsifal* in 1982. The strange thing is that Syberberg's 'romantic' view of *Parsifal* nevertheless ended up, like Berghaus's, as an obituary for the work. They both regarded the Grail community as terminally doomed. In Berghaus the fire turns to ice, in Syberberg it is as though the beauty of the enactment is to be preserved for ever in an icy tomb. There was something uncomfortably, eerily valedictory about both interpretations, virtually defying anyone to take the work further.

An extreme response to this challenge came in 1991 in Hamburg from the American stage artist Robert Wilson, who showed, if nothing else, that it is not only German directors who find the work peculiarly problematic. Wilson rejected the imagery of Grail and spear as too explicit, too reminiscent of the Christianity that had inspired it. He wanted to break through to a deeper layer of abstraction in order to complete what Nike Wagner has called the 'desanctifying, depsychologising and [even] desexualization' of the opera. Thus no spear, no Kundry kiss and the Grail as a black box retrieved from a glowing pyramid of ice. All problems over the identity of the knights were solved by banishing them from the stage, leaving their voices to sound unseen from the theatre's highest balcony. The principal characters were lost souls wandering in a stage space that was an image of their imaginations. Wilson's staging was cold, austerely beautiful in its lighting and its stylized choreography. It was a vision into which every spectator could project his or her feelings about primeval wounds, about an unhealable, aching pain at the heart of human existence.[78]

The endlessly problematic relationship between the composer's life and his art has been explored in productions all over the world – sometimes with aggressive intent, sometimes defensively. The hard questions asked by the intellectual prosecution, what might be called the negative critique, have paradoxically, I believe, had a positive effect. They have inspired productions that have been outstanding precisely because of the 'drama' of their interrogation of works which, *pace* Syberberg, have never been entirely innocent but always fraught with turbulence and subversion.

The radical new approaches staked out by Chéreau, Berghaus and, to a lesser extent, Syberberg effectively demolished all inhibitions over the interpretation of Wagner's works, unleashing new energies and new impulses far and wide. Writing in 1992 I noted 'Brechtian assaults on Wagner's theatre of illusion, overtly political interpretations, surrealistic fantasizing, deconstructions with extensive use of "quotation" techniques, multiple framing (play within a play), time-travelling between different periods, suspensions of belief, suspensions of disbelief, all-out critical fragmentation, antiheroic and deflationary presentations, the pursuit of unity, the pursuit of disunity, science-fiction fantasies, productions attacking, denouncing, debunking Wagner, and productions handing the burden of sense-making entirely over to the audience'.[79] More than ten years later this roll-call could be extended very much further. It would inevitably include a fair proportion of stupidities not worth dignifying with analysis, for I believe that it is only from productions of outstanding quality that there is anything to be learnt. Numbered among the latter would be Richard Jones's 1995 *Siegfried* at Covent Garden, in which a *Waiting for Godot* slant on the scene in which the Wanderer, Alberich and Mime squabble outside Fafner's cave made the best theatrical sense of it I have ever seen. At Bayreuth in 1999 Keith Warner and Stefanos Lazaridis discovered previously unplumbed symbolic and psychological depths in *Lohengrin*. Many more examples could be added.

The sheer diversity of Wagner stage interpretations at the beginning of the twenty-first century only confirms the capacity of his operas for perennial self-renewal. It is a measure of their enduring vitality that they can elicit such a wealth of enthralling and provocative responses. All the Wagnerian problematics are of course in the end swept away by the overwhelming power of the music. And if it was always the total dramatic conception – words, music and staging – that mattered to Wagner, in the end it is to the music that we return. Boulez surely has it exactly right when he says that he and Chéreau wanted their staging not to be an end in itself but always to lead back into the 'invisible theatre' of the music[80] – and, it should be added, on into the imaginary theatre of the mind.

NOTES

A key to the abbreviations adopted for frequently cited titles is included with the bibliography. All other titles are fully referenced at their first mention; thereafter they appear in shortened form.

Chapter 1

1 Eduard Hanslick, *Aus dem Opernleben der Gegenwart* (vol. III of Hanslick's collected writings, *Die moderne Oper*, 9 vols, 1875–1900), Berlin 1884, 324. The word 'regisseur' was in use at least as early as 1771, when it was used to describe the directorial role undertaken by Stephanie, a leading actor in a play in Vienna. Martina Srocke, *Wagner als Regisseur*, Munich/Salzburg 1988, 23. It does not diminish the hyperbole of Hanslick's description to point out that composers had attempted to direct stagings of their works long before Wagner did so. Obvious instances include in the seventeenth century Lully in France and in the eighteenth century Jommelli in Germany. The role of the regisseur in Germany in the nineteenth century, and particularly the transition from functionary stage manager to a director with a significant artistic role, is described in Arne Langer, *Der Regisseur und die Aufzeichnungspraxis der Opernregie im 19. Jahrhundert*, Frankfurt (Peter Lang) 1997. Langer discusses Wagner's part in this process on pp. 179–85 and pp. 244–7. For stage direction in Italy, see Lorenzo Bianconi and Giorgio Pestelli, eds, *The History of Italian Opera*, vol. IV, trans. Lydia G. Cochrane (*Opera Production and Its Resources*), Chicago 1998, and vol. V, trans. Kate Singleton (*Opera on Stage*), Chicago 2002.

2 'Das Wiener Hof-Operntheater' (The Vienna Opera-House) SSD VII, 283 (PW III, 374).

3 'Über die Aufführung des *Tannhäuser*' (On performing *Tannhäuser*), SSD V, 126–8 (PW III, 171–3).

4 John Warrack, *Carl Maria von Weber*, 2nd edn, Cambridge 1976, 205.

5 ML, 5. *Der Weinberg an der Elbe* was actually written to celebrate the marriage of Princess Maria Anna Carolina of Saxony and Grand Duke Leopold of Tuscany on 15 November 1817. Oswald Georg Bauer, *Richard Wagner Goes to the Theatre*, trans. Stewart Spencer, Bayreuth 1996, 12–13 (see n.26 below).

6 Ferdinand Avenarius (Cäcilie Geyer's son) in 'Richard Wagner als Kind. Nach Erinnerungen seiner Schwester Cäcilie Avenarius und anderer Jugendgenossen', *Allgemeine Zeitung* (Munich), 15 March 1883, quoted in Herbert Barth, Dietrich Mack and Egon Voss, eds, *Wagner: A Documentary Study*, trans. P. R. J. Ford and M. Whittall, London 1975, 151.

7 Karl Theodor von Küstner, *Rückblick auf das Leipziger Stadttheater*, Leipzig 1830, 235, quoted in Ernest Newman, *The Life of Richard Wagner*, 4 vols. New York 1933–46, repr. 1966, I, 137n.

8 Küstner, *Rückblick*, 44–154, quoted in Newman, *Wagner* I, 137n.

9 Eduard Genast, *Aus Weimars klassischer Zeit: Erinnerungen eines alten Schauspielers*, ed. Robert Kohlrausch, Stuttgart 1905, 58, quoted in Newman, *Wagner* I, 146. For Devrient, see p. 27 below.

10 Newman, *Wagner* I, 147.
11 Quoted in Newman, *Wagner* I, 145.
12 Warrack, *Weber*, 205.
13 From a review of an 1816 Berlin performance of E. T. A. Hoffmann's opera *Undine*, in Carl Maria von Weber, *Writings on Music*, ed. John Warrack, trans. Martin Cooper, Cambridge 1981, 201.
14 Weber, *Writings*, 205.
15 Weber, *Writings*, 224.
16 Weber, *Writings*, 226.
17 Warrack, *Weber*, 206.
18 Weber, *Writings*, 227.
19 Warrack, *Weber*, 206–7.
20 ML, 285.
21 John Warrack, 'The Musical Background', in Peter Burbidge and Richard Sutton, eds, *The Wagner Companion*, London 1979, 87–8.
22 Warrack, *Weber*, 206–7.
23 ML, 37. See also 'Über Schauspieler und Sänger' (On Actors and Singers), SSD IX, 219–30 (PW V, 217–28).
24 Bauer, *Wagner Goes to the Theatre*, 34–7 and 40. Wagner's own account of Schröder-Devrient as Romeo is in ML, 80–1.
25 ML, 26.
26 ML, 36–7. Wagner's experiences as a theatre-goer were chronicled in an exhibition at Bayreuth in 1996 accompanied by an outstanding illustrated study: Oswald Georg Bauer, *Richard Wagner Goes to the Theatre*, trans. Stewart Spencer, Bayreuth 1996. Although Wagner fails to include any works by Weber in his Leipzig listing there is no doubt that he was well acquainted with *Der Freischütz*, the Singspiel *Preciosa* and *Silvana*, in which Luise Wagner played the title role. He would also have seen *Oberon*, premiered in Leipzig in 1826. There were at least 162 performances of Weber's theatre works given in Leipzig before 1828. Bauer, *Wagner Goes to the Theatre*, 21.
27 Newman, *Wagner* I, 99.
28 ML, 73.
29 ML, 79.
30 ML, 100.
31 Newman, *Wagner* I, 178.
32 ML, 113 and 112.
33 ML, 124.
34 John Deathridge, *Wagner's 'Rienzi': A Reappraisal Based on a Study of the Sketches and Drafts*, Oxford 1977, 20.

35 Carl Friedrich Glasenapp, *Das Leben Richard Wagners in sechs Büchern*, repr. Vaduz/Liechtenstein 1977, I, 288–9, quoted in Barth, *Documentary Study*, 160. See also Carl Friedrich Glasenapp, *Richard Wagner in Riga*, Riga 1913.
36 The plans are reproduced in Carl-Friedrich Baumann, *Bühnentechnik im Festspielhaus Bayreuth*, Munich 1980, 19. See also Elmar Arro, 'Richard Wagners Rigaer Wanderjahre. Über einige baltische Züge im Schaffen Wagners', *Musik des Ostens* (Kassel), 3 (1965), 125–68.
37 William Ashton Ellis, *Life of Richard Wagner*, 6 vols, London 1900–8, I, 248n and 263–4n.
38 ML, 197.
39 Quoted in Jane F. Fulcher, *The Nation's Image: French Grand Opera as Politics and Politicized Art*, Cambridge 1987, 60.
40 Quoted in David Charlton, 'The Nineteenth Century: France', in Roger Parker, ed., *The Oxford Illustrated History of Opera*, Oxford 1994, 127.
41 Gösta M. Bergman, *Lighting in the Theatre*, trans. N. Stedt, Stockholm/Totowa (New Jersey) 1977, 202.
42 Carl Dahlhaus, *Nineteenth-Century Music*, trans. J. Bradford Robinson, Berkeley/Los Angeles 1989, 128.
43 Heinz and Gudrun Becker, *Giacomo Meyerbeer: A Life in Letters*, ed. Reinhard G. Pauly, trans. Mark Violette, London 1989, 71.
44 Fulcher, *The Nation's Image*, 180.
45 Becker, *Meyerbeer*, 71.
46 H. Robert Cohen, *The Original Staging Manuals for Twelve Parisian Operatic Premieres*, Stuyvesant 1991.
47 Quoted in Bergman, *Lighting*, 134.
48 Bergman, *Lighting*, 226.
49 For the involvement of such notable artists as Caspar David Friedrich and Karl Friedrich Schinkel, see Birgit Verwiebe, 'Transparent Painting and the Romantic Spirit: Experimental Anticipations of Modern Visual Arts', trans. David Britt, in Keith Hartley et al., eds, *The Romantic Spirit in German Art 1790–1990* (exhibition catalogue), Edinburgh/London 1994–5, 171–7.
50 Phyllis Hartnoll, ed., *The Oxford Companion to the Theatre*, 4th edn, Oxford 1983, 502–3.
51 Bergman, *Lighting*, 228–9. The only

known illustration of the Eidophusikon is a watercolour by E. F. Burney in the British Museum. It is reproduced and discussed by Sybil Rosenfeld in 'The Eidophusikon Illustrated', *Theatre Notebook*, 18, no. 2 (Winter 1963–4), 52–4. Argand lamps were used for the first time in the premiere of Beaumarchais's *Le Mariage de Figaro* at the Comédie-Française (27 April 1784). They made their debut at the Paris Opéra a year later. Bergman, *Lighting*, 200.

52 John Britton, *The Autobiography of John Britton*, 2 vols, London 1850, I, 97–101, quoted in Frederick Penzel, *Theatre Lighting before Electricity*, Middletown (Connecticut) 1978, 23.

53 Bergman, *Lighting*, 232, with good illustrations of the Diorama.

54 Warrack, 'Musical Background', 90.

55 Bergman, *Lighting*, 278, with illustration; David Charlton, 'Paris' (4), in Stanley Sadie, ed., *The New Grove Dictionary of Opera*, 4 vols, London 1992. See also Helmut and Alison Gernsheim, *L. J. M. Daguerre: The History of the Diorama and the Daguerreotype*, New York 1969.

56 Recent research on this by Karin Pendle is cited in Charlton, 'The Nineteenth Century: France', 145.

57 ML, 197; Bauer, *Wagner Goes to the Theatre*, 63.

58 'Erinnerungen an Auber' (Reminiscences of Auber), SSD IX, 42–60 (PW V, 35–55); 'Erinnerungen an Spontini' (Reminiscences of Spontini), SSD V, 86–104 (PW III, 123–43).

59 'Halévy und die Französische Oper', SSD XII, 131–48; '*La Reine de Chypre* d'Halévy', SSD XII, 406–13 (the two articles are combined as 'Halévy and *La Reine de Chypre*', PW VIII, 175–200).

60 CD I, 848 (25 May 1875), and II, 429 (17 January 1880).

61 'Über Meyerbeers *Hugenotten*', SSD XII, 22–30 (not published in full until 1911 and therefore not in PW).

62 ML, 197.

63 Oswald Georg Bauer, *Richard Wagner: The Stage Designs and Productions from the Premières to the Present*, New York 1983, 27–8. See also Deathridge, *Rienzi*, 20.

64 *The Memoirs of Hector Berlioz*, trans. David Cairns, 2nd edn, London 1977, 303.

65 Deathridge, *Rienzi*, 51.

66 Deathridge, *Rienzi*, 21 and 11.

67 Letter to Ernst Benedikt Kietz, 6 September 1842, SL, 95. I am unaware of any evidence that she actually did so.

68 Warrack, 'Musical Background', 90.

69 Bergman, *Lighting*, 230.

70 Warrack, 'Musical Background', 91.

71 Letter of 28 February 1841, quoted in Bauer, *Stage Designs*, 26.

72 'Über Eduard Devrients *Geschichte der deutschen Schauspielkunst*' (On E. Devrient's *History of German Acting*), SSD XII, 230–2 (PW VIII, 218–21).

73 MLg, 166.

74 ML, 244.

75 ML, 244 and 266–7.

76 ML, 242.

77 ML, 242–3.

78 Berlioz, *Memoirs*, 303.

79 'Die Königliche Kapelle betreffend', SSD XII, 151–204 (not in PW); 'Entwurf zur Organisation eines deutschen National-Theaters für das Königreich Sachsen', SSD II, 233–73 (PW VII, 319–60).

80 'Theater-Reform', SSD XII, 233–6 (PW VIII, 222–5); 'Nochmals Theater-Reform', SSD XII, 237–9 (not in PW).

81 Bauer, *Stage Designs*, 50.

82 Bauer, *Stage Designs*, 50.

83 ML, 263.

84 Bauer, *Stage Designs*, 50. Trained as an architect, Schinkel (1781–1841) studied painting in Italy and France (1803–5). Thereafter he worked in Berlin, painting panoramas and dioramas and using lighting and transparency effects for devising scenic spectacles with musical accompaniment. His best-known scenic designs are for *Die Zauberflöte* (1816). See Helmut Borch-Supan, *Karl Friedrich Schinkel: Bühnenentwürfe*, 2 vols, Berlin 1990 (text in German and English), and, for a general introduction, Michael Snodin, ed., *Karl Friedrich Schinkel: A Universal Man*, New Haven/London 1991.

85 'Bemerkungen zur Aufführung der Oper *Der fliegende Holländer*', SSD V, 160–8 (PW III, 207–17). For a much better translation, see Thomas Grey, ed., *Richard Wagner: 'Der fliegende Holländer'* (Cambridge Opera Handbook), Cambridge 2000, 193–200. Wagner's correspondence with Liszt is illuminating on the problems of realizing his intentions on the stage: *Franz Liszt–Richard Wagner Briefwechsel*, ed.

Hanjo Kesting, Frankfurt 1988. For an earlier, incomplete English selection, see *Correspondence of Wagner and Liszt*, trans. Francis Hueffer, 2 vols, London 1888. Liszt's Weimar performances, with an orchestra of about thirty-five and chorus of about twenty-five, dispelled the myth that Wagner's operas could only succeed in the largest theatres, and were therefore invaluable to the composer. But they still left much to be desired (see, inter alia, Newman, *Wagner* I, 136). Friends told Wagner that the first performance of *Lohengrin* (28 August 1850) left much to be desired, confirming his hunch that Liszt would not be able to effect the necessary reforms and inspiring the idea that he would have to build a festival theatre of his own.

86 ML, 243.

87 SSD V, 161–2 (PW III, 210) – and a great deal more in the same vein.

88 *Richard Wagner in Bayreuth*, in Friedrich Nietzsche, *Werke*, ed. Karl Schlechta, 5 vols, Frankfurt 1972, I, 418. See also Stefan Kunze, 'The Role of Nature in Wagner's Music Dramas', in BP *Siegfried* 1972, 25–44, and Roswitha Karpf, 'Die naturphilosophischen Elemente in Richard Wagners Bühnenfestspiel *Der Ring des Nibelungen*', diss. Karl-Franzens-Universität, Graz, 1972.

89 Quoted in Newman, *Wagner* III, 312.

90 'Bemerkungen zur Aufführung der Oper *Der fliegende Holländer*', SSD V, 160 (PW III, 209).

91 Wagner's annotations are in the C. F. Peters edition of the vocal score, ed. Gustav Brecher, Frankfurt 1914.

92 *Das Kunstwerk der Zukunft* (The Artwork of the Future), SSD III, 152 (PW I, 186): 'das lebendige Abbild der Natur'.

93 'Bemerkungen zur Aufführung der Oper *Der fliegende Holländer*', SSD V, 160 (PW III, 209).

94 'Bemerkungen zur Aufführung der Oper *Der fliegende Holländer*', SSD V, 161 (PW III, 209).

95 ML, 308–9.

96 'Meine Erinnerungen an Ludwig Schnorr von Carolsfeld' (My Recollections of Ludwig Schnorr von Carolsfeld), SSD VIII, 183 (PW IV, 233).

97 Newman, *Wagner* I, 397.

98 CD II, 996 (23 January 1883).

99 There are four recognizable versions of *Tannhäuser*, none definitive. See WWV, 257ff.

100 'Scenirung der Oper *Tannhäuser*' survives only in two manuscript copies, neither by Wagner himself: a copy by Heinrich Ploch in the Hessische Landes- und Hochschulbibliothek, Darmstadt (LaBi Hs. 3933), and a copy by an unknown hand in the Fritz Reuter-Richard Wagner-Museum, Eisenach (I 108 and 408). 'Costumbeschreibung zur Oper *Tannhäuser*' exists only in a copy by an unknown hand in the Fritz Reuter-Richard Wagner-Museum, Eisenach (I 109 and 409). These three copies, unquestionably of Wagner's instructions and including also material by his designer Ferdinand Heine, are reproduced in facsimile and transcribed in Dietrich Steinbeck, ed., *Richard Wagners 'Tannhäuser'-Szenarium*, Berlin (Gesellschaft für Theatergeschichte) 1968, respectively 31–75, 76–89 and 90–122. 'Über die Aufführung des *Tannhäuser*: eine Mitteilung an die Dirigenten und Darsteller dieser Oper', SSD V, 123–59 (PW III, 167–205).

101 See Newman, *Wagner* II, 317.

102 'Über die Aufführung des *Tannhäuser*', SSD V, 148 (PW, III, 194).

103 'Über die Aufführung des *Tannhäuser*', SSD V, 149 and 147 (PW III, 195 and 193).

104 Bauer, *Stage Designs*, 74.

105 Newman, *Wagner* II, 317.

106 *Das Kunstwerk der Zukunft*, SSD III, 151–2 (PW I, 185).

107 Quoted in Bauer, *Stage Designs*, 71.

108 Quoted in Bauer, *Stage Designs*, 76.

109 Bauer, *Stage Designs*, 73–4.

110 Ferdinand Heine, *Decorative und costümliche Scenirung der Oper 'Lohengrin' von Richard Wagner. In Auftrag des Dichters entworfen*, Leipzig 1854.

111 *Richard Wagner in Bayreuth*, in Friedrich Nietzsche, *Untimely Meditations*, trans. R. J. Hollingdale, Cambridge 1983, 206.

112 For a detailed discussion of the 1861 Paris *Tannhäuser*, see Carolyn Abbate, 'The Parisian "Venus" and the "Paris" *Tannhäuser*', *JAMS*, 36 (1983), 73–123, and Carolyn Abbate, 'The "Parisian" *Tannhäuser*', diss. University of Princeton, 1984.

113 Newman, *Wagner* II, 107.

114 ML, 625.

115 Newman, *Wagner* II, 63–4.

116 Quoted in Newman, *Wagner* III, 85, from Hans von Bülow, *Briefe*, 7 vols, Leipzig 1899–1908, III, 382.

117 Charles Baudelaire, *The Painter of Modern Life and Other Essays*, ed. and trans. Jonathan Mayne, London 1964, 126.

118 Newman, *Wagner* III, 105.

Chapter 2

1 *Die Kunst und die Revolution*, SSD III, 8–41 (PW I, 21–65); *Das Kunstwerk der Zukunft*, SSD III, 42–177 (PW I, 67–213); *Oper und Drama*, SSD III, 222–320, and IV, 1–229 (PW II, 1–376); *Eine Mitteilung an meine Freunde*, SSD IV, 230–344 (PW I, 267–392); letter to Liszt, 20 November 1851, SL, 234.

2 *Die Kunst und die Revolution*, SSD III, 26–7 (PW I, 50).

3 *Oper und Drama*, SSD IV, 64 (PW II, 191).

4 *Das Kunstwerk der Zukunft*, SSD III, 117–48 (PW I, 149–81).

5 See in particular the 'Besondere Bemerkungen für die Scene' (Special Remarks on the Staging), which includes sketches by Wagner for the layout of the opera's three acts (SSD XVI, 63–73; not in PW). Also the letters to Liszt and Genast in SB III, 291, 343, 353, 376 and 568.

6 *Das Kunstwerk der Zukunft*, SSD III, 153 (PW I, 186).

7 *Oper und Drama*, SSD III, 270 (PW II, 62).

8 *Eine Mitteilung an meine Freunde*, SSD IV, 321 (PW I, 367).

9 *Letters of Richard Wagner: The Burrell Collection*, ed. John N. Burk, London 1951, 309.

10 Arthur Schopenhauer, *The World As Will and Representation*, trans. E. F. J. Payne, 2 vols, New York 1969, I, 257 (translation amended).

11 *Das Kunstwerk der Zukunft*, SSD III, 60 (PW I, 88).

12 'Über Franz Liszt's Symphonische Dichtungen' (On Franz Liszt's Symphonic Poems), SSD V, 191 (PW III, 246).

13 SL, 324.

14 SB VIII, 230.

15 Arthur Schopenhauer, *Parerga and Paralipomena*, trans. E. F. J. Payne, 2 vols, Oxford 1974, II, 432.

16 Preface to the second edition (1863) of the *Ring* poem, SSD VI, 278 (PW III, 280).

17 The Court Theatre burnt down in 1869, but was rebuilt by Semper and his son Manfred, 1871–8.

18 See Newman, *Wagner* III, 412–21. The plans for the Munich festival theatre are documented in Heinrich Habel, *Festspielhaus und Wahnfried*, Munich 1985. For Semper, see Harry Francis Mallgrave, *Gottfried Semper: Architect of the Nineteenth Century*, New Haven/London 1996.

19 Patrick Carnegy, 'Landfall on the Stage: A Brief Production History', in Grey, *Der fliegende Holländer*, 100.

20 Wilfrid Blunt, *The Dream King*, London 1970, 29–30.

21 Quoted in Rupert Hacker, ed., *Ludwig II. von Bayern in Augenzeugenberichten*, Munich 1972, 77.

22 Hacker, *Ludwig II.*, 77.

23 Kurt Hommel, *Die Separatvorstellungen vor König Ludwig II. von Bayern*, Munich 1963, 168ff.

24 Letter to Ludwig, 21–2 July 1865, SL, 650.

25 Günter Metken, 'Wagner and the Visual Arts', in Ulrich Müller and Peter Wapnewski, eds, *The Wagner Handbook*, translation edited by John Deathridge, Cambridge (Massachusetts) 1992, 354.

26 The frescoes were destroyed in the Second World War; copies by Franz Heigel exist and are reproduced in Detta and Michael Petzet, *Die Richard Wagner-Bühne König Ludwigs II.*, Munich 1970, plates 349–78. See also pp. 183–4.

27 Michael Petzet, 'Ludwig and the Arts', in Blunt, *Dream King*, 239. For Wagner and Ludwig's attitudes to historicism, see Manfred Eger, 'The Patronage of King Ludwig II', in Müller, *Wagner Handbook*, 317.

28 Bauer, *Stage Designs*, 142.

29 'Über die Benennung "Musikdrama"', (On the Term 'Musikdrama'), SSD IX, 307 (PW V, 303–4).

30 Paul Bekker, *Richard Wagner: His Life in His Work*, trans. M. M. Bozman, London 1936, 512.

31 'Meine Erinnerungen an Ludwig Schnorr von Carolsfeld', SSD VIII, 186 (PW IV, 236).

32 Letter of 18 April 1865, SSD XVI, 39ff.,

quoted in Barth, *Documentary Study*, 207–8.

33 If Bülow is to be believed; see Newman, *Wagner* III, 381.

34 Letter to Joachim Raff, 21 June 1865, quoted in Newman, *Wagner* III, 381.

35 Eduard Hanslick, *Music Criticisms 1846–1899*, ed. and trans. Henry Pleasants, London 1963, 222–7.

36 See Stewart Spencer, 'Wagner's Nuremberg', *Cambridge Opera Journal*, 4, no. 1 (March 1992), 21–41.

37 Königsbriefe IV, 33, quoted in Spencer, 'Wagner's Nuremberg', 38.

38 Quoted in Bauer, *Stage Designs*, 181–2.

39 Quoted in Barth, *Documentary Study*, 214.

40 *Neue Freie Presse* (Vienna), 24–6 June 1868, quoted in Barth, *Documentary Study*, 215.

41 SL, 752.

42 Döll and the Brandts are discussed in chapter 3.

43 Quoted in Bauer, *Stage Designs*, 222.

44 Quoted in Newman, *Wagner* IV, 234.

45 SL, 759–60.

46 Bauer, *Stage Designs*, 224, after newspaper reports quoted in Petzet, *Wagner-Bühne*, 217–18.

47 Edwin O. Sachs, *Modern Opera Houses and Theatres*, 3 vols, London 1896–8, repr. New York 1968, III, Supplement 2, 85–140, quoted in Michael Forsyth, *Buildings for Music*, Cambridge 1985, 175.

48 Letter of 1 March 1871, quoted in Bauer, *Stage Designs*, 224, and in Newman, *Wagner* IV, 408.

49 Quoted in Bauer, *Stage Designs*, 224, and in Newman, *Wagner* IV, 408.

Chapter 3

1 CD I, 917.

2 SSD VI, 272–4 (PW III, 274–5). Wagner's development of his festival theatre from theory into bricks and mortar is thoroughly documented in Habel, *Festspielhaus und Wahnfried*.

3 SL, 216–17.

4 Letter of 17 December 1861, *Richard Wagner: Briefe an Hans von Bülow*, Jena 1916, 170ff., quoted in Barth, *Documentary Study*, 198.

5 Preface to the second edition (1863) of the *Ring* poem, SSD VI, 273–6 (PW III, 274–7).

6 Forsyth, *Buildings for Music*, 112.

7 Herbert A. Frenzel, *Geschichte des Theaters: Daten und Dokumente 1470–1890*, 2nd edn, Munich 1984, 520.

8 Manfred Semper, *Das Münchener Festspielhaus: Gottfried Semper und Richard Wagner*, Hamburg 1906, 108, quoted in Barth, *Documentary Study*, 206–7.

9 'Das Bühnenfestspielhaus in Bayreuth' (The Stage Festival Theatre in Bayreuth), SSD IX, 337–8 (PW V, 334–5).

10 Letter of 12 April 1872, SL, 793.

11 'Das Bühnenfestspielhaus in Bayreuth', SSD IX, 326–7 (PW V, 324–5), quoted in Barth, *Documentary Study*, 221.

12 'Das Bühnenfestspielhaus in Bayreuth', SSD IX, 337–8 (PW V, 335).

13 Petzet, *Wagner-Bühne*, 196.

14 Bergman, *Lighting*, 89–92.

15 Baumann, *Bühnentechnik*, 258, citing Pierre Patte, *Essai sur l'architecture théâtrale*, Paris 1782. See also Forsyth, *Buildings for Music*, 80.

16 Bergman, *Lighting*, 91, 133 and 135.

17 Bergman, *Lighting*, 298.

18 Heinrich Porges, *Wagner Rehearsing the 'Ring'*, trans. Robert L. Jacobs, Cambridge 1983, 26.

19 Letter to Ludwig, 13 September 1865, Königsbriefe I, 178, quoted in Petzet, *Wagner-Bühne*, 183.

20 Hoffmann's first name is sometimes misspelt as 'Joseph'.

21 Letter of 1 October 1874, Königsbriefe III, 40ff., quoted in Barth, *Documentary Study*, 226.

22 SSD VI, 75.

23 CD II, 113. For the influence on Wagner of Swiss mountain scenery, see Hans Erismann, 'Richard Wagner und die Schweizer Landschaft', in *Richard Wagner in der Schweiz*, *Ring* centenary number of *Schweiz*, journal of the Swiss National Tourist Office, Zürich, August 1976, 2–3.

24 Quoted in Petzet, *Wagner-Bühne*, 228.

25 CD II, 45.

26 Unpublished letter of 26 December 1873 in the Richard-Wagner-Museum, Bayreuth, quoted in Petzet, *Wagner-Bühne*, 229.

27 Letter of 28 July 1872, SL, 810–11.

28 Letter from Malwida von Meysenbug to Emil Heckel, 1 December 1873, quoted in Glasenapp, *Das Leben Richard Wagners* V, 117; CD I, 703–4 (29 November 1873).

29 Letter from Wagner to Hoffmann, 9 June 1874, *Bayreuther Briefe von Richard*

Wagner: 1871–1883, ed. Carl Friedrich Glasenapp, Berlin/Leipzig 1907, 2nd edn Leipzig 1912, 172–3.

30 Königsbriefe III, 57–58, quoted in Petzet, *Wagner-Bühne*, 230.

31 Glasenapp, *Das Leben Richard Wagners* V, 197.

32 Illustrations 499, 502, 505, 500, 503 and 506 in Petzet, *Wagner-Bühne*.

33 Illustrations 477–97 in Petzet, *Wagner-Bühne*.

34 For this caution I am indebted to Gudrun Föttinger of the Richard-Wagner-Museum, Bayreuth. See Claudia Balk, *Theaterfotografie*, Munich 1989, in which it is claimed that the first photographs showing actors on a complete set in an indoor theatre do not appear until 1899. Balk argues that the crucial technical developments necessary for 'on-stage' performance photography, such as flexible film and fast shutter speeds, did not occur until 1885 and 1888.

35 Srocke, *Regisseur*, 86. See also John Osborne, *The Meiningen Court Theatre 1866–1890*, Cambridge 1988.

36 SL, 846.

37 CD I, 840 (17 April 1875); Bauer, *Wagner Goes to the Theatre*, 138–40.

38 CD I, 915 (13 July 1876).

39 CD I, 917 and 918.

40 Richard Fricke, *Bayreuth in 1876* (entry for 28 July), trans. Stewart Spencer, in *Wagner* (Journal of the London Wagner Society), new series, ed. Stewart Spencer, 12, no. 1 (January 1991), 39. Fricke's *Bayreuth vor dreissig Jahren*, which consisted principally of diary entries for 1876, was first published in 1906. My references are usually either to the facsimile edition, *1876: Richard Wagner auf der Probe*, Stuttgart 1983 – 'Fricke 1983' – or to the valuably annotated translation by Stewart Spencer in *Wagner*, 1990–91.

41 Friedrich Kranich jr, *Bühnentechnik der Gegenwart*, 2 vols. Munich/Berlin 1929–33, I, 15.

42 Fricke, *Bayreuth in 1876* (26 June), in *Wagner*, 12, no. 1 (January 1991), 30.

43 Bergman, *Lighting*, 278; Baumann, *Bühnentechnik*, 224.

44 Paul Lindau, *Nüchterne Briefe aus Bayreuth*, Breslau 1876, 68ff. quoted in Baumann, *Bühnentechnik*, 224.

45 Baumann, *Bühnentechnik*, 230.

46 The magic-lantern slide show was a highly developed minor art of the nineteenth century. Images from Hoffmann and Doepler's designs were the basis of a magic-lantern version of the 1876 *Ring* presented on 10 November 1887 by the German showman Paul Hoffmann. In November 2002 Ludwig Vogl-Bienek and colleagues from the Frankfurt-based Institut für historische Projektionskunst recreated Paul Hoffmann's show as *Wagner's 'Ring': A Magic-Lantern Spectacular* in London at the Barbican Centre. The 'magic' extended to some ingenious animation of the figures in the painted slides.

47 Lindau *Nüchterne Briefe*, 56, quoted in Srocke, *Regisseur*, 83.

48 Bergman, *Lighting*, 277.

49 'Ein Einblick in das heutige deutsche Opernwesen' (A Look at German Opera Today), SSD IX, 286–7 (PW V, 283–4).

50 Letter of 12 May 1875, quoted in Fricke, *Richard Wagner auf der Probe*, 17.

51 Fricke, *Bayreuth in 1876* (28 July), in *Wagner*, 12, no. 1 (January 1991), 39.

52 Quoted in Newman, *Wagner* IV, 475.

53 Fricke, *Bayreuth in 1876* (14 August), in *Wagner*, 12, no. 1, (January 1991), 42. Ernest Newman relays a helpful suggestion that the neck may have mistakenly been despatched to Beirut in the Lebanon (*Wagner* IV, 475).

54 Fricke, *Bayreuth in 1876* (15 May), in *Wagner*, 11, no. 3 (August 1990), 106.

55 Unpublished notebook of stage directions for the 1876 *Ring*, Anton Seidl Papers, Columbia University, quoted in Srocke, *Regisseur*, 43.

56 Lilli Lehmann, *My Path through Life*, trans. Alice Benedict Seligman, London 1914, 222.

57 Letter of 6 November 1872, SL, 816.

58 Porges, *Wagner Rehearsing*, 4–5.

59 Fricke, *Bayreuth in 1876* (1 July), in *Wagner*, 12, no. 1 (January 1991), 31.

60 Porges, *Wagner Rehearsing*, 3.

61 'Erinnerungen an Richard Wagner: Die Bayreuther Vorproben 1875', *Die Wiener Freie Presse*, 1912, quoted in Srocke, *Regisseur*, 40.

62 Lehmann, *My Path*, 221ff.

63 Fricke, *Bayreuth in 1876* (10 May), in *Wagner*, 11, no. 3 (August 1990), 97.

64 Fricke, *Bayreuth in 1876* (29 May), in *Wagner*, 11, no. 4 (October 1990), 141.

65 Lehmann, *My Path*, 216.

66 Porges, *Wagner Rehearsing*, 52.

67 Fricke, *Bayreuth in 1876* (10 May), in *Wagner*, 11, no. 3 (August 1990), 97.
68 Porges, *Wagner Rehearsing*, 4.
69 Fricke, *Richard Wagner auf der Probe* (22 June), 107.
70 Porges, *Wagner Rehearsing*, 2–3.
71 Lehmann, *My Path*, 433; other similar testimonies include that of Emil Heckel in *Briefe Richard Wagners an Emil Heckel: Zur Entstehungsgeschichte der Bühnenfestspiele in Bayreuth*, Berlin 1899, quoted in Srocke, *Regisseur*, 37. See also Julius Hey, *Richard Wagner als Vortragsmeister*, Leipzig 1911.
72 Porges, *Wagner Rehearsing*, viii.
73 Porges, *Wagner Rehearsing*, 129.
74 'Ein Rückblick auf die Bühnenfestspiele des Jahres 1876' (A Retrospect of the Stage Festivals of 1876), SSD X, 109 (PW VI, 102).
75 Lindau, *Nüchterne Briefe*, 28, quoted in Baumann, *Bühnentechnik*, 257.
76 Lindau, *Nüchterne Briefe*, 28, and other sources, quoted in Baumann, *Bühnentechnik*, 259–60.
77 Baumann, *Bühnentechnik*, 185.
78 Petzet, *Wagner-Bühne*, 231.
79 *Musikalisches Wochenblatt* (Leipzig), 22 August 1876, quoted in Srocke, *Regisseur*, 76.
80 Fricke, *Bayreuth in 1876* (21 May), in *Wagner*, 11, no. 4 (October 1990), 137.
81 Kranich, *Bühnentechnik* I, 185.
82 Fricke, *Richard Wagner auf der Probe* (26 May), 81.
83 Baumann, *Bühnentechnik*, 181 and 269–72.
84 Fricke, *Bayreuth in 1876* in *Wagner*, 11, no. 4 (October 1990), 147.
85 Fricke, *Bayreuth in 1876* (15 August), in *Wagner*, 12, no. 1 (January 1991), 43.
86 CD I, 918 (13 August 1876).
87 Both descriptions quoted in Srocke, *Regisseur*, 77.
88 Max Kalbeck, *Das Bühnenfestspiel zu Bayreuth*, Breslau 1877, 32, quoted in Srocke, *Regisseur*, 79.
89 Fricke, *Bayreuth in 1876* (9 June and 29 July), in *Wagner*, 11, no. 4 (October 1990), 149, and 12, no. 1 (January 1991), 39.
90 Hanslick, *Music Criticisms*, 154.
91 Petzet, *Wagner-Bühne*, 215.
92 CD I, 44 (20 January 1869).
93 Lindau, *Nüchterne Briefe*, 29.
94 Fricke, *Bayreuth in 1876* (15 June), in *Wagner*, 12, no. 1 (January 1991), 26.

95 CD I, 912 (17 June 1876).
96 Fricke, *Bayreuth in 1876* (17–18 June), in *Wagner*, 12, no. 1 (January 1991), 27.
97 CD I, 915.
98 Lindau, *Nüchterne Briefe*, 56.
99 Fricke, *Richard Wagner auf der Probe* (26 June), 110.
100 CD I, 913.
101 Fricke, *Bayreuth in 1876* (26 June), in *Wagner*, 12, no. 1 (January 1991), 30.
102 CD I, 913.
103 Fricke, *Bayreuth in 1876* in *Wagner*, 12, no. 1 (January 1991), 30.
104 Quoted in Srocke, *Regisseur*, 59.
105 Lindau, *Nüchterne Briefe*, 68–9, quoted in Petzet, *Wagner-Bühne*, 241.
106 Joseph Kürschner, *Bayreuther Tagebuchblätter*, Leipzig n.d., 17, quoted in Srocke, *Regisseur*, 84.
107 CD I, 921 (9 September 1876).
108 Fricke, *Bayreuth in 1876* (2 July), in *Wagner*, 12, no. 1 (January 1991), 33.
109 Hanslick, *Music Criticisms*, 155.
110 Fricke, *Bayreuth in 1876* (18 August), in *Wagner*, 12, no. 1 (January 1991), 44.
111 'Nächstes Jahr machen wir Alles anders.' Fricke, *Bayreuth in 1876* (undated postscript), in *Wagner*, 12, no. 1 (January 1991), 44.
112 Lehmann, *My Path*, 227–9.
113 'Ein Rückblick auf die Bühnenfestspiele des Jahres 1876', SSD X, 113 (PW VI, 105).
114 CD I, 921 (9 September 1876).
115 'Ein Rückblick auf die Bühnenfestspiele des Jahres 1876', SSD X, 114–15 (PW VI, 106–7).
116 Quoted in Barth, *Documentary Study*, 234.
117 Quoted in Barth, *Documentary Study*, 233 – this is a fuller version of a passage abbreviated in Hanslick, *Music Criticisms*.
118 'Sehen Sie nicht zu viel hin! Hören Sie zu!' Quoted in Dietrich Mack, *Der Bayreuther Inszenierungsstil 1876–1976*, Munich 1976, 8.
119 Max Kalbeck, *Opernabende: Beiträge zur Geschichte und Kritik der Oper*, 2 vols, Berlin 1898, I, 139, quoted in Srocke, *Regisseur*, 89.
120 *Adolf von Hildebrands Briefwechsel mit Conrad Fiedler*, ed. Günther Jachmann, Dresden 1927, 65–7 and 69–75, quoted in Barth, *Documentary Study*, 234.
121 Wilhelm Mohr, *Richard Wagner und das Kunstwerk der Zukunft im Lichte der Baireuther Aufführung betrachtet*,

Cologne 1876, 63 and 65–8, quoted in Barth, *Documentary Study*, 233.

122 CD I, 921–2 (9 September 1876).

123 From an account by Franz Muncker in the *Richard Wagner Jahrbuch*, vol. I, ed. Joseph Kürschner, Stuttgart 1886, 205–8, quoted in Barth, *Documentary Study*, 239.

124 'Ein Rückblick auf die Bühnenfestspiele des Jahres 1876', SSD X, 111–12 (PW VI, 104).

Chapter 4

1 Inscription on the façade of Wagner's villa in Bayreuth.

2 Bauer, *Stage Designs*, 269 and 272.

3 CD II, 531 (2 September 1880).

4 'Religion und Kunst', SSD X, 211–53 (PW VI, 211–52).

5 Bauer, *Stage Designs*, 272.

6 CD II, 171 (13 October 1878).

7 Petzet, *Wagner-Bühne*, 271 and illustrations 653–6.

8 CD II, 194 (9 November 1878).

9 CD II, 64 (21 April 1878).

10 Mack, *Inszenierungsstil*, 17.

11 Hans B. Brand, *Aus Richard Wagners Leben in Bayreuth*, Munich 1934, 42, quoted in Srocke, *Regisseur*, 110.

12 CD II, 775 (22 December 1881), and annotations by Kniese in his vocal score, quoted in Baumann, *Bühnentechnik*, 260–1.

13 For the fascinating story of the *panorama mobile* in the nineteenth century and especially as used at Bayreuth in 1882, see Carl-Friedrich Baumann, 'Entwicklung und Anwendung der Bühnenbeleuchtung seit der Mitte des 18. Jahrhunderts', diss. Universität zu Köln, 1955, 334 and 369ff. and Baumann, *Bühnentechnik*, 154–5 and 163–4. In the 1840s an American scene painter, John Banvard, a rival of P. T. Barnum, invented a panorama viewing machine in which a two-mile-long cloth depiction of a journey down the Mississippi created a sensation when demonstrated in New York, Boston and London. Banvard also did a down-the-Nile panorama. See Paul S. Collins, *Banvard's Folly*, London 2001.

14 CD II, 183 (27 October 1878) and 154 (23 September 1878).

15 Bauer, *Stage Designs*, 276 (translation amended).

16 Letter of 17 May 1881, Königsbriefe III,

210, quoted in Gisela Zeh, *Das Bayreuther Bühnenkostüm*, Munich 1973, 30.

17 The notes are in SW XXX, *Dokumente zur Entstehung und ersten Aufführung des Bühnenweihfestspiels Parsifal*, ed. Martin Geck and Egon Voss, Mainz 1970.

18 Srocke, *Regisseur*, 99.

19 Luise Reuß-Belce, 'Persönliche Erinnerungen an das Jahr 1882', *Tägliche Rundschau*, 22 (1913), quoted in Srocke, *Regisseur*, 94.

20 Felix Weingartner, *Buffets and Rewards*, trans. Marguerite Wolff, London 1937, quoted in Robert Hartford, ed., *Bayreuth: The Early Years*, London 1980, 130.

21 Charles and Pierre Bonnier in the *Revue wagnérienne* (Paris), April 1887, quoted in extenso in Lucy Beckett, *Richard Wagner: 'Parsifal'* (Cambridge Opera Handbook), Cambridge 1981, 91–2.

22 CD II, 590 (4 January 1881).

23 Ernst Leopold Stahl, 'Parsifal: Beiträge und Bilder zu seiner szenischen Dramaturgie', *Die Scene: Blätter für Bühnenkunst*, 3, nos 1–2 (July–August 1913), 13, quoted in Srocke, *Regisseur*, 115.

24 CD II, 905, 909, 904 and 905.

25 SL, 926.

26 CD II, 948 (10 November 1882), 954 (16 November 1882), etc.

27 'Das Bühnenweihfestspiel in Bayreuth 1882' (The Stage Dedication Festival in Bayreuth 1882), *Bayreuther Blätter*, November–December 1882, SSD X, 297–308 (PW VI, 301–12).

28 *Beethoven*, SSD IX, 76–7 (PW V, 76).

29 'Über die Benennung "Musikdrama"', SSD IX, 305–6 (PW V, 302–3).

30 See Dieter Borchmeyer, *Richard Wagner: Theory and Theatre*, trans. Stewart Spencer, Oxford 1991, 39 and 45–50.

31 Forsyth, *Buildings for Music*, 192–3.

32 A. Oppenheim and E. Gethe, *Deutsches Theater-Lexicon*, Leipzig 1889, 92, quoted in Bergman, *Lighting*, 300.

33 Letter of 28 September 1882, *Richard Wagner an seine Künstler*, ed. Erich Kloss, Berlin/Leipzig 1908, 405.

34 CD II, 920–1 (2 October 1882) and 945 (7 November 1882).

35 CD II, 769–70 (15 December 1881) and 954 (16 November 1882).

36 CD II, 104 (1 July 1878).

37 John Deathridge and Carl Dahlhaus, *The New Grove Wagner*, London 1984, 106.

38 Newman, *Wagner* III, 148.

39 CD II, 112 (12 July 1878).
40 CD II, 662 (3 May 1881) and 663 (4 May 1881).
41 Letter of 16 May 1881, SL, 914.
42 Angelo Neumann, *Personal Recollections of Wagner*, trans. Edith Livermore, London 1909, 22.
43 Quoted in Neumann, *Recollections*, 25–6.
44 Neumann, *Recollections*, 58.
45 Neumann, *Recollections*, 72. Neumann gives no source for Liszt's verdict, which may have been a spoken comment to Wagner.
46 Neumann, *Recollections*, 74–5.
47 Neumann, *Recollections*, 147–8.
48 Letter of 15 June 1881, quoted in Neumann, *Recollections*, 173–4.
49 Letter of 16 June 1881, quoted in Neumann, *Recollections*, 178–9. The quotation 'Close packed our heads …' is from Schiller's *Wallensteins Tod*, Act II, scene 2.
50 Reported by Neumann from table-talk at a dinner at Wahnfried on 21 July 1881, *Recollections*, 184.
51 Neumann, *Recollections*, 208.
52 Letter of 16 January 1882, quoted in Neumann, *Recollections*, 209.
53 Neumann, *Recollections*, 243.
54 Letter from Wagner to Renz, 3 July 1878, first published by Egon Voss in 'Wagner konzertant oder Der Walkürenritt im Zirkus als Rettung vor der Oper', in Christoph-Hellmut Mahling and Ruth Seiberts, eds, *Festschrift Walter Wiora zum 90. Geburtstag*, Tutzing 1997, 553.
55 *Athenaeum*, 13 May 1882.
56 Felix Adler, 'Neumann als Operndirektor', *Bohemia*, 21 December 1910, quoted in Peter Heyworth, *Otto Klemperer: His Life and Times*, vol. I (1885–1933) Cambridge 1983, 31.
57 Neumann, *Recollections*, 289 and 224.
58 Ute Jung, *Die Rezeption der Kunst Richard Wagners in Italien*, Regensburg 1974, 172–8, quoted in Andrew Medlicott, 'A Man for All Theatres: Angelo Neumann', *Wagner*, 74 (February 1979), 5–11.
59 SL, 928.
60 Letter from Wagner to Neumann, 29 September 1882, SL, 928.
61 CD II, 898 (11 August 1882).
62 'Once again the Flying Richard Wagner Theatre sprang into life,' wrote Richard Rosenheim of the company's visit to Russia in 1889: *Die Geschichte der Deutschen Bühnen in Prag 1883–1918*, Prague 1938, 91.
63 Letter to Liszt, 8 September 1852, SL, 269.
64 Fricke, *Bayreuth vor dreissig Jahren*, Dresden 1906, 107, quoted in Srocke, *Regisseur*, 44.
65 'Über die Bestimmung der Oper', SSD IX, 142 (PW V, 143).
66 CD II, 246 (2 January 1879).
67 CD II, 861 (30 May 1882).
68 'Das Bühnenweihfestspiel in Bayreuth 1882', SSD X, 305 (PW VI, 310).
69 Pierre Boulez, *Orientations*, ed. Jean-Jacques Nattiez, trans. Martin Cooper, London 1986, 258.
70 Introduction to *Wagner on Music and Drama*, ed. Albert Goldman and Evert Sprinchorn, trans. W. Ashton Ellis, London 1970, 26.
71 *Richard Wagner's Letters to August Roeckel*, trans. Eleanor C. Sellar, Bristol 1897, 146–7.

Chapter 5

1 Quoted in *1876 Bayreuth 1976*, festival souvenir publication, Bayreuth 1976.
2 Lehmann, *My Path*, 224.
3 Lehmann, *My Path*, 424–5.
4 *Shaw's Music: The Complete Musical Criticism*, ed. Dan H. Laurence, 3 vols, London 1981, III, 283–4 (21 July 1894).
5 Lehmann, *My Path*, 430.
6 Felix Weingartner, 'Bayreuth (1876–1896)', in *Felix Weingartner: Recollections and Recordings*, ed. Christopher Dyment, Rickmansworth 1976, 105.
7 Quoted in Mack, *Inszenierungsstil*, 30.
8 Letter of 11 September 1891, *Cosima Wagner: Das zweite Leben, Briefe und Aufzeichnungen 1883–1930*, ed. Dietrich Mack, Munich 1980, 256.
9 Letter of 22 July 1887, *Cosima Wagner: Das zweite Leben*, 115.
10 Letter to Cosima, 24 August 1892, quoted in Mack, *Inszenierungsstil*, 90–2.
11 Quoted in Mack, *Inszenierungsstil*, 35.
12 *Shaw's Music* III, 322 and 324 (8 August 1894).
13 The term 'compliance' as applied to performance is a useful coinage of the philosopher Nelson Goodman in *Languages of Art*, London 1969, esp. 210–12. The proposed criterion, which of course begs many questions, is whether or not a performance is a legitimate representation of the text and score as

notated by the composer. Goodman
concludes that even in cases of the
strictest notation a performance may
enjoy a considerable degree of freedom
while still remaining a legitimate
'instance' of the work. The notion of
'compliance' is interestingly developed by
Jonathan Miller in his study of what he
calls the 'afterlife' of plays and operas,
meaning simply the history of their
performance and interpretation after
their creators' death. See Miller,
Subsequent Performances, London 1986,
32ff.

14 See *Cosima Wagner: Das zweite Leben*,
311, 813, 828–9.

15 *Shaw's Music* III, 287 (review of
Lohengrin, 21 July 1894).

16 Lehmann, *My Path*, 419, 422 and
434–5.

17 See, for example, Anton Seidl in the
Bayreuther Blätter, 1900, 292ff.,
quoted in Mack, *Inszenierungsstil*, 51.

18 Quoted in Mack, *Inszenierungsstil*, 90–2.

19 Weingartner, 'Bayreuth', 99 and 106.

20 Edward Gordon Craig, *Index to the Story
of My Days*, London 1957, 272.

21 Letter of 23 October 1888, *Cosima
Wagner: Das zweite Leben*, 166.

22 Letter of 13 May 1896, *Cosima Wagner:
Das zweite Leben*, 412–15.

23 Quoted in Edmund Stadler, *Adolphe
Appia* (exhibition catalogue), London
1970, 12.

24 Letter of 11 April 1903, *Cosima Wagner:
Das zweite Leben*, 629–32.

25 Letter of 11 April 1903, *Cosima Wagner:
Das zweite Leben*, 631.

26 Quoted in Hans Mayer, *Richard Wagner
in Bayreuth 1876–1976*, trans. Jack Zipes,
Zürich/Stuttgart/London 1976, 109.

27 Weingartner, 'Bayreuth', 108.

28 Peter P. Pachl, *Siegfried Wagner: Genie im
Schatten*, Munich 1988, 69.

29 Quoted in Mack, *Inszenierungsstil*, 20.

30 Baumann, *Bühnentechnik*, 191.

31 See Kurt Söhnlein, *Erinnerungen an
Siegfried Wagner und Bayreuth*, ed. Peter
P. Pachl, Bayreuth 1980, 22–7.

32 Letter from Siegfried to Söhnlein, 20
August 1927, quoted in Söhnlein,
Erinnerungen, 104.

33 Illustration in Söhnlein, *Erinnerungen*,
47.

34 Mack, *Inszenierungsstil*, 10.

35 Quoted in Mack, *Inszenierungsstil*, 35.

36 Quoted in Mack, *Inszenierungsstil*, 34–5.

37 Mack, *Inszenierungsstil*, 34–5.

38 *Berliner Tageblatt*, 5 August 1912, quoted
in Mack, *Inszenierungsstil*, 25–6.

39 Article in the 1931 *Festspielführer*, quoted
in Zeh, *Bühnenkostüm*, 57–8. Costumes
illustrated in plates 172–82.

40 *Hamburger Nachrichten*, 21 July 1927,
quoted in Mack, *Inszenierungsstil*, 23.

41 Quoted in Mack, *Inszenierungsstil*, 23.

42 Letter to Houston Stewart Chamberlain,
13 May 1896, *Cosima Wagner: Das zweite
Leben*, 413.

43 Mayer, *Wagner in Bayreuth*, 90.

44 Quoted in Mack, *Inszenierungsstil*, 99.

45 Well described in Söhnlein,
Erinnerungen, 60–3.

46 Rudolf Laban, *A Life for Dance*, trans.
Lisa Ullmann, London 1975, 172–3.

47 Quoted in Mack, *Inszenierungsstil*,
99–100. Laban is of course twisting the
facts in order to suggest that Wagner was
godfather to his own style of expressive
dance. Wagner actually had only classical
ballet steps in mind, even if the music he
wrote for them was very far from
classical. For a reappraisal of dance in
Wagner, see Theresa Cameron, 'The
Third Art of the "Gesamtkunstwerk": The
Significance of Dance within Total Art
Theatre', *Wagner*, 12, no. 1 (January
1991), 3–12.

48 Quoted in Mack, *Inszenierungsstil*, 52–3.

49 *Die Musik* (Berlin), May 1930, quoted in
Mack, *Inszenierungsstil*, 53.

50 *Mahler's Unknown Letters*, ed. Herta
Blaukopf, trans. Richard Stokes, London
1986, 201.

51 Quoted in Kurt Blaukopf, ed., with
Zoltan Roman, *Mahler: A Documentary
Study*, Oxford/New York 1976, 183.

52 Quoted in *Mahler's Unknown Letters*, 202
and 205.

53 Bruno Walter, *Theme and Variations*,
trans. James A. Galston, London 1947, 86.

54 Henry-Louis de La Grange, *Gustav
Mahler*, vol. II, trans. Johanna Harwood
et al., Oxford 1995, 357n.

55 Blaukopf, *Documentary Study*, 235.

56 Interview in *Fremden-Blatt*, 6 September
1903, quoted in Kurt Blaukopf, *Gustav
Mahler*, trans. Inge Goodwin, London
1973, 250–1.

57 *Illustriertes Extrablatt* (Vienna), 9
September 1903, quoted in Blaukopf,
Documentary Study, 235.

58 La Grange, *Mahler* II, 624–5.

59 Ernest Bartolo, *Die Wiener Oper: Die*

aufregenden Jahre seit 1625, Vienna 1992, 61–2.

60　Blaukopf, *Documentary Study*, 222.

61　Quoted in La Grange, *Mahler* II, 562.

62　Quoted in La Grange, *Mahler* II, 563.

63　For an English version of *Die Revolution des Theaters*, see Georg Fuchs, *Revolution in the Theatre*, ed. and trans. Constance Connor Kuhn, Port Washington (New York) 1972.

64　La Grange, *Mahler* II, 503.

65　Alma Mahler, *Gustav Mahler: Memories and Letters*, ed. Donald Mitchell, trans. Basil Creighton, 3rd edn, London 1973, 160.

66　Alma Mahler, *Memories*, 160.

67　See La Grange, *Mahler* II, 515.

68　La Grange, *Mahler* II, 561.

69　For a good discussion, see Bauer, '"… daβ der Ausdruck Eindruck werde" ', 55ff.

70　Peter Vergo, *Vienna 1900*, Edinburgh 1983, 44.

71　Illustrations in Peter Vergo, *Art in Vienna 1898–1918*, London 1975, 67 and 70.

72　Blaukopf, *Mahler*, 169, 164 and 164.

73　Alfred Roller, 'Mahler und die Inszenierung', *Musikblätter des Anbruch* (Vienna), 2 (1920) (Mahler issue), quoted in Heyworth, *Klemperer* I, 27.

74　La Grange, *Mahler* II, 565.

75　La Grange, *Mahler* II, 577n.

76　Quoted in Heyworth, *Klemperer* I, 27–8.

77　Interview in *Illustriertes Extrablatt* (Vienna), 9 September 1903, quoted in Blaukopf, *Documentary Study*, 235.

78　La Grange, *Mahler* II, 573n.

79　Ernst Decsey's 1911 recollection of seeing the production in December 1906, quoted in Norman Lebrecht, ed., *Mahler Remembered*, London 1987, 265.

80　Quoted in Blaukopf, *Mahler*, 173.

81　Egon and Emmy Wellesz, *Egon Wellesz: Leben und Werk*, ed. Franz Endler, Vienna 1981, 24.

82　Wellesz, *Leben und Werk*, 24–5.

83　Emil Lucke, quoted in La Grange, *Mahler* II, 573.

84　Ernst Decsey, quoted in Lebrecht, *Mahler*, 266.

85　Quoted in La Grange, *Mahler* II, 580 and 574.

86　'The Sorrows and Grandeur of Richard Wagner', in Thomas Mann, *Pro and Contra Wagner*, trans. Allan Blunden, London 1985, 96ff.

87　Wellesz, *Leben und Werk*, 25.

88　Quoted in La Grange, *Mahler* II, 573–85.

89　Quoted in Lebrecht, *Mahler*, 267.

90　Hermann Bahr, *Glossen zum Wiener Theater (1903–1906)*, Berlin 1907, quoted in La Grange, *Mahler* II, 583.

91　Max Graf, 'Der Sezessionistische Tristan', *Hamburger Nachrichten*, 15 March 1903, quoted in La Grange, *Mahler* II, 583–4.

92　Alfred Roller, 'Bühnenreform?', *Der Merker* (Vienna), 1, no. 5 (December 1909), 193, quoted in La Grange, *Mahler* II, 569.

93　Wellesz, *Leben und Werk*, 25.

94　Quoted in Heyworth, *Klemperer* I, 27–8.

95　Walter, *Theme and Variations*, 158–9.

96　Henry-Louis de La Grange, *Gustav Mahler: Chronique d'une vie*, 3 vols, Paris 1979–84, II, 541.

97　La Grange, *Mahler* II (French edn), 1037.

98　La Grange, *Mahler* II (French edn), 1038–9.

99　*Neue Freie Presse* (Vienna), 25 January 1905, quoted in Blaukopf, *Documentary Study*, 239.

100　La Grange, *Mahler* II (French edn), 548–9.

101　Otto Klemperer, *Minor Recollections*, London 1964, 15.

102　The lighting innovations in *Die Walküre* are detailed in Ludwig Hevesi, *Alt Kunst – Neu Kunst: Wien 1894–1908*, Vienna 1909.

103　La Grange, *Mahler* II (French edn), 1040ff.

104　*Selected Letters of Gustav Mahler*, ed. Knud Martner, trans. Eithne Wilkins, Ernst Kaiser and Bill Hopkins, London 1979, 300; Walter, *Theme and Variations*, 158; Lilli Lehmann, *My Path*, 388.

105　Quoted in Blaukopf, *Mahler*, 174.

106　Adolf Loos, *Trotzdem (1900–1930)*, Innsbruck 1931, quoted in La Grange, *Mahler* II, 585.

107　Letter of 22 January 1908, in Alma Mahler, *Memories*, 312–13.

Chapter 6

1　The phrase 'the opened eye of the score' in the chapter title is taken from Hans Werner Henze ('The stage is only the opened eye of the score') in his book *Music and Politics*, trans. Peter Labanyi, London 1982, 137.

2　Letter to Karl Reyle, 10 September 1926, quoted in Adolphe Appia, *Essays, Scenarios, and Designs*, ed. Richard C. Beacham, trans. Walther R. Volbach, Ann

Arbor/London 1989, 25. Wherever possible Appia's writings are cited from published translations, sometimes with necessary revision. The standard edition, whose editorial principles leave much to be desired, is the *Oeuvres complètes*, ed. Marie L. Bablet-Hahn, 4 vols, Bonstetten (Switzerland) 1983–91. A fifth and final volume, promised as a complete illustrated catalogue of Appia's designs, has at the time of writing yet to appear. Many of Appia's finest designs are beautifully reproduced in *Adolphe Appia: A Portfolio*, with an introduction by Henry C. Bonifas, Zürich 1929.

3   Adolphe Appia, *The Work of Living Art*, trans. H. D. Albright, Coral Gables (Florida) 1960, 85–7.

4   Appia, *Oeuvres* II, 124.

5   Appia, *Oeuvres* II, 114–24.

6   Appia, *Essays*, 58 (c. 1921).

7   Appia, *Living Art*, 50.

8   Quoted in Appia, *Oeuvres* II, 226.

9   Quoted in Walther R. Volbach, *Adolphe Appia: Prophet of the Modern Theatre*, Middletown (Connecticut) 1968, 126.

10   Adolphe Appia, *Music and the Art of the Theatre*, ed. Barnard Hewitt, trans. Robert W. Corrigan and Mary Douglas Dirks, Coral Gables (Florida) 1962, 10–16.

11   Quoted in Volbach, *Appia*, 27.

12   Appia, *Music*, 23n.

13   Appia, *Music*, 32–5.

14   Extracts from Egusquiza's article may be found in Baumann, *Bühnentechnik*, 225.

15   Appia, *Music*, 72–8.

16   Appia, *Music*, 21.

17   Donald Oenslager, quoted in Volbach, *Appia*, 66.

18   Appia, *Oeuvres* II, 249–65.

19   Appia, *Oeuvres* II, 124–5.

20   Appia, *Oeuvres* II, 125–7.

21   Appia, *Oeuvres* II, 192–202.

22   Appia, *Oeuvres* II, 199.

23   Appia, *Living Art*, 98.

24   Appia, *Oeuvres* II, 178.

25   Appia, *Oeuvres* II, 179–80.

26   Appia, *Oeuvres* II, 180.

27   In Appia, *Oeuvres* II, 382–7.

28   Volbach, *Appia*, 80.

29   Jacques Petit and Jean-Pierre Kempf, *Claudel on the Theatre*, trans. Christine Trollope, Coral Gables (Florida) 1972, 17ff.

30   The production was fascinatingly reconstructed (with some necessary creative licence) in January 1991 at the University of Warwick under the direction of David Thomas and Richard Beacham, with eurhythmic choreography by Selma Odom and conducted by Colin Touchin. A VHS video is available from the 3D Visualisation Group, Centre for Computing in the Humanities, King's College London, Strand, London WC2R 2LS.

31   Appia, *Oeuvres* III, 130; Richard C. Beacham, *Adolphe Appia: Theatre Artist*, Cambridge 1987, 77.

32   Appia, *Essays*, 18.

33   Quoted in Volbach, *Appia*, 143.

34   Letter to Oskar Wälterlin, quoted in Volbach, *Appia*, 141.

35   Volbach, *Appia*, 141–2. For a wider selection of the press response, see Appia, *Oeuvres* IV, 250–60.

36   Appia, *Oeuvres* IV, 247.

37   Appia, *Essays*, 27.

38   Appia, quoted in Volbach, *Appia*, 153.

39   Quoted in Volbach, *Appia*, 154.

40   Letter of 13 February 1894, HSC Nachlaß in Richard-Wagner-Gedenkstätte, Bayreuth, quoted in Geoffrey G. Field, *Evangelist of Race: The Germanic Vision of Houston Stewart Chamberlain*, New York 1981, 105.

41   Marie L. Bablet-Hahn in Appia, *Oeuvres* II, 35.

42   Houston Stewart Chamberlain, *Richard Wagner*, trans. G. Ainslie Hight, London 1897, 215.

43   Chamberlain, *Wagner*, 318.

44   Full text in French translation in Appia, *Oeuvres* II, 382–7.

45   Appia, *Oeuvres* II, 266.

46   *Der Türmer* was edited by Karl Storck, music critic of the *Deutsche Zeitung* (Berlin). Storck's enthusiasm for Appia and for the inventor of eurhythmics is evident in his *Emile Jaques-Dalcroze*, Stuttgart 1912.

47   Marie L. Bablet-Hahn in Appia, *Oeuvres* II, 269–70.

48   Fortuny's involvement is asserted by Volbach and Beacham and by Guillermo de Osma, *Mariano Fortuny*, London 1980, 75–8, but questioned by Marie L. Bablet-Hahn in Appia, *Oeuvres* II, 371.

49   *Le Ménestrel* (Paris) 15 April 1906, quoted in Appia, *Oeuvres* II, 377–8.

50   For a detailed description, see de Osma, *Fortuny*, 78–9.

51   Appia, *Oeuvres* II, 349.

52 Quoted in de Osma, *Fortuny*, 69.
53 Quoted in de Osma, *Fortuny*, 70.
54 *Siegfried*, trans. William Mann, London 1964, 90.
55 De Osma, *Fortuny*, 75; Beacham, *Appia*, 90.
56 Volbach, *Appia*, 196.
57 Beacham, *Appia*, 145.
58 Beacham, *Appia*, 148.
59 *Gazette des beaux-arts* (Paris), 23 March 1895, 103; text in Appia, *Oeuvres* I, 287–8.
60 *La Revue hebdomadaire* (Paris), October 1899, 130–1; text in Appia, *Oeuvres* II, 215.
61 Paris 1910; text in Appia, *Oeuvres* II, 293–8.
62 Oskar Wälterlin, *Bekenntnis zum Theater*, Zürich 1955.
63 John Dizikes, *Opera in America: A Cultural History*, New Haven/London 1993, 367–8.
64 14 August 1912, quoted in Irwin Spector, *Rhythm and Life: The Work of Emile Jaques-Dalcroze*, Stuyvesant (New York) 1990, 165.
65 'Shall We Realize Wagner's Ideals?', in Carl van Vechten, *Music and Bad Manners*, New York 1916, 147, quoted in Joseph Horowitz, *Wagner Nights: An American History*, Berkeley/Los Angeles/London 1994, 313.
66 Beacham, *Appia*, 149.
67 Donald M. Oenslager, *The Theatre of Donald Oenslager*, Middletown (Connecticut) 1978, 55.
68 Marie Rambert, *Quicksilver*, London 1972, 78.
69 Beacham, *Appia*, 150.
70 Anton Seidl, quoted in Spector, *Jaques-Dalcroze*, 166.
71 *Das Kunstwerk der Zukunft*, SSD III, 74–6 (PW I, 102–5).
72 Quoted in Edward Braun, *The Theatre of Meyerhold*, London 1979, 95.
73 Appia, *Essays*, 29.
74 Edward Gordon Craig, *On the Art of the Theatre*, London 1911, 2nd edn London 1912, vii.
75 Quoted in Denis Bablet, *The Theatre of Edward Gordon Craig*, trans. Daphne Woodward, London 1981, 174.
76 Quoted in Beacham, *Appia*, 65.
77 Richard C. Beacham, ed., ' "Brothers in Suffering and Joy": The Appia-Craig Correspondence', *New Theatre Quarterly*, 4, no. 15 (1988), 268–88.
78 Bablet, *Gordon Craig*, 180.
79 Quoted in Bablet, *Gordon Craig*, 176.
80 Christopher Innes, *Edward Gordon Craig*, Cambridge 1983, 163–4.
81 Quoted in Innes, *Gordon Craig*, 181.
82 Quoted in Innes, *Gordon Craig*, 176.
83 Lee Simonson, *The Stage Is Set*, New York 1932, repr. 1970, 341
84 Quoted in Innes, *Gordon Craig*, 108.
85 Appia, *Essays*, 58 (c. 1921).
86 Appia, *Living Art*, 87.
87 Appia, *Music*, 35–43.
88 Oskar Schlemmer, 'Mensch und Kunstfigur', in Walter Gropius, ed., *Die Bühne im Bauhaus*, Munich 1925, trans. Arthur S. Wensinger, *The Theater of the Bauhaus*, Middletown (Connecticut) 1961, 15–46.
89 Appia, *Music*, 35–43.
90 Appia, *Music*, 88.
91 Appia, *Living Art*, 65.
92 Appia, *Oeuvres* III, 376; Appia, *Living Art*, 35.
93 Appia, *Oeuvres* II, 267, 276ff. and 278–9.
94 Appia, *Oeuvres* III, 407.
95 Appia, *Oeuvres* III, 407.
96 John Willett, letter to the editor, *Kurt Weill Newsletter* (New York), 14, no. 1 (Spring 1996), 3.

Chapter 7

1 The avant-garde theatre of the Weimar Republic and its relationship with Russian developments are discussed in chapter 8.
2 Alexandre Benois, *Memoirs*, trans. Moura Budberg, 2 vols, London 1960–4, II, 78.
3 Benois, *Memoirs* II, 101; Rosamund Bartlett, *Wagner and Russia*, Cambridge 1995, 66. Benois seems to have been unaware of Wagner's unsuccessful attempts to get Böcklin to design the *Ring* at Bayreuth in 1876. The present chapter is greatly indebted to Dr Bartlett's ground-breaking study and I thank her most warmly for generously sharing her research in many personal communications.
4 Volkonsky's adventurous taste ran into resistance, and an unwise attempt to fine a prima ballerina, who happened to be a mistress of the Tsar's cousin, for refusing to wear a farthingale in a Louis XV period ballet, precipitated his resignation at the end of the 1900–1 season. He remained a powerful reforming influence and his interest in Appia and Craig has

already been noted.

5   Quoted in Bartlett, *Wagner and Russia*, 80.

6   Benois, *Memoirs* II, 201–2.

7   Quoted in Bartlett, *Wagner and Russia*, 80.

8   Camilla Gray, *The Russian Experiment in Art 1863–1922*, rev. Marian Burleigh-Motley, London 1986, 11.

9   Quoted in Charles Spencer, *The World of Serge Diaghilev*, London 1974, 73.

10 Gray, *Russian Experiment*, 51.

11 Bartlett, *Wagner and Russia*, 68.

12 Vassily Kandinsky, *Complete Writings on Art*, ed. Kenneth C. Lindsay and Peter Vergo, 2 vols, London 1982, I, 264.

13 For a selection of his writings on opera see *Stanislavsky on Opera*, ed. E. R. Hapgood, New York 1975.

14 Theodore Komisarjevsky, *Myself and the Theatre*, London 1929, 88.

15 Edward Braun, *The Director and the Stage*, London 1982, 67.

16 Quoted in Robert Cannon, 'Stanislavski and the Opera', *Opera*, November 1982, 1114.

17 For Meyerhold's remark to Chekhov about the importance of capturing the sound of *The Cherry Orchard*, see chapter 6, p. 199.

18 Quoted in Bartlett, *Wagner and Russia*, 95. See also the chapter 'Meyerhold and Music', in Paul Schmidt, ed., *Meyerhold at Work*, Manchester 1981.

19 Nikolai Ulyanov, quoted in Braun, *Director and the Stage*, 113.

20 Translations in *Meyerhold on Theatre*, ed. and trans. Edward Braun, London 1969, 39–64.

21 Komisarjevsky, *Myself and the Theatre*, 71.

22 Fuchs's innovations were briefly mentioned in chapter 5.

23 Braun, *Director and the Stage*, 117.

24 Komisarjevsky, *Myself and the Theatre*, 78–9.

25 Braun, *Director and the Stage*, 5.

26 *Petersburgskaya gazeta* (St Petersburg), 24 April 1908, quoted in *Meyerhold on Theatre*, 75.

27 Partial translation in *Meyerhold on Theatre*, 80–98.

28 *Meyerhold on Theatre*, 95–7.

29 *Meyerhold on Theatre*, 97–8.

30 *Meyerhold on Theatre*, 91–2.

31 *Teatr i iskusstvo* (Theatre and Art) (St Petersburg), 8 November 1909, quoted in

Brigitte Heldt, *Richard Wagner: 'Tristan und Isolde' – Das Werk und seine Inszenierung*, Laaber 1994, 166.

32 Quoted in Braun, *Theatre of Meyerhold*, 98.

33 Quoted in Heldt, *Tristan und Isolde*, 169.

34 Braun, *Theatre of Meyerhold*, 89–90; *Meyerhold on Theatre*, 75.

35 *Meyerhold on Theatre*, 81 and 85.

36 Richard Buckle, *Diaghilev*, London 1979, 165.

37 In the early 1920s Meyerhold developed 'Biomechanics', a system of physical training for actors which was introduced into every Soviet drama school. For his own rather cloudy account of Biomechanics, see *Meyerhold on Theatre*, 197–200, and for an excellent detailed exposition, Robert Leach, *Vsevolod Meyerhold*, Cambridge 1989, 52ff.

38 *Meyerhold on Theatre*, 83 and 82.

39 Lidiya Ivanova, quoted in Bartlett, *Wagner and Russia*, 100.

40 Bartlett, *Wagner and Russia*, 101.

41 Quoted in Konstantin Rudnitsky, *Meyerhold the Director*, ed. Sydney Schultze, trans. George Petrov, Ann Arbor 1981, 144 (for Russian edition, see n. 45 below).

42 Quoted in Bartlett, *Wagner and Russia*, 335, n. 193.

43 Diary entry for 28 January 1910, Bayerische Staatsbibliothek, Munich, quoted in Heldt, *Tristan und Isolde*, 169.

44 Bartlett, *Wagner and Russia*, 100.

45 Konstantin L. Rudnitsky, *Rezhisser Meierkhold*, Moscow 1969, 203, Quoted in Braun, *Theatre of Meyerhold*, 144.

46 The important role played in the advocacy of Wagner as a social revolutionary by Anatoly Lunacharsky, 'People's Commissar of Public Education', is described in chapter 10.

47 Bartlett, *Wagner and Russia*, 135.

48 Bartlett, *Wagner and Russia*, 96, 229, 225 and 259.

49 Mikhail Kolesnokov, quoted in Bartlett, *Wagner and Russia*, 221.

50 Bartlett, *Wagner and Russia*, 221.

51 Illustrations in Bartlett, *Wagner and Russia*, 222 and 234.

52 Tatlin, quoted in Gray, *Russian Experiment*, 226.

53 Bartlett, *Wagner and Russia*, 224.

54 Bartlett, *Wagner and Russia*, 237 and 239.

55 Bartlett, *Wagner and Russia*, 247; illustration of set model on 240.

56   Huntly Carter, *The New Spirit in the Russian Theatre 1917–1928*, London 1929, 144, quoted in Bartlett, *Wagner and Russia*, 248.

57   In 1935 it was rechristened the Kirov Theatre to honour the recently assassinated Communist Party chief of Leningrad. In 1991 the Mariinsky reverted to its original name, by which it is generally referred to in this book.

58   Bartlett, *Wagner and Russia*, 244–5, 243 and 245.

59   Carter, *Russian Theatre*, 170–1, quoted in Bartlett, *Wagner and Russia*, 246–7.

60   Bartlett, *Wagner and Russia*, 250.

61   Bartlett, *Wagner and Russia*, 250–1 and 251–3.

62   Bartlett, *Wagner and Russia*, 257–9 (Bartlett's quoted words are from A. Trabsky, ed., *Russki sovetskii teatr, 1921–26*, Leningrad 1982, 304) and 265–7.

63   Bartlett, *Wagner and Russia*, 243.

64   Bartlett, *Wagner and Russia*, 267–9 and 271.

65   Jay Leyda and Zina Voynow, *Eisenstein at Work*, London 1985, 111.

66   Leyda and Voynow, *Eisenstein*, 97.

67   Bartlett, *Wagner and Russia*, 273 and 281.

68   Quoted in Braun, *Theatre of Meyerhold*, 163, 179, 134ff. and 179.

69   Bartlett, *Wagner and Russia*, 281. The essay, 'Voploshchenie mifa', *Teatr* (Moscow), 10 (October 1940), 13–38, is translated as 'The Incarnation of Myth', in Sergei Eisenstein, *Selected Works*, vol. III, ed. Richard Taylor, trans. William Powell, London 1996, 142–69.

70   Quoted in Bartlett, *Wagner and Russia*, 280.

71   Bartlett, *Wagner and Russia*, 272.

72   Quoted in Rosamund Bartlett, 'The Embodiment of Myth: Eizenshtein's Production of *Die Walküre*', *Slavonic and East European Review*, 70, no. 1 (January 1992), 65.

73   Carl Dahlhaus, *Richard Wagner's Music Dramas*, trans. Mary Whittall, Cambridge 1979, 119. See also John Deathridge, '*Die Walküre*: A Tale of Two Stories', in the programme book for the 1991 production of *Der Ring des Nibelungen* at the Royal Opera House, London, 36.

74   Bartlett, 'Eizenshtein's *Die Walküre*', 67, 70–1 and 70.

75   Bartlett, *Wagner and Russia*, 272.

76   Quoted in Bartlett, 'Eizenshtein's *Die Walküre*', 67.

77   Quoted in Bartlett, 'Eizenshtein's *Die Walküre*', 71.

78   Quoted in Bartlett, 'Eizenshtein's *Die Walküre*', 72–3.

79   'Vertical Montage', in Sergei Eisenstein, *Selected Works*, vol. II, ed. Michael Glenny and Richard Taylor, trans. Michael Glenny, London 1991, 327–99.

80   Bartlett, *Wagner and Russia*, 281.

81   Quoted in Bartlett, 'Eizenshtein's *Die Walküre*', 74.

82   Quoted in Leyda and Voynow, *Eisenstein*, 114.

83   Quoted in Bartlett, 'Eizenshtein's *Die Walküre*', 59. Later, at the time of the *Walküre* production, Eisenstein describes *Götterdämmerung* as symbolizing 'the death of the whole "world of murder and plunder, legalized by falsehood, deceit and hypocrisy"'. Sergei Eisenstein, *Film Essays*, ed. Jay Leyda, London 1968, 86.

84   *Testimony: The Memoirs of Dmitri Shostakovich*, ed. Solomon Volkov, trans. Antonina W. Bouis, London 1979, 99.

85   Quoted in Bartlett, 'Eizenshtein's *Die Walküre*', 65.

86   Bartlett, 'Eizenshtein's *Die Walküre*', 64.

87   Quoted in Bartlett, 'Eizenshtein's *Die Walküre*', 62.

88   Quoted in Bartlett, 'Eizenshtein's *Die Walküre*', 68.

Chapter 8

1   Franz-Heinz Köhler, *Die Struktur der Spielpläne deutschsprachiger Opernbühnen von 1896 bis 1966*, Koblenz 1968, 38, quoted in Áine Sheil, 'The Politics of Reception: Richard Wagner's *Die Meistersinger von Nürnberg* in Weimar Germany', diss. King's College London, 2004. The basis for Köhler's statistics is principally opera houses in Germany and Austria, though it also includes German-speaking theatres outside German borders. I am grateful to Dr Sheil for drawing my attention to Köhler's book and for helpful comments on this chapter.

2   Quoted in Frederic Spotts, *Bayreuth: A History of the Wagner Festival*, New Haven/London 1994, 143.

3   One such 'rescue' attempt was Bernhard Diebold's 1928 pamphlet *Der Fall Wagner: Eine Revision* (Frankfurt 1928), which deplored the right-wing appropriation of Wagner and

extolled the composer as a social revolutionary.

4   Heyworth, *Klemperer* I, 279.
5   Köhler, *Spielpläne Opernbühnen*, 38.
6   Kim Kowalke, *Kurt Weill in Europe*, Ann Arbor 1979, 22.
7   See John Willett, *The Theatre of the Weimar Republic*, London 1988, 33 and whole chapter. I gratefully acknowledge this chapter's indebtedness to Mr Willett's book and to two other invaluable sources: Peter Heyworth, *Otto Klemperer: His Life and Times*, vol. I (1885–1933), Cambridge 1983, and Hans Curjel, *Experiment Krolloper 1927–1931*, ed. Eigel Kruttge, Munich 1975.
8   Willett, *Weimar Theatre*, 64.
9   Quoted in J. L. Styan, *Max Reinhardt*, Cambridge 1982, 108.
10   Quoted in Styan, *Max Reinhardt*, 110.
11   Willett, *Weimar Theatre*, 66.
12   Peter Gay, *Weimar Culture*, London 1969, 111.
13   Gay, *Weimar Culture*, 111.
14   Gay, *Weimar Culture*, 111.
15   Fritz Kortner, *Alle Tage Abend*, Munich 1959, 350–62 and 225, quoted in Willett, *Weimar Theatre*, 67.
16   Willett, *Weimar Theatre*, 79–81.
17   *Style and Idea: Selected Writings of Arnold Schoenberg*, ed. Leonard Stein, trans. Leo Black, London 1975, 337.
18   See the important chapter by Bryan Gilliam, 'Stage and Screen: Kurt Weill and Operatic Reform in the 1920s', in Bryan Gilliam, ed., *Music and Performance during the Weimar Republic*, Cambridge 1994, 1–12.
19   Willett, *Weimar Theatre*, 109.
20   Quoted in Gilliam, 'Stage and Screen', 2.
21   *Richard Strauss–Hugo von Hofmannsthal: Briefwechsel*, ed. Willi Schuh, Zürich 1978, 359, quoted in Gilliam, 'Stage and Screen', 2.
22   Arnold Schoenberg, 'Gibt es eine Krise der Oper?', *Musikblätter des Anbruch* (Vienna), 8 (1926), 209, quoted in Gilliam, 'Stage and Screen', 2.
23   Quoted in Mosco Carner, *Alban Berg*, London 1975, 62.
24   Quoted in Gilliam, 'Stage and Screen', 9.
25   Quoted in Gilliam, 'Stage and Screen', 10.
26   Willett, *Weimar Theatre*, 112.
27   Good sources on opera's filmic career include Richard Fawkes, *Opera on Film*, London 2000; Richard Evidon, 'Film', in *New Grove Opera*; Ken Wlaschin, *Opera on Screen*, Los Angeles 1997; and Marcia J. Citron, *Opera on Screen*, New Haven/London 2000.
28   Evan Baker, 'Parsifal for the Stage and Screen in New York City, 1904', in BP *Parsifal* 1996, 147.
29   Illustrations in Walter Panofsky, *Protest in der Oper*, Munich 1966, 101.
30   Illustration in Manfred Boetzkes, 'Sievert, Ludwig', in *New Grove Opera*.
31   Mike Ashman, 'Producing Wagner', in Barry Millington and Stewart Spencer, eds, *Wagner in Performance*, New Haven/London 1992, 37.
32   Illustration in Bauer, *Stage Designs*, 277.
33   Illustration in Bauer, *Stage Designs*, 279.
34   For a good contextual account of the 1920s Handel renaissance, see Panofsky, *Protest*, 69ff.
35   Winton Dean, 'The Recovery of Handel's Operas', in Christopher Hogwood and Richard Luckett, eds, *Music in Eighteenth-Century England*, Cambridge 1983, 104.
36   Panofsky, *Protest*, 75.
37   'Wer dabei war, hat den Geist des 20. Jahrhunderts gespürt.' Quoted in Curjel, *Krolloper*, 74.
38   'Berliner Opernmemorial', *Anbruch* (Vienna), June 1929, quoted in Heyworth, *Klemperer* I, 281.
39   Irmhild La Nier Kuhnt, quoted in Heyworth, *Klemperer* I, 83.
40   Heyworth, *Klemperer* I, 84.
41   Heyworth, *Klemperer* I, 85–6. See also Walter René Fuerst and Samuel J. Hume, *Twentieth-Century Stage Decoration*, 2 vols, New York 1967, I, 42, which dates the *Stilbühne* to 1912.
42   Heyworth, *Klemperer* I, 121.
43   Carl Hagemann, *Bühne und Welt*, Wiesbaden 1948, 101–3, quoted in Heyworth, *Klemperer* I, 247–8.
44   Heyworth, *Klemperer* I, 199–200.
45   Curjel, *Krolloper*, 13 and 47.
46   Quoted in Curjel, *Krolloper*, 47.
47   Ewald Dülberg, 'Musik und Szene', in Eigel Kruttge, ed., *Von neuer Musik*, Cologne 1924, quoted in Heyworth, *Klemperer* I, 200–1.
48   Curjel, *Krolloper*, 48.
49   Heyworth, *Klemperer* I, 202.
50   13 September 1924, quoted in Heyworth, *Klemperer* I, 202.
51   *Pult und Taktstock* (Vienna), October 1924, quoted in Heyworth, *Klemperer* I, 203.
52   Heyworth, *Klemperer* I, 211–12.

53   See John Rockwell, 'The Prussian
      Ministry of Culture and the Berlin State
      Opera, 1918–1931', diss. University of
      California (Berkeley), n.d.
54   Willett, *Weimar Theatre*, 68.
55   In all there were three opera houses in
      Berlin: the Staatsoper (whose conductors
      included Leo Blech and Erich Kleiber),
      the Städische Oper (Municipal Opera,
      where Bruno Walter was music director,
      1925–9) and the Krolloper. From 1926
      the coordination of the three theatres was
      entrusted to the conductor and producer
      Heinz Tietjen as Generalintendant.
56   Heyworth, *Klemperer* I, 271.
57   Heyworth, *Klemperer* I, 218.
58   Heyworth, *Klemperer* I, 261 and 260.
59   Quoted in Curjel, *Krolloper*, 74.
60   Heyworth, *Klemperer* I, 281.
61   Heyworth, *Klemperer* I, 256.
62   Curjel, *Krolloper*, 48.
63   Curjel, *Krolloper*, 60 and 69.
64   Heyworth, *Klemperer* I, 65.
65   Heyworth, *Klemperer* I, 285.
66   Heyworth, *Klemperer* I, 286–7.
67   Curjel, *Krolloper*, 58.
68   'Rettung Wagners durch surrealistische
      Kolportage', in Ernst Bloch, *Zur
      Philosophie der Musik*, Frankfurt 1974,
      176–84.
69   *Frankfurter Zeitung*, 18 January 1929,
      quoted in Curjel, *Krolloper*, 253–5.
70   *Melos* (Mainz), 7 (1929), 84, quoted in
      Curjel, *Krolloper*, 258–9.
71   *Berliner Tageblatt*, 16 January 1929,
      quoted in Curjel, *Krolloper*, 252–3.
72   Quoted in Curjel, *Krolloper*, 52.
73   Quoted in Curjel, *Krolloper*, 52.
74   Quoted in Curjel, *Krolloper*, 259.
75   Quoted in Curjel, *Krolloper*, 253.
76   Such an approach was castigated by
      Heinrich Strobel in his review of
      Holländer in *Melos*, quoted in Curjel,
      Krolloper, 258–9.
77   Quoted in Curjel, *Krolloper*, 257.
78   Quoted in Heyworth, *Klemperer* I, 280.
79   Heyworth, *Klemperer* I, 286.
80   Quoted by Heinrich Strobel in Curjel,
      Krolloper, 258.
81   Peter Heyworth, ed., *Conversations with
      Klemperer*, London 1973, 65.
82   Heyworth, *Klemperer* I, 270.
83   Heyworth, *Klemperer* I, 409–10.
84   Otto Klemperer, 'In eigener Sache',
      Berliner Tageblatt, 27 January 1931,
      quoted in Heyworth, *Klemperer* I, 377.

Chapter 9

1   Wieland Wagner, interview in the
      Hessische Nachrichtung, 27 July 1956,
      quoted in Geoffrey Skelton, *Wieland
      Wagner: The Positive Sceptic*, London
      1971, 134.
2   Nike Wagner, *The Wagners: The Dramas
      of a Musical Dynasty*, trans. Ewald Osers
      and Michael Downes, London 2000, 111.
3   Walter Panofsky, *Wieland Wagner*,
      Bremen 1964, 74.
4   For the basic idea of the production
      Wieland was indebted to Joachim Herz
      and Rudolf Heinrich's Leipzig staging of
      1960. See chapter 10.
5   Panofsky, *Wieland Wagner*, 74.
6   Panofsky, *Wieland Wagner*, 76.
7   Geoffrey Skelton, *Wagner at Bayreuth*,
      2nd edn, London 1976, 193. Sachs's
      closing words are: 'Drum sag' ich
      euch:/ehrt eure deutschen Meister!/Dann
      bannt ihr gute Geister;/und gebt ihr
      ihrem Wirken Gunst,/zerging' in
      Dunst/das heil'ge röm'sche Reich,/uns
      bliebe gleich/die heil'ge deutsche Kunst!'
      Wagner went to the trouble of deleting
      from his original text a couplet
      honouring the German warrior:
      see John Warrack, *Richard Wagner:
      'Die Meistersinger von Nürnberg'*
      (Cambridge Opera Handbook),
      Cambridge 1994, 29.
8   Nike Wagner, *The Wagners*, 114–15.
9   Quoted in Mack, *Inszenierungsstil*, 27.
10 The significance of Wieland's apprentice
      years in the 1930s is discussed with acuity
      by Nike Wagner in *The Wagners*, esp.
      103–17 and 147–52.
11 In the Siegfried era Hitler bought about
      two hundred tickets for each festival, but
      his ticket bill escalated once he became
      Chancellor. In most years he also
      contributed 100,000 RM to the festival's
      running costs, roughly one-tenth of its
      annual expenditure of about 1 million
      RM. From 1941 the festival was almost
      entirely funded through the Reich's Kraft
      durch Freude (Strength through Joy)
      programme for boosting morale among
      its workers. See Fred K. Prieberg, *Musik
      im NS-Staat*, Frankfurt 1982, 129 and
      307, and Michael Karbaum, *Studien zur
      Geschichte der Bayreuther Festspiele
      (1876–1976)*, Regensburg 1976, part II,
      152–3. I am indebted to Gudrun
      Föttinger of the Richard-Wagner-

Museum, Bayreuth, for detailed information on the festival's finances in the 1930s.

12 These included not only the Berlin Staatsoper, Krolloper and Staatstheater, but also the theatres in Wiesbaden, Kassel and Hanover.

13 Berndt W. Wessling, ed., *Bayreuth im Dritten Reich: Richard Wagners politische Erben: Eine Dokumentation*, Weinheim/Basel 1983, 217.

14 Quoted in Spotts, *Bayreuth*, 164.

15 Wolfgang Wagner, *Acts*, trans. John Brownjohn, London 1994, 68.

16 Skelton, *Wieland Wagner*, 23; Mayer, *Wagner in Bayreuth*, 144.

17 Spotts, *Bayreuth*, 168–9.

18 Quoted in Nike Wagner, *The Wagners*, 154.

19 Frederic Spotts, *Hitler and the Power of Aesthetics*, London 2002, 258.

20 Mack, *Inszenierungsstil*, 11.

21 Quoted in Bauer, *Stage Designs*, 248.

22 Reprinted in Mack, *Inszenierungsstil*, 54–6, and in Wessling, *Bayreuth im Dritten Reich*, 218–22.

23 Quoted in Wessling, *Bayreuth im Dritten Reich*, 221.

24 Quoted in Wessling, *Bayreuth im Dritten Reich*, 222.

25 Emil Preetorius, *Wagner: Bild und Vision*, 3rd edn, Godesberg 1949, 19–22, quoted from Stewart Spencer's translation in *Wagner*, 12, no. 2 (May 1991), 78–9.

26 Preetorius, *Bild und Vision*, 29, quoted from Stewart Spencer's translation in *Wagner*, 12, no. 2 (May 1991), 81.

27 Illustration 244 in Mack, *Inszenierungsstil*.

28 Illustration 268 in Mack, *Inszenierungsstil*.

29 Illustrations 274, 307, 294 and 285 in Mack, *Inszenierungsstil*.

30 Mack, *Inszenierungsstil*, 11.

31 Friedelind Wagner (with Page Cooper), *The Royal Family of Bayreuth*, London 1948, 84 and 134.

32 Skelton, *Wagner at Bayreuth*, 152.

33 Mack, *Inszenierungsstil*, 27.

34 Mack, *Inszenierungsstil*, 36.

35 24 July 1933, quoted in Wessling, *Bayreuth im Dritten Reich*, 196.

36 *BZ am Mittag* (Berlin), 22 July 1933, quoted in Wessling, *Bayreuth im Dritten Reich*, 196.

37 *Manchester Guardian*, 15 August 1933, quoted in Wessling, *Bayreuth im Dritten*

Reich, 189.

38 Spotts, *Bayreuth*, 179–80.

39 Heinz Tietjen, 'Emil Preetorius, der Szeniker', in Fritz Hollwich, ed., *Im Umkreis der Kunst: Eine Festschrift für Emil Preetorius* (published to mark Preetorius's seventieth birthday), Wiesbaden [1953], 262, quoted in Skelton, *Wagner at Bayreuth*, 155.

40 August Kubizek, *Young Hitler: The Story of Our Friendship*, trans. E. V. Anderson, Maidstone 1973, 66. Although Kubizek's book is deeply flawed there is little reason to doubt his account of Hitler's epiphany after the performance of *Rienzi* in Linz.

41 Spotts, *Hitler*, 58, illustrations on 238.

42 Spotts, *Bayreuth*, 141.

43 Albert Speer, *Inside the Third Reich*, trans. Richard and Clara Winston, London 1970. Citation from pbk edn, London 1978, 194.

44 Albert Speer, *Spandau: The Secret Diaries*, trans. Richard and Clara Winston, London 1976, 102.

45 Spotts, *Hitler*, 207.

46 Speer, *Spandau Diaries*, 103.

47 Speer, *Spandau Diaries*, 103.

48 Spotts, *Bayreuth*, 186.

49 Wolfgang Wagner, *Acts*, 10.

50 A 1937 Berlin exhibition, *Das deutsche Bühnenbild, 1933–1936*, honoured Roller and Preetorius's work alongside that of Arent. Other favoured designers included Adolf Mahnke, Traugott Müller, Leo Pasetti, Wilhelm Reinking and Hans Wildermann. The exhibits were published in book form with a foreword by Goebbels. Arent's introduction claims that 'the revolutionary ideas of National Socialism have decisively changed scenic design in Germany. It is no longer an art in itself but serves the German people as the visual link between the stage and the public'. One would have imagined that that had never ceased to be its function. Benno von Arent, ed., *Das deutsche Bühnenbild: 1933–1936*, Berlin (Leonhard Preiss) 1938.

51 Speer, *Spandau Diaries*, 313.

52 Mann modelled the morally irresponsible aesthete Sixtus Kridwiß partly on Preetorius. See also Mann's letter of 6 December 1949 thanking Preetorius for the 1949 reissue of the latter's *Wagner: Bild und Vision*, in Mann, *Pro and Contra Wagner*, 208–11.

53 See Patrick Carnegy, 'Stage History', in

Warrack, *Die Meistersinger*, 140–2.

54 Quoted in Herbert Barth, Dietrich Mack and Wilhelm Rauh, *Der Festspielhügel: Richard Wagners Werk in Bayreuth*, Munich 1973, 115.

55 Quoted in Mack, *Inszenierungsstil*, 36.

56 Karl Alfons Meyer, *Neue Zürcher Zeitung*, 7 August 1936, quoted in Mack, *Inszenierungsstil*, 36.

57 Spotts, *Bayreuth*, 178–9.

58 *Bayreuther Festspielführer* 1938, 89.

59 *Bayreuther Festspielführer* 1936, 83–6.

60 Spotts, *Bayreuth*, 184; Spotts, *Hitler*, 224.

61 Wolfgang Wagner, *Acts*, 42.

62 Karbaum, *Bayreuther Festspiele* II, 94.

63 In 1941 Hitler had Goebbels circulate photographs of the 1914 Roller designs to all opera houses with the instruction that they were to be followed and that the work 'was no longer to be done in the Byzantine-sacred style that was common up to then'. Spotts, *Hitler*, 236. Hitler's enthusiasm for the Roller designs was in large measure driven by his belief that they secularized the 'sacred festival drama'.

64 Spotts, *Bayreuth*, 184. Roller's designs are illustrated and described by Oswald Georg Bauer in 'Touchstone *Parsifal*: On the First Publication of Alfred Roller's Designs for the Bayreuth *Parsifal* of 1934', in BP *Parsifal* 1998, 59–67.

65 Paul Bülow, 'Ein Besuch bei Wieland Wagner', *Nordbayerische Zeitung*, 24 July 1937, quoted in Wessling, *Bayreuth im Dritten Reich*, 270.

66 Skelton, *Wieland Wagner*, 53.

67 Wolfgang Wagner, *Acts*, 41.

68 Quoted in Mack, *Inszenierungsstil*, 21.

69 Illustrations 298–300 in Mack, *Inszenierungsstil*.

70 Letter of 24 August 1937, in Mack, *Inszenierungsstil*, 102.

71 Ferdinand Staeger (1880–1976) enjoyed a considerable reputation as a painter, illustrator and teacher.

72 Overhoff's publications include *Richard Wagners 'Tristan'-Partitur*, Bayreuth 1948; *Richard Wagners 'Parsifal'*, Lindau 1951; *Die Musikdramen Richard Wagners*, Salzburg 1967; and *Wagners Nibelungen-Tetralogie*, Salzburg 1971.

73 Skelton, *Wieland Wagner*, 60.

74 The Richard-Wagner-Museum in Bayreuth has a photograph that may be of Act I, scene 1, of Wieland's *Götterdämmerung* in Nuremberg

(1943–4), and also a flyer based on a drawing by Wieland for Act I of *Der fliegende Holländer*, which he designed for the same city in 1942.

75 Skelton, *Wieland Wagner*, 69.

76 Skelton, *Wieland Wagner*, 70–1.

77 Richard Reinhardt in the *Bayerische Kurier* (Bayreuth), 30 June 1943, quoted in Skelton, *Wieland Wagner*, 67–8.

78 Quoted in Skelton, *Wieland Wagner*, 66.

79 Quoted in Skelton, *Wieland Wagner*, 66.

80 Spotts, *Bayreuth*, 183.

81 Illustrations 318–21 in Mack, *Inszenierungsstil*.

82 Overhoff, *Richard Wagners 'Tristan'-Partitur*, 28, n. 73.

83 Wolfgang Wagner, *Acts*, 45.

84 Speer, *Spandau Diaries*, 370.

85 Panofsky, *Wieland Wagner*, 14; Walter Erich Schäfer, *Wieland Wagner: Persönlichkeit und Leistung*, Tübingen 1970, 14.

86 Skelton, *Wieland Wagner*, 52.

87 Antoine Goléa, *Gespräche mit Wieland Wagner*, Salzburg 1968, 31 and 32.

88 Goléa, *Gespräche*, 32.

89 Michael H. Kater, *The Twisted Muse: Musicians and Their Music in the Third Reich*, New York/Oxford 1997, 38. (Kater's cited source is, inter alia, an article on Tietjen by Rudolf Augstein in *Der Spiegel* (Hamburg), 25 July 1994, 156.)

90 Karbaum, *Bayreuther Festspiele* II, 106–13.

91 'Überlieferung und Neugestaltung', in *Das Bayreuther Festspielbuch* 1951, 22–6. Reprinted in Wieland Wagner, *Sein Denken*, ed. Oswald Georg Bauer, Bayreuth 1991, 19–23. Translated as 'Tradition and Innovation', in Herbert Barth, ed., *Life, Work, Festspielhaus*, Bayreuth 1952, 22–5. Substantial extracts translated in Skelton, *Wieland Wagner*, 94–6.

92 Barth, *Life, Work, Festspielhaus*, 22–5.

93 Goléa, *Gespräche*, 24. Wieland's assertion that Hitler had 'effectively banned *Parsifal*' is incorrect. According to the records of the Deutscher Bühnenverein (Association of German Theatres), between 1933 and 1939 there were 714 performances in the Reich, though they did dry up with the outbreak of war. See Ulrich Drüner, ed., *Richard Wagner: 'Parsifal'* (libretto with extensive analysis and commentaries), Munich (PremOp)

1990, 205, and also Philippe Olivier, 'L'Equivoque Nazie', in Alain Duault, ed., *Wagner: 'Parsifal'* (*L'Avant-Scène Opéra*, 38–9), Paris 1982, 151–3.

94 'Das Parsifalkreuz: Ein psychologisches Schema', in *Das Bayreuther Festspielbuch* 1951, 68–9. Reprinted in Wieland Wagner, *Sein Denken*, 28–9.

95 Barth, *Life, Work, Festspielhaus*, 23.

96 Quoted in Skelton, *Wieland Wagner*, 104.

97 Quoted in Skelton, *Wieland Wagner*, 104.

98 The central role of Eberhardt in Festspielhaus technology is described in Baumann, *Bühnentechnik*, 82–4.

99 Spotts, *Bayreuth*, 199.

100 'Lieber Paul Eberhardt', in BP *Rheingold* 1966, 12–13. Reprinted in Wieland Wagner, *Sein Denken*, 56–7. Translated, in part, in Skelton, *Wieland Wagner*, 101–2.

101 Mack, *Inszenierungsstil*, 12–13.

102 Illustrations in Schäfer, *Wieland Wagner*, plates ff. 92, no. 4 (*Rheingold*, scene 2, 1956).

103 Illustrations in Schäfer, *Wieland Wagner*, plates ff. 92, no. 13.

104 Panofsky, *Wieland Wagner*, 41.

105 Panofsky, *Wieland Wagner*, 41.

106 Conversation with Geoffrey Skelton, quoted in Skelton, *Wieland Wagner*, 179.

107 Panofsky, *Wieland Wagner*, 40. Other Schadewaldt parallels which Wieland told Panofsky he considered to be important for contemporary Wagner interpretation were Prometheus–Brünnhilde, Io–Sieglinde and the Oceanides–Valkyries. Schadewaldt's 'Richard Wagner und die Griechen' was printed in BP *Lohengrin* 1962, 2–32; 'Richard Wagner und die Griechen. Zweiter Teil: Die Ringdichtung und Aischylos' *Prometheus* Interpretationen' in BP *Meistersinger* 1963, 24–44; and 'Richard Wagner und die Griechen. Dritter Teil: Nachlese' in BP *Meistersinger* 1964, 3–30. An English translation of the first lecture by Desmond Clayton was published in three parts in BP *Rheingold* 1964, 10–21; BP *Walküre* 1964, 18–23; and BP *Siegfried* 1964, 21–7. This first lecture, translated by David C. Durst as 'Richard Wagner and the Greeks' and with a commentary by John Deathridge, is in *Dialogos (Hellenic Studies Review)* (Ilford, Essex), 6 (1999), 108–40. Schadewaldt's 'Der "Homerische" Charakter der *Meistersinger*' is in BP *Meistersinger* 1969, 2–7. Many articles in the programme

books of the 1950s also emphasized the mythic and Greek elements in Wagner's works, as in Curt von Westernhagen's 'Die Auferstehung des Mythos' (1953) and 'Das Beispiel des Aischylos' (1955). The topic has continued to receive much attention, as in Hugh Lloyd-Jones, 'Wagner and the Greeks', *Times Literary Supplement*, 9 January 1976, expanded in Hugh Lloyd-Jones, *Blood for the Ghosts*, London 1982, 126–42; Michael Ewans, *Wagner and Aeschylus: The 'Ring' and the 'Oresteia'*, London 1982; and Simon Goldhill's 'Wagner and the Greeks', in the programme book for the 1991 production of *Der Ring des Nibelungen* at the Royal Opera House, London, 63–70.

108 Goléa, *Gespräche*, 88.

109 Goléa, *Gespräche*, 129.

110 Goléa, *Gespräche*, 80.

111 Quoted in Skelton, *Wieland Wagner*, 182.

112 Quoted in Victor Gollancz, *The 'Ring' at Bayreuth*, London 1966, 35.

113 Quoted in Skelton, *Wieland Wagner*, 181.

114 Panofsky, *Wieland Wagner*, 41.

115 Panofsky, *Wieland Wagner*, 41–2.

116 Schäfer, *Wieland Wagner*, 92.

117 Goléa, *Gespräche*, 79.

118 Wieland reinvented the production for theatres abroad, notably in Stuttgart and Copenhagen (1961) and in Hamburg (1966), whence it travelled to the Edinburgh Festival in 1968. It was still in the Copenhagen repertory in 1999. Wieland's ideas about the opera (from an essay in the programme book for Copenhagen 1961) are quoted in Skelton, *Wieland Wagner*, 145–6.

119 Panofsky, *Wieland Wagner*, 83.

120 Panofsky, *Wieland Wagner*, 83.

121 Panofsky, *Wieland Wagner*, 84.

122 See chapter 10.

123 'Wieland Wagner on Producing *Lohengrin*', interview with Geoffrey Skelton, *Listener*, 7 February 1963, 240.

124 Skelton interview, 240–1.

125 Skelton interview, 240.

126 Skelton interview, 240.

127 William Mann in the booklet to the Philips live recording of the 1962 Bayreuth *Lohengrin*, rec. no. 6747 241.

128 Panofsky, *Wieland Wagner*, 82.

129 Panofsky, *Wieland Wagner*, 80–1.

130 Wagner's autobiographical identification with the character is evident enough. Stewart Spencer has drawn attention to Wagner's fear of his own sensuality as

described in GS IV, 279, commenting that 'There is much to be said for the suggestion that the Venusberg is not so much a place as a representation of the hero's sexuality, which he himself is at pains to exorcise, but which may ultimately be exorcisable only through death.' 'Tannhäuser und der Tanhusaere', in Ursula and Ulrich Müller, eds, *Opern und Opernfiguren: Festschrift für Joachim Herz*, Anif (Salzburg, Ursula Müller-Speiser) 1989, 244–5.

131 GS V, 147, quoted in Spencer, 'Tannhäuser und der Tanhusaere', 245.

132 Nike Wagner, *The Wagners*, 247.

133 Mayer, *Wagner in Bayreuth*, 184. He argues that Wagner's stage, like Peter Brook's, is essentially an 'empty stage' and this 'is at the basis of the new dramaturgy and scenery of Bayreuth'.

134 Gollancz, *The 'Ring'*, 27.

135 Gollancz, *The 'Ring'*, 111–12. For another example of Wieland's response to interrogation by a veteran opera lover, see 'Wieland Wagner' by Willy Haas in the booklet to the Philips live recording of the 1962 Bayreuth *Lohengrin* (see n. 127 above). See also Goléa, *Gespräche*, passim.

136 For example, Goléa, *Gespräche*, 48: 'ich bin kein abstrakter, sondern nur ein werkgetreuer Regisseur, versuche wenigstens, ein solcher zu sein.'

137 Gollancz, *The 'Ring'*, 40.

138 Panofsky, *Wieland Wagner*, 18–19.

139 Interview with Geoffrey Skelton (see p. 417, nn. 123–6), 240.

140 Mack, *Inszenierungsstil*, 12.

141 Anja Silja, *Die Sehnsucht nach dem Unerreichbaren*, Berlin 1999, 61.

142 'Interview mit Anja Silja' by Martin Korn, *Gondroms Festspielmagazin* (Bayreuth), 1998, 36–44.

143 At the words 'der dort dir schimmert heil und hehr: des Grales heil'gen Speer'. Boosey and Hawkes vocal score, London 1914, 303.

144 Conversation with Patrick Carnegy, Bayreuth 1976. Jess Thomas gives a good account of working with Wieland in his autobiography, *Kein Schwert verhieß mir der Vater*, Vienna 1986.

145 Panofsky, *Wieland Wagner*, 56.

146 Herbert von Karajan, who had conducted Wieland's 1952 Bayreuth *Tristan*, was among those who were to lean heavily on his style. See, for example, Karajan's 1959

Tristan in Vienna with designs by Emil Preetorius, illustrated in Heldt, *Tristan und Isolde*, 205–6.

147 Mayer, *Wagner in Bayreuth*, 222.

148 Quoted in Skelton, *Wieland Wagner*, 109.

149 Nike Wagner, *The Wagners*, 112.

150 Letter of 11 July 1966, quoted in Wieland Wagner, *Sein Denken*, 141.

151 Nike Wagner, *The Wagners*, 117.

152 Schadewaldt, 'Richard Wagner and the Greeks' (see p. 417, n. 107), 131.

153 Deathridge, commentary on Schadewaldt, 'Richard Wagner and the Greeks' (see p. 417, n. 107), 139.

Chapter 10

1 Mann, *Pro and Contra Wagner*, 193.

2 Pernerstorfer's group of confused liberals was actually of German nationalist persuasion. Nevertheless, it took Wagner's revolutionary socialism more seriously than did the composer's right-wing adherents. Ernst Hanisch, 'The Political Influence and Appropriation of Wagner', in Müller, *Wagner Handbook*, 195.

3 Diebold, *Der Fall Wagner*.

4 Bartlett, *Wagner and Russia*, 227.

5 Bartlett, *Wagner and Russia*, 224 and 226.

6 Anatoly Lunacharsky, 'Richard Wagner', an essay written for the fiftieth anniversary of the composer's death, in Anatoly Lunacharsky, *On Literature and Art*, ed. A. Lebedev, Moscow 1965, 349–51.

7 Werner P. Seiferth, 'Wagner-Pflege in der DDR', in *Richard-Wagner-Blätter: Zeitschrift des Aktionskreises für das Werk Richard Wagners* (Bayreuth), 13 (1989), nos 3–4, 89–113.

8 Seiferth, 'Wagner-Pflege', 91–3.

9 Nike Wagner, *The Wagners*, 112.

10 Nike Wagner, *The Wagners*, 236.

11 Marion Benz, 'Die Wagner-Inszenierungen von Joachim Herz: Studie zur theatralen Wagner-Rezeption in der DDR', diss. Friedrich-Alexander-Universität, Erlangen-Nürnberg, 1998, 70. Dr Benz's study is richly illuminating not only on Herz but on all aspects of Wagner in the cultural and political context of East Germany. It is a pleasure to thank her for her invaluable help with this chapter.

12 Quoted in Peter Paul Fuchs, ed., *The*

Music Theatre of Walter Felsenstein, London 1991, xxii.

13 Quoted in Fuchs, *Felsenstein*, xxvi.

14 Quoted in Joachim Herz, 'Neubeginn und Neuorientierung', unpublished paper delivered at the International Richard Wagner Congress in Berlin, 3 June 2000.

15 Walter Felsenstein and Joachim Herz, *Musiktheater*, ed. Stephan Stompor, Leipzig 1976, 257.

16 Quoted in Fuchs, *Felsenstein*, 150.

17 Herz's lecture was published in *Richard Wagner 1883–1983: Gesammelte Beiträge des Salzburger Symposions* ed. Ulrich Müller, Franz Hundsnurscher and Cornelius Sommer, Stuttgart 1984, 3–32, and reprinted in Joachim Herz, *Theater – Kunst des erfüllten Augenblicks*, ed. Ilse Kobán, Berlin 1989, 186–99. It is translated by Stewart Spencer in *Wagner*, 19, no. 1 (January 1998), 3–33.

18 *Die Meistersinger* (Basel 1927), *Parsifal* (Basel 1928), *Rienzi* (Cologne 1932), *Parsifal* (Cologne 1933), *Tannhäuser* (Frankfurt 1934 and Aachen 1943). Felsenstein, *Musiktheater*, 536–50.

19 See Benz, 'Herz Inszenierungen', 85.

20 Brecht derided Stanislavsky's 'transfigured actors, the emotionally windswept audience, the too, too solid settings, the rigid formal framework of the plot'. Quoted in John Willett, *The Theatre of Bertolt Brecht*, London 1967, 207.

21 Michael Patterson, *German Theatre Today*, London 1976, 45.

22 Willett, *Theatre of Bertolt Brecht*, 204.

23 Benz, 'Herz Inszenierungen', 33.

24 Seiferth, 'Wagner-Pflege', 97 and 99.

25 Seiferth, 'Wagner-Pflege', 102–5.

26 Seiferth, 'Wagner-Pflege', 103–4.

27 P. Witzmann, 'Tönende Vorhalle des Faschismus', *Theater der Zeit* (East Berlin), (1958), 26–7.

28 Benz, 'Herz Inszenierungen', 34–5.

29 Quoted in Seiferth, 'Wagner-Pflege', 106.

30 Patterson, *German Theatre*, 61–2.

31 Patterson, *German Theatre*, 60.

32 Joachim Herz, 'Die Meistersinger von Nürnberg: Komödie in der Zeitenwende' (1960), in Herz, *Theater*, 99–101. The principal sources for my account of the Leipzig *Meistersinger* include this essay and personal communications. Unattributed quotations from Herz throughout this chapter are from conversations with him recorded in

London on 20 April 1994 and subsequently, as well as from correspondence.

33 Joachim Herz, 'Richard Wagner und das Erbe', in Herz, *Theater*, 129.

34 In a letter to me of 2 September 2000, Herz says he had always thought that the Brechtian elements had been the source of the very conservative Kayser's apprehension, the impudence not only in introducing a river but in labelling it as the Pegnitz. After his death in 1956 Brecht had been proscribed in Leipzig and Stanislavsky was the model held up for emulation. Doubtless another problem may have been Nuremberg's association with the Nazi Reichsparteitage. But for Herz himself, the word Nürnberg was not so much a reminder of West Germany as of the quintessential Germanness associated with its greatest citizens – figures like Hans Sachs, Dürer, Veit Stoβ and others whose tradition the GDR had inherited and would be carrying forward.

35 Benz, 'Herz Inszenierungen', 117.

36 Benz, 'Herz Inszenierungen', 111–12.

37 Benz, 'Herz Inszenierungen', 128.

38 Benz, 'Herz Inszenierungen', 126 and 130.

39 Benz, 'Herz Inszenierungen', 116, n. 73.

40 Benz, 'Herz Inszenierungen', 126.

41 Benz, 'Herz Inszenierungen', 130–1.

42 Joachim Herz, 'Zur filmischen Gestaltung von Richard Wagners Oper *Der fliegende Holländer*: Gespräch mit Horst Seeger', in Herz, *Theater*, 104.

43 'Remarks on the Performance of the Opera *Der fliegende Holländer*', trans. Thomas Grey, in Grey, *Der fliegende Holländer*, 200.

44 Personal communication, 5 February 1998, from which unattributed quotations from Herz in relation to his *Holländer* productions are also taken.

45 Behind his back, Karl Kayser was commonly known as 'Kaiser Karl' on account of his implacably imperious behaviour.

46 Following the 'thaw' at the end of the repressive Zhdanov years, *Der fliegende Holländer* had been the first Wagner opera to be chosen for production in the Soviet Union since the Second World War, the production in question taking place at the Maly Theatre in Leningrad in 1957, conducted by Kurt Sanderling. See Bartlett, *Wagner and Russia*, 290.

47 Herz, 'Zur filmischen Gestaltung', 107. I am grateful to Professor Herz for helping me to see a copy of his film and for answering my questions about it and about his stage productions of *Holländer*.

48 'From her dreams Senta at last finds the strength to leave the world of money-grubbing and strict convention, and to start a new life. In this way the folk legend also becomes an expression of hope for a better future.' Promotional brochure for the film of *Der fliegende Holländer*, Joachim Herz personal archive.

49 Michael Lewin, *Harry Kupfer*, Vienna 1988, 138.

50 Lewin lists 147 substantive reviews: *Harry Kupfer*, 442–5.

51 Lewin, *Harry Kupfer*, 135.

52 Benz, 'Herz Inszenierungen', 274, n. 165.

53 Sieglinde's melody was once defined by Wagner himself as 'the glorification of Brünnhilde'; see *Wagner*, 4, no. 3 (June 1983), 90.

54 The principal sources for my account of the Leipzig *Ring* are personal communications from Joachim Herz. Valuable documentation includes programme books for the production and the 'Arbeitshefte' (Workbooks) published by the Akademie der Künste der DDR entitled 'Joachim Herz inszeniert Richard Wagners *Ring des Nibelungen* am Opernhaus Leipzig', nos 21 (ed. Marion Reinisch) and 29 (ed. Eginhard Röhlig), Berlin 1975 and 1980.

55 Herz mentions his indebtedness to Mann's 'Ibsen and Wagner' in 'Das Romantische und die Wirklichkeit', *Theater der Zeit* (East Berlin), 8 (1962), 58.

56 CD I, 965 (25 May 1877).

57 '*Der Ring* als bürgerliches Parabelspiel', in *Bayreuth 1966* (festival publication). (The essay was first published in *Theater heute*, East Berlin, September 1965.) When Kurt Masur, music director of the Leipzig Gewandhaus Orchestra (which also played for the Opera), heard of the *Ring* project he sent Herz a copy of Shaw – a further demonstration that many were familiar with his ideas and looked forward to seeing them given an airing on the stage. Herz recalls going to Berlin to discuss a possible *Ring* co-production between his own Leipzig theatre and the Berlin Staatsoper with its Intendant,

Hans Pischner, who read aloud to him passages from *The Perfect Wagnerite* as though Shaw's own ideas of a socialist utopia had already been realized in the GDR (letter from Herz 14 February 2000). Nothing came of the co-production plan and Leipzig went ahead on its own.

58 Bernard Shaw, *Major Critical Essays*, London 1932, 179.

59 Dahlhaus, *Wagner's Music Dramas*, 131 and 140–1.

60 Ernst Bloch, *Das Prinzip Hoffnung*, Frankfurt 1954–9.

61 Benz, 'Herz Inszenierungen', 242.

62 Rudolf Heinrich, Arbeitsheft 21, 46.

63 Heinrich, Arbeitsheft 21, 43.

64 Herz, Arbeitsheft 21, 47.

65 Herz, Arbeitsheft 21, 47.

66 Herz, Arbeitsheft 21, 48.

67 Rudolf Heinrich, 'In verständlichen Bildern', in the programme book for the 1973 production of *Das Rheingold* at the Leipzig Opera.

68 Herz and Heinrich, Arbeitsheft 21, 40–9.

69 It will be recalled that Eisenstein, Herz's forerunner in illustrating the musical narrative, used mime groups extensively in the first act of *Walküre* (see chapter 5).

70 Arbeitsheft 21, 61. Ibsen was much performed in the GDR at this time. The production emphasis was on his plays' clinical exposure of the ills of bourgeois society. I am grateful to Marion Kant (formerly Reinisch, see n. 54), for this information.

71 Herz, Arbeitsheft 21, 44.

72 Compare this approach with that of Wieland Wagner, for whom the *Ring* was not primarily a social drama but a metaphor for the archetypal psyche.

73 The grandiloquent march, obviously enough, is to be read as Wotan's idea of his entry into Valhalla, not ours. Herz's principle was to follow the music as the only reliable guide to what is going on.

74 'Pritschenschwinger des Jahrmarktes'. Mann goes on to characterize him more roundly as also 'the son of light and Nordic sun myth – which does not prevent him … from being something very modern and nineteenth-century: the free man, the breaker of old tablets and renewer of a corrupt society – or "Bakoonin", as Bernard Shaw's cheery rationalism always terms him. Hans Wurst, god of light, and anarchistic social

revolutionary, all in the same person: what more could the theatre possibly ask for?' Mann, 'The Sorrows and Grandeur of Richard Wagner', in *Pro and Contra Wagner*, 131 (translation amended).

75 Herz, unpublished typescript, quoted in Benz, 'Herz Inszenierungen', 252.

76 Herz, *Arbeitsheft* 29, 30.

77 Eckart Schwinger, *Opera*, May 1974, 425.

78 Peter Wittig, *Die Union* (Dresden), 20 April 1974, quoted in Benz, 'Herz Inszenierungen', 281.

79 Manfred Haedler, *Der Morgen* (East Berlin), 27 April 1973; Hans-Jürgen Schaefer, *Neues Deutschland* (East Berlin), 16 April 1973; both quoted in Benz, 'Herz Inszenierungen', 280.

80 *New York Herald Tribune*, 10 April 1973.

81 *Kürbiskern* (Munich), April 1974.

82 *Opera*, July 1973, 595, and July 1976, 624–5. Schwinger's review of *Die Walküre* is in *Opera*, May 1974, 408 and 425–7.

83 Christoph Hamm, *Arbeitsheft* 21, 81, and Benz, 'Herz Inszenierungen', 279.

84 Eginhard Röhlig, *Arbeitsheft* 21, 81.

85 Herz, *Arbeitsheft* 21, 81–2.

86 See especially the debate 'Wagner und das realistische Musiktheater' that took place at the Akademie der Künste in Berlin on 2 May 1974 and is reported in *Arbeitsheft* 21, 63–83.

87 *Leipziger Volkszeitung*, 2 October 1991, quoted in Benz, 'Herz Inszenierungen', 280, n. 183.

88 For a perceptive recent positive account of Herz and particularly of the influence of his *Holländer*, see Ulrich Schreiber, 'Der Zeitgeist – ein sonderbar' Ding', in *Oper aktuell XXV: Die Bayerische Staatsoper 2002/2003*, Munich (Stiebner) 2002, 45–51.

89 T. W. Adorno, 'Berliner Opernmemorial', *Anbruch*, June 1929, quoted in Heyworth, *Klemperer* I, 281.

90 Benz, 'Herz Inszenierungen', 53–4.

91 Never consistent or clear-sighted in its cultural policy, the GDR was generally happy to sanction these excursions as good advertisements for the achievements of the socialist state, not worrying overmuch about what its radical directors were actually getting up to – very likely because they barely understood it. What *was* understood was that the directors brought back hard currency.

92 Herz's influence is also discernible on Jean-Pierre Ponnelle (*Ring*, Stuttgart 1977–9) and Peter Stein (*Das Rheingold*, Paris 1976).

93 Wolfgang Wagner, *Acts*, 274.

94 Wolfgang Wagner, *Acts*, 158.

95 Quoted in Paul Barz, *Götz Friedrich*, Bonn 1978, 94.

96 Barz, *Friedrich*, 93.

97 Heyworth, *Klemperer* I, 409–11.

98 Stefan Jaeger, ed., *Götz Friedrich: Wagner-Regie*, Zürich 1983, 47–8.

99 Friedrich's initial idea had been to keep the chorus out of sight, with Tannhäuser and Wolfram alone on the stage, and consequently no costumes had been made for them. When at the last minute it was decided that the chorus should after all be seen, the 'working clothes' were thus *faute de mieux*. The story behind this is as follows. Herbert Balatsch, in his first year as chorus master after taking over from the legendary Wilhelm Pitz, feared that if the chorus were off stage the consequent reduction in volume would redound badly on him, and so persuaded Friedrich 'that the pilgrims should enter in the dark, forming a tableau that was steeped in light only when they began to sing'. But such were the protests against the 'pilgrims shown as ordinary people' at the premiere that for a number of performances the chorus was concealed behind the scene. Regarding the Balatsch-inspired revision as an improvement on his original idea, Friedrich soon recalled the chorus to the stage, and that was where they stayed for all subsequent performances, as can be seen in the video from the television recording that was made in 1978, the production's last year – the first time that a full-length Bayreuth performance had been so recorded. Wolfgang Wagner, *Acts*, 159–61.

100 Barz, *Friedrich*, 98.

101 The Gliese design was for the Theateratelier Baruch in Berlin; see Bauer, *Stage Designs*, 92.

102 Spencer, 'Tannhäuser und der Tanhusaere', in Müller, *Opern und Opernfiguren*, 241–47.

103 Wolfgang Wagner, *Acts*, 159.

104 Wolfgang Wagner, *Acts*, 186.

105 Götz Friedrich, 'Utopia and Reality', trans. Eleanor Lewis, in *Richard Wagner: 'Der Ring des Nibelungen'*, booklet distributed for the 1975 production of

the *Ring* at the Royal Opera House, London. See also Götz Friedrich, *Musiktheater: Ansichten, Einsichten*, Frankfurt/Berlin 1986.

106 Friedrich, 'Utopia and Reality'.

107 Friedrich, 'Utopia and Reality'.

108 Interview with John Higgins, *The Times*, 21 September 1974.

109 Barry Millington, 'Friedrich, Götz', in *New Grove Opera*.

110 William Mann described George Shirley's Loge as 'a camp hippie descendant of Sammy Davis', sending up the gods with insolent gestures. *The Times*, 1 October 1974.

111 Friedrich, 'Utopia and Reality'.

112 *The Times*, 3 October 1974.

113 Peter Heyworth, *Observer*, 6 October 1974.

114 *The Times*, 18 September 1976.

115 Götz Friedrich, quoted in Walter Bronnenmeyer, 'Alberich und *Apocalypse Now*', *Beiträge zum Musiktheater*, 4 (1984–5 yearbook of the Deutsche Oper Berlin), 60; Peter Sykora, 'The Spatial Concept', in the programme book for the 1989 production of *Die Walküre* at the Royal Opera House, London.

Chapter 11

1 Jean-Jacques Nattiez, ' "Fidelity" to Wagner: Reflections on the Centenary Ring', in Millington, *Wagner in Performance*, 86.

2 Pierre Boulez, Patrice Chéreau, Richard Peduzzi and Jacques Schmidt, *Histoire d'un 'Ring': 'Der Ring des Nibelungen' (l'Anneau du Nibelung) de Richard Wagner, Bayreuth 1976–1980*, Paris 1980, 16. German translation by Monika Seehof and Josef Häusler, *Der 'Ring', Bayreuth 1976–1980*, Berlin/Hamburg 1980.

3 Nike Wagner, *The Wagners*, 268.

4 BP *Siegfried* 1977, 68.

5 BP *Siegfried* 1977, 82.

6 BP *Siegfried* 1977, 82.

7 BP *Siegfried* 1977, 83. The production played from 1976 to 1980 and was filmed for television and video (VHS, six cassettes, Philips 070 407–3). Across the four-year span there were changes in the staging and in the cast. The singers named are those I saw either in 1976 or on the film.

8 Elisabeth Bouillon, *Le 'Ring' à Bayreuth:*

La Tétralogie du centenaire, Paris 1980, 119.

9 BP *Rheingold* 1977, 50–1.

10 BP *Siegfried* 1977, 71.

11 BP *Siegfried* 1977, 80 and 84.

12 'Que ces rois de l'azur, maladroits et honteux,/Laissent piteusement leurs grandes ailes blanches/Comme des avirons traîner à côté d'eux.' Baudelaire, 'L'Albatros', 1859.

13 Tom Sutcliffe, *Believing in Opera*, London 1996, 113.

14 BP *Siegfried* 1977, 73–4.

15 BP *Siegfried* 1977, 73–4.

16 William Mann in the *The Times* (no date given), quoted in Sutcliffe, *Believing in Opera*, 108.

17 Boulez, *Orientations*, 228.

18 Quoted in Sutcliffe, *Believing in Opera*, 381.

19 Hans-Klaus Jungheinrich and Mara Eggert, *Durchbrüche – 10 Jahre Musiktheater mit Michael Gielen*, Berlin/Weinheim 1987.

20 See Lillian Karina and Marion Kant, *Hitler's Dancers: German Modern Dance and the Third Reich*, trans. Jonathan Steinberg, New York/Oxford 2003, 120ff.

21 Sigrid Neef, *Das Theater der Ruth Berghaus*, Berlin/Frankfurt 1989, 7.

22 I am very grateful to Frank Martin Widmaier of the Städtische Bühnen Frankfurt for making available to me production videos of the Berghaus *Parsifal* and *Ring*.

23 Hans Jürgen Syberberg, *Parsifal: Ein Filmessay*, Munich 1982, 11.

24 Quoted in Neef, *Theater Ruth Berghaus*, 165.

25 Quoted in Neef, *Theater Ruth Berghaus*, 164.

26 Interview with Andrew Clark, *Opernwelt* (Zürich), August 1987.

27 Quoted in Neef, *Theater Ruth Berghaus*, 159.

28 Quoted in Neef, *Theater Ruth Berghaus*, 162.

29 Quoted in Neef, *Theater Ruth Berghaus*, 158.

30 Quoted in Neef, *Theater Ruth Berghaus*, 160.

31 Ashman, 'Producing Wagner', in Millington, *Wagner in Performance*, 45. In *Le degré zéro de l'écriture*, Roland Barthes's first book (1953), he argues that the Word, stripped of any intentions its author may have had for it, 'is reduced to

a sort of zero degree, pregnant with all past and future specifications. … Nobody chooses for [words] a privileged meaning, or a particular use, or some service; nobody imposes a hierarchy on them, nobody reduces them to the manifestation of a mental behaviour, or of an intention.' Roland Barthes, *Selected Writings*, ed. Susan Sontag, trans. Annette Lavers and Colin Smith, London 1983, 58–9.

32 Quoted in Neef, *Theater Ruth Berghaus*, 158.

33 Hans Jürgen Syberberg, *Hitler: Ein Film aus Deutschland* (screenplay with additional material), trans. Joachim Neugroschel, Manchester 1982, 246.

34 For the cinema's interest in Wagner in its early years, see chapter 8. For a survey of film versions of Wagner's operas, see Ulrich Müller, 'Wagner in Literature and Film', in Müller, *Wagner Handbook*, 390–2.

35 Quoted in Alain Auffray, 'Doing the Reich thing', *Guardian*, 14 December 1990.

36 'Trauerarbeit' is a notion taken over by Syberberg from *Die Unfähigkeit zu trauern* (The Inability to Mourn, 1967), a psychoanalytic study by Alexander and Margarete Mitscherlich which argues that post-war Germany's melancholia is the result of its refusal to accept collective responsibility for the Nazi past and to mourn for it. See Susan Sontag's preface to Hans Jürgen Syberberg, *Hitler*, xiii.

37 Heinrich von Kleist, 'Über das Marionettentheater', 1810, translated as 'The Puppet Theatre', in Heinrich von Kleist, *Selected Writings*, ed. and trans. David Constantine, London 1997, 411–16.

38 *Nach meinem letzten Umzug* (After My Last Change of Address, 8 mm).

39 *Ludwig: Requiem für einen jungfräulichen König.*

40 *Theodor Hierneis, oder wie man ehemaliger Hofkoch wird* (Theodor Hierneis, or How One Became Ludwig's Sometime Court Cook), 1972.

41 *Karl May: Auf der Suche nach dem verlorenen Paradies* (Karl May: In Search of the Lost Paradise), 1974. Syberberg, *Hitler*, 267.

42 *Winifred Wagner und die Geschichte des Hauses Wahnfried, 1914–1975* (The Confessions of Winifred Wagner), 1975.

43 *Hitler: Ein Film aus Deutschland*, 1977.

44 Syberberg, *Hitler*, 231.

45 Syberberg, *Hitler*, 71.

46 Syberberg, *Hitler*, 109.

47 According to Alain Auffray ('Doing the Reich Thing'), Syberberg exonerated the composer from the 'curse of Hitlerism' in an article entitled 'Wagner war nicht schuldig' (Wagner Was Not Guilty) which he published in 1983, a year after the *Parsifal* film. Syberberg himself has no recollection of this piece (personal communication, September 2004).

48 Syberberg, *Parsifal*, 25.

49 Theodor Adorno, *In Search of Wagner*, trans. Rodney Livingstone, London 1985, 107.

50 Adorno, *In Search of Wagner*, 109.

51 Syberberg, *Parsifal*, 30.

52 Syberberg, *Parsifal*, 26.

53 The film is available on VHS video, Artificial Eye ART OP1.

54 Syberberg, *Parsifal*, 195–9.

55 Syberberg, *Parsifal*, 22–3.

56 'In diesen Kopftempel'. Syberberg, *Parsifal*, 97.

57 Syberberg, *Parsifal*, 96.

58 Syberberg, *Parsifal*, 228.

59 Syberberg, *Parsifal*, 230.

60 It is more than likely that Syberberg would have had in mind the essay on which Wagner was working on the day of his death – 'On the Feminine in the Human' ('Über das Weibliche im Menschlichen', SSD XII, 343–5; PW VI, 333–7, and VIII, 396–8). 'Would Richard Wagner not have been happy with a feminine portrayal of this androgynous Parsifal?' he asks. 'Had he not applauded the idea of Schröder-Devrient playing Romeo and spoken of tenors as little runts on the stage?' Syberberg, *Parsifal*, 35.

61 'Parsifal träumt, was er erlebt und sein Abenteuer als Traum von uns' ('Parsifal dreams what he experiences, and his adventures are a dream of ours'). Syberberg, *Parsifal*, 69.

62 Syberberg, *Parsifal*, 55.

63 Syberberg, *Parsifal*, 161.

64 Syberberg, *Parsifal*, 166.

65 Syberberg, *Parsifal*, 67.

66 Syberberg's first idea was actually that all the players should be actors, but he had to change his mind when there were problems of actor availability. Syberberg, *Parsifal*, 32–3.

67 Jean-Jacques Nattiez, *Wagner Androgyne*,

trans. Stewart Spencer, Princeton 1993, 290–1.

68   'Syberberg's *Hitler*', in Susan Sontag, *Under the Sign of Saturn*, London 1983, 157.

69   Syberberg, *Parsifal*, 233.

70   Syberberg, *Hitler*, 10.

71   Syberberg, *Parsifal*, 244.

72   Syberberg, *Parsifal*, 264.

73   Syberberg, *Parsifal*, 235.

74   Syberberg, *Parsifal*, 237–40.

75   The attacks were specifically provoked by his pamphlet *Vom Unglück und Glück der Kunst in Deutschland nach dem letzten Kriege* (About the Vicissitudes of Art in Germany after the Last War), Munich 1990, in which he had castigated left-wing intellectuals for insisting that the Nazis' appropriation of Germany's romantic heritage had polluted it beyond remedy. Auffray, 'Doing the Reich Thing'.

76   Auffray, 'Doing the Reich Thing'.

77   Boulez, *Orientations*, 229.

78   A good account and illustrations may be found in Gerd Albrecht, ed., *Der Hamburger 'Parsifal': Eine Provokation?*, Hamburg 1992.

79   Patrick Carnegy, 'Designing Wagner: Deeds of Music Made Visible?', in Millington, *Wagner in Performance*, 73–4.

80   BP *Siegfried* 1977, 64.

Bibliography

This is primarily a list of principal sources cited in the notes, though also includes some titles that have been consulted but not specifically cited. Sources mentioned en passant are referenced in the notes and are listed here only when of major relevance.

Details of publication

Publishers are named only when a publication might be difficult to identify from the place and date of publication alone. (This mostly pertains to institutions, such as the Akademie der Künste, Berlin.) Where a publisher has multiple offices, the place of publication is given as a principal office or sometimes as a combination of such offices. The place of publication of journals is generally London unless stated otherwise. In a few instances the place has remained elusive.

Abbreviated titles

BP   *Bayreuther Programmhefte* (the festival programme books, typically cited as 'BP *Rheingold* 1966'). The pre-1951 *Festspielführer* are cited without abbreviation

CD   *Cosima Wagner's Diaries*, ed. Martin Gregor-Dellin and Dietrich Mack, trans. Geoffrey Skelton, vol. I (1869–1877), London 1978, vol. II (1878–1883), London 1980

GS   Richard Wagner, *Gesammelte Schriften und Dichtungen*, 4th edn, 10 vols, Leipzig 1907, repr. 1976

Königsbriefe   *König Ludwig II. und Richard Wagner: Briefwechsel*, ed. Otto Strobel, 5 vols, Karlsruhe 1936–9

ML   Richard Wagner, *My Life*, ed. Mary Whittall, trans. Andrew Gray, Cambridge 1983

MLg   Richard Wagner, *Mein Leben*, ed. Martin Gregor-Dellin, Munich 1976

PW   *Richard Wagner's Prose Works*, trans. William Ashton Ellis, 8 vols, London 1895–9, repr. Lincoln (USA)/London (University of Nebraska Press) 1993–5. The standard English translation is far from lucid and is cited primarily for bibliographic orientation. It does not include all the items in GS and SSD. My translations are usually either drawn from better sources (gratefully acknowledged, and sometimes amended) or are my own.

SB   Richard Wagner, *Sämtliche Briefe*, ed. Gertrud Strobel, Werner Wolf, Hans-Joachim Bauer, Johannes Forner et al., Leipzig (from 1999 Wiesbaden) 1967–

SL   *Selected Letters of Richard Wagner*, ed. and trans. Stewart Spencer and Barry Millington, London 1987

SSD   Richard Wagner, *Sämtliche Schriften und Dichtungen*, 16 vols, Leipzig [1911–14]

SW   Richard Wagner, *Sämtliche Werke*, ed. Carl Dahlhaus, Egon Voss et al., Mainz 1970–

WWV John Deathridge, Martin Geck and Egon Voss, *Wagner Werk-Verzeichnis: Verzeichnis der musicalischen Werke Richard Wagners und ihrer Quellen*, Mainz 1986

Wagner's writings

Bayreuther Briefe von Richard Wagner: 1871–1883, ed. Carl Friedrich Glasenapp, Berlin/Leipzig 1907, 2nd edn Leipzig 1912

Briefe Richard Wagners an Emil Heckel: Zur Entstehungsgeschichte der Bühnenfestspiele in Bayreuth, Berlin 1899

Correspondence of Wagner and Liszt, trans. Francis Hueffer, 2 vols, London 1888

Franz Liszt–Richard Wagner Briefwechsel, ed. Hanjo Kesting, Frankfurt 1988

Letters of Richard Wagner: The Burrell Collection, ed. John N. Burk, London 1951

Richard Wagner an seine Künstler, ed. Erich Kloss, Berlin/Leipzig 1908

Richard Wagner's Letters to August Roeckel, trans. Eleanor C. Sellar, Bristol 1897

'Scenirung der Oper *Tannhäuser*' and 'Costumbeschreibung zur Oper *Tannhäuser*', both written with Ferdinand Heine, in Dietrich Steinbeck, ed., *Richard Wagners 'Tannhäuser'-Szenarium*, Berlin (Gesellschaft für Theatergeschichte) 1968, 31–75, 76–89 and 90–122

Siegfried, trans. William Mann, London 1964

Wagner on Music and Drama, ed. Albert Goldman and Evert Sprinchorn, trans. W. Ashton Ellis, London 1970

Other material

Abbate, Carolyn, 'The Parisian "Venus" and the "Paris" *Tannhäuser*', *JAMS*, 36 (1983), 73–123
    'The "Parisian" *Tannhäuser*', diss. University of Princeton, 1984

Adorno, Theodor, *In Search of Wagner*, trans. Rodney Livingstone, London 1981

Albrecht, Gerd, ed., *Der Hamburger 'Parsifal': Eine Provokation?*, Hamburg 1992

Appia, Adolphe, *Adolphe Appia: A Portfolio*, with an introduction by Henry C. Bonifas, Zürich 1929
    The Work of Living Art, trans. H. D. Albright, Coral Gables (Florida) 1960
    Music and the Art of the Theatre, ed. Barnard Hewitt, trans. Robert W. Corrigan and Mary Douglas Dirks, Coral Gables (Florida) 1962
    Oeuvres complètes, ed. Marie L. Bablet-Hahn, 4 vols, Bonstetten (Switzerland) 1983–91
    Essays, Scenarios, and Designs, ed. Richard C. Beacham, trans. Walther R. Volbach, Ann Arbor/London 1989

Arent, Benno von, ed., *Das deutsche Bühnenbild: 1933–1936*, Berlin (Leonhard Preiss) 1938

Arro, Elmar, 'Richard Wagners Rigaer Wanderjahre. Über einige baltische Züge im Schaffen Wagners', *Musik des Ostens* (Kassel), 3 (1965), 125–68

Auffray, Alain, 'Doing the Reich thing', *Guardian*, 14 December 1990

Bablet, Denis, *The Theatre of Edward Gordon Craig*, trans. Daphne Woodward, London 1981

Balk, Claudia, *Theaterfotografie*, Munich 1989

Barth, Herbert, ed., *Life, Work, Festspielhaus*, Bayreuth 1952

Barth, Herbert, Dietrich Mack and Wilhelm Rauh, *Der Festspielhügel: Richard Wagners Werk in Bayreuth*, Munich 1973

Barth, Herbert, Dietrich Mack and Egon Voss, eds, *Wagner: A Documentary Study*, trans. P. R. J. Ford and M. Whittall, London 1975

Barthes, Roland, *Selected Writings*, ed. Susan Sontag, trans. Annette Lavers and Colin Smith, London 1983

Bartlett, Rosamund, 'The Embodiment of Myth: Eizenshtein's Production of *Die Walküre*', *Slavonic and East European Review*, 70, no. 1 (January 1992), 53–76
    Wagner and Russia, Cambridge 1995

Bartolo, Ernest, *Die Wiener Oper: Die aufregenden Jahre seit 1625*, Vienna 1992

Barz, Paul, *Götz Friedrich*, Bonn 1978

Baudelaire, Charles, *The Painter of Modern Life and Other Essays*, ed. and trans. Jonathan Mayne, London 1964

Bauer, Oswald Georg, *Richard Wagner: The Stage Designs and Productions from the Premières to the*

Present, trans. Stewart Spencer, New York 1983 (*Richard Wagner: Die Bühnenwerke von der Uraufführung bis heute*, Frankfurt 1982)

Richard Wagner Goes to the Theatre, trans. Stewart Spencer, Bayreuth n.d. (*Richard Wagner geht ins Theater*, Bayreuth 1996)

' "… daß der Ausdruck Eindruck werde": Gustav Mahler und Alfred Roller – Die Reform der Wiener Wagner-Szene', in *Jahrbuch der Bayerischen Akademie der Schönen Künste*, Munich 1997, 55–95

'Touchstone *Parsifal*: On the First Publication of Alfred Roller's Designs for the Bayreuth *Parsifal* of 1934', BP *Parsifal* 1998, 59–67

Baumann, Carl-Friedrich, 'Entwicklung und Anwendung der Bühnenbeleuchtung seit der Mitte des 18. Jahrhunderts', diss. Universität zu Köln, 1955

Bühnentechnik im Festspielhaus Bayreuth, Munich 1980

Beacham, Richard C., *Adolphe Appia: Theatre Artist*, Cambridge 1987

Beacham, Richard C., ed., ' "Brothers in Suffering and Joy": The Appia–Craig Correspondence', *New Theatre Quarterly*, 4, no. 15 (1988), 268–88

Becker, Heinz and Gudrun, *Giacomo Meyerbeer: A Life in Letters*, ed. Reinhard G. Pauly, trans. Mark Violette, London 1989

Beckett, Lucy, *Richard Wagner: 'Parsifal'* (Cambridge Opera Handbook), Cambridge 1981

Bekker, Paul, *Richard Wagner: His Life in His Work*, trans. M. M. Bozman, London 1936

Benois, Alexandre, *Memoirs*, trans. Moura Budberg, 2 vols, London 1960–4

Benz, Marion, 'Die Wagner-Inszenierungen von Joachim Herz: Studie zur theatralen Wagner-Rezeption in der DDR', diss. Friedrich-Alexander-Universität, Erlangen-Nürnberg, 1998

Bergman, Gösta M., *Lighting in the Theatre*, trans. N. Stedt, Stockholm/Totowa (New Jersey) 1977

Berlioz, Hector, *The Memoirs of Hector Berlioz*, trans. David Cairns, 2nd edn, London 1977

Bianconi, Lorenzo, and Giorgio Pestelli, eds, *The History of Italian Opera*, vol. IV, trans. Lydia G. Cochrane (*Opera Production and Its Resources*), Chicago 1998, and vol. V, trans. Kate Singleton (*Opera on Stage*), Chicago 2002

Blaukopf, Kurt, *Gustav Mahler*, trans. Inge Goodwin, London 1973

Blaukopf, Kurt, ed., with Zoltan Roman, *Mahler: A Documentary Study*, trans. Paul Baker et al., Oxford/New York 1976

Bloch, Ernst, *Das Prinzip Hoffnung*, Frankfurt 1954–9

Zur Philosophie der Musik, Frankfurt 1974

Blunt, Wilfrid, *The Dream King*, London 1970

Borchmeyer, Dieter, *Richard Wagner: Theory and Theatre*, trans. Stewart Spencer, Oxford 1991

Bouillon, Elisabeth, *Le 'Ring' à Bayreuth: La Tétralogie du centenaire*, Paris 1980

Boulez, Pierre, *Orientations*, ed. Jean-Jacques Nattiez, trans. Martin Cooper, London 1986

Boulez, Pierre, Patrice Chéreau, Richard Peduzzi and Jacques Schmidt, *Histoire d'un 'Ring': 'Der Ring des Nibelungen' (l'Anneau du Nibelung) de Richard Wagner, Bayreuth 1976–1980*, Paris 1980. German translation by Monika Seehof and Josef Häusler, *Der 'Ring', Bayreuth 1976–1980*, Berlin/Hamburg 1980

Brand, Hans B., *Aus Richard Wagners Leben in Bayreuth*, Munich 1934

Braun, Edward, *The Theatre of Meyerhold*, London 1979 (rev. edn *Meyerhold: A Revolution in Theatre*, London 1995)

The Director and the Stage, London 1982

Buckle, Richard, *Diaghilev*, London 1979

Busoni, Ferruccio, 'Sketch of a New Esthetic of Music', trans. Th. Baker, in *Three Classics in the Aesthetic of Music*, New York 1962, 73–102

Carnegy, Patrick, 'Opera As Mystery Play' (article on Wieland Wagner), *Times Educational Supplement*, 27 September 1968

'With Helmet, Shield and Spear?' (review-article on Detta and Michael Petzet, *Die Richard Wagner-Bühne König Ludwigs II.*), *Times Literary Supplement*, 20 November 1970

'Damming the Rhine' (review-article on the 1976 Bayreuth *Ring*), *Times Literary Supplement*, 10 June 1977

'The Staging of *Tristan and Isolde*: Landmarks along the Appian Way', in Nicholas John, ed., *Tristan and Isolde* (English National Opera Guide), London 1981, 29–35

'Designing Wagner: Deeds of Music Made Visible?', in Barry Millington and Stewart Spencer, eds, *Wagner in Performance*, New Haven/London, 1992, 48–74

'Stage History', in John Warrack, ed., *Richard Wagner: 'Die Meistersinger von Nürnberg'* (Cambridge Opera Handbook), Cambridge 1994, 135–52

'Landfall on the Stage: A Brief Production History', in Thomas Grey, ed., *Richard Wagner: 'Der fliegende Holländer'* (Cambridge Opera Handbook), Cambridge 2000, 92–108

'Which Way to the Grail?', in the programme book for the 2001 production of *Parsifal* at the Royal Opera House, London, 44–51

'Swan's Way: A Brief Stage History', in the programme book for the 2003 revival of *Lohengrin* at the Royal Opera House, London, 37–44

Carner, Mosco, *Alban Berg*, London 1975

Carter, Huntly, *The New Spirit in the Russian Theatre 1917–1928*, London 1929

Chamberlain, Houston Stewart, *Richard Wagner*, trans. G. Ainslie Hight, London 1897

Charlton, David, 'The Nineteenth Century: France', in Roger Parker, ed., *The Oxford Illustrated History of Opera*, Oxford 1994

Citron, Marcia J., *Opera on Screen*, New Haven/London 2000

Cohen, H. Robert, *The Original Staging Manuals for Twelve Parisian Operatic Premieres*, Stuyvesant 1991

Craig, Edward Gordon, *On the Art of the Theatre*, London 1911, 2nd edn London 1912

Index to the Story of My Days, London 1957

Curjel, Hans, *Experiment Krolloper 1927–1931*, ed. Eigel Kruttge, Munich 1975

Dahlhaus, Carl, *Richard Wagner's Music Dramas*, trans. Mary Whittall, Cambridge 1979 (*Die Musikdramen Richard Wagners*, Velber 1971)

Nineteenth-Century Music, trans. J. Bradford Robinson, Berkeley/Los Angeles, 1989

Dean, Winton, 'The Recovery of Handel's Operas', in Christopher Hogwood and Richard Luckett, eds, *Music in Eighteenth-Century England*, Cambridge 1983, 103–13

Deathridge, John, *Wagner's 'Rienzi': A Reappraisal Based on a Study of the Sketches and Drafts*, Oxford 1977

Deathridge, John, and Carl Dahlhaus, *The New Grove Wagner*, London 1984

Diebold, Bernhard, *Der Fall Wagner: Eine Revision*, Frankfurt 1928

Dizikes, John, *Opera in America: A Cultural History*, New Haven/London 1993

Drew, David, *Kurt Weill: A Handbook*, London 1987

Eger, Manfred, 'The Patronage of King Ludwig II', in Ulrich Müller and Peter Wapnewski, eds, *The Wagner Handbook*, translation edited by John Deathridge, Cambridge (Massachusetts) 1992, 317–26

Eisenstein, Sergei, *The Film Sense*, ed. and trans. Jay Leyda, London 1953

Film Essays, ed. Jay Leyda, London 1968

Selected Works, vol. II, ed. Michael Glenny and Richard Taylor, trans. Michael Glenny, London 1991, and vol. III, ed. Richard Taylor, trans. William Powell, London 1996

Ellis, William Ashton, *Life of Richard Wagner*, 6 vols, London 1900–8

Fawkes, Richard, *Opera on Film*, London 2000

Felsenstein, Walter, *Schriften zum Musiktheater*, ed. Stephan Stompor, Berlin 1976

Felsenstein, Walter, and Joachim Herz, *Musiktheater*, ed. Stephan Stompor, Leipzig 1976

Field, Geoffrey G., *Evangelist of Race: The Germanic Vision of Houston Stewart Chamberlain*, New York 1981

Forsyth, Michael, *Buildings for Music*, Cambridge 1985

Frenzel, Herbert A., *Geschichte des Theaters: Daten und Dokumente 1470–1890*, 2nd edn, Munich 1984

Fricke, Richard, *Bayreuth vor dreissig Jahren*, Dresden 1906

1876: Richard Wagner auf der Probe, Stuttgart 1983 (retitled facsimile of *Bayreuth vor dreissig Jahren*, with an afterword by Joachim Herz)

Bayreuth in 1876, trans. Stewart Spencer, *Wagner*, 11, no. 3, (August 1990), to 12, no. 1 (January 1991)

Friedrich, Götz, 'Utopia and Reality', trans. Eleanor Lewis, in *Richard Wagner: 'Der Ring des Nibelungen'*, booklet distributed for the 1975 production of the *Ring* at the Royal Opera House, London

Musiktheater: Ansichten, Einsichten, Frankfurt/Berlin 1986

see also Jaeger, Stefan, ed.

Fuchs, Georg, *Revolution in the Theatre*, ed. and trans. Constance Connor Kuhn, Port Washington (New York) 1972

Fuchs, Peter Paul, ed., *The Music Theatre of Walter Felsenstein*, London 1991

Fuerst, Walter René, and Samuel J. Hume, *Twentieth-Century Stage Decoration*, 2 vols, repr. New York 1967

Fulcher, Jane F., *The Nation's Image: French Grand Opera as Politics and Politicized Art*, Cambridge 1987

Gay, Peter, *Weimar Culture*, London 1969

Genast, Eduard, *Aus Weimars klassischer Zeit: Erinnerungen eines alten Schauspielers*, ed. Robert Kohlrausch, Stuttgart 1905

Gernsheim, Helmut and Alison, *L. J. M. Daguerre: The History of the Diorama and the Daguerreotype*, New York 1969

Gilliam, Bryan, ed., *Music and Performance during the Weimar Republic*, Cambridge 1994

Glasenapp, Carl Friedrich, *Das Leben Richard Wagners in sechs Büchern*, repr. Vaduz (Liechtenstein) 1977
  Richard Wagner in Riga, Riga 1913

Goléa, Antoine, *Gespräche mit Wieland Wagner*, Salzburg 1968

Gollancz, Victor, *The 'Ring' at Bayreuth*, London 1966

Goodman, Nelson, *Languages of Art*, London 1969

Gorelik, Mordecai, *New Theatres for Old*, London 1947

Gray, Camilla, *The Russian Experiment in Art 1863–1922*, rev. Marian Burleigh-Motley, London 1986

Grey, Thomas, ed., *Richard Wagner: 'Der fliegende Holländer'* (Cambridge Opera Handbook), Cambridge 2000

Gropius, Walter, ed., *The Theater of the Bauhaus*, trans. Arthur S. Wensinger, Middletown (Connecticut) 1961 (*Die Bühne im Bauhaus*, Munich 1925)

Habel, Heinrich, *Festspielhaus und Wahnfried*, Munich 1985

Hacker, Rupert, ed., *Ludwig II. von Bayern in Augenzeugenberichten*, Munich 1972

Hagemann, Carl, *Bühne und Welt*, Wiesbaden 1948

Hanslick, Eduard, *Aus dem Opernleben der Gegenwart* (vol. III of Hanslick's collected writings, *Die moderne Oper*, 9 vols, 1875–1900), Berlin 1884
  Music Criticisms 1846–1899, ed. and trans. Henry Pleasants, London 1963

Hartford, Robert, ed., *Bayreuth: The Early Years*, London 1980

Hartnoll, Phyllis, ed., *The Oxford Companion to the Theatre*, 4th edn, Oxford 1983

Heine, Ferdinand, *Decorative und costümliche Scenirung der Oper 'Lohengrin' von Richard Wagner. In Auftrag des Dichters entworfen*, Leipzig 1854

Heldt, Brigitte, *Richard Wagner: 'Tristan und Isolde' – Das Werk und seine Inszenierung*, Laaber 1994

Herz, Joachim, *Theater – Kunst des erfüllten Augenblicks*, ed. Ilse Kobán, Berlin 1989
  see also Felsenstein, Walter, and Joachim Herz
  for Festschrift, see Müller, Ursula and Ulrich, eds.

Herz, Joachim, et al., 'Joachim Herz inszeniert Richard Wagners *Ring des Nibelungen* am Opernhaus Leipzig', Arbeitshefte nos 21 (ed. Marion Reinisch) and 29 (ed. Eginhard Röhlig), Berlin (Akademie der Künste der DDR) 1975 and 1980

Hevesi, Ludwig, *Alt Kunst – Neu Kunst: Wien 1894–1908*, Vienna 1909

Hey, Julius, *Richard Wagner als Vortragsmeister*, Leipzig 1911

Heyworth, Peter, *Otto Klemperer: His Life and Times*, vol. I (1885–1933), Cambridge 1983

Heyworth, Peter, ed., *Conversations with Klemperer*, London 1973

Hollwich, Fritz, ed., *Im Umkreis der Kunst: Eine Festschrift für Emil Preetorius*, Wiesbaden [1953]

Hommel, Kurt, *Die Separatvorstellungen vor König Ludwig II. von Bayern*, Munich 1963

Horowitz, Joseph, *Wagner Nights: An American History*, Berkeley/Los Angeles/London 1994

Innes, Christopher, *Edward Gordon Craig*, Cambridge 1983

Jaeger, Stefan, ed., *Götz Friedrich: Wagner-Regie*, Zürich 1983

Jelavich, Peter, *Munich and Theatrical Modernism*, Cambridge (Massachusetts) 1985

Jung, Ute, *Die Rezeption der Kunst Richard Wagners in Italien*, Regensburg 1974

Jungheinrich, Hans-Klaus, and Mara Eggert, *Durchbrüche – 10 Jahre Musiktheater mit Michael Gielen*, Berlin/Weinheim 1987

Kalbeck, Max, *Das Bühnenfestspiel zu Bayreuth*, Breslau 1877
    Opernabende: Beiträge zur Geschichte und Kritik der Oper, 2 vols, Berlin 1898
Kandinsky, Vassily, *Complete Writings on Art*, ed. Kenneth C. Lindsay and Peter Vergo, 2 vols, London 1982
Karbaum, Michael, *Studien zur Geschichte der Bayreuther Festspiele (1876–1976)*, Regensburg 1976
Karina, Lillian, and Marion Kant, *Hitler's Dancers: German Modern Dance and the Third Reich*, trans. Jonathan Steinberg, New York/Oxford 2003
Karpf, Roswitha, 'Die naturphilosophischen Elemente in Richard Wagners Bühnenfestspiel *Der Ring des Nibelungen*', diss. Karl-Franzens-Universität, Graz, 1972
Kater, Michael H., *The Twisted Muse: Musicians and Their Music in the Third Reich*, New York/Oxford 1997
Klemperer, Otto, *Minor Recollections*, London 1964
Köhler, Franz-Heinz, *Die Struktur der Spielpläne deutschsprachiger Opernbühnen von 1896 bis 1966*, Koblenz 1968
Komisarjevsky, Theodore, *Myself and the Theatre*, London 1929
Kortner, Fritz, *Alle Tage Abend*, Munich 1959
Kowalke, Kim, *Kurt Weill in Europe*, Ann Arbor 1979
Kranich, Friedrich jr, *Bühnentechnik der Gegenwart*, 2 vols, Munich/Berlin 1929–33
Kröplin, Eckhart, *Richard Wagner: Theatralisches Leben und lebendiges Theater*, Leipzig 1989. Drawn from this is Eckhart's 'Richard Wagner and Nineteenth-Century Theatricality', in BP *Parsifal* 1988, 87–108
Kubizek, August, *Young Hitler: The Story of Our Friendship*, trans. E. V. Anderson, Maidstone 1973
Kunze, Stefan, 'The Role of Nature in Wagner's Music Dramas', in *BP Siegfried* 1972, 25–44
La Grange, Henry-Louis de, *Gustav Mahler: Chronique d'une vie*, 3 vols, Paris 1979–84
    Gustav Mahler, vol. II, trans. Johanna Harwood et al., Oxford 1995
Laban, Rudolf, *A Life for Dance*, trans. Lisa Ullmann, London 1975
Langer, Arne, *Der Regisseur und die Aufzeichnungspraxis der Opernregie im 19. Jahrhundert*, Frankfurt (Peter Lang) 1997
Leach, Robert, *Vsevolod Meyerhold*, Cambridge 1989
Lebrecht, Norman, ed., *Mahler Remembered*, London 1987
Lehmann, Lilli, *My Path through Life*, trans. Alice Benedict Seligman, London 1914 (*Mein Weg*, Leipzig 1913)
Lewin, Michael, *Harry Kupfer*, Vienna 1988
Leyda, Jay, and Zina Voynow, *Eisenstein at Work*, London 1985
Lifar, Serge, *A History of the Russian Ballet*, trans. Arnold Haskell, London 1954
Lindau, Paul, *Nüchterne Briefe aus Bayreuth*, Breslau 1876
Littmann, Max, *Das Münchner Künstlertheater*, Munich 1908
Lunacharsky, Anatoly, *On Literature and Art*, ed. A. Lebedev, Moscow 1965
Mack, Dietrich, *Der Bayreuther Inszenierungsstil 1876–1976*, Munich 1976
Mack, Dietrich, ed. *Theaterarbeit an Wagners 'Ring'*, Munich 1978
Mahler, Alma, *Gustav Mahler: Memories and Letters*, ed. Donald Mitchell, trans. Basil Creighton, 3rd edn, London 1973
Mahler, Gustav, *Selected Letters of Gustav Mahler*, ed. Knud Martner, trans. Eithne Wilkins, Ernst Kaiser and Bill Hopkins, London 1979
    Mahler's Unknown Letters, ed. Herta Blaukopf, trans. Richard Stokes, London 1986
Mallgrave, Harry Francis, *Gottfried Semper: Architect of the Nineteenth Century*, New Haven/London 1996
Mann, Thomas, *Pro and Contra Wagner*, trans. Allan Blunden, London 1985
Mayer, Hans, *Richard Wagner in Bayreuth 1876–1976*, trans. Jack Zipes, Zürich/Stuttgart/London 1976
Medlicott, Andrew, 'A Man for All Theatres: Angelo Neumann', *Wagner*, 74 (February 1979), 5–11
Metken, Günter, 'Wagner and the Visual Arts', in Ulrich Müller and Peter Wapnewski, eds, *The Wagner Handbook*, translation edited by John Deathridge, Cambridge (Massachusetts) 1992, 354–72
Meyerhold, Vysevolod, *Meyerhold on Theatre*, ed. and trans. Edward Braun, London 1969
Miller, Jonathan, *Subsequent Performances*, London 1986
Millington, Barry, and Stewart Spencer, eds, *Wagner in Performance*, New Haven/London 1992

Müller, Ursula and Ulrich, eds, *Opern und Opernfiguren: Festschrift für Joachim Herz*, Anif (Salzburg, Ursula Müller-Speiser) 1989

Müller, Ulrich, and Peter Wapnewski, eds, *The Wagner Handbook*, translation edited by John Deathridge, Cambridge (Massachusetts) 1992

Nattiez, Jean-Jacques, *Wagner Androgyne*, trans. Stewart Spencer, Princeton 1993

Neef, Sigrid, *Das Theater der Ruth Berghaus*, Berlin/Frankfurt 1989

Neumann, Angelo, *Personal Recollections of Wagner*, trans. Edith Livermore, London 1909 (*Erinnerungen an Richard Wagner*, Leipzig 1907)

Newman, Ernest, *The Life of Richard Wagner*, 4 vols, New York 1933–46, repr. 1966

Nietzsche, Friedrich, *Richard Wagner in Bayreuth*, in Friedrich Nietzsche, *Untimely Meditations*, trans. R. J. Hollingdale, Cambridge 1983, 197–254

Oenslager, Donald M., *The Theatre of Donald Oenslager*, Middletown (Connecticut) 1978

Osborne, John, *The Meiningen Court Theatre 1866–1890*, Cambridge 1988

Osma, Guillermo de, *Mariano Fortuny*, London 1980

Pachl, Peter P., *Siegfried Wagner: Genie im Schatten*, Munich 1988

Panofsky, Walter, *Wieland Wagner*, Bremen 1964
    Protest in der Oper, Munich 1966

Parker, Roger, ed., *The Oxford Illustrated History of Opera*, Oxford 1994

Patterson, Michael, *German Theatre Today*, London 1976

Penzel, Frederick, *Theatre Lighting before Electricity*, Middletown (Connecticut) 1978

Petit, Jacques, and Jean-Pierre Kempf, *Claudel on the Theatre*, trans. Christine Trollope, Coral Gables (Florida) 1972

Petzet, Detta and Michael, *Die Richard Wagner-Bühne König Ludwigs II.*, Munich 1970

Petzet, Michael, 'Ludwig and the Arts', in Wilfred Blunt, *The Dream King*, London 1970, 229–54

Porges, Heinrich, *Wagner Rehearsing the 'Ring'*, trans. Robert L. Jacobs, Cambridge 1983 (*Die Bühnenproben zu den Bayreuther Festspielen des Jahres 1876*, first published in the *Bayreuther Blätter*, 1881–96)

Preetorius, Emil, *Wagner: Bild und Vision*, 3rd edn, Godesberg 1949
    for Festschrift, see Hollwich, Fritz, ed.

Prieberg, Fred K., *Musik im NS-Staat*, Frankfurt 1982

Rambert, Marie, *Quicksilver*, London 1972

Rockwell, John, 'The Prussian Ministry of Culture and the Berlin State Opera, 1918–1931', diss. University of California (Berkeley), n.d.

Rudnitsky, Konstantin, *Meyerhold the Director*, ed. Sydney Schultze, trans. George Petrov, Ann Arbor 1981

Sadie, Stanley, ed., *The New Grove Dictionary of Opera*, 4 vols, London 1992

Schäfer, Walter Erich, *Wieland Wagner: Persönlichkeit und Leistung*, Tübingen 1970

Schmidt, Paul, ed., *Meyerhold at Work*, Manchester 1981

Schoenberg, Arnold, *Style and Idea: Selected Writings of Arnold Schoenberg*, ed. Leonard Stein, trans. Leo Black, London 1975

Schopenhauer, Arthur, *The World As Will and Representation*, trans. E. F. J. Payne, 2 vols, New York 1969
    Parerga and Paralipomena, trans. E. F. J. Payne, 2 vols, Oxford 1974

Seiferth, Werner P., 'Wagner-Pflege in der DDR', in *Richard-Wagner-Blätter: Zeitschrift des Aktionskreises für das Werk Richard Wagners* (Bayreuth), 13 (1989), nos. 3–4, 89–113

Semper, Manfred, *Das Münchener Festspielhaus: Gottfried Semper und Richard Wagner*, Hamburg 1906

Shaw, [George] Bernard, *Major Critical Essays*, London 1932
    Shaw's Music: The Complete Musical Criticism, ed. Dan H. Laurence, 3 vols, London 1981

Sheil, Áine, 'The Politics of Reception: Richard Wagner's *Die Meistersinger von Nürnberg* in Weimar Germany', diss. King's College London, 2004

Shostakovich, Dmitri, *Testimony: The Memoirs of Dmitri Shostakovich*, ed. Solomon Volkov, trans. Antonina W. Bouis, London 1979

Silja, Anja, *Die Sehnsucht nach dem Unerreichbaren*, Berlin 1999

Simonson, Lee, *The Stage Is Set*, New York 1932, repr. 1970

Skelton, Geoffrey, *Wieland Wagner: The Positive Sceptic*, London 1971
    Wagner at Bayreuth, 2nd edn, London 1976

Snodin, Michael, ed., *Karl Friedrich Schinkel: A Universal Man*, New Haven/London 1991

Söhnlein, Kurt, *Erinnerungen an Siegfried Wagner und Bayreuth*, ed. Peter P. Pachl, Bayreuth 1980

Spector, Irwin, *Rhythm and Life: The Work of Emile Jaques-Dalcroze*, Stuyvesant (New York) 1990

Speer, Albert, *Inside the Third Reich*, trans. Richard and Clara Winston, London 1970
   Spandau: The Secret Diaries, trans. Richard and Clara Winston, London 1976

Spencer, Charles, *The World of Serge Diaghilev*, London 1974

Spencer, Stewart, 'Wagner's Nuremberg', *Cambridge Opera Journal*, 4, no. 1 (March 1992), 21–41

Spotts, Frederic, *Bayreuth: A History of the Wagner Festival*, New Haven/London 1994
   Hitler and the Power of Aesthetics, London 2002

Srocke, Martina, *Wagner als Regisseur*, Munich/Salzburg 1988

Stadler, Edmund, *Adolphe Appia* (exhibition catalogue), London 1970

Stanislavsky, Konstantin, *Stanislavsky on Opera*, ed. E. R. Hapgood, New York 1975

Stein, Jack M., *Richard Wagner and the Synthesis of the Arts*, Detroit 1960

Storck, Karl, *Emile Jaques-Dalcroze*, Stuttgart 1912

Strauss, Richard, *Recollections and Reflections*, ed. Willi Schuh, trans. L. J. Lawrence, London 1953
   Richard Strauss–Hugo von Hofmannsthal: Briefwechsel, ed. Willi Schuh, Zürich 1978

Stravinsky, Igor, *Poetics of Music*, trans. Arthur Knodel and Ingolf Dahl, New York 1956

Styan, J. L., *Max Reinhardt*, Cambridge 1982

Sutcliffe, Tom, *Believing in Opera*, London 1996

Syberberg, Hans Jürgen, *Hitler: A Film from Germany*, trans. Joachim Neugroschel, Manchester 1982
   Parsifal: Ein Filmessay, Munich 1982
   Vom Unglück und Glück der Kunst in Deutschland nach dem letzten Kriege, Munich 1990

Thomas, Jess, *Kein Schwert verhieß mir der Vater*, Vienna 1986

Vergo, Peter, *Art in Vienna 1898–1918*, London 1975
   Vienna 1900, Edinburgh 1983

Verwiebe, Birgit, 'Transparent Painting and the Romantic Spirit: Experimental Anticipations of Modern Visual Arts', trans. David Britt, in Keith Hartley *et al.*, eds, *The Romantic Spirit in German Art 1790–1990* (exhibition catalogue), Edinburgh/London 1994–5, 171–7

Volbach, Walther R., *Adolphe Appia: Prophet of the Modern Theatre*, Middletown (Connecticut) 1968

Volkonsky, Sergei, *Reminiscences*, trans. A. E. Chanut, 2 vols, London 1925

Wagner, Cosima, *Cosima Wagner: Das zweite Leben, Briefe und Aufzeichnungen 1883–1930*, ed. Dietrich Mack, Munich 1980

Wagner, Friedelind (with Page Cooper), *The Royal Family of Bayreuth*, London 1948

Wagner, Nike, *The Wagners: The Dramas of a Musical Dynasty*, trans. Ewald Osers and Michael Downes, London 2000

Wagner, Wieland, *Sein Denken*, ed. Oswald Georg Bauer, Bayreuth 1991

Wagner, Wolfgang, *Acts*, trans. John Brownjohn, London 1994

Waldschmidt, Ralf, 'Regietheater und Bühnenweihfestspiel: Eine Untersuchung zur Inszenierungsgeschichte von Richard Wagners *Parsifal* (1970–1985)', diss., Universität Frankfurt am Main, 1986

Walter, Bruno, *Theme and Variations*, trans. James A. Galston, London 1947

Wälterlin, Oskar, *Bekenntnis zum Theater*, Zürich 1955

Warrack, John, *Carl Maria von Weber*, 2nd edn, Cambridge 1976
   'The Musical Background', in Peter Burbidge and Richard Sutton, eds, *The Wagner Companion*, London 1979

Warrack, John, *Richard Wagner: 'Die Meistersinger von Nürnberg'* (Cambridge Opera Handbook), Cambridge 1994

Weber, Carl Maria von, *Writings on Music*, ed. John Warrack, trans. Martin Cooper, Cambridge 1981

Weingartner, Felix, *Buffets and Rewards*, trans. Marguerite Wolff, London 1937
   Felix Weingartner: Recollections and Recordings, ed. Christopher Dyment, Rickmansworth 1976

Wellesz, Egon and Emmy, *Egon Wellesz: Leben und Werk*, ed. Franz Endler, Vienna 1981

Wessling, Berndt W., ed., *Bayreuth im Dritten Reich: Richard Wagners politische Erben: Eine Dokumentation*, Weinheim/Basel 1983

Willett, John, *The Theatre of Bertolt Brecht*, London 1967

The Theatre of the Weimar Republic, London 1988
Willnauer, Franz, *Gustav Mahler und die Wiener Oper*, Vienna 1979
Wlaschin, Ken, *Opera on Screen*, Los Angeles 1997
    Encyclopedia of Opera on Screen, New Haven/London 2004
Zeh, Gisela, *Das Bayreuther Bühnenkostüm*, Munich 1973

INDEX

Illustrations are indicated in **bold** type

Illustration Credits

Grateful acknowledgement is made to the following sources, and especially to the archivists whose names are listed with them. Names of photographers are given after the relevant page number. Unlisted illustrations are from private collections or from sources I have not been able to trace.

Bayreuth: Bildarchiv, Bayreuther Festspiele (Peter and Frederike Emmerich, Roland Poellinger) Photographs by Rudolf Betz, Siegfried Lauterwasser, Wilhelm Rauh and Eduard Renner: 265, 266, 267, 269, 287, 289, 291, 292, 293, 294, 298, 299, 301, 303, 330, 347, 357, 358, 359, 360, 361, 362
Bayreuth: Nationalarchiv der Richard-Wagner-Stiftung (Gudrun Föttinger) 42, 74 (bottom), 91, 98, 112 (bottom), 125, 140, 141, 148, 150, 152, 191 (bottom), 271, 279
Berlin: Hans Curjel Archiv 253, 257
Berne: Fonds Appia, Fondation de la Collection théâtrale suisse 149, 182, 184, 188, 189
Cologne: Deutsches Tanzarchiv 142
Darmstadt: Landesbibliothek 38
Dresden: Joachim Herz private collection 321, 324 (Willi Saeger), 326 (DEFA – Wenzel), 327 (DEFA – Wenzel), 328 (DEFA – Wenzel), 333 (Helga Wallmüller), 335, 336 (Helga Wallmüller), 338 (Helga Wallmüller)
Eisenach: Fritz Reuter-Richard Wagner-Museum 35
Frankfurt: Mara Eggert 368, 369, 371, 373
London: Archives of the Royal Opera House (Julia Creed, Francesca Franchi) 72, 74 (top), 350 (Donald Southern)
Los Angeles: Doheny Memorial Library, University of Southern California 244
Lyon: Office National de la Propriété Industrielle 193
Moscow: Bakhrushin State Central Theatre Museum (Vera Pavlova) 223
Moscow: Bolshoi Theatre Museum 226, 230, 231
Munich: Bayerische Verwaltung der staatlichen Schlösser, Gärten und Seen 57 (top), 59, 62
Munich: Deutsches Theatermuseum (Babette Angelaeas, Andrea Hauer, Gabriele Jäckl, Susanne de Ponte, Johanna Renauer) 57 (bottom), 65, 66 (right), 117 (Hans Brand), 191 (top)
Munich: Hans Jürgen Syberberg private collection 384 (Dirk Franke), 387 (Natalie Maier), 388, 390 (Hans Peter Litscher), 392. Rights in Syberberg's film of *Parsifal* are owned by Gaumont (Paris)
Munich: Wittelsbacher Ausgleichsfonds (Brigitte Schuhbauer) 43, 66 (left)
New Haven, Connecticut: Oenslager Collection, Beinecke Library, Yale University 178, 198
Paris: Bibliothèque nationale 202
Paris: Bibliothèque nationale, Musée de l'Opéra 16, 21, 44
Paris: Collection Médiathèque Musicale Mahler (Henry-Louis de La Grange, Alena Parthonnaud) 168 (bottom, left and right)
St Petersburg: State Museum of Theatre and Music 216, 219
Vienna: Österreichisches Theatermuseum (Haris Balic, Varna Greisenegger) 168 (top), 172, 238
Zürich: Gottfried-Semper-Archiv der Eidgenössischen Technischen Hochschule 53

Zürich: Schweizerische Verkehrszentrale 79 (Philipp Giegel)

Josef Hoffmann's painting of the first act of *Die Walküre* is reproduced on the jacket in colour for the first time by generous permission of Cornelia and Henrik von Bodenhausen. I am also indebted to Karl Heinrich von Bodenhausen for information about the provenance of the Hoffmann paintings, and to Oswald Georg Bauer who first identified them.

For additional help in finding illustrations and resolving questions connected with them it is a pleasure to thank Elisabeth Agate, Rosamund Bartlett, Richard Beacham, Elizabeth Bowers, David Charlton, Victoria Cooper, Geoffrey Davies, Christopher Innes, Marion Kant, Barry Millington, Bruce Phillips, Simon Reynolds, Stewart Spencer, Daphne Stevens, Jean-Louis Tamvaco, Dmitry Trubotchkin and Keith Warner.

Every effort has been made to contact copyright holders, but if there are any inadvertent omissions or mistakes the author and publisheer will be glad to correct them at the earliest opportunity.